AN
INTRODUCTION
TO
LABOR

THE PRENTICE-HALL INDUSTRIAL RELATIONS AND PERSONNEL SERIES

Dale Yoder, Editor

AN INTRODUCTION TO LABOR

CLYDE E. DANKERT
Professor of Economics
Dartmouth College

PRENTICE-HALL, INC.
New York 1954

K. B. B.
Jan. 5, 1955
037
Ainsley Hund

$6.75

LIBRARY OF CONGRESS
CATALOG CARD NUMBER:

54-10893

PREFACE

In order to fulfill the special function of an *introduction* to our subject, a book should have certain characteristics. It should be comprehensive, but not superficial; scholarly, but not dull; interesting, but not frivolous; stimulating, but not exhaustive. It is the hope of the author that the present volume will measure up to these requirements.

A few words should be said about the comprehensiveness of the book, and of the various "approaches" used by the author in writing it. The specific matters dealt with are numerous due to the simple fact that the number of important questions in the field of labor is large, and it is becoming ever larger with each passing year. Many of these questions could have been set aside and a few representative ones picked out for detailed and extensive study. But for an introduction to labor it seems desirable that the reader have a general acquaintance with the field as a whole, or a large part of it, rather than a specialized knowledge of a few of its segments. The author attempts to present this larger view of the subject.

It should be pointed out, however, that the approach used is not solely one of "breadth." It is also one of "depth." At various points along the way significant matters in the field are dealt with at some length. The chief purpose of the first type of approach is to acquaint the reader with important facts; of the second, to encourage him to think—to reason carefully and objectively about issues in the field.

In addition to the "breadth-depth" manner of dealing with the subject the author uses another approach. The careful observer will note that the word "economics" is not in the title of the book. This omission does not mean that no use is made of economic analysis and of economic terminology; it means merely that the author has stepped far beyond the boundaries of economics (which is his natural habitat) into other territories in his examination of labor. He has ventured into the area of history, of sociology, of psychology, of government—and even of philosophy. His approach, therefore, is more that of the social scientist than that of the economist. But this particular way of dealing with labor is not new, as over the years most of the general books in the field have been an admixture of at least some of the ingredients just mentioned.

In the present volume numerous sources have been used, and the author has indicated the places from which many of his facts and ideas have come. His hope, and he trusts that it is not a vain hope, is that many readers interested in delving more deeply into some of the matters discussed will consult these references. It might be added, too, that at some points, particularly in the chapters on wages, footnotes are used for the purpose of indicating additional aspects, possibly of a theoretical nature, of the topic under discussion.

The author has worked in the field of labor for quite some years and has carried on certain original investigations the fruits of which may be seen occasionally in the chapters that follow. It will also be seen that he draws rather freely, but not too freely, upon the fields of comparative economic systems and the history of economic thought for pertinent data. Personal interests must be given at least a little consideration, even in such a book as this!

In addition to being indebted to the host of writers from whose works he has obtained material and inspiration, the author is also indebted to a number of his colleagues at Dartmouth. Professors Bell, Cusick, and Hines have read some of the chapters and have made useful suggestions; and the members of the library staff of The Amos Tuck School of Business Administration and of the reference department of Baker Library have also been of assistance. To them the author expresses his sincere thanks. At the same time, and after the fashion of the craft, he completely frees them from responsibility for any of the sins of omission or commission that may be found in the book.

CLYDE E. DANKERT

CONTENTS

Part I

EMPLOYMENT AND UNEMPLOYMENT

Part III

WAGES AND HOURS

FIGURES AND TABLES

FIGURES

TABLES

Part I

▼

EMPLOYMENT AND UNEMPLOYMENT

I

WORK—PAST AND PRESENT

It has always been necessary for man to work in order to survive. The no-work society has never existed; and there is no reason for expecting that it ever will exist, even in the imagination. Many changes have taken place, and will continue to take place, in the volume and the nature of the work man must perform, as well as in the conditions and arrangements under which he works. But the institution of work will always remain, and with it there will always be labor problems. A good point of departure for our present study of labor, therefore, will be a general analysis of work itself, an analysis that will point to many of the specific topics to be taken up in detail in the chapters that follow.

Why Work Is Necessary

The basic reason work is necessary is that man has wants that can be satisfied only by the expenditure of human effort. The amount of work that is necessary is dependent, at any given time, on the scope and the intensity of these wants and on the relative ease with which they can be met. Let us look into these two aspects of the question.

First there is the matter of human wants, viewed, for the moment, apart from their fulfilment. At the outset it should be noted that we are here considering only economic wants, wants that can be satisfied by commodities and services that possess exchange value. We are not taking into account such things as friendship, individual recognition, and freedom of speech; although, as we shall see later, some of these noneconomic wants have great significance in the subject we are studying. We must include leisure, however, in our present category of human wants, even though it is not sold in the market place like shoes and movies. The reason for this inclusion will become apparent as we proceed.

Man's wants are very extensive. It is true, of course, that his desire for a single good is definitely limited: in other words, the significance to a consumer, in terms of utility or satisfactions, of one unit of an article diminishes as the number of units increases. In fact the "marginal utility" might go to zero, or even below zero, and hence reflect a situation of complete satiation for the article. But man's desire for goods as a whole, including both commodities and services, is highly expansible—some would say indefinitely so. It is this magnitude of human wants that helps to make work an inescapable necessity and labor problems an unavoidable reality.

It is well to observe, however, that there are some persons to whom our generalization is only partially applicable. Thoreau, it may be recalled, had very limited wants. In fact, he taught that the way to achieve happiness was to minimize one's wants ("A man is rich in proportion to the number of things which he can let alone"), not maximize them as we are wont to do. Thoreau's contemporary, Agassiz, seemed to be of a similar turn of mind on this point. "I can't waste my time in earning money," that naturalist once asserted, or so Emerson tells us in his *Journal.*

The world, however, is not made up of persons like Thoreau and Agassiz. Most individuals are cast in a different mold, believing that men (especially themselves) are rich in proportion to the number of things they possess.

The great expansibility of human wants would not be such an important factor in the matter of work were it not for the difficulty that man experiences in trying to satisfy his wants. Most of the goods he desires do not come to him free of charge and in a form ready for immediate consumption, like fresh air and sunshine. If, for example, he wants bread, he must sow the seeds; cut, harvest, and mill the grain; and bake the flour. He, or someone else, must do all these things before his desire for bread is met. A similar expenditure of effort is needed before he can obtain the many other articles he wants to consume.

The difficulty of satisfying man's wants is further increased by the operation of that well known physical-economic principle, the law of diminishing returns. According to this principle, after a certain point is reached (and assuming no change in the methods of production) the application of labor to land and capital yields smaller and smaller returns per unit of labor used. Turning the principle around, it can be said that after a certain point more and more labor must be applied to the land and capital to yield the same sized unit of product. The point at which diminishing returns set in may be altered by improvements in the arts of production, but the principle itself cannot be done away with in this fashion. Diminishing returns, therefore, must to no small extent share the blame for the necessity of work, and for the creation of labor problems. Ordinarily we do not think of such issues as the closed shop, the union demand for social security legislation, and jurisdictional disputes as being tied up with the law of diminishing returns, but in actual truth they are.

Clearly, then, work is necessary. In a sense we are all engaged in forced labor; but this forced labor, it must be emphasized, is self-imposed. We undertake it voluntarily, for the purpose of keeping alive—which is no minor consideration! Behind the Iron Curtain there is another type of forced labor which, though it also may be connected with individual survival, is imposed by others. In our present discussion we shall not be able to deal at any length with the latter variety. Our concern will be with "voluntary" labor.

Other Reasons for Work

Our analysis so far has implied that work is merely a means to an end and never an end in itself. That is not always the case. Work is often a means *and* an end, not only yielding us funds to buy things we want but bringing us satisfactions in the process. When work assumes the second characteristic it partakes of the nature of play and is obviously of a highly desirable type. Since the whole question of work as an end is a fascinating one, a few additional observations must be made concerning it.[1]

Work has long been looked upon as essential not only to man's existence but to his excellence. Individual men may not always regard it in this light, but many of the sages of the past—poets, prophets, philosophers, and economists too—have proclaimed the noneconomic value of work. Browning advised us to "get work, get

[1] A historical account of the various attitudes toward work will be found in Adriano Tilgher, *Work (What It Has Meant Through the Ages)*. London: George G. Harap & Co., 1931.

work," but to be certain that the work we get is better than what we "work to get." The writer of Proverbs declares that "In all labor there is profit; but the talk of the lips tendeth only to penury." Thomas Burton looked upon idleness as an important cause of melancholy.[2] And Alfred Marshall, a most worthy economist, stated that work "is a necessity for the formation of character and, therefore, for progress." [3] In the light of these authoritative pronouncements (and many more could be added to the list), it would be rash indeed to deny the character-building attributes of work.

Not only does work contribute to the excellence or quality of man; it contributes also to his reputation. Certainly most people in the United States look with disfavor on persons who, though physically and mentally capable, have avoided work. The leisure class has never been popular in this country. In fact the United States is the only country in the world, Professor A. M. Schlesinger, Sr., tells us, [4] in which one is ashamed of not having anything to do. This statement sounds rather extreme, but it emphasizes our strong dislike of the loafer. Though we have never made work a legal necessity, as was done in the imaginary commonwealths of Sir Thomas More and other utopian writers, we have regarded work as something that everyone should experience. And the paradoxical thing is that while we have held this view we have never established work—in the form of a job—as a constitutional right.

Since work would seem to be necessary for the development of individual character and for social approval, it seems rather strange that we should exert so much effort and display so much technological ingenuity in an effort to escape from work. Instead of seeking freedom *in* work, as William Morris put it, we seek freedom *from* work. In this respect we differ from the backward Trobriand Islanders who, we are told, do a great deal of work for the sheer enjoyment of it, giving away three-quarters of what they produce.[5] We often tend to do the very opposite. We try to get as much as we can with

[2] These quotations, and much else relating to the question of work, will be found in Hugh Black, *Work*. Chicago: F. H. Revell Co., 1903.

[3] *Memorials of Alfred Marshall,* ed. by A. C. Pigou, p. 267. London: Macmillan & Co., 1925.

[4] *Paths to the Present,* p. 9. New York: The Macmillan Co., 1949.

[5] Adolf Lowe, *Economics and Sociology,* p. 51. London: George Allen & Unwin, Ltd., 1935. It is to be hoped that the Trobriand Islanders have not been induced, through modern progress, to give up their excellent custom.

as little work as possible, especially when the boss is not around. How can one explain this kind of behavior?

Part of the explanation is found in the fact that although work as an institution is of undisputed value, a great deal of work is valueless in the noneconomic sense—monotonous, enervating, sometimes dangerous. Such work does not yield any direct satisfactions; it is merely a means, a necessary evil. A nice problem, and one of concern both to the economist and the social philosopher, is the extent to which work under modern industrial conditions can be, and should be, made to serve as both an end and a means. Can the play element (defining *play* as an activity engaged in for its own sake) be introduced into work to any substantial degree? If so, what are the best means?

Systems of Work

From the standpoint of the legal status of the worker there are three main systems of work. These are slavery, serfdom, and freedom. The system of slavery has had a long and dishonorable career, dating back to the unrecorded period beyond the time of the ancient Sumerians. Slaves have been used, in times past, in most societies; [6] and slavery exists, in certain forms, in a number of countries today.

Under slavery the employer or master owns not only the product the worker turns out but the worker himself. The worker is a commodity or, better, a piece of property to which the employer has legal title; and the employer can sell him just like a horse or a bushel of wheat. The status of the worker is one of dependency and subserviency; he has duties but no rights.

Under slavery the economic lot of the worker may be very bad; his life, like that of the "state-less" people of Thomas Hobbes, may be poor, nasty, brutish, and short—and possibly solitary as well. But the worker need not necessarily live in this benighted fashion. If the master is benevolent, as many were in the southern states of this country during the period of slavery, his standard of living may be above the subsistence level.

The work of the slave may be of a very unskilled, manual char-

[6] A detailed discussion of slavery—primitive, ancient, medieval, and modern—will be found in *The Encyclopedia of the Social Sciences,* Vol. 14. New York: The Macmillan Co., 1934.

acter, but it need not necessarily be so. In ancient Greece, for example, many of the slaves were engaged in skilled occupations.[7] Furthermore, work done under the system of slavery is usually, though not invariably, inefficient.

The system of serfdom represents a partial freeing of the worker from bondage to the master. We ordinarily associate serfdom with the feudal period in Europe, though its application, both in place and time, has been more extensive. Under serfdom the worker generally had a certain amount of land on which he raised enough food to support himself and his family. The time not needed for this purpose was devoted to the service of the feudal lord. The serf could not leave the estate of the lord, and was often bartered with the estate. But the lord did not own him, as under the system of slavery.[8]

The system of freedom is marked by the absence of legal bonds tying the worker to the employer. The worker is free, *legally* free, to leave his employer, to change his occupation, to move to another town, to start his own store or factory. He does not belong to his employer, and his employer cannot sell him.

Today when we speak of a free worker we mean a person who has such legal rights. But we also apply the term in a more comprehensive fashion. We use it to describe a worker who has the right to join with others in forming a union and engaging in collective bargaining; who has the right to participate with others in a strike; who has the right to engage in political activities. The free worker of today possesses many rights.

The system of freedom must be viewed, however, in proper perspective. One should distinguish carefully between legal freedom and economic freedom. A worker may be legally free to leave his employer, but if the employer is the only one in the community or if jobs are scarce, this freedom may mean very little. Again, a worker may be legally free to move to a job in another town, but home ownership and the ties of family and friends may constitute formidable obstacles in the way. He may also be legally free to start a factory, one that makes, say, automobiles or steel rails, but this freedom is of no practical significance to him. Despite these limita-

[7] *The Cambridge Journal,* November, 1949.

[8] Maurice Dobb, *Wages,* p. 3. London: Nisbet & Co. Cambridge Economic Handbooks, 1928.

tions, however, the legal freedom under which we work today is a possession of incalculable value. It is one of the indispensable features of a democratic society and of our particular way of life.

The Environment of Work

With the exception of prison labor, work in the United States is done in an atmosphere of legal freedom. But work in this country is also done within a highly complex and varied institutional environment. In the following paragraphs we shall examine several particularly important parts of this work environment.

Legal-Economic Organization of Work. To begin with there is the legal-economic organization of work—or of economic activity, as work is more commonly described. Work is carried on under three different legal-economic arrangements. First, and by all odds the most important, is the arrangement known as private enterprise. Under this scheme the means of production—the tools and machines, the barns and factories—are privately owned. And these means, along with the labor that is associated with them, are used for the making of private profits.

Private gain is the prime motivating factor of the private enterprisers, though other considerations may, and frequently do, play a very significant role. In viewing the pursuit of private gain we ordinarily assume that such gain is not incompatible with the public good. Though we do not go as far as Adam Smith and the Physiocrats in our belief in the beneficent social results of individual self-seeking, nevertheless we subscribe as they did to the doctrine of economic harmonies. The only difference is that we, living in a very different world, recognize more numerous exceptions to the doctrine.

All private enterprise is not of the same character. It manifests itself in several forms: the single enterpriser, represented by the farmer and the village grocer; the partnership, illustrated by the legal firm of Green, Jones, Knight, Shaw and McDonald; and the corporation, for example General Motors.

A great deal of the work done in this country is carried out under the first two of these three forms. But it is the third form, the corporation, that is especially important to us. The circumstances under which corporation work is done differ greatly from the circumstances associated with the work under the other forms, as we shall see later; and these circumstances give rise to, or intensify, all sorts of labor problems.

The second legal-economic arrangement under which work is done in this country is known as governmental, or public, enterprise. Except under pure anarchism there is always some work to do for the government. The amount of government work has been increasing at a very rapid rate during recent years. The "agenda" of government, to use Bentham's term, has been increasing, while the "non-agenda" has been declining. To some extent the expansion of public activity has been due to a penetration by the government into fields formerly occupied by private enterpise; but to a much larger degree the expansion reflects the assumption by government of tasks that private agencies never perform at all, or perform on a very small scale.

It should be emphasized, however, that in this country very little of the work associated with the production of commodities and services is performed under governmental auspices. The workers in our automobile factories, steel mills, and stove foundries do not work for the government. They work for private enterprise. In this respect there is a vast difference between Russia and the United States. In Russia almost all enterprise is public enterprise or cooperative enterprise.

Cooperative enterprise, which is the third of the legal-economic arrangements in our list, is not highly developed in this country. To be sure there are numerous cooperative organizations, some of them quite sizable; but they do not bulk large in the over-all economy of the nation. In recent years, however, there has been considerable growth in the scope of cooperative activity.

Physical Environment of Work. Another aspect of the institutional environment of work is the physical surroundings under which the work is carried on. In the pioneer days in this country, most work was home work, done not in factories or stores, but in and around the home. Although agriculture was the chief occupation, people on the farms produced a variety of nonagricultural items: for example, furniture, clothing, and tools. At the time the United States became an independent nation about 90 per cent of the workers were engaged more or less in agricultural pursuits.[9] The

[9] Holland Thompson, *The Age of Invention,* pp. 24-25. New Haven: Yale University Press, 1921.

hours of work were often very long and the work itself was frequently strenuous; but there was a certain freedom and independence that gave the worker a sense of security, something the worker of today does not always possess.

As the years went by, agriculture, though it grew absolutely, became of less relative importance in the economic life of the nation. Manufacturing and commerce developed rapidly, and much of the nonagricultural work that had been performed on the farm was shifted to the factory and the store. This shift, which has been of outstanding economic and social significance, is still going on. In some cases it is being pushed to what might once have been considered very extreme lengths: farm wives now are even giving up the baking of bread!

As the amount of home work has declined over the years, the volume of work performed outside the home has increased. Factories have greatly grown in number and size; and a vast multitude of service establishments—stores, theatres, gasoline stations—has come into being. The result is that today work is performed in a physical environment very different from that of a century ago. And it is this environment that has created or rendered more serious many of our contemporary labor problems.

Technology and Work. The outstanding difference between work today and work in earlier times is the extent to which work is now mechanized. Hand methods have been superseded more and more by machine methods. The Industrial Revolution, which had its formal beginning in England during the latter part of the 18th century, and which still continues, has had phenomenal effects on the nature and results of work. *Manu*-facture has given way more and more to *machino*-facture, though the former term, despite its inappropriateness, continues in use.[10]

The development of machine industry has been closely linked

[10] *Manufacture,* which is derived from the Latin words *manus* and *facio,* means to make by hand. Thus a manufacturer, literally interpreted, is a person who makes things by hand. Adam Smith used the word in this fashion, and as late as 1819 the first American edition of Dr. Johnson's dictionary defined a manufacturer as "a workman, an artificer." For a brief and exploratory discussion of the effect of mechanization on the English language see the present author's article "Machinery and Words," in *The American Federationist,* August, 1939.

with the growth of power; in fact, the latter is an indispensable condition of the former. Man-power and animal-power, which for many centuries constituted the chief source of industrial energy, and which placed obvious limitations on the results of man's efforts, have been replaced to an increasing extent by other forms of power: steam, electric, gas. And now we seem to be on the verge of utilizing atomic energy to turn the wheels of industry. It is power,[11] along with the tools and machines to which the power has been applied, that has enabled man—"feeblest of bipeds," as Carlyle called him —to make granite mountains melt "into light dust before his eyes" and to achieve so many miracles of production.

To achieve by the old methods of production the amount of work we actually perform today would require a work force many times the size of the one we now have. Some years ago it was estimated that if the *Europa,* a large ship of the 1930's, had used the type of power that Eurybiades used at the battle of Salamis, it would have needed 3,000,000 sweep-pullers.[12] It is easy to see what a fantastically large work force we would need to do all the world's work by hand.

The technological advances in industry have encouraged the development of large factories. In the earlier years a great many factories, if not most of them, were dull and unattractive. They were often dirty and dangerous and unhealthy. To some extent these conditions still exist, but there has been a definite change for the better. More and more attention is being given to factory construction and design. It has been found that work carried on in attractive surroundings is likely to be of a very efficient nature. Aesthetics and economics are by no means mutually exclusive.

Cooperation and Conflict in Work

Cooperation in Work. Although in satisfying his economic wants man has generally found it expedient to cooperate with his fellows, the extent to which he has cooperated has varied greatly from time to time and from place to place. Cooperation in work involves a

[11] For a provocative discussion of the significance of nonhuman power in industry, see Fred Henderson, *The Economic Consequences of Power Production.* London: George Allen & Unwin, Ltd., 1931.

[12] *Fortune,* December, 1932, p. 25.

division of work; or, to use the more common term, a division of labor. In its simplest form the division of labor assumes the character of specialization in tasks, sometimes of a very minute nature. Thus, to use Adam Smith's famous pin illustration, one man may draw out the wire from which the pins are made, another man may straighten it, a third may cut it, and so on. Today there is an immense amount of task specialization, a much greater amount than existed in the days of the "father of political economy."

A second type of division of labor is that between trades, and between professions. This division is very common and it goes back to the early years of human history. In recent decades there has been an increasing amount of specialization *within* separate trades and professions. This is true of the building industry, for example. And in the medical field the "all-round" doctor has been replaced more and more by specialists. One doctor may concentrate on ailments of the bones, another on those of the skin, another on those of the nose. (According to rumor, specialization has been carried to the extent of concentration on individual nostrils.)

Work is divided not only on the basis of tasks and of trade or profession, but also according to product (furniture, bicycles, and shoes); according to stage of production (logging camps, sawmills, furniture factories, wholesale and retail outlets); and according to geographical area (Michigan with its automobiles, Pennsylvania with its steel).

Because work is carried on in a highly specialized fashion, it is highly cooperative. The individual workers—the individual "cooperators"—may not always be aware that they are engaged in a vast cooperative undertaking, but they are nevertheless. The great advantage of the cooperative method of production, of course, is that it leads to greater production.

Conflict in Work. The fact that most work today is of a cooperative character does not mean that it is always carried on in an atmosphere of harmony and good will. There is, unfortunately, a great deal of disharmony in work; and much of this, interestingly enough, stems from its cooperative nature.

When two or more persons work together in any economic undertaking, the question of what share each should get of the joint product invariably arises. Very often there is disagreement on this point.

This disagreement is frequently seen in the relations between labor and capital in modern industry. Both labor and capital are needed in the productive process, but how much should each receive for its contribution?

There is no completely satisfactory standard to use in making the decision. Even if we could measure accurately—in terms of marginal productivity, or economic worth—the contribution that each makes to the joint product, there is no reason for believing that we would have found the solution. Noneconomic factors, including ethical considerations, are involved in the question, and hence there is no final and absolute economic key to it. The fact that there are difficulties does not mean, of course, that there must be constant conflict between labor and capital, that work must always be carried on under conditions of friction and ill will. It does mean, however, that joint effort has within it the seeds of discord.

In addition to differences over the sharing of the joint product of industry there are also differences over the sharing of control. To an ever increasing extent the sole right of capital and management to govern industry is being called into question. Labor, through united action, is more and more asserting its right to participate in the governing process. The result is that many of the old prerogatives of the employer have been curbed. A bilateral type of industrial government has come to replace, over a wide area of our economic life, the old unilateral type. As we shall stress later, this development has been one of the most significant social changes of the last century.

The claim made by labor for a share in the control of industry has inevitably led to disagreements and to conflict. Here, too, there is no absolute solution, not even the complete replacement of private enterprise by public enterprise. However, it is ordinarily possible to prevent this disagreement from resulting in open conflict.

One of the most important and fascinating problems to the student of labor is that of formulating policies for reducing the area of conflict between workers and employers and for increasing the area of cooperation—of *conscious* cooperation—between them. Numerous techniques are already available and in use, but new techniques must be discovered and the old and effective ones must be more extensively adopted.

Monotony. One of the specific consequences of excessive division of work is monotony. Concentration on some narrow task—from which all the unnecessary "therbligs" have been firmly discarded—enables us to increase output, but it exposes us to a type of work activity that is likely to be repetitive, uninteresting, and monotonous.

That there is a great deal of monotony in work at the present time is a fact that cannot be denied. Two observations on the monotony issue should be made, however. In the first place, though the amount of monotony "per man-hour" in industry has probably increased over the years, the sum total of monotony has likely decreased. Owing to the extensive use of machinery and of the division-of-work principle, the worker now has leisure to engage in a variety of nonmonotonous activites. One authority, Bertrand Russell, is of the opinion that the amount of boredom in the world has been "enormously" decreased by the coming of the machine age.[16]

The fact still remains, though, that there is a great deal of monotonous work in industry. And this brings us to our second observation, namely that more attention should be given by management, and also by organized labor and the public at large, to the reduction of work monotony.

Some steps have already been taken to cope with the problem of monotony, and we shall pause briefly to note a few of them. A considerable number of employers have introduced music into their plants. This policy works best in a relatively quiet work environment. Moreover, careful thought must be given to the nature of the work and the nature of the music: they must harmonize. It is quite possible that certain musical types, such as boogie woogie, would have a devastating effect on some kinds of production.

An increasing amount of attention has also been given in recent years to color in industry. Some colors are more restful to the eyes than others, and a decrease in eye strain may reduce monotony. Even apart from the question of eye strain, a change of color combinations often makes the work place more attractive and interesting.

Monotony may also be reduced by the use of rest periods in industry. If a four-hour stretch of work can be broken up at half time by a ten- or fifteen-minute break, the worker can return to his job refreshed and in a happier frame of mind. The use of rest periods

16 *The Conquest of Happiness,* p. 58. New York: H. Liveright, 1930.

has become increasingly common in American industry, and has unquestionably been a factor in reducing monotony.

Finally, the proper placement of workers, a question we shall deal with at length in Chapter 3, can reduce monotony. When workers hold jobs for which they are not well fitted by temperament, training, or experience, they are likely to find their work monotonous and themselves unhappy. If, on the other hand, they find jobs suited to their nature and qualifications, they will experience much less monotony. Moreover, their output will be greater. Graham Wallas goes so far as to say that "an almost unimaginable increase of personal happiness, social contentment and economic efficiency" would follow if modern society systematically and effectively achieved a more complete relationship between the capacity of individuals and their work.[17]

Insecurity. Modern production methods have been a basic factor in unemployment. If work were of a nonspecialized, nonmechanized nature, there would be little involuntary idleness. Seasonal unemployment would be of small proportions because of the diversity of tasks undertaken by many of the workers. Technological unemployment would be of minor significance because of the slight changes in the methods of industry. Cyclical unemployment would be absent because the business cycle would not exist. Under such a system of work there would be some dislocations in employment, to be sure, but these would be produced largely by natural phenomena and wars.

The mechanization of industry and the extensive division of work have also led to an increase in the pace of work. No group has felt the impact of this change more than the older members of the labor force. That they have been the chief victims is clearly seen in the discrimination that is now practised against older workers in wide areas of American industry. It is true that age discrimination is due to a variety of factors. But the inability of many older workers to stand up under the strain of highly specialized operations performed at a high rate of speed is probably one of the most important of the factors.

Much of the discrimination against older workers is unwarranted, and there are jobs in which age (and experience) may be a

[17] Quoted by William A. Robson, *The Relation of Wealth to Welfare,* p. 100. New York: The Macmillan Co., 1925.

definite asset. But the fact remains that the advantages of age frequently do not weigh as much as the great advantage of youth, its ability to stand physical strain and its greater adjustability to changing methods and techniques.

Another way in which modern production methods have contributed to insecurity is through their effect on industrial accidents and industrial diseases—matters we shall investigate later on in our analysis.

Whatever the benefits of our highly developed methods of production may be, it remains true that such methods have often produced a great deal of individual economic insecurity. As Robert Lynd, the English essayist, put it, "By a curious paradox, machines at once marvelous instruments for producing wealth are equally marvelous instruments for producing poverty." [18]

The Advantages of the Modern Work Process

The advantages of modern production methods may be viewed in terms of the different ways in which we have "consumed" their benefits (or fruits). First, these benefits have been consumed partly in the form of higher material living standards. There has been a vast increase in the output of goods and hence in the material well-being of the populace. So great, indeed, has been this increase, and so great is the possibility of still further increases in output, that some people have declared that we have solved the problem of production.[19] Like the report of Mark Twain's demise, this seems a little exaggerated.

It is impossible to say precisely how much higher material living standards are today than they were fifty or a hundred years ago. It has been estimated that during the last century they have been raised three- or fourfold, and looking at the matter in a broad fashion this estimate is probably correct. Any such estimate must, however, fail to give due recognition to changes in the composition of living standards. One cannot compare, statistically, automobiles with buggies, nor electric lights with candles and oil lamps.

[18] *New Statesman and Nation,* February 25, 1933, p. 217.

[19] Back in 1886, before the day of the automobile, the radio, the refrigerator, and many other things, Richard T. Ely stated that "The problem of production is well on the way to solution. What now agitates the public is the problem of distribution." *The Labor Movement in America,* p. 77. New York: T. Y. Crowell & Co., 1886.

An interesting aspect of the change in living standards has been the shift in the meaning or content of the terms "luxuries" and "necessities." Things that at one time were regarded as in the luxury class are now looked upon as being necessary to a decent existence. Shoes, for example, were considered a luxury in Adam Smith's time in certain parts of Scotland; they are not so considered today. In this country automobiles were once a luxury, but they are not in that category any more.

It is sometimes said that modern production methods result in a poorer quality of goods. This is probably true in some instances, but, in general, machine-made goods are definitely superior to the hand-made variety. Often the alleged qualitative superiority of hand-made goods grows out of their scarcity value rather than their inherent characteristics.

The second form in which the benefits of modern production methods have been consumed is leisure. Over the years there has been a very marked decrease in the length of the work day and the work week—and, considering the rapid growth of paid vacations, the work year. During the first part of the last century the 12-hour day was quite common, and the 14-hour day was not unknown. Gradually, however, the number of working hours decreased. Today the average work day is only slightly more than half that of a century ago.

The unions claim, and quite correctly, a great deal of credit for this phenomenal reduction. Had it not been for constant union pressure on employers, and to some extent on the government, the decrease in the length of the work day and work week would have been much slower. The basic reason for the reduction in hours, however, has been improvements in the methods of industry. Technological progress rather than union pressure has been the fundamental cause of shorter hours.

Labor, and particularly organized labor, has ordinarily placed more emphasis on higher wages as an objective than on shorter hours, though these aims often go hand in hand. The general primacy of higher wages is suggested in the common triumvirate of union aims: "higher wages, shorter hours, and better conditions." According to an estimate made some years ago, the workers of the United States tended at that time to take from two-thirds to three-quarters of the gains in productivity in the form of higher material living standards, and from one-quarter to one-third in the form of an increase in leisure either for themselves or their families.[20]

The relative amount of emphasis placed on leisure, in contrast to wages, depends on a variety of factors: such things as the standard of living during the period in question, the nature of the work process, the kinds of leisure-time activities in existence, and the availability of facilities for enjoying these activities. There is some reason for believing that in the future, if international relations should become more amicable, the emphasis on leisure time will increase. In view of the frequent abuses of leisure, such a shift in emphasis is not without its disquieting features.

It should be noted that in many instances the union demand for shorter hours is an indirect effort to obtain higher wages. If the *standard* work day can be reduced, overtime rates become applicable at a lower level. Thus, without a change in the actual length of the work day, wages or earnings can be higher.

The benefits of the mechanized and specialized methods of production have been consumed, in the third place, in the form of a larger population. Emerson said, apropos of England, that "The steampipe has added to her population and wealth the equivalent of four or five Englands." [21] It was a somewhat similar point that John Stuart Mill had in mind when (in 1848) he made his frequently quoted, and generally misinterpreted, statement that "it is questionable if all the mechanical inventions yet made have lightened the day's toil of any human being. They have enabled a *greater population* to live the same life of drudgery and imprisonment, and an increased number of manufacturers and others to make fortunes." [22]

The number of people that any country can support depends

20 Paul Douglas, *The Theory of Wages,* pp. 313-314. New York: The Macmillan Co., 1934.

21 *English Traits,* new and rev. ed., p. 155. Boston: Houghton, Mifflin & Co., 1892.

22 *Principles of Political Economy,* p. 751. Ashley ed. London: Longman's Green & Co., 1926. Italics mine. The point referred to above, or at least one related to it, was made by James Bonar many years ago, but it has gone by unobserved. Bonar says Mill's statement is in reality "a protest against over-population." See James Bonar *Philosophy and Political Economy,* p. 257. London: George Allen and Unwin, Ltd., 1927. Professor J. E. LeRossignol has collected several misinterpretations of this passage, to which others could be added. See *The American Economic Review,* March, 1940, pp. 115-116.

on "the state of the industrial arts." As the arts of production improve a larger population is possible. It is clearly evident that the United States, for example, could not support a population of 160,000,000 people if we still used the production methods employed in colonial America.

In concluding our appraisal of modern industrial methods, it can be said that whatever the benefits of a simpler type of industrial society might be—and these benefits are not inconsequential—it is foolish to think of returning to such a condition. We cannot go back to any ideal "golden age" of the past. Rather we must work toward modifications in the present system, along lines that combine the ideal and the practicable.

2

THE WORK FORCE

The present book relates largely to a comprehensive analysis of the labor force in its manifold aspects. Though we started our study by examining the institution of work, our main concern is with those who do the work—not that work and the workers can be kept separate, of course. In this chapter we shall devote our attention to the labor force, using the term in its narrow, technical sense.

The labor force of the nation includes, in general, all persons above 14 years of age who are working for an income or who are desirous of working for an income (persons in jail or asylums who are gainfully employed are not included). The labor force includes, then, not only the employed but those of the unemployed who are able to work and desirous of work. It also includes the members of the armed services (though in statistics relating to the labor force these "workers" are very often shown in a separate category). Since part-time workers, such as students, are also included, the size of the labor force is exaggerated relative to the rest of the population.[1] Unfortunately it seems impossible to transform the statistics of part-time workers into full-time equivalents.

The Labor Force

The total labor force of the nation is divided into a number of broad categories. The changes in the numerical composition of these categories for a number of selected years can be seen in Table 1.

The labor force of the country has exhibited a continuous expansion. In war periods its growth has been particularly rapid. During such periods there is a marked shift of persons from the civilian

1 See C. D. Long's discussion in *Insights into Labor Issues,* ed. by Richard A. Lester and Joseph Shister, p. 335. New York: The Macmillan Co., 1948.

labor force into the armed labor force; and at the same time the civilian labor force attracts many persons who are not ordinarily interested in gainful employment. There is, in other words, a sharp increase in "labor force participation." The changes in the size of the labor force from year to year in normal times are due chiefly to population growth. To some extent, however, there may be variations in the participation of the population in gainful occupations. (A case in point, this time involving "exits," would be a lowering of retirement ages.)

Table 1

The Total Labor Force of the United States, According to Major Groupings *

(1000's)

Year	Total Labor Force	Armed Forces	Civilian Labor Force		
			Total	Employed	Unemployed
1950	64,599	1,500	63,099	59,957	3,142
1945	65,140	11,280	53,860	52,820	1,040
1940	56,030	390	55,640	47,520	8,120
1935	53,140	270	52,870	42,260	10,610
1930	50,080	260	49,820	45,480	4,340

* *Statistical Abstract of the United States,* 1952, p. 178. Bureau of the Census, United States Department of Commerce.

Between 1940 and 1950 the average annual increase in the nation's labor force was 790,000, representing an annual rate of growth of 1.4 per cent. Looking ahead to 1970 the rates of annual change, in five-year periods, will be approximately as follows: [2]

Years	*Annual Increase*	
	Number	*Percentage*
1950-1955	560,000	0.9%
1955-1960	680,000	1.0
1960-1965	920,000	1.3
1965-1970	780,000	1.1

The especially high birth rate during World War II accounts for the exceptionally large annual additions to the labor force during the period 1960 to 1965.

[2] See *Investment for Jobs,* p. 7. Bulletin, Chamber of Commerce of the United States, 1950.

The size of the labor force varies not only from year to year but monthly and even daily as well. For example, at the end of the school and college year there is a large shift of younger persons into the labor force, many of whom will be permanent members. Again, the labor force at any given time is made up in part of persons who do not want steady employment and who, as a consequence, are employed for only part of the year. Thus if the labor force for a given year is 60 million, it is possible that as many as 70 million different persons may have been in it at one time or another.[3] During cyclical slumps there is a tendency for the labor force to increase. The loss of his job by the breadwinner of the family (who would still be a member of the labor force though unemployed) may cause one or more members of the family who normally are not in the labor force to seek employment. The labor force also increases under the impact of war, when many persons (adolescents, married women, old people, "marginal" workers) are drawn into gainful employment who in normal times would not be interested in it. In 1945, to cite an illustrative year, there were about seven million "emergency workers" in the United States labor force.

If the influence of seasonality and of cyclical and war factors is excluded from one's calculations, it appears that the labor force remains highly stable over short periods. Allowance must be made, of course, for regular growth in the size of the force due to population increases.

Women in the Labor Force

One of the most notable changes that have taken place in the composition of the labor force is the growing importance of women workers. Over the years an increasing percentage of women have turned to gainful employment. At the same time the percentage that women workers form of the total labor force has shown a remarkable expansion. These two developments are clearly brought out in Table 2.

During major war periods there is a large increase in the number of women workers (see Table 2). In 1945 well over one-third of the total labor force was composed of women.

It is interesting to note that in Russia the percentage of women

[3] Writing in 1945 Professor Slichter used the figures 55 million and 65 million or more. See *Fortune,* October, 1945, p. 160.

in the labor force is much larger than in the United States. In 1947, for example, women constituted 47 per cent of the wage and salary earners of the Soviet Union [4]; in the same year women constituted slightly more than 25 per cent of the labor force in this country.

Table 2

Women Workers in the United States, in Selected Years *

Year	Number	Per Cent of All Workers	Per Cent of All Women of Working Age
1870 †	1,917,446	14.8	13.3
1900	5,114,461	18.1	20.4
1930	10,679,048	22.0	24.3
1940	13,840,000	25.4	27.4
1945	19,570,000	36.1	36.8
1952	18,798,000	30.4	32.7

* *Handbook of Facts on Women Workers,* Bulletin No. 225, p. 1; No. 242, p. 1. Women's Bureau, United States Department of Labor.

† Figures for 1870 cover workers 10 years of age and over. Other figures relate to workers 14 and over. Not all the entries in the table are strictly comparable, but they are satisfactory for showing the general trend.

The steady expansion in the number of women in the labor force of the United States has been due to various causes. Probably the most important has been the great changes that have taken place in industrial technology, changes that have transformed industry and have had profound effects on the composition of the nation's work force. Many occupations once performed in the home, by women, have been shifted to factories. This change in the *locus* of the work has brought with it a shift of women away from the home and into the factory.

The technological revolution has also given rise to a wide variety of jobs that are within the competency of women, even relatively untrained women. There are numerous factory jobs of an unskilled or semiskilled nature for which women are well fitted. Moreover, the technological revolution has led, indirectly, to a large increase in white-collar employment in industry: office staffs have been

[4] This figure is presented by Solomon M. Schwartz in the *Modern Review,* June, 1948, p. 285. In Russia the number of women in the medical profession exceeds the number of men. And women, apparently, have a monopoly on painting and plastering (see *The New York Times,* May 4, 1952).

greatly enlarged and many of the new employees have been women. A subordinate cause of the growth of office employment has been the increasing demand on the part of the government for reports of one kind or another. Another indirect effect of the technological revolution has been the great increase in selling jobs, especially in retail stores.

A second development is the great growth that has taken place in the service industries. As the nation has become more and more efficient in the production of material goods, it has shifted its interests—and its labor force—to an ever greater extent into the making of nonmaterial goods: that is, into the provision of services. In this way the field of women's work has been greatly expanded, since many of the jobs in the service industries are so clearly suited to the capabilities and talents of women.

The increase in the employment of women has not been due wholly to the increase in the number of jobs suitable for women. One other factor is the change that has occurred in the status of women in society. Women have been emancipated; they have won rights and privileges that at one time were denied to them completely, or granted to them meagerly and with reluctance. It would be misleading and unjust to say that women have won the privilege of working. That privilege, and duty, has long been theirs—man's bread, to no small extent, has long been provided by the sweat of woman's brow. But the propriety of women's working outside the home has now been widely granted, even for married women, although in times of depression some married women's rights to a paying job may be questioned.

Let us digress from our main theme for a moment to note the change that has taken place over the years in the labor force participation of married women. In 1900 there were 769,477 married women in the labor force, and they constituted 15 per cent of the total number of women 14 years of age and over in gainful employment. By 1930 the number of working married women had increased to 3,071,302, 29 per cent of the woman labor force; and by 1951 there were 10,182,000 married women working, representing 55 per cent of all working women.[5]

5 Statistical data from two publications of the Women's Bureau of the United States Department of Labor: Bulletin No. 218, *Women's Occupations Through Seven Decades* by Janet M. Hoaks, p. 39; Bulletin No. 242, *Handbook of Facts on Women Workers,* p. 17.

The acceptance of the idea that women have the right to engage in work outside the home would not have led to the large increase in the number of women workers had it not been for a very keen desire on the part of many women to engage in gainful employment. This desire has been a product of two factors.

Most women work because of economic necessity. This has always been true. The degree of necessity has probably increased, however, over the years. Living standards have gone up but so have desires: there are many things that people feel they *must* have. This seems to be especially true of women. Of greater significance, perhaps, is the insecurity that has accompanied the development of modern industry and the breakdown of the largely self-sufficient home.

Another factor that has induced women to get jobs outside the home is the desire for a more varied, more interesting manner of life. A considerable number of women join the labor force to escape the dullness and monotony of housework.

A final factor that helps to account for the increase of women in the labor force is the change in the relative number of women in the country's population. The 1950 census showed, for the first time, more females than males in the United States. This being the case, some women—more than in times past—must of necessity shift into the labor force rather than marry.

The extensive employment of women in modern business and industry has given rise to many problems of a legislative character. Numerous laws have been passed relating to the conditions under which women are to be employed; some of these we shall discuss in the chapters that follow. Women unionists in the United States are now numerous, although (as we shall see in Chapter 11) their influence in the labor movement is not in keeping with their numbers.

Child Labor

During the early period of industrialization there were enormous numbers of children working in factories, usually at jobs of a simple, repetitive type that children could easily perform. It has been stated that during the period from 1800 to 1860 probably 40 to 60 per cent of the factory workers in this country were children.[6]

[6] Harry J. Carmen, *Social and Economic History of the United States,* Vol. 2, p. 51. Boston: D. C. Heath & Co., 1934.

The large-scale employment of children, often under dangerous and unsanitary conditions, was one of the most serious evils of the Industrial Revolution both in England and in this country. Loud and eloquent protests were made against it. Elizabeth Browning, in *The Cry of the Children,* wrote feelingly of the young workers with "their pale and sunken faces." And in America Sarah Cleghorn, in a verse that has since become a classic, wrote of the little children looking out from the mill and seeing the men at play on the nearby golf links.

Chiefly as a result of the passing of regulatory legislation, the relative number of children in the nation's labor force has sharply declined over the years. The child labor problem has not been completely solved, however. According to a 1952 report of the National Child Labor Committee, many of the more than 2,000,000 children of school age who are working on either a full-time or a part-time basis are illegally employed, especially in agriculture.[7]

The first state to restrict the use of child labor was Pennsylvania, which in 1848 passed a law prohibiting textile mills from employing children under 12 years of age. Since that time great progress has been made in the legislative control of child labor. Today all states have laws placing limitations on the employment of young workers. As of June, 1950, twenty-three states specified a basic minimum hiring age of 16 years; the other states provided for a basic minimum of less than 16 years.[8] In addition the federal government, through its Fair Labor Standards Act, prohibits in plants engaged in interstate commerce the employment of anyone under 16. If the occupation is especially dangerous the limit is 18.

Older Workers

During recent years there has been a great deal of discussion concerning the position of older workers in modern industrial society. Older workers constitute a sizable portion of the nation's labor force, yet we seem to have great difficulty in using them to the best advantage. Let us try to see why this is so.

For one thing, the age structure of the population is undergoing a marked change. In 1860 persons aged 65 and over made up 2.7 per

7 *The New York Times,* November 27, 1952.

8 For most recent information at any time see latest *Social Work Yearbook,* under "Labor Standards."

cent of the population of the country; in 1900 the percentage was 4.1; in 1930, 5.4; and by 1950, 8.2. According to one estimate this percentage by 1970 will be slightly over 10, and during the three decades after 1970 it will rise to over 12 per cent.[9] This change in the age structure of the population has been due to several influences: the decline in the birth rate; the increase in the life span; and the drop in immigration and the consequent decline in large accretions of relatively young persons to the native-born population.

At the same time that the population has been aging there has been a notable decrease in the percentage of older persons in the labor force. Thus in 1940 less than 50 per cent of the male members of the population 65 years of age or over were gainfully employed. Fifty years earlier, in 1890, the percentage was over 70.[10] For women 65 and over the *rate* of decline was even greater. During the war period, from 1940 to 1947, a period characterized by high employment, there was a notable increase in the labor force participation of older workers, and the long-time trend was halted.[11]

The long-time trend in the number of older workers actually engaged in gainful employment has been due chiefly to the decrease in the number of employment opportunities open to older persons. This decrease has resulted largely from changes in the industrial pattern of the nation. The agricultural industry, in which older persons can generally find a niche, has become of less relative importance; and nonagricultural industries, in which older persons cannot as easily find employment, have increased in importance. Moreover, the growth of large establishments in industry and commerce has lowered the number of opportunities for self-employment, often the recourse of older persons in the past.[12]

The increasing mechanization of industry has been another factor that has helped to reduce the number of older persons in the work

[9] A number of estimates of future population changes have been made. The one above is from *Social Security in America*, p. 141, published by the Social Security Board in 1937.

[10] J. Frederic Dewhurst and Associates, *America's Needs and Resources*, p. 544. New York: The Twentieth Century Fund, 1947. There was no appreciable change, however, in the percentage of the work force composed of persons 65 and over. In both it was about 4 per cent. See John D. Durand, *The Labor Force in the United States, 1890-1960*, p. 41, New York: Social Science Research Council, 1948.

[11] See the *Monthly Labor Review*, October, 1951, p. 441.

[12] See Durand, *op. cit.*, p. 110.

force. The pace of work has been stepped up and the strain of effort increased, to the disadvantage of older workers.

This change in industrial methods helps to account for the discrimination against older workers. Other factors also contribute. Among these is a certain amount of unwarranted prejudice, based on ignorance of all the facts concerning the production capabilities of older workers. Whether the reasons are good or bad, age limits on hiring are common in industry. In many companies a job seeker is old at forty, or even at a lower age. For a great many persons trouble, rather than life, begins at forty.

Older persons also have difficulty very often in *retaining* employment—that is, if they reach certain age limits. It has become common for companies to establish compulsory retirement plans, and older persons may be squeezed out of the labor force, or at least out of employment, through the operation of these plans.

The decrease in the number of older workers in the labor force is due, in part, to voluntary action. Federal and private pension plans and state old-age assistance programs have induced some older persons to shift out of the labor force. In many cases the increase in individual financial resources has encouraged voluntary retirement, as has the wide variety of outlets for spending money.

In so far as older persons leave the labor force voluntarily—and the number of such persons should not be exaggerated—there is no great economic problem involved. The serious problem arises in connection with older persons who want to work but who, for one reason or another, cannot find employment. Here is a situation that needs correcting, both in the interest of individual well-being and in terms of the welfare of society as a whole. This situation is made the more serious because of the increase in the life span and the changing idea among the populace (but not among most employers) as to what constitutes old age. A nice problem for the student of labor is to figure out a program of action for making better use of our older workers.[13]

[13] Useful information on the problem of older workers will be found in *Employment and Economic Status of Older Men and Women,* Bulletin No. 1092, Bureau of Labor Statistics, United States Department of Labor, May, 1952.

Other Groups within the Labor Force

Foreign-born Workers. During recent years the number of foreign-born members in the United States labor force has been declining, both absolutely and relatively. This change reflects the drop in the number of foreign-born persons in the population at large: between 1920 and 1950 the foreign-born population as a percentage of the total population decreased from 7.8 per cent to 3.4 per cent. The decline in the number of foreign-born workers, due primarily to the restrictive immigration laws of the last few decades, has brought about greater homogeneity in the labor force, a development that has had considerable influence on the country's utilization of its workers and on labor-management relations.

Negro Workers. Negro workers constitute an important segment of the nation's labor force, and the likelihood is that during the years ahead the Negro labor force will increase in size and importance. The increase will be due to the continuing absence of large-scale immigration, which was made up predominantly of white people, and to the relatively rapid rate of population growth among the Negroes.

Negroes join the labor force at an earlier age than whites do, and Negro women tend to stay in the labor force longer than white women. A serious problem that has faced Negro workers in general has been the existence of employment discrimination against them, an abuse practised by both employers and unions. By 1953 twelve states had passed laws setting up Fair Employment Practice Commissions and barring discriminatory practices against Negroes and other minority groups. Nine of these laws are compulsory, three voluntary. A number of attempts were made in the early 1950's to place a federal compulsory FEPC law on the statute books, but without success.

Union Workers. Unionized workers have become increasingly numerous in the nation's labor force over the years, particularly from the middle 1930's on. At present unionists constitute approximately 25 per cent of the labor force, and about 33 per cent of the organizable workers. More will be said about the growth of organized labor in later chapters. Here we want to note merely that this growth has taken place and that it involves a change in the composition of the nation's labor force that is of great significance.

Industrial Distribution of the Labor Force

The industrial distribution of the labor force has exhibited numerous changes during the last century. Many old industries have disappeared or declined greatly in importance. Many entirely new ones have come into existence, and some of the old ones have grown rapidly. In this brief survey it will not be possible for us to trace in statistical terms the life history of all these industries. Instead we shall devote our attention to the three major *groups* of industries: manufacturing, agriculture, and service.

Manufacturing. In the early stages of the country's history manufacturing industry was relatively unimportant. Agriculture was the chief pursuit of the people, and many of the things that were later made in factories were produced in the home. As time went on, however, manufacturing developed, and the number of workers engaged in manufacturing activity rapidly increased (see Table 3).

Table 3

Workers Engaged in Manufacturing Pursuits *

Year	Number †	Per Cent of Gainful Workers	Per Cent of Population
1820	350,000	12.2	3.6
1860	1,930,000	18.3	6.2
1900	6,250,000	21.5	8.2
1910	8,250,000	22.5	9.0
1920	10,890,000	26.2	10.3
1930	10,990,000	22.5	9.0
1940	11,940,000	22.4	9.1
1950	14,370,000	22.2	9.5

* *Historical Statistics of the United States, 1789-1945,* pp. 25, 64; *Statistical Abstract of the United States,* 1952, pp. 10, 178, 747; Bureau of the Census, United States Department of Commerce. Percentage calculations by author.

† 1820 and 1860 figures include "construction."

The especially rapid growth in manufacturing industry during the 19th century reflects the expansion in population, the shift of work from the home to factories, and the increase in the living standards of the people—expressed not so much in terms of more food as in terms of more manufactured articles. Between 1900 and

1920 (remember that these dates must not be looked upon as marking exactly the time of changes in developments) manufacturing employment continued its growth; but since 1920 it has remained remarkably stable. Because of defense activity the figure for 1950 should be "deflated" a little to show the normal trend. In view of the great increase that has taken place in the output of manufactured goods since 1920, and in view also of the increase in population, the relative stability of manufacturing employment during the last three decades may appear strange. One must keep in mind, however, that during these years many labor-saving improvements were made in manufacturing industries.

Agriculture. One of the most notable changes in the labor force of the nation has been the reduction in the relative number of workers engaged in agriculture. In recent decades there has been not only a relative decline in numbers but an absolute decline as well (see Table 4). It will be seen that in 1820 more than 70 per cent of the persons in gainful work were found in the agricultural industry. By 1950 the percentage had fallen to less than 15. The absolute number of persons in the industry, it will be noted, was smaller in 1950 than in 1900. In future years the figures, both absolutely and relatively, are likely to decline still further, as the estimates in the table show.

Table 4

Workers in Agricultural Pursuits *

Year	Number (in 000's)	Per Cent of Labor Force
1820	2,069	71.8
1860	6,208	58.9
1900	10,912	37.5
1920	11,449	27.0
1940	9,162	17.6
1950	9,320	14.7
1960 est	7,785	10.9
1970 est.	5,850	7.1

* Figures for 1820 to 1940 are from the *Historical Statistics of the United States, 1789-1945,* p. 63. Bureau of the Census, United States Department of Commerce. Figures for 1950 to 1970 are from *Manpower, Chemistry and Agriculture,* p. 9, Senate Report, Document 103, 82nd Cong., 2nd Sess. The figures before 1940 are not exactly comparable with those for the previous years, nor are the figures for 1950 to 1970 exactly comparable with the preceding ones.

The drop in agricultural employment over the years has been due to two basic sets of influences. First, vast improvements have been made in the methods of farming, including such diverse things as contour plowing, modern mechanized equipment, and the extensive use of chemical fertilizers. As a result of these changes there has been a great saving in the amount of manpower (and especially of animal power) needed on farms.

The second influence has been the relatively inelastic nature of the demand for agricultural products. Consumers do not show any large response, in the form of increased purchases, to lower agricultural prices; or, to state this idea in a form that is more pertinent in this age of agricultural price supports, as people's income increases they do not expand their purchases of agricultural products to any marked extent. The reason for the inelasticity of the demand for the chief agricultural product, food, was given classic expression by Adam Smith many years ago. "The desire for food," said Smith, "is limited in every man by the narrow capacity of the human stomach, but the desire of the conveniences and ornaments of building, dress, equipage, and household furniture, seems to have no limit or certain boundary."

Service Industries. Employees in the manufacturing and agricultural industries are engaged in the production of "form" utilities—a type of effort some of the earlier economists thought to include all productive activity. A great many employees in modern industrial societies, however, are engaged in creating other types of utilities: place, possession, time, and service utilities. The number of such employees, considered collectively, has been increasing in both absolute and relative terms during recent decades. Table 5 shows the numerical changes that have taken place in some of the more important of these groups. It will be observed that in the thirty-year period covered by the table the increase in employment in the trade, service, and governmental categories was more than 100 per cent. This rate of growth was much larger than the rate of growth of the country's population or that of the labor force over the same period. The increase in the number of persons in service categories reflects the expansion of our "market economy"; the greater and greater prominence of nonmaterial goods in the consumption pattern of consumers; and the further development of the "positive state."

Table 5

Employees in Service Occupations *
(in 000's)

Year	Trade	Finance	Service	Government
1920	4,623	1,110	2,142	2,603
1930	6,064	1,398	3,084	3,149
1940	6,940	1,419	3,477	4,192
1950	9,524	1,812	4,761	5,910

* *Statistical Abstract of the United States,* 1952, p. 182. Bureau of the Census, United States Department of Commerce. The figures in the table do not include proprietors, self-employed persons, and domestic servants. For 1940 and 1950 "Service" includes automotive repair work, which was formerly under "Trade."

The statistics presented in the preceding pages bear out the idea that in economically progressive societies such as the United States there are three stages of production. In the primary stage agricultural pursuits are of the utmost importance, giving employment to a large percentage of the people. In the secondary stage agriculture experiences a decline in relative importance and manufacturing industries grow rapidly. In the tertiary stage service industries and employments come into prominence and goods of the comfort and luxury classes become increasingly common. The pattern of production thus undergoes a number of large-scale changes as well as innumerable small ones. These changes necessitate many shifts in the distribution of labor, shifts that are not always easy to achieve.[14]

The Short-Run Supply of Labor

In discussing variations in the supply of labor in the present section we shall limit ourselves very largely to one causal factor, namely changes in the price of labor. We shall have a little to say about certain nonpecuniary factors, such as patriotism, and their influence on labor supply; but our chief problem is to try to determine the relationship between wage rates in the labor market and the amount of labor offered for sale. In other words we are concerned with the slope of the supply curve for labor.

[14] The general theme touched on in the above paragraph is discussed at length in Allan G. B. Fisher, *The Clash of Progress and Security.* London: Macmillan & Co., 1935.

This problem must be looked at from two different points of view, depending upon the length of the time period involved. These are the traditional short-run approach, which is basically static in nature, and the long-run approach.

The short-run point of view does not inquire into the possible effect of higher wages on population growth; that is a province of the long-run discussion. Our short-run analysis will take the present population as a datum and inquire into the effect of higher wages on the number of persons who work or want work.

Instead of speaking of labor supply in terms of workers we shall speak of it in terms of man-hours. Obviously the number of man-hours offered for sale in the market is based largely on the number of workers; but there can easily be an increase or decrease in the number of man-hours without any change in the number of workers. The man-hour approach, therefore, is more comprehensive, and also more meaningful, than the worker approach. One might go farther and think of labor supply not simply in terms of man-hours but in terms of the intensity and efficiency with which the man-hours are worked. Such an approach, however, would introduce into our discussion elements that are extremely difficult to measure, and that for our present purpose need not be taken into account.

The specific questions before us, then, are these: What relationship is there between the wage rates paid per hour (assuming the cost of living to remain unchanged) and the number of man-hours of work offered in the labor market? Will more man-hours be offered, per week, if wage rates are higher than if they are lower? In brief, does the short-run supply curve for labor look like the short-run supply curve for a commodity—sloping upward to the right? If so, what degree of slope does it possess? (It should be added at this point, though the matter will be dealt with at length in Chapter 4, that there are in reality many separate labor "supplies." Here we are dealing with the very useful, but still somewhat metaphysical, concept of an aggregate supply.)

These questions cannot be easily answered. Higher money wages induce some persons to work who, at lower wages, prefer to be idle. Moreover, higher wages per hour make some workers who are already in the labor force willing to work longer hours. In both of these instances leisure is sacrificed for higher pay. If these were the only two types of reactions to a higher hourly wage, we could say that the supply curve of labor had a positive slope. But there are other reactions.

In some cases higher wages induce workers to drop out of the labor force. Consider a family with a number of wage earners, all of whom had to work at the lower wage levels to provide the standard of living that the family wants to have. Now, at higher rates, one or more of the members might stop working, the others being able to earn enough to meet the desires of the family. In some cases higher wages per hour might induce the worker to work fewer hours. Obviously he could not offer only seven hours of work a day when the standard work day in his place of employment is eight. But he could achieve his objective by absenting himself from his work with greater frequency and for longer periods (there is good reason for believing that the high absentee rate in industry during World War II was in part a result of the high wage rates). If these latter two types of reaction were the only ones, the supply curve of labor would have a negative slope—like the slope of an ordinary demand curve.

The problem we are faced with, then, relates not to individual situations but to the over-all conditions, not to individual supply curves of labor but to the aggregate supply curve.

The slope of the aggregate supply curve is not uniform throughout its whole length. It varies from one wage level to another. At lower wage levels it *may* be somewhat negative, sloping downward to the right. This was the view held by some of the Mercantilist writers and by others, [15] and given classic and extreme expression by Arthur Young. "Everyone but an idiot," said Young, "knows that the lower classes must be kept poor or they will never be industrious—they must be in poverty or they will not work." Without advocating poverty as an incentive to work, one can still say that (if living standards are low) more man-hours of work may be offered at lower wages than at higher wages. The fact must be recognized, however, that the intermediate and the long-run effect of very low wages may decrease both the absolute number of workers and the number who are able to work.

In the medium wage range the slope of the supply curve would seem to be close to a vertical position. Whereas higher wages would

[15] For a discussion of the views of the Mercantilists and others see Paul H. Douglas, *The Theory of Wages*, pp. 270-272. New York: The Macmillan Co., 1934. See also footnote 5 in Chapter 21 of the present book.

induce some workers to offer more man-hours of work and possibly encourage some persons to enter the labor force, they would also induce some workers to offer fewer hours and possibly impel some persons to drop out of the labor force. One cannot be too sure of the over-all situation, but it appears that variations in wage rates have little effect in the middle range of wages upon the aggregate number of man-hours offered.

In the upper range of wages the supply curve becomes either completely vertical or slopes back to the left. After a certain point is reached no more persons can be drawn into the labor force no matter how high the wages are. This is due to the fact that all possible workers are in the labor force; and these workers cannot work more than so many hours a week (168 hours at the most, and this for not more than a week!). Moreover, the points made previously about some persons dropping out of the labor force and an increase in absenteeism are especially applicable here. The probability, then, is that the supply curve assumes a negative slope, indicating that higher wages per hour eventually called forth *fewer* hours.

We do not know at what point the aggregate supply curve (under given conditions) assumes this backward slope; but we can make a few observations on the factors that influence the thinking and behavior of the individual worker, and that in turn affect this curve. These factors are: (a) the nature of the work; (b) the number of dependents the worker has; (c) the material living standards he desires for his dependents and for himself; (d) the nature of the worker—his physical and psychological make-up—and his general attitude toward work and leisure; (e) the size of his outside income, if he has any. Because of the different patterns produced by these factors, there are marked differences in both degree and direction in the man-hour response of individual workers to higher wage rates.

A word of caution should be uttered at this point concerning our experience during World War II in the matter of labor supply. During the war wage rates increased (we shall include here the element of overtime pay) and the number of persons in the labor force and the number of man-hours worked greatly increased. Although these facts might be taken as proof that the supply curve of labor has a positive slope, such a conclusion does not follow. The patriotic motive could well account for much of the increase in the number of workers and man-hours. The fact that many women, with their husbands in the armed service, were freed from part of their household obligations could also have had some effect. Another extraneous factor that could have been of influence was the increase in the cost of living (in thinking about the short-run supply curve of labor, however, we must assume this to be constant).

Finally, there is the so-called "additional worker" theory, which in recent years has received a considerable amount of attention from students of the labor market.[16] W. S. Woytinsky, perhaps the outstanding champion of the idea, has applied it especially to depression periods. By "additional worker" Woytinsky means "the person who is in the labor market because of the unemployment of the usual bread winner in his family and who otherwise would not be seeking work" (Father Jones loses his job, so Daughter Jones, who had been helping Mother Jones around home and who was not interested in outside employment, decides to seek a job). Thus, says Woytinsky, during depressions the number of persons seeking jobs tends to outrun the number of persons who have lost their jobs. During recovery, additional workers are likely to withdraw from the labor market as the regular workers again get jobs. The consensus among economists who have carefully studied the additional worker thesis is that it lacks positive proof.

On the whole question of the *exact* nature of the short-run supply of labor we seem to be in a state of profound uncertainty; [17] it is to be hoped that studies now going on in the field will help to improve this situation.

The Long-Run Supply of Labor

The long-run supply of labor (in aggregative terms) may be looked at from a number of angles, the most common being the relationship between wages and population. Do higher real wages lead to larger families and hence to a larger population?

16 The following references may be advantageously consulted: (1) C. D. Long's observations on pp. 344-349 of *Insights into Labor Issues,* ed. by Richard A. Lester and Joseph Shister. New York: The Macmillan Co., 1948. (2) Durand, *op. cit.,* pp. 86-105. (3) *Industrial and Labor Relations Review,* July, 1950, article by Herbert G. Heneman.

17 Durand believes that "the *a priori* arguments and the fragmentary data" on "the effects of peacetime fluctuations in employment and income upon the size or composition of the labor force" are "inconclusive and controversial." *Op. cit.,* p. 104.

Thomas Robert Malthus, whose name is inseparably connected with discussions of population problems, gave an affirmative answer to this question. According to the Malthusian principle of population, first set forth during the latter part of the eighteenth century, population tends to increase up to the limits set by the means of subsistence. It cannot go beyond this point because of the operation of two sets of checks: positive checks, which increase the death rate; and preventive checks, which decrease the birth rate. Malthus believed that the potential rate of population growth was much greater than the potential rate of subsistence (food) growth. To illustrate the difference in rates of growth he expressed the former in terms of a geometrical ratio (1, 2, 4, 8) and the latter in terms of an arithmetical ratio (1, 2, 3, 4). Were it not for the postponement of marriage and the exercise of "moral restraint" (the preventive checks), and the occurrence of wars, pestilences, and famines (the positive checks), population would grow at a very rapid rate. But these checks hold it back, to within the walls of subsistence. Population growth is always rapid enough, according to Malthus, to cause many people to be at or near mere subsistence.

With respect to the United States and to most other industrialized nations the Malthusian principle is today either not applicable at all or applicable to only a limited degree. There are some married couples, to be sure, who will have one or more extra children if the family income increases, and there are couples that will postpone marriage and the begetting of children until the husband-to-be is earning a certain income. On the other hand there are many couples who prefer higher material living standards to larger families. The net result seems to be that while higher incomes have led to some increase in population size, the rate of population growth has not, on the whole, been so rapid as to pull the standard of living down to the subsistence level.

Since higher real wages have over the years led to some increase in population size, they have probably also led to some increase in the size of the labor force. But the increase in the latter has not been so large as the increase in the former, owing to the effect of higher wages on labor force participation. Younger persons are now staying in school longer, partly as a result of the higher incomes received by the heads of families. Older workers are voluntarily retiring earlier—in many cases they are being forced to retire earlier—than formerly; many retirements are influenced in part by higher incomes. Of the effect of higher incomes on the labor force propensity of women, one cannot be at all certain.

On the whole, it would seem that the degree of labor force participation has declined with the raising of real incomes. The actual size of the labor force has not shrunk as a consequence, since, as we have already noted, population has increased somewhat as a result of higher incomes. Looking at the matter from a long-run point of view, it would seem that the supply curve of labor, in terms of number of persons, and taking into account both population changes and changes in labor force participation, has a positive slope. But much research work remains to be done in connection with this matter.[18]

Again it should be emphasized that we are here dealing with only one causal factor producing changes in population and in labor force participation, namely increases in real wages. In actual practice there are various other influences in operation: such things as company retirement policies; changing public and private attitudes concerning the employment of women, children, and older persons; and technological changes, especially with reference to home work.

The *actual* percentage of labor force participation (reflecting the operation of all causal influences) increased from about 35 per cent to more than 40 per cent between 1890 and 1940, and rose during World War II to 46 per cent. It has been estimated that in 1960 it will be about 41 per cent. It would be beyond the compass of this work to discuss all the factors that have had, and will have, a bearing on these changes.

We must now consider the long-run labor supply in terms of man-hours. Here we must take into account the effect of changes in real wages both on population growth and on the length of the work day, or work week. (In reality, it would be better to think in terms of the length of the work year or, still better, in terms of the length of the work life.) It is clear that as the productivity of industry has increased, the benefits of this increase have to no small extent been consumed in the form of shorter hours. If one takes into

[18] The question of higher incomes and labor force participation is discussed briefly by Durand, *op. cit.*, pp. 107-109. The general problem of labor force participation receives extended treatment in Durand's book.

account the decrease in the length of the normal work week, the widespread existence of vacations with pay, and the later entry into and earlier departure from the labor force on the part of the members of the population, it would seem that the long-run supply of labor, in terms of man-hours, has not been greatly altered during recent decades. This conclusion seems to hold despite the increase in population and number of workers.

There is one final point to be noted. Some nations have taken positive action in connection with population matters, usually with a view to increasing the size of the labor force or the military force. Family allowance plans may be adopted with one or more of these objects in view; special taxes may be placed on bachelors, as is done in Russia; liberal immigration policies may be employed, as in Australia.

3

THE PLACEMENT, DISTRIBUTION, AND ALLOCATION OF LABOR

From the standpoint of both individual and social well-being it is desirable that the unemployed members of the nation's labor force be brought into contact with job openings as rapidly as possible; that the members of the labor force in general be placed in the jobs for which they are best fitted (and also that they be trained for those jobs); and, finally, that the jobs into which the members of the labor force move be those that contribute most to human welfare. These three conditions are all indispensable to the achievement of a good economic society, and they all may be looked upon as important topics in the study of labor.

In the present discussion we shall give attention to all three of the *desiderata,* concentrating on the first one in the list. It has the clearest labor "imprint" on it, and for this reason merits more attention than the other two.

Labor Mobility and Obstacles in the Way

The question of bringing workers and jobs together with as little delay as possible leads us to a study of what is commonly called "the organization of the labor market." This expression has nothing to do with unionism, except in one or two ways that we shall take up shortly, and does not relate to the organization of labor. The organization of the *market* for labor (in reality there are many labor markets) is a very different matter.

In general terms the organization of the labor market involves the establishment of means whereby workers seeking jobs and employers seeking workers may be brought into rapid contact with each other. As we shall soon see, it involves other aims too; but the paramount one is getting workers jobs, and getting employers workers.

If the labor market is to be well organized the workers must possess some degree of mobility: since the jobs do not come to the workers, the workers must go to the jobs. The workers must also be fitted for the jobs, or be willing to get fitted for them, since the jobs ordinarily are not adjusted to the particular qualifications of the workers. Two kinds of labor mobility, then, are required: geographical and occupational.

Geographical mobility relates to the willingness and ability of workers to move to new job locations. These locations may be no farther away than a block or two; or they may be in a different part of the city, a different part of the state, or a different part of the country. Geographical mobility is generally of a short-run nature: if a worker is able and willing to move, he can usually do so quickly.

Occupational mobility has to do with the willingness and ability of workers to change occupations. Sometimes a change can be made easily and with rapidity, as when a worker moves down the occupational scale. But horizontal, and particularly upward, occupational mobility may take time, involving as it does the acquisition of new skills or qualifications.

The organization of the labor market relates principally to the matter of geographical mobility, as we have defined it. It is highly desirable that such mobility be of the proper amount; it must not be either excessive or inadequate. In the words of Beveridge, what we want is "not simply the fluidity of labor, but the organized and intelligent fluidity of labor." [1] Such a fluidity is not easy to achieve; there are certain obstacles in the way, obstacles which we shall now examine.

To begin with, it is obvious that workers cannot always move easily to new job locations. Adam Smith truthfully stated, many years ago, that man is "of all sorts of luggage the most difficult to be transported." A person without a job may be very reluctant to go to another town ten, twenty, or a hundred miles away for employment. Such a shift often means that he will have to sell his home, move his furniture, and leave many of his friends and rela-

[1] *Unemployment, a Problem of Industry,* 1930 ed., p. 209. London: Longmans, Green & Co., 1931.

tives behind. Under these circumstances he may prefer to remain idle, hoping that "something will turn up" shortly.

This particular obstacle is a formidable one, and society cannot do much to remove it. It should be pointed out, however, that American workers have perhaps been more willing to move than workers in other countries. Succeeding censuses of the United States have shown a very sizable interstate shifting of population. In 1950, for example, 25.2 per cent of the native population was born outside the state of residence. In 1930 this percentage was 23.4; and in 1900 it was 20.6.[2] These figures do not show the intrastate shifting of population, which has also been large. Although it is clear that many people in this country are not opposed to moving, the fact remains that many people are inclined to stay where they are.

Another obstacle in the way of labor mobility is the lack of knowledge a worker may have concerning employment opportunities. There may be an opening very close at hand that he knows nothing about. This is doubly unfortunate: the employer has an unfilled job and the worker an unsatisfied desire for a job. This obstacle can cause economic and social loss, but fortunately it is quite possible for society to remove it or at least diminish its proportions.

A further obstacle to labor mobility grows out of certain union practices. For example, high initiation fees, jurisdictional rules, and union shop arrangements may discourage workers from moving into certain areas, also into certain occupations. A system of employment offices cannot do much to remove such obstacles. Legislation like the Taft-Hartley Act (with provisions that exercise control over just such union practices) may have some effect, however. Moreover, in periods of full employment the impact of such restrictions is lessened.

Unemployment compensation may also act to hinder labor mobility, even though under our unemployment insurance laws workers out of jobs are supposed either to accept "suitable" employment when it is offered or to forego benefits. Some workers prefer to live off their benefits, even though the money is just a fraction of what their regular pay would be, rather than search for new jobs. Our

[2] *1950 United States Census of Population,* Special Report P-E No. 4A, p. 4A-11. Bureau of the Census, United States Department of Commerce.

public employment offices, however, do much to prevent this type of immobility.

State old-age assistance plans, with their residence rules, also tend to discourage mobility. An older worker might be unwilling to risk taking an uncertain job in another state for fear of losing his right to old-age assistance should he become unemployed.

Private pension schemes that do not carry transferable rights—that is, which do not provide for "vesting"—also constitute an obstacle in the way of labor mobility. A worker temporarily unemployed may be strongly disinclined to move if his transference to another company means a loss of his pension credits. This particular obstacle to mobility applies to the employed worker as well. Its significance with respect to employed workers should not be exaggerated, however, since older workers, who may have large pension credits, do not ordinarily desire to change jobs as much as younger workers with small pension credits.

What has just been said concerning the possible effects of old-age assistance and private pensions on labor mobility does not apply to the Federal Old-Age and Survivors' Insurance program. Workers under OASI carry their rights with them when they shift from employer to employer and from state to state.

So far we have concentrated on obstacles to labor mobility, particularly to geographical labor mobility. Let us now examine the factors which, at least in the United States, increase the amount of geographical and occupational mobility that is necessary.

Seasonal changes in industrial activity, which are very common in this country, call for a high degree of mobility. Sometimes workers shift hundreds of miles—even from Puerto Rico to Michigan, to help with the strawberry crop—to meet seasonal labor requirements. Mobility of this sort, unless carefully controlled, can be very wasteful.

Again, geographical shifts in industry may call for a considerable amount of labor mobility. These shifts may or may not be to areas where labor is plentiful. Companies that locate in other areas may want all or some of their workers to go with them.

Technological improvements necessitate a considerable degree of labor mobility, both geographical and occupational. Especially if the monetary gains from these improvements are retained as profits or dispersed in the form of higher wages, the employment opportunities that will result from the spending of the gains will be diffused in terms of place and also of industry. Hence it follows that in a dynamic economy in which technological improvements are constantly being made, a high degree of price inflexibility (which may result from enterprise monopoly and strong unionism) makes it essential that labor possess no small amount of mobility.[3]

Many developments in recent decades have increased the geographical mobility of labor. The expansion of the automobile industry and the increase in the number of commuter trains may be cited as examples. Television, on the other hand, has decreased, on a small scale, the amount of mobility necessary to its performers (they do not need to shift around as much as formerly to earn a living). Most work, however, cannot be done in this "absentia" manner.

Private Employment Institutions and Techniques

The bringing of jobs and workers together is a highly important function in society; various agencies, private and public, contribute toward its performance.

Types of Private Agencies. In dealing with private agencies we shall examine not only organizations that aid in bringing jobs and workers together but also the employers themselves and the means they use. We shall begin with the latter.

(1) Large numbers of workers are hired directly by employers, with no intermediary agency assisting in the process. Direct hiring is done in a number of ways. The simplest method is for the employer to make his selections from the workers who apply for jobs "at the gate." Or the employer may run advertisements in newspapers and magazines, indicating that he has certain jobs open. Workers may also use the advertising method to inform interested employers that they are seeking jobs. Or the employer may learn of available workers through his employees; just as workers may learn of job openings through their friends.

Direct hiring carried on by these methods may be done in a rather haphazard way. On the other hand, it may be accompanied by elaborate hiring procedures—the employer may have a specialized

3 This point is discussed at greater length in an article by the author on "Labor Immobility and Technological Unemployment," in *Social Forces,* March, 1941.

employment office that "processes" the candidates for jobs. If the employment office has detailed job specifications showing the qualities in the worker that the various jobs require, it may question the worker, and possibly subject him to certain tests, to find out the particular qualities he possesses. Use of these techniques often results in a better adjustment between jobs and workers.

The method of direct hiring has its advantages, but it has at least two serious disadvantages. First, it does not give the employer a large market from which to select his workers; nor does it give the workers a large market in which to sell their services. The result is that employers may not obtain the best workers that are available, and workers may not obtain the best jobs that are open. In the second place, hiring of this sort tends to result in the establishment of separate labor reserves or labor "pools." The formation of labor pools may not represent a serious loss to the individual employer, but it definitely involves a serious loss to society. Scattered and decentralized labor reserves are wasteful in the same way that scattered and decentralized banking reserves are wasteful. They lead to an excessively large *aggregate* reserve, in this case to an excessively large number of idle workers.

(2) Various private organizations help to bring jobs and workers together. Colleges and universities often have employment bureaus. YMCA's and YWCA's may also have employment divisions. Fraternal groups and other organizations may also function as placement agencies. These bodies do not charge fees for their work, and within the limits in which they operate they may render a very valuable service.

(3) Unions may aid in the placement of workers if the workers are, or are about to become, union members. Where the closed shop exists—that is, where a worker must be a union member before he begins a job—the union is almost of necessity required to act as an employment agency. If the employer can hire none but union men, he must resort to the union for help. In the building trades, where the closed shop has been widely adopted, unions commonly act as employment agencies.

In some of the maritime trades the so-called hiring halls figure prominently. These halls may be under the direct control of the union, or they may be jointly controlled by the union and the employer. The status of the hiring halls under the Taft-Hartley Act (with its ban on discrimination against nonunionists) was at first very uncertain; but since 1950 such halls have been looked upon as legal if they register and place both union and nonunion workers. The hiring halls have done much to de-casualize labor in the maritime industry and have eliminated serious abuses that used to be found under the old methods of hiring workers. The industry used to be a prize example of the evils of casual labor, of what happens when the labor market is not well organized. The New York waterfront is still—or at least was until comparatively recently—an outstanding example of a poorly organized labor market.

(4) Fee-charging private employment agencies are business enterprises, just like furniture factories and steel mills, and their business is the placement of labor. For the performance of this service they charge a fee, sometimes from the employer but much more often from the worker.

Private employment agencies are often found in the larger cities, where it is a common sight to see work seekers scanning the job announcements posted outside an agency's office. Many of the agencies are specialized in nature, concentrating their efforts on a limited range of employments.

Appraisal of Fee-Charging Agencies. In times past considerable attention was given by students of labor to the abuses of which some of the agencies were guilty. These abuses included misrepresenting jobs; fee-splitting with foremen, who would discharge workers after a short duration of employment and then be ready for a new crop; collecting exorbitant fees; and sending applicants to nonexistent jobs. Abuses like these are probably still perpetrated, but they do not command the attention they once did.[4] Many states now have laws regulating the fee-charging agencies, and there is a national organization of such agencies that encourages ethical practices. Some persons feel that there is need for federal legislative control, but they have found it difficult to interest Congress.

In the United States there has been no attempt to do away completely with private profit-making employment agencies. This step has been taken by some countries, and there is considerable feeling

[4] For a discussion of abuses, written in the early 1930's, see Paul H. Douglas and Aaron Director, *The Problem of Unemployment,* pp. 266-273. New York: The Macmillan Co., 1931.

in others in favor of it.[5] The general question has been discussed at various sessions of the International Labor Conference. In 1949 the Conference changed its 1933 convention, which called for the abolition of profit-making agencies and the regulation of other private agencies not set up for profit, so that the member nations of the organization could endorse either the principle set forth in the 1933 Convention or simply the principle of regulating private agencies, both profit-making and otherwise.[6]

Private employment agencies, if properly operated, perform a useful function in society, at least in American society. By themselves, however, they cannot bring about a proper organization of the labor market, since they are not integrated into a closely-knit system, and since their geographical and occupational coverage is inadequate. If the labor market is to be properly organized, there must be a system of public employment offices.

Public Employment Offices

Compared with other countries the United States was rather slow in establishing a good system of public employment offices. This step was not taken until 1933, when the Wagner-Peyser Act was passed. There had been public employment offices in the country some decades before then, but their numbers had been very small, except during World War I. At that time the United States Employment Service was established and grew to sizable proportions. The Service greatly shrank, however, after the war, owing to the withdrawal of a large part of its financial support. During the 1920's many states set up employment services of their own or continued their work in this field. In 1932 the federal employment service went through a partial reorganization; but it was not until 1933, when the Wagner-Peyser Act was passed, that the service was refashioned and placed on a solid foundation. That year marks the beginning of a new era in the history of the organization of the labor market in this country.

5 In general, the governments of Canada, Chile, Egypt, Finland, France, India, Italy and a number of other countries have expressed themselves in favor (1) of progressively eliminating fee-charging agencies that are operated for profit purposes, and (2) of regulating nonfee agencies. *Revision of the Fee-Charging Employment Agencies Convention, 1933*, p. 15. International Labor Conference, 32nd Sess., 1949, Report X (2).

6 See *International Labor Review*, October, 1949, pp. 345-348

The United States Employment Service (USES) is a federal administrative organization that ties together and unifies the work of the separate state employment systems. In addition to its headquarters in Washington it has a number of regional offices. Under the plan set up in 1933 the federal government made grants-in-aid to the states for the operation of their employment offices. These funds were forthcoming only if the states operated their employment offices in accordance with certain standards. In 1942, when the USES was linked up with the War Manpower Commission, the grants-in-aid arrangement was suspended and the federal government took over the whole task of financing the work of the state employment offices. This plan exists at the present time, and the same arrangement obtains with respect to unemployment insurance. At the present time the employment services of all the states, comprising about 1800 permanent employment offices and more than that number of temporary offices, are affiliated with the USES.

The public employment office system in the United States is pyramidal in structure. At the top is the headquarters in Washington, the USES; directly below are the employment service headquarters of the states; and at the bottom are the local offices.

The USES aids its affiliates in a variety of ways. It devises and promotes techniques relating to placement work; issues bulletins; promotes, with the cooperation of the state unemployment services, the hiring of workers of various minority groups (the young, the old, the physically handicapped, and members of certain racial and other minority classes); collects statistical data relating to the labor market and makes such data available to other governmental agencies and the public at large; and publishes a monthly periodical, *The Employment Services Review.*

In addition to these activities the USES is in charge of a program designed specifically for the placement and counseling of veterans. The body directly entrusted with this work is known as the Veterans' Employment Service. This service supplies to each state an employment representative and one or more assistants who work with the state employment service in the placement of veterans. The USES also has the responsibility of maintaining a placement service for farm workers: the Farm Placement Service. Because of the changing seasonal demand for labor the placement of farm workers is a highly important undertaking, and the USES has developed an extensive program to meet the responsibility.

The chief function of the local employment offices (the work of which cannot always be easily separated from that of the USES) is bringing jobs and workers together. Unemployed workers are encouraged to register at the offices; and in case they are eligible for unemployment compensation they are *required* to register. Employers are also encouraged to use the employment offices, to get in touch with them whenever they need help. The effectiveness with which any system of public employment offices functions is largely dependent on the extent to which workers and employers use the system's facilities. The wider the use, the better the mobility of labor and the more effective its allocation. It is not surprising, therefore, that the public employment offices frequently try to sell themselves to the public and to special employer and worker groups.

When an unemployed worker registers at a public employment office, he is asked to supply the office with information concerning his age, experience, and so on. If the worker needs help in deciding upon the proper type of employment, a counseling specialist is ready to serve him. All the local employment offices now provide counseling service, and hundreds of thousands of counseling interviews are held each year (in 1952 the number was 1,296,000). To aid the local offices in this work the USES has issued a series of *Occupational Guides,* each of which describes the nature of a given occupation and its present and possible future "economic characteristics."

The USES has also published a *Dictionary of Occupational Titles,* with over 40,000 job titles and 20,000 job definitions. This publication is used extensively both inside and outside the employment office system. In their placement and counseling work the local offices make frequent use of aptitude tests. The Employment Service uses more than 200 aptitude "batteries" in trying to discover the fitness of job applicants for specific occupations, and it has also developed a General Aptitude Test Battery. Oral tests relating to numerous occupations are also given. The resulting improvement in the occupational allocation of labor is a boon to worker and employer alike.[7]

The public employment offices are not only ready to help the

[7] For a brief description of the tests, and of counseling, see *Labor Information Bulletin,* December, 1949, pp. 6-7; and March, 1949, p. 7.

employer in obtaining workers, the proper kind of workers; they are also ready to aid him in dealing with various personnel problems, such as labor turnover and absenteeism. An increasing number of employers are availing themselves of this assistance.

The public employment offices in the United States have been placing about 10 million workers each year. In 1952, however, they placed 15,555,000 workers, of whom 6,501,000 were in nonagricultural employments. (Strictly speaking we should speak of "placements" rather than of "workers placed," since a single worker may be placed more than once in a given time period.) In connection with the matter of placement it should be pointed out that a certain amount of cooperation exists between the employment services of the various states and also between the employment offices within the separate states.

No information is available on precisely what percentage the placements made by the USES form of total national placements (or hirings). The percentage is probably rather small.[8] However, there is every likelihood that in the years ahead the public employment offices will play an increasingly important part in the task of bringing jobs and workers together.

There is one other public agency in the United States that engages in placement work, the Railroad Retirement Board. As one of its chief duties the Board certifies claims for unemployment insurance in the railroad industry, but also, through its subordinate field offices, it acts as a placement agency in the industry.

Gains from a Well Organized Labor Market

A well organized labor market leads to a variety of beneficial results. To begin with it reduces the volume of unemployment. It does this not by increasing the number of jobs available but by bringing work and workers together with greater speed, by cutting down the *duration* of unemployment.

The employment offices can play a particularly useful role in connection with seasonal and technological unemployment. They can also aid significantly in reducing unemployment caused by separate labor reserves—such as has existed on the New York waterfront. Employment offices cannot do much about cyclical unemploy-

[8] See *Employment Service Organization,* Report V (1), pp. 192-193. International Labor Conference, 1947.

ment. There are too few jobs into which the many unemployed can be shifted.

The organization of the labor market may be looked upon as the initial policy to be adopted in any systematic attack on unemployment. As Beveridge has stated, the "deliberate organization of the labor market," which means the establishment of a good system of public employment offices, "is the first step in the permanent solution of the problem of unemployment." [9] It is so for two very good reasons. In the first place, before programs are adopted for creating new jobs it is desirable to fill the jobs that are already available. And secondly, the success with which certain other means for dealing with unemployment operate depends on the existence of a well organized labor market. When such a market exists it is possible to gather useful statistics relating to employment and unemployment in various parts of the country. If a public works policy is used to meet the problem, the offices can tell where the need for jobs is particularly acute and can help to mobilize the workers accordingly. In the matter of unemployment insurance a system of public employment offices is an indispensable requirement. The employment offices not only act as disbursing agencies but, by helping to find the workers jobs, take them off the unemployment insurance rolls.[10]

A second beneficial result from a well organized labor market relates to the volume of production. The speed with which vacancies are filled, and the high-quality occupational allocation resulting from testing and vocational guidance, mean an increase in national output.

A third desirable result follows: workers in general will be better satisfied with their employment. There will be less danger of square pegs getting into round holes, and vice versa. The psychological advantages that accrue to a person from having a job suited to his

[9] *Unemployment: A Problem of Industry,* 1930 ed., p. 198. London: Longmans, Green & Co., 1931. In a later discussion Beveridge included "the controlled mobility of labor" in his list of three conditions for full employment. See *Full Employment in a Free Society,* pp. 125, 170-175. New York: W. W. Norton & Co., 1945.

[10] A comprehensive discussion of the contributions that a well-organized labor market can make toward the handling of the unemployment problem will be found in Chapter V of *Action Against Unemployment,* International Labor Office, Studies and Reports, New Series, No. 20, 1950.

interests and abilities are very important. That many workers are not suitably placed is a fact that is widely recognized; clearly any agency that helps to overcome misallocation of this type is conferring a definite benefit upon society.

A fourth beneficial effect of a well organized labor market is a reduction in labor turnover. If workers are placed in jobs for which they are fitted, they will be less likely to quit and seek employment elsewhere. Although some labor turnover in a plant is desirable, too high a turnover is not. A well organized labor market makes possible a closer approach to the optimum rate of turnover.

A final advantage of such a labor market relates to the matter of wage differentials. If the public employment offices are closely tied together, wage differences for work that is essentially the same should be reduced. Such differences do exist; but if the workers have a larger market in which to sell their services, and if employers have a larger area from which they may select their workers, differentials should be cut down. Low differentials are likely to be more logical and more just.

The Distribution of Labor

The effective use of a nation's labor force involves not only the prompt placement of workers and their placement in the jobs for which they are best fitted, but also the training of workers for the jobs they are to follow. Vocational guidance and vocational training are thus highly important considerations in the wise utilization of labor. Both constitute genuine labor problems.

The individual and social gains that can be derived from a joint program of vocational guidance and vocational training are large. Professor Wallas (see p. 18) possibly exaggerated the gains that would follow from a nice adjustment between the capacity of the individual worker and his work, but that such gains would be very substantial cannot be denied. In proof of this contention one has only to think of his own satisfactions and high productivity when employed at work for which he is well adapted, and his dissatisfactions and low productivity when he is engaged in tasks for which he is not fitted.

We must think not only of the actual but also of the potential capabilities of the individual. It is important, of course, for a person to utilize his present capacities to the best advantage, but it is often more important to develop any latent talents he may possess and put them to the best use. Unfortunately this is not an easy task, but it is a task society should undertake, and undertake on a large scale. Professor Taussig once declared that "The removal of all artificial barriers to the choice of occupation is the most important goal of society." [11] Through vocational guidance and vocational training we have already made some progress in removing these barriers, but much remains to be done.

The magnitude of the task is suggested by the present large degree of dissatisfaction that exists among workers with respect to their jobs. In a poll taken by *Fortune* magazine some years ago, more than half of the factory workers quizzed said that they would not choose the same trade or occupation again if they were 15 years of age.[12] More recently a Gallup poll revealed that 43 per cent of the manual workers queried said they would not follow the same line of work again if they had a second chance. The percentage of misallocated white-collar workers was considerably better (lower), and that of professional and business workers very much better.[13] Making due allowance for the fact that distant fields often look greener, it still remains true that there is a great deal of occupational maladjustment.

Vocational Guidance and Education. Numerous agencies, both public and private, aid in the work of vocational guidance in the United States.[14] A point might be raised concerning the specific objectives that these agencies should strive to attain. Is the goal of vocational guidance merely economic, in the sense of greater output for the factory or the economy as a whole? Or is it to be thought of in terms of the general welfare, both economic and noneconomic, of the individual workers? These two goals are by no means completely exclusive, but they are not exactly harmonious.

Under conditions of national emergency emphasis should be on the first of the objectives; in other times the latter should be given primacy. A few years ago the committee on vocational guidance of

[11] Frank W. Taussig, *Principles of Economics,* Vol. II, 3rd ed., rev., p. 149. New York: The Macmillan Co., 1923.

[12] *Public Opinion Quarterly,* Fall, 1947, p. 488.

[13] *Business Week,* June 3, 1950, p. 85.

[14] A brief description of these agencies will be found in H. A. Jager, "Vocational Guidance in the United States," *International Labor Review,* April, 1948, pp. 300-314.

the International Labor Conference adopted a number of general principles concerning vocational guidance, one of which implied that the first objective of such guidance "is to give the individual full opportunity for personal development and satisfaction from work, with due regard for the most effective use of national manpower resources." The worker members on the committee wanted to have this principle included. It was their view that vocational guidance should be centered on the individual worker primarily, and not on considerations of a national or economic character.[15] It will be noted, however, that the principle, as adopted, does not completely rule out considerations of the latter type.

In vocational education, as in vocational guidance, a combination of economic and noneconomic ends, and of individual and social goals, should be set up. Usually the interests of the individual should be given paramount consideration, since in this way the good of society as a whole will be best promoted.

Numerous professional and trade schools are engaged in the work of vocational education. Many business enterprises carry on educational activities of a vocational nature. An elaborate apprenticeship system exists, in which the federal government plays an important role. Despite the efforts of the agencies just mentioned, however, our general system of vocational training has at least two weaknesses: it lacks facilities and it lacks proper coordination among the various agencies.

The Allocation of Labor

Bringing jobs and workers together with as little delay as possible is obviously of great importance. So too is the placement of workers in positions for which they are best fitted, and the training of workers for jobs for which they *can be* best fitted. But there is another type of "placement problem," and one of great significance, namely the determination of the channels into which labor, and also the other factors of production, are to move. In our discussion so far we have taken these channels for granted. Now we must ask about the desirability of the particular channels selected. This problem is ordinarily not dealt with, at least at any length, in the gen-

[15] *International Labor Review,* October, 1949, p. 344.

eral discussions in the field of labor. Nevertheless it is a labor problem of great scope and one that deserves attention.

The question involved may be thought of in terms of the best means for determining the particular uses to which labor shall be put. Viewing the matter broadly, and in terms of a national economy, the issue is one that exists on two different levels. First there is the plant level. Within each plant or enterprise the proper articles should be produced and the proper amounts of labor should be directed into the various "article" and "department" channels. This is a management problem, a problem in business administration, and we shall not delve into it here. We should point out, however, that the problem is generally handled with direct reference to the well-being of the plant or enterprise.

The second level on which our problem exists relates to allocation not within a single plant but within the economy as a whole. The factors of production should be directed into those industries, or branches of industry, in which they will do the most good. In this instance the "good" is that of the country as a whole, and may be thought of in terms of the size of the national output or, more accurately, per capita output (or income). The allocation problem at this level is not one of internal plant management. It is one of economy management. This is the allocation issue that we shall discuss in the concluding part of our present chapter.

There are three means or methods by which a nation may direct its labor and other productive factors into their various possible uses. One is the so-called price mechanism, which is in operation in the United States. At the other extreme is centralized planning, the best example of which is found in Soviet Russia. There is a third method of a hybrid or mixed character, in which use is made of both the price mechanism and centralized planning; here Great Britain serves as a good example. Actually almost all economies are of a mixed character, though there are immense variations in the weight of the ingredients. In the brief discussion that follows it will be the economies at the extremes to which we shall direct our attention.

The Price Mechanism and Centralized Planning. In a free enterprise economy such as we have in the United States, the price mechanism is inevitably the chief allocation guide. This mechanism works more or less automatically. There is no governmental department to decide what shall be produced and how much. These decisions are made by private businessmen acting in response to real or anticipated prices and price movements. Prices are not set by fiat or decree; they do not spring from the brain of some governmental bureaucrat. Rather, they are esablished in the market through the operation of supply and demand forces.

Centralized planning does not function in any automatic manner. Under it the major decisions relating to production and prices are made arbitrarily by a small number of persons, the planners. The planners cannot be oblivious to what goes on in the market; they cannot completely disregard the behavior of consumers. But in deciding what to produce and how much—two decisions which, it will be remembered, have highly important effects on the particular uses made of labor—they do not react to market prices, since they themselves decide what the prices are going to be.

Under a price-guided economy there are planners, to be sure. But they are "little" planners. Although they must often make decisions similar to those made by the big planners under a controlled economy, their decisions are much narrower in scope and, viewed individually, of much less significance. Decision-making in an economy that uses the price mechanism as guide is greatly diffused. In an economy operating under centralized planning it is highly concentrated. In the former type of economy there are many entrepreneurs, and hence many planners. In the latter type there is for the most part only one entrepreneur, the state, and it is the great planner. It is the visible hand, and the all-powerful hand, that guides production.

Pros and Cons. Both methods of allocation have their strong points and their weak points; the student of labor should know what these are and be able to discuss them intelligently. Here we cannot do much more than point to one or two of the chief aspects of the question.

As we have already noted, the price mechanism works more or less automatically. It also works in a rather simple manner. No complex, interrelated system of output quotas, price controls, and priorities, need be established. Hence no large governmental bureaucracy is required to make and enforce decisions in these matters. Moreover the price mechanism reflects, more accurately than can centralized planning, the wants of the consumer. This is probably its greatest merit—under the price mechanism the consumer is sovereign. He is not an absolute sovereign, it is true, nor always a wise and efficient one. Because of his vulnerability to high-pressure salesmanship, exaggerated advertising, and certain forms of ignorance or indifference on his own part, the consumer has only limited sovereignty. The fact remains, however, that through casting his "dollar votes" the consumer is ordinarily the chief determinant of the direction of production. This is not so under centralized planning. The consumer in Russia has no corresponding "ruble votes" to determine the course of production after the fashion of his American counterpart.[16]

Under the price mechanism, therefore, labor is usually drawn into industries and occupations that the consumers favor. Under a planned economy labor is indirectly forced into certain channels by the decisions of the planners concerning what should be produced. If the economy is extremely totalitarian, some of the labor may, usually on the basis of political unorthodoxy, be directly forced.

Though under the price mechanism the consumers guide production by the dollar votes they cast, they do not all have the same number of votes. This inequality of purchasing power is reflected in the pattern of production and employment; through high income taxes, however, this distortion has been greatly decreased. Under the price mechanism, too, socially undesirable things (*illth,* to use Ruskin's term) may be produced; natural resources may be wasted; and cyclical instability is engendered. Under a highly planned economy these weaknesses may be largely if not wholly removed. But centralized planning means the elimination of private enterprise over a wide range of the nation's economy; and this, in turn, could mean the curtailment of human incentives and freedom.

The issue we have opened up here is indeed a complex one. Though the point that we are especially concerned with in the present chapter is the effect of the two methods of economic guidance on the general allocation of labor, it is clear that the problem is one that greatly transcends this particular consideration.

[16] The above statement suggests a nice problem which economic theorists have discussed at considerable length, namely, the extent to which it is possible to have a "rational" allocation of productive factors in a highly planned economy. An excellent brief presentation of the controversy will be found in E. H. Phelps-Brown, *A Course in Applied Economics,* Chap. VII. London: Sir Isaac Pitman & Sons, Ltd., 1951.

4

UNEMPLOYMENT—GENERAL AND SEASONAL

What does the term "unemployment" mean? Or, to ask the question in a form more useful for our present purpose, who is an unemployed person? As with most definitions, this particular one depends in part on the use to which it is going to be put. In the present case we shall start with a definition that in terms of inclusiveness is moderate in character.

Who Is an Unemployed Person?

An unemployed person is one who is able to work, willing to work, and desirous of work but cannot obtain work. Examining our unemployed person in detail, in the first place he is capable of work. A person who is idle because of physical or mental deficiencies is not unemployed in the strict, technical sense. He is idle, to be sure, probably involuntarily idle; but his idleness is not due to a scarcity of jobs.

Secondly, an unemployed person is willing to work. The ne'er-do-well who is interested in avoiding work is not unemployed, though he is idle.

A person may be both able and willing to work and yet, because of his satisfactory economic condition, not desirous of work. He may not be looking for a job, though, in contrast to the ne'er-do-well, he is not opposed to work "on principle." An able-bodied person who is living retired is not unemployed.

So far our definition seems reasonable enough; but now we begin to run into difficulties with it. Is a worker who is out on strike to be counted as one of the unemployed? We have indicated that an unemployed person is *involuntarily* idle. A striker is voluntarily idle. For our purposes it would seem desirable to exclude strikers from the unemployed category, though under some of our unemployment insurance laws they are looked upon, at least to some extent, in the same way as workers who are out of jobs because of a drop in business activity.

But should we also exclude workers who are idle, not because they are on strike but because other workers (on whom they may be dependent for materials, for example) are on strike? These persons, unlike the actual strikers, are involuntarily idle. It seems desirable, nevertheless, to exclude them from the unemployed.

Finally, is a person *strictly* unemployed if, though idle, he refuses to accept a job because the wage rate it carries is not satisfactory judged by local standards, or because the job is outside the area or community in which he lives, or because he is not fitted for the job? Such a person is definitely marginal in terms of our interpretation of unemployment. Under the unemployment insurance laws of this country he would be eligible for insurance benefits since the job does not meet the "suitability" test. We shall follow the practice used in these laws and look upon an unemployed person as one who cannot find a *suitable* job, recognizing however that it is not always easy to say whether a job is, or is not, suitable.

It should be clear that unemployment is not the same as idleness. It is not even the same as involuntary idleness, since this term includes persons who are not able to work. We may say, in summing up our discussion, that an unemployed person is one who is able to work, is willing to work, and wants to work, but cannot obtain a suitable job.

Personal Weaknesses and Unemployment

Early in the last century a writer strongly imbued with the physiocratic principle of laissez-faire made the following observation concerning an unemployed person:

> Under a government which does not interfere with the direction of industry, it is impossible that a man in health and strength can be without employment, unless his vices make employment intolerable to him. Let the workman be allowed to choose the market for his labor, and you may be sure that he will find one, and more and more certainly in proportion to

the wealth of the country. The complaint of want of work is the threadbare excuse of the idler who prefers relief to wages.[1]

Whatever validity this statement may have had at the time it was made, it is evident that it has little applicability to the situation today. At the present time we recognize, or at least *should* recognize, that unemployment is not the result of personal weaknesses or vices. It is not caused by individual deficiencies. To be sure, there are some persons who try to avoid work, but the great bulk of the workers who are idle definitely want work.

This initial generalization suggests that the problem of unemployment will never be solved by improving the morality of the individual worker. The problem goes far beyond the worker. To some extent it is "a problem of industry," to use Sir William Beveridge's expression; but for the most part it is a problem of the economy as a whole. In other words, unemployment is basically a social problem and not an individual one.

Labor Demands and Supplies

Viewing the matter in terms of direct causation, it may be said that all unemployment is due to maladjustments between the demand for and the supply of labor.[2] If these two elements were always kept in close alignment, as would be the case in a simple type of economy, unemployment would be almost unknown. But the two elements are not always found in close alignment; and in modern industrial nations, especially those in which the chief guide to economic activities is the price mechanism, it is no easy task to bring them into this relationship. However, as we shall see in the discussion that follows, some policies do contribute to the desired end.

In one sense, and it is a very important sense, there is no such thing as *the demand* for labor or *the supply* of labor. Rather, there are numerous demands and numerous supplies. When an employer desires help he wants workers of a certain kind. He is interested

[1] Quoted in Nassau W. Senior's *Political Economy,* 3rd ed., p. 218. London and Glasgow: Richard Griffin & Co., 1854.

[2] "Unemployment is always a symptom of some maladjustment of the demand for labor of different kinds and the supply of workers." Majority Report of the Royal Commission of Great Britain on Unemployment Insurance, *Final Report,* p. 87.

not in "labor in the abstract," such as was imagined in the old labor theory of value, but in workers who possess the ability to perform specific jobs. Moreover, he wants the workers to be at a definite place at a definite time.

Because of the various types of specialization in modern industrial society, including geographical specialization, the demands for labor are specialized. This means that there are many separate demands for labor, a condition that intensifies the complexity and the seriousness of the unemployment problem. These separate or particular demands often change independently of one another. But frequently they change together, though not necessarily to the same degree. During a seasonal slump in a given industry, all or most of the demands for labor represented in that industry may experience a decline. Similarly, during a cyclical slump in business, demands for labor in all industries undergo a shrinkage.

When we speak of the demand for labor, we want to think of it as a sum of many individual demands. As Henry Clay once put it, "The demand for labor as a whole is normally an aggregate of particular demands, for discontinuous, dispersed and changing pieces of work." [3]

It should be noted, further, that the demand for labor is not so much a demand for workers as it is a demand for man-hours. If an employer desires to increase his output, he can do so by taking on more workers or by having his present employees work longer hours (he could also try to induce them to work harder). An increase in the demand for labor, therefore, may not mean an increase in the number of workers employed. And on the other hand, a decrease in the demand for labor may not involve a decrease in the number of persons unemployed.

When the hours of work are increased, there may be overemployment; that is, the workers may have to work longer hours than they would have worked had they had a free choice in the matter. When the length of the work week is shortened, there may be underemployment.

The supply of labor, like the demand for it, is composed of many separate units. Workers differ greatly in their ability and inclination to perform specific jobs; in their situation or location with

[3] *The Post-War Unemployment Problem,* p. 3. London: Macmillan & Co., 1929.

respect to these jobs; and, to some extent, in the hours per week they are willing to work at the jobs. As a result of these supply differences, especially the first two, there are definite limitations on the extent to which workers can shift from one particular supply group to another. The various supplies of unskilled workers merge rather easily, and movement between them is not difficult. In the semiskilled class, where the work is somewhat specialized, movement is more difficult. In the skilled class the work is still more specialized, the separate supplies are more distinct, and movement from occupation to occupation is still more difficult.

If movement within given strata of labor—we might follow Cairnes and call these strata "non-competing groups"—is sometimes difficult, movement from one stratum to another is even more difficult; that is, if the movement is *upwards.* The ditch digger cannot apply for a job as tool maker; and he cannot obtain the necessary training to be a tool maker in any short period of time. The movement of labor *downwards,* on the other hand, may on occasion be very rapid. If the tool maker is out of a job, and if he is physically able, he can compete with the ditch digger for the unskilled job of digging ditches.

During a time of widespread unemployment the individual supplies of labor are not as distinct as they are at other times. During such a period occupational shifts, especially downwards, are very common.[4] Moreover, the workers are willing to travel farther from home if jobs are available for them. But even during a general depression there are still many individual supplies of labor, and their existence adds to the seriousness of the unemployment problem.

Fluctuations in the individual supplies of labor occur independently of one another. These changes do not occur as quickly as changes in demand, however, except in downward shifts during depressions, and also when workers are willing to work longer hours (bear in mind that the supplies of labor, as well as the demands for labor, are reducible to man-hours).

As for changes in the aggregate supply of labor, or rather of workers, they are extremely sluggish compared with changes in the aggregate demand for labor. The latter are economically determined, at least in the first instance; the former are biologically

[4] See *Labor Information Bulletin,* May, 1935, p. 21.

determined, or rather are subject to biological limitations. And here economic forces operate with greater speed than biological processes.

We can now revert to our original statement that unemployment is a result of supply and demand maladjustments. Whereas some of the maladjustments are very general in nature, affecting the whole economy, many of them are specific in character, relating to special demands for labor and special supplies.

It should be added, and this is a point of real significance, that when maladjustments occur, and unemployment ensues, the disturbance comes chiefly from the side of demand. In other words, most of our unemployment is due not to changes in the number of workers, either in specific occupations or in occupations in general,[5] but to changes in the demands for workers. Hence in our discussion of unemployment we shall give primary emphasis to the factors that produce such changes in demand. Some unemployment, however, *is* due to supply influences—lack of adaptability on the part of individual workers to jobs that are open for them, and excessive mobility of labor to points of limited employment opportunities are examples—and these influences should not be overlooked.

Modern Industry and Unemployment

In Chapter 1 we noted that unemployment is largely a product of modern industry. If industry were of a nonspecialized, nonmechanized nature, there would be little unemployment. There would be some dislocations, some maladjustments between the demands and the supplies of labor, but these would be due largely to the operation of natural forces and to wars. In such a simple type of economy the maladjustments would not be as numerous nor as serious, and when they occurred it would be much easier to correct the situation.

Unemployment, then, is largely a product of the machine age.[6]

5 The contention of the Keynesians that equilibrium in the economy may be reached at less than full employment does not invalidate this statement. There is no reason for expecting that mere change in the size of the population and the size of the work force will lead to changes in the *average* volume of unemployment.

6 The author has discussed, in popular terms, the relationship between the mechanization of industry and insecurity (including unemployment) in *The American Federationist,* April, 1940.

The machine has led to the establishment of a type of economic order in which the causes of unemployment, both the indirect and the direct causes, have an excellent environment in which to operate. Among the characteristics of this order are extensive specialization, the widespread use of the roundabout method of production, the production of goods for markets that are distant both in time and place, and an elaborate money and credit system.

The unemployment problem cannot be solved, of course, by reestablishing the simple productive methods of our ancestors, unless we are willing to have our living standards drastically lowered and see the population of the country reduced to a mere fraction of its present size.[7]

Unemployment and Full Employment

Unemployment always exists. At no time do all who are able and willing to work, and desirous of obtaining work, have jobs. Even during the most prosperous periods, when business is booming, there is some unemployment. For example, in October, 1952, a month in which industry was operating at a very high level, there were approximately 1,284,000 persons unemployed. The unemployed constituted about 2 per cent of the civilian labor force, a percentage much lower, by the way, than is commonly expected even during times of heavy industrial activity.

In 1952 we had a condition of full employment—yet we had unemployment. This may seem paradoxical until we realize that full employment really does not mean *full* employment, at least not in the ordinary meaning of the word. What, then, does the expression mean?

Full employment has been defined in various ways. Beveridge uses the term to cover a situation under which there are more job openings than there are job applicants—job openings "at fair wages, of such a kind, and so located that the unemployed men can reasonably be expected to take them." As a result of the above conditions, the time lag between jobs is very short. Beveridge further

[7] Nassau Senior, writing in a somewhat different connection, sagely and satirically remarked that "If the thing required be *employment,* we should abandon ploughs and even spades. To scratch up a rood with the fingers would give more employment than to dig an acre." *Political Economy,* 3rd ed., p. 169. London and Glasgow: Richard Griffin & Co., 1854.

states that full employment involves a sellers' labor market and not a buyers' market.[8]

The Group of Experts appointed by the Secretary-General of the United Nations to probe into the problem of full employment defined the term as "a situation in which unemployment does not exceed the minimum allowances that must be made for the effects of frictional and seasonal factors." [9]

Full employment, as is apparent from the two sample definitions just noted, does not mean 100 per cent employment. And it is important to observe that if it did involve 100 per cent employment we would not want it! Full employment in this sense could be achieved only at the loss of a great deal of personal liberty. It would mean complete labor conscription.[10] In any free society a certain amount of unemployment is not only inevitable but desirable. However, it behooves society to see to it that the unemployed persons get jobs with as little delay as possible, and also that these persons move into the most suitable jobs available.

The ideal of full employment as a broad social objective has been widely established. Thus, for example, there is a full employment pledge in the Charter of the United Nations, which the Group of Experts declares "marks a historic phase in the modern conception of the functions and responsibilities of the democratic state." In the United States' Employment Act of 1946 there is a declaration of policy relating to the provision of useful employment "for those able, willing, and seeking to work," though the statement is worded in such as manner as to furnish a way out for a government opposed to the extreme measures that may be necessary to achieve full employment. (The term "full employment," it is interesting to note, is not used in the Employment Act.) In general the responsibility of providing "high," if not "full," employment has been widely recognized by governments throughout the world.

8 *Full Employment in a Free Society,* pp. 18-19. New York: W. W. Norton & Co., 1945.

9 *National and International Measures for Full Employment,* United Nations, Department of Economic Affairs, 1949, p. 13.

10 See Joan Robinson, *Collected Economic Papers,* pp. 105-106. New York: Augustus M. Kelley, Inc., 1951.

The Causes of Seasonal Unemployment

Turning now to specific types of unemployment, we shall begin with the seasonal variety, taking up the causes first. The causes of seasonal unemployment are of two kinds: the basic, indirect, *unseen* causes; and the immediate, direct, *seen* causes. The latter are the causes usually discussed in treatments of seasonal unemployment.

Fundamentally, much of our seasonal unemployment is due to the nature of modern industry. Workers of the Colonial period were much less concerned about seasonal slumps. They were more versatile, better able to shift employments in accordance with changes in the seasons. They did not carry all their labor power in one basket. Like the wise investor of today, they diversified their "holdings."

Today, however, our work is highly specialized. We concentrate our efforts on narrow tasks—cutting cloth, plastering walls, or tightening nut number 3—and if these tasks experience a seasonal decline we may have difficulty turning to something else. Basically, then, seasonal unemployment is a result of the division of labor in modern industry.

But it is with the immediate causes of seasonal unemployment that we are chiefly concerned. First there is the weather. Most seasonal unemployment is due directly to weather changes, or, more accurately, to changes in the seasons.

These seasonal changes in the weather lead to slackness and unemployment through their effect either on the supplying or producing of goods, or on the demanding or consuming of goods; that is to say they act through two different channels of influence. In agriculture, seasonal unemployment is not due to changes in consumers' buying habits; bread, for example, is eaten during all months of the year. Seasonal employment comes, rather, from the farmer's inability to grow and harvest agricultural crops throughout the year. In this case the weather operates on the *supplying* of goods. In the bathing suit industry it is just the opposite. Bathing suits can be made during any month of the year, but consumers (in the northern part of the country) do not buy them every month in the year. Here the weather operates on the *demanding* of the goods.

The second direct cause of seasonal unemployment is found in the existence of certain "institutions." These either may exist independently of the weather or in one way or another may be associated with it. Previous to July 4 there is a spurt in the firecracker industry, and then a decline sets in. This slump has nothing to do with the weather—independence could just as well have been declared on March 4 or October 4. Moving Day, on the other hand, shows seasonal influences. It is not on May 1 by sheer accident. The moderate days of May are much better for moving than the hot days of July or the cold days of January. In addition to July 4 and Moving Day there are other institutions, such as Christmas, Easter, and Thanksgiving. In connection with all of these there is a certain amount of seasonal activity, followed by seasonal inactivity.

Mitigating Factors

Seasonal unemployment is widespread in the United States. Certain of its characteristics, however, reduce its seriousness, though they do not by any means render it of no consequence. These characteristics deserve some attention.

In the first place seasonal unemployment is highly regular, and therefore predictable. The employer and his workers, knowing what months are going to be slack, may be able to make plans for meeting the contingency. It is to be noted, however, that the individual worker may not always be certain of his own situation during the lean months. He may know that the employer will temporarily reduce his staff by 30 per cent, or cut the man-hours worked by 50 per cent, but he may not know definitely whether he will be one of those laid off or one of those whose hours have been reduced.

A second mitigating factor is the limited duration of seasonal unemployment. Unlike the worker who is idle for cyclical or technological reasons, the seasonally displaced worker knows that he will not be unemployed for more than a fraction of the year. His enforced idleness may last for a few weeks or a few months; only in exceptional cases is it for a substantial part of the year. The relatively short duration of seasonal unemployment lessens the drain on the worker's resources. Moreover, it helps to preserve the credit standing of the worker under our unemployment insurance laws. Unless he should be idle for four or five months he is not likely to exhaust his benefit rights for unemployment insurance. It should be observed, too, that some workers who are laid off during seasonal slumps are not desirous of having steady employment. Certain housewives, for example, are willing and eager to work for part of the year only.

A further mitigating factor may be the wage rates the seasonally employed workers are paid. On *a priori* grounds one would expect that wages in seasonal employments would have a compensatory element in them. This point was made by Adam Smith in his well-known discussion of wage differences. In recent years serious doubt has been raised concerning the general validity of the notion Smith advanced.[11] The determining factor, it should be pointed out, is the effect of seasonality in specific occupations on the supply of labor in these occupations.

In addition to the factors noted, which mitigate the seriousness of seasonal unemployment, there are certain other factors that reduce the extent to which seasonality in industry causes unemployment. One of these is the staggered nature of the active and the inactive months. If all the slack periods in industry came at the same time, the amount of seasonal employment would be much larger than it is. However, while some industries are experiencing a seasonal slump others are having a seasonal rush, so that workers from the slack industries may be able to obtain jobs in the busy ones. A certain amount of this dovetailing of jobs is found in the farming and the lumbering industries, for example. One should not exaggerate the degree to which such shifts take place, however. A seasonally idle worker cannot shift temporarily to another job unless the job is within his capabilities and conveniently located. He must also know of its existence.

Unlike cyclical swings in business activity, seasonality in industry is much more subject to control by employers. There are various preventive or ameliorative policies that the employer may be able to adopt. Under some conditions these policies may merely result in greater seasonal instability in other businesses; but, as we shall see shortly, this is not necessarily the case.

[11] See Joseph Shister, *Economics of the Labor Market,* pp. 448-450. Philadelphia: J. B. Lippincott Co., 1949. Consult also *Economic Analysis of Guaranteed Wages,* by Alvin H. Hansen and Paul A. Samuelson, p. 12, Bulletin No. 907, Bureau of Labor Statistics, United States Department of Labor.

Coping with Seasonal Unemployment [12]

Reducing Hours. Possibly the simplest way to cope with seasonal unemployment is for the employer to reduce the length of the work week during the period in which business is slack. This policy is one of spreading work or work-sharing; it substitutes underemployment for unemployment. Instead of laying off, say, 25 per cent of the work force, the employer reduces the length of the work week to 30 hours and retains a full work force. A policy of this sort has distinct advantages. From the employer's standpoint, it means that his workers will not be as likely to seek jobs elsewhere and that he will therefore not be exposed to the various costs—hiring expenses, training costs, lower and poorer production, and so on—involved in taking on new help. There will be no loss of skill on the part of the employer's work force, no "getting rusty" as a result of temporary idleness. Such a policy, moreover, may contribute to improved morale in the business. The workers know they will not be laid off completely, and hence their attitude toward the employer may well be improved.

But the work-sharing policy is not without its problems for the employer. Adoption of the policy means that poor workers may be kept on who otherwise would be laid off. The retention of poor workers could have an adverse effect on the quality and quantity of output, resulting in higher unit costs. Moreover, the application of the policy (assuming it to be on a plant-wide basis) can be complicated if different departments in the business are not all affected to the same degree by the seasonal decline. Finally, administrative costs, including payroll calculation expenses, may be increased. Despite these possible disadvantages, however, the work-sharing policy is usually applied with definite gain to the employer.

It is clear, of course, that some workers, those who would have been employed on a full-time basis had the work-sharing plan not been adopted, suffer under the policy. But there is good reason for believing that any loss to them (in terms of "utils" of satisfaction)

12 An extensive discussion of means for coping with seasonal (and other) fluctuations in employment, with numerous illustrations drawn from industry, will be found in Herman Feldman, *Stabilizing Jobs and Wages.* New York: Harper & Bros., 1940. See also the valuable discussion in Paul H. Douglas and Aaron Director, *The Problem of Unemployment,* Chapters VII & VIII. New York: The Macmillan Co., 1931.

is more than offset by the gains accruing to those who otherwise would have been laid off. Certainly society as a whole benefits through the preservation of the workers' skills and the probable improvement in general worker morale.

The policy of work-sharing should not be pushed too far, however. If business falls off to such an extent that the length of the work week must be reduced to 15 or 20 hours in order to provide work for everyone, the policy should be applied in a modified form. Under many union agreements there are provisions which place a floor under hours when the work-sharing policy is applied. The length of the work week for all employees may be reduced to 25 or 30 hours. Then, if further curtailment is necessary, the layoff policy is used, with the seniority principle determining the order of layoff.

Producing for Stock. When an employer's volume of business experiences a seasonal drop, it may be possible for him to iron out his production and employment "curves" by producing for stock during the slack months. Stating the matter differently, he may be able to cope with the seasonality problem by budgeting production over each twelve-month period.

Certain conditions must be present before the production-for-stock policy can be put into successful operation. For one thing, the product, or products, must be standardized. It would be hazardous indeed for an employer to produce for stock an article that would be out of style by the time it was to be put on the market. Although it may be feasible to build up a supply of soap, it would undoubtedly be very risky to produce ladies' hats or dresses for stock.

The product must obviously be of a nonperishable character, or at least refrigerator facilities must be available and not too costly. Moreover, the article must be valuable relative to its bulk; otherwise high storage costs would more than offset the gains achieved through the regularization of production.

An employer who finds it possible to adopt the production-for-stock policy stands to gain in a number of ways. The amount of machinery a plant requires is determined by its peak load; if, through the policy of production for stock, the top of the peak can be lopped off, the amount of machinery needed is naturally less and overhead is lower. The same saving would result if hours were lengthened (instead of extra workers' being taken on) during periods of high seasonal activity. To be sure the machinery would be used more intensively—the depreciation caused by wear and tear would increase. However, the depreciation due to obsolescence would decrease. The net effect would be a gain. If storage costs are very high, however, any gain involved in the more regular and intensive use of machines may be wiped out.

Production for stock also involves a steadier labor force. There is a smaller amount of labor turnover, and the various costs associated with labor turnover, particularly with reference to skilled workers, are consequently reduced.

Dovetailing Products. Seasonality in production and employment may be lessened by the introduction of new products, products that are in strong demand at the time the demand for the regular line is low.

Here again, however, there are certain conditions necessary. For one thing, members of the regular work force must be used for the most part in producing the new products. Otherwise the switch to new products would not contribute to the solution of the unemployment problem in the plant in question. In fact the problem might be intensified, since the number of workers exposed to seasonal slumps might be increased.

To be economically feasible, the policy of dovetailing products should not involve large expenditures for new machinery. In other words, it is desirable that the machinery already in the plant be used for the production of the new items. Moreover, the regular sales channels should be used for the marketing of the new products. If a special sales force is required, the desirability of the dovetailing policy is open to question.

In connection with this policy one must make a clear distinction between the plant or company and the economy as a whole. The *X* Corporation may be able to reduce seasonality in its operations and cut down the extent to which its employees are subject to seasonal unemployment by introducing new products. But it by no means follows that the amount of seasonal unemployment in the economy is thereby reduced. What the over-all result is depends on the nature of the products introduced.

There are three general possibilities. The products may be entirely new, in which case the attainment of seasonal stability in the *X* Corporation would also mean higher seasonal stability in the economy as a whole. Or they may be products that other companies are making—making, let us assume, along with other goods and under conditions of general month-to-month stability. In these circumstances the achievement of stability by the first company brings instability to the other companies, and the total amount of seasonality in the economy as a whole either has not been reduced at all or has been reduced very little.

Finally the new products introduced may be the sole output items of other companies. These companies, of course, would also be operating on a seasonal basis, but with their peaks and valleys opposite to those of the *X* Corporation. Competition from the *X* Corporation will either force the companies into bankruptcy, because of lack of business, or compel them to operate at lower levels of output. Under either condition the short-run effect will be dislocation and unemployment in the companies thus adversely affected. However, in the long run, the economy as a whole will be benefited. The concentration of two (or more) seasonal products, with diametrically opposed peaks and valleys, in one (or more) plants rather than in two (or more) would represent a social gain. The displaced workers would probably experience some hardship in obtaining new jobs, just as do technologically unemployed workers. But ultimately society would benefit. Labor would be more efficiently and more steadily employed.

Building Up Off-Season Demands. A company may reduce seasonality in its operations by building up the demand for its products during the slack period. The company may be able to move into markets that are active during the months its present markets are dull, possibly by expanding sales into other countries. Granting price concessions—for example, in coal during the summer months—often stimulates off-season buying. Special sales, as in the furniture industry during the slack months of February and August, may be used for the same purpose. Sometimes a company or an industry can change the habits of people so that they will continue buying during normally slack months. The sale of ice cream in the winter is a good example.

The possibility of a diversion of trade from other companies, and the possibility of increasing seasonal instability in other companies, must again be recognized. The reasoning used on this point in our discussion of the method of dovetailing products is largely applicable here, although with respect to some of the policies there is a new "angle" posed by a possible shift in general purchasing power. There may be a shift of money spending toward some commodities (the seasonal ones) and away from others. On the whole, however, it would seem that this factor would not be very influential in producing offsetting losses, not in an economy in which credit is so widely used.

Organization of the Labor Market. Since seasonal slumps in some industries and seasonal peaks in others to some extent coincide, the volume of seasonal unemployment can be reduced somewhat by an extensive and efficient organization of the labor market. The United States Employment Service, with its hundreds of employment offices scattered over the country, is doing much to solve the seasonal unemployment problem. Were it not in existence the number of separate labor pools throughout the nation would be much larger, and the amount of seasonal unemployment substantially greater.

5

TECHNOLOGY AND TECHNOLOGICAL UNEMPLOYMENT

The expression "technological unemployment" is of relatively recent origin. It was first used, apparently, by Professor Sumner Slichter in the latter part of the 1920's,[1] when interest in the effects of mechanization on labor was at a high level. The term soon achieved great popularity, and the ability to use it became one of the marks of enlightened citizenship. During the late 1920's and early 1930's the subject of labor displacement was widely and vigorously discussed—especially during the heyday of the technocrats [2]—and many articles and books were written on the question. Interest in the subject waned as business activity recovered, but it did not disappear.

[1] See Professor Slichter's article in *The New Republic,* February 8, 1928. It is interesting to note that Thorstein Veblen, who used the adjective "technological" in a multitude of ways, never once, it would seem, linked it up with the word "unemployment."

[2] The technocrats were greatly interested in the mechanization of industry and the labor displacement that it caused. They were very unorthodox, however, in their general beliefs and recommendations. They attempted to explain and solve some of our most pressing economic problems in a way that was indeed radical. They relied very little on the logic of economics and had little sympathy or admiration for economists. In fact, Mr. Howard Scott, the rather mystical leader of the group, had a disrespect for them which, according to Stuart Chase (*Technocracy, an Interpretation,* p. 7. New York: The John Day Co., 1933) was not only profound but profane. Only two were excepted, Thorstein Veblen and Wesley Mitchell. The technocrats, who were physicists, biochemists, technologists, and so on, felt the price system was obsolete and advocated a new type of exchange system, one based on such things as ergs and joules. By substituting such a system for our present one, no longer would we have poverty in the midst of plenty, and no longer would we have unemployment. For a critical appraisal of technocracy, by an economist, see Aaron Director, *The Economics of Technocracy,* Public Policy Pamphlets, No. 2, the University of Chicago Press, 1933.

Recently there has been increased concern about the problem and there is a strong likelihood that this concern will continue.

If the term "technological unemployment" is relatively new, the phenomenon to which it relates is by no means of recent origin. Workers have been displaced by machines for centuries; Queen Elizabeth and James I, for example, refused to grant William Lee a patent for his knitting machine ("I have too much regard for my people who obtain their bread by knitting," said Good Queen Bess). It was not until the late 18th century, however, that the question became of any real significance. With the remarkable improvements in industrial technology made at that time, represented by the inventions of such men as Watt, Arkwright, Hargreaves, and Crompton, the struggle between men and machines became much more intense and ruthless. The volume of labor displacement increased, and attention became more and more focused on labor problems. In the main, therefore, technological unemployment grew out of the Industrial Revolution, which had its formal beginning near the end of the 18th century.

The Matter of Definition

In its narrowest sense, and in the sense in which the term is widely used, technological unemployment is unemployment caused by the introduction of new and improved machinery; in the discussion that follows we shall use the term for the most part in this restricted fashion.

It is well to realize, however, that other changes in industry are motivated by the same general desire (to reduce costs) and have the same results (economy in the use of labor) as technological improvements. In this nontechnological group we may include changes in the internal organization and methods of a plant, for example the elimination of unnecessary motions in productive operations. We may also include mergers and combinations among plants, as well as geographical shifts in industry. There is some virtue in using the term "technological unemployment" to cover the unemployment resulting from all such changes, even though some of the changes are of a nontechnological character,[3] since the reasoning used in

[3] J. M. Keynes defines the term much after this fashion. See *Essays in Persuasion,* p. 364. New York: Harcourt, Brace & Co., 1932. The term "rationalization," which is commonly used in Europe, largely relates to changes of the same

explaining the volume of labor displacement and the speed of labor reabsorption is the same in all cases. However, in the discussion that follows we shall use the term in its more limited sense.

Certain other expressions bear a close kinship to the term "technological unemployment." Isador Lubin has used the term "transitional unemployment," including as causes not only the changes mentioned in the preceding paragraph but also changing habits of consumers, and bankruptcy.[4] Professor Hansen has used the term "structural unemployment," and has it cover not only the unemployment caused by changes in the techniques of production, in the location of industry, and in demand, but also unemployment resulting from the appreciation of the monetary unit, uneconomic wage levels, overpopulation, and the scarcity of capital.[5] Professor Daugherty has used the expression "secular unemployment," including under it unemployment caused by the decline of industries, geographical shifts in industry, mergers and consolidations, the development of excess capacity, the invention of new machinery, and improvements in productive processes.[6] All these terms have merit; we shall, however, adhere to "technological unemployment."

Views on Technological Unemployment

Writers on economic questions have discussed the problem of technological unemployment for more than a century and a half.[7] On the whole the earlier writers assumed an optimistic view concerning the displacement of men by machines, and toward the effects of mechanization in general. Their view was more optimistic than the attitude of the general populace. J. B. Say declared that

type as those indicated above. See The International Labor Office, *The Social Aspects of Rationalization,* p. 1. Geneva, 1931.

[4] *Unemployment in the United States,* Hearings before the Committee on Education and Labor, United States Senate, 70th Congress, 2nd Session, Sen. Res. 219, p. 500. One could also include under the term the unemployment resulting from obstacles in the way of labor mobility.

[5] Alvin H. Hansen, *Economic Stabilization in an Unbalanced World,* p. 148. New York: Harcourt, Brace & Co., 1932.

[6] Carroll R. Daugherty, *Labor Problems in American Industry,* p. 90. Boston: Houghton, Mifflin Co., 1933.

[7] For detailed treatment of these views see Alexander Gourvitch, *Survey of Economic Theory on Technological Change,* National Research Project, WPA, 1940; and the following articles by the present writer: "Views on Machinery and Unemployment," in *The Scientific Monthly,* February, 1940; and "Labor Immobility and Technological Unemployment," in *Social Forces,* March, 1941.

he had "always found, practically, that new machines produced more alarm than injury." [8] And the now-forgotten Caroline, the brain-child of Mrs. Jane Marcet, begged the pardon "of Mr. Watts for having ventured to doubt the beneficial effects of his steam-engine, and of Sir Richard Arkwright for having found fault with his spinning jennies." [9]

The early writers recognized that mechanization could lead to temporary hardship on the part of displaced workers, but in general they did not consider the problem a serious one. In the long run, they felt, things would work out satisfactorily. Malthus stated that "the most usual" effect of the use of machinery was such an increase in the demand for the article produced that "notwithstanding the saving of labor, more hands, instead of fewer, are required in the manufacture." [10] Some time later an American writer, Professor Arthur L. Perry, declared in very optimistic tones that "the application of machinery to all departments of production, and the introduction of improved processes of every name, can hardly in the first instance be prejudicial to any, and are sure ultimately to be beneficial to all." [11]

Among those who emphasized the possible serious effects of mechanization on the employment of individual workers may be mentioned William Godwin and John Stuart Mill. Godwin, writing in 1797 (*The Enquirer*), emphasized the time that was needed by a displaced worker to learn a new job and the suffering to which he would be exposed in the meantime. This was a situation, declared Godwin, "that requires kindness and soothing." And Mill, in referring to the technologically unemployed, said "There cannot be a more legitimate object of the legislator's care than the interests of those who are thus sacrificed to the good of their fellow citizens and posterity." [12]

The earlier writers recognized that technological improvements

[8] *Letters to Malthus,* Letter No. 4. London: Printed for Sherwood, Neely, and Jones, 1821.

[9] *Conversations on Political Economy,* 3rd ed., p. 116. London: Printed for Longman, Hurst, Rees, Orme, and Brown, 1819.

[10] *Principles of Political Economy,* 2nd ed., p. 352. London: William Pickering, 1836.

[11] *Elements of Political Economy,* 14th ed., p. 126. New York: Scribner, Armstrong & Co., 1877.

[12] *Principles of Political Economy,* Ashley ed., p. 99. London: Longmans, Green & Co., 1926.

could decrease the demand for *particular groups* of workers. A number of them went farther, however, and maintained that such improvements could decrease the *total* demand for labor. David Ricardo, for example, thought that this was possible. In one of his letters to Malthus, [13] he said that this result was "absolutely demonstrable"; and in his famous chapter, "On Machinery," which he added to the third edition of his *Principles,* he attempted to give such a demonstration.

Whether or not it is theoretically possible for machinery to lead to a decrease in the total demand for labor is a nice question. However, in actuality the mechanization of industry has not had such an effect. There has been no constantly increasing "industrial reserve army" as a result of mechanization, no general and increasing superfluity of labor. Labor in particular occupations has been rendered superfluous but not labor in the aggregate. If the total demand for labor were reduced as a consequence of industrial mechanization, the average amount of unemployment (the volume of unemployment relative to the size of the work-force) should have greatly increased over the years, but there has been no such increase. Or the general wage level should have dropped as a consequence of the strong competition for jobs on the part of the allegedly superfluous workers. But wages have not fallen.

In a dynamic economy there is no need to fear a decline in the *total* demand for labor as a result of technological change. There is a great need, however, to give thought to the problems created by declines in *specific* demands for labor. We must devise policies for aiding those who, in Mill's phrase, "are sacrificed to the good of their fellow citizens and posterity." No optimism concerning the beneficial long-run effect of technological improvements in industry should blind us to the serious short-run consequences.

The student of labor should distinguish clearly between the static approach to the problem of technological unemployment and the dynamic approach. Both approaches throw light on the general nature of the problem, and both should be used. The discussion of technological unemployment has suffered grievously because of the failure to distinguish between and make proper use of the two approaches.

[13] *Letters of Ricardo to Malthus,* ed. by James Bonar, p. 184. Oxford: At the Clarendon Press, 1887.

Factors Determining the Amount of Labor Displacement

A clear distinction must be made between the terms "labor displacement" and "technological unemployment." Since the two terms are intimately related, in any general discussion of the subject not much harm will be done by using them interchangeably. It is quite possible, however, to have labor displacement without technological unemployment.

Professor Harry Jerome, in his study of mechanization,[14] classified labor displacement into the following five types: (1) operation; (2) plant; (3) occupational; (4) industrial; (5) complete. The first four types need not necessarily involve unemployment. Thus a worker who, as a result of a technological improvement, loses his job performing a given operation may find immediate employment in the same plant, or outside of the plant, either in his regular occupation or in another. A given improvement may involve all of the first four types of displacement, as a matter of fact, without leading to unemployment.

The distinction we have just noted is a useful one, especially in considering the larger aspects of mechanization and employment. In our present analysis, however, we shall assume—and our assumption is by no means purely hypothetical—that displacement, whether it be operation, plant, occupational, or industrial, or a combination of these, does involve a time lag between jobs: that is, that it involves technological unemployment, or, in Professor Jerome's terminology, complete displacement.

To begin our analysis let us assume that a number of new machines are introduced into Department 20, where operation 35 is performed, of the Super-Miraculous Corporation. What factors determine how many workers are going to be squeezed out of the department? There are two: (1) what effect the new machines have on the price of the end, or final, product of the plant; and (2) whether the demand for the product is elastic or inelastic.

The older writers stressed the importance of lower prices as a factor governing the amount of technological unemployment. They assumed that the lower costs resulting from the use of machinery would be reflected in lower prices. With prices reduced there would

[14] *Mechanization in Industry,* pp. 30-31. New York: National Bureau of Economic Research, 1934.

be an increase in the volume of sales and therefore in the volume of production. The increase in production would help to prevent the destruction of jobs. In fact the increase in sales and production, consequent upon the lower prices, might be great enough to bring about an actual increase in the number of jobs.

This reasoning is valid if one assumes that reductions in cost are followed by reductions in price. But prices may remain the same or not fall commensurately with the drop in costs—when prices are "administered," for example, or when there is an element of monopoly. Under such circumstances the amount of technological unemployment, following the introduction of cost-reducing improvements, will be greater than it would have been had there been strong competition and hence flexible prices. In general, the volume of technological unemployment resulting from a given improvement varies inversely with the degree of competition in the industry involved.[15]

If the monetary gains resulting from technological improvements are not passed on to the consumer in the form of lower prices, they accrue either to the owners of the business or to the workers. These gains will lead ultimately to the creation of jobs. In terms of aggregate spending power the gains offset the loss sustained by the displaced workers. This aspect of the problem will be considered in the next section.

The second factor that governs the volume of displacement is the nature of the demand for the article in the production of which the new machinery is used. Here let us assume that the price of the good is reduced in keeping with the lower costs of production. If the lower price causes a large increase in purchases, the amount of labor displacement will be small; there may even be an increase in the amount of labor required. On the other hand, if the lower prices evoke little response on the part of the buyers, the volume of displacement will be large. In other words, the more inelastic (or less

[15] For a pioneer discussion of this and other pertinent points see Paul H. Douglas and Aaron Director, *The Problem of Unemployment,* Chapter X. New York: The Macmillan Co., 1931. Early in the present century J. B. Clark maintained that when hardships occurred on a large scale as a result of mechanization and a discharging of workers they were due chiefly to monopoly—"an abnormal influence" which "now shows itself in ugly and disquieting ways throughout the industrial system." *Essentials of Economic Theory,* pp. 297-298. New York: The Macmillan Co., 1907. Whether or not the degree of monopoly has increased over the years is debatable. For a negative view on the question see David McCord Wright's remarks in *The Saturday Review,* September 19, 1953, p. 26.

elastic) the demand for the article produced by the new machines, the larger the amount of displacement.

Consider the agricultural industry. Speaking in broad terms, the demand for farm products (through the relevant price range) is rather inelastic. A lower price per loaf of bread, for instance, will not bring about a large increase in the number of loaves purchased, and hence a large increase in the demand for wheat. As might be expected labor displacement (and particularly *animal* displacement) on farms has been large as a result of mechanization.

The demand for automobiles, on the other hand, is elastic. Lower prices on cars have brought about a large increase in the number sold, so that despite the extensive mechanization of the industry the volume of employment in it has increased. Of course this increase must not be wholly ascribed to the nature of the demand for automobiles.[16] The automobile industry has enjoyed the benefits of a secular or long-time growth in the popularity of its product. Automobiles now stand very high on the consumers' preference list, partly because of the shorter work day, longer weekends, and vacations with pay.

When new machines are introduced into a plant or industry, there may be no change in the number of workers needed: that is, there may be no labor displacement. But there may be some *laborer* displacement. That is, some new workers may be hired and some old ones fired.[17] The new machines may call for skills the present employees do not possess, or less skillful workers may be used to replace skilled workers, or women may replace men. Thus the machines lead to labor turnover though not to any *net* labor displacement.

The Reabsorption of Unemployed Workers

Though some of the workers who lose their jobs as a result of mechanization find employment at once, or in a very short time, others are forced to remain idle for long periods. Professor Mentor

[16] It is to be remembered that the demand curve in economics relates to a given time period, and does not cover "historic" or "time" changes such as population growth, shifts in consumer buying habits, and changes in the size of the national income.

[17] For early discussions of this point see the article by Davis R. Dewey in *Publications of the American Economic Association,* Vol. IX, 1894, pp. 64-65; and J. Shield Nicholson, *The Effects of Machinery on Wages,* rev. ed., especially pp. 43-44. London: S. Sonnenschein & Co., 1892.

Bouniatian's statement[18] that under normal conditions the displaced workers easily find jobs suggests unwarranted optimism. For one thing conditions are not always normal; also, a situation of general normality in the country as a whole may be accompanied by a condition of grave abnormality in particular localities. The reabsorption problem, therefore, is an important one.[19]

The length of time displaced workers are unemployed depends in part on the way the monetary gains resulting from technological improvements are distributed. If they are passed on to the consumer in the form of lower prices, there may be little displacement in the first place. However, it is possible that some workers may be laid off at the time the improvements are introduced, since the employer may not know accurately what the response of the consumers will be to the lower prices. Moreover, there may be some lag in the response. However, the consumers will soon react; orders will increase; and some of the workers who were let out may be rehired, or new ones may be taken on.

If the gains are retained by the employer or paid to the workers in higher wages, the reabsorption process will not be as rapid. An employer who keeps his gains will either use them in the business, for fixed or working capital purposes, or disburse them as dividends. Whatever he does, the funds may be idle for a period, and idle funds do not create jobs. In time, however, the funds will be spent on either producers' or consumers' goods and will thus give rise to employment opportunities. But, and this is the important point, these opportunities may not be in the same industry, or in the same locality, in which the displaced workers were employed.

When the gains are passed on to the workers, there is a greater likelihood that the funds will be used immediately; but they will probably be used only to a negligible extent in buying goods made in the plant or industry in which the improvements have been made. Unlike when the employer gets the gains, more of the workers' new funds, perhaps all of them, will be used for buying consumer goods. Hence there is small likelihood of any great delay in

[18] *The International Labor Review,* March, 1933, p. 332.

[19] Statistical data concerning the length of time technologically displaced workers are unemployed will be found in an article by Robert J. Myers in *The Journal of Political Economy,* August, 1929; and in an article by Otis E. Young in *The Personnel Journal,* June, 1934.

their use. In both cases, however, there is a new demand pattern, the influence of which is felt outside the industry and perhaps outside the locality.

The second factor governing the speed with which technologically unemployed workers are reabsorbed is the degree of mobility possessed by the workers. The problem of technological unemployment is primarily a "demand problem," since it has to do chiefly with the creation of new jobs for those that have disappeared. However, to some extent it is a "supply problem," relating to the ease with which displaced workers can move into jobs that are open for them.[20]

The new jobs are often different from those the displaced workers have left, and they may be in a different locality. To take advantage of them the workers may have to be both occupationally and geographically mobile. If a worker is disinclined, or finds it difficult, to learn a new type of work, or if he is opposed to moving to another community, he may be out of work, technologically unemployed, for a long time. His idleness will be due not to a lack of jobs but to his lack of availability.

Another factor governing the speed of reabsorption is the nature of business conditions in general and in the particular community in which the technological improvements have been made. If business is booming, many new jobs are being created and the displaced workers should not have great difficulty in getting into gainful employment if they are adequately mobile. If business is depressed, the reabsorption process is greatly hindered and workers remain unemployed longer. Moreover, if the depression is of a cyclical variety, we have a nice problem of terminology and classification. Are the workers technologically or cyclically unemployed? We should probably call them cyclically unemployed even though the original cause of their idleness was technological in nature.

Speed of reabsorption is also affected by the flexibility of wages. If wages are kept at arbitrarily high levels, either by governmental action or, as is more likely, by union action, displaced workers may have difficulty finding jobs. An employer may be willing to hire them at, say, a dollar an hour, but not at a dollar and a half. Inflexible

20 The author has dealt at length with this aspect of the problem in an article entitled "Labor Immobility and Technological Unemployment," in *Social Forces,* March, 1941.

wage rates, whatever advantage they may possess, retard the reabsorption of the technologically unemployed.

In a dynamic economy, and one in which labor possesses an adequate degree of mobility, there need be no fear of a large and growing pool of technologically unemployed workers. However, as we said before, no belief in the favorable long-run consequences of technological change should blind us to a realization of the unfavorable short-run effects. For many workers these effects are very serious. The loss of job and income, however temporary, is a serious matter. And when there is added to that loss the loss of marketable skill and experience, both of which may be made worthless by the improvements, the burden on the worker is especially great. Well may we say with William Godwin that "It is a serious hardship, after having devoted myself to one profession, and accomplished myself with one species of skill, to be driven in pursuit of another."

Coping with Technological Unemployment

Proposals for dealing with the problem of technological unemployment may be divided into three principal categories: those that aim at controlling the rate at which new machinery is introduced and the extent to which machinery is used; those that try to effect a reduction in the time lost by displaced workers; and those that aim at ameliorating the lot of displaced workers while they are out of jobs. We shall use this classification in the discussion that follows.

Controlling the Introduction and Use of Machinery. (1) The suggestion has been made that if new machines were introduced gradually rather than spasmodically the volume of technological unemployment would be reduced. Many years ago a writer in an English publication[21] declared that "Machinery then, like the rain of heaven, is a present blessing to all concerned, provided it comes down by drops and not by tons together." The proposal of gradual introduction does not imply that a permanent restriction should be placed on the quantity of machinery used, but simply that the machinery should be put into operation at a steadier, more regular rate.

Considered in the abstract this policy has much to commend it,

[21] *Westminster Review,* January, 1831, p. 194.

but it is difficult to apply. An employer who feels that new or improved machines will enable him to reduce his costs is not likely to limit himself to buying and introducing a few machines at a time, particularly if there is any appreciable competition in the industry. Even if an employer is in a monopolistic position, he is under strong pressure to introduce the new machines in whatever quantity seems desirable from a financial point of view.

If an employer is benevolent, if he is interested in social costs as well as private costs, he may make some use of the gradual introduction policy.

Clearly, then, to expect all employers to adopt the gradual introduction policy is out of the question. And to have the government pass a law requiring its use is clearly undesirable. Not only would such a law be difficult to administer, but it would be almost impossible to fix satisfactory rates at which new machinery is to be introduced. Despite the limitations on the gradual introduction policy some employers have become interested in it and have applied it. And in a number of collective bargaining agreements, notably in the men's clothing industry, the policy has become established.

(2) Sometimes unions propose and apply the policy of placing limits on work loads as a means for coping with the adverse effects of technological change. This policy not only helps to preserve jobs but may also, so the unions commonly argue, promote the safety of the general public and protect the health of the worker. One of the best illustrations of this policy in operation is found in the railroad industry in connection with the running of Diesel engines. The policy of controlling work loads is often very desirable, but there is a real danger that it will be applied too rigidly and extensively and result in a waste of labor power.

(3) Another approach to the problem of technological unemployment involves the making of public investigations. Arthur Penty suggested that before any new machinery is introduced a public inquiry should be made for the purpose of obtaining evidence concerning such things as its effects on unemployment and on the condition of labor generally. If the investigators found that the application of the machinery would be socially beneficial, its use would be permitted.[22] Apparently Mr. Penty thought that a considerable

22 *Post Industrialism,* p. 56. London: G. Allen & Unwin, Ltd., 1922. See also *The American Review,* December, 1935, p. 215.

amount of machinery would not meet the test, for he believed the machine to be the most powerful agency for the disintegration of society—its family life, its religion and its art, its politics, its industry, and its technical skill.

The policy of public investigation, if applied on an extensive scale, would be clearly unfeasible. A more modest proposal, but one along the same general line as that suggested by Mr. Penty, was made by Professor Slichter back in the early 1930's.[23] Professor Slichter suggested that a federal labor board be established, partly for the purpose of investigating the various problems arising from such technological and geographical changes in industry as seem likely to lead to a substantial amount of labor displacement. This board would be empowered to make recommendations to industry. Needless to say many employers would not act on the board's suggestions. Professor Slichter further suggested, however, that the board could be given the power to exercise control over the issuance of patents, which would be granted only on condition that labor be adequately protected.

(4) Another way of restricting the use of machinery would be to impose a tax on all the new machines introduced. This proposal is not of recent origin—it was suggested and discussed as far back as 1822 in Great Britain.[24] Early in 1939 a resolution was introduced into the United States House of Representatives directing the Secretary of the Treasury "to investigate the desirability and practicability of imposing a tax on the use of labor-saving and labor-displacing machinery," and asking him to report on the matter at the next session of Congress. Some time later a bill was introduced into the Senate providing for the imposition of a tax on employers who made "more than average" use of machines. It would appear that no such study as was proposed in the House was made, and certainly no such tax as was proposed in the Senate was levied.

For administrative and other reasons the use of the taxing power for coping with technological unemployment is on the whole undesirable. It is interesting to note, however, that some use of private taxing power is made in this country in connection with technological improvements. The levy placed on record producers by the

[23] *The American Economic Review,* March, 1932, Supplement, pp. 48-49.

[24] *Quarterly Review,* 1828, p. 410; 1830, pp. 256-261. See also William Smart, *Second Thoughts of an Economist,* p. 59. London: Macmillan & Co., 1916.

American Federation of Musicians is a good example. The proceeds of this levy are used to benefit the live musicians who are obliged to compete with "canned music."

(5) Still another proposal recommends the declaration of an "Inventors' Holiday." During the vacation period the inventors would keep away from their regular work—presumably, like all good vacationists, they would not even think of it. In this way society would have a chance to catch up with the discoveries and inventions that had already been made. This policy, although ingenious, has little to commend it.

(6) Another suggestion is to return to a simpler type of economic society. It may be recalled that Samuel Butler's Erewhonians adopted this policy, destroying a great deal of machinery in the process (all that had not been in existence for 271 years). The effect of such a retrogression on present living standards and the size of the population has already been thoroughly discussed.

It is well to recall, however, that this policy has sometimes been used by real people. In the early 19th century some workers were so averse to the conditions produced by the mechanization of industry that they launched direct, physical attacks on the machines. The machines had too many legions behind them, however, to be greatly disturbed by the scattered attacks of Ned Ludd and his friends.[25]

Today direct opposition to machinery takes more subtle forms. A union may refuse to permit its members to work on a new machine, or may threaten the employer with a strike if he should use it. A policy of this nature was followed by the National Window Glass Workers' union when window-glass-making machines first came into use, about 1908. In using this policy the union courted and finally achieved disaster. A union may try to have laws or ordinances passed to debar certain machines from use. The Street Railway Workers' union tried for legislation against one-man street cars —and succeeded only in encouraging the use of buses.

[25] These attacks were only in part directed against the actual introduction of new machinery. To a large extent they were made for the purpose of raising wages, improving the conditions of work, and lowering the price of foodstuffs. See F. A. Darvall, *Popular Disturbances and Public Disorder in Regency England,* Chapter X. London: Oxford University Press, 1934. The Hammonds state that the struggle was carried on not so much against the machine as against the power behind the machine, the power of capital. See J. L. and Barbara Hammond, *The Town Laborer,* p. 15. London: Longmans, Green & Co., 1918.

Occasionally a union will attempt to cope with the machine by making wage or other concessions. Though such concessions may lessen the impact of technological change, they will inevitably give way to some policy of control over the new devices, as either a supplement to or a substitute for the concessions.[26]

Sometimes, however, unions cooperate with management in the introduction of improved methods and equipment. The International Ladies' Garment Workers' Union and the United Mine Workers have been outstanding in this respect.

Reducing the Time Lost Between Jobs. Any satisfactory attack on the problem of technological unemployment must attempt to reduce the length of time the displaced workers are involuntarily idle. Policies toward this end may be divided into two general classes: plans that can be put into operation by the individual employer or group of employers, and plans that should be sponsored and applied by the government.

(1) Let us first consider what employers can do. Sometimes the time of unemployment can be shortened by shifting displaced workers within or between plants. Intraplant shifting has its limitations: the displaced workers may not be fitted for the jobs that are open, or there may be no jobs open. However, under certain circumstances—for example, if the plant has a high rate of labor turnover—the policy is feasible; and not a few employers in times past have adopted it. Sometimes a benevolent employer can find jobs for his displaced workers in other plants in the community. Formal and informal contacts between employers may clear the way for such transfers.

If jobs are available for displaced workers in the plants or in the community in which they have been employed, but they are not fitted for the jobs, they will need education and retraining. Although such a vocational rehabilitation program involves certain costs, the employer should benefit from it through the appreciation and loyalty of the retrained workers and through better cooperation from the working force in general.

When union members are threatened with displacement the un-

[26] For a detailed discussion of the method of competition and of other methods used by unions in connection with technological change, see Sumner H. Slichter, *Union Policies and Industrial Management,* Chapters VII, VIII, and IX. Washington: The Brookings Institution, 1941.

ions sometimes attempt to have their members transferred to other jobs. This policy was tried with some degree of success by the Glass Bottle Blowers' Association during the years that the industry was being technologically transformed. It was tried, with still more success, by the International Typographical Union when the Mergenthaler Linotype was introduced, during the latter part of the last century. In the railroad industry, too, the policy of shifting displaced workers to new jobs has been tried on a large scale.[27] Unions have also shown some interest in the retraining of displaced union members.

In rare circumstances the employer might be able to fit the jobs to the workers, instead of the reverse. Conceivably the costs involved could be overbalanced by the good will engendered.

Another policy open to the employer is to give his workers advance notice of likely or certain displacement, so that the workers can look around for other jobs. From the employer's standpoint, obviously, this practice has its dangers.

Finally, the employer could reduce hours (and earnings) temporarily, to spread the work. Professor Carver believed the reduction of hours to be the easiest temporary expedient for dealing with normal technological unemployment.[28] This policy is of limited value only, as we shall see in Chapter 28.

(2) Let us turn now to a brief consideration of what society can do for the technologically unemployed. Since labor immobility is one of the chief reasons for the continued idleness of displaced workers, a well organized labor market is again shown to be essential. In this country the United States Employment Service has greatly improved the general functioning of our labor markets and aided in the placing of the technologically unemployed.

Another social policy, or rather set of policies, for aiding technologically displaced workers is the establishment of a program of vocational training, guidance, and rehabilitation. In directing displaced workers to employments in which their services will be needed, and in supplying significant information concerning labor

27 For a more detailed description of the policy as applied to the above cases, and to others not mentioned, see Harry Ober, *Trade Union Policy and Technological Change,* pp. 17-45. W.P.A. National Research Project, Report L-8, April, 1940.

28 Thomas Nixon Carver, *The Essential Factors of Social Evolution,* p. 539. Cambridge: Harvard University Press, 1935.

market conditions, the public employment offices have an important part to play in the functioning of any such plan or program. At the present time we have national, state, and local agencies carrying on vocational training activities.[29]

Caring for the Technologically Unemployed. Technologically unemployed workers, like other unemployed persons, are entitled to unemployment insurance if they meet the eligibility requirements. Since the middle of the 1930's, when our unemployment insurance laws came into operation, many workers displaced by machines have been helped by such insurance. (The question of unemployment insurance is discussed at length in Chapter 29.)

Another policy for ameliorating the lot of the displaced worker is that of dismissal compensation, by which workers whose services are no longer required are paid a certain sum of money, either in a lump sum or over a period of time. The size of the sum is regulated either by predetermined formal standards or by informal reckoning at the time the workers are dismissed.

An early use of this policy is supplied by the men's clothing industry. Back in the 1920's the Hart Schaffner & Marx Company, operating under an agreement with the Amalgamated Clothing Workers' union, introduced cutting machines in large numbers. Jobs were wiped out and the curtailment of the working force was necessary. The company and the union entered an agreement under which the company set aside $50,000, and from the unemployment insurance fund (built up jointly by the company and the union) there was taken an additional $25,000. From the amount thus established each of the dismissed workers received $500. It was understood that those who received this parting gift were not to re-enter the industry.[30]

Dismissal compensation has also been paid to workers dismissed as a result of the closing of plants and of mergers, because of personal obsolescence, and for other reasons unconnected with technological improvements.

Labor organizations have become increasingly interested in dis-

[29] See *Vocational Education and Changing Conditions,* United States Department of the Interior, Office of Education, Vocational Educational Bulletin No. 174, p. 7, 1934; and *Report of the Secretary of Labor's Committee on Technological Unemployment,* p. 553.

[30] A detailed study of the employment experience of the displaced cutters was made by Robert J. Myers. See *The Journal of Political Economy,* August, 1929.

missal compensation; more and more collective bargaining agreements make provision for it. One of the most notable agreements of this nature was concluded in the railroad industry in 1936 between 21 railroad unions and most of the railroads in the industry. Under this agreement employees who are displaced as a result of railway consolidation receive a "coordination allowance" based on their length of service and their recent pay.

When collective bargaining agreements provide for dismissal pay, they commonly specify the conditions under which such pay is required. In many agreements the term "technological changes" is specifically mentioned. The amount of an employee's dismissal pay is usually based on his length of service, with a minimum period generally stated; in a considerable number of agreements there is an upper limit to the amount that can be received. In a few agreements provision is made for the payment of uniform amounts (such as two weeks' pay), with no distinction made between the variations in length of service.[31]

[31] Further information on dismissal pay will be found in *Labor Management Contract Provisions,* 1949-1950, pp. 12-15, Bulletin No. 1022, Bureau of Labor Statistics, United States Department of Labor. See also the Bureau's Bulletin No. 908-5, *Collective Bargaining Provisions.*

6

CYCLICAL UNEMPLOYMENT

If seasonal and technological unemployment were all we had to contend with, the unemployment problem would be much less serious than it is. But in addition to the numerous, scattered, and more or less continuous changes in the economy that result from seasonal influences and technological improvements and that, in turn, cause unemployment, we have general, cyclical changes in the economy that lead periodically to *mass* unemployment. This cyclical unemployment has been with us intermittently in times past and has caused an immense amount of economic loss and social distress. There is some reason for believing that the volume of such unemployment will be less in the future than it has been in the years gone by. There is no reason for believing, however, that serious cyclical slumps are a thing of the past.

The business cycle has not had a long history. Estey observes that business cycles made their first appearance in England "at the beginning of that modern period ushered in by the end of the Napoleonic Wars"; and Carl Snyder states that in this country the real beginning of the cycle (in the widely used, present-day sense) appears to go back to about the end of the 1860's.[1] The business cycle, then, is a product of modern industrial society; it did not exist in the pre-industrial era. There were fluctuations in economic activity, to be sure, before the modern industrial era began; but in the matter of causality and in other key characteristics these fluctuations differed from those associated with the contemporary business cycle. Pre-industrial era fluctuations were a product not of the prevailing

[1] See James A. Estey, *Business Cycles*, 2nd ed., pp. 42, 44. New York: Prentice-Hall, Inc., 1950. Carl Snyder, *Business Cycles and Business Measurements*, p. 17. New York: The Macmillan Co., 1927.

industrial system, but of natural disasters (famines, pestilences, and floods), wars, and miscellaneous secondary causes (including certain governmental policies). In varying degrees these factors still influence fluctuations in business activity, but they are not the causes of the business cycle. There can be cyclical fluctuations in business activity without them.

The earlier fluctuations, it should further be noted, were not as regular as the modern fluctuations. They were more of a random, nonperiodic nature. In brief they did not constitute what we now refer to as business "cycles."

Products of modern industrialism, business cycles are also products of the "market economy" or free enterprise system. Under a highly planned economy, in which private business is of little account, it is possible to eliminate both cyclical swings in business and cyclical unemployment. A planned economy, however, may still be exposed to noncyclical fluctuations: crops may fail, wars may occur, there may be lack of close coordination in planning. Such fluctuations may lead to ups and downs in production and in employment; but they will never bring on the mass unemployment associated with cyclical fluctuations. The bulk of the working force can be given steady employment. Whether or not the workers can be as effectively employed in a controlled economy as under a free enterprise system is another question.[2]

Characteristics of the Business Cycle

What *are* business cycles? Burns and Mitchell have stated, tentatively, that they are "a type of fluctuation found in the aggregate economic activity of nations that organize their work mainly in business enterprises." [3] The authors go on to point out that a cycle is made up of expansions that occur in many different economic activities at about the same time; that these expansions are followed by recessions, contractions, and revivals, with the revivals developing into new expansions; and that this order of events repeats itself

[2] This question relates to allocation of the productive factors at a given time and over a period of time. This allocation is tied up intimately with the problem of economic growth. For a good discussion of capitalism and communism in terms of growth possibilities, and also in terms of employment, see David McCord Wright, *Capitalism*. New York: McGraw-Hill Book Co., Inc., 1951.

[3] Wesley C. Mitchell, *What Happens During Business Cycles,* p. 6. New York: National Bureau of Economic Research, Inc., 1951.

in cycles varying in length from about two years to ten or twelve years. It will not be possible to examine and elaborate upon all the characteristics of the business cycle as thus defined, but we shall pause to discuss a few of them.

(1) To begin with, most types of business activity move in cycles. The National Bureau of Economic Research has studied hundreds of time series, covering such things as industrial production, factory payrolls, common stock prices, and bank clearings, and has found that approximately 97 per cent of them experience cyclical fluctuations.[4]

It must be emphasized, however, that these series do not all expand and contract at the same time. While some are expanding, others are contracting; and quite often when some are at their high point, others are at their low. The turning points in the general cycle are determined by the kind of movement that predominates in the individual series. As Professor Burns indicates, the turning points in the individual or specific cycles appear in "clusters," which generally have "definite points of concentration," and "when the peaks are bunched the troughs are few, and *vice versa*." [5]

(2) The various series change not only at different times but also to different degrees; that is, the amplitudes of their fluctuations vary. Fluctuations in profits are much more pronounced than fluctuations in wages, as can be seen in Table 6. If a depression is extremely serious, profits for the economy as a whole may be nonexistent, or even of a minus character, as they were for corporations at the bottom of the Great Depression. Some companies, of course, make profits even though business in general is sorely depressed, just as some sustain losses when the economy as a whole is prosperous. The volatile nature of profits is very pertinent in connection with certain labor matters (such as profit-sharing and the ability-to-pay principle of wage-setting) that we shall consider later.

[4] Arthur F. Burns, *New Facts on Business Cycles,* 30th Annual Report of the National Bureau of Economic Research, Inc., May, 1950, p. 4.

[5] Professor Burns has further indicated that in the early stages of an expansion in aggregate economic activities the *proportion* of expansions in individual series is also moving upwards; but in the later stages of the aggregate expansion the proportion moves downwards. The same relationship obtains in periods of general contraction. Thus, as Professor Burns has pointed out, there are two cycles, rather than only one, in economic activities. The "proportion" cycle foreshadows the "aggregate" cycle. See *Ibid.,* pp. 10-22.

Table 6

Unemployment, Corporate Profits, and Wages and Salaries in the United States *

Year	Unemployment (000's)	Corporate Profits Before Tax (billions)	Private Wages and Salaries (billions)
1929	1,550	$ 9.8	45.2
1930	4,340	3.3	40.7
1931	8,020	—0.8	33.6
1932	12,060	—3.0	25.3
1933	12,830	0.2	23.7
1934	11,340	1.7	27.4
1935	10,610	3.2	30.0
1936	9,030	5.7	33.9
1937	7,700	6.2	38.4
1938	10,390	3.3	34.6
1939	9,480	6.5	37.5
1940	8,120	9.3	41.1
1945	1,040	19.7	82.1
1950	3,142	41.4	123.4

* *Historical Statistics of the United States, 1789-1945,* p. 12; *Statistical Abstract of the United States,* 1952, pp. 178, 255, 448; both published by the Bureau of the Census, United States Department of Commerce.

Fluctuations in output are much more marked in the durable goods industries than in the nondurable goods industries. Production of durable goods declines sharply during a recession, and is usually at a very low ebb during the depression phase of the cycle. In 1932 the index for machine tool orders, according to the National Machine Tool Builders' Association, stood at 19.6 as against 155.8 in 1929 and 186.9 in 1937.

The decline in production and employment is generally more severe in durable producers' goods than in durable consumers' goods. For example, the drop in passenger car production between 1929 and 1932, though sharp, was not as sharp as the drop in the production of machine tools.

Since it is the durable goods industries—particularly those of a capital-building character—that experience the most drastic contractions during general business slumps, as well as the most rapid expansion during general business prosperity, it is not surprising that economists should direct major attention to those industries in their discussions of cycle theory and cycle policy. It is in the field of investment that the most spectacular and significant developments of the cycle occur. This fact has been recognized by the Keynesians, but also by the Swedish "pre-Keynesians."

(3) In terms of duration business cycles may last from around two years to around ten or twelve years. In the period from December, 1854 to May, 1938 there were, according to Mitchell, 21 business cycles in the United States. Counting from trough to trough, the shortest was 29 months (from April, 1919 to September, 1921) and the longest was 99 months (from December, 1870 to March, 1879). Fourteen of the cycles had durations of from 30 to 48 months.

Sometimes a distinction is made between "minor" and "major" cycles.[6] It has been found that in this country there are "cycles within cycles," particularly during periods of expansion. During the 73 years between 1865 and 1938 there were, according to Hansen, seven major cycles and eleven minor ones.

(4) The major cycles, as one would expect, are the ones in which production and employment show marked declines and in which there is a serious volume of unemployment. The amplitude of the cyclical swings in the major cycles (and also in the minor cycles) varies from one to another; so does the duration of the various phases of the cycles. In terms of depression severity, therefore, the major cycles differ considerably. At the head of the list, however, must be placed the Great Depression, which reached its low point in the early 1930's. The second most severe was the depression of the 1870's, which "hit bottom" in 1876.[7]

(5) Although it is generally agreed that business cycles are generated by factors operating within, and produced by, the economic system, external forces also affect cyclical movements. The most important external force has been wars. During war periods production rises and unemployment decreases. Any tendency that may have existed for business to decline is counteracted by the artificial pros-

[6] See Alvin H. Hansen, *Business Cycles and National Income,* Chapter 2. New York: W. W. Norton & Co., 1951.

[7] For a "severity ranking" of six major depressions, by A. R. Echler, see Estey, *op. cit.,* p. 120.

perity of the war boom. After the war is over, the drop that takes place in war production, and the demobilization of great numbers of servicemen, may exert a very strong pull downwards to depression and unemployment. (The period immediately after World War II was largely an exception to the common sequence of events.)

Another external factor that may have an effect on business fluctuations is the weather, especially in the influence that it exerts on agricultural production. It may be that this paricular factor has some relationship to the appearance of spots on the sun, as some reputable scholars have contended. It certainly has no relationship to the type of economic system that prevails.

Business Cycle Theories

A great many theories have been advanced in explanation of why (in Wesley Mitchell's picturesque language) "the whole congeries of squirming entities," which constitute the components of the business cycle, "manages to swell in volume for a while, then to shrink for a while, only to repeat what it has already done time and again."

Most of the theories are partial theories, in the sense that they do not contain a complete explanation of the cycle. Each points to a specific force, or set of forces, which is supposed to be of major and possibly of overwhelming influence in leading to cyclical fluctuations.

Some cycle theorists have emphasized psychological factors; others have given chief weight to monetary influences; others have stressed underconsumption. In more recent years savings and investment factors have been increasingly emphasized.[8]

It may well be that it is now possible to construct an integrated theory of the cycle. Such is Professor Hansen's contention, and he has constructed such a theory, one in which savings and investment influences are given a primary place.[9] Using the tools of analysis fashioned by Wicksell, Aftalion, and Keynes, and bringing into the picture a variety of ideas advanced over the years by various cycle theorists, Hansen sets forth a "modern" cycle theory. This theory (which accounts for changes in national income) makes use of (1) the notion of a marginal efficiency schedule of capital relative to the

[8] For detailed discussions of various business cycle theories, see Estey, *op. cit.*, Chapters 8-17; and Hansen, *op. cit.*, Chapters 13-24.

[9] *Ibid.*, Chapter 24.

interest rate; (2) the principle of acceleration—the effect on the rate of investment of changes in consumption spending; and (3) the so-called "investment-multiplier" (which is based upon the "consumption function") in its relationship to the formation of income.

In his theory of the cycle Hansen emphasizes the point that in both the expansion and the contraction phases of the cycle there are self-limiting factors. These phases of the cycle, in other words, are not self-reinforcing; they do not go on and on, like Tennyson's celebrated brook. To understand why this is so one has to probe into the marginal efficiency schedule, the principle of acceleration, and the scope of the consumption function. The modern business cycle theory, it is evident, is not a simple matter! But neither is the phenomenon with which it purports to deal.

In its essentials the Hansen theory would probably meet with widespread support among economists. There is a great deal of agreement on the basic influence of saving and investment processes upon cyclical fluctuations, and there is general agreement also on the importance of the aggregate-demand consideration. However, differences of opinion still exist among cycle theorists, and the riddle of the cycle has by no means been completely solved.

Complete and Partial Unemployment

Unemployment in any country may be envisaged as a large, ever-changing pool (in a sense it is more accurate to speak of many pools, but we shall use the notion of a single one). The pool of unemployment is always in existence; it never dries up. The level of the pool varies from time to time—daily, weekly, monthly, and yearly. On some occasions the level will be quite low; on other occasions it will be very high. When business is experiencing a cyclical depression, for example, the volume of unemployment is especially large and the pool level is high.

The yearly changes in the size of the unemployment pool in this country for certain selected years are clearly revealed in Table 6 (p. 99). It will be noted that in 1929 the average amount of unemployment was about 1.5 million. After business started its cyclical toboggan slide in the latter part of that year, the volume increased, until in 1933 the figure amounted to almost 13 million. (This figure is an average; during some weeks in 1933 the number of unemployed totaled considerably more than 13 million.) Table 6 shows the effect on unemployment of the slow process of recovery after 1933, as well as the effect of the short recession beginning in 1937.

During 1933 approximately one-quarter of the labor force was unemployed. The unemployed pool was indeed full. However, more than one-quarter of the members of the work force experienced unemployment during the year, since there is a more or less constant change in the personnel of the unemployed pool, even when the level of the pool is constant. In a sense, then, the seriousness of the unemployment situation is a little less than the 25 per cent figure would seem to indicate, since the burden of unemployment is not concentrated wholly on a fixed, specific 25 per cent of the workers.

The burden of unemployment is nevertheless concentrated to some extent. In 1933 each worker in the labor force did not spend one-quarter of his time in the unemployment pool. A great many were not in it at all. Many, however, were in it for a large fraction of the year; and some were in it all year long. This unequal distribution of the unemployment burden is a matter that we shall discuss in the next section.

The full impact of a cyclical depression on unemployment cannot be gauged from unemployment statistics, for in addition to the workers who are fully unemployed there are many who are partially unemployed. Partial unemployment—or partial employment—is preferable to complete unemployment; but it is subject to many of the evils that accompany complete unemployment, though to a lesser degree.

The number of part-time workers is much smaller than the number of unemployed, but it is sizable nevertheless. A general idea of the extent of partial unemployment during a period of low economic activity can be formed from the following figures on Philadelphia, a city that was particularly hard hit by the depression.[10]

Year	*Full Time*	*Part Time*	*Unemployed*
1930	79.8%	5.2%	15.0%
1931	60.7	13.8	25.5
1932	37.1	20.8	42.1
1933	34.1	19.9	46.0
1934	49.2	14.6	36.2

10 *Monthly Labor Review,* October, 1939, p. 838. Persons employed on work relief undertakings were included in the unemployed category. For Cincinnati the part-time and unemployed percentages were considerably smaller. See p. 836.

Variations in the Burden of Unemployment

When one-quarter of the labor force is idle, the decline in national output and in material living standards is certain to be serious. But over-all figures do not reveal clearly the loss that many individual workers suffer as a consequence of depression. In the following paragraphs we shall give some attention to variations in the incidence of unemployment, using statistics to illustrate the general points. Since the figures speak rather loudly, words may be kept to a minimum.

(1) During a cyclical slump there is more unemployment among workers in the durable goods industries than in the nondurable goods industries. In 1932, 42 per cent of the AFL unionists in the metal trades were unemployed; 64 per cent of those in the building trades; and 32 per cent of those in all trades. In the printing trades, which to a very considerable extent turn out nondurable products, the percentage was 19.[11]

(2) Some towns, cities, and geographical regions experience a much larger amount of cyclical unemployment than others. The difference is due largely to the relative importance, in terms of numbers employed, of the durable and nondurable goods industries found within their limits. In Albany, Schenectady, and Troy, New York, centers that are outstanding in the production of durable goods, the employment index fell from 110 in 1929 to 54 in 1932; whereas in New York City, where durable goods industries are relatively less prominent, the employment index fell only from 92 to 59.[12]

(3) Young workers bear a disproportionate share of the burden of cyclical unemployment, as the figures in Table 7 indicate. At a time when 20 per cent of the total labor force of the nation was idle (or engaged in relief work) 41 per cent of the available workers in the age group 15 to 19 years were similarly situated. Although the number of young persons was at a maximum level in 1937 (owing to the high birth rate during World War I), for the most part their unemployment was due to "age discrimination." When it becomes necessary to lay off workers many employers let out the younger ones

[11] *American Federationist,* June, 1935, p. 635.

[12] *Hearings,* Sub-committee, Committee on Labor, House of Representatives, 74th Cong., 1st Sess., on H.R. 2827, etc., p. 94.

first; and they rehire younger workers last when business improves. To make the lot of young workers still worse, professional associations and unions during the Great Depression raised the minimum-age level for membership and imposed greater restrictions on job opportunities for apprentices and beginners.

Older workers frequently benefit from seniority arrangements and the common tendency of employers to retain workers with long service and experience. Nevertheless, older workers experience more unemployment than the workers in the 25 to 54 age group. The figures in Table 7 may possibly understate the degree of unemployment of older workers during a depression.[13]

Table 7

Workers Unemployed or Engaged in Emergency Work, November 30, 1937, by Age Group *

Age Group (years)	Estimated Per Cent of Available Workers Unemployed
All ages	20%
15-19	41
20-24	24
25-34	16
35-44	16
45-54	17
55-64	20
65-74	19

* *Monthly Labor Review,* January, 1940, p. 72. Figures are from the November, 1937 Census of Unemployment.

(4) Cyclical unemployment is generally more severe among Negro workers than among white workers. This fact is illustrated in the following figures, which show, for the month of May in 1933 through 1937, the percentage of unemployment in the two groups in the city of Cincinnati.[14]

[13] In a study made in Bridgeport, Conn., in 1934—when business was more depressed than in 1937—34.4 per cent of the workers 65 years of age and over were unemployed. *Monthly Labor Review,* March, 1935, p. 632.

[14] *Monthly Labor Review,* October, 1938, p. 772. The above figures include as unemployed persons employed on various governmental employment projects.

Year	*White*	*Colored*
1933	28.04%	54.32%
1934	21.19	53.40
1935	17.80	51.00
1936	17.52	49.45
1937	8.00	35.97

The figures for Cincinnati may not reflect accurately those of the country as a whole, but they at least indicate in a general way a situation that is known to exist.

(5) Some workers are unemployed much longer than others. In Table 8, based on the registration of unemployed workers with the United States Employment Service during the fiscal year 1935-36, it will be seen that over 600,000 workers were (at the time they registered) idle for over 4 years. A simple calculation will reveal that over a million and a half were idle for over a year; close to two and a half million were idle for six months or less.

Table 8

Classification of Unemployed Applicants for Jobs in Terms of Duration of Unemployment *

Unemployed	Number
1 month or under	1,225,792
2 to 6 months	1,181,847
7 to 12 months	592,010
13 to 24 months	446,342
25 to 36 months	283,406
37 to 48 months	134,099
Over 48 months	645,878
Recent students	474,196
Without work experience	323,564
Total:	5,307,134

* *Monthly Labor Review*, December, 1936, p. 1527.

The Costs of Cyclical Unemployment

There are various ways in which the cost of serious depressions may be indicated. One of these is the loss in income to the nation at large. The total loss in income from 1930 to 1937, inclusive, has been estimated at more than $200 billion.[15] This figure does not

[15] *Monthly Labor Review*, November, 1939, p. 1075.

include any loss from "residual unemployment," estimated at approximately two million workers, but relates solely to depression unemployment. To make the loss appear more graphic the National Resources Committee, which made the estimate, states that if the idle men and machines could have been used in making houses, the use of the lost income would have given every family in the country a new $6,000 home. (When the Committee made its calculation new $6,000 homes were well within the realm of possibility.) The Committee also pointed out that the country's whole railroad system could have been scrapped and rebuilt, not once, but at least five times.

The loss in income to the nation from a serious depression may indeed be staggering. But the loss to specific persons may be relatively much greater. As we have emphasized in our preceding discussion, the burden of cyclical unemployment is not evenly distributed over the populace. Some persons suffer little, if at all, while others suffer a great deal.

The losses to which individual workers are exposed when their wages disappear are numerous and painful. Workers and their dependents may have to live without adequate food and clothing. They may have to forego various activities of a cultural or recreational nature. Their accumulated savings will dwindle, and if the period of unemployment is protracted, may completely disappear. That many persons thus suffered during the Great Depression is suggested by the stark figures relating to the decline in savings accounts from 1928 to 1932—a decline of nine million.[16] Workers may lose their homes through inability to keep up mortgage payments; they may be compelled to let insurance policies lapse because they cannot pay the premiums; they may be driven deeper and deeper into debt.

The visible losses resulting from unemployment are accompanied by extremely serious invisible consequences, consequences that are registered not in the economic balance sheet of the unemployed

[16] Clarence J. Enzler, *Some Social Aspects of the Depression, (1930-1935)*, p. 19. Washington: The Catholic University of America Press, 1939. The general topic discussed in Enzler's book is also taken up in Chapter 5 of *Unemployment, an International Problem,* Royal Institute of International Affairs. London: Oxford University Press, 1935. A briefer and more theoretical treatment of the subject will be found in A. C. Pigou, *The Theory of Unemployment,* Chapter 3. London: Macmillan & Co., 1933.

worker, but in his heart and mind. Though a short spell of unemployment may not have any serious psychological results, long idleness may embitter the unemployed worker toward the economic system, and not without cause. He may, indeed, join with others in seeking a new type of system. It was no accident that the Communist appeal carried increased power during the Great Depression.

The unemployed are likely to be driven to worry, and some to despair, as is clear from the increased suicide rates during the depression years. When a man is forced to seek aid from his friends or relatives, or from the government, he may feel degraded; if he accepts such aid without qualms, he may well be in a condition of moral deterioration. Even relief work can be morally injurious to a worker—particularly if he is given a job of little or no social value, like chasing certain birds out of Washington parks by rattling stones in tin cans.

Protracted unemployment has other invisible effects. Being idle, and probably exposed to physical undernourishment and psychological strain, the workers are almost certain to lose some of their mental and manual agility. Even workers fortunate enough to retain their jobs may be subjected to loss and suffering. Their wages may be cut and they may be placed on short time; thus their earnings may seriously decline. With lower earnings they may be called upon to make many of the sacrifices experienced, generally to a more pronounced degree, by the totally unemployed.[17]

Coping with Cyclical Unemployment

Back in 1916 Samuel Gompers thought the day would come when unions, with increased membership and greater benefit programs, would solve the problem of unemployment.[18] Some years later Henry Ford expressed the view that if a dozen of the country's largest companies were to cooperate "in certain essentials," depressions could be prevented.[19] Today there is still disagreement concern-

[17] For a study of the condition of 1,000 employed railway employees during a serious part of the Great Depression, see *Monthly Labor Review,* October, 1934, pp. 853-856.

[18] *Labor and Employer* (ed. by H. Robbins), p. 151. New York: E. P. Dutton & Co., 1920.

[19] *Moving Forward,* p. 78. Garden City: Doubleday, Doran & Co., 1930. Views of a somewhat similar, though less extreme, nature were held by other businessmen at the time.

ing the best methods to use in coping with cyclical unemployment, but few persons would maintain that the problem can be solved either by the unions or by businessmen.

Policies for dealing with cyclical unemployment may be divided into two categories: preventive and ameliorative. These two categories are not completely distinct, since ameliorative measures can have preventive effects; however, we shall keep them separate, giving most of our attention to the preventive measures.

If cyclical unemployment is to be avoided or kept at a low level, wide fluctuations in production must be avoided: in other words, the economy must be stabilized—not static, but moving ahead at a steady rate. Numerous policies for promoting economic stability have been advanced, and partial use has already been made of some of them. Let us examine some of these policies.

(1) *Fiscal Policy.* Through its tax and expenditure policies the government can exert a large amount of influence over private industry. If it aims to stabilize economic activity and maintain a high level of employment, there are certain procedures it should follow.

At a time of prosperity, when production and employment are at a high level, the government should keep its expenditures down as much as possible. It has its regular functions to perform, of course, but it should not embark on other spending ventures. The government should not compete unduly with private industry for labor and capital. At the same time taxes should be kept at a level high enough to enable the government to reduce the size of the national debt (which may have been built up to large proportions during a previous depression), and to limit the strong tendency, growing out of heavy private spending, toward higher and higher prices and overemployment.

During a time of depression the opposite procedures should be followed. At such a time the aim of the government, and of other agencies, should be to maintain "effective demand," especially by increasing investment spending.

When business in general is depressed taxes should be kept down, so that private spending may be maintained or even go up; and governmental expenditures should be increased, so that general industrial activity will be stimulated. During a depressed period the budget will be unbalanced, with expenditures in excess of revenues. The difference will be made up by public borrowing.

This fiscal policy has a number of implications. First, the idea of an annually balanced budget is discarded. Not that there should be a continuous piling up of deficits; the budget should be balanced over a period of years, perhaps a decade or so.

Secondly, if the government is to increase its expenditures by a large amount during times when private industry is in the doldrums, it behooves the government to do some very careful planning ahead of time so that its greatly enlarged spending can be done wisely and without undue delay. Whether the government in this country has been doing enough in the way of making such plans is questionable.[20]

Thirdly, the carrying out of such a policy as we have described is beset with difficulties. This is due to the fact that economics and "politics" can very easily come into conflict. It requires considerable courage for a legislator to advocate high, or higher, taxes even when conditions are prosperous. And yet at such a time it is not enough to balance the budget; it must be overbalanced, or the deficit financing of depression periods will lead to a constantly growing national debt. And despite possible expressions to the contrary, such a development is not to be viewed with equanimity.

Another way in which the fiscal weapon could be used to combat business depressions and mass unemployment would be to increase the number of built-in, automatic stabilizers in our fiscal system. Already there is an automatic response in federal income and federal spending to changes in the national income. For example, tax yields from personal income taxes increase when the national income goes up; and governmental expenditures for unemployment insurance and farm relief go up when the national income goes down. There are other possible built-in stabilizing procedures: for example, to provide that the tax rate for unemployment insurance should go automatically up, and benefit rates automatically down, when business is prosperous; when business is depressed, then the taxes could go down and the benefits up. Another step would be to alter the withholding rate of the income tax in accordance with certain prescribed changes in the price level.

[20] For a harsh criticism of the Council of Economic Advisors for its alleged failure to prepare a definite (comprehensive) depression program, see Henry H. Villard's communication in *The American Economic Review*, September, 1950, pp. 600-604.

Although some economists look upon built-in stabilizers with a great deal of favor, believing that they alone are adequate to promote stability, the majority feel that such stabilizers must be supplemented by specific, discretionary stabilizing policies.[21]

Federal taxation in general can probably be manipulated in such a way as to have far-reaching effects on business activity. Professor Hansen has declared that in view of our vast federal budget "the anti-cyclical possibilities in our tax program are enormous"; and the group of experts appointed by the Secretary-General of the United Nations to look into the problem of promoting full employment has stated that variations in tax rates seem to offer for many countries (including, presumably, the United States) "a most effective and prompt method for maintaining the level of effective demand in the economy." [22]

Two final points should be made about fiscal policy and the maintenance of economic stability. Since there are numerous governmental disbursing agencies, the spending activities of these should be closely coordinated. Any spending measures adopted should be flexible in nature and prompt in execution, as well as large enough to give the necessary fillip to private industry. Often prompt spending can cut down the size of the required expenditures.

(2) *Monetary Policy.* Monetary policy can be planned in a way to promote economic stability. During periods of prosperity the supply of "money" should be curtailed; during periods of depression it should be increased. The most effective means available for achieving these ends is called "quantitative" credit control: that is, control aimed at the use of credit throughout the economy in general, not in specific employments only ("qualitative" control). Quantitative credit control is more influential in restricting excessive credit expansion in prosperous periods than in promoting expansion in bad times: you can lead the horse to water, but you cannot make him drink. Despite this weakness quantitative credit control is a very useful method.

Open-market operations constitute another effective means of

[21] See *The American Economic Review,* September, 1950, pp. 520-525 for a discussion of this general problem by the American Economic Association's Sub-Committee on Economic Instability.

[22] *Saving American Capitalism,* ed. by Seymour E. Harris, p. 223. New York: A. A. Knopf, 1948. *National and International Measures for Full Employment,* p. 38. United Nations, Department of Economic Affairs, 1949.

monetary control.[23] When the Federal Reserve Banks or the Treasury buy government securities in the open market, they tend to promote an expansion of credit. The sellers of the securities receive checks which, when collected by a member bank from a Reserve bank, build up the reserves of the member bank thus enabling it to extend more credit. When the Federal Reserve Banks sell securities in the open market, member bank reserves are pulled down and credit is thereby curtailed.

Open-market operations should be meshed with appropriate rediscount rate changes. Thus when the Federal Reserve Banks are trying to encourage credit expansion through buying securities in the open market they should lower their rediscount rates. This makes possible lower discount (interest) rates and thus encourages borrowing, which in turn promotes industrial activity and employment. When the banks' aim is to discourage borrowing, the rediscount rate should be raised.

The Federal Reserve Banks can exercise some degree of control over credit by changing the reserve ratios: lowering them when expansion is desired, and increasing them (if they are not already at the maximum) when contraction is required. Moral suasion may also be used by the Reserve Banks in an effort to affect the use of credit. The United States Treasury can also exercise control over bank reserves, especially by means of the control it exerts over the money in its own vaults and over its deposits with the Federal Reserve banks and the commercial banks.

Other monetary techniques for promoting economic stability have been suggested. Among these are the commodity-reserve currency plan, the 100 per cent money plan, and the social credit plan.[24]

Students of the problem of economic stability believe that the fiscal and monetary policies we have described should be integrated (some economists, like Professor Lester V. Chandler, use the term "monetary policy" in a very broad sense to include fiscal policy). Thus, to take a single illustration, when deficit financing is resorted to during a period of serious unemployment, the money should be

[23] This is the view of the Sub-Committee on Economic Instability of the American Economic Association. See *The American Economic Review,* September, 1950, p. 527.

[24] For a discussion of these plans see Estey, *op. cit.,* pp. 354-355, 389-391, 453-454.

raised in ways that promote monetary ease, not monetary stringency. The government should borrow chiefly from the Federal Reserve Banks, or from the member banks (which, at the same time, receive the aid of the Federal Reserve Banks in the form of additional reserves).[25] In general, private borrowers should not be discouraged, by higher interest rates or credit limitations, as a result of the public borrowing.

It might be added that the government could obtain the needed funds by printing paper money, a policy mentioned, though not advocated, by the sub-committee on economic instability of the American Economic Association. Such a policy, regardless of its economic merits, places too much of a strain on frail humanity and is definitely undesirable.

Although closer integration, both between and within fiscal and monetary policies, seems very desirable, the fact that the agencies exercising control over the two policies are not the same complicates the issue. The legislature controls fiscal policies; the Federal Reserve System, the Treasury, and other governmental bodies control monetary policies (this dispersion of control over monetary policies is also an obstacle to integration).

(3) *Wage Policy*. The view was once widely held, particularly by economists and businessmen, that an effective way to pull down the volume of depression unemployment is to reduce wages. It was thought that more units of labor would be purchased if the "price" were lower.[26] As a suitable policy for coping with mass unemployment the wage reduction policy now meets with little approval, certainly among economists.

The theoretical weakness of the wage reduction policy is that it fails to give adequate attention to the influence of wage rates on total, or aggregate, demand. In specific cases a wage reduction can increase employment—and it must be granted that a policy of selective wage cuts in a depression is often desirable. It does not follow, however, that a general wage reduction will increase general employ-

[25] See Professor Chandler's remarks (included in his general discussion of monetary policies) on pp. 250-251 of *Saving American Capitalism*, ed. by Seymour Harris. New York: A. A. Knopf, 1948.

[26] Professor F. A. Burchardt discusses at some length "three different strands of thought that appear to give support to the argument that wage reductions promote employment," in *The Economics of Full Employment*, pp. 7-12. Oxford University Institute of Statistics, 1944.

ment. The older view, as Professor Hansen has pointed out,[27] took aggregate demand for granted and favored the manipulation of wages. According to the newer view, which Keynes strongly advocated, aggregate demand should be increased (by the use of fiscal and monetary measures) and wage rates should remain largely unchanged. This shift in view is indeed an important one. It represents, in Hansen's words, "a major change in cycle policy." It should be added that the new or "modern" view not only indicates that general wage cuts during a depression lead to deflation, but that during booms general wage increases that outrun the over-all increase in labor productivity lead to inflation (see Chapter 23).

Selective wage cuts may be made, in fact probably must be made, in plants that are on the verge of bankruptcy. There may also be cuts in plants where wages are exceptionally high. A case can be made for reducing wages—rapidly and "once and for all"—in certain investment industries; but Bertil Ohlin, who has examined this possibility, is of the opinion that it would be impracticable in Western societies.[28]

Admitting the desirability of selective wage cuts during a depression, there remain two practical problems. First, how are we to determine in what plants or industries wages should be cut? In some instances this might not be a difficult problem; in others it could be very difficult. The criteria of keeping up aggregate demand and of maintaining a healthy psychological attitude on the part of workers and businessmen are useful in making the decision, but only in a very general way. Secondly, what about union opposition to wage cuts? Though in some cases unions have willingly, though not enthusiastically, accepted wage cuts, union willingness to accept wage cuts can rarely be counted upon.

(4) *The Annual Wage.* During recent years unions have to an increasing extent advocated the annual wage (or guaranteed employ-

[27] For a discussion of depression wage-policy, see Alvin H. Hansen, *Business Cycles and National Income*, pp. 518-520. New York: W. W. Norton & Co., 1951.

[28] *The Problem of Employment Stabilization*, pp. 34-35. New York: Columbia University Press, 1949. Professor Haberler supports the idea of selective wage cuts even though they would lead to a decline in the general wage level. He strongly supports monetary and fiscal policies, however, for stimulating expansion. See *The Impact of the Union*, ed. by David McCord Wright, pp. 53-54, 74. New York: Harcourt, Brace & Co., 1951. See also Professor Wright's remarks on pp. 290-291 of the same book.

ment, which is virtually the same) as a means for promoting economic stability and steadier employment. "The annual wage plan," Philip Murray once said, "will help to achieve the goal of continuing prosperity. If employers will agree to give labor regular work and pay, the whole community will benefit. When factories are full-blast, farmers and storekeepers prosper. When plants and men are idle, farm prices fall and business loses. A floor under the income of wage-earners would mean a floor under national income." [29]

In making their request for an annual wage the unions do not feel that their plans would harm employers. Indeed, they believe the plans would bring the employers certain advantages that would enable them to pay higher wages. The guaranteed wage plans "cut down losses from labor turnover. They remove much of the fear of unemployment, which is one thing that keeps workers from putting forth their best efforts. They increase the workers' interest in solving production problems." Moreover, these plans, according to union argument, increase buying power and, by making possible more production, result in lower costs. What is more, the necessity of paying wages on an annual basis is an incentive to employers to introduce regularizing devices into their industrial operations.

The prospect of seeing workers paid on an annual basis (the same as many salaried employees) is pleasing. But is industry able to assume such a responsibility? Employers, not oblivious to certain benefits that a policy of annual wages would bring, feel that most industries are not stable enough to warrant the payment of wages on this basis; nor are most employers convinced by the union argument that such wages would promote stability.

Though it seems likely that the annual wage plan will be used more widely in the future than in the present, progress in its adoption will probably be slow. The plan can undoubtedly make some contribution to the attainment of economic stability, but in view of the great difficulties in the way of its widespread use the contribution is not likely to be large.

(5) *Miscellaneous Policies.* In conclusion, let us consider a few miscellaneous policies for dealing with cyclical unemployment. A temporary reduction in the length of the working-week is sometimes effective, but the reduction should not be pushed too far

[29] *Guaranteed Wages the Year Round.* Foreword, Publication No. 124, C.I.O. Department of Research and Education.

(see p. 74). Our unemployment insurance system, which was nonexistent during the Great Depression, is a useful means for ameliorating the lot of the cyclically unemployed worker and for reducing, to a small extent, the amount of cyclical unemployment. Our Old-Age and Survivors' Insurance plan and our old-age assistance programs also ameliorate the condition of some of the unemployed, and, by helping to maintain spending, serve as a small obstacle in the way of the cyclical decline. As a last line of defence there is private and public charity.

Miscellaneous Types of Unemployment

Some unemployment is due to the fact that workers are not in the right place or the right occupation to take advantage of job openings. They are not adequately mobile, either occupationally or geographically. This type of unemployment is sometimes referred to as "frictional unemployment." Unemployment of this nature presupposes, as Beveridge points out,[30] the existence somewhere of unsatisfied demands for labor.

Some unemployment is due to "structural" changes in the economy. Most such unemployment can be included accurately under the term "technological unemployment"; but some of this unemployment—such as that due to a drop in the demand for a particular good—must be given separate recognition. It can be called "structural unemployment" (see p. 80). However, it might also be thrown into a broad category of "Miscellaneous Unemployment," a category which can be looked on as a sort of residuary legatee, receiving all the unemployment that is not placed in the seasonal, technological, and cyclical categories.

There is some merit in having such a broad category as there are many minor causes of unemployment in addition to the "Big Three" suggested by the three categories just mentioned. Among such causes are bankruptcies, fires, floods, hurricanes, unavailability of materials, and breakdowns in power supply.

Had this book been written in the 1940's it probably would have contained a few pages on the problem of secular stagnation and the unemployment that would have accompanied such stagnation. At

[30] Sir William Beveridge, *Full Employment in a Free Society*, p. 409. New York: W. W. Norton Co., 1945.

that time the prospect of our economy's "running down" was under serious discussion. At the present time the view that secular stagnation of the economy is present or imminent meets with little support, so we shall not probe into the old controversy.[31]

[31] The question is discussed in many places, but the following two sources may be mentioned. Alvin H. Hansen, *Fiscal Policy and Business Cycles,* especially Chapter XVII. New York: W. W. Norton & Co., 1941. George Terborgh, *The Bogey of Economic Maturity*. Chicago: Machinery and Allied Products Institute, 1945.

Part II

▼

UNIONS, MANAGEMENT, AND INDUSTRIAL RELATIONS

7

AN HISTORICAL SURVEY OF AMERICAN UNIONISM

A Century of Uncertainty

Unions, in the sense in which we now use the term, first appeared on the American industrial scene late in the 18th century.[1] It is true that there were labor organizations during the Colonial period, but these bodies did not possess the distinguishing features of unions. They were "friendly" (or "benevolent") societies, and their chief purpose was to help those of their members who experienced financial distress.

The achievement of national independence set in operation the forces that led to the establishment of union organizations. The elimination of internal tariff walls and the setting up of tariff barriers against goods from abroad hastened the expansion of manufacturing. At the same time the so-called merchant-capitalist rose to prominence in the economic life of the nation. Acting in the capacity of middleman, the merchant-capitalist sought to buy at the lowest possible prices, either at home or in other countries, and sell at the highest prices. The resulting pressure on manufacturers to cut wages helped to drive a wedge between master and men and greatly

[1] The author has presented an historical survey of American unionism at somewhat greater length in Chapters 2 and 3 of *Contemporary Unionism in the United States*. New York: Prentice-Hall Inc., 1948. Much more detailed accounts will be found in the following well known books, which students of labor (including the present writer) have long relied upon. J. R. Commons and Associates, *History of Labor in the United States*, Vol. I, New York: The Macmillan Co., 1918; Mary Beard, *A Short History of the American Labor Movement*. New York: Harcourt, Brace & Howe, 1920; Selig Perlman, *A History of Trade Unionism in the United States*. New York: The Macmillan Co., 1922.

promoted the growth of a distinct wage-earning class. And so, in 1792, the first genuine union, established by a group of Philadelphia shoemakers, came into existence. This organization collapsed before a year passed by; but in 1794 the shoemakers reorganized, setting up the Federal Society of Journeymen Cordwainers. In the same year another local union was established, by the printers in New York.

In the years that followed other local labor organizations were formed, but they did not achieve permanency. With one or two exceptions,[2] not a single present-day local union dates back continuously to the first half of the last century, and very few go back beyond the 1880's.

Tender Years. The early decades of the trade union movement in this country were uncertain ones. There were times of great activity in the labor field, during which many unions, principally locals, were established. At other times the whole union movement fell into a conditon of suspended animation. The periods of inactivity coincided very closely with periods of business depression and hard times.

A very important issue that faced the early unions was the charge of conspiracy. The issue at stake was whether or not combinations of workers trying to raise wages through collective action, and particularly through the use of the closed shop, were criminal conspiracies. Opinion on this matter was sharply divided, as were the decisions of the courts. Of the six conspiracy cases on record involving shoemaker organizations during the period from 1806 to 1815, four judgments went against the workers, one was for them, and the other was a compromise. As time went on, however, legal opinion shifted, and the right of workers to combine and seek higher wages became firmly established. A landmark in this shift was the famous decision handed down by Chief Justice Shaw of Massachusetts in the case of Commonwealth *v.* Hunt. Although unions as such came to be legally accepted, the legality of the various means they use to achieve their ends remained, and remains today, a question.

During the latter part of the 1820's labor embarked on an extensive program of political action. In view of the circumstances at the time such a move was not surprising. By 1827 the religious and

[2] The Columbia Typographical Union of Washington, D. C. is apparently the oldest local union in the country, possibly in the world. This organization was formed in 1815. See *American Federationist,* February, 1945, p. 23.

property qualifications for voting had largely been discarded in the various states, and manhood suffrage became an actual and important fact. The winning of the ballot at a time when industrial conditions were bad and a wave of democratic idealism was sweeping the country directed the attention of the workers to politics.

Other factors reinforced this influence. The workers had grievances—the conspiracy cases and long hours—which, to their way of thinking, could best be settled by political means. Finally, the concentration of large aggregations of labor in the growing industrial cities promoted greater political consciousness. The political efforts of the workers at this time were not very successful, however. The local labor parties that had been set up soon disappeared, and most of their demands went unsatisfied.

An important development of this period was the formation of the Mechanics' Union of Trade Associations in 1827, in Philadelphia. This organization, which was very active politically, was made up of the various local unions in the city. Today it would be called, in AFL parlance, a city central. It was the first organization of this type in the country and presumably in the world.

In the early 1830's labor swung back to economic action, and for a while unionism made marked progress. Then, in 1837, a serious panic occurred; hard times wrought great havoc among the unions, and most of them disappeared. For more than two decades unionism remained in a state of quiescence.

Although there was little trade union activity during the 1840's, there were a great many nonunion attempts at social and economic betterment. Three reform groups were particularly outstanding. One group sought to improve the lot of man by establishing utopian communities. More than thirty such communities were actually established, one of the most important being Brook Farm. Most of these modern utopias went out of existence shortly after their formation, but some lasted for a number of years.

A second group, the "cooperators," were interested in establishing producers' or consumers' cooperatives. The producers' cooperatives that were set up did not last long. The consumers' cooperatives did better, particularly in the New England area, but on the whole their success was moderate. During the Civil War period almost all of the cooperative enterprises then in existence collapsed.

The third reform group, under the leadership of George Henry Evans, supported a policy of land reform known as agrarianism. There was a long struggle over the reforms the agrarians sought. Finally, in 1862, the campaign that Evans and his followers had started in the 1840's bore fruit in the Homestead Law. Although this law did not include everything the agrarians had suggested, it did provide that settlers were entitled to a free homestead of 160 acres.

Late in the 1840's industry revived, and once again "pure and simple" unionism began to stir. For the first time, a number of national unions were formed: some of the earliest by the printers (in 1850) and by the locomotive engineers and the hat finishers (both in 1854). Although organizations embracing the locals in a small number of trades had been established in the 1830's, their geographical coverage could not be called national. It was not until the fifties, therefore, that this very important structural type made its appearance.

That the unions were still immature was brought out by the panic of 1857. As had happened before, and was to happen again, unionism suffered a serious setback, with a large loss of membership and the disintegration of numerous organized groups.

The Civil War Period and After. The outbreak of the Civil War seriously disturbed both industry and unionism, but not for long. The demands of war led to great industrial activity, and also to the printing of large volumes of inflation-producing Greenbacks, both of which stimulated the growth of unions. Many local unions were established. Numerous local trades' assemblies, or city centrals, were formed. These assemblies, which in terms of membership differed somewhat from the city centrals of today, were the most important structural units of the labor movement at that time. The Civil War period also witnessed the formation of a number of national unions; during the years 1862-1865 twelve such organizations were set up. Weak and decentralized, these early national unions did not occupy the position of commanding importance in the labor movement that they were to occupy after the formation of the AFL. The year 1866 saw the formation of the National Labor Union, a forerunner of the AFL, though it differed from the AFL both in structure and in policies. This organization, which lasted until 1872, had a precursor in the International Industrial Assembly which was formed in 1864 but disappeared after having held one convention.

The remarkable expansion of the 1860's was followed by an equally remarkable contraction during the 1870's. The panic of 1873 set off a depression that lasted until almost the end of the decade, and during this period unionism again disintegrated. Most of the national unions fell to pieces; their number declined from around 30 in the early 1870's to eight or nine in 1877. The number of collapses clearly demonstrates the inherent weakness of the early national unions. In contrast to the nationals and internationals of today, they had little in the way of benefit programs; they were highly decentralized; they had slender financial resources; their leaders were easily swept into the bypaths of political action; their members were exposed to the "Call of the West."

Amid the hard times of the period extremism in the behavior of labor manifested itself. (Men's actions as well as their judgments are "a parcel of their fortunes.") The notorious Molly Maguires, operating in the anthracite counties of Pennsylvania, resorted to violence on a large scale.[3] Using such techniques as the destruction of property, manhandling, and ordinary murder, and yet, at the same time, sincerely believing in the justness of their cause, they spread terror through the anthracite area. The collapse of the Molly Maguires, which was accompanied by severe legal punishment to some of the group's members, was accomplished by a Pinkerton detective who had worked his way into a position of authority in the organization.

In 1877, not long after the Molly Maguire episodes, another manifestation of extremism, the Great Railroad Strikes, took place in numerous American cities.[4] The outbreak at Pittsburgh was especially serious and destructive, involving a considerable loss of life and a great deal of property damage. Seldom has industrial warfare more closely resembled actual military warfare than in the 1877 railroad strike at Pittsburgh.

During the 1870's two further attempts were made to form a

[3] Detailed treatments of the Molly Maguires will be found in Louis Adamic, *Dynamite,* Chapter 2. New York: The Viking Press, 1931; and in J. Walter Coleman, *The Molly Maguire Riots.* Richmond: Garrett & Massie, 1936.

[4] For discussions of these strikes see Adamic, *op. cit.,* Chapter 3; and Samuel Yellen, *American Labor Struggles,* Chapter 1. New York: Harcourt, Brace & Co., 1936.

national federation of labor. In 1873 a National Industrial Congress was established, but the panic of that year destroyed it. Another attempt, in 1876, also failed.

The Rise and Decline of the Knights of Labor. The most important labor body in this country before the AFL was the Knights of Labor. Started as a secret society in 1869 by a few tailors in Philadelphia, the Knights made little progress during the first ten years of their existence. Then the Order began to grow rapidly, until by the middle of the 1880's it numbered over 100,000 members. The most rapid growth, however, came during the 12-month period from July, 1885 to July, 1886. On July 1 of the latter year membership in the Knights of Labor amounted to more than 700,000. At that point the Knights began to go down hill, and at a rapid pace. By the early 1890's their numbers had fallen to less than 100,000, and the order ceased to be of any real significance. Gradually it faded out of the union picture entirely.

The Knights' organization surpassed the AFL and the CIO in the geographical scope of its membership, and probably in the occupational scope as well. It took into its fold anyone over 18 years of age who was working for wages or who had "at any time worked for wages," with a very few exceptions, among them lawyers. In geographical scope the Knights of Labor went far beyond the limits of the United States. They had members in Canada, England, Belgium, France, Italy, Australia, and other countries as well.

The range of interests and activities of the Knights was as broad as their membership. They carried on ordinary trade union activities, applying pressure directly on employers and sometimes calling strikes (which they ordinarily tried to avoid). They also engaged in political action and experimented with numerous cooperative enterprises. Moreover, they were interested in the dissemination of "education," or propaganda. The slogan of the Knights was noble in character: "An injury to one is the concern of all." This spirit of solidarity was an outstanding feature of the organization's ideology.

The name most intimately associated with the Knights of Labor is that of its second president (its second "Master Workman"), Terence V. Powderly. Powderly, who stepped into leadership after the chief founder and first head of the organization, Uriah S. Stephens, stepped out, has been one of the most harshly criticized of American labor leaders; the appellations applied to him were perhaps even more severe than those applied by AFL and CIO leaders to one another in the middle 1930's. Although he merited some of the criticism, Powderly was not completely lacking in good qualities. He was a fine orator and a prolific letter writer, two capabilities which gave him power in the Knights' organization.

The decline of the Knights of Labor was due in part to its failure to achieve an adequate degree of internal harmony. A shrewd observation on the Knights' membership was made by Powderly in a letter he wrote in 1889, when the organization was in its decline: "In 1885 we had about 80,000 members in good standing, in one year the number jumped up to 700,000 of which at least 400,000 came in from curiosity and caused more damage than good." [5]

Other factors also contributed to the decline of the Knights. Most of the organization's attempts to establish cooperatives were unsuccessful, and so were its strikes—although it won a notable victory in the Gould strike of 1885, which gave it a great deal of prestige and contributed substantially to its phenomenal growth in the succeeding months. Strong opposition from employers help to undermine the organization. The Haymarket Riot in 1886, with which the name of the Knights was unjustly associated, also promoted the weakening process.

A particularly important element in the downfall of the Knights was the emergence of competition from the American Federation of Labor. The AFL, although a smaller organization than the Knights, had a more homogeneous and a more unified membership, a more capable set of officers, and a more limited and achievable body of objectives. In the contest between the two groups the Knights went down to defeat.

The Achievement of Stability

The Formation of the AFL and the Aftermath. In November, 1881 an organization known as the Federation of Organized Trades and Labor Unions of the United States and Canada was formed at a meeting held in Pittsburgh. The new organization was primarily a political or legislative body, closely resembling in its purpose the British Trade Union Congress. Its legislative committee, of which Samuel Gompers became the head in 1883 (he also became head of

[5] See Powderly's autobiography, *The Path I Trod,* ed. by Harry J. Carman, *et al.,* p. 7. New York: Columbia University Press, 1940.

the federation in general) constituted the essence of the organization. Apart from this committee the federation was little more than an annual convention.

In December, 1886 a convention was held at Columbus, Ohio at which there were delegates not only from the Federation of Organized Trades and Labor Unions but also from various other labor organizations. The unions represented at this meeting decided to unite forces under the name "The American Federation of Labor." Gompers was chosen president. In the new federation the nationals and internationals became the basic structural and functional units; and the organization, although interested in political matters, decided to direct its efforts mainly into economic channels.

With the formation of the AFL, unionism of a new kind, sometimes called "business unionism" or "unionism pure and simple," became definitely established in this country, and a new era in the country's labor history commenced. Composed of skilled workers and based on the principles of craft organization, voluntarism, and exclusive jurisdiction, the AFL represented a type of unionism more in keeping with the social and economic conditions of the time than the Knights of Labor.

A number of spectacular and violent labor episodes occurred during the latter part of the century. In 1886 there was the Haymarket Riot in Chicago, one of the most tragic chapters in American labor history.[6] In 1889 there was the bitter Homestead Strike, involving the steelworkers and the Carnegie Steel Company, and in 1892 the destructive Pullman strike, led by Eugene Debs. The Pullman strike involved the American Railway Union and the Pullman Company as well as the railways running out of Chicago. Both of these strikes were failures from the workers' standpoint.[7]

During the first years of the 1890's business experienced another depression. This depression was significant not only because of the industrial strife associated with it but because for the first time the labor movement did not collapse when confronted with hard times. By the nineties, and after the formation of the AFL, unions

[6] An exhaustive study of the Haymarket Riot is contained in Henry David, *The History of the Haymarket Affair*. New York: Farrar & Rinehart, Inc., 1936.

[7] For accounts of the Homestead and Pullman strikes, see Adamic, *op. cit.*, and Yellen, *op. cit.*

in the United States had become firmly entrenched. A new period in trade union history had unquestionably commenced.

That a new period had started was also demonstrated by the development of more refined methods in the labor movement. The trade agreement (or collective bargaining contract) became an important instrument in industrial relations at this time. Although trade agreements had been in effect before the 1890's, the one negotiated on a national scale by the Molders' Union and the Stove Founders' National Defense Association in 1891 marked the real beginning of the trade agreement era in this country.

For a period of half a century dating from the decline of the Knights of Labor in 1886, the AFL was by all odds the most powerful labor organization in the country. There were other labor bodies, notably the Big Four Railroad Brotherhoods and the Industrial Workers of the World, but the AFL was supreme. Although its growth during the first ten years of its existence was slow, the Federation began to expand rapidly during the closing years of the 19th century. By 1900 its members numbered 548,000; and by 1904 its membership had jumped to 1,676,000, a figure that was not to be equaled or surpassed until 1911.

Along with the rapid growth in union membership during the last years of the old century and the first years of the new went a corresponding increase in industrial strife. Notable battles of the time were the Steel Strike of 1901, which the workers lost, and the Anthracite Coal Strike of 1902, which they won. The period was also characterized by a struggle within the AFL between socialists and nonsocialists.

During the years immediately following 1904, the AFL made no progress. For a while, in fact, the Federation lost ground. Opposition from employers, which was given organized expression in the formation of the National Association of Manufacturers, the Citizens' Industrial Association of America, the American Anti-Boycott Association, and other bodies, was strong. This was the period of the celebrated Danbury Hatters' case and the Buck's Stove and Range Company case. The use of the injunction by employers and the government was a great threat against which unions fought at this time. The passing of the Clayton Act in 1914 was the culmination of a vigorous struggle by labor for greater legal protection, including additional protection against the use of injunctions. Although this act was called the Magna Charta of Labor, it did not, as events turned out, provide the protection labor had anticipated.

Spectacular episodes of the decade following 1904 included the McNamara case of 1910-1911, still another chapter in the history of violence in America; the Lawrence strike of 1912, in which the IWW assumed a position of leadership; and the Colorado Fuel and Iron Company strike of 1913-1914, a violent strike out of which arose the first outstanding company union in the country.[8]

World War I and the 1920's. From 1915 to 1920 membership in the American Federation of Labor more than doubled, rising from 1,946,000 to 4,079,000. This phenomenal growth reflects the great wartime increase in industrial activity and the very favorable position that labor occupied, for both economic and political reasons, during the war period.

After the war ended a wave of serious strikes swept the country. Among the more notable were the Boston Police Strike, in dealing with which Calvin Coolidge, then Governor of Massachusets, first gained nationwide fame; the Seattle Strike, which assumed the nature of a local general strike; the Great Steel Strike, in which 24 different unions participated and which led to a famous report; and the Soft Coal Strike. The first two of these strikes, which all took place in 1919, were failures from the workers' point of view; the third largely a failure; the fourth substantially a success.

In 1920 a serious depression commenced from which the country did not fully recover until about two years later. Business activity declined and union membership fell sharply. The AFL lost almost a million members. Membership continued to decline slightly for a short time after the depression was over, settling for the rest of the decade at a figure somewhat less than three million.

The post-depression era of the 1920's is a significant one, not for what labor achieved but for what it failed to achieve. During these years economic activity was at a relatively high level, although there were minor recessions in 1924 and 1927. Yet the labor movement, certainly the AFL, merely marked time. In fact, it did worse than mark time: the percentage of workers organized in regular unions actually declined during the years 1923 to 1930.

No single, all-sufficient explanation can be given for this back-

[8] Descriptions of these three episodes will be found in Malcolm Keir, *Labor's Search For More,* Chapters 4 and 13. New York: The Ronald Press, 1937.

sliding; a variety of influences contributed. For one thing, opposition from employers was both strong and effective. During the 1920's employers conducted a vigorous open-shop campaign under the appealing and misleading title "The American Plan." They also established company unions, which tended to keep workers from joining the outside organizations. Moreover, the employers carried on an extensive program of welfare activities—Welfare Capitalism, the program has been called—which, by providing workers with many things they desired, made them less interested in unions. The economic position of the skilled workers, and they were the ones to whom the AFL unions and the other labor organizations largely limited their efforts, was often so satisfactory that they saw no need for becoming unionists. The great body of unskilled workers, whose wages were low and to whom unionism could have been sold with greater ease, were for the most part overlooked or sadly neglected.

The weakness of the craft union as a basis for organizing the mass production industries, which were expanding at the time, also hindered union expansion. The technological and geographical changes in industry constituted still another factor. The large-scale introduction of new machines and new methods displaced numerous skilled workers, many of them unionists. The shift of industry—the cotton textile and shoe industries, for example—from the East to the South or Middle West resulted, to some extent, in the unemployment of unionists and the employment of non unionists. Finally, the lethargy of many union leaders and their lack of labor-consciousness, possession of which would have made them keenly interested in organizing the unorganized, militated against progress.

Miscellaneous developments in the labor field during the 1920's included the venture of unions into banking, which, with few exceptions, turned out to be a failure; the death of Samuel Gompers, the great leader of the AFL, in 1924 and the elevation of William Green to the presidency of the organization; the attempt of the AFL to organize the southern textile industry, and the textile strikes at the end of the decade; a growing concern on the part of the unions and of the public at large with the problem of techological unemployment.

The Early 1930's. In late 1929 the "new era of permanent prosperity" that had been established during the 1920's came to an end. The terrific stock market crash in October of that year ushered in a newer era, the era of the Great Depression. Many workers dropped out of the unions during the early part of this period. Membership in the AFL increased slightly in 1930 over 1929 and then fell sharply. In 1933 there were 2,127,000 workers in the organization, compared with 2,961,000 in 1929. Since 1933, however, when AFL membership began again to increase, its growth has been continuous year after year except for the year when the CIO unions were expelled.

Two factors were of special significance in accounting for the growth in union membership in the years immediately following 1933. One was the improvement in the economic condition of the country; the other was the passing in 1933 of the National Industrial Recovery Act, with its famous Section 7(a). Under this section of the act the right of the workers to organize and bargain collectively was given definite legal recognition, and with the encouragement conveyed by this recognition many of the unions went out and conducted successful organizing campaigns.

The Attainment of Power

The Formation of the CIO. Although the AFL as a whole made marked progress under the encouragement given to it by the NIRA, some of its leaders felt that the Federation was not taking full advantage of the organizational opportunities it had been given. A prime reason for this failure, in their opinion, was the unwillingness of the AFL to see the mass production industries organized on an industrial union basis. Dissatisfaction within the ranks of the AFL manifested itself very noticeably at the Federation's 1934 convention. Numerous resolutions relating to the question of organization, particularly with reference to industrial unionism, were introduced. After a great deal of vigorous discussion, in which John L. Lewis took a prominent part, the convention agreed that the executive council should establish national or international unions in the automobile, cement, and aluminum industries and in "such other mass production and miscellaneous industries as in the judgment of the Executive Council may be necessary to meet the situation." The council was also to "inaugurate, manage, promote and conduct" an organizing campaign in the iron and steel industry as soon as such a campaign seemed practicable.

In the months that followed, the convention's declaration of policy was not applied very effectively, and unrest and friction over organizational matters reached a new high. Matters came to a head in the 1935 AFL convention. As at the previous gathering resolutions relating to organization were submitted and were taken under advisement by the resolutions committee. This time, however, the committee did not submit a unanimous report on the subject matter of these resolutions. The majority recommended nonconcurrence in the resolutions and a reaffirmation of the 1934 declaration. The minority group pointed out the lack of progress made by the AFL in organizing the great body of American workers and declared that the time had arrived "when common sense demands the organization policies of the American Federation of Labor must be molded to meet present needs." A prolonged and lively debate, in which feelings ran high, followed the submission of the two reports. Finally a roll call vote on the minority report was taken. The report was rejected by a vote of 18,024 to 10,933, with 788 abstaining. The 1934 pronouncements stood unchanged.

The outcome of the convention convinced minority leaders "that the craft stand-patters would not yield, and that if any more years were spent trying to convince them, the opportunity of the century to build a real labor movement in the country would be lost." [9] Not long after the convention, therefore, eight of these leaders met and set up a committee "to encourage and promote organization of the workers in the mass-production and unorganized industries of the nation and affiliation with the American Federation of Labor." The group adopted the name Committee for Industrial Organization and elected John L. Lewis chairman.

The formation of this committee within the confines of the AFL was viewed with disfavor by other leaders of the Federation. The executive council decided, by a vote of 11 to 6, to request the CIO to dissolve; at the same time the council appointed a committee to meet with the CIO leaders. The CIO refused to dissolve and went ahead with its organizing campaign. At a meeting in August, 1936, the AFL executive council ordered the unions attached to the CIO to break away from the committee and cease their organizing work, on pain of suspension. The CIO unions again disregarded this order, and in September ten of them were suspended by the AFL executive council. The suspension order was ratified at the conven-

[9] *The CIO, What It Is and How It Came to Be,* CIO publication, No. 12, p. 10.

tion in November (at which the suspended unions were without representation and voting power). The CIO unions, which had been acting more or less independently since the 1935 convention, were now definitely outside the Federation.

The formation of the CIO, and the consequent struggle between it and the AFL, largely grew out of a basic difference in principle on the question of organizing workers in the mass-production industries. Personal elements, manifesting themselves in a variety of ways, undoubtedly played a significant part in the struggle—as they do in most group encounters. The influence of John L. Lewis, in particular, was profound. But the "great man" interpretation of the CIO is very inadequate. The ground had to be ready, the time had to be suitable, or Lewis and his fellow "rebels" would have met with failure.

During the years since the AFL and the CIO parted company there has been a widespread feeling, both inside and outside the labor movement, that the two factions should reunite. At times this feeling has been particularly strong, and on a number of occasions formal peace conferences between representatives of the two organizations have been held. As the result of one such conference in 1953, a no-raiding pact (effective in June of 1954 for those unions signing the agreement) was adopted. As the years have gone on, personal obstacles in the way of unity between the two labor groups have diminished in importance, but the basic issue of the conditions under which the organizations should merge has remained. The AFL has insisted on "organic unity" at once. The CIO, fearing the dismemberment of its unions, has favored a more gradual approach.

It should be noted that in 1942 the United Mine Workers, led by John L. Lewis, left the CIO—largely as a result of political differences growing out of the presidential election of 1940. In 1946 the union rejoined the AFL, only to break off again in 1947. The latter step was marked by one of the shortest notes of withdrawal ever submitted in any organization: "Green – we disaffiliate. Lewis."

Organized Labor's Magna Charta. The year 1935 marks the beginning of another new era in the history of American unionism. In that year the CIO was formed. In that year, too, another momentous event took place: the National Labor Relations Act (Wagner Act) was passed. Under the NLRA the right of employees to engage in collective bargaining without interference from employers was again asserted. The law listed five unfair labor practices that employers must not engage in and, in addition, provided for the holding of elections (or the use of payroll checks) to determine which union, if any, the workers wanted as their official collective bargaining agency.

The Wagner Act (like the Clayton Act) has been called the Magna Charta of labor, and the expression in this case is highly appropriate. The act brought *organized* labor to new and unparalleled heights of numerical strength and economic and political influence. By 1940 union membership had increased to 8,500,000.

Unionism and World War II. During World War II unionism continued to grow, until by 1945 membership amounted to approximately 15,000,000. As in World War I the great increase in industrial activity, particularly in the mass-production industries, expanded the "market" for unionism. Other causes of the membership increase were the vigorous organizing activities carried on by the unions, prompted by continued AFL-CIO rivalry, and the favorable governmental attitude toward unions.

The National War Labor Board, which was given wartime control over wages and industrial disputes, exerted a profound, diverse, and to no small extent permanent influence on American unionism.[10] The influence of the board on union status was especially significant. Under its operation the maintenance-of-membership principle became a commonplace and the check-off a widely adopted procedure.

During the war the unions were represented on a variety of private and governmental bodies engaged in promoting the war effort. Union representation on these bodies improved the status of unions in the community and in the nation at large. Union standing was raised, too, by labor's wartime no-strike pledge.

Other important developments of the war period included the formation of the CIO's Political Action Committee in 1943; the spread of unionism among foremen resulting in the founding, in 1941, of the Foremen's Association of America; widespread advocacy by labor of the annual-wage plan, or guaranteed employment; the continued expansion of the area of collective bargaining—that is, the

[10] See the informative article by Paul Fisher on "The War Labor Board and Post-War Industrial Relations," in *The Quarterly Journal of Economics,* August, 1945.

continued shift toward industry-wide bargaining; and the passage of labor control bills by the legislatures of a considerable number of states.

The Postwar Period. The ending of military warfare in August, 1945 was followed by the beginning of extensive industrial warfare. Strikes, although not much more numerous than they had been, became larger and longer. The amount of lost time caused by strikes rose from 8,720,000 man-days in 1944 (despite the no-strike pledge given by the parent unions, numerous local unions engaged in "wildcat" strikes during the war period) to 38,000,000 in 1945, and to the unprecedented total of 116,000,000 in 1946. Notable work stoppages of the early postwar period included the General Motors strike, the industry-wide steel strike, and the bituminous coal strikes. During the whole post-war period strikes in the bituminous coal industry occurred with unerring frequency.

The most frequent cause of industrial strife during the postwar years was the failure of management and labor to agree on wages. With a reduction in the length of the work week (and the consequent lowering of take-home pay), with labor's no-strike pledge rescinded, with price control discontinued, and in view of an immense pent-up demand for consumer's goods, it is not surprising that wage controversies developed. After winning a "first round" of increased wages the workers, finding that prices continued to increase, pressed for still higher wages. This process continued (with the Korean conflict in the meantime increasing the inflationary pressure) until in 1953 the seventh round had been reached.

The postwar period was marked by numerous efforts, state and federal, to regulate unions. Many of the states passed labor control bills, and in 1947 Congress passed the highly important Labor Management Relations Act, commonly called the Taft-Hartley Act after its two Congressional sponsors. (We shall deal with this measure at length in some of the chapters that follow.) Labor was strongly opposed to the passing of the act and later exerted vigorous efforts to have it repealed. Outright repeal was out of the question, but its revision was spoken of as essential by both major parties in the 1952 presidential campaign and afterwards.

A notable development in the postwar history of unionism was the explusion by the CIO of 11 of its affiliates on the alleged grounds that the affiliates were Communist-dominated. This step temporarily decreased the membership of the CIO by 800,000. CIO unions were organized to compete with the expelled units and intense rivalry and bitterness followed.

During the years following World War II, total union membership remained around 16,000,000, about a million more than it had been at the end of hostilities. The labor organizations maintained that this lack of growth was due in no small measure to the Taft-Hartley Act. Others felt that it was because the field of unionization had become increasingly difficult to cultivate.

If the unions made little progress in adding to their total membership during the postwar years, they remained "in the news," and their place in industry and in society at large continued to be important. The election of 1952 indicated some shift in the political balance of power between organized labor and business; but there was no question of the continuation of union influence in the realm of politics.

Other outstanding union developments in the postwar period include the deaths of William Green and Philip Murray (heads of the AFL and CIO respectively) and the succession of George Meany and Walter Reuther to the posts they left vacant; the clamping down by the AFL on racketeering in one or two of its affiliates, especially the International Longshoremen's Association; and the establishment of plans for dealing with jurisdictional disputes, which had continued to be serious during the postwar years.

Causal Factors

Having surveyed the history of unionism in this country, we might now ask ourselves why unions are formed in the first place. How can we account for their existence? It is clear that unions are not accidental growths, though accident may play an important part in their development. They are not a product of individual ingenuity, or perverseness, though specific persons may exercise immense influence in their formation and subsequent progress. They are not a foreign importation, though foreign ideas and foreign-born members may modify and color their behavior. Unions come into existence for reasons that are much more basic.

Unions represent a reaction, in institutional form, to several features of modern industrial society. Foremost among these features is the capitalistic basis of industry. Generally speaking, the means of production are privately owned; and the owners appoint those who manage or control the means of production. Thus, under our capitalistic system, the labor-supplying group and the capital-supplying and management-appointing group (the "capitalists") are not the same. If the two groups *were* the same, there would be little need for unions because there would be no serious clash of interests, at least of the type now common.[11] Since the two groups are not the same, and since the services of both are necessary to production, a conflict arises over what share of the joint-product is to go to each. The labor-suppliers—the workers—long ago concluded that unless they combined and acted cooperatively they would not receive a fair share: their wages would be too low, their hours would be too long, and the conditions under which they work would be unfavorable.

The capital vs. labor conflict relates not only to what we might call the *product* of industry but to the *processes* of industry; that is, it relates to the matter of industrial control. This aspect of the conflict is probably not of much significance to many workers, but to many others, especially if they are in leadership posts, it is highly important. Through united effort workers are able to participate in the exercise of industrial control, as they could not do if unions were nonexistent.

Helping also to account for unionism is the competitive nature of modern industry. In the struggle for more business and higher profits that is carried on by employers, labor standards are in danger of being undermined unless the workers are in a strong defensive position. Acting individually the only defense they can offer is the threat to quit. Since full employment is not common, especially in specific labor markets, this threat is frequently very weak. Should the worker leave under such conditions, the employer will be able to get another worker without much difficulty. Moreover, since many jobs are highly specialized and since there are many obstacles in the way of shifting, especially to another town or city, the worker may be reluctant to make the threat in the first place.

A combined threat to quit, however, or rather a threat to stop working temporarily, made through the agency of a trade union, is much more effective in protecting or raising labor standards than is

[11] Unions of a worker-owner variety, if one can imagine such, could serve purposes other than that of collective bargaining. For one thing they might become important political agencies.

a series of individual threats. As one writer has pointed out, a union aims to give to the individual worker "something of the indispensability of labor as a whole." [12] If we could assume full employment as a permanent condition, of course, the individual worker would be competed for and in a sense would be indispensable. Under such a situation the *economic* case for unions would be seriously weakened, though not destroyed.

The impersonal nature of modern industry, resulting from the growth of large, mechanized producing units, also helps to explain the development of unions. The bonds of intimacy that linked employer and employee in small-scale enterprise have been greatly weakened. The cash nexus, to use Carlyle's expression, has replaced them. A chasm separates the employer and his men, and communication between them is difficult. Since it is not easy, and perhaps not even possible, for an employee to discuss matters personally with his employer, employees are receptive to the idea of sending union representatives to meet with him and carry on discussions and negotiations. Moreover, through their union workers are able to achieve a feeling of importance, of recognition, and of psychological stature that nonunion workers in larger establishments (and in some smaller ones too) often cannot acquire.

The basic reasons for the existence of unions are very much the same in all free, industrialized nations. But the union movement of each country bears the imprint of a variety of conditioning influences. A fascinating exercise for the student of unionism is to try to discover, with respect to the United States, what these particular influences have been and how they have been reflected in the structure, the policies, and the ideology of our labor movement.[13] Unfortunately in our present analysis we shall have to bypass this undertaking. All we can do is to affirm that geographic, economic, and political influences have affected unionism in this country in various

[12] John Davidson, *The Bargain Theory of Wages*, p. 267. New York: J. P. Putnam's Sons, 1898. A new and extensive discussion of the relative bargaining strength of individual workers and individual employers will be found in Fritz Machlup, *The Political Economy of Monopoly*, pp. 344-379. Baltimore: Johns Hopkins Press, 1952.

[13] A suggestive discussion in the general area indicated above, a discussion in terms of ethnic factors, will be found in an article by Jack Barbash in *Interpreting the Labor Movement*, Publication No. 9, Industrial Relations Research Association, 1952.

ways; so have demographic, social, and religious and philosophical factors; so too have international and other factors. American unionism, like unionism elsewhere, exhibits the influence of both its material and nonmaterial environment.

The preceding observations, especially those relating to the fundamental reasons for unions, would seem to suggest the desirability of a *theory* or *interpretation* of unionism. We shall set aside such a venture, however, until we have learned more about the chief "ideological" factors of the unions in this country.

8

UNION AIMS AND PRINCIPLES

Organizations of any sort are by their very nature "purposive" institutions. They are established in order to attain certain objectives. Unions are no exception to this rule. They have been set up to achieve a number of goals.

The specific goals of labor unions are numerous, but most of these goals may be divided into two major groups. Stating the matter in a somewhat different form we may say that unions have two central objectives, namely the attainment of a higher degree of economic security and of betterment for their members, and the winning of an improved status for their members both in industry and in society at large. Another union objective, and one that differs greatly from the two just mentioned, is the preservation (and, if possible, the increase) of the power of the union and of its leaders. This "political" purpose of unions has received considerable attention from students of labor in recent years, and we shall discuss it later on in our analysis.

Union Aims

Economic Security and Betterment. That unions are vitally interested in promoting the economic security of their members is clearly evident from a glance at the various activities in which they engage and the causes they espouse. Unions are constantly seeking higher wages, an effort which in large part represents an attempt to achieve greater security. This is particularly true of the annual wage, which has become an important union objective. They are greatly concerned about unemployment (probably the most formidable obstacle in the way of security). And for the purpose of coping with this problem they advocate such things as increased wages, shorter hours, and more liberal unemployment insurance benefits. The unions are keenly interested in industrial accidents and the insecurity caused by such accidents. They are desirous of seeing workmen's compensation laws liberalized. They are concerned with old-age insecurity and have taken various steps of an economic and political nature to deal with it. These aims, and others that could be mentioned, indicate the great interest unions have in the matter of economic security.

But to economic security as a goal we must add economic betterment, which, though it goes along with security, may also go beyond it. There is still a great deal of worker insecurity in our economy, but not as much as there once was. Many workers, particularly union members, now have a reasonable income, and in addition are protected by a variety of social security measures. These workers may not feel that they are subject to any serious threat of economic insecurity. Yet they are dissatisfied with their wages, and quite understandably so. Workers want not only economic security but higher, and still higher, standards of living. In other words they are interested in economic betterment. No interpretation of unionism is adequate that fails to take this aim into account.

With the change that is taking place in the distribution of wealth as a result of government fiscal policies and union action; with the increasing development of our social and private security programs; and with the growing productivity of industry and the resulting improvement in real wages—with these changes the objective of economic betterment will become increasingly important. It should be added that economic betterment is a dynamic aim, without definite limits. Economic security, on the other hand, is more absolute in character, at least as the term has ordinarily been used, and can be achieved by reaching a certain stable level of income. Since the meaning of "necessities" of life undergoes change from time to time, of course, economic security is not completely absolute in nature.

Industrial and Social Status. To an ever greater extent unions are attempting to improve the status of their members, both as participants in the activities of industry and as members of organized society. Radical unionists have for many years sought to raise the status of the worker, not by tampering with the present economic system and making it more tolerable, but by sweeping the system out of existence entirely. The radical view has not been predominant in

American trade unionism, however. Most unionists have been totally unconcerned about establishing a wholly new type of economic and social order, one which, for example, would do away with the institutions of private enterprise, free competition, and the institution of private property in production goods. Although most unionists have not been perfectly satisfied with the present system, they have nevertheless accepted it and have limited their objectives to such things as can be achieved within its general limits.

Union interest in the question of status manifests itself in a variety of ways. It is clearly evident in the demand of the unions for grievance machinery to be used in handling issues that arise between management and men. It is seen in the demand for control over hiring and discharging. The whole process of collective bargaining, which of necessity places some degree of influence and control in the hands of employees, represents interest in, and the attainment of, an improved status for workers in industry.

Union participation in various civic undertakings and union representation on such civic bodies as school boards, municipal governments, and community chests indicate interest in the matter of status. So, too, does union representation on state and federal governmental bodies.

By means of their unions workers achieve an improved status. This status, it is interesting to note, is largely though by no means solely obtained through the mechanism of a contract, the collective bargaining contract. The workers thus move from contract to status! This is a sort of reversal of the well known evolutionary process in society pointed out by Sir Henry Maine.[1] It should be stressed, however, that the status achieved by present-day unionists is not the same as the status associated with the workers in the Middle Ages. It is not as restrictive, and the unionists' place in society is not as rigidly fixed. Moreover, their position, in contrast to that of their precursors, is more powerful. The unionists of today have status; but, through their unions, they have influence as well.

Unions as Political Institutions. Unions are institutions—"political" institutions—and as such are interested in the extension of their power and influence. This interest is particularly manifested in the

[1] See R. G. Hawtrey, *Economic Destiny,* p. 64. London: Longmans, Green & Co., 1944. In reality the reversal referred to above is to no small extent verbal in nature.

activities of the union leaders. In fact it is the leaders who are the "prime movers" in the generation of power, power for their organizations as well as for themselves. The important notion of unions as political bodies is comparatively recent in the study of labor. It throws a great deal of light on the behavior of unions and their leaders, and, as will be evident later, helps the student understand and interpret this behavior.

Have American Unions a Philosophy?

It may appear a little pretentious, if not absolutely inaccurate, to speak of American unions as having a philosophy; and yet they *do* have a philosophy. Their day-to-day activities are for the most part carried on in accordance with certain well established principles. And these principles may be looked upon as the constituent elements of the unions' philosophy.[2]

The fact that these principles do not involve the radical transformation of the present economic system does not preclude reference to the principles as a philosophy. A set of principles does not have to be radical in nature to constitute a philosophy. The principles may be neutral or even very reactionary in character and yet still be a philosophy.

It should not be assumed that there is complete agreement on the principles that constitute the basic philosophy of American unionism. Minority views are found in all or most organizations, including unions. Thus, for example, some unionists in this country favor socialism, but they are of little influence and their views are unrepresentative. It should not be assumed, moreover, that all the rank-and-file members of the unions are clearly aware of the basic principles to which we have alluded. Neverthless, if questioned on these principles they would generally endorse them. The union leaders and the more enlightened active members—and these are the

[2] Some students of unionism believe that American labor organizations have a philosophy in a more basic sense, one that involves long-range and broad objectives and "a sense of direction." J. B. S. Hardman, for example, leans toward this view. The "inherent aim of unionism," Hardman maintains, is "to create and to accumulate power by organization." See his article on "Labor in Midpassage," in the *Harvard Business Review*, January-February, 1953. At this point the reader might refer to the discussion of theories of unionism at the end of this chapter.

influential persons in the unions—are aware of the principles and will speak vigorously in defense of them.

In the discussion that follows we shall examine the chief principles of American unions. We shall note as we go along, however, significant departures from these principles by specific union groups and particularly variations in the degree of allegiance to them exhibited by the two labor federations, the AFL and the CIO.

Union Principles

Business Unionism. During the early years of the labor movement in this country unions frequently took an active interest in political undertakings and in various reform schemes. With the formation of the AFL, however, a new type of unionism came into the forefront, a type that limited its efforts largely to the economic field and to the achievement of objectives within reach. In short, business unionism, to use Professor Robert F. Hoxie's term, became supreme.

This principle of unionism, which abhors utopian aims and cleaves to the policy of exerting pressure on employers in the expectation of gaining higher wages and other concessions, has been adhered to by the AFL since its formation. AFL unions are business unions, endeavoring to sell their product, namely labor, on the most advantageous terms possible. The typical AFL unionist is business-conscious much more than he is reform-conscious, though he is interested to some degree in moderate reform policies. He is generally practical in his outlook. "We are practical men, dealing with practical questions, keeping in mind practical solutions for our economic problems," said William Green in 1930. Essentially the same statement could be made today although the interests of the AFL have been somewhat broadened since the 1930's.

Business unionism is also a fundamental principle of non-AFL unions. The Big Four Railroad Brotherhoods subscribe to the doctrine, perhaps even more faithfully than the AFL, and the CIO is no exception. Though CIO affiliates are in general farther to the left than most AFL unions, exhibiting greater interest in the question of economic and social reform, their chief interest is nevertheless the advantageous selling of their product. Collective bargaining is their principal method of advancement, just as it is for the AFL unions.

Though the principle of business unionism is of paramount significance in American unionism, it has decreased in relative importance during the last two or three decades. Unions today are more active politically than they were earlier in the century; they are more interested in community matters; they are more concerned about international affairs; they are more power-conscious. With the development of these other interests the relative amount of emphasis placed on collective bargaining, on the marketing of labor, has of necessity diminished.[3]

Capitalistic Unionism. American unions are capitalistic, in the sense that they favor the preservation of the key institutions of capitalism. There are, of course, unionists in this country, particularly in the left-wing unions that were expelled from the CIO in 1949-50, who are opposed to capitalism and favor another type of economic order. However, these persons constitute a very small minority.

Though there was strong socialistic sentiment in the AFL during the early years of its existence, the Federation has been a strong supporter of capitalism. It is "against every ism except Americanism" and has for years carried on a struggle against revolutionary and radical groups. It combated the Industrial Workers of the World (the IWW); it opposed the One Big Union (OBU), and other socialistic groups that have sought to establish themselves among organized workers. Since the 1920's it has carried on an incessant struggle against the Communists, and during the 1930's and 1940's it assailed the Fascists and Nazis. Although the AFL is in favor of capitalism, it does not believe that the system is perfect, and it suggests various improvements. One or two of these improvements, it is true, if adopted on a large scale, would involve serious interference with the system of private enterprise; but on the whole the AFL aims are quite compatible with private enterprise and the other features of capitalism.

The Big Four Railroad Brotherhoods closely resemble the AFL in their attitude toward the present system. The fact that these unions after World War I supported the so-called Plumb Plan, which

[3] Collective bargaining should not be looked upon merely as an *economic* process. It has to do with numerous matters that do not have a direct tie-up with dollars and cents. Many of these relate to "improving or reforming human relations in the process of work" and are, as J. B. S. Hardman has argued, essentially *political* in terms of aim. They relate to workers as "political citizens." *Ibid.,* pp. 41-42.

called for the nationalization of the railroads (the same plan was temporarily endorsed by the AFL), is not to be taken as a sign of radicalism among the brotherhoods. Nor is the endorsement of government ownership of the railways by the Railway Labor Executives' Association, as late as 1948, a sign of radicalism. The fact of the matter is that the brotherhoods and the other unions in the industry are conservative organizations.

The CIO has always officially supported capitalism. Previous to 1949, however, a sizable amount of radical sentiment within the CIO favored the elimination or extensive renovation of the present system. But with the expulsion of eleven left-wing unions in 1949-1950, after an internal struggle of considerable duration and intensity, the size of the "militant minority" within the organization was greatly reduced. It is now of small consequence.

Though supporting the capitalistic system, the CIO, like the AFL, favors certain changes in it. It believes in the redistribution of the wealth of the nation (this feeling is not, of course, confined to the CIO). "Out of the bountiful benefits that flow from the increased productivity and increased efficiency the workers should be assured a larger proportion of the financial benefits that pour from industry in the United States." Thus the CIO believes that (in relative terms) the rich should get poorer and the poor richer. But it does not believe (with the Marxians) that the method for achieving this goal is the destruction of the present system.

The CIO supports the idea of economic planning. Like the AFL it does not favor the establishment of a *highly* planned economy. It does favor, however, certain rather extensive planning schemes, including the Murray Plan (see Chapter 19). The CIO, like the AFL, is interested in consumers' cooperation. It is also interested in credit unions.

One cannot say how many unionists in this country favor a new type of economic system. There is no national or international union in this country, except the Industrial Workers of the World (now seldom heard of), that officially advocates the replacement of capitalism. But within some of the unions there are appreciable numbers opposed to the capitalistic system.

It should be pointed out, however, that some labor students, such as Charles Lindblom, believe that the unions are undermining the present system though this is far from their intention. According to this view, unions with their great power, and with their pressure for higher and higher wages, which in turn lead to higher and higher prices, are preparing the way for the downfall of the free-enterprise economy. This aspect of the question is a highly important one; we shall deal with it later.

Group Consciousness. American unions are essentially group-conscious rather than class-conscious. This particular principle is very closely allied with the two we have just discussed; in fact it is inseparably connected with them. It is desirable nevertheless to give it the advantage of separate treatment.

"Society as a whole," said Marx and Engels in the *Communist Manifesto,* published in 1848, "is more and more splitting up into two great hostile camps, into two great classes directly facing each other: Bourgeoisie and Proletariat." This statement suggests the existence of an ideologically homogeneous class of workers engaged in mortal combat with the class of capitalists. From this combat the workers will emerge victorious, and the classless society—the absolute synthesis of Marx's dialectical materialism—will become a reality.

That American workers are so little concerned with the class struggle philosophy has seemed rather strange to some observers, who have assumed that unions which have used violent methods as frequently as American unions should be receptive to the Marxian doctrine of the class struggle. But militancy and radicalism need not go hand in hand.[4]

One of the reasons class consciousness, in the Marxian sense, is weak in this country is the fact that a great many American workers look upon themselves as members of the middle class. They do not regard themselves as members of the downtrodden proletariat, sinking "deeper and deeper below the conditions of existence" of their own class, as the *Communist Manifesto* has it.

American unionists are group-conscious rather than class-conscious: that is, in so far as they look beyond individual interests, as they very commonly do. they have the interest of their own group (not their class) in mind. The group they consider most meaningful

[4] See Alfred Bingham, *Insurgent America,* pp. 12, 33-34. New York: Harper & Bros., 1935. A non-Marxian type of class struggle has been very important in this country, namely the struggle to get out of one's class. Professor Arthur M. Schlesinger, Jr., has stated, perhaps with some exaggeration, that "the class struggle in America has consisted in the struggle to climb out of one class into a higher one." *Paths to the Present,* p. 16. New York: Macmillan Co., 1949.

to them is probably either their immediate shop group or their local union, especially if the latter is the bargaining unit. The workers may also be interested in their parent organization as well as in the other structural units which compose the two large labor federations. They may be interested, too, in the federations themselves, and in international labor groups. The likelihood is, however, that the ripples of interest become smaller and smaller as one moves outward from the point where the workers throw their chief support. An examination of union activities and policies in this country will furnish numerous illustrations of the group consciousness thesis.

The fact that unions typically assume a group point of view does not mean that the rest of society necessarily suffers as a consequence. If this were so, it would be difficult to justify the existence of unions. Although numerous instances can be found in which the private interests of the unions do not coincide with public interests, *on balance* the self-seeking of the unions (in the manifold forms that this takes) is not hostile to the general welfare.[5] In fact it is not only not hostile but favorable. The same generalization can be made of business enterprises, though socialists and communists would deny it, and of most other types of private organizations.

Political Nonpartisanship. Labor organizations do not support any political party as such, nor do they support the idea of a separate labor, or labor-farmer, party. Instead the unions support "principles" and "persons."

This nonpartisan idea has been a cardinal one in AFL philosophy from the beginning of the organization. It is given clear expression in the following statement: "Stand faithfully by our friends and elect them. Oppose our enemies and defeat them, whether they be candidates for President, for Congress, or other offices, whether executive, legislative, or judicial." The friends are those who support, or come closest to supporting, the policies the AFL advocates. Although more of its friends have been Democrats than Republicans, it has never given its support to the Democratic party as such. Only twice has the AFL departed from the nonpartisan policy,

5 In times of peace, and with some exceptions, unions in their regular, day-to-day activities do not look far beyond their own interests to the well-being of society as a whole. The promotion of the latter is merely coincidental with their success in achieving the former. However, when the nation is confronted with a great emergency, such as a world war, then the unions may frequently, and at sacrifice to themselves, consciously endeavor to promote the common good.

and these were only partial departures. In 1924 the executive council endorsed the candidacies of La Follette and Wheeler, who ran for president and vice-president as Progressive-Independents. Gompers pointed out, however, that this endorsement did not mean that the AFL was in favor of a third party. In 1952 the AFL (this time the convention) endorsed the Stevenson-Sparkman ticket.

The political philosophy of the CIO is somewhat less conservative than that of the AFL, but the CIO also holds to the nonpartisan political principle. There is more third party sentiment in the CIO than in the AFL or in the Railroad Brotherhoods, whose political outlook is similar to that of the AFL. Since the exclusion from its ranks of the group of left-wing unions, however, the amount of this sentiment in the CIO has been considerably less. In general it can be said that there is a larger amount of political consciousness in the CIO than in the AFL.

The country's most politically conscious unionists, however, are the extreme left-wingers, whose concept of political reform involves the elimination of the capitalistic system. As we noted before, the influence of this group is not great, though in specific localities or situations it may be of some weight.

Voluntarism. The principle of voluntarism relates to the internal affairs and government of the AFL and the CIO; it also relates to the attitude of the two organizations toward politics.

In connection with the second aspect of the doctrine we should add one or two further observations. According to the principle of voluntarism the unions should make most of their gains through the process of collective bargaining. In this process the government, with its powers of compulsion, should not be represented. Employment relationships should be worked out voluntarily by labor and management.

Voluntarism, as applied to government, thus involves a sort of laissez-faire philosophy in labor matters. In times past there was good reason for organized labor to be suspicious of government. But with the growing strength of unions the laissez-faire attitude has been altered. The AFL is more receptive to the idea of making gains through the use of political methods than it once was (at one time Samuel Gompers even opposed minimum-wage legislation); and, as we have already noted, the CIO is quite willing to make gains on the political front. However, even the CIO puts its chief emphasis on voluntary collective bargaining. The notion that what the government can give it can also take away is still embedded in labor's thinking.

The other aspect of the doctrine of voluntarism relates to the government of the AFL and CIO. Both organizations are federations of self-governing units. The national and international unions that make up the federations are independent commonwealths, not colonies. They came into the federations voluntarily and may leave them voluntarily at any time they wish.

In the CIO, however, the doctrine of voluntarism is not quite as strong as in the AFL. There is more centralization of power in the CIO. The head office of the CIO collects a larger per capita tax than the AFL, a fact which, in accordance with the axiom of the "purse strings," suggests greater power; the CIO has been willing to go farther than the AFL in trying to modify the behavior of its affiliates, as can be seen for example in the plan adopted in 1951 for handling jurisdictional disputes. If CIO affiliates were as guilty of race discrimination as a small number of AFL unions are, it is certain that the organization would do more to cope with the problem than the AFL has done. The AFL however is beginning to modify its adherence to the voluntarism doctrine. Thus, in 1952, its executive council set up a committee to probe into the affairs of a number of its affiliates—specifically the issuance of local charters to ex-convicts. A still better example was its expulsion in 1953 of the International Longshoremen's Association, chiefly because of that union's racketeering elements in the New York area.

In both federations affiliates may be expelled if their "crime" warrants expulsion. For example, the original CIO unions were expelled from the AFL for starting a dual movement within that federation. A group of left-wing unions were expelled from the CIO because of alleged communistic ideas and policies. Unless the crime is serious, however, the two federations do not interfere with the operation of their affiliates. For the most part they give these affiliates assistance rather than orders.[6]

[6] Under President Meany there has been some shift toward "presidential leadership" in the AFL. As A. H. Raskin has pointed out, Mr. Meany has "established the idea" among his associates that the president of the organization "should be a real leader and not merely a mouthpiece for the heads of powerful international unions, who used to dominate the federation's executive council." *The New York Times,* June 15, 1953.

Other Principles. In the matter of union structure there is a marked difference of opinion between the CIO and the AFL. The former supports the principle of industrial unionism, though not all its affiliates are industrial unions. The latter endorses the principle of craft unionism; or rather, it prefers what we might call "structural narrowness." In the AFL there are as a matter of fact very few pure craft unions, most of the Federation's affiliates being at least multiple-craft bodies. Moreover, there are in the AFL four quasi-industrial organizations, namely, the four industrial departments. The most accurate way of stating the difference between the CIO and the AFL in the matter of structure is to say that the CIO prefers wide coverage, as wide as the industry if possible, whereas the AFL prefers unions of a narrow coverage, at least narrower than that desired by the CIO.

Another principle that the AFL has long adhered to is that of exclusive jurisdiction. Holding that there should be only one union to a jurisdiction (and that one an AFL union), it is strongly opposed to what is commonly called dual unionsm. Within its own ranks it will not grant charters to two unions in the same field (as does the British Trade Union Congress, for example), despite the omnipresent problems arising from shifting and partially overlapping jurisdictional claims. The CIO, like the AFL, refuses to issue charters to two unions in the same field; and like the AFL it has had its jurisdictional difficulties, though not on the same scale.

The principle of antidiscrimination should also be noted. "One of the bedrock principles of the CIO," the official paper of the organization declares, "is its policy of no discrimination—equal rights for all." The CIO has done notable work in applying this principle to Negro workers. The AFL is also opposed to discrimination, but as an organization it has not done much to eliminate it from its affiliates, a number of which are guilty of the practice. This AFL principle comes into conflict with the principle of voluntarism (union autonomy), and the latter prevails. As we shall see in Chapter 11 certain independent unions, particularly in the railroad industry, also engage in discrimination, especially against Negroes.

Finally, there is the principle of the short-run viewpoint. In viewing their problems and in deciding upon their policies and methods, American unions, whether they be AFL, CIO, or independent, generally place much more emphasis on short-run or immediate considerations than on considerations of a remote or long-run nature. They are much more interested in the here and now than in the distant future.

As long as unions have to struggle for existence they are not likely to place much emphasis on the long-run point of view. They are not likely to make any elaborate plans for an uncertain future, particularly if the living standards of the union members are low. Under such circumstances the unionists' "rate of time preference," if one may use the expression in this connection, will tend to be high: in other words, the emphasis placed on present considerations will be relatively great.

Short-run considerations will also prevail if job scarcity is a serious threat. The unionist who may become unemployed tomorrow, or next week, is not likely to be interested in union policies aimed at objectives to be achieved in a year, or five years. When job scarcity is not a factor, the unions can then, without any danger, stress long-run considerations. They may safely pursue, in the words of Bastiat, "a great good to come, at the risk of a small present evil."

Unions are now giving more and more attention to the long-run effects of their policies.[7] To an increasing extent they are looking beyond immediate results, realizing that the ultimate and total effect of a policy that yields an immediate gain may be distinctly harmful. This shift in interest is manifesting itself, for example, in union discussions concerning social and economic planning. Planning necessarily involves thought for tomorrow as well as for today.

Theories of Unionism

In the preceding analysis we have examined the chief characteristics of American unionism. Now we shall don the mantle of labor philosopher and try to interpret the union movement. This is a rather common intellectual exercise—and it is an exercise of the utmost importance.

A theory of unionism relates to the basic purpose of unions and hence to their general significance in society. A considerable number of such theories have been advanced. We shall not attempt to

[7] Professor Sumner Slichter, in his extensive studies in the field of trade unionism, has observed a discernible trend among unions to "explore the facts" in determining their policies, and to give "more careful and realistic consideration" to long-run results in connection with these policies.

survey all of them but shall concentrate on a few that have a distinctly American flavor.[8]

The Job-Security Theory. The most outstanding American theory of unionism is that advanced by Professor Selig Perlman, friend and associate of John R. Commons at the University of Wisconsin. (The theory is sometimes referred to as the "Commons-Perlman" theory or the "Wisconsin" theory.)

Professor Perlman believes that the underlying factor in American trade unionism is the quest for job security on the part of the workers.[9] Unionism in the United States became a stabilized institution, Professor Perlman argues, only when the workers became "security conscious," job-scarcity-conscious. As long as American workers held optimistic notions about the attainment of economic salvation through such things as ideal communities, free land, cooperative production, and greenbackism, unionism was of an unstable, uncohesive, vacillating nature. Only when the idea of job scarcity came to be widely recognized did the unions become firmly established institutions. This belief, implying as it did a recognition of the fact that economic security was limited and uncertain, became both the basis for a permanent type of unionism and the center around which most trade union policies revolved.

The Perlman theory has been subject to some criticism during the last few years,[10] but it probably still sheds more light on present-day American unions (and certainly on past American unions) than any other theory. At the same time, however, it seems desirable to give more weight now to the element of power as a feature of American unionism and as a determinant of union policy. This element is closely related to the objective of status, which we discussed at the beginning of the chapter, just as the element of job security is inseparably connected with what we called economic security and betterment.

[8] For an historical survey of "Theories of the Labor Movement," see Philip Taft's article in *Interpreting the Labor Movement,* Publication No. 9, Industrial Relations Research Association, 1952.

[9] See Selig Perlman, *A Theory of the Labor Movement,* particularly Chapter I and Part II. New York: The Macmillan Co., 1928.

[10] For a critical appraisal of Perlman's theory see J. B. S. Hardman's article, "From 'Job-Consciousness' to Power Accumulation," in *Proceedings* of the Third Annual Meeting, Industrial Relations Research Association, December, 1950. This publication contains a general discussion, by a number of writers, of the "theory" of unionism.

Power Theories. A number of variations in the power theory of unions may be noted. In the first place there is the general notion that unions of necessity are power organizations, and that inevitably they are interested in exerting more and more influence in industry and in society. According to J. B. S. Hardman "the 'core-substance' of unionism is an ever-evolving contest for a satisfying share in carrying on the business of living within the reach or the outlook of the nation and the time."[11] Though Mr. Hardman is by no means oblivious of the importance of job consciousness and of job opportunities, he believes that in the running of their organizations and in "shaping of long-range policies" labor leaders are thinking primarily in terms of "building power in industry."

Another variation in the power theory of unionism is advanced by Professor J. K. Galbraith in his general theory of countervailing power under capitalism.[12] Galbraith finds his general theory most fully developed in the labor market, where unions have arisen (in most instances) to oppose the "original" power possessed by the employers. The Galbraith theory is based on the assumption that the individual worker is in no position to match the power of the employer; but if he acts unitedly with other workers he can build up effective power groups of a countervailing character and obtain gains which he would not have won otherwise, at least not as readily. In some instances, and with reference to commodity markets, the two power groups may work together for mutual gain.

A final version of the power theory views unions as agencies for bringing about the more or less complete elimination of the present employer group. In other words, unions are seen as instruments for bringing in a wholly new type of society, namely socialism or one of its variants. This is the Marxian view of unions. (The first version of the power theory may also be pushed to the Marxian consummation.)

It seems clear that any general theory of unions should give considerable weight to the element of power, though not to the extent

[11] *Ibid.*, p. 157. Mr. Hardman also deals with the power thesis in his article "Labor in Midpassage," *Harvard Business Review*, January-February, 1953. The power theory is also supported by C. Wright Mills, who looks upon unions as organizations "established to accumulate power and to exert it." *The New Men of Power*, p. 7. New York: Harcourt, Brace & Co., 1948.

[12] J. K. Galbraith, *American Capitalism—The Concept of Countervailing Power*, especially pp. 121-123. Boston: Houghton Mifflin Co., 1952.

of substituting power for economic security as the most significant factor in American unionism.

Though the present writer cannot detect in American unionism any "historic mission" involving the use of unions as instrumentalities for bringing about the destruction of our present economic society, he can see in them an important means for modifying, in a gradual and limited fashion, the capitalistic system.

The Counterrevolutionary Theory. Standing in direct contrast to the more extreme power theories of unionism is the counterrevolutionary theory advanced by Frank Tannenbaum.[13] Professor Tannenbaum views unions as agents that by concentrating on limited objectives—"tinkering with little things"—are gradually bringing about change in the system without overthrowing it. Through the process of collective bargaining a "society of status" is being created. The unions represent an "unconscious rebellion against the atomization of industrial society," and through them the workers achieve a "fellowship," a "society" that they would otherwise not possess.

That unions are bringing about a notable change in the status of the worker is true, as we have argued earlier in the chapter. That the extent of the change is, or will be, as great as the Tannenbaum theory implies may be questioned. Moreover, one might maintain, with Professor Charles E. Lindblom (whose view may be looked upon as a still further theory),[14] that unions, instead of unconsciously representing a counterrevolutionary force, represent (also unconsciously) a destructive force—a force that will lead to the destruction of the system of free enterprise and the introduction of a planned economy. This ultimate result is also embodied in the extreme power theories of unionism.

[13] Frank Tannenbaum, *A Philosophy of Labor.* New York: Alfred A. Knopf, 1951. For a criticism of the Tannenbaum theory see J. B. S. Hardman's observations (and Mr. Tannenbaum's reply) in *Labor and Nation,* Winter, 1951, pp. 67-71.

[14] *Unions and Capitalism.* New Haven: Yale University Press, 1949.

9

MAJOR UNION ORGANIZATIONS

There are two major union organizations in the United States, the American Federation of Labor and the Congress of Industrial Organizations. Both are complex bodies composed of a variety of constituent units that possess varying degrees of autonomy. The most important of the structural units in both the AFL and the CIO are the national and international unions. These unions are for the most part self-governing bodies which, for the purpose of achieving certain objectives, have found it expedient to federate. Thus both the AFL and the CIO are, in essence, federations of autonomous unions.

In addition to the AFL and the CIO unions there are many nonaffiliated organizations. Though these unions, which vary widely in size and coverage, sometimes act in a cooperative fashion, there is no over-all body that unites them into a structural and functional whole.

In the present chapter we shall deal mostly with the two federations, examining their structure, government, and activities. We shall also consider briefly the more important unions in the unaffiliated group and a number of international labor organizations. A detailed analysis of the nationals and internationals, which are of such outstanding significance in American unionism, will come in the chapters that immediately follow.

The American Federation of Labor

Structure. A glance at Figure 1 will reveal the fact that the AFL when viewed in its totality is indeed a complex body. At the very center of the organization, and constituting its heart, so to speak, are the nationals and internationals. The former are unions com-

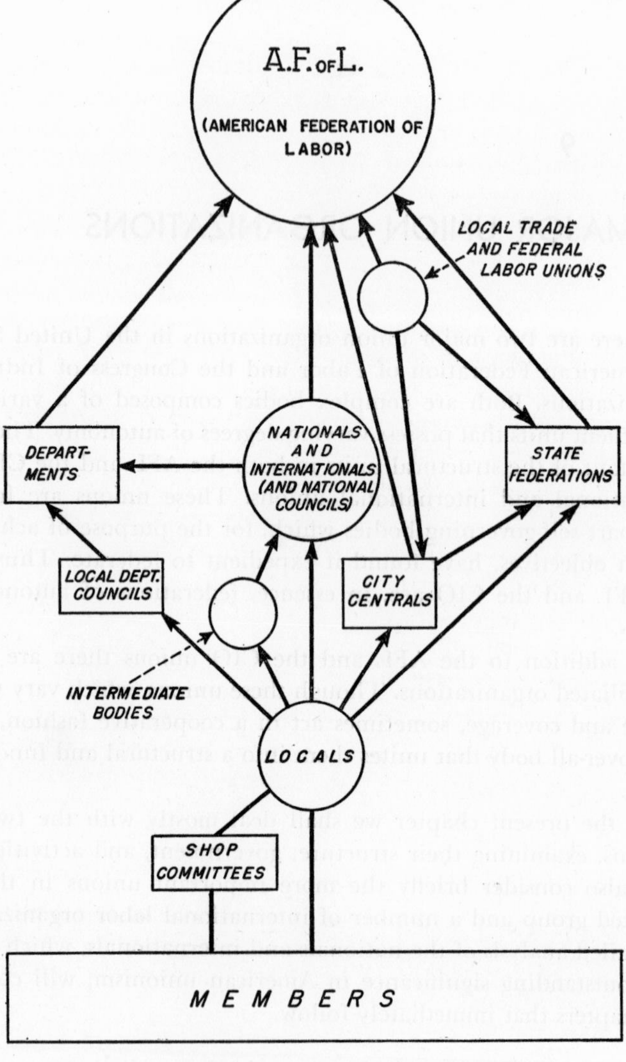

Fig. 1. Structure of the American Federation of Labor.

posed of locals found exclusively in the United States. The latter are unions that have locals not only in this country but also outside of it, chiefly in Canada.

There are slightly more than a hundred nationals and internationals in the AFL, most of them having a membership of less than 50,000. Among the largest of the affiliates are the Teamsters' Union, with approximately 1,350,000 members (Dave Beck, president of the union, expects to increase the membership to at least 3,000,000 by the early 1960's), and the Machinists' Union, with more than 700,000 members. At the other extreme from these mammoth organizations is the International Association of Siderographers with its 48 members divided among three locals. Between the parent nationals and internationals and the local unions of which they are composed there are sometimes intermediate units, made up of a number of locals in a given geographical area.

Some local unions have no parent organization apart from the AFL itself. These are the so-called local trade unions and the federal labor unions. The former are composed of workers (at least seven) in specific trades, the latter of workers in a variety of trades. In AFL circles the two types are ordinarily spoken of together as federal labor unions. In the case of a local trade union there is generally no national or international in the field. In the case of a federal labor union, however, national or international organizations may exist, but the number of unionists in the community in any of the occupations covered by these nationals and internationals is too small to make possible the formation of separate locals. A federal labor union may exist, of course, in a field in which no national or international has so far been established.

Generally local trade unions and federal labor unions are looked upon by the AFL as temporary bodies; in time the members of such locals are expected to come under the aegis of a national or international. This change in status may be brought about in two ways: by the establishment of new nationals and internationals, or by the parceling out of the members of the directly affiliated locals (when the members become sufficiently numerous) among already existing nationals and internationals.

Of all the units in the AFL structure, local trade unions and federal labor unions possess the smallest degree of independence. The AFL has unquestioned authority over them, as it does not have over the locals that are directly affiliated to the nationals and internationals.

When the number of local trade unions or federal labor unions in any "trade, calling or industry" is sufficiently large to warrant a cooperative bond between them, a national council is established. These councils are temporary bodies; they are nationals or internationals "in the making," and as long as they are in the council stage they remain directly subordinate to the Federation. In 1952 the AFL had four such councils, or "organizing committees," as they have been called. One of these was transformed in early 1953 from the "Aluminum Workers' Council" to the "International Council of Aluminum Workers."

Another unit in the AFL structure is the city central. These organizations are found in hundreds of cities and go under such names as Central Labor Union, Trades and Labor Council, and Federation of Labor. In a sense they are miniature AFL's. They are composed of the AFL locals in the city or area, though in many unions the locals are not compelled to affiliate with their city centrals. The fact that a considerable number of locals do not seek such affiliation is looked upon in AFL circles as somewhat of a problem.

In the matter of activities the city centrals attempt to do on a local level what the AFL tries to achieve on the national level. They engage in municipal politics as well as in other political activities; they aid their affiliated locals in organizing work and in the collective bargaining process; they extend help to locals during strikes; they promote the sale of union-made goods; and they may play an important role in community affairs through their representatives on school boards, city councils, community chests. Many city centrals publish journals, and at least one has a radio station.

The city central is a delegate body, with representatives from its affiliates coming to its periodic meetings and serving on its various committees. It is an old unit in the AFL, having existed as a form long before the Federation was established (the first city central was set up in 1827). The city central is not as important, relatively, as it once was; nor is it as important as its present-day counterpart in Great Britain. With the formation and growth of the nationals and internationals, city centrals diminished in stature, and this condition has been perpetuated by the lukewarm and at times suspicious attitude of the AFL toward them. (Some of the city centrals have been radical in their political activities.)

In each state of the country, and in Alaska and in Puerto Rico, there is an AFL organization known as the State Federation of Labor. These federations have as their affiliated bodies the local AFL unions within the state, the city centrals, and sometimes other union bodies comprising groups of locals. As with city centrals affiliation is not compulsory, and again there is a problem of non-affiliation.

The state federations are delegate bodies, holding annual conventions. Each has a set of officers. Just as the nationals and internationals are the units possessing most voting power at the AFL convenions, so the locals belonging to these organizations possess the great bulk of the voting strength at the state conventions.

The state federations direct much of their effort into political channels. They try to see that the "proper" persons are elected to the state legislatures and that the "proper" legislation is passed. Sometimes they aid the AFL headquarters in national political elections. The state federations may also engage in organizing work—chief responsibility was given to them in a special organizing drive in 1950, for at least 1,000,000 members, launched by the AFL. The state federations participate in educational activities, including the organization of institutes or summer schools for the special benefit of union members; they supply their affiliates with information and advice concerning labor legislation; and they render assistance in such matters as collective bargaining, the carrying on of strikes, and the promotion of the sale of union-made goods. They commonly publish a paper or magazine. A state federation may cooperate with other groups in the state, as when the Minnesota federation (one of the most enlightened in the country) in 1952 participated in an effort to get subcontracts for small businesses in the state.

There are five so-called departments in the AFL structure.[1] Four of these are of an industrial character and may be looked upon

[1] There is a "Government Employees Council" in the AFL (to be differentiated from the "national councils" referred to previously), which to some extent resembles a department. This council, which was set up in 1945, has over 20 unions associated with it. There is also an International Allied Printing Trades Association composed of five printing trades unions. Its primary purpose is to promote the use of union printing, as designated by the Allied Printing Trades Council label.

as quasi-industrial unions. These departments are the Building and Construction Trades Department (formed in 1908), the Metal Trades Department (1908), the Railway Employees Department (1909), and the Maritime Trades Department (1946, becoming active in 1952). Each department is composed of the AFL unions in its field. Each has a set of officers, holds conventions, and tries to promote the interests of its members. In each departmental structure there are units between the department itself and the local unions belonging to the nationals and internationals that make up the department. These intermediate bodies are especially important in the building industry. The departments, including their intermediate units, may engage in collective bargaining, in organizing work, and in the settlement of jurisdictional disputes.

The other department in the AFL is the Union Label and Service Trades Department, composed of over 50 unions that use the union label (or shop card, or button). This department, with its subordinate units, promotes the sale of union-made goods and services by educational and publicity activities. It issues news releases, editorials, and cartoons, which are used in labor and other periodicals; broadcasts messages on the radio; sponsors Union Label Weeks in various cities; and organizes Union Label Industrial Exhibitions (one held in Minneapolis in 1953 was visited by almost half a million persons). The department tries to "sell" union-made goods by such arguments that these goods are made under sanitary conditions, that they "represent economic justice for the human element in industry," and that the various insignia of these goods are "the emblems of a wage adequate to buy *back* the full production created by union labor, thereby eliminating the cause of industrial depressions." The department's job is not an easy one, since a great many persons, including not a few unionists, seem to be indifferent to whether the goods they buy are union-made or not. Incidentally, it might be pointed out that some unions supply labels to manufacturers gratis; others make a charge.

Government. The AFL has two principal agencies of government: the annual convention, which is the supreme body of control; and the executive council, which is composed of a president, a secretary-treasurer, and 15 vice-presidents.

The convention is made up of delegates from the five directly connected groups shown in Figure 1, plus a few fraternal delegates.

The group that sends the most delegates and wields the most power is the nationals and internationals. This fact is clearly brought out in Table 9. For the national and international unions both the number of delegates and the number of votes are based on membership, or rather on the membership on which these unions have paid per capita tax to the AFL—which may be something different.

Table 9

Number of Union Groups Represented, Number of Delegates, and Number of Votes, AFL Convention, 1952 *

Number of Unions	Names	Number of Delegates	Number of Votes
97	Nationals and Internationals	396	71,383
4	Departments	4	4
39	State Federations	39	39
159	City Centrals	159	159
69	Local Trade and Federal Labor Unions	67	499
2	Fraternal Organizations	3	3
		668	72,087

* *Proceedings,* AFL Convention, 1952, p. xxix.

Clearly the voting power at AFL conventions, which is given full, outward expression only intermittently, is predominantly in the possession of the nationals and internationals. There is more concentration of power, however, than Table 9 reflects. Since the voting strength of these organizations is based on their paid-up membership, the unions with the largest numbers naturally exercise the most power.

To aid in the work of the convention the president of the AFL appoints some 15 different convention committees, each one composed of 15 or more members. Among the more important of these are the Resolutions Committee, the Committee on Legislation, and the Committee on Organization. Much of the work of the convention is carried on by the committees in separate and private sessions. The convention resolutions are referred to the appropriate committees, as are the various sections of the report that the executive council makes to the convention. The committees, after their sessions, report to the convention on the resolutions and the parts of the report referred to them. Ordinarily they comment briefly and favorably on the latter; as for the former they recommend concurrence or nonconcurrence. Almost invariably the convention agrees with the committees' recommendations.

The executive council of the AFL is composed of 17 members. The term of office is one year, but the members of the council are usually re-elected. The council meets four times a year. Since 1886 the AFL has had four presidents. Samuel Gompers served in that capacity from 1886 until he died in 1924 (except for 1895, when he was replaced by John McBride of the United Mine Workers' Union, who had defated him at the 1894 convention by a vote of 1,170 to 976). William Green, also of the miners' organization, succeeded Gompers in 1924 and continued in office until his death in 1952. He was succeeded by George Meany, who grew up in the plumbers' union.

The executive council is supposed to carry out the decisions reached at the annual conventions and to act as the ultimate authority in the AFL between the convention sessions. Its work is partly administrative in nature and partly of a policy-making character—the executive council has become exceedingly influential in directing and determining AFL policy.

The larger unions, in turn, exert great power over the council, and over the AFL in general. Most of the larger unions have representatives on the council (although some representatives come from smaller organizations), so that in reaching its decisions the council cannot be too unmindful of the wishes of the unions with the large battalions.

To carry on its diverse activities the AFL must have a regular income, and provision for such an income is made in the Federation's constitution. Most of the revenue comes from the nationals and internationals, which pay a per capita tax on their "full paid-up membership" of four cents per member per month. (In times past this rule was not always followed. To cite an extreme example, the Teamsters' Union, which in the middle of 1953 had 1,250,000 members, had been paying per capita tax on only 650,000. In 1953 the AFL executive council decided that the under-payment of dues must cease.) The local trade unions and federal labor unions pay 38 cents per member per month, part of which goes into a special defense fund. The total receipts of the AFL for 1952 were $3,621,119.

The principal expenditures of the AFL are for organizational work. Office-employee salaries, publicity expenses, and a great variety of other items make up the expenditure list.

The power of the AFL is not due to its financial strength. Its annual income and its money reserve are both quite modest. In the field of industry an enterprise with gross receipts of less than four million dollars a year would not be looked upon as big business. But the AFL, in a certain sense, *is* big business, and it is powerful, since with its large membership it is capable of exerting strong political and economic pressure. The real financial strength of the labor movement, in both the AFL and the CIO, is found in the nationals and internationals. The head office of the AFL, like that of the CIO, is comparatively poor.

Activities. In considering the activities of the AFL we must remember that the AFL is primarily a unifying agency, linking together about a hundred national and international unions which, although AFL affiliates, retain their independence. Not only do they retain their independence; they retain most of the money they collect as dues. Hence they, and their locals, are the chief disbursing bodies, and the most active bodies, in the general AFL structure. There are various activities, however, in which the Federation itself engages. To some extent these supplement similar activities carried on by the nationals and internationals, but they also involve work that the affiliates cannot perform effectively and hence do not undertake themselves, or undertake on a small scale only.[2]

Though most of the effort and money devoted to organizational work is expended directly by the nationals and internationals and their locals, the AFL also carries on activities in this field. It has a special organizing department of its own, and as we have already suggested it spends a sizable amount each year on organizing work. Some of this money is spent in establishing and aiding local trade and federal labor unions, but other units in the AFL structure are also aided by it.

The Federation devotes no small amount of time and energy to political affairs. The AFL is very active in elections, particularly on the national level; it acts as a pressure group trying to influence the course of national legislation; it takes a keen interest in the administration and interpretation of the legislation that is placed

2 A detailed account of the activities of the AFL will be found in the report of the Executive Council, contained in the annual convention *Proceedings*.

on the statute books. In its political work the AFL took a notable step in 1947 when it established Labor's League for Political Education.

The AFL is also interested in economic activities. It aids its affiliated unions in their quest for higher wages, shorter hours, and better working conditions. The aid it extends may be both direct and indirect, both applied and theoretical. The local trade unions and federal labor unions are the special beneficiaries of its help, but the Federation also extends substantial aid to the nationals and internationals, particularly those that are newly established and need outside assistance.

Since the early 1930's the AFL has had a full-fledged research department. In addition to acting as an information supply service the department carries on investigations in such fields as taxation and workmen's compensation, and uses the results of its studies "as a guide in formulating and presenting to the proper authorities labor's views and concern in their problems." The department also issues a research report for the special benefit of union officials and union organizers, and members of its staff frequently appear before governmental committees.

The AFL also sponsors a certain amount of educational activity, particularly through its Workers' Education Bureau. It has two different "student bodies." One is the general public, and the other is the members of the Federation itself. Part of its educational work is carried on through the columns of *The American Federationist,* a monthly magazine, and the *AFL News-Reporter,* a weekly newspaper.

The AFL also engages in a number of other tasks. It has a legal department and a general legal counsel, working in a field that has become increasingly important in recent years. The Federation takes an active interest in international labor affairs and in promoting labor solidarity in the free world. It acts, along with the CIO, as a spokesman for labor on domestic and foreign issues.

The Congress of Industrial Organizations

Structure. Like the AFL, the CIO is essentially a federation of autonomous unions. Like the AFL, it has other structural units in addition to the powerful nationals and internationals. Except that there are no departments as such in the CIO, these structural units are of the same general character in the two organizations, though there is some difference in the terms applied to them.

As in the AFL, the most important units in the CIO are the nationals and internationals, which number approximately 35. The two largest of these units are the Automobile Workers' union, with well over a million members, and the Steel Workers' union, with approximately a million members.

Organizing committees have figured rather prominently in CIO history. These committees are embryonic nationals or internationals. Instead of being autonomous bodies, however, they are subordinate organizations, set up temporarily and controlled by the CIO. The number of organizing committees fluctuates from time to time, the general trend being downwards.

Within the CIO structure there are local unions with no parent organization apart from the CIO itself. Like the local trade unions and federal labor unions in the AFL, they are not attached to any national or international union. These unions, known as local industrial unions, are under the direct control of the CIO. The make-up of the group of local industrial unions is constantly being altered. While new ones are coming into existence, others are passing out of existence: that is, they are changing their status by becoming affiliated with nationals and internationals, which have perhaps just been formed.

In the CIO there are also units called local industrial union councils. Like the city centrals in the AFL, these operate on a city, county, or district basis. These councils are in a general sense under the control of the CIO, but the CIO does not force the local unions, either directly or indirectly, to become affiliated with them. The local councils are coordinating agencies designed to serve the unions within their area. They participate in organizing work; engage in municipal, state, and national politics; carry on public relations work; and promote educational and other activities. Since the establishment of the Political Action Committee by the CIO, the political activities of the local industrial union councils (and also of the state councils) have increased in importance.

The state industrial union councils in the CIO are similar in structure and function to the state federations of labor in the AFL. The councils are composed of the various CIO organizations (local unions and citywide bodies) within their respective states, and their chief work has to do with the promotion and the unification of the interests and activities of these units.

The CIO state councils aid in organizing activities, probably to a greater extent than the AFL state units. They try to cultivate a favorable public opinion toward CIO unions. Some form study classes and encourage the formation of education committees in local unions. The state councils also act as political pressure groups at the state capitals, working for the passage of "good," and the defeat of "bad," legislation. They are also active in state and federal elections and engage in other activities.[3]

In the CIO the departmental unit has not assumed the significance it has in the AFL, although it is present, at least in a modified form. Since so many of the CIO unions are organized on an industrial union basis, there is not the same need for departments as there is in the AFL with its craft and multiple-craft organizations.

The CIO has a Maritime Committee, established in 1939, that somewhat resembles the industrial departments in the AFL. This committee acts as "the Washington arm" of its affiliated unions, its interests and activities being political in nature.

Although the CIO has not had a label department since the earlier years of the organization, at its 1952 convention a resolution was passed instructing the executive board to study the feasibility of establishing such a department. The CIO has, however, a Standing Committee on Union Labels. This committee attempts to "coordinate and intensify [the] activities of the CIO in support of the union labels of its affiliates." Its work is not as extensive as that of its AFL counterpart, nor are there as many label-using unions in the CIO as in the AFL. Among the label-using organizations in the CIO, however, there is one that deserves special mention, namely the Amalgamated Clothing Workers. This union has carried on extensive campaigns to influence the buying habits of unionists and of the general public. In the early 1950's it ran advertisements in more than 40 of the country's leading daily papers, and also presented its appeal in some of the national magazines. The union also used the radio and the labor and trade journals, and distributed "hun-

[3] The CIO also has a Department of Industrial Union Councils, which promotes the work of the state and local councils. For example, in 1952 it had a series of seven regional conferences, which dealt with certain kinds of state labor legislation and with the duties and methods of the state councils.

dreds of thousands of pieces of literature." [4] No other union has carried its label appeal to the public as vigorously as the ACW.

Government. The CIO has a number of governmental bodies, including the annual convention. As in the AFL most of the delegates to the convention come from the nationals and internationals. Voting at the conventions is also much the same in principle as at the AFL gatherings. The nationals, internationals, organizing committees, and the local industrial unions have one vote for each member.[5] Various committees, smaller in number than in the AFL, aid in the convention's work. Many resolutions are sent in by the affiliated bodies, but in contrast to AFL procedure they are not presented to the convention in the form in which they are submitted. The resolutions committee sorts and groups them and then formulates substitute resolutions on each of the subjects involved.

Next to the convention the highest governing body in the CIO is the executive board. This is a large body, greatly exceeding in size the AFL's executive council. It is composed of the officers of the CIO plus one representative from each of the nationals, internationals, and organizing committees. The officers are the president, an executive vice-president (who is also Director of Organization and Councils), eight vice-presidents, and a secretary-treasurer.

The CIO officers are *ex-officio* members of the board, but they constitute a separate and very influential governing body in themselves, a sort of inner cabinet—closely resembling the AFL's executive council—that meets frequently to deal with the more detailed affairs of the organization.

The CIO's chief source of income is the per capita tax or membership dues. The nationals, internationals, and organizing committees pay a tax of 5 cents per member per month, and the local industrial unions pay a per capita tax of 50 cents per member per month; both figures are higher than the corresponding AFL dues. The most important expenditure item is organization, especially salaries, traveling expenses, and regional and field office expenses. Other sizable items include officers' salaries, general organizational supplies, office expenses, and publicity.

[4] *General Executive Board Report and Proceedings,* 18th Biennial Convention, 1952, Amalgamated Clothing Workers of America, pp. 28, 29.

[5] In the CIO the organizing committees as such have votes on the same basis as the nationals and internationals. In the AFL the national trades councils do not have voting power of their own, although their subordinate units do.

Activities. During the first years of its existence the chief task of the CIO was organizing the unorganized. The early emphasis placed on the work of organization has by no means disappeared, though as more and more workers have been brought into the union fold the *relative* importance of this activity has at least declined, and other activities, some of which can appropriately be referred to as "union servicing," have increased in significance.[6]

The CIO has an Organizing Department with a director and other staff members. This department not only does organizing work on its own but assists the affiliated unions in their organizing activities, and also helps them in negotiating agreements with employers and in handling problems of interunion and intraunion friction. In 1953 the Organizing Department underwent a major change, involving a consolidation of regional offices and the separation of the organizing function and the servicing function of its field representatives.[7] The most outstanding organization drive of the CIO in recent years, the one launched in the South in 1946 and carried on more or less continuously since then, has been only moderately successful. Southern employers, with the valuable aid of the Taft-Hartley Act, have in many instances shown vigorous opposition to the organizing effort.

The CIO is a politically conscious organization that is firmly convinced of the desirability of supplementing economic action with political action. Although it is more politically conscious than the AFL, its political activities in their main outlines are much the same as those of the AFL. It might be added that at election times the "friends" of the CIO are usually the same as those of the AFL, but not always. The requirements of friendship are a little more severe in the case of the CIO; a good labor record alone may not be enough to insure CIO support of a candidate for political office. In its attempts to influence the course of national legislation directly the CIO uses the ordinary pressure technique. Since 1943, when it was formed, the Political Action Committee of the CIO has played a key role in the election and general political activities of the organization.

[6] For a description of the current activities of the organization see the annual report of the president of the CIO, included in the annual convention *Proceedings*.

[7] The new plan is described briefly in *The CIO News,* June 1, 1953, p. 3.

The CIO extends considerable economic assistance to its affiliates. Like the AFL it engages in research work and supplies its member unions with various economic data that may be of use to them in their collective bargaining activities. Over the radio and through printed material it extends indirect assistance to its affiliates in their attempts to win higher wages. Information placed by CIO leaders in the hands of Congressional committees may contribute toward the same end. The CIO aids its affiliates in planning bargaining strategy, and it may also help in settling serious strikes.

A publicity department, established in the early days of the CIO, has been an important part of the CIO organization and has carried on its work with vigor, subtlety, and intelligence. In addition to its general public relations work the department has helped to educate CIO unionists or potential unionists. The department's chief avenues of communication are *The CIO News* and radio programs. In 1952 it made a start in the use of television.

The CIO also has a Department of Education and Research, a fact-finding and fact-analyzing agency dealing with economic data that have a bearing on the welfare of labor and are related to CIO policies. This department is responsible for the publication of *The Economic Outlook,* a monthly "survey of current problems from labor's point of view." The department supplies CIO unions with information relating to the financial standing of corporations with which they are dealing. It prepares speeches for radio broadcasts and meetings, and articles for magazines. In general the department aids the CIO itself, some of its departments and committees, and the CIO affiliates.

The CIO has a legal department and various committees to deal with specific matters. The names of these committees—an International Affairs Committee, a Committee on Social Security, a Community Services Committee, to name three—suggest in a general way the scope of the organization's interests and indicate some of its activities.

Finally the CIO shares with the AFL the task of being the chief public spokesman for organized labor. During recent years there has been some talk, much of it idle rumor, about the formation of a third federation of unions, comparable to the present AFL and CIO. In the proposed group the United Mine Workers would occupy a strategic position. Mentioned as possible affiliates have been the CIO Steelworkers' Union and the AFL Teamsters' Union (the presidents of both organizations have denied any interest in the plan). To date nothing has come of the "Phantom Phederation," as it has been called.

Independent Unions

The unions outside of the AFL and the CIO are generally spoken of as independent unions. The word "independent" is not to be interpreted as meaning that these unions always exist for and by themselves and that there are never any connecting links between them—it merely connotes nonaffiliation with either of the Big Two. Some of the independent unions have been members of the AFL or the CIO in times past, but most of them, particularly the small ones, have had an independent status from the beginning.

The unions in the independent category may be classified, roughly, as follows: (1) company unions (some of which belong to federated bodies); (2) railway unions; (3) left-wing unions; (4) miscellaneous unions.

Company Unions. The history of company unionism in the United States may be divided into two distinct parts. The first part covers a period of about forty years, extending from 1898, when the Filene Cooperative Association was established, until 1937, when the National Labor Relations Act (which was passed in 1935) was declared constitutional. The second part covers the years since 1937. Before 1937 company unions were in most cases under management control, the term "company" indicating not only the scope of their membership but also, generally, the *locus* of ultimate power and authority. Since 1937 company unions, to be legal, have had to be independent of the employer, except in companies doing an intrastate business in states that have no "little Wagner Acts" of their own.

Company unions of the present period possess greater strength than their pre-1937 counterparts, but they usually do not have the power of the locals associated with the nationals and internationals. Their financial resources are likely to be slender, and their leaders usually lack broad experience in collective bargaining, although they may be assisted by legal experts. In dealing with grievances in the plants, these leaders, because of their intimate knowledge of plant conditions, may be able to serve their union very efficiently; but in taking up the larger issues of wages and hours, they are not in a strong position. For the above reasons the gains achieved by the independent locals may not be as large as those won by outside unions, though this does not invariably follow.

Workers may prefer belonging to an independent company union, however, and for various reasons. They may favor an inside organization because it is much less likely to call strikes; they may attach considerable significance to the lower dues of the company union; they may feel that in such a union they will not have graft or racketeering; they may prefer local autonomy to centralized power; furthermore, they may prize the greater harmony with management that an independent union makes possible. Because of these possible advantages it seems likely that there will always be a considerable number of company unions.

It is impossible to say accurately how many company unions exist at the present time. But there are hundreds of them—possibly more than two thousand.[8]

Independent Federations. A great many company unions exist wholly by themselves, but many others have contacts of one sort or another with other similar organizations. These unions may be in other plants or divisions of the same company or they may come from various companies and various industries.

The Confederate Unions of America (CUA), which was organized in 1942, is composed of affiliated unions in a wide variety of industries scattered over the country.[9] The organization is highly decentralized, the unions associated with it having complete local autonomy. The principle of voluntarism, in the matter of union government, operates 100 per cent. One of the chief aims of the CUA has been to obtain representation for independent unions on governmental committees and agencies. Its efforts have met with only minor success. According to its president, testifying in Wash-

[8] During the period of World War II there was a section of the Wage Stabilization Board that handled cases affecting independent unions. According to one estimate more than 2,200 independent unions had business relations with the section. See *Taft-Hartley Act Revision,* Part 2, April, 1953, Hearings, Committee on Labor and Public Welfare, United States Senate, 83rd Cong., 1st Sess., p. 680.

[9] Information relating to the CUA, and to the National Independent Union Council, will be found in the volume of hearings cited in footnote 8, and in *Labor Management Relations,* Part 4, March, 1953, Hearings, Committee on Education and Labor, House of Representatives, 83rd Cong., 1st Sess., H. Res. 115.

ington in 1953, the Confederation has about 125,000 dues-paying members.

A second federation of independent unions, and one that has amicable relations with the first, is the National Independent Union Council, founded in the early 1950's. Unions associated with the Council are found in the telephone industry (e.g. the Connecticut Union of Telephone Workers, which itself has 65 locals), the shipyards, the electrical industry, and other industries. The affiliated organizations, like those in the CUA, have complete autonomy. The Council seeks to provide its unions "with a sort of a united front and a stronger voice, and, of course, our objective is to obtain national recognition and equal representation for them." The program of the council has been endorsed by more than 300 unions, which represent about 500,000 workers. (These, presumably, are not all dues-paying members.)

The CUA and the NIUC are greatly overshadowed by the AFL and the CIO. Lacking as they do the coherence, the size, and the power of the older organizations, their influence in the American labor movement has not been large. Nevertheless, within the limits in which they have operated they seem to have performed a useful service, and their demand for greater recognition appears to be warranted.

Independent Railroad Unions. Unions in the railroad industry may be divided into three groups. In one relatively unimportant group are the independent company or system organizations, which are not very numerous in the industry. In a second group are the national and international unions that are affiliated with the AFL (or the CIO). The membership of some of these organizations is found wholly within the railroad industry, but others have most of their membership outside the industry. This group of organizations is a very important one. The third group consists of the independent, or nonaffiliated, nationals and internationals. This group too is very important, containing among other organizations the Big Four Brotherhoods. In the present section we shall devote our attention primarily to the unions in the last group, and especially to the Big Four organizations.

The Big Four Brotherhoods, which are among the oldest unions in the country, are good examples of business unionism. They are highly practical in their point of view, shunning any utopian schemes of social betterment. They are interested in achieving higher wages, shorter hours, and improved working conditions here and now.

Although the Big Four Brotherhoods, and the other unions in the railroad industry, place most of their emphasis on economic action, to an increasing extent they have resorted to the use of political means. Through political activity they influence not only the course of legislation but the course of collective bargaining as well. In the railroad industry there is a closer tie-up between legislation and collective bargaining than in any other industry, since Congress possesses sweeping powers over the railroad industry and is thus in a position to grant favors to the industry's workers if it feels so inclined. In this situation the increase in the political activity of the railroad unions is not surprising.

The members of the Big Four Brotherhoods and of other railroad unions seem to be more security-conscious, or at least more active in taking steps to achieve security, than the members of most other labor organizations. Over the years the Brotherhoods have placed great emphasis on benefit programs, and the principle of seniority had its first extensive application in the railroad industry. The railroad unions have been more successful than most others in protecting their members against technological unemployment. The interest of railroad unions in safety measures may be mentioned as a final aspect of their security-consciousness.

It would be inadvisable to end our discussion of the characteristics of the railroad unions without mentioning the matter of racial discrimination, particularly as it affects Negro workers. In no other union group have Negroes been subjected to such a high degree of discriminatory action.

The independent railway unions cooperate to some extent among themselves and with the railroad unions affiliated with the AFL. The chief agency through which this cooperation is achieved is the Railway Labor Executives' Association. Composed of approximately 20 unions (not including any of the Big Four Brotherhoods at the present time, but including a small number of unions in the maritime industry), the RLEA plays an active role in both the legislative and the collective bargaining activities of its affiliates. In 1947 the chief leaders of the Association established, as an independent body, Railway Labor's Political League to take over and extend the work of the railway unions in the political sphere. As another example of cooperative effort among the railway unions one might mention the joint publication of the weekly newspaper, *Labor.*

Left-Wing Unions. A militant minority in the American labor movement has long sought to bring about the downfall of the capitalistic system and the introduction of some new type of economic order. The most popular of the substitute orders has been socialism, although in the earlier years anarchism and syndicalism had their supporters, just as communism has today.

The best known radical labor organization in the country is the Industrial Workers of the World, formed in Chicago in 1905 and familiarly known as the IWW. The ideology of the new organization was given picturesque verbal expression in the constitution it adopted. "The working class and the employing class have nothing in common," the IWW constitution declared. "There can be no peace so long as hunger and want are found among millions of the working people and the few who make up the employing class have all the good things of life." After the fashion of the Communist Manifesto, the constitution, in an addition made later, declared that "Between these two classes a struggle must go on until the workers of the world organize as a class, take possession of the earth and the machinery of production and abolish the wage system."

Soon after its formation the IWW became involved in internecine warfare. A rebel group under the leadership of Daniel De Leon in 1908 established a second IWW, which lasted until 1925. The IWW has always been numerically weak; its membership probably never exceeded 35,000. But as with militant minority groups in general it exerted in times past a degree of influence out of keeping with its numbers. The IWW still exists but in contrast to its earlier years it seldom gets in the news.

Early in the 1920's the communists came into leadership in the radical union movement. Whereas the IWW favored the policy of dual unionism, the communists originally preferred the technique of "boring from within"; in 1921 they established the Trade Union Educational League to educate their supporters in the use of this technique. After making little headway in their efforts to gain control in existing unions, the communists decided to shift their emphasis to the policy of dual unionism and accordingly organized the Trade Union Unity League in 1929.

Then in 1934 the communists decided to change their tactics again; they dissolved their unions and directed the members to join other labor organizations. The boring-from-within technique was taken up once more, and it has been used ever since. At the present time there are no avowedly communistic unions, but there are ordinary unions in which the communists or fellow travelers are influential.

These unions at the present time are of an independent nature. Until a few years ago they were in the CIO. In 1949 and 1950 the CIO charged them (11 organizations) with being under communistic influence and expelled them from its ranks. In one or two cases, including the United Electrical, Radio and Machine Workers of America, the unions withdrew before their formal expulsion. To what extent these organizations were, and are, under communist control it is not easy to say.[10] The CIO clearly found them wanting in the attributes it believed its affiliates should possess. To the CIO, at least, they were definitely under communist domination.

Miscellaneous Unions. Among the independent unions there are some that cannot be fitted into any of the preceding categories. The very powerful United Mine Workers of America, which has been in both the AFL and the CIO, is a good example. Other examples, to name a few of varied character, are the Authors' League of America, the International Die Sinkers' Conference, the National Federation of Federal Employees, and the Foremen's Association of America.

International Labor Bodies

During the last hundred years numerous international labor organizations have been established. American workers and American unions have been connected with a considerable number of

[10] For the reports of nine of the committees established by the CIO to investigate affiliates under alleged communist influence, see *Communist Domination of Certain Unions,* Report of the Subcommittee on Labor and Labor-Management Relations of the Committee on Labor and Public Welfare, United States Senate, 82nd Cong., 1st Sess., Document 89 (1951). See also *Public Policy and Communist Domination of Certain Unions,* a report from the same subcommittee, 82nd Cong., 2nd Sess., Document 26 (1953).

these bodies, though the intimacy and the significance of the relationship has varied a great deal. In recent years American unions have shown more interest in international affairs than ever before, and this interest is reflected in their more extensive representation in international labor organizations and their greatly increased participation in world political and economic affairs.[11]

The first of the international labor organizations to which we shall give attention are the so-called Internationals.[12] The First International (Working Men's Association), with which Karl Marx was closely associated, was formed in 1864 and lasted until 1876. The Second International was established in 1889 and continued to exist until 1914 when, with the outbreak of World War I, the nationalistic and belligerent sentiments of many of its leaders and members triumphed over their internationalism and pacifism. In 1919 the Second International was revived but did not become immediately active. However, in 1923 it was rejuvenated under the name of the Labor and Socialist International and it continued to exist until 1939. In 1951 the Second International (or Socialist International, as it is sometimes called) was revived again. Early in 1952 friction appeared in the organization over the question of European unification, with nationalistic sentiments once more coming to the fore.[13]

The Third International, which was communistic in character, was established in 1919. It was widely known as the Communist International or Comintern. This organization went out of existence, presumably, in 1943 when the communists and the capitalist West were jointly engaged in the struggle against the Nazis.

The WFTU. In 1945 a new international labor organization was formed under the name World Federation of Trade Unions, and this body still exists. When the WFTU was established it was

[11] For a brief but informative account of "American Labor and World Affairs," see W. J. Handley's article in *The Annals of the American Academy of Political and Social Science,* March, 1951.

[12] For a detailed treatment of the First and Second Internationals, and of the earlier years of the Third International, see Lewis L. Lorwin, *Labor and Internationalism,* New York: The Macmillan Co., 1929. For information on recent developments in the field of international labor see Lorwin's later book, *The International Labor Movement.* New York: Harper & Bros., 1953.

[13] *The New York Times,* July 8, 1951, and February 19, 1952. A successor to the Second International was also announced as having been established on March 4, 1951. *The New York Times,* March 5, 1951.

referred to by some persons as the Fourth International, but this name is not commonly used.

Before saying more about the WFTU it should be noted that in 1947 the Comintern was re-established under the name Cominform (Communist Information Bureau). The Cominform apparently still exists, though the existence of the now wholly communist WFTU would seem to make its existence unnecessary.

The WFTU was originally a world-wide organization of unions dedicated to the improvement of the lot of the workers, but not specifically to the overthrow of capitalism. Among its affiliates were the Russian unions, the British Trade Union Congress, and the CIO. Almost from the beginning friction developed between the Russian-led unions and those of the United States and Western Europe. Ideological differences became numerous. The communist unions assumed a highly critical attitude toward the European Recovery Program, voicing their opposition in the WFTU. Finally, in January, 1949 the CIO, the British Trade Union Congress, and the Dutch unions withdrew from the organization, refusing, in Sir Walter Citrine's felicitous phrase, "to conform to the cominform."[14] These bodies were followed shortly by other free trade-union groups. The WFTU came wholly under the domination of the communist unions, and remains so today.

The ICFTU. For some time before the split actually occurred in the ranks of the WFTU there was talk of the formation of a new international labor organization in which communist influence would be absent. Mention was made in this country of a Freedomtern and also of a Deminform (Democratic Information Bureau). In view of the definite limits to verbal ingenuity it is fortunate that no organization bearing either of these names was established. In the latter part of 1949 a new organization of the type that had been envisaged did come into being, under the name International Confederation of Free Trade Unions.[15] This body was set up at a

[14] *Labour,* February, 1949, p. 176.

[15] For an account of the founding of the ICFTU see the article by Adolf Sturmthal in the *Industrial and Labor Relations Review,* April, 1950. A word should be said at this point about another international labor body, the International Federation of Trade Unions (IFTU). This organization was formed early in the century and embraced many of the unions throughout the world. The AFL was affiliated with the IFTU for two periods during its existence. With the formation of the WFTU, the IFTU ended its history.

conference held in London attended by delegates from over 50 countries and representing about 48,000,000 workers. (At its July, 1953 convention, delegates representing 73 countries and 54,000,000 workers were present.) Both the AFL and the CIO, and also the United Mine Workers, participated in the formation of the ICFTU, and both federations are very influential affiliates of it.

Though the constitution of the ICFTU places great emphasis on the attainment of what are regarded as definitely trade union objectives, in its deliberations and its work the organization reaches out into matters that are broadly social and political. At its second congress it passed resolutions on such matters as the development of economically undeveloped countries, social rights, peace and democracy, and full employement.[16] The ICFTU advocates a wide range of reform measures, but unlike the present WFTU and the earlier Internationals it does not recommend the destruction of the capitalistic system. There is a great deal of socialistic sentiment found in the organization, however.

In general the ICFTU may be looked upon as a counter influence to the WFTU, and one of the great bulwarks against communist aggression. It proclaims the doctrine that "only through democracy can the spiritual and material needs of the people be met," and by democracy it does not mean the "democratic centralism" of the communist nations. Especially important in the functioning of the ICFTU are the regional organizations that have been established, each covering a segment of the world and giving special attention to the area under its jurisdiction. An example is the Inter-American Regional Organization of Workers (ORIT), formed in 1951.

Other International Labor Organizations. Mention should be made of the International Trade Secretariats (ITS), which are organizations that cover a given trade or industry and endeavor in various ways to promote the interest of their members.[17] The first secretariats were set up during the latter part of the last century. In 1952 there were 20 such organizations, 14 of them having American unions (with a membership of about 6,000,000) among their affiliates. Two of the more important of the secretariats are the In-

[16] See *Industry and Labour* (ILO), January 1, 1952, pp. 39-43.

[17] An informative treatment of the International Trade Secretariats by Melvin J. Segal will be found in the *Monthly Labor Review,* April, 1953, pp. 372-380.

ternational Transport Workers' Federation and the International Metalworkers' Federation. Although there is cooperation between the ITS and the ICFTU, the former are autonomous bodies. The establishment of a Coordinating Committee by the ITS organizations in the late 1940's has led to greater activity on the part of many of the secretariats, including stronger opposition to the communists.

There are three international labor organizations in the western hemisphere that are worthy of note. First is the Latin American Federation of Labor (CTAL). This organization has affiliated bodies in most of the South and Central American countries and is definitely left-wing in character. The second organization is the Inter-American Confederation of Workers (CIT). This body, anticommunist in character and with affiliates in most of the countries in which the CTAL is represented, has in its membership the AFL. In November, 1952, a third organization, the Latin-American Unionized Workers' Association (ATLAS), was set up. This association, with a nice show of impartiality, is both anticommunist and anti-United States (anti-United States policy) in nature. Its headquarters are in Buenos Aires.

Another organization, the International Labor Organization (ILO), was founded after World War I, as an adjunct of the League of Nations. Today, as an integral part of the United Nations, it has more than 60 member nations (now including Russia). The ILO has collected and published statistics relating to labor matters; has conducted various studies; has held periodic meetings attended by labor, management, and governmental representatives, and has passed numerous "conventions" and "recommendations." The United States linked up with the ILO in 1934, and representatives from this country play an important part in its affairs.

10

UNION STRUCTURE AND JURISDICTION

With this chapter we begin our detailed analysis of national and international unions, the most important units in the American labor movement. We shall defer, however, our analysis of their chief activity, collective bargaining, until after our discussion of management.

The Structure of the Nationals and Internationals

In terms of structural appearance, national and international unions resemble a pyramid. Making up the base of the pyramid and serving as the main foundation for the whole structure are the local unions. Above the locals there are usually intermediate units. These are less numerous than the local units and help to knit them together. At the top of the pyramid is the national or international itself, which rests on, and gets its support from, the intermediate and local bodies beneath it.

Actually in many labor organizations there are structural units smaller than, and subordinate to, the locals. These are the so-called shop committees, which are under the leadership of shop stewards; and it is with these committees, and particularly with the shop stewards, that we shall begin our discussion.

Sublocal Units—Shop Stewards. Sublocal units are always intraplant, or at least intracompany, in nature (local unions in most instances cover a number of plants or companies). The sublocal units may be on a plant or shop level or, in the case of large businesses, on a departmental level. On both levels the units are led by union functionaries known as shop stewards.

The shop steward—he is also referred to as the shop committeeman, the shop chairman, and the union committeeman—is either elected to his job by the workers he represents or appointed by the officers of the local or parent union. He has the status of an employee, just like the workers he represents, although by virtue of his job he may be given preferential treatment in the matter of seniority.

In a large plant each department will probably have a steward of its own; it may even have more than one. In addition, many plants have a "plant grievance committee," which is composed of all or some of the shop stewards. The members of such a committee may be elected by the departmental stewards, who as a whole may constitute a "stewards' council," or by the union membership in the plant. They may also be appointed by the union.

The chief task of the shop steward is handling grievances. This important work demands for its successful performance both knowledge and tact on the part of the steward. In addtion to dealing with grievances, the shop steward may collect union dues, carry on organizing work within the department or plant, and try to stimulate the workers to a keener interest in the activities of the local and in politics. In general the shop steward acts as spokesman for the workers under him.

Shop stewards, acting individually or through a shop committee, are of importance in the union set-up.[1] But it must be emphasized that they *apply* union policy rather than determine it. In other words, the work of the shop stewards is administrative and judicial in nature, not legislative. The legislative units in the union structure are on (and above) the local union level.

Local Unions. The basic structural and governmental unit in the labor movement is the local union. In point of origin the local antedates the national or international, although many of the locals existing at the present time were established through the efforts of already functioning parent organizations.

As its name implies, the local union operates in a given locality, usually a town or city, but sometimes a larger area. The members of a local may come from one plant or company or from more than one. If the plants are large, and if the union is set up on an industrial or semi-industrial basis, there will probably be one local for

1 According to studies made by the New York State School of Industrial and Labor Relations there is evidence that the power of shop stewards in some unions is diminishing. *The New York Times,* April 27, 1952.

each plant, as there is in many automobile factories and steel plants. If, on the other hand, the plant or the employing units are small, as in the clothing and trucking industries, a given local may have within its membership workers from a large number of different enterprises. In some unions it is customary, particularly in the larger centers, to establish specialized locals of one sort or another, on the basis of such factors as occupation, race, and language.

Most local unions are relatively small, with not more than two or three hundred members. There are some mammoth locals, however, with thousands of members. Local 600 of the United Automobile Workers (the Ford River Rouge local) is the largest in the country, if not in the world. At one point during World War II it had 80,000 members.

Local unions, like local or municipal governments, have certain powers. Ordinarily they have the right to levy taxes on their members, although very often the parent organization exercises some control over the taxation rate. The locals pass laws or adopt rules, which must be consistent with those of the parent body; they also engage in various activities, the range of which is sometimes wide.

Intermediate Units. Unless a national or international is very small it is likely to establish a number of intermediate structural units between the locals and the head office. These units are convenient for administrative purposes and facilitate the work of the organization. In some unions they perform important functions and occupy an outstanding place in the general union structure.[2] The intermediate units are for the most part geographical in scope.

Intermediate units may be on a local (or district) basis. A good example is furnished by the "joint boards" in the ladies' clothing industry. These bodies are very significant in the organization; one of their jobs is to serve as collective bargaining agencies. Moreover, they enable the union to achieve a sort of industrial form since through them different craft, trade, and language locals are brought together into a unified body. Numerous other unions, including the Teamsters', the Carpenters', and the Hod Carriers' organizations,

[2] Herbert J. Lahne has a detailed discussion of intermediate structural units, with special reference to collective bargaining, in *Industrial and Labor Relations Review*, January, 1953.

also have city or district bodies. Other unions have intermediate units on a geographical scale extending beyond the city or narrow district.

Intermediate units are sometimes of a nongeographical nature. District 50 of the United Mine Workers, for example, a subordinate unit in the miners' union, has within its ranks workers from many industries and from many parts of the country. In its structure there is a Chemical Division, a Dairy Farmers' Division, a Utility Workers' Union—to name just a few of its subordinate units. The jurisdiction of District 50 extends, under its charter, to workers in all industries; and there are few major industrial categories in which it is not represented.

Parent Organizations. At the apex of the structural pyramid, heading up all the subordinate units, is the national or international union. This parent unit draws together and harmonizes the activities of its various member organizations. Quite often it is a very dictatorial and firm parent, but sometimes its authority is rather weak.

In the trade union world a national or international union is an entity in itself. It is an autonomous body. In authority and in structure it resembles an independent, self-governing nation. And just as independent nations have found it desirable to work together, through leagues and alliances, for the attainment of certain objectives, so have unions found it desirable to combine—witness the existence of the AFL and the CIO. Smaller leagues or alliances are the five departments, the local department councils, the state federations and the city centrals in the AFL, and the state and local industrial union councils in the CIO.

The word "international" that is associated with most of the unions does not mean that the organizations bearing the title are revolutionary in character and desirous of overthrowing the present economic system, like the First International, for example. Nor does the term mean that these unions espouse an international point of view and are interested in, say, a world state. As applied to American unionism the word "international" has no broad ideological or philosophical implications; it is simply a geographical concept indicating, to an exaggerated degree, the spatial or territorial composition of a union's membership. An "international" union is one that has affiliated locals, or at least members, outside the United States and its dependencies, especially in Canada.[3]

Structural Types and Union Developments

A Classification. Most national and international unions fall into five principal categories. These categories tend to shade into one another, however, so that it is not always possible to classify particular unions with ease and precision. Moreover, more than one structural type may be found within a single national or international. For example, an organization that is commonly looked upon as an industrial union may have a considerable number of nonindustrial locals. A classification of parent unions on the basis of structure must therefore be somewhat arbitrary in character, and its usefulness is consequently limited. Such a classification nevertheless seems helpful.[4]

A *craft union* is composed of skilled workers who perform a given industrial process. The International Wood Carvers' Association may be cited as an example.

A *multiple-craft union* is composed of skilled workers in a number of different, but nevertheless closely allied, crafts. The Journeymen Barbers, Hairdressers, and Cosmetologists' Union is an example; its members include journeymen barbers, hairdressers, wavers, marcellers, cosmeticians, and manicurists. Many of the unions in this category have been formed through the amalgamation of separate crafts.

A *semi-industrial* union covers skilled, semiskilled, and unskilled workers in the basic production occupations of an industry. Workers in auxiliary employments, such as maintenance, are not included. The United Hatters, Cap, and Millinery Workers' International Union is an example of a semi-industrial union.

An *industrial union* includes all the workers, in both the pro-

[3] For a discussion of this aspect of unionism see Paul Norgren, "The Labor Link Between Canada and the United States," *Industrial and Labor Relations Review,* October, 1950.

[4] The following classification (with its definitions and illustrations) is based substantially but not wholly on the one presented in a study made by the Division of Research of the National Labor Relations Board, *Structure of A.F. of L. Unions,* by David J. Saposs and Sol Davison. Among the changes made is the exclusion of one entry in the classification (the *trade union,* coming after the *multiple-craft union)* and the inclusion of the *multiple-industrial union* entry.

duction and the auxiliary employments, engaged in providing a given service or in making a given commodity. The Progressive Mine Workers' Union is an example.

A *multiple-industrial union* is a comprehensive organization covering workers in a number of industries. An example is the International Union of United Brewery, Flour, Cereal, and Soft Drink Workers.

A *labor union* takes in all workers regardless of their occupation or the industry in which they are engaged. Some of the so-called federal labor unions in the AFL are in reality labor unions. So is District 50 of the United Mine Workers' union.

To be all-inclusive our classification must have one final entry, namely *miscellaneous unions,* to cover all the organizations that cannot easily be placed, or forced, into the preceding categories.

A given national or international union may have a number of structural types represented in its composition. The Carpenters' union, for example, acts as a craft (trade) union in the construction field, as a semi-industrial union in furniture and wood-working plants, and as an industrial union in lumber and logging camps.

Union Structure and Union Developments. The question of union structure has played an important part in the history of the American labor movement. As was pointed out in Chapter 7, the division within the ranks of the AFL in the middle 1930's was mostly a result of disagreement over the structural set-up to be assumed by the new unions in the mass-production industries. The formation of the CIO represented a spectacular triumph of the principle of wide coverage in union structure.

Even within the AFL itself this principle has become more extensively accepted. Through the process of amalgamation, either voluntary or enforced, and through the constant reaching out of unions into adjacent tasks or occupations, many of which have been newly created, the structural basis of AFL unions has been steadily enlarged.

There is a strong likelihood that the structural foundation of American unions, and particularly of AFL unions, will continue to broaden out in the future. The process of industrial mechanization, which has shattered so many of the old crafts and has created so many new jobs (thereby greatly aiding the growth of industrial unionism), will continue. The power that industrial unions can muster in dealing with employers, their relative immunity from jurisdictional strife, the economy with which they are able to operate, and the solidarity and unity of action they engender—these and other elements of strength that industry-wide unions possess will pull strongly for the expansion of industrial unionism. Finally, the desire of some union leaders to build up their "empires" is pulling toward more multiple-craft unionism, if not toward industrial unionism.

But this country is not likely to turn completely to industrial unionism as Russia has done. Many multpile craft and other non-industrial unions will remain in existence. The presence of vested interests in the unions and the reluctance of the rank-and-file members to have the identity of their organizations destroyed can easily outweigh in influence the potential benefits of amalgamation. Moreover, there are situations in which a union with a narrow occupational coverage can reap greater gains for its members than could an organization of wider coverage. Sometimes workers all in a given industry reap greater benefits if there are several unions, each with a limited occupational coverage, than if there were only one.

Functional Types

The functional approach to the study of unionism is likely to be more fruitful than an approach merely in terms of structure. This was the lesson taught with great emphasis and brilliancy by Professor Robert F. Hoxie several decades ago. In his analysis of the American labor movement Hoxie not only used the functional method of approach but formulated a functional classification, not of unions but of *unionism.*[5]

According to Hoxie, American unionism is divisible into four chief types: business unionism, uplift unionism, revolutionary unionism, and predatory unionism. The last two were further subdivided: revolutionary unionism into socialistic and quasi-anarchistic unionism, and predatory unionism into hold-up and guerilla unionism.

This classification points to the chief things in which unionists are immediately interested. It may seem abstract and unreal because of the great difficulty of pinning down actual unions under

[5] For a detailed discussion of these functional types see *Trade Unionism in the United States,* Chapters II and III. New York: D. Appleton & Co., 1926.

the various headings; but it must be remembered that Hoxie was trying to classify not unions but unionism or union functions.

The functional types Hoxie set forth do not exist in pure form. Since unions are set up on the basis of occupation or industry, one should not expect to find in any single organization a complete, unmixed embodiment of any one function. However, in many unions one or two of the functions are of outstanding significance: business unionism, for example, is found in all American labor organizations; but in some, notably the Railroad Brotherhoods, it is especially marked. We may follow Hoxie, therefore, in looking upon the Brotherhoods as examples of business unionism, though other functions are represented in them as well. Not a few unions are keenly interested in welfare projects; the International Ladies Garment Workers' Union, an outstanding example, approaches in character Hoxie's "uplift" unionism. But it also illustrates business unionism.

Union Jurisdiction

A sovereign labor organization, like a sovereign nation, is interested in having its boundaries definitely and clearly defined. Like a sovereign nation, too, it is very jealous of its "territorial" integrity, and resists strongly any attempts by other unions at invasion. At the same time unions are generally on the lookout for new, unclaimed "lands" to conquer; and very often they become involved in open conflict with one or more unions that are similarly bent on conquest.

Boundary-line struggles between unions, commonly called jurisdictional disputes, bear a striking resemblance indeed to the struggles that occur between nations. They also resemble the struggles that are carried on in competitive business, in which each business unit attempts either to hold its established volume of trade or to obtain more.

Jurisdictional disputes are in a sense collective struggles for jobs and income. As such they represent a departure from the "atomistic" competition that used to prevail in the labor market, when worker competed with worker for employment and employer competed with employer for help. Ordinary collective bargaining also represents a departure from atomistic competition, but it differs from bargaining (and fighting) over jurisdiction in that the employer is directly a party to the process. Jurisdictional disputes involve collective action *within* the labor movement, whereas collective bargaining involves collective action *between* units in the labor movement on the one hand and employer or management units on the other. The shift from atomistic competition to collective competition, it should be added, has not been confined to the labor field. It is a common phenomenon in the field of business.[6]

Kinds of Jurisdictional Disputes

There are two chief types of jurisdictional disputes: trade or job disputes, and membership disputes.[7] Job disputes arise when two or more unions claim the right to perform a specific task or set of tasks. Membership disputes arise when two or more unions claim the same individuals as members.

Innumerable examples of disputes between (or among) unions over the right to do a certain task or piece of work could be cited. Such disputes have been especially common in the building trades. A quarrel between the Carpenters' union (which includes millwrights in its membership) and the Machinists' union over the right to install and dismantle machinery was a notable one, not only because it involved two powerful unions but because it led, a few years ago, to a famous Supreme Court case, U.S. *v.* Hutcheson.

Membership jurisdictional disputes, which until the formation of the CIO were not as important as job disputes, are not based on differences of opinion over which workers are to do the task or job, but grow out of conflicting claims over the union affiliation of the workers who are already doing the work and whose right to it is not questioned. There are two kinds of membership disputes. The first involves unions whose jurisdictional claims are for the most part clearly distinct but which, at the same time, overlap to a small degree. The bitter, long drawn out quarrel between the Teamsters' Union and the Brewery Workers' union over the drivers of beer

[6] See Professor John R. Commons' acute discussion of "Jurisdictional Disputes," especially p. 119, in *Wertheim Lectures on Industrial Relations.* Cambridge: Harvard University Press, 1929.

[7] Sometimes a third type is distinguished, namely "territorial" disputes. See Carroll R. Daugherty, *Labor Problems in American Industry,* 4th, rev. ed., pp. 410-411. Boston: Houghton Mifflin Co., 1938. The line between the so-called territorial disputes and the two types discussed in the text is not a very clear one; hence the above classification seems adequate.

wagons and trucks is a good example of this type. It might be added that the Teamsters' Union claims that numerous organizations (including the following AFL affiliates: the retail clerks, the butchers, the plumbers, the electrical workers, the carpenters, the laborers, and the building service employees) are trespassing on its jurisdictional preserves.[8]

The second kind of membership disputes, the ones between unions with jurisdictions that completely or very largely overlap, came into great prominence with the formation of the CIO. A considerable number of CIO unions invaded fields that AFL organizations looked upon as their own. Interunion warfare inevitably developed. Affiliates of the two federations have clashed in the automobile industry, the timber and logging industry, and the electrical and radio industry, to name but three. Membership disputes of this kind involve dual unionism, sometimes called "rival unionism."[9]

Reasons for Jurisdictional Disputes

Basic Causes. There are two basic reasons for jurisdictional strife. One is the desire of unionists to achieve as large a degree of economic security as possible; the other, a less important one, is their desire (at least the union leaders' desire) to make their organization as strong and as influential as possible. Other reasons given for jurisdictional disputes generally have meaning only in terms of these two fundamental causes.

To union members, and to workers in general, economic security is a matter of the utmost importance. The amount of security achieved by the members of any labor group is largely a matter of their wage rates and the amount of employment they have. If a union can bring more tasks within its jurisdiction, the amount of

[8] *The New York Times,* September 22, 1953.

[9] Objection may be taken to applying the adjective "jurisdictional" to disputes between rival or dual unions. See Florence Peterson, *American Labor Unions,* pp. 259, 266. New York: Harper & Bros., 1945. The present writer believes it is desirable to use the term "jurisdictional dispute" in a broad sense—as it is used in the text above—and not limit it to struggles between unions in the same central organization. Another term that has been used in discussions of the present subject is "organizational disputes." Thus, George Meany has said (in testifying in Washington in April, 1953, on revision of the Taft-Hartley Act), "You see, a dispute between the CIO and the AFL is not a jurisdictional dispute; it is an organizational dispute." While recognizing that this term has some merit, we shall use the more comprehensive one.

employment available for its members will be increased and their earnings will be greater.

The desire of a union to build up its strength can be achieved if more jobs and more workers, and more initiation fees and more membership dues, are brought under the control of the union. When the attempt to achieve greater union power is pursued without proper respect for the rights of smaller unions, it constitutes a type of "imperialism." [10]

Intensifying Factors. In addition to the two basic causes of jurisdictional disputes there are various intensifying factors that increase the seriousness of the disputes. Some of these factors could be listed as separate causes, but it seems preferable to look upon them as influences—in a number of cases very important influences—that enlarge the scope and power of the basic causes.

One such intensifying factor is the highly complex and interdependent nature of modern industry. There are literally millions of different operations involved in present-day production, and the union jurisdiction under which each of these tasks or operations should come is by no means always clear. Is the installation of a glass shelf in a bathroom a job for a carpenter or a plumber? It would be a rash man indeed who would attempt to answer that question without careful thought.

The narrow structural set-up of many American unions also causes trouble: a great many jurisdictional disputes involve craft or multiple-craft unions. It would be a mistake to assume, however, that these disputes would disappear if all unions were of the industrial type. Quarrels over jurisdiction can take place, and do take place, between industrial unions. It should be added, too, that the coexistence of craft unions and industrial unions is a fruitful source of jurisdictional strife, since this coexistence almost of necessity involves some overlapping of boundary lines.

A third factor intensifying the seriousness of jurisdictional controversy is the incessant flux of modern industry. Production methods are in constant process of change. New materials are continually being developed and placed on the market. These changes not only open up new territory for union exploitation, but also render the

[10] See Philip Taft, *Economics and Problems of Labor,* p. 552. Harrisburg: Stackpole Sons, 1942.

boundaries around the old territories less clear and definite. The result is jurisdictional friction.

The highly group-conscious character of American unionism also promotes jurisdictional disputes. If unionists in this country were more class-conscious (not that this is to be advocated), union imperialism would exist on a much smaller scale, and jurisdictional warfare as a means of protecting or promoting economic security would be of less consequence. This conclusion is borne out by labor experience in Great Britain.[11]

The "economism" of American unionism, which is inseparably associated with its group consciousness, is another intensifying factor. By emphasizing economic methods and objectives and placing those of a political nature in a secondary position, American unions have found it relatively easy to fall into jurisdictional controversy.

The fear of establishing a precedent may be a factor in jurisdictional strife, accounting at times for great tempests over what to the outsider may seem picayune issues.

As a final intensifying factor we may point to the small degree of union organization that has heretofore existed in this country. With many jobs and many workers not under the control of any organization, unions have had little difficulty in becoming embroiled in jurisdictional battles. Even where there is a high degree of organization, of course, there may still be a certain amount of jurisdictional strife, in the form of "raiding."

Effects of Jurisdictional Disputes

In terms of their participants jurisdictional disputes are internal problems of the unions. In terms of their effects, however, these disputes extend far beyond the unions and their members. They reach to employers and to the general public as well.

There is no need to develop the point that individual unionists and individual union groups may frequently benefit from jurisdictional struggles. It is conceivable that the labor movement as a whole may also benefit on occasion from such struggles. Generally speaking, however, jurisdictional disputes are harmful to the unions, and for a number of reasons.

11 See W. A. McConagha, *Development of the Labor Movement in Great Britain, France, and Germany*, pp. 9, 10. Chapel Hill: University of North Carolina Press, 1942.

Like family quarrels, jurisdictional disputes give rise to ill feeling and bitterness. Brother unionist is set against brother unionist, and extreme statements and extreme actions—threats, strikes, violence, boycotts—often follow. Another disadvantageous effect of jurisdictional disputes is the loss of time and energy. Union leaders and rank-and-file members involved in jurisdictional strife obviously cannot carry on their regular union duties with the same degree of effectiveness. Disputes often involve substantial cash outlays on the part of the unions engaged.[12]

In addition to actually spending money, one organization, as a means of getting additional members, may underbid its competitor in the field in the matter of union dues or initiation fees. Again, jurisdictional disputes may force individual unionists to join more than one union as a means of retaining their jobs. Furthermore, such disputes tend to create an antiunion attitude on the part of the public, which may manifest itself in common action for the legal control of unions.

Jurisdictional disputes may be harmful to unionists not only as workers but also as consumers. Since some of these disputes are settled on a might-makes-right basis, jobs may be given to unqualified or poorly qualified workers at the expense of capable workers. This poor allocation of labor power damages the real income of the nation.

A few words should be said about the general effects of jurisdictional strife on employers and the public. A membership dispute in which the more docile or more cooperative union wins may be advantageous to the employer; but apart from exceptions of this sort disputes by unions over jurisdictional matters are distinctly harmful to the employer. He is the innocent bystander who, with no direct interest in the struggle going on before his eyes, is harmed by it, sometimes to the extent of serious economic losses. And these effects are not always restricted to the employers in whose establishments the disputes occur.

Jurisdictional strife is generally harmful to the public because of its adverse effect on production and hence on the real income of society. When a jurisdictional dispute involves loss of time, dissipa-

[12] In 1952 an official of the AFL stated that "Raiding between the AFL and CIO costs us more money than all the money spent on organizing." *The New York Times,* December 21, 1952.

tion of effort, and improper allocation of labor power, production suffers and material living standards sink. Although it is possible that jurisdictional struggles may sometimes bring noneconomic advantages to society (for example, when a progressive union wins over a reactionary one), on the whole the noneconomic results of these struggles are definitely harmful.

The Settlement of Jurisdictional Disputes

AFL Agencies. Since the AFL has long had to contend with jurisdictional strife within its ranks, it is not surprising that it has adopted various means for dealing with such strife. Of special importance in this connection are the industry departments and their subordinate units, the local department councils. The Building and Construction Trades Department is particularly outstanding as a settlement or adjudicating agency, for the simple reason that a large percentage of the job jurisdictional disputes take place between unions affiliated with it. In the late 1940's a national joint board was created in the building industry, made up of an impartial chairman, two union representatives, and two employer representatives. The union and employer representatives are selected by the chairman, for each dispute that comes before the board, from a joint panel of twenty-four persons. Before a dispute reaches the national board it must first be examined by a board of trustees, composed of four union and four employer members, who determine whether or not the dispute has already been settled by an earlier decision or agreement. The trustees, it should also be noted, select the impartial chairman. Minor disputes in the building trades over jurisdiction may, of course, be settled by the contending unions without resort to the above machinery.[13]

Some of the more important jurisdictional disputes between AFL unions reach the AFL's executive council. In attempting to bring about settlements the council may act either as a whole or through a subcommittee. If the disputes still remain unsettled, they may be brought before the AFL convention, which is the ultimate authority in jurisdictional matters. Sometimes the convention

[13] An effective plan for settling jurisdictional disputes in the building trades of New York City has been in operation for many years. The plan calls for final arbitration by *employer* representatives in cases of unsettled disputes. *The New York Times,* June 27, 1952.

merely expresses the hope that a peaceful settlement will be reached. At other times it hands down a positive award, which may or may not be accepted. If a union is dissatisfied with an AFL award and is not willing to accept it, it may decide to drop out of the Federation. If it remains within the organization but at the same time disobeys the award, its charter may be revoked. The AFL seldom exercises this power until every attempt to reach a settlement has been made, and only occasionally will it revoke the charter of a strong union.[14]

Sometimes individual unions within the AFL establish their own machinery for handling jurisdictional disputes. A notable example is the arrangement entered into by the Teamsters and Machinists in early 1953 for dealing with jurisdictional differences that might arise in a large-scale, cooperative organizing drive about to be launched by the two unions in the garage and service station industry. The Teamsters have also entered into pacts of a like nature with other AFL unions.

Still further means for handling jurisdictional disputes within the AFL seem desirable. This need was clearly brought out in 1953 when the powerful Carpenters' union temporarily pulled out of the Federation (which on this occasion made no attempt to discourage the act). The union, or rather the union officers, criticized the no-raiding pact that the AFL had agreed to sign with the CIO, and alleged that the Federation had not given enough attention to its own internal jurisdictional problems. The agreement concerning the return of the Carpenters to the Federation provided that the latter "should adopt some policy definitely designed to prevent raids within our own organization." The AFL convention directed the executive council to appoint a committee to study the matter.

CIO Agencies. Because of the broader structural basis of the CIO unions, and probably also because of the larger degree of labor consciousness in the organization, jurisdictional strife is much less common in the CIO than in the AFL. Nevertheless such strife occurs and a number of steps have been taken to cope with it. The most important was the one taken at the 1951 CIO convention. At

[14] See *The Yale Law Journal,* January, 1940, p. 434, for a discussion by Professor Louis L. Jaffe of interunion disputes, including a detailed historical account of AFL policy in dealing with such disputes.

that time almost all the CIO unions signed an "agreement governing organizational disputes," which outlawed jurisdictional disputes and provided for an arbitration arrangement for unsettled controversies. Early in 1952 Professor George W. Taylor was appointed arbitrator and served in that capacity until early 1953 when he was succeeded by Professor Nathan Feinsinger.

According to the CIO plan, "responsible representatives" of the unions involved in a jurisdictional dispute must first try to bring about a settlement. If they fail, then a second step is taken: the Director of Organization (and Executive Vice-President) of the CIO brings national officers or representatives of the unions together in an effort to effect a settlement. If this step fails, either union involved or the Director of Organization submits the dispute to the "organizational disputes director," who hands down a decision. All the CIO unions that ratify the plan are legally bound to accept any decision the arbitrator makes. During the first year's operation of the plan 32 jurisdictional disputes were brought to the CIO's attention; 19 of these were settled before the arbitration process came into play (these settlements, which were aided by the Director of Organization, were looked upon by Professor Taylor as the "outstanding success of the machinery"); 7 were arbitrated; and 6 cases were pending.[15]

Other Agencies. To a certain extent the National Labor Relations Board aids in the settlement of jurisdictional disputes. It is empowered to hold elections for the purpse of determining which union, if any, the workers in a given collective bargaining unit desire. Sometimes more than one union from the AFL, or the CIO, will be on the same ballot. Three entries from the same federation are not unknown. The NLRB may also directly settle jurisdictional disputes of a job character. If, within a short space of time, the unions engaged in such a dispute (involving a stoppage of work) cannot settle the issue themselves, the NLRB is not only empowered to hear the dispute but directed to "determine" it.

The Railway Mediation Board has conducted similar elections in the railroad industry, but it has done so reluctantly. Among other

[15] *The CIO News,* June 1, 1953, p. 3. *Proceedings,* CIO Convention, 1952, p. 337. A description of the "organizational disputes program," which includes a few more details than those presented above, will be found in *The CIO News,* February 18, 1953, p. 2.

agencies that may be used in settling jurisdictional quarrels are arbitration tribunals and conciliation bodies.

Unions engaged in jurisdictional disputes, and with different affiliations, sometimes work out settlements or arrangements between themselves. A good example is furnished by the Automobile Workers' union of the CIO and the Machinists' union of the AFL. In 1953 these two organizations extended a no-raiding agreement that they had previously assigned, at the time time including in it a provision for united action in bargaining with multiplant employers. An even better example, and one on a much larger scale, is the no-raiding agreement made in 1953 between the AFL and the CIO. Under this plan, groups of workers already unionized by either one of the organizations and possessing collective bargaining rights are not to be raided—in attempts to win them over—by the other one. The plan does not cover situations involving unorganized workers, nor does it cover affiliates that do not sign the pact.

Types of Settlements. Solutions of jurisdictional disputes, whether suggested by adjudicating bodies or arrived at by the contending parties themselves, are of two main types. The first is amalgamation, in which unions eliminate the conflict over membership jurisdiction by combining into a new organization, possibly with a new name. Amalgamation as a solution to jurisdictional controversy has been common in American trade union history. Disputes solved by amalgamation are ordinarily serious: the "territory" over which there are rival claims is likely to be extensive, and the contestants are usually substantially equal in power, although not necessarily in numbers. If there is a marked difference in the power of the parties to the dispute, and if there is little that the weaker one can do but give in to the stronger, the solution is more likely to be liquidation or confiscation.

Under the second main type of solution to jurisdictional quarrels the unions maintain their identity, but the territory—in this case the *job* or *task* territory—in dispute is awarded to the one or the other or, as often happens, it is divided between them. Solutions of this character are very numerous in the disputes in the building trades, for example.

11

UNION MEMBERSHIP AND GOVERNMENT

Membership and Degree of Organization

Before the formation of the AFL, union membership in this country was subject to wide fluctuations, particularly as a result of changing industrial and employment conditions. From about 1890 on unions were more successful in buffeting the recurring economic storms than they had been. Except for a brief period after the turn of the century and the period of World War I, however, the numerical strength of the unions increased only gradually during the ensuing decades. By 1929 total union membership amounted to less than 3,500,000 (it had been slightly more than 5,000,000 in 1920); and in 1933, at the bottom of the Great Depression, it was slightly less than 3,000,000. A phenomenal change was soon to take place. For the reasons given in Chapter 7 union membership started to grow; by 1940 it was 8,500,000. It kept on growing during the war period, reaching about 15,000,000 in 1945. Since then the growth has been much slower; during the early 1950's union membership was in the neighborhood of 16,000,000.

Despite the extremely rapid growth in the American labor movement between 1935 and 1945 (and the relative stability of the membership since then), the degree of union organization in this country is still relatively small compared with that of some of the other nations of the world. Only about 33 per cent of our nonagricultural employees, most of whom may be looked upon as organizable, are unionized. In Great Britain the percentage is approximately 45, in Denmark 53, in Norway 60, and in Sweden 77.[1]

[1] *Monthly Labor Review,* May, 1951, p. 529. About 25 per cent of the total work force in this country is unionized.

The degree of union organization in the United States varies greatly from industry to industry. Some, like the railroads, building and construction, and the clothing industry are very highly organized. Others, like the service industries and such manufacturing industries as textiles and lumber, are organized only to a small or moderate extent.[2]

The degree of union organization also varies from one labor market to another, largely because of the types of industries found in the various markets. Such major labor markets as Detroit and Pittsburgh are very highly organized; others like Atlanta and Houston are only moderately organized.[3] In general it can be said that the degree of unionization is greater in large labor markets than in small ones. It is also greater among plant workers than among office workers.

Membership Control

As a rule unions are desirous of increasing their membership, believing that in numbers there is strength. They are not, however, willing to take into their membership everyone who applies. To be admitted into a union a person must ordinarily possess certain qualifications.[4]

Almost all nationals and internationals set forth in their constitutions rules or requirements concerning membership in their constituent locals. These written rules and regulations are not always accurate indicators of the degree of membership control, however: there may be departures in either "direction" from them. There may be unwritten laws to reckon with; and other exclusionary devices—such things as negative votes by members, high initiation fees, apprenticeship rules, and skill tests—may be used.

Concentrating our attention chiefly on constitutional provisions concerning membership control, we shall note some of the rules that prevail. Often unions have age requirements for admittance to membership—minimum age levels, maximum levels, or combi-

[2] See Leo Wolman, "Concentration of Union Membership," in *Proceedings of the Fifth Annual Meeting, Industrial Relations Research Association,* 1952.

[3] For data on this matter see the study by A. N. Jarrell in the *Monthly Labor Review,* January, 1953, pp. 26-29.

[4] An extensive and useful study of this topic is Clyde M. Summers, "Admission Policies of Labor Unions," *The Quarterly Journal of Economics,* November, 1946, pp. 66-107.

nations of these two. In occupations and industries in which skill and dexterity are essential, it is common for unions to have training qualifications for membership. Many unions require citizenship. Some require membership in the white race. The Order of Railway Conductors states in its constitution that prospective members must be "sound in mind and body." The Railroad Trainmen's Union specifies that its members must be "sober and industrious." Some unions have membership requirements of a physical nature. A few have religious standards. In some instances, however, the statements in constitutions relating to membership qualifications are ignored in practical application.[5]

It should be added that not all unions provide equality of status for their members. Different membership categories or separate locals are sometimes established for those who have not been taken into full "citizenship." Differentiation is often based on differences in skill, sex, or color.

Unions and Race

The type of membership control that has most attracted public attention during recent years is that having to do with nonwhite workers. Although Negroes have been the chief victims of this control, other groups—Asiatics, Mexicans, and American Indians—have also been injured by it.

The unions that discriminate against Negroes may be divided into three categories. Those in the first category exclude Negroes from membership by provisions in their constitutions or by their rituals. In the second category are those whose locals generally exclude Negroes, without provisions in the constitutions of the parent organizations authorizing such a policy. Those in the third category set up special, auxiliary locals for their Negro members. In the early 1940's Professor Herbert R. Northrup found that there were 15 unions in the first category, five in the second, and nine in the third. Since then the extent of discrimination has been noticeably reduced. In the decade following the publication of Professor Northrup's figures, eight unions, seven of them AFL affiliates and four of them railway unions, have removed racial restrictions (in

[5] The general membership requirements of American unions, as set forth in their constitutions, will be found in Florence Peterson, *Handbook of Labor Unions*. Washington: American Council on Public Affairs, 1944.

the form of exclusion provisions and auxiliary-status provisions) from their constitutions; ten unions, five of them AFL affiliates and eight of them railway unions, have made their constitutional restrictions inoperative in states that have Fair Employment Practice legislation. These states, it might be added, have almost one-third of the total population of the country.[6]

Most discrimination against the Negro has been in AFL unions, and in unions wholly or partly associated with the railroad industry (a considerable number of these are AFL organizations). From the figures that have been presented it is clear that the amount of discrimination among unions in both of these groups has been substantially reduced. The general problem of discrimination has been a difficult one for the AFL because the Federation, though it has long been opposed to the principle of race discrimination, adheres to the philosophy of craft autonomy, which prevents interference in the affairs of its affiliates. It should be noted, however, that since about the middle of the 1890's the Federation has not felt induced to refuse requests for affiliation from unions that exclude Negroes.

In no industrial group has there been as much discrimination against Negroes as in the railroad industry. Despite the progress evident from the preceding statistics, the industry still retains its primacy in this respect. All of the Big Four Brotherhoods, for example, have retained discriminatory clauses in their constitutions.

The unions in the CIO have been relatively free of race discrimination, partly because there is more of an "equalitarian" philosophy and less skilled work and craft consciousness in the CIO than in the AFL and the railway unions.

During recent years the number of Negro unionists in the country has been growing rapidly. According to a survey made in 1952 the figure stood at 1,500,000.[7] In the matter of leadership positions in the union movement the Negroes are underrepresented; very few of the really important positions in the movement are held by Negroes, although a considerable number of Negroes occupy positions

[6] For discussions of the subject by Professor Northrup, see his articles in *The Nation*, August 14, 1943, and *The Journal of Political Economy*, June, 1943. Northrup deals with the problem in greater detail in his book, *Organized Labor and the Negro*. New York: Harper & Bros., 1944. The more recent facts cited above are from *The Negro Yearbook*, 11th ed., 1952, p. 121. New York: Wm. H. Wise & Co., Inc.

[7] *The Labor Leader*, March 16, 1953, p. 4.

of secondary importance. Of course, in unions composed wholly of Negroes, and there are a few such unions in this country, Negroes are in top leadership positions.

Women Workers

Until comparatively recently there were three outstanding groups of "forgotten men" in the American labor movement: Negroes, unskilled workers, and women. One may also add white-collar workers, who have come to be looked upon as organizable. Despite the fact that racial discrimination still exists, Negroes are emerging from the state of neglect. So are unskilled workers and white-collar workers. Women, too, have been rescued from the state of neglect, and to some extent from their own indifference to unionism. Hundreds of thousands of women are now union members.

It must not be inferred, however, that women have just recently become participants in union activities. More than one hundred years ago, during the first third of the last century, women workers formed unions (societies) of their own.[8] These organizations were of a transient nature, however. In the latter part of the 1860's the women in the shoe industry had a national union, known as The Daughters of St. Crispin, but it did not last long. With the upsurge of unionism after the period of disintegration in the 1870's, women once more, and to a greater extent, participated in union affairs. The Knights of Labor accepted them into membership, and at one time may have had as many as 50,000 women workers within their organization. The American Federation of Labor, which superseded the Knights, declared its intention of organizing women workers, but for many years it did little in the way of carrying out its intention. In recent years, however, the Federation has been devoting more and more attention to women workers and it has succeeded in bringing many of them into its fold. But much of the credit for the expansion of unionism among women must go to the CIO.

The coming of World War II and the phenomenal expansion that took place in American industry at that time drew thousands of women into gainful jobs, many of them in industries in which

[8] F. E. Wolfe, *Admission to American Trade Unions*, p. 75. Baltimore: Johns Hopkins Press, 1912. The first strike of women workers, it is interesting to note, occurred in 1828.

unions were active. The inevitable consequence was a large growth in the female membership of the unions. This membership was estimated at 3,500,000 early in 1943. In 1953 the figure was placed at nearly 3,000,000, out of a total of somewhat more than 19,000,000 women in the labor force.

In a survey made in 1952-1953 by the United States Bureau of Labor Statistics it was found that of 213 organizations studied 43 had no women members; 82 had less than 10 per cent of their membership composed of women; 28 had 50 per cent or more women members. Close to 2,500,000 of the total number of women unionists were in 45 unions. Heading the list was the International Ladies Garment Workers' Union with 292,500 women members, followed by the Amalgamated Clothing Workers with 261,800.[9] At their 1952 convention both the AFL and the CIO resolved to increase the attention given to women unionists and workers.

Although the growth in the number of women unionists during the last two decades has been rapid, up to the present time women have not occupied a very prominent place as union leaders. Both the AFL and the CIO have been distinctly men's organizations. It will be a red letter day for women when they succeed in winning a place on the executive council of either of the federations (The CIO has had one woman on its executive board). At the conventions of the national and international unions, however, women delegates are usually numerous and participate actively in the work of the gatherings. Moreover, in not a few of these unions women occupy positions of leadership. It is in local unions that women appear to achieve the highest degree of representation in official positions. Many locals have women on their executive bodies.

Looking at the situation as a whole it is abundantly clear that women are underrepresented in the councils of the labor movement. As time goes on the degree of underrepresentation will probably decrease, but it will be a long time before anything approaching "proportional representation" is achieved.

The National Women's Trade Union League (founded in 1903), existing not within but very close to the American labor movement, and including members from outside the ranks of labor, has rendered great help to women wage earners. Mention should also be

[9] *Directory of Labor Unions in the United States, 1953,* Bulletin No. 1127, Bureau of Labor Statistics, United States Department of Labor, pp. 5, 46.

made of the women's auxiliaries, which aid the regular union organizations in many ways—for example, in strikes, in political campaigns, and in the sale of union-made goods.

Supervisory Employees

Most unionists in the United States, and elsewhere, have the status of ordinary employees. They are order receivers, not order givers or order transmitters. But some *extraordinary* employees, mostly foremen or supervisors, belong to unions. In some instances supervisors are found in unions that they themselves have established.

Many national and international unions in their constitutions specifically exclude supervisory employees from membership; many more say nothing about the matter; some, however, are very desirous, even to the point of compulsion, of having supervisors become members.[10]

The position of supervisors in the last-mentioned group has been altered somewhat under the Taft-Hartley Act. The Act states that "Nothing herein shall prohibit any individual employed as a supervisor from becoming or remaining a member of a labor organization," but it goes on to say that such individuals are not considered "employees . . . for the purpose of any law, either national or local, relating to collective bargaining." The implication here is that supervisors, whether they are members of regular unions or members of their own unions, do not have the protection of the Taft-Hartley Act. It might be expected that under such a provision supervisors would be inclined to drop out of the regular unions. Apparently this has not happened.[11]

Some unions are composed exclusively of supervisory employees. In 1953 the number of such organizations was placed (by the Executive Director of the Foremen's Association of America) at 29. Nine of these unions have been in existence for a long time: three in the maritime industries, two in the railroad industry, one in naval yards, and three in the postal and railway mail service.

Probably the best known supervisors' union is the Foremen's

[10] *Monthly Labor Review,* June, 1943, p. 1050.

[11] See remarks of Carl Brown, Executive Director of the Foremen's Association of America in *Labor Management Relations,* Part 8, p. 2559. Hearings, Committee on Education and Labor, House of Representatives, 83rd Cong., 1st Sess., H. Res. 115, (April, 1953).

Association of America. In 1941 this organization was founded by a small group of Ford foremen, led by Robert H. Keys.[12] By March, 1947 the membership of the Association totaled 33,000. But 1947 was an unfortunate year in the history of the FAA. In May the Association called its 3,800 Ford members out on strike. Early in July the members voted to go back to work, without a contract and with none of their demands met. This ended a contractual relationship that had been established three years previously.

The other unfortunate event for the FAA was the passing of the Taft-Hartley Act. As we have already noted, this Act withdrew legislative support and encouragement from foremen and foremen's unions in the realm of collective bargaining. The FAA and the other supervisors' unions were left with no more status than ordinary unions had had previous to the passing of the Wagner Act: they had to stand on their own feet. Membership in the FAA fell by more than 50 per cent during the first six months after the Taft-Hartley Act became operative. In early 1953 its paid-up membership was between 20,500 and 22,000, and its formal contracts numbered "about 15." In addition the FAA had informal agreements with a "good many" employers who prefer such agreements because of "the retaliation they could get . . . from employers they supply to." [13]

The interest of supervisors in unionization is not an accidental development. There are good reasons why many supervisors have turned their thoughts to unions. One reason, operative in larger enterprises, has been the growth of industrial relations departments and the increasingly extensive powers exercised by shop stewards and other union functionaries in the conduct of industrial operations.

In connection with the general problem of unionization among supervisors a nice question can be asked of the student of labor: Can foremen and other supervisory employees who form unions of their own or become members of other unions adequately represent the interests of management? Whatever the answer one gives to this question, it is evident that a considerable number of fore-

[12] A detailed account of the early period of the FAA, by Herbert R. Northrup, will be found in the *Harvard Business Review*, Winter, 1945, pp. 187-202.

[13] *Labor-Management Relations*, Part 8, p. 2570 (cited in footnote 11); see also Part 3, p. 1412.

men have been dissatisfied with their status and with the way the employers have treated them. During recent years some employers, notably Ford, have attempted to establish a closer bond between their foremen and themselves.[14]

Severance of Union Membership

The connecting bond between a worker and a union may be severed in a number of ways. One way is withdrawal, which may be either voluntary (e.g., if a worker is leaving the trade) or compulsory (e.g., if a worker becomes a supervisor or an employer). A second way is through suspension. Suspension, which is always involuntary, may arise from the worker's failure to meet his financial obligations to the union, or from his inability to abide by the rules and regulations of the organization. A third way out is expulsion. This is the extreme penalty, and the unions generally try to avoid applying it. It is a general rule to give any union member who is threatened with expulsion a fair hearing. Moreover, the parent union may specify the relative number of votes that must be cast in favor of the sentence of expulsion before it can be carried out by the local. The expelled worker may also be given the right to appeal his case to the executive board of the parent union and to the union convention.

The power to suspend or expel members is a necessary one, though it is a power that may be abused. As Clyde Summers has pointed out, "Discipline is essential for the maintenance of the union as an effective and orderly organization, but it is also the potential instrument of oppression when misused by overzealous or corrupted leaders." [15] The courts have granted injunctive relief to

[14] It is interesting to note that in Sweden about 90 per cent of the foremen and supervisors are unionized. See *Management Record,* July, 1951, pp. 252-253. A presentation of the case against foremen's unions, by John S. Bugas of the Ford Company, will be found in *Taft-Hartley Act Revisions,* Part 3, pp. 1354 ff. Hearings, Committee on Labor and Public Welfare, United States Senate, 83rd Cong., 1st Sess. (April, 1953). The testimony of the Foremen's Association of America, which of course supports such unions, will be found in the same volume. See also the sources cited in the previous footnote.

[15] Two excellent articles by Professor Summers on the question of union discipline will be found in the *Industrial and Labor Relations Review,* July and October, 1950. Professor Summers believes that the number of cases in which unions abuse their disciplinary powers is "probably very small." For a somewhat different opinion see Wellington Roe's article in *The Reader's Digest,* January, 1947.

suspended or expelled members, but ordinarily they will not interfere unless the action taken represents a departure from the rules of the union. Moreover, the courts generally will not review an expulsion case until the union member involved has used all the remedies afforded by the union. To this rule there are a few exceptions.[16]

It is pertinent to add that under the Taft-Hartley Act a union with a union shop contract can compel an employer to discharge expelled members for one reason only—failure to meet financial obligations to the union. This means that a worker who is expelled from his union for nonfinancial reasons does not, when employed in a union shop, lose his job.

In most union constitutions the major union crimes are not listed specifically. The basis of expulsion is stated in general terms—for example, conduct that is "disloyal," or conduct that "brings the union into discredit or disrepute." However some unions do list such specific crimes as working while a strike is on, disclosing union secrets, and criticizing excessively union officers or members.

As a rule unions are willing, if not pleased, to take back into their fold workers whose membership has been severed. For suspended or expelled workers, however, readmission must not be too easy; otherwise the disciplinary value of these policies may be weakened. It is common, therefore, to levy readmission charges or fines on such workers, and to punish them in other ways.[17]

Union Government—Local Unions

Any organization that attempts to be democratic has two supremely important governmental problems. The first is how to discover, accurately, what the wishes of its members are; and the second is how to transform these wishes into reality. In our discussion of union government we shall give attention to these problems as well as to another important governmental question, the matter of finances.

Each local union has a set of officers, usually elected for one year

[16] *Democracy in Trade Unions,* p. 30. New York: American Civil Liberties Union, 1943. *Columbia Law Review,* January, 1943, p. 48 of article by Ralph A. Newman.

[17] For a treatment of this matter and of the other questions dealt with in the present section, see Florence Peterson, *American Labor Unions,* pp. 102-108. New York: Harper & Bros., 1945.

at a time. Nominees for office must be members of the union in good standing and may have to possess certain other qualifications. In small locals the officers usually continue at their regular jobs. In large unions the top officers, such as the president and especially the secretary-treasurer, often relinquish their jobs and serve the union on a full-time basis at a definite salary.

Local officers must act in harmony with the constitution and with the convention and referendum decisions of the parent organization; if they act otherwise, they are subject to expulsion. If they are expelled by the locals, or if other disciplinary action is taken against them, they have the right to appeal to higher bodies in the union. With the growing centralization of control in unions, the influence of the local officers and of the locals as a whole has decreased. In many instances, however, powerful local officers have successfully defied the leaders of the parent organization.

Regular meetings of the local's membership are generally held once a month, and special meetings are occasionally called. Sometimes, unfortunately, membership meetings are seldom held (this was true of some International Longshoremen's Association locals until reforms were introduced in 1953). A serious problem facing many locals—especially large and medium-size locals, in which normal attendance usually runs from one to eight per cent [18]—is the small number of members who come out to the meetings. Many locals are trying to increase attendance at their meetings by introducing positive and negative incentives.

A local union may have a variety of committees dealing with such matters as politics, education, recreation, and the union label. In addition to its regular officers it may, in some industries, have a business agent. Although the business agent is not an elected *officer* of the union (he probably has been one in times past), he is an important person in the organization.

Little need be said about the government of the units between the locals and the parent organizations, except to point out that they are delegate bodies and have a set of officers. As we have already noted, however, some of these intermediate bodies are important units in the union structure.

[18] See George Strauss and Leonard R. Sayles, "The Local Union Meeting," *Industrial and Labor Relations Review,* January, 1953, p. 209.

Government of the Nationals and Internationals

The Convention. A national or international union is a miniature political state with its own citizens, its own laws, and its own government. Like the government of a political state, its government has three principal functions to perform: legislative, executive, and judicial. The convention is the chief legislative body, although in some unions important legislative matters are settled by referendum vote. On occasion the convention may be called to act in a judicial capacity, but its chief work is legislative.

The convention is a periodic gathering of delegates from such chartered locals as are in good standing. Regulations provide either for delegations in direct proportion to membership, or for a more than proportionate representation for small locals.

There are various rules for voting at the conventions. Sometimes there is one vote for each delegate, an arrangement that lessens somewhat the power of the large locals when the small locals are more than proportionately represented. Sometimes voting is on the basis of membership, the relationship being either directly proportional or regressive. Just as there may be a limit placed on the number of delegates a local may send to the convention, there may be a limit on its voting power.

Most unions hold regular conventions every year or two. The United States Bureau of Labor Statistics found that of 209 national and international unions, 56 met annually, 74 every two years, 19 every three years, 29 every four years, and 11 every five years. Among the remainder seven unions used the referendum to determine when conventions were to be held, and 11 had no provision in their constitutions concerning the holding of conventions.[19]

The work of the convention consists of such things as hearing the president's or executive council's report; listening to the reading of resolutions and disposing of them; hearing speeches by eminent outsiders; and electing officers for the period between conventions. The performance of the legislative activities of the convention is facilitated by the appointment of a number of committees to

[19] *Directory of Labor Unions in the United States, 1953,* Bulletin No. 1127, Bureau of Labor Statistics, United States Department of Labor, p. 6.

which resolutions and sections of the president's or executive council's report are referred for preliminary study.[20]

The Referendum. Another legislative device used by unions is the referendum. By submitting questions, not to the convention or to the executive board, but to the membership at large, the union is able to ascertain the real wishes of its members—if, of course, the majority of the members vote. A few years ago Joseph Shister, in a study of union constitutions, found that 74 out of 167 organizations provide for the use of the referendum and the initiative.[21]

Many unions resort to the referendum when constitutional changes are proposed. In some instances the proposed changes are voted on by the convention and then submitted to the membership for approval. In other cases no convention action is taken; and in still other cases the convention alone decides on the alterations to be made.

Some unions use the referendum in electing their officers, although this particular use is not too common. Some unions also make use of the "recall." Some unions use the referendum for ordinary legislative purposes. Legislation may be passed without resort to the convention or, as is sometimes done, it may be submitted to a referendum vote after the convention has adopted it. Sometimes the referendum is used to determine if special conventions are to be called or, as we have already noted, if the regular convention is to be held.

Various rules prevail concerning the "initiation" of the referendum. The most common appears to be a request from a given number of locals or a given percentage of the total number of locals. Sometimes these locals must be scattered, and sometimes they must contain at least a certain percentage of the total membership of the union. In some unions the referendum may be initiated by the executive council or board; in other organizations it may be initiated by the convention. Sometimes two, or even three, of the initiating methods just indicated may be used as alternatives.

Operating at its best, when the percentage of the membership

20 For further information on the work of union conventions and on the question of union conventions in general, see Joseph Kooner, "Union Conventions," *Labor and Nation,* June-July, 1946.

21 *The Quarterly Journal of Economics,* November, 1945, p. 92.

that votes is large, the referendum has great merit.[22] The real wishes of the members can be determined. The majority opinion of the membership can be gauged more accurately than in a convention. If the percentage of the members that vote is small, however, the referendum is of questionable value. No statistics are available that would make it possible to generalize on the voting response in union-conducted referendums. The fact that unions will specify a minimum membership vote of as low as 15 or 20 per cent suggests that in many instances the response must be weak.

The Union Executive. During the periods between conventions the affairs of a national or international are managed by its full-time officers and its executive board. The chief full-time officer is generally the president, who occasionally serves as secretary-treasurer as well. Along with the president there is ordinarily a full-time secretary-treasurer, however, and sometimes there are still other full-time officers.

The structural relationship between the group of full-time officers and the executive board varies from union to union. In some organizations the two groups are the same (though this is not usually the case), and in others there is a complete separation between the officers and the executive. In most unions there is partial overlapping, the board containing all, or some, of the officers and possibly a number of ordinary members as well.[23] Sometimes nonactive members are placed on the union executive board because of their former service.

The executive board is entrusted with a wide range of responsibilities. In most unions the board is empowered to do such things as issue and revoke local charters; remove incompetent and negligent officers; pass upon claims, grievances, and appeals of the subordinate units in the organization; and control the actions of the officers of the union. The board's work is general and supervisory in nature rather than detailed and administrative. When the board is not in

[22] Possibly no union has used the referendum with greater frequency and greater success than the International Typographical Union. Since 1889 this organization has held more than 500 referendums. See Seymour M. Lipsett, "Democracy and Private Government," *The British Journal of Sociology,* March, 1952. (Also issued as Reprint No. 42 by the Institute of Industrial Relations, University of California.)

[23] Statistical data on these arrangements will be found in Professor Shister's discussion referred to in footnote 21.

session, authority in a union rests in the hands of the president and the other full-time officers.

Since the executive board has control over the actions of union officers, it is in a position to check the derelictions of those officers. It may fail to do so, however, because of its intimate relationship with the officers. Where this happens democracy and efficiency are impaired. Some years ago it was stated by the American Civil Liberties Union that "The close links which usually exist between executive board, national officers and powerful local leaders are perhaps the most serious barrier to genuine democracy in many American trade unions." [24]

Although there has been, and still is, great diversity in the distribution of power between the locals, the intermediate units, and the parent organizations, authority has been shifting more and more from the base of the union pyramid to the top. The trend in union government, as in political government, has been definitely away from decentralization of authority and in the direction of centralization. The strength of national and international union leaders has been increasing while that of the local leaders has been diminishing. There also appears to be an increasing willingness on the part of union conventions to let the executive officers "do it."

The Problem of Union Leadership [25]

The question of union leadership has received an increasing amount of attention in recent years. The union leader has been surveyed, examined, diagnosed, tested, and tried—and in many cases found wanting.

Requirements of Union Leadership. From the preceding discussion it should be apparent that the duties of labor leaders, on both the local and the national levels, are becoming increasingly complex. To be sure, the tasks that have faced these leaders have never been easy ones. But various developments have rendered the tasks more involved and at the same time have called for a higher caliber of union leadership.

For one thing collective bargaining is much less simple than it

[24] *Democracy in Trade Unions,* p. 47. New York, 1943.

[25] Among the more outstanding books on this subject are C. Wright Mills, *The New Men of Power.* New York: Harcourt, Brace & Co., 1948; and Eli Ginsberg, *The Labor Leader.* New York: The Macmillan Co., 1948.

once was. It deals with more matters, and more complicated matters. Moreover, the spatial scope of collective bargaining has been expanded, with a definite trend in the direction of multiple-unit bargaining. Although this particular development may lessen the burden on the subordinate union leaders, it increases the problems of the top leaders.

The increasing extent to which employers are using experts in their handling of personnel problems makes the job of the union leader more exacting. In order to deal with personnel experts effectively he must possess other qualities besides determination and belligerency.

The political tasks confronting the union leader have also increased. Labor leaders are now being called upon to serve on various national governmental agencies; they frequently give testimony on labor matters before governmental investigating committees; they represent the rank-and-file members before judicial or semijudicial bodies. This active union participation in governmental affairs is in effect not only on the national level but on the state and municipal levels as well.

Another type of "political" responsibility that faces the union leader, of course, is seeing to his own continuance and advancement in office and striving for the preservation and growth of the union. These essentially political objectives are not always easy to achieve.

The increasing participation of unions in community activities makes new demands upon the union leader. He may be called upon to serve on the school board; he may be appointed to the committee in charge of the community chest; he may be asked to serve on the local planning board. Such service calls for a new kind of knowledge and a modified outlook and behavior.

Although the requirements of union leadership have become more exacting, union leaders have become better equipped to meet these requirements. The leaders of today may not always possess as much technical knowledge about their craft or industry as their predecessors did, but in terms of general education (which has become increasingly valuable in the field of industrial relations) they are much better equipped. Some unions, it is interesting to observe, have taken steps to provide their actual or potential leaders with educational programs designed to improve their efficiency in leadership positions. Outstanding in this connection is the International Ladies

Garment Workers' Union. Other unions active in this field include the Steel Workers and the Amalgamated Clothing Workers.[26] The quality of union leadership has also been raised by the functioning of union research departments. These departments give union leaders various statistical data and other informative material for use in collective bargaining and other activities. Union legal advisers also help improve union leadership by making the leaders better acquainted with the legal and legislative aspects of the problems with which they deal.

Clearly the nature of union leadership is undergoing a marked change. Leadership qualities that were once of great significance are now of much less importance, and qualities that were once largely if not wholly unnecessary for successful leadership are now indispensable. This change is well suggested in a remark made by a prominent English trade union leader, Charles Dukes: "Every officer in this union knows that whereas some thirty years ago your job was at the street corner, today it is in the conference room." [27] Union leaders in this country have to spend more time on the "street corners" than their English colleagues, but more and more of their time is spent in the "conference room."

Leadership Tenure. There is a strong tendency for labor leaders to remain in office for many years. As in politics and elsewhere, this has become a controversial issue. Long tenure of office is not wholly an unmixed evil, though it certainly has its dangers. The chief argument against long tenure is that it presents difficulties in getting rid of leaders who are incompetent or in other ways undesirable.[28]

Racketeering Leadership. The extent of racketeering leadership in American unions has been greatly exaggerated, but such leadership has existed to some extent in the past and it still exists. It came into some prominence in the early 1950's (as it had in the early 1930's when the repeal of prohibition brought about an occupa-

[26] The Bureau of Labor Statistics of the United States Department of Labor has made a number of studies in the field, including studies of the training programs sponsored by the CIO and the American Labor Education Service. See its Bulletin No. 1114, *Case Studies in Union Leadership Training,* 1951-52.

[27] *British Trade Unionism,* p. 23. London: PEP (Political and Economic Planning), 1948.

[28] For a longer discussion of the tenure question, see the author's *Contemporary Unionism in the United States,* pp. 431-434. New York: Prentice-Hall, Inc., 1948.

tional shift of many gangsters) when public attention was directed to various sordid practices on the east coast waterfront, involving the International Longshoremen's Association.[29] Because of the attention given to union racketeering in this country, a few words on the subject at this point are warranted. Let us begin by asking ourselves what racketeering leadership is.

The distinguishing feature of the racketeering union leader is that he uses his position and power to levy tribute on employers or workers for the primary purpose of personal gain. Ordinarily he is not interested in unionism as a means for improving the economic position and social status of the workers, although these ends may be incidental effects of his activities. The mere fact, therefore, that a labor leader forces an employer to "come across" with very high wages and short hours is no reason for calling him a racketeer. The distinguishing features of the racketeer are coercion and personal gain, and (sometimes) violence. The personal gain in which he is interested must be of some size; mere padding of expense accounts, for example, is not enough in itself to warrant our calling a person a racketeer.

The racketeering labor leader exploits the workers under his authority in a variety of ways. He may introduce the so-called "kickback," forcing the members of the union, and perhaps nonunionists as well, to hand over a portion of their wages to him. He may levy high dues and initiation fees. He may distribute favors unfairly among union members. He may take large sums out of the union treasury. He may sell out the union members by agreeing to wages and other conditions which are satisfactory to the employer but not to them.

Although the racketeer has left conspicuous tracks across the pages of American trade union history during the last half century,[30] he has by no means confined his activities to labor organizations or to the labor field. The racketeer, therefore, should not be looked upon as a product of unionism. If he were, racketeering, or

[29] A good account of the recrudescence of union gangsterism in the New York area, by A. H. Raskin, will be found in *The New York Times,* April 24, 1952. See also Malcolm Johnson's detailed discussion of the subject in *Crime on the Labor Front.* New York: McGraw-Hill Book Co., 1950.

[30] A comprehensive account of labor racketeering, published some years ago but still well worth reading, is Harold Seidman's *Labor Czars.* New York: Liveright Publishing Corp., 1938.

at least attempts at racketeering, would be common (as it is not) in the labor movements of Canada, Great Britain, and Sweden. The racketeer in this country is a product not of unionism but of our general social-economic environment. The unions, of course, are not totally without responsibility for the presence of racketeers in their ranks.

Unions are trying more and more vigorously to cope with the racketeering menace. The AFL, departing somewhat from its principle of craft autonomy, is now applying pressure to force racketeers out of its affiliates—the best illustration of the new policy is the action the Federation took in ousting the International Longshoremen's Association. The CIO, which has not been bothered much by racketeers, adopted a "statement of ethical practices" at its 1951 convention declaring that its policy is that "every affiliate shall always act with dispatch to stamp out any infiltration by criminal or racketeering elements anxious to prey upon our members." In 1953 President David Dubinsky of the International Ladies Garment Workers' Union appointed a confidential investigator to aid in keeping grafters and racketeers out of that union.

Union Finances

Union Income. When a worker becomes a unionist he generally pays an initiation fee to the local union. After he is in the organization he must pay regular membership dues to it, unless he is excused. In addition the worker may be called upon to make irregular contributions known as special assessments.

The funds for operating local unions come wholly or very largely from the individual unionists. The funds for running the parent organizations come for the most part from the individual unionists too, but in an indirect way. Of the initiation fees and the membership dues collected, part goes to the parent body. Each local pays to the national or international with which it is affiliated a "per capita tax" of so much per member per month. Occasionally, in a union in which power is highly concentrated, all the membership dues go to the parent organization, which, in turn, pays the expenses of the locals. In addition to the funds received from initiation fees and membership dues, the parent union may also receive considerable amounts from special assessments. Other sources of revenue are the charter fees paid by the locals at the time of affiliation, membership reinstatement fees (part of which go to the local), and interest on investments.[31]

The initiation fee is a sort of initial sales charge made by the union for what it turns over to the new member—the higher wages, shorter hours, and better conditions that it has already won. Or, if the union is a new one, the fee is an advance payment given in anticipation of these gains. The membership dues may be regarded, at least in part, as a service charge—a regular payment made to preserve and extend the benefits already won.

The size of the initiaton fee is sometimes determined by the local union, but much more frequently it is determined, either in whole or in part, by the parent organization. This body may specify the exact fee to be charged, or, as is much more common, it may set up a maximum or minimum amount, or both. The nationals and internationals establish minimums more often than they do maximums. Occasionally the amount of the initiation fee in a given union varies with such things as occupation, income, and sex. The actual initiation fees levied vary a great deal. They may be as low as $1 or as high as $100 or more. In times past there have been examples of initiation fees (determined by local unions) ranging from $300 to $3,000. It should be pointed out that under the Taft-Hartley Act it is now an unfair labor practice for a union to charge, *where a union shop exists,* an initiation fee "in an amount which the Board finds excessive or discriminating under all the circumstances."

Membership dues may be determined by the local union, or they may be regulated in whole or in part by the parent organization. As with initiation fees, the parent organization commonly specifies a minimum amount; rarely does it set a maximum alone, although it sometimes establishes both a minimum and a maximum. Sometimes, too, the membership dues are fixed completely by the parent body.

Membership dues are smaller than initiation fees, as one would expect. Most range from $2 to $4 a month. Within a given union the amount may vary according to employment status, union benefits, occupation, and salary.

Unions sometimes resort to special assessments as a means for raising extra funds. Generally, however, the unions try to avoid such assessments because of the dissatisfaction they are likely to arouse.

[31] See Kirk R. Petshek and William Paschell, "Financing of Union Activities," *Monthly Labor Review,* October, 1952, pp. 373-380. See also Peterson, *op. cit.*

Special assessments are usually imposed by the parent organization, although the local unions (and sometimes intermediate units) may share the right.

Unions use special assessments either to build up their general funds or for specific purposes. These purposes include the carrying on of particularly costly strikes or the building up of strike funds (in 1952 the convention of the United Mine Workers approved a special assessment of $20, payable in four instalments, to strengthen the union treasury for "future contingencies"); the provision of relief for unemployed members; and the provision of funds for meeting the costs of special organizing campaigns.

Unions may have other sources of revenue—from permit fees, fines, and reinstatement fees, for example—but these sources of income are usually of little significance. Finally a number of unions receive a sizable income from investments.

Union Expenditures. The money paid into local unions by their members is disbursed by two principal agencies, the locals themselves and the parent organizations. Some of these funds are usually turned over to other units in the general union set-up—to the AFL or the CIO, for example, or to central labor unions—but most of the money remains with the locals and the nationals or internationals.

The locals and the parent unions spend their income for a variety of purposes, the actual expenditure patterns differing from one organization to another. In addition to its contribution to the head office, a contribution that tends to vary with the degree of union centralization, a local may pay out a sizable amount for administrative expenses. It may also spend money on organizing work, on recreation, for charity, and for other purposes. The parent union pays administrative expenses, including salaries of officers; organizing expenses; and certain expenses for research, education, legal services, strike benefits, charitable donations, publication of the union paper, and so on.

The question of union salaries has attracted considerable attention in recent years. Compared with the salaries of outstanding business leaders (whose annual pay the labor papers like to publish!) the salaries of top union officers are not large. In terms of the responsibilities of the leaders of the two groups, it is difficult to account for the difference in salary. However, it must be borne in mind that union leaders, though businessmen of a sort, are not quite like business leaders. Most of them feel they are engaged in a "cause," and many would gladly take a salary cut to continue serving that cause. It is not surprising, then, that their incomes—like the incomes of those serving other causes, including the cause of education—are often moderate.

Some union leaders, nevertheless, are paid quite substantial salaries. The president of the United Mine Workers receives an annual stipend of $50,000, plus expenses (as well as "a custom-built Cadillac and a liveried chauffeur"), [32] and the vice-president and secretary-treasurer both receive salaries of $40,000. The president of the Teamsters' Union receives $50,000 a year, as does the president emeritus. A small number of other union leaders receive similar amounts. To come down to a lower level, one might mention that the head of the International Ladies Garment Workers' Union is paid $23,400 a year, an amount considerably lower than that which the union in 1953 wanted to give him; and the president of the Automobile Workers, with more than a million members, receives $18,000, also less than what convention delegates in 1953 wanted to pay him.

With the exception of a few cases the salaries of union leaders are not large. In the vast majority of unions (nationals and internationals) the salaries of the top leaders probably range between $7,000 and $20,000. And one can safely assume that none of these leaders has a custom-built Cadillac and a liveried chauffeur.

Union Assets. One of the noteworthy developments in unionism in recent years has been the remarkable growth in union assets. No exact figures covering all unions, including parent and subordinate units, are available; and estimates vary a great deal, partly because they are based on different interpretations of "assets" or "resources." [33] There is no question, however, concerning the way unions keep their assets. Nathan Belfer, in a study of 42 major unions, discovered that 72.9 per cent of their assets were in bonds, largely United States Government bonds, and 10.9 per cent were in cash. Only a small portion of the assets, 1.6 per cent, was invested in stock.

[32] *Management Record,* July, 1951.

[33] For a number of estimates, and for a general discussion of the question of union assets, see Nathan Belfer, "Trade Union Investment Policies," *Industrial and Labor Relations Review,* April, 1953. See also J. B. S. Hardman, "'Dollar Worth' of the Unions" in *The House of Labor,* ed. by J. B. S. Hardman and Maurice F. Neufeld. New York: Prentice-Hall, Inc., 1951.

The ownership rights of labor organizations in American industry are thus extremely small, much smaller, as Belfer points out, than the rights of some of our educational institutions.

Union Government and Federal Law

The Taft-Hartley Act contains a number of provisions relating to union government and finance. Under the Act unions are compelled to supply the federal government with various kinds of information concerning their finances: salaries and allowances of the three chief officers, initiation fees, membership dues, and so on. As we have already observed the Taft-Hartley Act exercises control over the size of initiation fees where the union shop exists. There are also provisions governing the use of the check-off, as we shall see in Chapter 16. The Act also provides that each union must annually send to the Secretary of Labor copies of its constitution and by-laws and a report stating the way in which all officers and agents receiving over $5,000 a year are "elected, appointed, or otherwise selected," and setting forth other types of nonfinancial information. It might be mentioned, finally, that if a union is to enjoy the rights set forth in the Taft-Hartley Act its officers (local and parent) must sign a noncommunist affidavit.

12

UNION ACTIVITIES

American unions are primarily collective bargaining agencies, and most of their activities relate either directly or indirectly to this particular interest. There are other activities, however, in which they engage—political action and the establishment of union-financed benefit programs are two examples. In recent years the unions have ventured into other fields. New policies and programs, directed toward the achievement either of the traditional union objectives or of more current objectives, have been adopted.

The extent to which the unions are entering the fresh fields of endeavor varies greatly from one organization to another. Some unions adhere rather closely to the old policies; "new-fangled" ideas have little appeal to them. Other unions launch out eagerly in new directions—research work, counseling, radio broadcasting, pamphleteering, art classes, book stores, baseball leagues, and education classes. In this chapter we shall discuss the newer activities as well as the older ones.[1] Since we shall deal comprehensively with collective bargaining, and also with strikes, in later chapters, we shall not take these topics up in detail at the present point.

Organizing Work

National and international unions have usually been formed from already existing locals; but once formed they are usually inter-

[1] Some persons believe that union activities should be limited largely or wholly to those of a "social" nature. Thus Willford I. King has argued that if the workers "want to have social unions it is all right, but not to interfere with wages or hours." Professor King is a staunch supporter of the "free market" and some of his ideas are not only provocative but, to many persons, exasperating as well. See his testimony in *Labor Management Relations,* Part 5, pp. 1568 ff. Hearings, Committee on Education and Labor, House of Representatives, 83rd Cong., 1st Sess., H. Res. 115 (March, 1953).

ested in establishing new locals and in increasing the size of the old ones. These parent bodies ordinarily have a number of organizers on their payrolls who devote all or part of their time to organizing work. The officers of the unions may also devote some of their time to this purpose, although generally their organizing activities are limited to particular occasions. Organizing work may also be carried on by local unions if, within their jurisdiction, there are workers outside the fold. The citywide and statewide units of the AFL and the CIO may also assist in organizing work, and the two federations themselves are important organizing agencies.

Sometimes unions engage in special organizing campaigns. Thus in 1946-1947 AFL and CIO organizations started vigorous campaigns in the South, in "Operation Dixie." The organizing work done in the mass-production industries during the latter half of the 1930's was also of a special nature. Much of the organizing work of the unions, however, is of a diffused, day-to-day nature.

Collective Bargaining and Strikes

Nationals and internationals have become increasingly important as collective bargaining agents. This development has been caused partly by the growing complexity of the problems involved in collective bargaining, and partly by the broadening of the geographical coverage of the bargaining agreements. The collective bargaining activities of the parent unions take various forms. The unions may simply supply their locals with information that will be helpful to them when they meet employers around the bargaining table. Or officers and staff members of the parent unions may directly aid the locals in negotiating agreements. If collective bargaining is on a nationwide or regional basis, the part played by national and international officers will of necessity be extensive. Finally, in some unions local agreements must be approved by the officers of the parent body.

As parent organizations the nationals and internationals are interested in the strikes in which their locals engage. In some unions the locals must first receive authorization from the parent body before going on strike. Although the locals generally obey this rule, sometimes they call a strike without the proper authorization and the parent union is obliged to exercise discipline. In legitimate strikes the parent organization may furnish the locals with financial aid, leadership assistance, sound trucks, and so on. If a strike is a large one involving a number of locals and a number of employers, and if the issue at stake is particularly vital, the national or international may assume complete or partial control over it. An increasing number of strikes are the complete responsibility of the parent organization from the very beginning. The periodic stoppages in the coal industry are of this nature.

Political Activities

The political interests of American unionists are given organized expression through various channels. In the AFL the central organization performs political functions, and so do the state federations and the city centrals. In the CIO the comparable structural units carry on political activities. The nationals and internationals and their locals are also politically active. The more progressive unions, like those in the clothing industry, are especially interested in politics; but so also are the conservative unions in the railroad industry. In our present discussion we shall deal with political action in a comprehensive manner, extending our analysis beyond the work of the nationals and internationals.

The AFL and Politics. Although it is true that in the AFL the philosophy of "economism," manifested in collective bargaining, has always taken unquestioned precedence over the philosophy of "politicalism," the organization has always given attention to political matters. The amount of this attention has varied from time to time, but it has never even approached zero. Preferring to make most of its gains through negotiations with, and pressure upon, employers, the AFL has never been oblivious to the gains to be made through the use of political methods.

Within the ranks of the Federation there have always been persons desirous of having the organization launch an independent political party, but support for such a step, although fairly substantial at times, has never been strong enough to be effective. Instead the AFL has rigidly adhered to its nonpartisan policy, preferring to work through the two major political parties.

The AFL in its totality, with all of its structural units included, conducts its political activities on three levels: municipal, state, and national. The city centrals deal especially with municipal politics, the state federations particularly with state politics, and the AFL central organization concentrates upon national politics. At the present point we shall limit our discussion to the political activities of the AFL itself.

The political activities of the AFL take three forms. In the first place the Federation tries to see that the "proper" persons are elected to Congress. To this end it makes a biographical study of the candidates, finding out their attitude toward important labor issues (possibly as these have already been expressed in votes in Congress) and appraising their general suitability for office. In carrying on its work the committee obtains assistance from local and state nonpartisan committees.

Since the AFL is partisan to principles and not to parties, the candidates it endorses are neither all Republicans nor all Democrats. It is true, however, that more Democrats have been endorsed than Republicans, the reason being, of course, that more Democratic nominees have been sympathetic to AFL political objectives. In most instances the AFL has refrained from supporting specific presidential candidates, as we noted in Chapter 8.

The endorsement of a candidate by the AFL in no way insures that all AFL unionists in the candidate's constituency will vote for him. The position taken by the Federation may have some influence on the individual member's vote—the AFL hopes it will—but no member is under compulsion to support the AFL-approved candidate.

After the passing of the Taft-Hartley Act the AFL felt the need for making a change in its political methods, though not in its fundamental political principles. The 1947 convention therefore ordered the setting up of a special political agency, and in December of that year Labor's League for Political Action was established. The League is financed by voluntary contributions, which in 1952 amounted to the modest sum of $252,002. In 1953 the AFL took a further step into systematic politics when it announced a plan for enlisting the aid of women unionists and the wives of unionists in its political activities.

A second type of political activity in which the AFL engages is lobbying. It was no accident that the organization moved its headquarters to Washington in 1897, nor is it an accident that the CIO and many nationals and internationals have their headquarters there. The AFL, like other labor bodies, is keenly interested in the course of national legislation, and it is a very important body in determining what that course will be. In carrying on its lobbying activities the AFL often cooperates with other groups, not only with other labor groups but with such groups as the farmers and the American Legion. Frequently there is overlapping in the legislation desired by these groups, and by acting together they bring about a greater likelihood that such legislation will be passed. Sometimes cooperation is on a *quid pro quo* basis—"We'll support you if you support us."

Finally, there is the effort on the part of the AFL to influence the administration and interpretation of laws and of executive decrees. To achieve these aims the organization may send representatives to Congressional hearings. It may also try to bring about the appointment of suitable persons to administrative and judicial posts. It is a matter of concern to the AFL who is Secretary of Labor, who serves on the National Labor Relations Board, and who is appointed to the Supreme Court.

The CIO and Politics. Political action is an important article of faith in the CIO, the prevailing attitude in the organization having long been that the political interests and the economic interests of labor are closely intertwined, if not inseparably connected. The CIO early showed its interest in politics by establishing Labor's Non-Partisan League in 1936. During the first part of its existence the League embraced, and was controlled by, AFL organizations and independent railway unions as well as by CIO affiliates, but it soon came under CIO (perhaps one should say John L. Lewis') domination. In 1943 the CIO took a step of the utmost political significance. In July of that year the executive board of the Congress established a Political Action Committee, soon to be known as the CIO-PAC, or simply as the PAC. Sidney Hillman, president of the Amalgamated Clothing Workers' union, was appointed chairman of the committee, a post he held until his death in 1946. At that time management of the organization passed into the hands of an executive board of five members, headed by Jack Kroll. In its initial foray in the field of politics in 1944 the PAC carried on its activities with great vigor, and since 1944 it has remained an active political agency.

The pattern of political action followed by the CIO is essentially the same as the AFL pattern. The CIO seeks to exert influence at election times, following the nonpartisan policy that has long been used by the AFL; it tries to influence the course of legislation by acting as a pressure group; it is interested in the administration and interpretation of whatever legislation is passed. Like the AFL, too, the CIO is active in municipal and state politics as well as national politics.

There are several differences between the two federations, however, in political matters: the CIO is probably more politically conscious than the AFL; there is more third-party sentiment in it than in the AFL, although in both organizations such sentiment is at low ebb; and it has always followed the policy of endorsing presidential candidates, which the AFL over its long history has done only twice.

Political Activities of the Nationals and Internationals. The political interests of the nationals and internationals are given expression through various channels, including the AFL and the CIO and their statewide and citywide units. In addition, the nationals and internationals sometimes engage in political activities on their own. One of the most politically active labor organizations in the country is the International Ladies Garment Workers' Union. There is a great deal of political consciousness in this union, as well as a certain amount of third-party support. The Teamsters' union is another organization that is very active politically. So too are the United Mine Workers of America. And, as we noted in an earlier chapter, the railway unions are keenly interested in politics, and for a very good reason.

Independent Political Action. The desirability of establishing a third major party in the United States has long been a subject of debate both inside and outside labor circles. Up to the present time the negative arguments have prevailed.

The negative arguments are numerous and weighty. To begin with there is the strong allegiance of many union members to the Republican and Democratic parties. What percentage of unionists are tied to the two major political parties it is impossible to say, but there can be no doubt that the percentage is large. Because of the loyalty of so many union members to the old parties, the setting up of an independent labor party might lead to serious cleavages within the labor movement. In this connection it might be pointed out that the withdrawal of the United Mine Workers from the CIO was due in part to political differences between John L. Lewis and other CIO leaders in the 1940 elections.

The heterogeneity of the American working population has been, and to some extent still is, a factor militating against a labor party. Differences of color, race, and nationality have interfered seriously with labor solidarity in this country, and without almost complete labor solidarity a separate labor party could not succeed.

Attempts on the part of the workers to set up their own party would meet with strong opposition. The program of a labor party would involve marked changes in the *status quo*. It would narrow the power of the financial and industrial leaders of the country and further restrict their income. Naturally these men would fight back, and they would probably fight harder against a labor party than their fathers fought against unionism.[2]

To become a strong force politically labor would have to conduct campaigns on 49 different fronts. To concentrate on Washington alone would not be sufficient, since much of the jurisdiction over matters in which labor is interested resides not with the federal government but with the states. To contest both federal and state elections it would be necessary for the unions to select a large number of suitable candidates. This would be a difficult task, and there is a danger that leadership in the unions would suffer as a consequence of the diversion of outstanding men into politics. On the other hand, there is a possibility that a labor party would sometimes elect men to political office not so much because of their statesmanlike qualities but because they have well served the union cause.

Can the workers and the farmers cooperate and set up a permanent farmer-labor party, one that can seriously enter the lists with the Democratic and Republican parties? There have been examples of cooperative action between the two groups in times past. Such ventures, however, have been short-lived or of limited geographical scope. The country has yet to see the farmers and workers cooperate on an extensive front and for a protracted period of time.[3]

[2] See R. R. R. Brooks, *When Labor Organizes*, p. 305. New Haven: Yale University Press, 1937.

[3] See Selig Perlman's remarks in *Justice*, December 15, 1943, p. 14.

It is true that the workers and the farmers have interests in common, but they also have certain conflicting desires. Both groups wish to increase their own economic welfare: the farmers want high prices for their products, and the workers want high prices for theirs. It is at this point that friction is likely to develop. Although many farmers are like ordinary industrial workers, having little or no ownership in the means of production, for many others the entrepreneur and capitalist point of view predominates in their thinking. It is interesting to note that when farmers have engaged in collective action (and here reference is not made to farm employees), they have done so primarily as capitalists and not as workers.[4]

For the above reasons, and others that might be mentioned, any possibility of a national labor party, or a national farmer-labor party, seems far away at the present time. However, despite the obstacles in the way some people still believe that it would be desirable to establish an independent party. They believe that in the long run labor would gain more by having its own party, or one involving cooperation with the farmers, than by using the nonpartisan policy and working through the Democratic and Republican parties.

Benefit Plans and Counseling

Union-Financed Benefit Plans. The fear and the painful reality of economic insecurity have exerted a profound influence on trade unionism. To meet this insecurity unions have adopted a variety of policies, with their chief aim, of course, the struggle for higher wages. The particular policy we are concerned with at the present moment, however, is the establishment of union-financed benefit programs. But it should be pointed out first that in addition to these programs there are others that are financed, either in whole or in part, by employers. These employer programs, which represent a comparatively recent development in the realm of "union social security," and also in the realm of collective bargaining, we shall discuss shortly.

[4] See Kenneth H. Parsons, "Farmers and Organized Labor," *The Journal of Farm Economics,* May, 1943, p. 368. For examples of friction between farmers and organized labor, see Arthur Moore, *The Farmers and the Rest of Us,* Chapter X. Boston: Little, Brown & Co., 1945.

Table 10 shows the principal benefit disbursements made by the nationals and internationals affiliated with the AFL, plus those made by the Big Four Railroad Brotherhoods, during 1951.

Table 10

Benefit Payments of AFL Unions and the Big Four Railroad Brotherhoods, 1951 *

Type of Benefit	Total Amount
Death benefits	$23,307,484
Sick benefits	14,470,397
Unemployment benefits	1,054,793
Old-age benefits	20,378,512
Disability benefits	1,216,032
Miscellaneous benefits	23,969,393
Total	$84,396,611 †

* Report of the Executive Council, *Proceedings* of American Federation of Labor, 1952, p. 225.

† Included in the total of $84,396,611 is the figure of $26,291,611 for the International Ladies Garment Workers' Union and covering benefits paid out of contributions made by employers as well as by union members. The sick benefits of the same union, amounting to more than 8½ million dollars, include benefits paid by local unions. The same is true of the total benefits ($16,000) paid by one of the other unions in the list.

In addition to their benefit plans American unions have adopted other measures of a benefit nature. A few organizations have established health programs and facilities; outstanding in this connection are the Union Health Centers established by the International Ladies Garment Workers' Union and the Amalgamated Clothing Workers. Some unions have established homes or sanitariums for their members; the Union Printers' Home at Colorado Springs, erected and maintained by the International Typographical Union, is particularly notable. Moreover, in addition to the benefit programs of the parent unions there are the smaller plans that many local unions have set up.

Although union benefits in the United States have been of limited extent, they have contributed significantly to the well-being of many unionists. They have met needs that the individual union member has been unable (and possibly sometimes unwilling) to meet himself, and for which society as a whole has not, at least until comparatively recently, made adequate provision.

The unions themselves have also reaped distinct gains from their benefit programs. These programs have acted as a stimulus to union membership, certainly before the passage of the Social Security Act, and probably to some extent even now. In addition the benefit plans have helped to keep workers in the unions once they have joined. Since union benefit plans have to be financed out of the contributions of the union members, contributions that are regular and may be quite large, the members tend to develop a "paying attitude." The unions may also gain from their ability to draw on the benefit funds for other purposes, such as strikes. This is not an unmixed blessing, to be sure; it is unsound actuarially, and some unions avoid it. But in numerous cases benefit funds are not reserved exclusively for the payment of benefits. Through their benefit plans the parent unions are able to exercise a certain amount of control over both their individual members and their locals. All in all the payment of benefits promotes union solidarity and adds to union power. At the same time, however, benefit plans may make unions more conservative and less militant.

Union-Employer Benefit Plans. Until a few years ago the benefit plans in American industry were all of a unilateral character. They were set up either by the unions or by the employers. In recent years a new type of benefit plan has come into prominence, established by the union and the employer acting jointly. That is to say, this type of plan is established through the process of collective bargaining.

In contrast to the plans we have just discussed, union-employer plans are financed either in whole or in part by the employers. The employers' contributions are obtained in two ways. In most instances a payroll levy or tax, ordinarily of 2 or 3 per cent, is imposed. Sometimes, however, the employer does not contribute a definite percentage of the payroll but pays whatever is necessary. The second method used in obtaining the funds involves the imposition of a royalty charge. This is well illustrated in the plans under which the musicians and coal miners operate (the current royalty charge on bituminous coal is 40 cents a ton).

Under the Taft-Hartley Act union-administered and employer-financed welfare plans are ruled out. The Act permits employer-financed plans only under certain conditions. First, the employer must participate in the administration of any such plan: to be more specific, employees and employer must be equally represented on the administrative board, together with a number of neutral persons. Moreover, there must be a written agreement made with the employer in which the "detailed basis on which . . . payments are to be made" from the accumulated trust fund under the plan is set forth; and in addition the trust fund must be audited each year. Another condition is that the resources of any trust fund must be used for "the benefit of employees, their families and dependents," and for purposes specified in the law: medical or hospital care, pensions on retirement or death of employees, compensation for occupational injuries and illness, and so on. The law, furthermore, states that employer's contributions for pensions and annuities must go into a separate trust fund and be used only for these two purposes.

The type of benefits provided for under the union-employer benefit plans varies from one plan to another, as does the size of the benefits. Many of the plans provide for the payment of weekly cash benefits in case the worker is ill or if he is disabled by an accident of a nonoccupational nature (occupational accidents are covered by workmen's compensation laws). Many plans also provide for the payment of hospital and surgical costs, and some of them cover doctor bills. Other benefits found in the plans include X-ray examinations, death benefits, optical examinations, and dismemberment benefits.[5]

Union Counseling. A new type of union activity, counseling, came into existence during World War II.[6] The purpose of counseling is to aid the union members in such matters as housing advice, child care and family problems, health questions, and legal problems. Union counselors are for the most part not social workers but "referral" specialists. Their function is not so much to solve matters as to refer the workers who have nonplant problems to the agencies that are fitted to deal with them.

[5] Further information on union-employer benefit plans will be found in Bulletin No. 1017 (*Employee-Benefit Plans Under Collective Bargaining*) and Bulletin No. 1113 (*Wages and Related Benefits*) of the Bureau of Labor Statistics, United States Department of Labor.

[6] See "Union Counseling—Bridge or Gap?" in the *Survey Midmonthly*, April, 1945, pp. 106-108; and Mark Starr's discussion in *Industry and Society*, ed. by William F. Whyte, pp. 161-163. New York: McGraw-Hill Book Co., Inc., 1946.

From the standpoint of the individual unionist counseling may be of great value. It does not add to the size of his pay envelope, at least not directly, but it increases his and his family's happiness. From the standpoint of the union itself counseling is a means not only for bringing benefits to the individual members of the organization but for keeping the members interested in, and loyal to, their organization. Counseling also brings the union into closer contact with the community. It should be added, incidentally, that union counseling may indirectly promote *community* action upon some of the problems, such as housing, that face the workers.

Educational, Cultural, and Recreational Work

Educational and Cultural Activities. From the standpoint of procedure followed and also, to some extent, from the standpoint of specific objectives and scope, workers' education as carried on by the unions may be divided into three types.[7]

First there is mass education, which is for the benefit of the general membership of the unions. It is more or less informal and popular in nature. Through mass education unionists not only become more closely associated with, and more loyal to, their organizations ("the organized are unionized," to use an expression of Walter Reuther's), but become better informed and more intelligent citizens as well.

Mass education may involve the giving of lectures, to which all members are invited; the organization of conducted trips or tours to places of interest in the immediate locality; the arrangement of theatre and concert parties; the showing of moving pictures. Mass education may also be promoted by the establishment of union libraries; by the inclusion of educational material of a technical or cultural nature in the official magazines of the unions; by the publication of pamphlets; by radio programs; by union book clubs. Most of the above activities have been undertaken by the International Ladies Garment Workers' Union, probably the most outstanding union in the country in the field of educational and cultural work. Mass education—in which we might include the "indoctrination" courses that are occasionally given to new unionists—has been

[7] The titles for this classification and some of the content for the separate categories are taken from Florence H. Schneider, *Patterns of Workers' Education,* pp. 28-29. Washington: American Council on Public Affairs, 1941.

making considerable headway during recent years in a number of unions.

A second way in which educational work is carried on by unions is through classroom instruction. Classroom education is more formal than mass education and is carried on for smaller and more select groups. It is for the more serious-minded unionists who are genuinely interested in improving themselves culturally, or in becoming better fitted for positions of leadership in their organizations, or in gaining further technical knowledge of the trade in which they are employed. Subjects that have been taught in union classrooms include trade union history, economics, parliamentary law, and public speaking. Occasionally, as in the Amalgamated Clothing Workers' union, courses in these or similar subjects are given by correspondence. Classroom work may be directed at least in part toward vocational objectives. Thus the Federal Workers of America have a school in Washington in which governmental employees gain technical knowledge that will improve their chances for advancement.

The third type of educational work, which has been growing in importance, is designed for union leaders; it has been referred to as "training for trade-union service." The extent and the complexity of the problems with which labor leaders must deal have been constantly expanding, just as the responsibilities attached to their jobs have been steadily increasing. Some unions are clearly aware of these facts and have taken steps to provide their leaders, or potential leaders, with educational opportunities. The ILGWU has gone so far as to rule that all new candidates seeking paid office in the union must finish a course of study either given by the Education Department of the union or approved by it. Education of this third type usually makes use of training courses, summer camps and training institutes, and bulletins of a technical or semitechnical nature.

Workers' education in the United States has been carried on not only by national and international unions and their locals but by numerous other organizations as well. A few of these may be singled out for brief attention. First there is the Workers' Education Bureau, which was established in 1921 by a group of trade unionists and teachers. In 1951 it became an organic part of the AFL, although almost from its beginning it had been intimately associated with the Federation. The Bureau's educational activities relate chiefly to "the stimulation and integration of union education in AFL organizations at all levels." [8]

The American Labor Education Service is another such educational agency. Covering in its membership residence schools, local unions, local labor colleges, and workers' educational committees, it helps to unify the work carried on by various groups interested in workers' education. It aids in starting educational programs, furnishes advice and information, and arranges conferences and seminars.

To an ever increasing extent the facilities of the colleges and universities of the country have been used for workers' education purposes, and the number of institutions participating in this work is now considerable. The pioneer work of the University of Wisconsin is especially worthy of mention.

Two general observations may be made concerning the educational activities of unions. One is that such activity, on any sizable scale, is limited to a rather small number of unions. The ILGWU and the ACW, to name two of the leading unions in the field, must not be looked upon as representative—it should be pointed out, however, that a certain amount of educational work is carried out by other units in the union structure, such as the state-wide labor organizations. Also the "curriculum" of unions in the field of education could be expanded to make ample provision for the study and discussion of the internal policies of the union by the ordinary union members. Today, as Kermit Eby has pointed out,[9] "it is not considered necessary [under] the average union educational program . . . to develop in the rank and file the ability to criticize policy." An educational program of this sort has been referred to as the "percolator" system rather than the "drip" system; that is, ideas percolate "from the rank and file up rather than dripping down from the top." Present union education is to a considerable extent of the drip type.

[8] An account of specific activities of the WEB will be found in *The American Federationist,* March, 1953.

[9] See his article on "The 'Drip Theory' in Labor Unions," *The Antioch Review,* Spring, 1953. The two terms cited by Eby are those of Myles Horton of the United Packing House Workers. Eby, with his emphasis on rank-and-file discussion of union policies, favors the development of "parties" within the union.

Recreational Activities. The advantages of providing recreational facilities and establishing recreational programs for their members is more widely recognized by unions today than ever before, and the scope of their activities in this field is greater than it has ever been. Sometimes the recreational work is closely allied with educational programs. In fact some activities are both educational and recreational in nature. Union-sponsored concert parties, for example, may serve this twofold end, particularly if they are preceded by lectures on the history and meaning of the symphonies, operas, or plays performed. An outstanding example of a recreational program with educational overtones was the series of symphony concerts sponsored by the Steel Workers' union during 1953, which prompted the statement that "It isn't unusual these days to hear steelworkers in Braddock, Pa., or Canton, Ohio, or half a dozen other steel towns humming the strains of Tchaikovsky's Fourth Symphony." [10] Although recreational and educational work may go hand in hand, much recreational work is pure fun.

Recreational activities are generally sponsored by local unions rather than by the parent organizations, although the latter may take an interest in them. Many locals have baseball, softball, and basketball teams organized into leagues. Many have bowling teams. Even such a highbrow game as golf is quite within the competency of the unions, as is tennis. Other sports and pastimes sponsored by unions include swimming, skating, dancing (aesthetic, tap, and social), card playing, smokers, picnics, boat rides, and singing. Some unions present plays and concerts, and others sponsor painting as a recreational activity. A number of locals in the ILGWU have been active in painting, especially Local 22, which in 1942 "made" the Ferargil Gallery in New York with its exhibits. In an art exhibit at one of the branch libraries in New York early in 1952 five unions in addition to the ILGWU were represented.

Some unions provide excellent physical facilities for carrying on their recreational work. Unity House, owned and operated by the ILGWU and located in the Pocono Mountains of Pennsylvania, is particularly outstanding. The headquarters of the locals and of other union organizations are often well equipped for recreational activities, with clubrooms, assembly halls, and the like.

[10] *Steel Labor,* February, 1953, p. 5.

Research, Publications, and Public Relations

Research. Unions have long been interested in factual information, but it was not until comparatively recently that they set up agencies to collect and disseminate such information. Now about 90 unions have research directors; in some cases the same person serves as director both of research and education.

Two chief groups use the findings of the union research departments: the union executive officers and the local and intermediate structural units within the union organizations. The information made available to the officers is usually, because of the interests of these officers, of a general character. The information supplied to the subordinate structural units is generally more specific, relating to the issues that confront them individually.

Research departments, with the information they gather, aid the unions in the collective bargaining process. They may also be of value in arbitration cases and in hearings before Congressional committees and governmental administrative agencies. They usually contribute material to the official organ of the union and publish pamphlets or bulletins.

From the standpoint of society the growth of union research is desirable. Although the research departments may sometimes be selective in their choice and presentation of data, the net effect of their work, and of the work of similar management organizations, is to place industrial relations on a higher plane.

Publications. Although unions depend a great deal on the spoken word as a means of communication, they have long recognized the importance of the written word. For many years it has been their custom to publish official papers or journals, and more recently they have supplemented their publishing activities by issuing pamphlets.

Most nationals and internationals publish a regular (usually monthly) journal or paper. In most unions the members receive the official organ free of charge, the cost being covered by their regular membership dues. This arrangement encourages wider readership, but it probably leads to some editorial disregard of the desires of the readers. The union journals print news of activities and developments within the union, and usually also contain news relating to the trade. Some contain technical articles; some have articles of a cultural nature; some publish poetry contributed by the members; some contain a great deal of political material; some run household columns in an effort to capture the interest of the housewife.

Local unions sometimes publish official organs of their own. In addition, union groups in some plants issue mimeographed or printed papers, "union shop-papers." And, of course, many of the higher units in the union structure also publish journals.

The publishing of pamphlets has become an increasingly important activity of some of the nationals and internationals. It might be added too that a start has been made in the issuance of plays, sheet music, records, film strips, and posters.

Publicity and Public Relations. The influence of public opinion on social and economic developments is often uncertain and indefinite, but it may be very powerful, particularly if public opinion is hostile in nature. Unions, more and more aware of the importance of public opinion, are adopting various measures to reduce public hostility to, and increase public support of, unionism in general and specific union policies in particular.

Leaders of the AFL and the CIO, as well as of smaller union groups, often present labor's point of view over the radio. Union leaders and employees with writing ability contribute articles both to popular magazines and to more learned publications. Some unions, as we have just noted, publish pamphlets that are available to the public. Some insert advertisements in the daily press in connection with strikes or threatened strikes. In carrying on their public relations work unions often obtain outside professional aid.

Business Ventures

A number of unions have embarked on business ventures, and in a few cases with marked success. At the present time there are four labor banks in this country, the two largest of which are owned by the Amalgamated Clothing Workers. Labor banking has had an interesting and unfortunate history in the United States. The movement started in the 1920's. At that time interest in banking was at a high level in union circles and a number of organizations decided to enter the field. Various factors induced the unions to take this step; possibly the most influential was their desire to increase their power and influence in industry and in society at large. By the first quarter of 1927 the labor banking movement was at its peak. At that time there were 36 labor banks in existence, with aggregate deposits of approximately $110,000,000 and resources totaling $128,000,000.

Then the banking movement started to go down hill. The most spectacular part of the decline was the collapse of the grandiose banking ventures of the Brotherhood of Locomotive Engineers. By the middle of 1929 the number of labor banks had declined to 22, and by the middle of 1932 the number had fallen to seven. Shortly thereafter it fell to four, where it remained until 1942, when it fell to three. In 1944 the number rose to four again, and it has remained there ever since.

Although the labor banks are obviously not of outstanding importance in the total banking system of the country, in their limited sphere they appear to be rendering a useful service. Viewing the labor banking movement as a whole, however, and in retrospect, it is clear that the unions have not been successful in this field.

The failure of the labor banking experiment, although in part due to the beginning of the Great Depression in 1929, stemmed mainly from the general administrative incompetency of the union leaders who were responsible for directing the policies of the banks, and from their specific incompetency in the specialized field of banking. It should be added, possibly in partial extenuation of the sins of the union leaders, that not a few of the banks were "sold" to local labor groups by professional promoters, who later bought them back at lower prices. Other factors that helped to bring about the collapse of the labor banking movement were inadequate support from rank-and-file unionists; lack of time on the part of the union leaders; union politics; and failure to make use of capable and sympathetic nonunionists.[11]

A less ambitious union venture into finance has been the establishment of credit unions. Requiring less in the way of support and less in managerial ability, credit unions, in contrast to banks, can be successfully operated by reasonably competent union officials.

Another business venture of the unions has been in the field of cooperative housing. One organization, the Amalgamated Clothing Workers, has been pre-eminent in this field, and its work has re-

[11] An extensive treatment of labor banking during the earlier years will be found in *The Labor Banking Movement in the United States*. Industrial Relations Section, Princeton University, 1929.

ceived world-wide attention. The ACW has three cooperative housing projects, made up of 18 apartment buildings, in New York. These projects provide low-rent accommodations for 2,500 families; they function on a consumer-cooperative basis, paying rent rebates when profits permit. Community activities are sponsored by the housing units.[12]

During recent years there has been some interest in a number of other unions in the matter of housing. One might mention the United Automobile Workers, the Textile Workers' union, and the ILGWU. The last-named organization introduced a new element in union housing in 1952 when it decided to use $7,500,000 of its own funds to finance a mortgage in a cooperative and union-sponsored housing development in New York. In other housing ventures the unions have generally resorted to outside financing.

Another venture of unions into the field of business is the Union Labor Life Insurance Company, founded in 1925 by unions affiliated with the AFL. At the end of 1951 the company had $350,810,000 of individual and group life, accident, and health insurance in force. Its president, Matthew Woll, has declared that the company can be looked upon not only as a venture "but as an established institution, financially sound and secure." [13]

[12] See *General Executive Board Report and Proceedings,* 18th Biennial Convention, 1952, pp. 76-77. Illustrations of ACW projects will be found in the union's paper, *The Advance,* December, 1951.

[13] *The American Federationist,* July, 1952, p. 15.

13

MANAGEMENT CHARACTERISTICS AND PERSONNEL POLICIES

In the five preceding chapters we have described and analyzed some of the outstanding aspects of American unionism. In this chapter we shall examine management, especially the characteristics and policies of management that relate to industrial relations. Then, in the chapters that immediately follow, we shall bring unions and management together in our detailed discussion of collective bargaining.

We shall use the word "management" in a broad sense to cover all those connected with a business enterprise who have the authority to give orders. Thus the president and the general manager represent, or constitute, management. So does the plant superintendent. So do the department managers and the foremen. Although we shall ordinarily think of management in this comprehensive manner, much of our discussion in the present chapter has special reference to the characteristics and policies of "top" management.

Forms, Size, and Ownership of Business Enterprise

Forms of Business Enterprise. There are three principal forms of private business enterprise. First there is the individual proprietorship under which an individual owns, or at least operates, a particular business undertaking. He may have one or more persons helping him; or, as is often the case, he may carry on the undertaking himself, acting as a more or less composite figure: owner, manager, employee. There are millions of individual proprietorships in this country, especially in farming and retailing and in the professions. Problems in industrial relations may arise under this type of business organization; but since not many persons involved have the sole status of employees, and since there is usually a close bond between employer and employee, the problems are not extensive nor of outstanding importance.

The partnership is the second form of business enterprise. Partnerships are usually larger and have more employees than individual proprietorships; and therefore the former are more subject to problems in industrial relations. But it is under the third form of business enterprise, namely the corporation, that these problems especially develop.

In a corporate enterprise, ownership is vested in stockholders. These stockholders elect a board of directors who are charged with the general responsibility of running the enterprise successfully. The directors, who may or may not play an active part in the operation of the enterprise, ordinarily appoint the top management officials. And it is these officials who have the specific responsibility of carrying on the day-to-day activities of the business.

It will thus be seen that under the corporate form of business enterprise the owners do not actually and directly operate their business. Any control they exercise is applied indirectly, through the directors, who in turn exercise influence on such officials as the president and general manager.

Although most business enterprises in the United States are of a private character, two nonprivate categories should be mentioned. First there is governmental enterprise. Our various governmental units—federal, state, and municipal—have in recent years undertaken an increasingly wide range of activities. In the process they have become large employers of labor, and as a result they have had to face more and more problems of an employee-management nature. One such highly important problem is the status and functions of unions in governmental employments. The other nonprivate category of business enterprise is the cooperative. If a cooperative business is of sizable proportions, with a staff of employees, it too may have its problems in industrial relations, including the "union problem."

Size of Business Enterprise. Restricting our analysis now to private enterprise, particularly in its corporate form, let us consider briefly the question of size. Many businesses are quite small, with very few employees. At the other extreme are the business mammoths with thousands, sometimes hundreds of thousands, of employees. (Table 11 relates solely to the field of manufacturing and has to do with "establishments"—single plants or factories, as a rule—and not necessarily with companies.)

Table 11

Size of Establishments, Manufacturing Industry, 1950 *

Average Number of Employees	Number of Establishments
1- 249	236,891
250- 499	5,817
500- 999	2,714
1,000-2,499	1,379
2,500 and over	506
Total	247,307

* *Statistical Abstract of the United States,* 1952, p. 750. Bureau of the Census, United States Department of Commerce.

As one would expect there is great variation in size of establishments from one industry to another. Such industrial groups as transportation equipment (which includes automobiles), machinery, metal, and textiles include a relatively large number of establishments with 1,000 or more employees. Other industries, such as printing and publishing, furniture and fixtures, lumber, apparel, and food, although they include some large establishments, run mostly to smaller units.

As enterprises grow in size (and growth has been the long-time trend in the United States), new management problems are created or old ones are rendered more complex. It becomes increasingly difficult for top management to know their employees, even by name. Direct, personal contacts give way to an indirect, impersonal relationship, which tends to reduce the feeling of community in the enterprise, and to decrease the interest of the employees in the business and possibly direct it to outside organizations and activities. Management is not unaware of this problem, and in a variety of ways it is trying to cope with it. It must not, of course, be assumed that large employers are less generous to their employees than small ones.

Ownership and Management of Business Enterprise. The fact that any management control exercised by the owners of corporations is ordinarily indirect (especially if the corporations are large) may cause a gap between the owners and the managers: their interests and the policies they favor may not exactly coincide. The size of this gap is larger than one might suspect.

For one thing many stockholders never exercise their prerogatives as owners. They do not attend stockholders' meetings, and often they do not even send in their voting proxies. Sometimes stock is of a nonvoting character: that is, no management rights accompany those of ownership. Sometimes, too, there is a pyramiding of stock ownership in such a way that control is centralized in the hands of a few persons.

The actual owners of a corporate enterprise, then, may do very little in the way of controlling it. And therefore in industrial relations it is much more appropriate to speak of labor and management than of labor and ownership—or, to use the older term, labor and capital. In a certain, basic sense the expression "labor and capital" is still very meaningful and hence should not be discarded; but labor (or employees) and management are usually the two parties that come together in the actual operation of industry. For the most part we shall use the term "labor and management" in our present discussion.

Developments in Management

Over the years a number of developments have occurred in the management of business enterprise. We have already pointed to the gap that often exists between ownership and management. This is to be viewed as a highly important development. But there are still others.

Development of a Management Class. As an outgrowth of the preceding development there has grown up a separate management class. Managers, particularly those on the higher levels, are often stockholders in the companies that employ them, but their holdings are usually relatively small. Their chief source of income is not dividends but salaries.

The increasing importance of managers in our economy, and throughout the world, has appeared to some observers as a highly significant development. James Burnham feels that a "managerial society" is emerging, that power is shifting more and more from the capitalists to the managers. Not only, we are told, is the "managerial revolution" just around the corner—the corner has already been turned, and the managers are now emerging as the new ruling class. That managers are becoming increasingly important in our society few will deny. That they are becoming the ruling class is not so certain, however. Some persons, like Professor Slichter, would argue that our society is becoming "laboristic" instead of "managementistic" (if we may coin a coordinate term). But discussion of this aspect of the problem we shall defer until Chapter 20.

Scientific Management. Another development, and one that goes back quite some years, is the growth of "scientific management." This development is inseparably associated with the name of Frederick W. Taylor. Taylor advocated the application of the scentific method to the problems of industry (especially those of a technical nature) rather than rule-of-thumb or hearsay methods. He sought the maximum development of each worker's inherent abilities; he tried to place workers in the work for which they were best fitted; he emphasized the merit of functional organization in industry; he extolled the achievement of maximum production rather than restricted production.[1]

Taylor was unqestionably one of the most influential figures in the country's history. The principles that he and other persons such as H. L. Gantt and Mr. and Mrs. Frank Gilbreth (of "Cheaper by the Dozen" fame) advocated have profoundly affected American industrial development. The notion that there is an optimum-sized shovel for handling iron ore; that the laying of brick can be speeded up greatly if the bricks are brought to the bricklayer on a frame with their better side up (Frank Gilbreth's study of the science of bricklaying is a fascinating one)—notions such as these have revolutionized production methods.

Labor has not always looked with favor on these innovations, but much of its earlier hostility to scientific management has disappeared. It is interesting to note, however, that there has grown up some opposition in management's own ranks to the use of certain techniques of scientific management. Thus there is a feeling that the principle of functional organization can be pushed too far, and

[1] A detailed description of Taylor's principles will be found in his book *The Principles of Scientific Management.* New York: Harper & Bros., 1911.

that the principle of "integrated organization" often has distinct advantages.[2]

Increasing Scope of Management Activities. Over the years the work of management, particularly of top management, has broadened in scope and increased in complexity. Now more than ever before management leaders are expected to be well informed about matters outside of their business. They must be aware of political and legislative developments, of changes in the general economy of the nation, of trends in the field of labor relations.

To deal intelligently with the many problems that now confront them, line managers are making more and more use of staff specialists and outside experts. This application of scientific management to the administrative field makes possible more enlightened and more rapid decision-making. At the beginning of this century the number of staff jobs in business was small, but with the growth in the size of our business enterprises staff work has become increasingly important and increasingly effective in raising industrial output.[3]

In response to the growing complexity and importance of management functions there have grown up increasing facilities for management training. The weakness of the school of experience as the sole educational institution for management has been revealed, and the value of more formal and more general training in the field has become apparent. Numerous schools of business administration have been established, and a great many educational institutions offer courses in business administration problems. The work offered by colleges and universities in the field is not a substitute for the practical experience gained "on the ground"; but, in view of the present-day nature of management functions and responsibilities, it is a highly useful supplement.

Some companies offer in-plant management training, and various management organizations also contribute to the development of management competency. The American Management Association and the National Industrial Conference Board are particularly in-

[2] A very able discussion of this problem is contained in James C. Worthy's article in the *Proceedings* of the Fifth Annual Meeting, Industrial Relations Research Association, December, 1952.

[3] See Sumner H. Slichter, *What's Ahead for American Business?* p. 7. Boston: Little, Brown & Co., 1951.

fluential, through their conferences and publications, in promoting efficient management. There are also a number of periodicals devoted to the subject of management.

Management as a Profession. Another development in the field of management is the growing feeling that the occupation is a profession. The term "profession" is used here to indicate not the long period of training to which managers may be exposed but the attitude that managers have toward their work. One who follows a profession is supposed to be imbued with the idea of service to his fellow men; he does not look upon his work as a mere means of making money; he is interested in doing a good job rather than a barely adequate one. As one business leader has put it, "The hallmark of a profession is its sense of duty." [4] This duty, in the case of business managers, is not confined to the stockholders alone; it is a duty to the employees, to the customers, and to the general public as well.

It is not an easy matter to say how these various claimants to the fruits of managerial duty should rank. The business leader quoted above gives special emphasis to employees, for he says that "modern business management might well measure its success or failure as a profession in large part by the satisfaction and opportunities it is able to produce for its employees." Another outstanding business leader, who is thinking not of professional management but of "business," says the first responsibility is to the customers. Employees come next, then management, and finally the stockholders.[5] Frederick Taylor declared that the chief aim of management should be to obtain "the maximum prosperity for the employer, coupled with the maximum prosperity for each employee." [6]

In general we can say that no manager is acting professionally unless his actions show a marked sense of duty to others besides the stockholders. In actual practice it seems that the amount of attention given to employees, customers, and stockholders usually varies "on the basis of which one demands it most at a particular time." [7]

4 Frank Abrams, in *Harvard Business Review,* May, 1951, pp. 29-31.

5 Robert Wood Johnson, *Or Forfeit Freedom,* pp. 79-81. New York: Doubleday & Co., 1947.

6 *Op. cit.,* p. 9.

7 *Partners in Production,* p. 65. New York: The Twentieth Century Fund, 1947. Pages 62-68 of this volume contain a discussion of the goals of management and the attitude of labor toward them.

Moreover, as the economic situation changes, the direction of management benevolence tends to change also.

One should not exaggerate the extent to which management has taken on the attributes of a profession; there remains a vast amount of nonprofessional behavior in business. Nevertheless, there is good reason for believing that the professional spirit is developing among management men, and that they are to an increasing extent giving thought to some of the wider social consequences of their acts.[8]

A possible danger involved in the professionalization of management is the growth of paternalism. This is not an inevitable result, but it is one that must be guarded against. The great weakness of paternalistic management is not that it fails to make profits but that it fails to "make men"—which, if we may follow the unpopular sentimentality of Ruskin, should be the chief aim of industry.

Responsibilities and Aims of Management

Although lofty aims are not uncommon among management men, traditionally and legally the primary responsibility of management is to make profits. Let us now consider the question of profit-making, especially in its relationship to union policies.

Making Profits. It does not follow that the interests of other groups in society are harmed when management seeks the economic well-being of the owners. In fact, economists believe that *in general* the welfare of society is promoted by the quest for private profits.

If profits are to be made in any enterprise, the average cost of production must be below the selling price. The key problems of the business manager and his subordinates thus center around these two magnitudes, with the core problem that of maintaining a satisfactory relationship between them. If a business enjoys monopolistic privileges, the desired relationship between cost and selling price is not too hard to attain. If, however, the business is in a highly competitive industry, both the achievement and the maintaining of the relationship are difficult. In competition management must be constantly on the alert, constantly trying to surpass its competitors in productivity. Competition in industry, which is so beneficial to the consumer, makes great and compelling demands on management.

[8] See Howard R. Bowen, *Social Responsibilities of the Business Man.* New York: Harper & Bros., 1953.

If competition is very keen, profits will tend to be low, and vice versa. At times, indeed, competition may be so keen as to reduce profits to zero, the situation that prevails under the economist's assumption of pure competition. At other times the force of competition, and especially of unfavorable external factors, may force them below zero. Where competition is very keen in the product market, management is under strong pressure to reduce costs, including labor costs. Relatively low wages may result, unless there is strong competition among the managers for labor, or unless the workers in question are covered by an industry-wide collective bargaining agreement. Bargaining on an industry-wide basis (which we shall discuss in detail in Chapter 14) tends to limit the extent to which strong competition in the product market leads to downward pressure on wages. At the same time it may serve to direct management's attention to other means of reducing costs.

Costs may be kept low and profits high if management commands a plant that is technically well equipped. There may be financial obstacles in the way of acquiring adequate equipment, however; and on occasion unions may place obstacles in the way, though, as we have seen, they sometimes encourage technical change.

Another condition for the realization of profits is a capable, mobile working force. Through careful employee selection and training, and through a well planned promotion policy, management can do much to build up such a force. But it can easily run into difficulties with work jurisdiction rules, seniority, and perhaps the union shop. There can be no doubt that certain union rules reduce the flexibility of the work force, and in some instances they also reduce the quality of the work force.

A still further factor having a bearing on costs and profits is the state of employee morale. This is a rather abstract quality but it is extremely important. Good morale is a product of many influences, including such things as fair dealing on the part of management, congenial working companions, pleasant working conditions, and monetary incentives.

Finally, the quality of management itself is important. Excellent machinery and a fine labor force are not enough to ensure profits. These must be combined and used in the optimum fashion, and that task belongs largely to management. Management, therefore, has an immense responsibility placed upon it.

Other Management Aims—the Question of Power. Management is also pledged to ensure the survival, and if possible further the growth, of the enterprise with which it is associated. Here, as in the previously noted objective, there is a high degree of similarity between the aim of management and the aim of union leaders.[9] The leaders in both cases are keenly interested in the survival and expansion of their particular institution. The best way to achieve this goal is to make the institution a profitable undertaking.

The desire for personal power is often an important motivating influence among managers, as among union leaders. The wish to exercise control over others serves as an incentive among men in management ranks and also helps to explain management policy.

The influence of the power factor in management is well brought out in the struggle with unions over prerogatives. Management is reluctant to give up, or even share, controls that it has long exercised, even when such relinquishment or sharing would have no appreciable effect on efficiency. If efficiency would be impaired by a union proposal, management opposition is likely to be especially strong, because then both the power aim and the profit aim are involved.

We have already noted (in our discussion of the development of a professional attitude among managers) that narrow economic considerations, and now we should add power considerations, are not the sole determinants of management policy. The idea of service to the community, to the customers, and to the employees is becoming more deeply embedded in management's thinking. One may exaggerate the social consciousness of business managers, of course; but one may also exaggerate their cupidity. It would seem, moreover, that the amount of social consciousness among them is capable of development; that the extent of "economic chivalry" (about which Alfred Marshall wrote early in the century)[10] is capable of greater growth.

[9] A good discussion of the similarities and dissimilarities between business and union leaders, between the business firm and the union, will be found in Arthur M. Ross, *Trade Union Wage Policy,* pp. 24-31. Berkeley: University of California Press, 1948.

[10] Marshall's article is reprinted in *Memorials of Alfred Marshall,* ed. by A. C. Pigou. London: Macmillan & Co., 1925.

Management, Employees, Unions

The important changes that have occurred over the years in the manager-worker relationship in American industry bear a striking resemblance to those that occur in the human family. From a parent-child type of relationship, which lasted roughly until the beginning of the present century, there evolved a teacher-child relationship, which predominated during the first two decades of the century (when welfare plans of various sorts blossomed forth). Then, during the 1920's and the first part of the 1930's, when employee representation plans were common, the relationship resembled that between father and adolescent. Finally, with the great growth in the power and influence of organized labor, beginning in the middle 1930's, the relationship has been more that of adult to adult, or man to man.[11] In this stage the workers are no longer mere subjects. To some extent they are co-rulers, participating in the governing of the enterprise in which they work. It is not to be inferred, of course, that *all* managers now deal with their employees on a man-to-man basis, only that many do and many more will in the foreseeable future.

This change in the status of labor and in the general pattern of industrial relations has given rise to a number of problems. One of the most important of these is the divided loyalty that tends to grow up among employees when the man-to-man stage is reached. Management obviously wants a work force that is loyal to the enterprise; the union, equally obviously, wants its members loyal to it. Both company loyalty and union loyalty are good ideas (though class-conscious workers may deny the value of the former, and class-conscious employers may deny the desirability of the latter). A union can make available to its members benefits, especially nonmonetary benefits, that management cannot provide; and a company can make available benefits that a union cannot.

Can these two loyalties be reconciled? Or does loyalty to the one party mean disloyalty to the other? It seems clear that the two loyalties are not incompatible. "There is no basic conflict between workers' loyalty to their company and their allegiance to their union,"

[11] The above paragraph follows closely an enlightened discussion of the changing pattern of industrial relations in Sara E. Southall, *Industry's Unfinished Business,* Chap. 2. New York: Harper & Bros., 1950.

declares an enlightened group of businessmen.[12] But the problem is how to sell the idea of compatability to both management men and unionists and, furthermore, how to strike a proper balance between the two loyalties.

If there is to be "mutual survival" of unions and management, some sort of balance, some sort of compromise, must be worked out. Professor E. Wight Bakke believes that such a compromise can be reached.[13] Pointing out the primary interest of both management and unions in survival, Bakke stresses the great need for each party to understand thoroughly "the kind of job the other has to do." Mutual survival involves mutual understanding, and mutual understanding will contribute to industrial peace and to the strengthening of our free economic system.

Mutual understanding, it should further be noted, helps to pave the way for a still higher type of industrial relations, a type in which there is not only mutual toleration and good will but active cooperation, particularly in the field of production (see Chapter 19).

Personnel Aims and Organization

Management's chief aims in matters relating to personnel may be listed as follows: to have an adequate number of employees, to have these employees well qualified, to have them placed in the jobs for which they are best fitted, to have the employees work diligently, to have them on the job as steadily as possible. To achieve these particular aims management has adopted various practices, all of which are aimed primarily at maximizing the efficient use of manpower. This general objective may be looked upon as "the basic purpose of all personnel management and administration" [14] and the chief goal to which all personnel policies are directed.

The importance of personnel work has been more and more recognized in American industry. For a long time this work was neglected. A great deal of attention was given to the financial, manufacturing, purchasing, and marketing aspects of business but relatively little to personnel matters. Now, however, the contribution that good personnel policies can make to successful business opera-

[12] See pamphlet entitled *Human Relations in Modern Business,* p. 28. New York: Prentice-Hall, Inc., 1949.

[13] *Mutual Survival.* New York: Harper & Bros., 1946.

[14] Dale Yoder, *Personnel Management and Industrial Relations,* 3rd ed., p. 5. New York: Prentice-Hall, Inc., 1948.

tions is widely granted, and work in the field has been greatly expanded.

To an ever increasing extent the application of personnel policies has become the work of specialists. Usually in large enterprises a separate department, called a Personnel, or Employee Relations, or Industrial Relations Department, performs the various personnel functions. The department is headed by a manager or director, who in some cases is a vice-president of the business. If the company is of considerable size, the department may be broken down into specialized divisions, each concentrating on the performance of a single personnel function. Recently some companies have been establishing specialized personnel research sections within their personnel departments.

In small companies there will probably not be a separate personnel department, but there may be a person who devotes all or much of his time to personnel work. In some small companies certain personnel functions are performed by persons whose major work is in other parts of the business. In general, however, work in the field of personnel has been concentrated increasingly in the hands of specially qualified persons and taken out of the hands of persons whose main interests and responsibilities are in other fields. Foremen, for example, do not perform as much personnel work as they once did, nor do top management men.

Personnel Policies

The range of personnel activities in American industry is wide, and in the limited space at our disposal we shall not be able to take more than a general, panoramic view of them.[15]

Employment. In Chapter 5 we discussed the various means by which workers and jobs are brought together. In the present section we shall assume that the worker has appeared on the scene and is now being considered for possible employment.[16]

[15] In writing the above section the author has used a considerable amount of information from the research study on *Personnel Activities in American Business,* published by the National Industrial Conference Board (Report No. 86, Studies in Personnel Policy). The Bureau's monthly magazine, *Management Record,* has also been useful, as has Yoder's book cited in footnote 14. See also Dale Yoder, *Personnel Principles and Policies.* New York: Prentice-Hall, Inc., 1952.

[16] An informative research study on the relative amount of emphasis placed on 19 different personnel functions (in different industries and in firms of different

In many small enterprises the hiring procedure is quite simple. The boss, who may be the owner-manager of the enterprise or a foreman, talks with the applicant, and if the latter seems to have the requisite qualifications for the opening he is hired. This method of hiring is informal and in most small companies is probably adequate. But more systematic methods must be used in medium-sized and large enterprises. It is here that the personnel department, which in plants of such size will probably have a special employment section, has a key role to play.

To facilitate the proper selection of workers a number of techniques may be used. The various jobs in the factory may be studied with a view to finding out their essential characteristics. This is called job analysis. Such analyses not only aid in the selection of workers but may be used in connection with training programs, work simplification, and wage determination.

After a job is analyzed a description of it is drawn up and the particular worker characteristics that the job calls for are set forth on a job specification form. It is now relatively easy to check the qualifications of a job applicant with the worker characteristics on the form and to make an intelligent selection from among the applicants.

In picking workers the personnel department may ask each job applicant to fill out an application blank. Following this there may be an employment interview, in connection with which a checklist or rating scale may be used. Tests may also be given, including general intelligence tests and trade tests.

Mention should be made of the exit interview as a personnel practice. By systematically interviewing persons who are leaving the company the personnel department may be able to discover weaknesses in the enterprise which, if corrected, will reduce the amount of labor turnover. Many companies now look upon the exit interview as a definite, planned function of the personnel department. The employment function of the department may also cover transfers, layoffs, and leaves.

---

sizes) has been made by Dale Yoder and Lenore N. Wilson. See *Employment-Relations Functions and Budgets,* printed in *Personnel,* November, 1952 (also issued as No. 10 in the Reprint Series, Industrial Relations Center, University of Minnesota).

Training, Promotions, Merit Rating. Recently hired employees (and also employees who have been on the job for some time) are very often inadequately qualified to perform their daily tasks. It may be to management's interests therefore to establish a training program or to cooperate with other groups and agencies in providing training facilities, or simply to encourage its workers to take advantage of training opportunities that are already available.

A very common technique used by management to equip workers for specific posts is on-the-job training. Such training is very much of an applied nature and is ordinarily given by older employees. Sometimes on-the-job training is supplemented by classroom instruction.

Apprenticeship training is of a broader character, since it relates not to one job but to a whole trade. Unions generally play an important part in this type of training, since most of the crafts are organized. The federal government has taken a keen interest in apprentice training and has sponsored the establishment of numerous joint apprenticeship committees.

In addition to their training programs for plant employees, many companies have established programs for training foremen and some have set up programs for training executives. A considerable number have programs designed especially for college graduates entering their employment. It might be added, too, that in addition to carrying on or aiding training programs of a vocational nature some companies have conducted programs of "economic education," under which employees study the nature and the operation of the free enterprise system.

An important factor in establishing and preserving morale in an enterprise is the adoption of a good set of principles governing promotions. These principles should be clearly stated, so that the employees know on what basis promotions are made. An essential condition to a satisfactory promotion scheme is a careful study of jobs so that the responsibilities associated with each job are made clear. The interrelationship of the various jobs should be studied and routes of promotion from job to job should be set up. Management's powers in the matter of promotion have been curtailed in recent years owing to the success with which unions have obtained seniority provisions in their contracts (see Chapter 15).

A promotion policy that has become increasingly common among

American companies is that of merit rating. Although this policy is most widely used with respect to factory workers and clerical employees, it is sometimes applied to supervisors, salesmen, and executives.

Incentive Plans. A common personnel function is that of devising and applying new methods of remuneration, other than the simple plan of straight time rates. These methods ordinarily involve a close relationship between output and earnings and, as we shall see in Chapter 25, they take various forms. In the establishment of such methods of wage payment it is common to use the joint techniques of motion study and time study in an attempt to make the determination of wages more scientific and also to stimulate efficiency. A plan closely allied to incentive wages is that of profit sharing. Under the latter plan the relationship between output and earnings is not so direct or intimate; but profit sharing, which we shall deal with later, has definite incentive characteristics.

Wage and Salary Administration. Under the impetus of World War II, when the government issued numerous wage and salary orders and regulations, it became common for companies to establish separate divisions in their personnel departments for the purpose of setting up and administering wage and salary scales. Other functions of such sections may include job analysis and classification and the formulation of job descriptions.

Employee Security, Benefits, and Safety. Many plans exist for giving employees greater security—and for improving employee-management relations. These plans, in part, are designed to cope with the typical insecurity hazards to which workers and their dependents are exposed.

Many companies have group insurance plans in operation. The most common type is ordinary life insurance, possibly carrying accidental death benefits. Another common plan provides for sickness and accident benefits. Hospitalization benefits are also frequently paid. Surgical benefits, though not as common, are often provided.

Old-age pensions, another type of security plan, are not new in American industry, but during recent years they have become very prominent, largely as a result of union pressure. As an adjunct to their pension plans some companies have introduced programs designed to aid their employees in adjusting themselves to retirement.

To an increasing extent companies are providing direct medical and health services. These services take such forms as treatment for on-the-job accidents and illness; physical examinations for new employees; assistance in placing workers in suitable jobs; and health education. Occasionally dental and optical services are provided. In large companies there may be one or more physicians and one or more nurses employed on a full-time basis.

Other types of security plans (using the term in a comprehensive fashion) include thrift plans, credit unions, employee stock ownership, profit sharing, dismissal compensation, employment stabilization plans, and annual-wage plans.

Since industrial accidents represent a huge loss to employers, it is to their interest to try to reduce both the frequency and the severity of such accidents. Safety programs may be conducted by the employer himself, or if there is a union in the plan it may participate. In many companies there is a special safety division within the personnel department, and in numerous larger plants there are safety committees.

Recreational Activities. It has long been the custom of some companies to sponsor recreational activities among their employees. Not a few companies employ a recreation director, on either a full-time or a part-time basis. This director serves under the agency or group that administers the program, usually an over-all employee association or the personnel department (possibly working through groups of employees concerned with specific recreational activities). Most programs are jointly financed by employers and employees. Though extensive use is made of outside recreational facilities, many companies provide facilities of their own, usually bearing the whole of the maintenance cost.

In a survey of employee recreational activities among 264 companies made by the National Industrial Conference Board, [17] it was found that 158 different types of activities were sponsored, including pinochle, weight-lifting, and boccie. The five most common were bowling, softball, golf, basketball, and picnics. The fact that interdepartment competition is more common than interplant competition suggests extensive employee participation.

In recent years the unions have become increasingly active in the field of recreation, and to some extent they have taken over this

[17] *Employee Recreation Activities,* Studies in Personnel Policy, No. 102, pp. 9, 10, 11. New York: National Industrial Conference Board, 1949.

particular personnel function. This trend will probably continue in the future.

Other Personnel Functions. To convey information to their employees concerning such matters as activities in the business, production operations, and labor policy, companies employ a variety of techniques. The ordinary bulletin board is most commonly used, but many companies issue employee manuals or handbooks in which the privileges and responsibilities of the employees and the operations of the company are set forth; many send out letters, either to the ordinary employees or to the supervisors, or to both, in which company plans and policies are described; many publish magazines or papers. Some companies give copies of their annual financial report to the employees, often with additional information relating to such things as new products and the business outlook. Still other techniques include policy and procedure manuals, organization manuals, and statements of labor policy. It is quite common, particularly among larger companies, to have a specialized employee information section within the personnel department. The whole problem of communication in industry has become highly important in industrial relations work.

The policy of asking employees for suggestions on how to improve methods of production is fairly widespread among American companies. Some enterprises have paid out large sums for useful suggestions they have received.[18]

Some companies establish libraries for the use of their employees. Though many of these libraries are of a technical nature, some have books and periodicals of a nontechnical type in them. Some companies also make arrangements by which reading matter from public libraries can be obtained through the company library.

Many companies extend advice or assistance to their employees—for example, in making out income tax returns, in real estate deals, and in making out wills.

Some companies conduct morale surveys, using either the questionnaire or the interview method or both, for the purpose of finding out what the employees' attitudes are toward the company. This

[18] A few years ago it was stated that the Illinois Central Railroad had paid out $680,000 for suggestions, having found 54,000 usable out of over 312,000 received. *The Management Review,* April, 1951, p. 201.

relatively new personnel practice is apparently yielding worth-while results.

As a final entry in our list of miscellaneous personnel functions we shall mention public relations. The famous dictum of Commodore Vanderbilt is falling more and more into discard, and both employers and unions usually do their best to win the interest and the favor of the public.

Labor Relations. All or most of the personnel functions so far described have in a sense related to labor relations. But there is a set of functions to which the term "labor relations" in a narrower sense is applied. These functions have to do especially with union relations, such as the negotiation of collective bargaining agreements, the administration of such agreements, and the handling of grievances (in non-union plants as well as union plants). In numerous companies there is a special division in the personnel department that concentrates on the performance of these functions. In addition this division deals with governmental agencies operating in the field of labor.

14

COLLECTIVE BARGAINING—PRINCIPLES AND PRACTICES

The Nature and Significance of Collective Bargaining

The expression "collective bargaining" is now well established in the English language and has in fact become an indispensable part of labor terminology. But, interestingly enough, the expression apparently does not date back beyond 1891, when Mrs. Sidney Webb coined it.[1] Though for more than a century and a half workers have been banding together for the purpose of acting unitedly in dealing with their employers, for less than half of that time has the act been called "collective bargaining."

Meaning of Collective Bargaining. The process of collective bargaining is joint in nature. Instead of the workers dealing separately with their employers they act *together,* as more or less *permanent* units. These units generally carry on the bargaining process through duly elected or appointed representatives, who deal either with single employers or with groups of employers. Both parties may use outsiders in carrying on the bargaining process. The workers' units, or unions, may use the services of officers of their parent organizations (if, of course, the parent organizations themselves are not the actual bargaining units). Either side may hire lawyers to assist it in the negotiations.

The "joint" or "collective" aspect of collective bargaining refers only to the workers. The word does not imply that employers act together in the bargaining process. As a matter of fact, however, employers frequently do unite for bargaining purposes, and unions are

[1] See Sidney and Beatrice Webb, *Industrial Democracy,* new ed., p. 173. London: Longmans, Green & Co., 1902.

often desirous that they should. But multiple-unit action by employers is in no way an essential condition of collective bargaining in the usual sense.

If collective bargaining means that the workers act as a collectivity or group, it also means that they, and in this case the employers too, actually bargain. The statements of policy drawn up by employers and setting forth the rules governing the employment relationship within their plants are not instruments of collective bargaining. Nor, on the other hand, are the rules that unions sometimes arbitrarily establish for employer observance. Under collective bargaining the employment-relationship, in its manifold aspects, is determined *bilaterally,* by actual bargaining.

Collective Bargaining a Law-Making Process. The bilateral determination of wages, hours, and the like may be looked upon as a legislative act. When a union and an employer enter into a collective agreement they are in reality adopting a law. This law, which is private in nature, sets forth the rules that are to govern the employment relationship for a given period of time.

The law established by the process of collective bargaining is usually called a trade agreement, though it may be referred to as a collective bargaining agreement, an employment contract, a labor contract, or a schedule. In a somewhat wider sense the collective bargaining agreement has been spoken of in still other terms: a constitution, a treaty, a pact, a formal compact, and a "form of constitutional government." All these expressions throw light on the essential nature of the process of collective bargaining and on the law or agreement that grows out of the process.

A collective bargaining agreement, like ordinary laws, must often be interpreted. The rights of the workers and of the employer under the law must often be examined and set forth. This process, in contrast to the adoption of the agreement in the first place, is judicial—not legislative—in nature, and is carried out by the grievance machinery that is ordinarily provided for in the trade agreement.[2]

[2] Strictly speaking the handling of grievances is not collective bargaining. The determination of rights under a set of predetermined rules is something that should not be carried out by the method of bargaining. However, following common usage, we shall look upon the settlement of grievances as part of the general collective bargaining process. For an excellent discussion of the difference between contract-making and grievance-handling, see Neil Chamberlain's article in *The Quarterly Journal of Economics,* June, 1944. Contract-making,

The Significance of Collective Bargaining. To the casual observer the full significance of collective bargaining is not likely to be apparent. He probably views the process simply as a means whereby the workers are able to obtain better wages, hours, and working conditions. It is such a means, to be sure, but its importance extends far beyond the achievement of these goals. The introduction of collective bargaining into the field of industrial relations represents one of the most outstanding social changes of the modern era: the decline of one type of industrial government and the emergence of another.

Without collective bargaining the system of government found in industry is essentially autocratic in nature. Authority in the matter of industrial relations is vested in the employer. True, a benevolent employer may voluntarily give his workers more than they could force from him through collective bargaining. True, many workers are very well satisfied. But the fact remains: the system is autocratic, and like all autocratic systems it is open to grave objections.

In the first place the benevolence of the employer is uncertain. Secondly, even if the employer were to continue his benevolence, and even if the workers were to remain satisfied, industrial autocracy is the very antithesis of democracy. If it is desirable that the citizens of the state should determine the political rules under which they live, it appears to be a good thing for the citizens of industry to play some part in determining the rules under which they work. And the only satisfactory way of their playing this part is through collective bargaining. This does not mean, of course, that everything that is done in the name of collective bargaining is economically and socially good. It does mean, however, that on balance collective bargaining, as a system of industrial government (and where the majority of workers voting in a given employment unit want it), is definitely superior to its alternative.

Stages and Developments in Collective Bargaining

Stages. Collective bargaining in industry has developed gradually. There have been times when its progress has been very fast—

---

says Mr. Chamberlain, has to do with "decisions of interests," whereas grievance-handling has to do with "decisions of rights." Mr. Chamberlain would limit the application of the term "collective bargaining" to the process of law-making. He would not apply it to that of law-interpreting.

when union membership has increased with phenomenal speed—but there have also been times of stagnancy and decline. Its long-time growth has been relatively slow.

Four outstanding stages can be discerned in the development of collective bargaining. The first stage, which began with the formation of the early, isolated unions and extended until the 1840's, was characterized by the uncertain legal status of labor organizations. During this period there was a tendency to look upon combinations of workers seeking higher wages as criminal and civil conspiracies, and in a number of instances judges handed down verdicts to this effect. As time went on, however, legal opinion on the issue changed, and the right of workers to combine was no longer called into question. Important in this connection was the decision handed down by Chief Justice Shaw of Massachusetts in 1842 in the case of Commonwealth *v.* Hunt. Although this decision did not settle the matter completely, we may look upon it as a rough dividing line between two stages in the history of collective bargaining in this country.

The second stage in the development of collective bargaining lasted, roughly, from the 1840's until the middle of the 1930's. This stage was marked not so much by the right of unions to exist and engage in collective bargaining—that right had been admitted—but by the lack of any legal duty on the part of employers to engage in collective bargaining activities with their employees. Employers were under no legal compulsion to recognize the unions of their workers, even though all or the vast majority of the workers were union members. Moreover, if the employers desired to undermine the influence of the unions, there were various policies (some of a highly reprehensible nature) they could adopt without running any risks of legal punishment.

The third stage in the development of collective bargaining began with the passing of the National Labor Relations Act in 1935. Under this act employers for the first time were obligated to bargain with their employees if the latter, in sufficient numbers, so desired. The employer was not forced to accede to all the demands made by the union nor, for that matter, to come to any agreement with it, but he was compelled to make a genuine effort to come to an agreement. Moreover, he was debarred from engaging in various unfair labor practices.

The fourth stage started in 1947, when the Labor Management Relations Act was passed, and comes down to the present. The significance of the LMRA is that it sets forth a list of unfair labor practices that *unions,* and not merely employers, must not engage in. The NLRA gave the unions important rights and imposed on the employers important duties; the LMRA gives the employers important rights and imposes on the unions important duties.

Developments. Four recent developments in the field of collective bargaining, all of a more or less general nature, are of special significance. The first and most obvious of the developments is the phenomenal growth that has taken place (especially between 1935 and 1946) in the number of persons who work under collective bargaining agreements. This change has been of the utmost importance, not only industrially but economically, politically, and socially as well.

The second general development has been the expansion that has occurred over the years in the contents or subject matter of the bargaining agreements. Although some of the changes in the contents of the agreements are changes in degree, representing a widening of union control along established lines, others are changes in kind. Both represent a definite shift, or rather a further definite shift, in the balance of power in industry.

The third development in collective bargaining is the growth of multiple-unit bargaining by employers (and by unions). Although many bargaining agreements still relate to a single plant or a single employer, many others have been extended to include more than one plant or employer.

The fourth development is an aspect of the third. During recent years the follow-the-leader principle has been making its way into the field of collective bargaining. A union will enter into an agreement with one of the large companies in the industry, and this agreement, or part of it, will serve as a pattern for other agreements concluded in the industry and possibly outside of it as well.[3]

[3] The use of the principle by the United Automobile Workers' union appeared to one business paper in 1946 as a demonstration "that the old argument whether or not there should be industry-wide bargaining" was now "thoroughly unrealistic." See *Business Week,* June 1, 1946, p. 42.

The Collective Bargaining Agreement

When a number of workers form a union, it is their intention to engage in collective bargaining; and they hope that as a result of the process of collective bargaining they will obtain a written agreement with their employer covering wages, hours, and the like. This agreement is the immediate goal, therefore, to which unions direct their efforts.

Development and Nature. The collective bargaining or trade agreement has gone through an interesting metamorphosis. The first agreements took the form of "price lists" or "bills of prices" submitted by the workers to their employers for acceptance.[4] The prices referred to were wages, of course. As time went on the agreements were broadened out to cover hours and working conditions as well. Although a considerable number of trade agreements were in operation before the 1890's, it was not until then that the trade agreement era really started. This era was ushered in by the signing of the famous national agreement between the Iron Molders' Union and the Stove Founders' Association in 1891. Since that period progress in the use of trade agreements has matched the progress of unionism itself.

In times past employers sometimes objected to having their understandings with the union put down in black and white. They were willing, under pressure, to come to an agreement with the union, but they did not want the details of the agreements in writing. Under very simple industrial conditions oral understandings, such as these employers favored, may have been tolerably satisfactory. But today, with industry highly complex and with more and more matters subject to the process of collective bargaining, oral understandings are obviously no substitute for written agreements. Under the Labor Management Relations Act it is an unfair labor practice for either unions or employers to refuse to have agreements put in writing.

It should not be inferred that oral understandings are no longer of any significance in industrial relations. As a *substitute* for written agreements such understandings are not of any significance, but as a

[4] The earliest agreement of this type on record dates back to 1795. See *The Annals of the American Academy of Political and Social Science,* September, 1910, p. 321.

supplement to them they are of some importance. This is true in the men's clothing industry, for example.[5]

Contents. Although collective bargaining agreements have certain general features in common, they vary in comprehensiveness or scope. The degree of this variation depends on a number of factors, including the extent to which the collective bargaining process is used in determining personnel and other plant policies, and the nature and complexity of the industry.

Ordinarily the provisions in the agreements are divisible into a number of groups. In the first group are introductory statements relating to such things as the principles and purposes of the agreement, the meaning of the terms that are used in the agreement, and the status of the bargaining union. In the second group are provisions, often very numerous and very detailed, relating to wages, hours, and conditions of work. In the third group are provisions for the administration and interpretation of the agreement; and in the fourth are provisions concerning the duration and renewal of the agreement.[6]

How detailed should the trade agreement be? Should it just touch the high spots, so to speak, of the employer-employee relationship or should it deal with minor as well as major matters? An agreement set forth in general terms is undoubtedly more flexible. On the other hand, such an agreement is likely to make the task of grievance-handling more difficult.[7]

Duration and Renewal. In terms of duration collective bargaining agreements are of two types: those that last for a specific period and those (known as "open-end" agreements) that continue indefinitely.[8] When an agreement is of indefinite duration (most are not), negotiations for changes in it may be reopened or the agreement may

[5] See *How Collective Bargaining Works,* p. 416. New York: The Twentieth Century Fund, 1942.

[6] See *Written Trade Agreements in Collective Bargaining,* p. 39. Bulletin No. 4, Division of Economic Research, National Labor Relations Board, November, 1939. In his classic work on American unionism, referred to in an earlier chapter, Professor Hoxie described the "essential parts of a trade agreement" as a preamble; a legislative code; a judicial code; an executive part. Hoxie recognized exceptions to this pattern and was aware, of course, that the provisions of agreements do not always fall nicely into his four categories.

[7] See Neil Chamberlain's remarks in *The Quarterly Journal of Economics,* May, 1944, p. 370.

[8] On duration of agreements see *Collective Bargaining Provisions,* Bulletin No. 908-19. Bureau of Labor Statistics, United States Department of Labor.

be ended if either the employer or the union so desires. But advance notice must be given, and in some cases the agreement must have been in operation for a certain minimum period.

The most common time period found in the definite-duration agreements is one year. Some run for less than a year; others run for two, three, or more years (during 1947 two-year agreements became rather popular, and a little later five-year agreements made an appearance, especially in the automobile industry). Some agreements, particularly in shipbuilding and the building industry, last a year plus the time necessary to complete the particular project on which the union is working.

If the duration period is too short, the union and the employer may waste valuable time in negotiation proceedings. Difficulties may arise from the turmoil preceding the frequent negotiations.[9] If the duration period is too long, and there are no modification provisions in the agreement, either the union or the employer may suffer because of unforeseen developments. Just what the optimum duration period is, it is hard to say. It may be stated, however, that one very significant influence having a bearing on the length of the period is the degree of economic and price stability that is anticipated during the months and years ahead. Incidentally, it might be pointed out that long-term agreements may give the union more security than it otherwise would have. This is especially true since the National Labor Relations Board handed down a ruling (in February, 1953) that five-year agreements could be employed to bar representation elections during the time the agreement is in force. Previously the Board had not granted that privilege for longer than three years.[10]

Definite-duration agreements usually provide for automatic yearly renewal; that is, the old agreement continues in force unless either party (or both) desires to change or end it. If either party should fail to abide by the terms of the collective bargaining agreement, it may be provided that the agreement ends. Since it would be very unwise to have an agreement end before negotiations for a new one are begun, most agreements provide for the giving of advance

[9] The labor relations director of General Motors, in discussing the company's five-year contract with the UAW, has pointed out that under one-year contracts the union has "to get the pot boiling once a year, and sometimes it gets so hot that plants are struck whether or not the union wants a strike." *The New York Times,* September 16, 1951.

[10] *The New York Times,* February 9, 1953.

notice if either party desires changes in the old agreement or wants to end it. The Labor Management Relations Act provides that in industries of an interstate nature this period has to be at least sixty days.

Some agreements are given flexibility by the inclusion of modification provisions. Such an arrangement is always found in agreements of indefinite duration. These provisions are especially useful in case significant new developments arise during the time the agreement is in force. Although flexibility helps to make agreements "living documents," the modification provisions may add a certain amount of instability to the bargaining and uncertainty to the agreements.[11]

Enforcement. Successful collective bargaining is obviously dependent on general adherence to the terms of the bargaining agreement. If either the employer or the union takes the agreement lightly and breaks its terms at will, friction is bound to arise and chaos in the employment relationship is likely to develop. American employers and unions have, for the most part, adhered to the agreements they have made, but neither side has had a perfect record.

Compliance with the terms of collective bargaining agreements has been almost wholly a matter of intraindustry sentiment and action. Very seldom have employers or unions resorted to the courts for agreement enforcement, although they themselves have adopted judicial techniques for the achievement of this end. The widespread system of grievance-handling, which generally culminates in arbitration, is an important means for ensuring adherence to the terms of bargaining agreements. But other means, such as penalties, for achieving adherence to the agreements are also used.[12]

The passing of the Labor Management Relations Act removed any doubt concerning the legality of damage suits in federal courts over the matter of agreement violation. In inter-state industries both the employer and the union have the right to bring suit for such violations in federal courts "without respect to the amount in controversy or without regard to the citizenship of the parties." Both

[11] For a good discussion of the continuous contract (as opposed to the definite-duration contract) see the article by John W. Teele in the *Harvard Business Review*, May-June, 1953.

[12] See latter part of *Collective Bargaining Provisions* (Strikes and Lockouts, Contract Enforcement), Bulletin No. 908-13, Bureau of Labor Statistics, United States Department of Labor.

unions and employers are responsible for the acts of their representatives. If a union is guilty of violating a contract, any money judgment against it is "enforceable only against the organization as an entity and against its assets, and shall not be enforceable against any individual member or his assets."

The Settlement of Grievances

The drawing up and signing of a collective bargaining agreement does not mean that for the duration of the agreement the workers and management are going to live in an industrial atmosphere of sweetness and light. Dissatisfaction and friction on the part of either party, or both, may easily arise, even under an agreement that was deemed highly satisfactory when it was signed. This dissatisfaction may be due to uncertainty and difference of opinion concerning the precise meaning of provisions in the agreement; and differences of opinion are not uncommon, since provisions are often left in a general form. Trouble often arises from the entry of new, unforeseen, unprovided for elements into the employment situation.

It is desirable, therefore, that some means be decided upon beforehand to take up the grievances, the misunderstandings, and the disputes that may arise while the agreement is in operation—to decide, in short, what the *rights* of the workers (and of management) are under the agreement. If this is not done the workers may become extremely dissatisfied and belligerent, and industrial strife may follow.

Because of differences in the size of bargaining units, because of differences in the extent of collective bargaining experience, and because of variations in the economic structure of plants and industries, uniformity in the methods used in handling grievances would not be expected.[13] Speaking very generally, however, in the majority of union agreements the grievance provisions provide for two broad procedural steps. First, direct efforts are made by the two parties concerned to settle the points at issue. Secondly, failing settlement by this method the questions are carried to arbitration, in which case an outside person (or persons) renders assistance. Sometimes, how-

[13] See "Settlement of Grievances Under Union Agreements," *Monthly Labor Review,* February, 1940. The Division of Labor Standards of the U. S. Department of Labor has issued a pamphlet on the handling of grievances (under collective bargaining) entitled *Settling Plant Grievances.* Bulletin No. 60, 1943.

ever, the second step is omitted. Whatever the set-up, it is understood that work shall not be interrupted, either by strikes or by lockouts, during the time that the grievance machinery is in operation. This is a cardinal principle in every grievance-handling arrangement.

Direct Settlement. The smaller the plant, the simpler the grievance machinery provided. In a small factory, with two or three hundred workers, there may be only two steps (or even only one) involved in direct settlement. The aggrieved worker himself, or the shop steward, may contact the foreman. Failing settlement at this point the grievance may be taken up by a higher union representative and the manager or owner of the plant. In large plants there are more than two steps involved before arbitration; four appears to be a common number.[14] On the union side the representatives may extend from the shop steward or the worker himself to officers of the parent union. On the employer's side the representatives may extend from the foreman to the top officers of the corporation.

Business agents sometimes serve as important cogs in the grievance machinery. Joint employer-union committees, officers of employers' associations, and "joint boards" (as in the clothing industry) also aid in the work. It should be added that the union, or at least the union officers, is sometimes very insistent that a union representative submit the grievances instead of the individual workers.[15] This is one way of demonstrating the value of the organization to the workers.

Various rules prevail concerning the form in which grievances are to be presented, the time limits for one or more of the processing steps, and the employment status of the union grievance men.

Arbitration. If a grievance cannot be settled by direct negotiation, the matter is often referred to arbitration. When a grievance reaches this stage, it is probable that an important issue is involved, one that may lead to a strike if it is not settled.

When arbitration is used, it is the second and final *major* procedural step involved in the settlement of grievances. The most fre-

[14] For statistical data relating to grievance-handling steps see the *Monthly Labor Review*, July, 1951, p. 37.

[15] See R. R. R. Brooks, *As Steel Goes*, p. 205. New Haven: Yale University Press, 1940; and W. H. McPerson, *Labor Relations in the Automobile Industry*, pp. 46-47. Washington: The Brookings Institution, 1940.

quent arbitration arrangement takes the form of a joint committee with an impartial chairman selected by the committee members. Before the joint or bipartisan committee calls in an impartial outsider it may first attempt to settle the question in dispute. If it fails, then, with its newly selected chairman, it becomes an arbitration board, although even before it calls in an outsider it may already function (or try to function) as an arbitration body. Sometimes the chairman (the umpire or the arbitrator) is decided upon ahead of time; sometimes he is selected only when the actual need arises. Ordinarily the grievance is settled by a majority vote of the arbitration committee, although once in a while the verdict is handed down by the chairman alone.

Some union agreements provide for the setting up of arbitration committees made up solely of impartial outsiders, usually three or five persons, occasionally seven. Very often, however, agreements provide for a single outside arbitrator. In some instances, where bargaining is carried on by a union with a very large employer, or with a group of employers working through an association, permanent arbitrators (or "impartial chairmen") are used.

Just as there are various rules concerning the first step in grievance handling (direct negotiation), so too are there rules concerning the use of arbitration. These rules relate to time periods for the various arbitration steps, the order in which different types of cases are to be handled, and the acceptance of the arbitration award.

The Scope of the Bargaining Unit

One of the most important problems in present-day collective bargaining is the matter of size, or make-up, of the bargaining units. One aspect of this problem involves the old issue of craft unionism versus industrial unionism (to state the issue in simplified form) and has been brought into prominence by two developments: the split in the ranks of labor and the passing of the National Labor Relations Act, both dating back to the middle of the 1930's. A second aspect involves the question of industry-wide bargaining, which has been pushed into the forefront by various influences.

The NLRB and the Size of the Bargaining Units. The National Labor Relations Board has a number of key functions to perform. One of these is to determine, in the cases that come before it, the official bargaining agency for the workers. In performing this function the board not only has to conduct elections for determining what union, if any, the workers prefer as their official bargaining agent, but also has to decide in numerous cases what the size of the election constituency shall be. In other words, the NLRB has to determine the size of the bargaining unit. Had it not been for the division in the ranks of labor this task would have been much simpler, although difficulties would have arisen with the expansion of unionism into the unorganized, and particularly the mass-production, fields.

In deciding the size of the bargaining unit the NLRB's primary aim (as it points out in its Sixteenth Annual Report) is to bring together "only employees who have substantial mutual interests in wages, hours, and other conditions of employment." In attempting to achieve this objective the Board gives attention to such matters as "(1) extent and type of union organization of the employees involved; (2) any pertinent history of collective bargaining among the employees involved; (3) similarity of duties, skills, and working conditions of the employees; and (4) the desires of the employees." These criteria are very fair, but in applying them to cases the Board obviously cannot completely satisfy the two or more unions involved, since their opinions on the matter of unit size are certain to differ.

It should be added that under the LMRA professional employees are not to be included in any bargaining unit with nonprofessional employees unless a majority of the professional employees vote in favor of such an arrangement. Furthermore, plant guards must not be included in any bargaining unit with other workers.

The Changing Union Pattern in Bargaining. In its simplest form collective bargaining may be thought of as a process involving a small number of workers enrolled in a local union and a single employer. This is the pattern it assumed in its early stages of development, and it is still a widespread pattern today.[16] But there has been a definite trend away from collective bargaining of this type. The size of the bargaining units, both on the union side and on the employer side, has been growing. As a result of this expansion toward industry-wide bargaining, the influence of the local union as a bargaining agency has diminished. Power has passed increasingly from its hands into the hands of the parent organization or the coopera-

[16] Information on this point will be found in the *Monthly Labor Review*, July, 1951, pp. 33-34.

tive bargaining group of which it is a part. Even where a local unit does perform the bargaining function, its influence may be restricted by rules and regulations laid down by its parent organization.

Though collective bargaining by local unions is still very common, a great deal of bargaining is now done by the locals acting together. This cooperative, group bargaining may be classified either according to the scope or extent of the crafts or industries covered by the collective agreements, or according to the size of the geographical areas covered.

(1) A common type of group collective bargaining is that carried on by locals of one craft or set of crafts. Thus various teamsters' locals in a given city or region may unite in their collective bargaining activities. A second type of such bargaining involves a variety of local craft unions within the same industry. In the building and construction industry, for example, carpenters', plasterers', bricklayers', and other local building trades unions may bargain unitedly. Sometimes local unions go rather far afield in their cooperative bargaining ventures. Thus an agreement was concluded some years ago in New York City between the Hotelmen's Association on the one side and hotel and restaurant workers, electrical workers, firemen and oilers, operating engineers, and building service employees on the other.

(2) In the second classification of group collective bargaining the city is at the head of the list. Most of the bargaining carried on by union and employer groups is conducted on a metropolitan or citywide basis. It was stated in early 1947 that there are probably 5,000 local or city employer organizations in the United States that deal with unions.[17] The building and construction industry and the metal industry, with their local department councils, are outstanding in citywide bargaining. In the needle trades, to cite another example, there is also a great deal of this type of bargaining.

Some collective bargaining is conducted on a region-wide basis; examples are found in the hosiery, textile, and maritime industries, and a number of others.

National (or nationwide) collective bargaining is not common in the United States, but there is some likelihood that it will become more common in the years ahead. From the early years of the present

[17] See "Collective Bargaining With Employers' Associations," *Monthly Labor Review,* August, 1939, and March, 1947.

century there have been annual meetings of a collective bargaining nature between representatives of the United States Potters' Association and the National Brotherhood of Operative Potters. In the coal industry there is a single agreement for the anthracite mines, and in the bituminous fields there is what virtually amounts to a single agreement. Collective bargaining on a national scale is found on the railroads; the matter of wage changes for railroad workers is handled in this way. National collective bargaining is also carried on in the wallpaper industry and the sprinkler-fitting industry.

Group Bargaining by Employers. Group bargaining by local unions is very often accompanied by group bargaining among employers, but the two need not necessarily go hand in hand. A single employer may bargain with several local unions acting jointly, just as a single local may, conceivably, bargain with several employers acting together.

In a study of over 3,300 collective bargaining agreements, covering more than four million workers, made by the Bureau of Labor Statistics in 1950, the following results relative to the size of the employer bargaining unit were obtained: [18]

Bargaining Unit	*Per Cent of Agreements*	*Per Cent of Workers*
Single plant	68	28
Multiplant	12	39
Multi-employer	20	33

It will be seen that almost 70 per cent of the agreements related to single plants (or a number of plants of the same employer located in the same city), but that these agreements covered less than 30 per cent of the workers. Multiplant units (covering a number of plants of the same employer but located in different cities) were not nearly as numerous but covered almost 40 per cent of the workers. It might be added that in the manufacturing industry 81 per cent of the agreements were of the single plant type, as compared with 37 per cent in nonmanufacturing.

Multi-employer or association bargaining in this country, although fairly extensive, is still far less common than in Great Britain

[18] *Labor-Management Contract Provisions, 1949-50,* pp. 30-31. Bulletin No. 1022, Bureau of Labor Statistics, United States Department of Labor. Information is presented in this bulletin concerning specific industries, etc.

and Sweden. In both of these nations such bargaining, especially on a nationwide basis, is of predominant importance.[19]

The Question of Industry-Wide Bargaining

Because of the increasing importance of industry-wide bargaining it is desirable to give some attention to its actual and potential effects. The term "industry-wide" is misleading in that it suggests that such bargaining must be nationwide in scope. Some industry-wide bargaining is of a nationwide character, but most of it is either citywide or region-wide. All industry-wide bargaining involves a group of employers who bargain collectively with a union or a group of unions. These employers generally represent the whole or a substantial part of the industry in the competitive area in which it operates. This is true of the industry-wide bargaining in the pottery industry (where the competitive area is the nation) and in the building industry (where the competitive area is the community or city). Our generalization does not apply to the industry-wide bargaining in the men's and women's clothing industries, however. Here the separate employer groups constitute only a minor part of the competitive coverage, which is the whole country.

The term "industry-wide bargaining" must be used with flexibility. It does not lend itself to precise definition, since it can be, and has been, applied to various situations. It can safely be stated, however, that in all cases (except a pure monopoly) industry-wide bargaining involves more than one employer.

Effects and Implications of Industry-Wide Bargaining. Collective bargaining on an industry-wide basis is likely to be of a higher quality than bargaining conducted on a narrower basis. In general, the larger the bargaining unit, the better qualified the actual bargainers. Bargainers for a large unit will probably be more tactful, broader in their point of view, and more willing to compromise, since failure on their part to reach an understanding may tie up a whole industry. Industry-wide bargaining is not, however, an absolute preventive of industry-wide stoppages, as the history of the bituminous coal industry definitely proves. Moreover, when an

19 Two-thirds of the workers in Sweden under union agreements are covered by national contracts—on an industry-wide basis. See *Labor-Management Relations in Scandinavia,* p. 10. Bulletin No. 1038, Bureau of Labor Statistics, United States Department of Labor.

industry-wide stoppage occurs it is likely to have more serious consequences than a number of scattered stoppages involving, over time, the same direct man-hour loss. However, the total number of man-hours lost as a result of industry-wide strikes may be less than the number of man-hours that would be lost in the same circumstances under small-unit bargaining.[20]

Industry-wide bargaining may promote industrial stability, as it has done in the bituminous coal industry and the ladies' dress industry. It may eliminate cutthroat competition and place employers on a more even footing, at least in the matter of wages. The achievement of greater stability may be distinctly advantageous to the employers as a group and to the workers. The public too may benefit; whether or not it does depends on the level at which the production in the industry is stabilized. If stabilization involves restrictionism, the public is likely to be worse off than before. Industry-wide bargaining has within it the germs of this social evil. It is monopolistic in character and, as with monopolies in general, production may be held down rather than increased. As this type of bargaining increases, therefore, it may be necessary for the government to introduce controls of one sort or another to prevent production curtailment.

Although industry-wide bargaining may cause great hardship to employers in the marginal or submarginal categories, if it is extensively adopted it may benefit employers in the aggregate by reducing fluctuations in business activity. By diverting a larger portion of the income stream of society to the workers, it is likely (following Keynesian analysis) to contribute to greater stability.

Industry-wide bargaining may reduce wage differentials not only between plants but, if industrial unions are involved, within plants also. There is good reason for believing that wage differences in this country are (or at least have been) greater than they should be.[21] But here, too, there are problems involved. Too great a re-

[20] Max Danish has declared that "Industry-wide bargaining, while occasionally resulting in industry-wide strikes, has had over the long run a far more stabilizing effect on our economy than a fragmented, multi-hundred system of shop parleys and shop strikes could possibly have on production and price structures in industry." *The New York Times,* May 24, 1952. This contention may well be true of the clothing industry. Its validity is doubtful if applied to bituminous coal and to steel (with its pattern bargaining).

[21] See Edwin G. Nourse, *Price Making in a Democracy,* p. 474. Washington: The Brookings Institution, 1944.

duction of interplant, and also intraplant, differences may lead to injustice to some of the workers. Excessive reduction in the differences may also lead to an unwise allocation of labor power, which is bad from the public standpoint. Standardized wage rates may have an effect, in the matter of labor allocation, similar to protective tariffs.[22] Moreover, if wage differences between plants are evened out too much, some employers will be paying higher, and others lower, wages than they can afford. As the president of International Harvester has said, "pattern bargaining" (and the same applies to industry-wide bargaining) is "an attempt to make everyone wear the same pair of shoes, whether or not they fit his feet." [23] In industry-wide bargaining, therefore, there should be some provision made for a certain amount of wage flexibility.

Industry-wide bargaining, although it may promote both intra-industry and interindustry stability, may, if it involves extensive standardization of wage rates, retard general industrial growth. Prospective employers may hesitate to build plants in new locations if they have to meet the wages paid in well established plants elsewhere.[24] If this happens, society is definitely harmed, and so is labor, although specific union groups, of course, may be benefited. If unions that engage in industry-wide bargaining make wage concessions to new enterprises, this danger need not exist.

Collective bargaining on an industry-wide basis resembles to some extent the corporate set-up in Italy during the Mussolini regime. This similarity in structure suggests the possibility that such bargaining may lead to a fascist type of economic order. An outcome of this sort must not be viewed as wholly fantastic, although the democratic traditions and institutions in this country constitute very formidable obstacles in its way.

Industry-wide bargaining can easily lead to excessive centralization of power, however. As one writer has pointed out, such bargaining "will constitute a form of regimentation for both unions and employers which will in a large measure disregard local conditions

22 "If standard wage rates are desirable," argues Professor Henry C. Simons, referring to intercommunity wages, "then tariffs should everywhere be adjusted to offset all difference in labor cost between domestic and foreign producers." *The Journal of Political Economy,* March, 1944, p. 10.

23 *The New York Times,* May 29, 1953.

24 Professor Simons discusses the question of monopoly unionism in the article referred to in footnote 22, pp. 13-18.

and individual rights."[25] Both on the union side and on the employer side power passes from the bottom toward the top: from the local unions to the nationals and internationals and from the single employers to employer associations. Centralization of power and the regimentation that accompanies it are not necessarily bad, but, as with stability, they have their dangerous aspects. They promote uniformity and inflexibility, both of which may be harmful to production.

It should be obvious from the preceding discussion that industry-wide bargaining is neither all good, from the standpoint of the public, nor all bad. Its *net* social effect cannot easily be gauged. Whether, on balance, it is good or bad, the fact remains that such bargaining is spreading, and society should do what it can to remove or reduce the disadvantages and dangers that may accompany it. Geographical and numerical limitations on the size of bargaining units hardly seem a feasible remedy.[26]

[25] Almon E. Roth, in *The Atlantic Monthly,* August, 1943, p. 73. In giving testimony before the Senate Labor and Public Welfare Committee in February, 1947, however, Mr. Roth (acting as a spokesman for the shipping industry) opposed the banning of industry-wide bargaining, declaring that such a ban would result in "a diversification of wage rates and working conditions among ships operating from the same coast, plying between the same ports, tying at the same docks, and employing in turn the same men." *The New York Times,* February 12, 1947.

[26] For the text and a discussion of a bill (the "Lucas Bill," H.R. 2545) directed toward such an end, see *Labor-Management Relations,* Part I, pp. 23 ff., Hearings, Committee on Education and Labor, House of Representatives, 83rd Cong., 1st Sess., H. Res. 115 (February, 1953).

15

COLLECTIVE BARGAINING—AGREEMENT PROVISIONS

In the preceding chapter we gave some attention to the contents of collective bargaining agreements, and at other points in our discussion we have dealt with specific matters covered in these agreements. In the present chapter we shall describe and discuss in a comprehensive fashion contract provisions *as such,* rather than as parts of a larger topic. These provisions are of such a diverse and extensive nature, however, that we shall not be able to deal with all of them, not even with all of those relating to the topics selected for analysis. Moreover, though we shall discuss some of the provisions—particularly a few of a highly controversial nature—at considerable length, others we shall be compelled to note very briefly.[1]

Wages

We shall begin our analysis of contract provisions by examining some provisions relating to wages; then we shall pass on to some having to do with hours. A number of the provisions relating to these two matters are so closely related that it is a matter of arbitrary judgment into which of the two categories they are placed.

(1) Some collective bargaining agreements contain elaborate

[1] The Bureau of Labor Statistics of the United States Department of Labor carries on a more or less continuous study of contract provisions. In addition to separate articles and bulletins dealing with the subject (such as Bulletin No. 1091, *Labor-Management Contract Provisions, 1950-51,* composed of articles that appeared originally in the *Monthly Labor Review*), it has published a very comprehensive series of bulletins entitled *Collective Bargaining Provisions* (Nos. 908, 908-2, etc.). In writing the present chapter the author has found some of these bulletins very useful.

lists of wage rates for the various jobs they cover. Others, much simpler in character, set forth one or perhaps several minimum rates, sometimes making allowances for payments either above (for skilled workers) or below (for minors, handicapped workers, and the like) the minimum.

(2) Collective bargaining agreements may provide for a detailed evaluation of jobs, followed by a classification of workers with respect to these jobs. This process has met with mixed reactions from the unions. Accurate and satisfactory job evaluations are not easy to make, as we shall note in Chapter 25, and unions often view evaluations with suspicion. In some agreements the introduction and administration of the job evaluation program is placed in management's hands; others provide for joint action, with unions and management and sometimes an outside agency (generally an engineering company) participating.

(3) Where jobs are evaluated the workers receive a variety of wage rates. These rates usually bear a more or less close relationship to such factors as the skill and experience of the worker, the responsibility attached to the job, and the physical and mental effort the job requires. In some cases, however, factors of a different type have a bearing on the wage-rate differentials, factors such as sex, race, age, physical condition, and type of product. It should be noted at this point that in many collective bargaining agreements the principle of equal pay for equal work is definitely recognized. Sometimes, however, qualifications are introduced (see Chapter 24).

(4) Under most collective bargaining agreements the general wage level (not individual wage rates) decided upon during the negotiating period remains unchanged for the duration of the agreements. This rule has the great merit of administrative simplicity, but it may cause a certain amount of dissatisfaction on the part of one of the two parties involved. The workers may become dissatisfied if, for example, the employer's profits should rise rapidly or if the cost of living should go up. The employer, on the other hand, may become dissatisfied if the opposite conditions develop. To counteract such dissatisfaction, wage adjustment provisions are sometimes inserted in collective bargaining agreements.

Wage adjustment provisions are of two general types: permissive and automatic. Under permissive provisions the question of wages *may* be reopened and reconsidered. This may be done at stated intervals, as it is when agreements are of indefinite duration, or, as is more frequently the rule, at such times as changes in certain conditions—cost of living, price of the product, profits, wages paid by competitors, general business conditions—warrant. Automatic wage adjustment provisions are compulsory in the sense that if certain changes take place wages must also be changed. Occasionally an agreement will combine the automatic and permissive features. Automatic changes will be made within certain limits, then the wage question may be opened up for renegotiation.[2]

A type of automatic wage adjustment that came into great prominence during the period following the outbreak of war in Korea was the "escalator" wage plan. Under such a plan wages are tied to changes in the cost of living, as indicated by the Consumers' Price Index compiled by the United States Bureau of Labor Statistics. Between June, 1950 and March, 1951 the number of workers covered by agreements with escalator clauses in them increased from about half a million to an estimated minimum of 2,650,000.[3] Still further increases took place later in the Korean conflict, though a limit was placed (by the Economic Stabilization Administration) on upward wage increases under agreements signed after January 25, 1951. In most of the agreements adjustments in wages were made quarterly, and in the great bulk of the cases a change of either 1 point or 1.14 points in the price index brought about a change of 1 cent per hour in wages. A particularly notable agreement providing for an escalator clause was the five-year contract signed in 1950 by the United Automobile Workers' union and General Motors. Most agreements with escalator clauses have been signed by large companies.

(5) In addition to the types of wage provision to which we have just given attention, there are several other important types that we consider elsewhere in our discussion. Wage adjustment provisions in terms of an "annual improvement factor"—which we shall discuss in Chapter 23—have been embodied in a considerable number of agreements. The guaranteed annual wage, which is now found in a few agreements and will probably become more common in the

[2] *Union Agreement Provisions*, pp. 49-50. Bulletin No. 686, Bureau of Labor Statistics, United States Department of Labor.

[3] *Monthly Labor Review*, May, 1951, pp. 509, 510. The figure of 2,650,000 did not include a quarter of a million salaried employees who received adjustments in their pay similar to those made in the pay of production workers.

years ahead, is taken up in Chapter 6. Dismissal wage provisions, which relate to unemployment and have been included in a considerable number of agreements, are dealt with in Chapter 5. Welfare provisions, which we may include in our wage category, we discussed in Chapter 12.

There are still other types of wage provisions in collective bargaining agreements that we can only mention. These relate to such diverse matters as minimum call-pay, transfer rates, traveling expenses, pay periods, and pay "extras."

Hours

(1) The standard work period—the work day, the work week, or the work shift—is the most important hour provision in collective agreements. The standards specified however are not always the same as the actual work periods. The latter may be longer than the former, in which case many workers will receive overtime rates, but it may also be shorter.

Collective bargaining agreements may specifically provide for exceptions to the normal standards. During seasonal rushes, for example, longer hours without the necessity of paying overtime rates may be permitted, in line with the policy of the Fair Labor Standards Act. Legislation in some states reduces the length of the work period for women and minors below the normal standard for adult males, and these regulations are taken into account in the bargaining agreements. In numerous agreements the work period is definitely scheduled: that is, the time of its beginning and ending is stated.

(2) Union control of overtime takes various forms. In some collective agreements the control is rigid, overtime work being completely prohibited. Under some agreements overtime, though not prohibited, is nevertheless restricted by provisions limiting it to peak seasons (if the plant is working at capacity) or to cases of emergency. Another type of restriction is the prohibition of overtime as long as there is unemployment in the union. Overtime may also be ruled out if the plant is not working to capacity.

Unions usually insist on extra pay for overtime. The overtime rate may be anywhere from slightly more than the regular rate to three times its amount. Time-and-a-half, however, is the usual rate, but double time (and even more) is sometimes insisted upon, particularly when the overtime work is done on holidays or if it occurs at a very late hour.

(3) Unions have taken various steps to protect their members against the disadvantages that work on extra shifts may entail. In a few agreements extra shifts are entirely ruled out. Generally, however, prohibitions on the use of extra shifts are of a conditional nature. Such shifts may be ruled out, for example, until the shifts already in use are working so many hours a week. Sometimes extra shifts are prohibited unless they will last a certain period of time. Occasionally a union may permit a second shift but prohibit a third.

Since work on the second and third shifts is not as desirable as work on the first or regular shift, those who are engaged in such shifts are often given extra compensation, in the form of higher wages (the usual arrangement) or shorter hours. Although numerous agreements specify the same differential for both shifts, a great many require a higher differential for the third than the second. Among the most common differentials are 4 and 6 cents, and 5 and 10 cents.[4] The hour differentials may amount to as much as one and a half or two hours a day, with the differential on the second shift usually less than that on the third. Sometimes an agreement has both a wage and an hour differential.

Instead of embodying the policy of differentials in connection with second and third shifts, some agreements, applying chiefly to continuous-process plants that regularly use the shift system, provide for a rotation of shifts. Other provisions in bargaining agreements concerning shifts relate to the question of split shifts, which are often prohibited; to shift partners; and to the place of seniority in the choice of shifts.

(4) Since the policy of paid holidays has become widespread in industry, a great many bargaining agreements have provisions relating to such holidays. The number of paid holidays may be as low as one and as high as ten. Six is by far the most common. The most frequently specified paid holidays can easily be imagined, but included in the list may be such days as Bunker Hill Day, Jefferson Davis Day, and Mardi Gras Day.

Agreements may also mention a number of unpaid holidays—

[4] *Monthly Labor Review,* November, 1952, p. 497. See also *Collective Bargaining Provisions,* Bulletin No. 908-18, Bureau of Labor Statistics, United States Department of Labor.

under some agreements all holidays are unpaid. Work on both paid and unpaid holidays is generally remunerated at a special rate, with paid holidays usually commanding a higher rate than unpaid holidays.[5]

(5) In addition to the hour provisions just described there are still others found in collective bargaining agreements. These relate to such things as rest periods, lunch periods, travel time (this issue came into great prominence in 1946 in connection with the "portal-to-portal" controversy), and leaves of absence. In the same category we may place the provisions relating to work-sharing (see Chapter 4) and vacations with pay (see Chapter 27).

Hiring—Union Security

In their quest for power and security unions have long been interested in exercising control over the hiring policies of management. Their efforts to gain such control have met with strong opposition, but their persistence in the matter has yielded them no small amount of success. The degree of control the unions exercise over hiring is by no means uniform. It varies markedly from one company to another, depending largely on the relative strength of the employer and the union. A number of more or less specific and clearly differentiated degrees of control may be distinguished, however. These are commonly expressed in terms of different types of "shops."

The Closed Shop.[6] Under the closed shop union control over hiring reaches its highest point of development, for under this arrangement the employer is compelled to hire union members exclusively. Workers must belong to the union before they start to work. Where the closed shop exists the employer usually hires his men through the union.

Under the Labor Management Relations Act the closed shop is ruled out. In intrastate industries in states that do not have laws prohibiting the closed shop, of course, such shops can still exist. And, as a matter of fact, even under the LMRA the closed shop is still found, especially in the building and construction industry. Though

[5] See *Labor-Management Contract Provisions,* 1949-50, p. 35. Bulletin No. 1022, Bureau of Labor Statistics, United States Department of Labor.

[6] A long discussion of the origin of the closed shop end of the different definitions given to the term will be found in J. L. Toner, *The Closed Shop,* Chapter 2. Washington: The American Council on Public Affairs, 1942.

closed shops are technically illegal, it has been found feasible in some instances to continue them.

The Union Shop. Under the union shop the workers need not be union members before they start to work but (with possible exceptions to be noted shortly) must join the union within a certain period of time—the LMRA states "on or after the thirtieth day" the worker starts to work. Ordinarily the thirty-day rule is found in collective bargaining agreements but sometimes longer periods, such as sixty or ninety days, are specified; and occasionally, in intrastate employments, shorter periods are established.[7] The regular union shop, which is the most common, provides that all workers shall be in the union. But some union shops are of a modified character, the modifications taking a number of forms:

(a) Sometimes workers who are in the union at the time the collective bargaining agreement is signed, or who start to work thereafter, are covered by the union shop provision; but workers who are employed at the time the agreement is signed but who are not in the union are not compelled to join it.

(b) It may be provided that only a certain percentage (e.g. 90 per cent) of the new employees are compelled to join the union. Such agreements have been entered into by the American Newspaper Guild.

(c) By another modified arrangement workers who do not want to join the union are not compelled to do so, but they must pay union dues. This so-called "agency shop" is at least a partial answer to the free-ride argument widely used by unionists in their advocacy of the union shop. It allows workers who are opposed to joining unions either for religious reasons (and there are certain sects which take this position) or on other grounds simply to pay the union a service charge for acting as their agent.

(d) Sometimes there is inserted in the collective bargaining agreement a "harmony clause," in which the employer goes on record as looking upon union membership as desirable.

In a 1950-51 study made by the Bureau of Labor Statistics it was found that 1,612 agreements out of 2,651 provided for the union shop (as the Bureau has defined it). Of these 1,612 agreements 62 per cent called for the regular type of union shop. Fourteen per cent

[7] *Management Record,* March, 1951, p. 93. This issue contains an informative article on different types of "shops."

went farther and provided that union members be given preference in the matter of hiring, thus establishing a type of preferential shop. An additional 14 per cent made provision for a modified union shop; and the remaining 10 per cent for a closed shop.[8]

The Maintenance-of-Membership Shop. The maintenance-of-membership shop came into prominence during World War II. Under this type of shop a worker need not belong to the union to obtain a job (as under the closed shop), nor need he join the union to hold his job (as under the regular union shop). But if he is a member of the union on the date the collective bargaining agreement becomes effective, or should he join the union after that date, then he must remain in the union or he will lose his job.

Agreements providing for a maintenance-of-membership shop include in the majority of cases an "escape clause," which specifies the period during which present workers may make up their minds concerning union membership. During World War II the National War Labor Board prescribed 15 days, and this period is still the most common. In the 1950-51 study already referred to, 13 per cent of the agreements included a maintenance-of-membership provision. This percentage represents a marked decline from the level attained in the war period.

The Preferential Shop. In some collective bargaining agreements provision is made for the preferential shop. Under this type of shop union members are given prior consideration over nonunionists. In the matter of hiring (and the preference may relate to other matters as well) the employer, although not bound to take on only union workers, gives preference to them. The preferential shop can exist without the simultaneous existence of the union shop, but not many such arrangements are actually found. Under the LMRA the preferential shop as such is banned, but indirectly (through such devices as preference to previous employees) it may be established.

The Exclusive Bargaining Shop Only. Still further down the scale is the exclusive bargaining shop. Under this arrangement the union possesses none of the specific rights indicated in the previous paragraphs, but it does possess the right to represent all the workers,

[8] *Monthly Labor Review,* November, 1951, p. 553. The closed shop agreements did not state specifically that workers must belong to the union before starting to work, but other stipulations—e.g., training qualifications—made union membership mandatory for most of the workers.

including the nonunionists, in the plant or department or whatever the bargaining unit may be.

In the 1950-51 study to which we have been referring 26 per cent of the collective bargaining agreements provided for recognition, and sole bargaining, only. Industries in which this type of agreement was quite common were tobacco, petroleum products, electrical machinery, and communications.

Other Variations in Union Status. All the entries in our classification so far involve union recognition and the right of the union to bargain for all the workers. A few other arrangements that may be added to the list do not involve these conditions. Occasionally a union in a minority position is granted the power by the employer to bargain for its own members. This degree of recognition is likely to lead to additional union progress and the achievement of one of the previously mentioned types of status.

The next lowest type of status is for the union to have its members in a minority and in no way recognized in a plant. Obviously the union hopes to increase its membership to the point where it will gain recognition. Finally there is the situation where the union has no members. In this case it has no status whatever.

Arguments for and against the Closed Shop. One of the most controversial topics in the whole field of labor is the closed shop. The term "closed shop" is not always carefully defined: sometimes the expression is used in the narrow sense noted earlier in the chapter (the worker must belong to the union before he *starts* to work); but very often it is given a broader meaning to include the union shop, and possibly the maintenance-of-membership shop as well. In the discussion that follows verbal precision will be sacrificed to popular usage: we shall use the term to include the union shop. It might be added that the arguments for and against the closed shop, defined in its narrow sense, are essentially the same as the arguments for and against the union shop.

(a) In a great many cases unions favor the closed shop because they are opposed to giving free rides to nonunionists. When a union wins concessions from an employer, these concessions are usually granted not only to members of the union but to nonmembers as well. This being so it is only fair, the unions argue, that the nonmembers should join the union and help to support the organization that has been responsible for the benefits they have received. As

William Green once stated "The worker who spurns the union is like the man in a community who gets all the benefits of free schools, free police and free fire protection but who refuses to pay taxes, preferring that others shoulder the cost of his protection and welfare." [9] The free ride argument is a strong one, probably the strongest that can be advanced in support of the closed shop. Since it is closely tied up with the "democracy" argument on the other side of the case, we shall defer further discussion of it until a little later.

(b) It is sometimes argued that the closed shop is necessary from the standpoint of union security. The presence of nonunionists in the department or plant in which the union is the official bargaining agency may result in the weakening of the union, if not its collapse. Moreover, because of the constant turnover of labor the union is forced to carry on a more or less constant organizing drive, something that even the employers may not like.[10]

It cannot be denied that unions have had good reason for giving serious thought to the matter of security. Antiunionism has been widespread and the possibility of the employer's undermining the position of the union has been more than a theoretical one. Since the middle 1930's, however, the possibility of employer tampering has been greatly reduced, and the union security argument has lost much of its force.

Another aspect of the union security question relates to interunion competition: the closed shop may protect one labor organization from the competition of another. Of course, such protection may not always be a good thing, particularly if the competing union is clearly more "desirable" than the union that is already entrenched.

In addition to giving a union security through the protection it affords against the competition of nonunionists and of other unions, the closed shop also contributes to union security by increasing the income and hence the financial power of the union.

(c) When a union embraces only a portion of the working force, there is a tendency for the number of grievances to increase excessively. The union officers, or grievance-committee members, as a means of inducing workers to join the union may spend a great deal

[9] *The New York Times Magazine,* August 2, 1942, p. 6. A nice problem for discussion is whether or not union dues *are* comparable to taxes.

[10] *The International Teamster,* September, 1951, p. 12.

of time trying to "sell" the grievance procedure; and they may also exhibit a willingness to take up any and all sorts of grievances. If all the workers must belong to the union, the union officers can refuse to deal with grievances that are imaginary in nature or without solid substance.

(d) Closed shop arrangements, it is sometimes contended, contribute to greater responsibility on the part of the working force. In an open shop, the union cannot very well exercise control over those workers who have remained outside the fold; if they are in the union, the union can keep them in line. This argument has merit. Although the increased authority and disciplinary power of the unions may sometimes be abused, the chances are they will not be. The responsibility record of unions having the closed shop (or possessing conditions that amount to the closed shop) has generally been of a high order.[11]

(e) In a discussion of the closed shop Ernest T. Weir has argued that the closed shop leads to productive inefficiency.[12] This view is in striking contrast to that commonly held by unionists, who argue that in a closed shop the leaders of the union will be in a better frame of mind and will be more willing to cooperate with management in promoting production. They will be able to devote more of their time to that purpose, and less time to thinking about the security and preservation of the union. The idea that union security may contribute to greater production underlay the many World War II decisions in which the National War Labor Board prescribed the maintenance-of-membership shop.

(f) Opinion is sharply divided on the relationship between the closed shop and democracy. The element of force associated with the closed shop (including the union shop, and to some extent the maintenance-of-membership shop as well) is sometimes regarded as being extremely undemocratic in nature. "The closed shop is a deeply illiberal device," ex-Senator Ball has stated. "It turns over to an outside agency, the union, very often dominated by a militant minority or even a single official, absolute control over the individ-

[11] Toner, *op. cit.*, pp. 157-158. The president of a company who says he would not want anything except a union shop in his plant points to the self-imposed discipline it leads to, and hence to a minimization of supervisory costs. See *Advanced Management*, March, 1951, p. 10.

[12] *The New York Times Magazine*, August 2, 1942, p. 23.

ual's right and opportunity to work and earn a living in his chosen occupation." [13] Others, however, believe that such a shop is not incompatible with democracy; that, in fact, it is essential to a wide and efficient application of the democratic principle. Thus Alfred M. Bingham, pointing out the equivalence between citizenship and union membership under the union shop, feels that without union membership industrial democracy is impossible, and that to require every worker to join the union and pay his dues is no impairment of his freedom.[14]

The issue here is indeed a highly controversial one, with notable authorities found on each of the two sides. Possibly a way of giving at least some recognition to the democracy argument, and at the same time taking into account the force of the free ride argument, is to have an agency shop. As we pointed out before, under such a shop workers are not compelled to join the union, but they must support it with dues in return for its support of them.

(g) In their brief presented to a panel of the National War Labor Board in the Little Steel Companies case, the United Steel Workers argued that without the union shop there would be ill feeling and disharmony in the working force because of the fact that the nonunionists would receive benefits without paying for them. The Republic Steel Company, in its brief, maintained the very opposite: that ill feeling would follow if the nonunionists were compelled to join the union.

Obviously, discord may arise in either of these situations. One important factor determining the extent of the discord in each case would be the relative number of unionists and nonunionists involved. Another is the degree to which the union is a responsible organization. If the bulk of the workers are already in the union when a union shop agreement is signed and if the union is well aware of its duties as well as its rights, there will probably be less ill feeling and disharmony with a union shop than without it. If conditions of a contrary nature prevail, the scales may be tipped the other way.

From the preceding arguments it is obvious that the closed shop issue is a very debatable one, and one on which it is not easy to reach

[13] *The New York Times,* February 21, 1947.

[14] *The Techniques of Democracy,* pp. 237-238. New York: Duell, Sloan and Pearce, 1942. Mr. Bingham emphasizes that a necessary concomitant of the enforced union shop is enforced constitutional democracy in the union.

a definite conclusion. The writer would suggest only that before one forms an opinion on the matter he should take into account all the pertinent considerations.

The Check-off

The term "check-off" refers to deductions made by an employer from the pay due to the worker. Used in a broad sense the expression covers all such deductions regardless of their nature: union dues, payments toward government bonds, social security payments, bills at company stores. In the narrow sense, which is most frequently used in labor parlance, the expression ordinarily relates only to deductions destined for the union. Generally these deductions cover regular union dues, but they may also cover initiation fees, special assessments, and fines.

In the study of 2,651 collective bargaining agreements made by the Bureau of Labor Statistics in 1950-51, the following "percent distribution of agreements," relative to the use of the check-off, was found: dues only, 30 per cent; dues and initiation fees, 18 per cent; dues and assessments, 3 per cent; dues, initiation fees, and assessments, 16 per cent; no provision, 33 per cent. It is interesting to note that check-off provisions are more frequent in agreements that are without union security clauses than in agreements with such clauses.

Types of Check-off. Check-offs may be either voluntary or compulsory (automatic). In voluntary check-offs the consent of the individual worker is required before any deduction may be made from his pay; in the compulsory or automatic check-off deductions are made from the pay of all union workers with or without individual authorization. Of course the union must win the check-off privilege from the employer.

Although the compulsory check-off has been common in this country in times past, at the present time it is of little significance. It is banned by the Labor Management Relations Act, which states that no "membership dues" (including, according to the Department of Justice, initiation fees and special assessments) may be deducted from a worker's pay by the employer unless the worker has given his consent in writing. The consent originally applied for a year, or until the end of the collective bargaining agreement if its expiration date were less than a year. Since 1948, however, the check-off authorization may be renewed automatically each year if the employee does not revoke it.

Arguments for and against the Check-Off. From a broad point of view the check-off may be looked upon as a means of contributing to the general welfare of the community. That was the point of view adopted by the National War Labor Board during World War II in numerous cases in which it prescribed adoption of the principle. During a time when a rapid increase in industrial output is of paramount importance, when industrial friction must be reduced as much as possible, when manpower should be utilized to the best advantage, the use of the check-off may very well be of genuine social value. In its brief submitted to the War Labor Board in the Little Steel Case, the Steel Workers' union pointed out that it devoted the equivalent of 242,000 man-days a year to the task of collecting dues. In a time of great national emergency the expenditure of so much time for such a simple task represents an unwise use of manpower.

In their attitude toward the check-off unions and employers do not think so much in terms of the general welfare as in terms of their own welfare. Thus many unions want the check-off because it will save them time and money, particularly if the union is a young one in which the members have not yet formed the dues-paying habit. Employers, on the other hand, are often opposed to the check-off because they feel that they should not act as a collection agency for the union. They may also be against the policy because of the extra expense it means to them (ordinarily the unions do not reimburse the employer for any costs involved in making pay deductions).

Some employers, however, favor the check-off. They believe that it is better from their standpoint to have union dues collected in this way than by union officers in the plant. They may also believe that the granting of the check-off may put the union in a more cooperative mood. Whether the employer gains or loses through the check-off depends upon the spirit that animates his behavior and that of the union.

Within the union itself there may be opposition to the principle, especially from workers who have been forced into the union through union shop arrangements or as a result of informal pressure. But even workers who have joined the union voluntarily may oppose the check-off because of its arbitrary nature. Leaders may be against it because it lessens their contacts with the rank and file, and possibly because it diminishes their chances of a steady job with the union.

Layoffs and Discharges

Layoffs. In their quest for greater job security unionists have become interested in exercising control not only over management's right to hire but also over its right to lay off. Collective bargaining agreements contain various provisions relating to layoffs.[15]

A very common provision is for work-sharing in times of business curtailment. This policy may be adhered to rigidly and completely or it may be applied in a limited manner. Another common provision has to do with the application of the seniority principle. This principle may be used after the length of the work week has been reduced to a specified level under the operation of the equal-division-of-work policy, or it may be applied right from the beginning of the curtailment. The seniority principle is usually applied to reemployment as well as to layoff.

In numerous cases the union and the employer agree that the latter is to give advance notice of layoffs (to the employees or the union, or to both of them), or enter into consultation with the union on the matter. It should be noted, too, that sometimes agreements provide that workers must give advance notice when they quit their jobs. When the labor force is temporarily curtailed, it is sometimes provided that nonunionists and probationary employees be laid off first.

Two or three new types of layoff control have received an increasing amount of attention in recent years. Guaranteed employment (the annual wage) is one of these; it is now found in a few collective bargaining agreements and will probably be found in still more in the years to come. The policy of dismissal pay, or severance compensation, has come into prominence and has been embodied in agreements in a number of industries. In only a few of these, however, has it been applied on any considerable scale.

[15] The topic of layoffs is dealt with at length in Sumner H. Slichter, *Union Policies and Industrial Management,* Chapters 4 and 5. Washington: The Brookings Institution, 1941. The topic is also covered in *Collective Bargaining Provisions,* Bulletin No. 908-7, Bureau of Labor Statistics, United States Department of Labor.

Discharges. Arbitrary discharging is something the unions are keenly desirous of preventing. Since the passing of the Wagner Act and a few state acts of a similar nature, most union members have been protected against discharge for union activity. But there exists a wide range of other reasons or excuses for discharge, and it is over these that the unions want to exercise control.

Unions generally recognize the justification of discharging for cause, but they are opposed to taking the employer's word that a legitimate cause exists. In numerous agreements, therefore, there are provisions relating to the matter of discharge.[16] Discharge cases constitute grievances, but they are often treated in a different way from other types of grievances. Time limits are set up for handling discharge cases more commonly than for handling ordinary grievances; and special lists are sometimes drawn up covering legitimate reasons for discharge. Sometimes workers who need disciplining instead of being discharged are first warned, and some times nondischarge penalties (such as suspension) are used in discipline cases.

Seniority

One of the most notable developments in union-management relations during recent years has been the rapid growth in the application of the seniority principle, whereby certain aspects of the worker's status in his place of employment are determined by length of service.[17] Before the middle of the 1930's little was heard of seniority outside of two or three industries, the most important of which was the railroad industry. Today a substantial percentage of unorganized as well as organized workers in American industry are keenly interested in the principle, and in a great many collective bargaining agreements one finds seniority provisions.

Application of Seniority. Before the seniority principle can be applied a number of very specific questions must first be settled. To begin with there is the method of computation. How is length of service to be reckoned? The general rule is to figure it from the time that employment begins. A probationary period is usually estab-

[16] See *Collective Bargaining Provisions,* Bulletin No. 908-5, Bureau of Labor Statistics, United States Department of Labor.

[17] Detailed treatments of seniority will be found in Slichter, *op. cit.,* Chapters 4 and 5; and in *Collective Bargaining Provisions,* Bulletin No. 908-11, Bureau of Labor Statistics, United States Department of Labor.

lished, however, during which the worker is on trial. If his services are found to be satisfactory he becomes an accepted member of the "family," and his seniority standing is calculated from the beginning of his employment.

Closely allied to the matter of computation of seniority is that of retention. Under what conditions can seniority be lost? There are a number of such conditions, some of which we shall note. Generally if a worker quits his job or is fired, he loses his seniority. The same rule applies if he stays away from work without receiving permission, or if he is laid off for a protracted period of time. Various arrangements are found in collective bargaining agreements with respect to the length of the period of layoff after which seniority is lost. Some agreements have absolute limits; others adjust the limits to the length of time the worker has been employed. Some do not have any limits at all—the employee retains his seniority indefinitely, though he may have to report periodically to the company that he wants to retain his seniority and be re-employed.

If a worker obtains leave of absence because of union activities, or because of sickness, or because he is in the armed forces, or for certain other reasons, it is commonly specified in union agreements that his seniority rights will be retained. Under provisions of this sort, as under those relating to layoffs, two important matters must be settled: the length of absence, under each of the cases, during which seniority rights will be retained; and whether or not the period of absence should be counted in when seniority standing is calculated.

Scope and Types of Seniority. Another problem that has to be settled before seniority can be applied relates to the size of the area to be used in reckoning seniority. Should it be the occupation, the department, the division, the plant, or the company? This is a debatable issue.

If the enterprise is small, plant-wide seniority is usually preferable. (Our discussion will largely center around plant seniority versus department seniority.) When the scale of operations is limited, the work is not likely to be highly specialized, and workers can frequently be shifted from job to job without any great difficulty. If, however, the enterprise is large, the workers cannot be as easily transferred from one type of work to another, and department seniority (or occupational or job seniority) is likely to prevail.

Plant seniority is distinctly advantageous to senior employees. It gives these workers a large area over which they may exert their rights; at the same time, however, it limits the area over which the younger workers may exert theirs. A situation of this sort may be disadvantageous both to the employer and to the majority of his employees: to the former it may involve heavy labor turnover costs; to the latter it may mean a high degree of uncertainty. However, since plant seniority tends to increase the versatility and flexibility of the working force, it is possible that the employer may be better able to stabilize employment in his plant.[18]

If the unit for calculating seniority is the department, difficulties can also arise. Depending upon which departments are slack and which departments are busy, a man with 20 years of employment to his credit could be laid off at the same time that a man with only two years to his credit would be kept on. Moreover, unless provision is made for the transference of seniority rights from one department to another, interdepartmental shifting will be discouraged by departmental seniority. It should be pointed out, however, that enforced departmental shifting, often a feature of the plant-wide seniority basis, may involve retraining, which in turn may entail a considerable outlay for the employer.

Plant-wide seniority has its advantages and disadvantages. So has department-wide seniority. As a result, attempts have been made to combine the two varieties in such a way as to retain the advantages and eliminate the disadvantages of each. To this end plant-wide seniority is sometimes limited in its application to layoffs, whereas promotions and transfers are carried out on the basis of department seniority. Sometimes a distinction is made between permanent reductions of the labor force and temporary layoffs, with plant or company seniority used in the former and department seniority in the latter.

There are two sorts of seniority: straight (or strict) seniority and modified (or contingent) seniority. Straight seniority involves the use of length of service alone as the criterion of policy. Modified seniority takes into account factors such as ability, experience, age, and need.

[18] F. H. Harbison, *Seniority Policies and Procedures as Developed Through Collective Bargaining*, p. 25. Industrial Relations Section, Princeton University, 1941.

Matters to Which Seniority Is Applicable. The chief matter to which the seniority principle applies is layoffs. Sometimes the principle is adhered to completely in determining layoffs; sometimes certain exceptions are made. Although from an administrative standpoint the strict application of seniority has great merit, it may entail laying off men who are exceptionally valuable to the employer and whom he would very much like to retain. Because of this possibility numerous collective bargaining agreements provide that the employer has the right to keep on certain exceptional or indispensable workers who, if the seniority principle were strictly applied, would have to be laid off. A right of a similar nature is sometimes granted to the union. Important men in the union (grievance committee members and shop stewards) may be given priority in the seniority classification.

The application of the seniority principle to layoffs is modified in still further ways. The employer may be permitted to use criteria other than length of service in determining the order in which men are to be let out. In numerous union agreements seniority applies only after adequate weight is given to ability. Occasionally such factors as the employee's place of residence, his citizenship standing, and the size of his family are taken into account. The emphasis placed on these factors varies greatly, however, from one agreement to another. As we have already noted, when severe curtailment of the work force is necessary layoffs may be regulated by a combination of the share-the-work policy and the seniority principle.

In addition to its application to layoffs, and to rehiring, seniority is sometimes applied to promotions. Because employers usually desire to promote the best qualified men, regardless of the length of their service, they are generally opposed to the basis of straight or strict seniority. In most union agreements, therefore, skill and ability are mentioned as important qualifications for promotions; only rarely does straight seniority apply.[19] Sometimes seniority is used when intershift or interdepartment transfers are made. Other matters that may be dealt with on the seniority basis include overtime work, piecework jobs, and vacation dates.

Seniority and Efficiency. The most important aspect of seniority is its relationship to productive efficiency. Does seniority help or

[19] *Monthly Labor Review,* August, 1951, p. 154.

hinder such efficiency? This is a question like the one Sir Roger de Coverly had in mind: there is much to be said on both sides. Let us look at some of the aspects of the question.

(a) One of the commonest arguments in favor of seniority is that it helps to do away with favoritism and discrimination in industry. It appears that many bosses, particularly those in the lower strata, indulge in discriminatory practices. Seniority helps to correct this condition: the workers know definitely where they stand, and as a consequence are in a better frame of mind. This psychological benefit has a favorable influence on production.

(b) On the other hand, it can be argued that although favoritism is undesirable (since it often penalizes the more efficient man), seniority is no solution to the problem (since it penalizes the good worker also, and probably more so). The man with the longest service record is not necessarily the most productive worker, and giving the breaks to him may result in an uneconomic utilization of labor. This argument undoubtedly points to one of the greatest weaknesses of the seniority principle. This weakness is greatest with straight seniority. Possible exceptions would be in occupations in which there is a close tie-up between length of experience and capability and in cases in which the seniority rule may lead to a more versatile and flexible working force.

(c) Seniority may result in a decrease in labor turnover, and such a decrease is often beneficial to production. First, it may make employers more careful in their hiring policies, since their freedom in such matters as layoffs and promotions is curbed. Second, seniority reduces the desire of employees to leave of their own volition. Rather than sacrifice their accumulated seniority many of them will stay in their present jobs. Thus the employer is saved the expense involved in training new help and is not exposed to other turnover costs.

(d) There is a distinct possibility, however, that seniority may lead to an excessive decline in labor turnover. A considerable amount of turnover, of labor mobility, is desirable; it is a condition essential to the proper allocation of labor. When seniority freezes workers to their present jobs and, in the case of strict departmental seniority, to their present departments, it tends to force the mobility of labor down from the optimum point. Labor should be neither excessively mobile nor inadequately mobile. Seniority may lead to a situation of inadequate mobility.[20]

(e) If seniority is on a plant-wide basis it may, when layoffs are necessary, lead to a great deal of shifting around within the plant. To cite what is probably an extreme example, in one company with a plant-wide seniority plan 1,323 job transfers were involved in laying off 255 workers.[21] A certain amount of "internal" labor mobility is desirable in a plant, just as it is desirable to have a certain amount of "external" mobility, but there should not be too much of either.

(f) Seniority, by keeping a worker at his job longer than he might otherwise have stayed at that job, extends the duration of his working life. Although the employer may not be particularly interested in this result, society as a whole benefits. To society the important consideration, as Professor Slichter has stated, is not what the worker's output is per hour or per day, but what it is per lifetime.

The question of seniority and efficiency is extremely important and extremely complex. The specific lines of influence between the seniority policy and industrial output are numerous and intertwined, partly positive and partly negative, and of varying character and weight, depending on the kind of seniority adopted and the type of work involved. These considerations suggest the desirability of taking up each case or situation by itself, although they do not debar one from reaching conclusions, or possessing hunches, on the aggregate effect of seniority throughout the whole field of industry.[22]

[20] In a study made in 1942 by the U.S. Employment Service the loss of seniority rights was the most frequent reason (given by 41 per cent of those interviewed) for refusal to shift to new jobs. *Monthly Labor Review*, August, 1951, p. 152.

[21] *Business Week*, April 9, 1949, p. 108.

[22] An extensive treatment of the subject matter of the present chapter and of other topics in collective bargaining will be found in Harold W. Davey, *Contemporary Collective Bargaining*. New York: Prentice-Hall, Inc., 1951.

16

COLLECTIVE BARGAINING—GOVERNMENTAL PROTECTION AND REGULATION

Under a system of anarchism there would be no labor laws; labor relations, and all other types of human relations, would be on a voluntary basis. In our complex and highly integrated society such a condition is impossible to imagine. The whole course of events is in the opposite direction, the direction of more and more state interference. The state, or government, has been applying its authority over larger and larger areas of human affairs, particularly of labor affairs. The body of labor law is vast, as well as intricate and controversial. In later chapters we shall give attention to laws relating to wages, hours, industrial disputes, and social security. In the present chapter we shall concern ourselves primarily with laws that have a bearing on collective bargaining, particularly on its principles and processes.

Historical Background

Laws relating to collective bargaining are not entirely new in this country, although the most important ones have been passed during the last few decades. One of the most significant collective bargaining laws, the Railway Labor Act, which was passed in 1926 and has been amended a number of times since then, has a history of antecedent legislation that extends back to the 1880's. The Sherman Anti-Trust Act, with its controversial applicability to labor, goes back to 1890. And the Clayton Act, which was supposed to have removed labor from the control of the Sherman Act, was passed in 1914.

It was in the 1930's, however, that collective bargaining (or labor relations) legislation really made progress. In 1932 the Federal Anti-Injunction Act, commonly known as the Norris-LaGuardia Act and a landmark in the new era of collective bargaining, was passed. There followed the National Industrial Recovery Act of 1933, with its section 7(a) under which the right of workers to engage in collective bargaining was given clear legal recognition, recognition that was not revoked when the NIRA was declared unconstitutional in 1935. Not only was this right reasserted but the process of collective bargaining itself received governmental benediction in the National Labor Relations Act, popularly called the Wagner Act, which was passed in 1935. Under the Wagner Act the unions grew rapidly and the principle of collective bargaining became widely established.

The NLRA provided machinery and policies for determining which union, if any, was to be the official bargaining agent of the workers; and it listed five unfair labor practices in which employers must not engage. It did not mention as unfair any labor practices engaged in by unions and employees.

In 1947 the NLRA was amended with the passage of the Labor Management Relations Act (Taft-Hartley Act), which included nearly all of the NLRA and a great deal more besides.

Some of the states have also passed labor relations acts, beginning back in the 1930's. We shall say a little about these state laws later on in our discussion, but now we shall turn to a detailed analysis of the LMRA.

The National Labor Relations Board

The National Labor Relations Act was administered by a nonpartisan board of three members known as the National Labor Relations Board. Under the LMRA the size of this board is increased from three members to five, although the board may delegate any or all of its powers to three or four of its members. In addition, the LMRA provides for a general counsel of the board. The general counsel has extensive powers. He has general supervisory control over all the board's attorneys and over the regional officers and employees. Moreover, he has final authority in the investigation of unfair labor practices, the issuance of complaints in connection therewith, and the prosecution of these complaints. The board itself is no longer entrusted with the power of prosecuting the unfair labor practices that come before it, as it was under the Wagner Act. It has the task, however, of reaching and handing down the decisions in these cases.

The work of the NLRB largely centers around the handling of the many representation cases and unfair labor practice cases that come before it. Most of this work, however, is done not by the five-man group in Washington but by the regional offices of the board. The terms "Board" and "NLRB" often refer to these offices as well as to the central board.[1]

Union Representation and the LMRA

One of the most important developments in the history of collective bargaining in this country was the inclusion in the Wagner Act of a plan for determining (in cases that were duly submitted to the NLRB) what union, if any, should be the official bargaining agent of the workers. This particular intrusion of the government into the field of industrial relations was highly desirable. That it is still highly desirable is given recognition in the LMRA and the Railway Labor Act.

Limiting our analysis to the LMRA let us see how the question of representation is handled. To begin with the NLRB, which is charged with the responsibility of dealing with the matter of representation, acts not on its own volition but only after it has been petitioned. The petition for board action in the matter may be filed by "an employee or group of employees or any individual or labor organization acting in their behalf"; or the petition may be filed by an employer if he has been presented with a claim for recogni-

[1] In the 1953 Congressional hearings on proposed changes in the LMRA it was suggested that the Board be increased to seven or nine members. An enlargement of the Board would speed up its work, though as Chairman Herzog pointed out a still larger staff would be necessary really to expedite the processing of the cases. See *Labor Management Relations,* Part I, p. 214. Hearings, Committee on Education and Labor, House of Representatives, 83rd Cong., 1st Sess., H. Res. 115. It should be pointed out that the five-man NLRB and its staff have been cutting down appreciably the average time required to process cases.

tion as official bargaining agent. If the board believes "that a question of representation affecting commerce" exists, it holds a hearing. If the hearing reveals that a question of representation is present —a question, that is, of certification or decertification of a union as the official bargaining agent—the board is directed by the LMRA to hold a secret-ballot election.

Before holding an election on the basis of a petition from employees or their representatives, the board tries to make sure that there is adequate interest in such a step. The board's policy is to require that the petition be supported by no less than 30 per cent of the workers in the bargaining unit. In some cases the board (regional directors) dismisses the petition, and very often the parties that submit petitions withdraw them before the board makes its decision.

The NLRB may certify a union as official bargaining agent only on the basis of a secret-ballot election, and the union thus certified becomes the exclusive representative of all the workers in the bargaining unit, both union and nonunion. Nonunion workers, however, may present grievances directly to the employer, if (a) the adjustment of these grievances is in harmony with the provisions of the collective bargaining agreement, and (b) the union is given a chance to be represented at the adjustment proceedings.

The question of frequency of elections is an important one. The LMRA provides that "No election shall be directed in any bargaining unit within which, in the preceding twelve-month period, a valid election shall have been held." The frequency problem presents complications when, for example, friction leads to splinter groups or to a shift by a local to another parent union.

To decide how long a current collective bargaining contract can act as a bar to a new election the NLRB has used the "reasonable period" criterion. Until the latter 1940's a reasonable period was generally considered to be a year, except in unusual circumstances or when agreements in the industry were customarily of longer duration. During World War II the board shifted to the two-year rule, recognizing exceptions. Early in 1953 the board decreed that elections could be barred in certain circumstances for as long as five years.

On the ballot there is always a "no union" entry in addition to the one or more unions. If there are three or more choices on the ballot and none receives a majority of the votes cast, the law provides for a run-off election between the two top choices in the first election.

In the matter of representation elections a number of questions must be settled. First, who is eligible to vote? The LMRA states that "Employees on strike who are not entitled to reinstatement shall not be eligible to vote." Workers who are on strike because of unfair labor practices of the employer could not thus be excluded from voting. However, workers who have struck in order to win higher wages or shorter hours or better conditions, and who have been replaced—i.e., who have lost their status as employees—do not have the right to vote in representation elections.

This rule has aroused widespread criticism from organized labor. Philip Murray called it "one of the most outrageous provisions" of the Taft-Hartley Act, pointing out that under the Wagner Act both "strikers and scabs" could vote. The LMRA provision, Mr. Murray felt, makes it possible for the employer "to write his own ticket of sub-standard terms of employment and to discredit the union." [2] The unions fear that the provision will encourage employers to foment strikes and in this way get rid of the unions. No such outbreak of union-busting has become apparent, however, possibly because of the existence of high employment.

Except for the requirement already noted the LMRA leaves the matter of eligibility in the hands of the NLRB, and the board has in general limited the voting privilege to workers who have been on the payroll in the representation unit "during the payroll period immediately preceding the date of issuance of the direction of the election."

Another question that must be settled when the issue arises, and it is often an extremely difficult question, is the size of the bargaining unit. The NLRB has the task of making the decision in such instances, and in reaching its conclusion it takes into account, the various criteria noted in Chapter 14.

The law states that professional employees are not to be included in a bargaining unit with nonprofessional employees unless the majority of the former vote in favor of such an arrangement. The law also provides that plant guards must not be included in a

[2] *Proceedings*, CIO Convention, 1951, pp. 127-128.

collective unit with other employees. If plant guards want to engage in bargaining, and be certified by the NLRB as bargaining agent, they must have a unit, and a union, of their own. Since the law does not cover supervisory employees, they cannot have a certified bargaining unit under it. The same is true of "confidential employees" and "managerial personnel."

A controversial issue associated with the question of representation is the matter of free speech, especially as it relates to the employer. The LMRA (in contrast to the Wagner Act in its earlier years) does not consider an expression of opinion by the employer as an unfair labor practice unless it contains a "threat of reprisal or force or promise of benefit." Employers may hand out pamphlets criticizing unions; they may urge that their employees remain nonunionists; they may deny claims made by unions. They may *not* express fears that there will be strikes and unemployment if the union wins representation rights; that any employee holding communication with the union organizer will be discharged; that the business might close up because of the union.[3]

Table 12 shows the results of the representation elections conducted by the NLRB during the year ending June 30, 1952. It will be observed that in over 1,800 of the elections the workers voted for "no union," and that in over 450 they voted for an unaffiliated organization.[4]

[3] For other examples and for a general discussion of the question of free speech see the annual Prentice-Hall *Labor Course* (1953, pp. 4055-4059). A widely discussed case that had a bearing on the free-speech policy related to an employer (operating a store) who had a "no-solicitation rule" governing union organization and who made an antiunion speech to his employees on company time and property, two days before a representation election. The union requested a similar right but the employer refused. This was looked upon by the NLRB as an unfair labor practice and the election was set aside. (Bonwit-Teller, Inc., 96 NLRB 608.) The stand of the NLRB was upheld by a lower court and also (virtually) by the Supreme Court, when it refused to review the case. In December, 1953, however, the NLRB reversed the position it had taken in the Bonwit-Teller case. It denied the right of unions to the "reply privilege"—on company time and property. At the same time it took away the right of employers to make speeches to their employees, on company time, during the 24 hours preceding a representation election (Livingston Shirt case and Peerless Plywood case). *The New York Times*, December 22, 1953.

[4] In connection with the election figures it should be pointed out that AFL affiliates participate in more contests than do CIO unions. The elections engaged in by the latter are ordinarily larger in size, however. The figures for the different entries in Table 12 vary somewhat from year to year.

Table 12
Results of Representation Elections Conducted by the NLRB, Year Ending June 30, 1952 *

Total number of elections	6,765
Elections won by:	
AFL affiliates	3,075
CIO affiliates	1,394
Nonaffiliated organizations	464
No union	1,832

* *Seventeenth Annual Report of the National Labor Relations Board*, 1952, p. 289.

Employer Unfair Labor Practices

Before the passing of the Wagner Act in 1935 there were numerous policies, some of a decidedly shady nature, that employers could adopt to undermine the influence of unions. The Wagner Act banned five such practices. This part of the act was a great boon to the unions and their membership grew rapidly under its beneficent influence.

When the Taft-Hartley Act was passed in 1947 the unfair labor practices banned by the Wagner Act were also banned by the new measure, with one significant change to be noted shortly. In addition, however, the Taft-Hartley Act listed a number of unfair labor practices in which unions must not engage. Let us examine these two lists, which are highly important in present-day union-management relations.

The unfair labor practices proscribed for employers are five in number. (1) Employers must not interfere with the right of their employees to "engage in, or refrain from, collective bargaining and self-organizational activities." This particular unfair labor practice is general in nature; employers who are guilty of any of the other four practices are automatically guilty of this one too. However, an employer may be guilty, or allegedly guilty, of the first unfair labor practice without being guilty of any of the other four: for example, if he questions his employees or prospective employees "concerning their own or other employees' union membership, sympathies, or activities." [5] The NLRB has interpreted this act as an infraction of the first unfair labor practice.

(2) Employers must not dominate, interfere with, or support financially or otherwise, any labor organizations in their plants. This unfair labor practice is significant in that it definitely rules out employer-controlled company unions. Company unions are still permissible, but they must be independent of the employer. As will be seen in Table 13 a considerable number of cases arise involving this unfair labor practice. The number (relative number) is larger than during the years immediately preceding the passing of the Taft-Hartley Act, though smaller than during the first years of the Wagner Act.

(3) Employers must not encourage or discourage membership in any union by acts of discrimination, such as discharging and demoting. An employer, however, can take action against a worker for such things as incompetency and absenteeism even though he is an active unionist. Under the Wagner Act both the closed shop and the union shop—both of which involve employer encouragement of union membership on the part of job applicants—were permissible. Under the Taft-Hartley Act the closed shop is banned and the union shop is subject to some control. This particular unfair labor practice is by all odds the most common, as is shown in Table 13.

(4) Employers must not discriminate against workers because they have filed charges or have given testimony under the law. Infractions of this rule are not common.

(5) Employers must not refuse to bargain collectively with the official bargaining agent of the workers. A similar unfair labor practice is included in the union list, and for both the law sets forth a statement indicating what it means to bargain collectively (included are such things as willingness "to meet at reasonable times and confer in good faith"). If an agreement is reached, the provisions of it must be put in writing if either party so requests. The law, however, does not "compel either party to agree to a proposal

[5] *Sixteenth Annual Report of the National Labor Relations Board,* 1951, p. 142. Other types of infractions are described in each annual report of the board. In 1950, the last year for which separate data are available, there were 352 cases involving only unfair labor practice number 1, out of a total of 4,472. *Fifteenth Annual Report,* p. 222.

or require the making of a concession." A nice problem sometimes arises as to whether or not a particular matter is "bargainable" under the act. Finally, procedural steps are specified in the event that either party wants to terminate an existing bargaining agreement (see Chapter 18).

Here the "free speech" provision that is found in the Taft-Hartley Act should be recalled. Employers now are much freer to express opinions about unions than they were during the first part of the Wagner Act era.

Table 13 indicates the relative importance of the various types of employer unfair labor practices. A given case may involve more than one unfair labor practice (exclusive of the first practice, which is always involved). On occasion one case may involve all five of the practices. The classified figures in the table, therefore, do not add up to the total.[6]

Table 13

Unfair Labor Practices Alleged in Charges Filed Against Employers under the LMRA, Year Ending June 30, 1952 *

Unfair Labor Practice	Number of Charges Filed
No. 1	4,306
2	406
3	2,972
4	62
5	1,226
Total cases	4,306

* *Seventeenth Annual Report of the National Labor Relations Board,* 1952, p. 281.

Union Unfair Labor Practices

The LMRA contains a list of six proscribed unfair labor practices as engaged in by unions or their agents. In terms of number of cases these are not as important as the unfair labor practices of employers; nevertheless they are of real significance and merit our attention.

(1) The LMRA provides that unions must not coerce an em-

[6] The number of unfair labor practices charged against employers remains large, and for this there are several reasons. See Professor Slichter, *The Quarterly Journal of Economics,* May, 1953, p. 152.

ployee into union membership, except in the case of a legitimate union shop; nor may unions coerce employers in the selection of their collective-bargaining and grievance-handling representatives. This particular unfair labor practice is relatively common, as Table 14 shows. Most instances of it relate to coercion of employees. Very often such coercion is found in connection with strikes and involves violence or the threat of violence.

(2) Unions may not force, or attempt to force, employers to discriminate against employees (by insisting, for example, on a closed shop). Under a duly established union shop, however, a union can force the employer to discharge any worker who does not pay the initiation fee of the union and the periodic dues. This unfair labor practice has been the most common, even more so than the first.

(3) Unions must not refuse to bargain collectively. A considerable number of alleged infractions of this provision arise. These cases, however, ordinarily involve not any outright refusal of the unions to bargain but their insistence on bargaining on certain illegal matters (such as a closed shop).

(4) Unions must not participate in secondary strikes and boycotts. The LMRA specifies four proscribed objectives of such illegal strikes and boycotts. The first of these, which is the one that is involved most frequently, includes the aim of compelling an employer or other person to stop doing business with someone else. The second objective is that of forcing an employer to recognize or bargain with a union that has not been certified. The third objective, which is somewhat similar to the second, is the forcing of an employer to recognize or bargain with a union when another one has already been certified. The fourth objective is that of forcing employers to assign work to a union not entitled to it. This last objective involves the question of "job jurisdiction"; and the act provides that if the union parties to such a dispute cannot settle it within ten days the NLRB must hand down a decision on the matter.

(5) Unions with union-shop agreements must not levy excessively high initiation fees. The NLRB in deciding whether or not such fees are excessive, or discriminatory, is to consider "among other relevant factors, the practices and customs of labor organiza-

tions in the particular industry, and the wages currently paid to the employees affected." Very few cases of this type arise, and very seldom do they go as far as the NLRB.

(6) Unions must not compel an employer to pay for services not rendered. Not many cases arise under this "featherbed" provision. Not all featherbedding is ruled out, only that which involves payment for work "not performed or not to be performed."

Table 14 shows the number of charges filed under each of the unfair labor practices during 1952. As in Table 13 the separate figures of alleged infractions do not add up to the total cases shown.

Table 14

Unfair Labor Practices Alleged in Charges Filed Against Unions under the LMRA, Year Ending June 30, 1952 *

Unfair Labor Practice	Number of Charges Filed
No. 1	668
2	675
3	105
4	302
5	13
6	16
Total cases	1,148

* *Seventeenth Annual Report of the National Labor Relations Board,* 1952, p. 281.

Procedure and Remedial Action—Unfair Labor Practices

Having given attention to the nature of the unfair labor practices under the LMRA, let us now turn to the question of board procedure in connection with these practices, and to the question of remedial action in case of infractions of the law.

The first step is the filing of a charge of an unfair labor practice. This may be done by an employee, a union, an employer, or some other private party. The charge must be filed with the regional office of the NLRB in the area in which the practice is supposed to have taken place. A representative from the regional office may visit the plant where the violation has allegedly taken place and in an informal manner may be able to settle the case without further action. A case may be settled by the process of adjustment, withdrawal, or dismissal.[7] However, if the matter is not disposed of in this way the board may issue a formal "complaint," including a notification of a hearing on the issue. The board cannot issue a complaint based on any unfair labor practice that occurred more than six months before the charge of such a practice was filed, unless the aggrieved party could not file such a charge because of military duty. It should again be noted that the general counsel has the final authority over the making of the initial investigation and over the issuance of the formal complaint.

After the formal complaint is issued there is a hearing under a "trial examiner," each regional office having a number of such examiners associated with it. After the hearings are over the trial examiner makes an intermediate report and submits a recommendation for the disposal of the case. This recommendation serves as a board order unless, within 20 days, exception is taken to it. If exceptions are taken, the case goes to the board in Washington, which reconsiders it and hands down a decision. The board does not have the legal power to enforce its decisions but may petition a United States Court of Appeals to perform the function.

If on the basis of the hearings the board (trial examiner) feels that an unfair labor practice has been or is being committed, it issues a cease-and-desist order in the manner indicated. If it feels that an unfair labor practice is not involved, it dismisses the complaint.

A person who is dissatisfied with a final order of the board has the right to have the order reviewed in the appropriate circuit court of appeals (or in the Court of Appeals for the District of Columbia). He also has the right to take the case still further up the court ladder, to the United States Supreme Court.

It should be added that the board has the power to obtain a temporary restraining order (injunction) in connection with any unfair labor practice. Priority in the matter of preliminary investigations is given to unfair labor practices involving secondary boycotts (Sec. 8(b), 4A,B,C); if there appears to be reasonable grounds for believing that a secondary boycott charge is valid, the NLRB official dealing with the case *must* obtain an injunction, which is

[7] The percentage of "withdrawn" or "dismissed" unfair labor practices against employers has increased under the LMRA, and the number of "adjusted" cases has decreased. See Slichter, *loc. cit.*, p. 154.

limited to five days, while the board settles the issue. In the case of a union unfair labor practice having to do with job jurisdictional disputes (Sec. 8(b), 4D) the board is directed to determine the dispute unless the parties themselves settle it within ten days. Professor Slichter is of the opinion that the "most important result" of this latter rule has been the setting up of the "excellent" machinery (described in Chapter 10) for dealing with job jurisdictional disputes in the construction industry.

If the NLRB finds that a person charged with an unfair labor practice is guilty, it is directed by the law to issue a cease-and-desist order, as we have already noted, and "to take such affirmative action including reinstatement of employees with or without back pay, as will effectuate the policies" of the act. The law also provides that the cease-and-desist order may require periodic reports from the person who has received it, indicating the extent of the compliance. In issuing its orders the board in each case tries both to remedy the practice in question and to prevent further recurrences of it.

The NLRB requires that the party—employer or union--guilty of an unfair labor practice post notices in which it states its intention of stopping the practice and of abstaining from such a practice in the future. Generally these notices state the remedial action taken by the party guilty of the practice.

The awarding of back pay to workers who have been illegally discharged is sometimes an important part of the remedial action taken. In figuring out the amount of back pay the board aims both at making up any financial loss the workers have sustained and at restoring the workers to the employment status they had when they were discharged. Since the early 1940's the board has insisted that a worker who has been illegally discharged should, during the discrimination period, make "a reasonable effort" to get a new job.[8]

In the vast majority of cases it is the employer who must furnish the back pay. However, occasionally the union may have to pay the sum involved. Sometimes, too, there may be joint liability of em-

[8] In figuring back pay the calculations (regarding what a worker has earned in a new job and what he would have earned in his old job) are now on a quarter-by-quarter basis. Thus, high wages received by a worker (who was illegally discharged) in a new employment cannot "liquidate" the back-pay liability of the employer extending over other quarters. See *Fifteenth Annual Report of the National Labor Relations Board,* 1950, p. 156.

ployer and union, though the NLRB may make it possible for the union to escape its liability by withdrawing its objection to the reinstatement of the employees who were discharged partly because of union influence. In 1952 employers paid out $1,345,882 in back-pay awards; unions paid out $23,910. Sometimes workers who have been discriminated against receive substantial amounts in back pay. Possibly the largest individual payment ever made was the $28,500 turned over to a worker (a director of research) in 1941.[9]

The Norris-LaGuardia Act—The Injunction

The Norris-LaGuardia Act, or Federal Anti-Injunction Act, was passed in 1932, before the period of the New Deal. The passing of this important measure represents a definite landmark in the history of labor relations legislation in this country. In fact Charles O. Gregory, writing in 1946, thought it fair to call the act "the most revolutionary piece of labor legislation ever adopted by Congress," and Lloyd K. Garrison has stated that "Actually, it was the Norris-LaGuardia Act which gave the great impetus to union organization." [10]

Before the passing of this act the injunction had been used with considerable frequency and with great effectiveness in labor disputes. The unions became strongly opposed to the injunction and exerted pressure to have the government rule out or restrict its use in labor controversies. The Clayton Act (1914) included provisions that the unions thought would deal a serious blow to the labor injunction, but this belief was badly shattered by a number of court decisions, including the Duplex Printing Press Company case, the Coronado Coal Company case, and the Bedford Cut Stone Company case.[11] Later on judicial opinion changed somewhat and labor's disillusionment with the Clayton Act disappeared, or at least greatly diminished. However, during the period of the early court decisions the unions started a drive to have a really effective anti-injunction law adopted, and finally in 1932 the Norris-LaGuardia Act was passed.

In this act the public policy of the country with respect to in-

[9] *The CIO News,* September 29, 1941, p. 6.

[10] *The Saturday Review of Literature,* November 16, 1946, pp. 11, 12.

[11] A discussion of these cases, and of the Norris-LaGuardia Act, will be found in the Prentice-Hall *Labor Course,* issued annually.

dustrial disputes and employer-employee relationships was set forth. Specifically the Norris-LaGuardia Act proclaimed the right of workers to establish organizations of their own, to engage in collective bargaining, and to be free from employer interference in the matters of organizing and bargaining.

The Norris-LaGuardia Act sets forth a list of acts in connection with which injunctions may not be issued. One section of it denies the use of injunctions in attempts to enforce the so-called "yellow dog" contract under which workers agree, as a condition of employment, not to join a union. Under the Wagner Act such a contract was made an unfair labor practice and it remains so under the Taft-Hartley Act. Another section in the Norris-LaGuardia Act provides that the charge of unlawful combination or conspiracy cannot be used as a basis for an injunction in labor disputes.

The act, however, does not completely rule out the use of injunctions in labor disputes. It contains a list of circumstances under which it may be employed, including "when unlawful acts have been threatened and will be continued unless restrained" and "when substantial and irreparable injury to complainant's property will occur."

The Norris-LaGuardia Act also contains a number of definite statements relating to injunction procedure. For one thing injunctions are to be granted only on "the basis of findings of fact made and filed by the court." Moreover, and this is important since it rules out the old type of omnibus injunction, injunctions (or restraining orders) "may prohibit only the acts complained of and expressly included in the facts found and filed by the court."

After the passing of the Norris-LaGuardia Act not much was heard in labor circles about the use of the injunction. But with the adoption of the Labor Management Relations Act in 1947 the injunction "menace" again came into prominence, and again the unions lined up in battle against their old foe.

Use of the injunctive procedure is provided for in a number of places in the LMRA. First it may be used in connection with national emergency disputes, as we shall see in Chapter 18. Second, provision has been made for use of the injunction (both mandatory and permissive) in cases involving secondary strikes and boycotts. Third, the act provides for use of the injunctive process on a still wider basis. After issuance of a formal complaint having to do with *any* unfair labor practice, the board (general counsel) has the right to petition for a temporary restraining order. This right is not frequently exercised, however.

Injunctions under the LMRA are issued not at the request of employers but on the initiative of the federal government. Thus the injunction may be looked upon "more as the expression of the public's impartial condemnation of the defendant's conduct than as the employer's weapon in a private economic quarrel." [12] The unions are nevertheless opposed to the injunctive process—to "government by injunction"—and would like to see it either abolished or its use greatly restricted. They feel that the LMRA has not only brought about the return of this undesirable legal instrument to federal courts but that it has "encouraged the state court judges to resume the issuance of injunctions." [13]

The Railway Labor Act

The Railway Labor Act, which was passed in 1926 and which has been amended a number of times since then, is a product of long development. A great deal of legislation having a bearing on labor relations in the railroad industry had been adopted during the 40 years previous to the passing of the act. This legislation included a law passed in 1888, which provided for voluntary arbitration and for the investigation of labor disputes; the Erdman Act of 1898, which provided for mediation and conciliation as well as for voluntary arbitration; the Newlands Act of 1913; the Adamson Act of 1916; the control measures adopted during World War I; and the Transportation Act of 1920.[14] The labor provisions in the last-mentioned act were unsatisfactory both to employers and unions. The act of 1926, however, was introduced with the approval of both parties and was composed, to a substantial extent, of provisions that both groups had proposed.

[12] Archibald Cox, *Proceedings of the Fifth Annual Conference on Industrial Relations,* April 30, 1953, p. 8. Department of Industrial Relations, School of Business Administration, University of Buffalo.

[13] *Proceedings,* CIO Convention, 1952, p. 454.

[14] A sketch of the labor provisions of these acts will be found in the chapter on the Railway Labor Act in the Prentice-Hall *Labor Course,* issued annually. See also *Fifteen Years Under the Railway Labor Act, Amended, and the National Mediation Board.* Washington: United States Printing Office, 1950. These sources also contain details of the present Railway Labor Act.

To begin with the Railway Labor Act contains a brief statement of general purposes. These purposes have to do with the avoidance of interruptions to interstate commerce; the right of workers to join unions; the right of both employers and workers to complete independence in the matter of self-organization; and the "prompt and orderly" settlement of industrial disputes. There then follows a list of general duties, which give substance to the general purposes. These "duties" to some extent resemble a number of the unfair labor practices found in the LMRA. For example, there is a company union provision under which the employer-dominated union is ruled out. The provision by which the Railway Labor Act obligates both employers and unions "to exert every reasonable effort to make and maintain agreements concerning rates of pay, rules and working conditions" is somewhat similar to the obligation "to bargain collectively" imposed by the LMRA.

Included in the general duties is a statement concerning the question of representation, which, it will be recalled, is an important matter dealt with by the NLRB. When occasions arise the National Mediation Board holds elections, or checks authorizations, to determine which union, if any, is to be the official bargaining agent. Once in a while it has to determine the size of the bargaining unit—specifically, what occupations are to be included in the collective bargaining craft or class.

For failure on the part of the employers to carry out a number of the listed general duties relating to the right of the workers to bargain collectively, the law provides for fines and imprisonment. But no such penalties have ever been imposed.[15]

The Railway Labor Act provides elaborate machinery for the handling of industrial disputes on the railroads and in the air transportation industry. Under the act there is a National Railroad Adjustment Board, which deals with unsettled grievance disputes and unsettled disputes over the interpretation or application of collective bargaining agreements. There is also the National Mediation Board, previously mentioned, which has as one of its functions the handling of disputes over new collective bargaining agreements. We shall discuss the work of the NMB in Chapter 18.

A significant change was made in the Railway Labor Act in Jan-

[15] Glenn W. Miller, *American Labor and the Government,* p. 406. New York: Prentice-Hall, Inc., 1948.

uary, 1951, when union-shop agreements and the check-off were made permissible in the industry. Both had been ruled out in the 1934 amendments to the act. The similarity of the new arrangements to the comparable ones in the LMRA will be noted.

Although the Railway Labor Act is one of our most important pieces of labor legislation, it is not looked upon as enthusiastically as it once was. There is a widespread feeling that as far as serious disputes in the transportation field are concerned the act has not been too successful. There is also some feeling that the adjustment board provided by the act has not worked out too well.[16]

State Labor Relations Acts

Shortly after the Wagner Act was declared constitutional in 1937, five states—Massachusetts, New York, Pennsylvania, Utah, and Wisconsin—passed labor relations acts of their own.[17] These acts were modeled on the federal measure, including a declaration of the rights of the workers to organize unions and bargain collectively and a list of certain unfair labor practices engaged in by employers.

In 1939 two of the states, Pennsylvania and Wisconsin, changed their laws by placing restrictions on employees and unions, eight years before a similar step was taken by the federal government. And when Minnesota (1939), Michigan (1939), Colorado (1943), Kansas (1943), Hawaii (1945), and Puerto Rico (1948) adopted labor relations acts, they too placed restrictions on employees and unions. Utah did the same thing in 1947 when it amended its act. When Rhode Island (1941) and Connecticut (1945) passed their labor relations acts, however, they included only employer unfair labor practices.

Many other states have laws that bear upon the matter of labor relations, including measures that place restrictions on unions and provide means for conciliating and mediating industrial disputes.

The labor relations laws of the states we have mentioned specifically may be divided into two groups. First are the "Little Wagner Acts," found in Connecticut, New York, and Rhode Island, which do not include union unfair labor practices. Massachusetts

16 An extensive critical analysis of the NRAB, with suggestions for improvement, will be found in articles by Herbert R. Northrup and Mark L. Kahn in the *Industrial and Labor Relations Review,* April and July, 1952.

17 See *Monthly Labor Review,* August, 1952, pp. 214-217, for a treatment of the state labor relations acts.

could be added to this group, though a 1947 amendment to its law introduced (on a small scale) certain prohibited union practices, Puerto Rico could also be included. In the second group are the laws which, like the federal LMRA, include unfair labor practices of both employers and unions.

Most of the laws in the two groups provide machinery for holding elections to determine which union, if any, is to be the official bargaining agent. Like the LMRA the state laws provide that the designated union becomes the bargaining agent for all the workers. Except in one of the states, they also provide that individual workers may submit grievances to the employer. Some of the state laws follow the LMRA in having provisions relating to such things as internal union operations (e.g. financial reports), the closed shop, and the check-off.

Union Security and the LMRA

As we noted earlier in the chapter the Wagner Act permitted both the closed shop and the union shop, as well as other types of "union security" shops. Under the LMRA, as it was initially passed, the closed shop was banned in interstate businesses, though in some cases, as in the building industry, it continued *de facto*. The preferential shop was banned as well, though it has come back into use. The union shop, and the maintenance-of-membership shop, were deemed to be legal but certain conditions were necessary for their establishment.

In the first place the union had to be the duly designated collective bargaining agent. Second, a majority of the workers in the bargaining unit (a majority of those eligible to vote, not merely of those who voted) had to signify in a vote conducted by the NLRB that they favored the union shop. Third, the union officers had to sign noncommunist affidavits, and the union had to submit financial reports to the NLRB. It should be added, too, that there was one other condition: that no state law exist prohibiting the union shop. If these conditions were met, a union shop was legal, though the employer was not legally compelled to grant it. Under legal union-shop agreements newly hired workers were to have at least 30 days in which to join the union.

Many elections on the union-shop issue were held. During the period from August, 1947 to October, 1951, over 46,000 elections, or polls, were held. In 97.1 per cent of the elections the union shop was authorized. Affirmative votes made up 77.5 per cent of the total votes that could have been cast, and 91.4 per cent of the actual votes cast.[18]

Because the workers were predominantly in favor of the union shop, and because the holding of elections was a costly process, the law was amended in 1951, doing away with the election procedure as a prerequisite to a legal union shop. The other conditions we noted a moment ago for the establishment of a union shop remained, however. The law still retained the old provision concerning the holding of polls for "de-authorizing" the union shop. Before such a poll is held there must be evidence that at least 30 per cent of the employees concerned favor a withdrawal of authorization.

It should be observed, too, that the 1951 amendment concerning the union shop did not eliminate the 30-day requirement. That is, workers could not be compelled to join the union before 30 days after they had started to work, or after the union-shop clause became operative. This provision continued to arouse dissatisfaction, particularly in the movie industry and the building industry. Because of short engagements in these fields employers, operating under union-shop agreements, can use the services of workers ("free riders") who never had to join the union.[19] There has been strong advocacy, therefore, that the length of the grace period be reduced—seven days has been suggested.

Shortly before the provisions in the LMRA relating to union-shop elections were amended, the Railway Labor Act was changed, making it possible for the union shop to be legally established in the railway industry. Prior to early 1951 such shops had been illegal. It should be added that under some state labor relations laws the union shop is still illegal. In 1953 there were 13 states in this category, plus four others that placed "restrictions" of one sort or another on the union shop.

[18] *Sixteenth Annual Report of the National Labor Relations Board*, 1951, p. 301.

[19] Trade unionist Walter Pidgeon gives some convincing statistical evidence on this point relating to the movie industry. See *Taft-Hartley Act Revisions*, Part 3, p. 1722, Hearings, Committee on Labor and Public Welfare, United States Senate, 83rd Cong., 1st Sess. (April, 1953). See also Part 1, p. 506.

17

THE NATURE OF INDUSTRIAL DISPUTES

Because of the nature of the employment relationship disharmony between management and labor can easily arise. The degree of disharmony is likely to be greater and its manifestations much more spectacular in unionized than in nonunionized enterprises; workers become more aggressive when organized into groups and endowed with the power that groups can apply. Fortunately the disharmony does not often lead to open warfare. Though it causes frequent disputes, some of which are bitter and vigorously contested, most of these disputes do not result in strikes or lockouts. Each year there are thousands of collective bargaining agreements made, just as there are millions of minor grievances settled, without resort to force. In view of the wide area over which disharmony between labor and management can arise, the surprising thing is not that we have so many strikes but that we have so few.

This situation is largely due to the attitude of unions and management toward work stoppages. "No body of men," Samuel Gompers once declared, "deplores strikes more than organized workers, and one of their chief aims is to endeavor to reduce their number, if not entirely eliminate striking." This statement may be somewhat exaggerated, but it indicates in a general way the feeling of American unionists toward the use of the strike weapon.

Some unionists, it must be admitted, do not share this peaceful attitude. Highly class-conscious unionists are inclined to believe that every strike, whether it succeeds or fails, is a "victory." In their estimation strikes keep the fires of class consciousness burning and hasten the coming of the general conflagration that will wipe out the capitalistic system. The bulk of American unionists, however, favor peace in industrial relations—though not peace at any price.

Employers, too, are ordinarily opposed to strikes and lockouts, and for a number of good reasons. During a work stoppage the strikers' wages need not be paid, but other costs must be met and these may be very large; moreover, the employer may lose business to competitors. However, employers, like unions, may conclude that the price of peace is too high and hence reconcile themselves to a period of industrial war, a period (they hope) that will not be of long duration and that will make the unionists more "reasonable" in their demands.

It is not, of course, to be inferred that strikes are of little consequence in our economy and can be disregarded. Strikes occur with sufficient frequency to cause considerable economic loss, and for this and other reasons deserve our close attention.

Table 15 reveals the extent of work stoppages in this country in a number of selected years. It will be noted that in 1946, after World War II was over, strikes were especially serious, resulting in more man-days of idleness than in any other year before or since. Even in 1946, however, the days of idleness constituted a very small fraction of the total working time. In most years the man-days lost—and here, it should be noted, we are dealing only with *direct* losses—are less than half of one per cent of the working time; but the absolute loss is still considerable.

Table 15
Work Stoppages in the United States *

		Man-days Idle	
Year	Number	Number	Per Cent of Estimated Working Time
1930	637	3,320,000	.05
1935	2,014	15,500,000	.29
1940	2,508	6,700,000	.10
1945	4,750	38,000,000	.47
1946	4,985	116,000,000	1.43
1947	3,693	34,600,000	.41
1948	3,419	34,100,000	.37
1949	3,606	50,500,000	.59
1950	4,843	38,800,000	.44
1951	4,737	22,900,000	.23
1952	5,117	59,100,000	.57

* *Monthly Labor Review,* May, 1953, p. 505.

General Characteristics of Strikes

Strikes are concerted and temporary stoppages from work by employees who have grievances to be settled, standards to be defended, or goals to be attained. This definition, which could be broadened to cover "slowages" (i.e., slowdowns) as well as stoppages, points to the outstanding characteristics of strikes.

Strikes are *concerted* stoppages from work; that is, they involve more than one person.[1] It is very uncommon for a single worker to give up his job temporarily as a means of exerting pressure on his employer. Workers often exhibit their displeasure with an employer's policies by quitting, but quitting is not the same as striking. When workers go on strike they expect to return to their old jobs—the stoppage is *temporary* only. Moreover, they are generally looked upon as still being members of the employment force.

Strikes have meaning and importance because they involve groups of workers. Although a stoppage of work by one person is not likely to disrupt production seriously, a stoppage by a group of workers can easily bring production to a complete halt. A temporary cessation of work by one person, moreover, is not likely to achieve any worth-while results for the worker involved, but if a whole group stops work the results may be distinctly favorable to the participants.

Present-day strikes, in contrast to those of earlier periods in American history, are ordinarily initiated and carried on by organized groups of workers rather than by unorganized groups. However, strikes by unorganized workers do occur occasionally.

In our definition of strikes we have indicated the general aims of the strikers, namely to protect what they have already gained, to achieve objectives that are still outside their grasp, and to bring about the redress of grievances. In a sense the last of these aims is covered by the other two, but it should be kept separate. The grievances referred to are those of a minor nature; they do not involve such key issues as wage rates.

From a very broad standpoint strikes may be regarded as attempts on the part of labor to bring about a shift in the balance of power in industry, that is, to reduce the prerogatives of management

[1] That there are exceptions to almost every rule—and definition—is evidenced by the decision of an Ohio court that there can be a one-man strike. See *The International Teamster,* November, 1950, p. 27.

and increase the amount of control in the hands of the workers. Not that in all strikes the workers have this particular object in mind; to make such an assumption would be to push the struggle-for-power interpretation of strikes to extremes. Most workers who go on strike do so because they want their employer to treat them better, not because they want to reduce his power. The achievement of better treatment, in turn, represents a change in the balance of power between management and labor.

One might add that in some strikes the struggle-for-power interpretation has little or no application, either directly or indirectly. In jurisdictional strikes, for example, no attempt is made to reduce the power of the employer. What is attempted is an increase in the power of one union at the expense of a rival union.

Kinds of Strikes

Strikes do not all follow the same pattern; they have various forms of expression. These forms are not always clearly differentiated from one another, but they lend themselves to a number of suggestive classifications.

(1) *Classification on Basis of Initiation.* Under this classification there are only two possible types: authorized and unauthorized. *Authorized strikes* are strikes that are called only after the proper union consent has been given. *Unauthorized strikes,* ordinarily termed wildcat strikes, are strikes that are called without the necessary union approval. These strikes represent rebellion, either by the rank-and-file membership against the union leadership or by part of the membership against the total membership. Most strikes during World War II were wildcat strikes.

(2) *Classification on Basis of Scope.* Classifying strikes according to scope, there are again only two types: the general strike and the "particular" strike. The *general strike* has wide coverage.[2] But there is great variation in the nature of the coverage; that is to say, the degree of "generality" is by no means always the same. There are at least three possible types of general strikes.

[2] A detailed account of the general strike, both in theory and in practice, will be found in W. H. Crooks, *The General Strike.* Chapel Hill: The University of North Carolina Press, 1931. Mr. Crooks divides general strikes into three categories: political, economic, and revolutionary.

The most extensive type covers a wide range of industries and all, or a large part, of the country. This is the kind of strike that extreme radicals sometimes envisage as the final means of bringing about the downfall of capitalism: workers in general will lay down their tools; the owners of industry will be utterly helpless and forced to capitulate; the new economic and social order will be established. Such a strike exists largely in the imagination (a description of it will be found in William Morris's *News from Nowhere*), although the General Strike of 1926 in England (which had little or no revolutionary content) and the general strike in France in 1938 may be cited as approximations to it.

A second type of general strike is citywide in scope. This type, although limited geographically, is extensive industrially. The Seattle Strike of 1919, the San Francisco Strike of 1934, and the Oakland Strike of 1946 are examples of this variety.

A third type of general strike covers all, or a large percentage of, the employers in a given industry. The larger strikes in the coal industry are "general" in this sense.

In contrast to the general strike there is what one might call, for want of a better term, the *particular strike*. This type of strike is limited in scope, although it is often carried on by large numbers of workers and may be very serious in nature. The particular strike is confined to a single plant or, at most, to a few plants, and often to a single trade or occupation. Usually it is also confined to a single town or city. The particular strike is ordinarily carried on by a single union group, although the group may receive encouragement and aid from other unions. Most strikes are of this character.

Closely allied to general strikes are "emergency strikes." A national emergency strike, according to the Taft-Hartley Act, relates to a whole industry, or a substantial part of it; it relates, moreover, to an industry that is engaged in interstate or foreign commerce; and finally it involves stoppages that "imperil the national health or safety." The first and third types of general strikes are definitely of a national emergency character.

Though the above-mentioned characteristics of national emergency strikes may seem to be precise, there has been marked difference of opinion on the question of what *really* constitutes such strikes. Some persons believe that a number of the so-called national emergency strikes of recent years have not been emergency strikes at all.[3] From 1947 to 1953 the procedure provided in the Taft-Hartley Act for dealing with emergency disputes was invoked ten times. Seven of these occasions were in 1948, and three related to the bituminous industry.

(3) *Classification on Basis of Means and Purpose.* Strikes may be classified in terms of the means or tactics used in conducting them and the purpose or purposes for which they are carried on. This classification is somewhat heterogeneous in nature and should not be applied too rigidly.

The *slowdown strike* is different from all other types of strikes in that it does not involve an actual stoppage of work. This unique feature causes its exclusion from the formal definition of a strike given earlier in the chapter. Since, however, the word "strike" is sometimes coupled with the concerted and possibly organized process of slowing down, it is not inappropriate to include it in the present classification.

The *quickie strike* is closely related to the slowdown strike; in fact, from one point of view it is a variant of the slowdown. In a quickie the workers remain in the plant, but they stop work for a brief period, possibly a few hours, or perhaps only a few minutes. Ordinarily such strikes are called without proper authorization.

The *sitdown strike* is similar to the quickie and to slowdown in that the strikers remain in the plant. In the sitdown strike, however, the stoppage period is much longer than in the quickie. The sitdown strike came into prominence in this country during the extensive organizing campaigns launched about the middle of the 1930's, and it reached its highest point of development in 1937 (about one-tenth of all strikes in that year were of the sitdown type). In 1939 the Supreme Court of the United States (in the case of Fansteel Metallurgi-

[3] See Irving Bernstein and Hugh G. Lovell, "Are Coal Strikes National Emergencies?" *Industrial and Labor Relations Review,* April, 1953. See also Edgar L. Warren, "Thirty-six Years of 'National Emergency' Strikes," *ibid.,* October, 1951. Professor Warren defines a national emergency strike as "one which has resulted in a dangerous curtailment of supplies of necessary goods or services where substitutes are not available," and declares that "few strike situations can result in national emergencies during peacetime." Professor Warren further states, quite logically, that his definition has to be "substantially broadened" during times of war.

cal Corporation *v.* NLRB) viewed the sitdown with disfavor, and since then it has very largely fallen into disuse.

The *ordinary strike* is the common, everyday type of strike. Unlike the strikes already mentioned, it involves a withdrawal on the part of the workers from their place of employment. Unlike those yet to be mentioned, it is carried on for the purpose of achieving objectives that are directly and intimately associated with the strikers themselves.

The *sympathetic strike* is carried on by workers who have no immediate grievance against their employer. They strike, nevertheless, out of sympathy for another group of workers who are on strike, or who are about to go on strike, and who, presumably, have a just cause for stopping work. The participants in this type of strike hope that their employer will be able and willing to bring pressure upon the "unfair" employer to effect a satisfactory settlement for their fellow workers.

The *jurisdictional strike,* like the sympathetic strike, does not involve any particular grievance against the company upon which the burden of the strike falls. But, unlike the sympathetic strike, it is not an example of labor solidarity; in fact it is just the opposite. Jurisdictional strikes, like sympathy strikes, are particularly distasteful to the employer because they grow out of causes that are not of his making. As we noted in the preceding chapter, jurisdictional strikes (of certain types) are ruled out under the Labor Management Relations Act.

The *general strike,* as we have already observed, is broad in scope and may be either revolutionary or nonrevolutionary in intent. The general strikes that have taken place in this country have been nonrevolutionary, although not always nonviolent, in nature. *National emergency strikes* are also broad in scope and of a nonrevolutionary character.

The *political strike,* a new type of work stoppage, bears some resemblance to the general strike as it is envisaged by extreme radicals. The purpose of the political strike is not to win concessions from employers, at least not directly, but to exert pressure on the government. Some of the recent strikes in Italy and France have been of this character.

Causes of Strikes

In any single stoppage there may well be more than one cause (i.e., more than one issue) involved. It is not always easy to discover what the particular causes are; surface manifestations of unrest and dissatisfaction that appear to be responsible for a strike may cover deep-seated and more basic causes that cannot be observed at first sight. Moreover, the relative importance of the causes, when more than one is present, is often very difficult to gauge.

Most strikes are due to differences between management and labor over one or more aspects of the employment relationship. In other words, there are specific issues involved in a strike; and a difference of opinion on these issues may be looked upon as the immediate cause of the strike. These issues, and the other elements that may have a bearing on work stoppages, may be divided into four chief categories.[4]

To begin with there are the economic issues. These include demands for wage changes,[5] shorter hours, job security, pensions, and a variety of other changes, including those relating to the physical conditions of work.

Second, there are disagreements over union status and union prerogatives. Numerous work stoppages occur over the question of union recognition, especially during prosperous periods, when the typical union is in a strong position to force the employer to recognize it as the official bargaining agent. In this category also are the differences that arise between the employer and the union over the type of "shop" that is to prevail, and over such questions of prerogative as contract work and apprenticeship rules. To an increasing extent unions are desirous of having a voice in decision-making, with respect not only to wages and hours but to other matters as well.

Third, there are differences arising between the unions them-

[4] Statistics relating to the major issues involved in the strikes occurring each year in this country will be found regularly in the May issue of the *Monthly Labor Review*. The classification used is somewhat different from the one above.

[5] A larger degree of stability in the general price level would help to reduce the number of strikes due to wage factors. Professor John R. Commons once declared that "The fluctuation of currency is the greatest of all the labor problems," and that "The first great method of bringing about industrial peace is the stabilization of the dollar." See *Trade Unionism and Labor Problems*, p. 4. Boston: Ginn & Co., 1921.

selves, and not from allegedly unsatisfactory employment conditions. In this category are jurisdictional differences over jobs, union rivalry, and union "politics."

Fourth, and finally, there are differences in ideological politics and beliefs. Strikes are sometimes brought about by left-wing groups in a direct attempt to hinder or sabotage certain specific policies such as national and international defense. Ideological differences have been a cause, or at least a very important issue, in strikes not only in a number of European countries but in the United States as well. The general desire for a new type of economic order, which has been mentioned as being at the basis of one type of general strikes, may also be of some influence in ordinary strikes.

Since by itself the preceding classification of strike causes is not adequate, a few additional observations are in order. It should be noted that psychological influences, divorced (at least directly) from specific aims of economic betterment, often play a very significant role. Strikes are danger signals; they indicate that the workers want not only such things as higher wages and shorter hours, but better recognition of their rights as human beings. In modern industry it is a simple matter for these rights to go unrecognized or be seriously neglected. Hence tensions and frustrations can arise, paving the way for unrest and industrial strife.[6]

There is a common notion that work stoppages are often caused by union officials. That these officials are sometimes the direct cause of strikes is a fact that cannot very well be denied. A number of factors, including social ostracism [7] and internal political matters, may induce union leaders to promote strikes. But strikes are not to be interpreted solely, or even largely, in terms of the whims and opinions of particular persons; there are other, more basic, elements involved. Union leaders may often take the initiative in bringing these elements into the open, but they are not responsible for their existence.

Certain strike "factors" operating with special force in the United States have led to greater strike participation in this country

[6] The psychological basis of industrial strife is discussed at length in *Industrial Conflict,* the 1939 yearbook of the Society for the Psychological Study of Social Issues, edited by George W. Hartmann and Theodore Newcomb. New York: The Cordon Co., 1939.

[7] A provocative discussion of this theme by A. A. Imberman will be found in the *Harvard Business Review,* January, 1950.

than in other free nations. Among these factors are the still widespread management opposition to unions, the division in the union movement, union jurisdictional disputes, and the absence of a labor party.[8] Some of these factors will lose part of their force as elements in strike situations as time goes on; others, including the absence of a labor party, will probably continue to operate unchanged into the indefinite future.

Strike Rules and Methods

It is customary for unions to set up rules of procedure before they launch strikes. Many national and international unions provide in their constitutions that locals may not go on strike without first receiving permission from the parent organization. The locals, moreover, before requesting this permission must usually have the support of at least two-thirds of the members who would be affected by the contemplated strike. Sometimes union officers have the power to call strikes. This authority may be conferred upon them by the union, or (in nondemocratic, boss-ridden organizations) it may be assumed by the leaders themselves. When strikes are launched for organization purposes, a strike vote among the workers, most of whom are nonunionists, cannot very well be taken. In such cases the strikes may be ordered by union officials.

Just as there are variations in the policies followed in calling strikes, so there are differences in the policies used in stopping them. Sometimes the president of the parent organization has the power to end a strike, but in most instances the decision rests with the local involved. However, the opinion of the higher officers in the organization is usually of considerable influence in the decision reached. In ending a strike the fraction of membership support necessary may be less than the fraction required in calling it.[9]

Many unions grant financial aid to strikers, in the form either of prefinanced strike benefits or of hastily improvised strike relief. To receive strike benefits a worker must meet certain eligibility re-

[8] For a discussion of these and other factors in relation to strikes in Australia, Canada, Great Britain, Sweden, and the United States, see the article by Arthur M. Ross and Donald Irwin in *Industrial and Labor Relations Review,* April, 1951. See also the comments by Adolf Sturmthal on this article, and the reply of Arthur Ross, in the April, 1953 issue of the same journal.

[9] An informative discussion of strike rules will be found in Florence Peterson, *American Labor Unions,* pp. 226-228. New York: Harper & Bros., 1945.

quirements: he must be in good standing in the union; he must report regularly to the union or strike headquarters; and he must be ready to perform whatever strike duties are given to him. In most instances there is a waiting period, usually of one or two weeks, before benefits are payable. Some unions establish a maximum period for benefit payments, sometimes as low as four weeks, sometimes six months or more. The size of the strike benefits paid by unions varies considerably. Probably the most generous union is the International Typographical Union, which pays married men 60 per cent of their wage scale when they are on strike and single men 40 per cent.

Unions that accumulate strike funds (or "defense funds," as they are often called) follow several practices in obtaining the necessary revenue. In some organizations a certain portion of the dues or per capita tax is set aside for the fund. In other organizations special strike fund assessments are levied. In some unions that have no separate strike fund, the general funds of the union are used for strike purposes until they are reduced to the danger point. Then a special assessment is imposed.

Sometimes a union involved in a strike appeals to other labor organizations for assistance. A local in need of aid may request help from other locals in the union or from the city central with which it is affiliated. Sometimes it will even appeal to the public. On occasion one national or international will aid another that is involved in a serious strike. A new policy for obtaining strike funds was put into operation in 1953 when the United Hatters' union decided to sell a $500,000 issue of bonds to its members to help finance a strike being carried on by one of its locals against a New England hat manufacturer who was contemplating moving some of his operations to the South.

Some unions furnish strike relief instead of paying fixed strike benefits. Soup and food kitchens may be established; clothes may be provided. Ladies' auxiliaries often play a significant role in dispensing strike relief.

Strikes are more carefully organized today than they were in the earlier history of the labor movement. Less is left to chance and more is based on definite planning. In this respect the battles in industry resemble those among nations—"progress" has been made in both cases. A strike is ordinarily under the control of a strike committee. If the strike is of considerable size, this committee is likely to have various specialized subcommittees working under it. There may be a subcommittee on strategy, one on picketing, one on law, one on relief, one on publicity, and one on settlement. Each subcommittee has specific duties entrusted to it, and the outcome of the strike is largely dependent on the effectiveness with which the duties are performed. If the strike is of very large proportions, it may be under the direct control of a small number of the leading members of the general strike committee.[10]

The Cost of Strikes

Cost to Workers and Unions. Whatever gains workers may ultimately achieve out of strikes, there are certain costs (or losses) to which they are immediately and directly exposed. In the first place there is an immediate wage loss. If the strike is of long duration the individual worker may forego a sizable amount of wages, and if the number of workers on strike is large the aggregate wage loss may be very substantial. For example, it was estimated that during the General Motors stoppage in 1945-1946 the strikers lost between $128,000,000 and $140,000,000 in wages.[11] These figures, it must be emphasized, are the *direct* and *immediate* wage losses. They do not include wage losses suffered by those indirectly affected by the strike; nor, on the other hand, do they show to what extent the wage losses of those who directly participated in the strike were later recouped. For these reasons the preceding figures, and any other figures relating to wage losses sustained by strikers, are of only limited value.

A second kind of strike cost is the actual money outlay that may be involved. In every strike there are various expenses to be met, such as strike benefits and relief, publicity outlays, and possibly legal expenditures. These costs are ordinarily small compared with the direct wage losses that the strikers suffer, but they may on occasion amount to large sums. In its "Taft-Hartley" strike in Chicago in the early 1950's the International Typographical Union spent "some $7,000,000."

There may be still other costs resulting from strikes, costs of a less definite but nevertheless important nature. "Every time a union takes a licking in a strike, it loses prestige," a union paper has

[10] For a brief discussion of the question of strike organization see Philip Taft, *Economics and Problems of Labor,* pp. 516-518. Harrisburg: Stackpole Sons, 1942.

[11] *The New York Times,* March 14, 1946.

pointed out.[12] "The members lose wages. They also lose confidence in the union and the employers get a little tougher because of their victory."

Thus the workers and their unions are exposing themselves to possible losses when they go on strike; and they are generally averse to such action unless the potential gains from the strike seem considerable and relatively certain.

Cost to Employers. Employers too are exposed to certain losses by strikes. While a strike is taking place employers do not need to pay wages to the absent workers, although in states where workers on strike are entitled to partial unemployment insurance benefits employers must make payments *indirectly*. There are other costs, however, that employers must meet even though their plants are idle, costs such as bond interest and property taxes. Employers may also spend money in combating a strike. Moreover, they may lose money through the shifting of business to competitors.

Employers, then, like unions, generally want to avoid strikes if they possibly can. The extent of the losses sustained by employers should not be exaggerated, however. They may be able to shift part or all of these losses on to the public in the form of higher prices. Moreover some of the losses may be shifted to the government (and the public at large) through a reduction in the amount payable in taxes, as when profits are reduced.

Cost to the Public. The cost of strikes to the public may be thought of in money terms or in "real" terms. The second approach is the more direct and meaningful one, and we shall use it in our analysis.

First of all, however, it should be pointed out that in one sense strikes are socially beneficial: that is, the very fact that there is a strike indicates that the cost of the concessions the unions are seeking will not be passed on to the public. If the employers could pass along the cost, they would very likely give in. Thus a strike may, in J. K. Galbraith's words, indicate "that countervailing power is being used in a sound context." [13] Strikes are a sign of health in the capitalistic system, a sign that the public is not going to be "gypped" (by harmonious, price-increasing action on the part of the union and the employer). This fact, however, does not remove the need for

[12] *The International Teamster,* November, 1946, p. 6.

[13] *American Capitalism,* p. 138. Boston: Houghton Mifflin Co., 1952.

probing into the various social losses that strikes entail; it means only that in some cases the results might be worse.

Do strikes reduce the total real income or (what is the same thing) the total real output of the nation? Samuel Gompers once affirmed that "production in the aggregate of an entire year has never yet been diminished by a strike." Is this statement correct? Before we can give a definite answer there are certain "unseen" elements we must examine.

To begin with, there are several reasons why the loss of production growing out of strikes may be *less* than appears at first sight. A strike in the plant of employer *A* that involves a thousand men for a work period of ten days appears to represent a loss of 10,000 man-days. And a loss of 10,000 man-days would seem to lead inevitably to a decrease in the industrial output of the country. This decrease is not inevitable, however, for several reasons.

For one thing, the loss in output in employer *A*'s plant may be offset by an increase in the production of competing plants. In addition, if *A* was expecting a strike, he may have speeded up production ahead of time in order to be able to fill his orders while the workers are idle. Moreover, after the strike is over *A* may increase output by having his labor force work overtime (probably at time-and-a-half). Finally a strike may have the effect of cutting into the amount of free time that *A*'s workers had rather than into their work time.[14]

For the reasons just noted, the direct, immediate loss of 10,000 man-days in employer *A*'s plant may not involve a decrease in the total output of the nation and in its total income. But we have not examined all the unseen elements. There are others that make the loss *greater* than it might seem at first sight.

Industry today is highly interdependent; when one plant is idle, as a result of a strike, other plants may also be forced into idleness. Thus, a strike in a plant in the steel industry, or a strike in the steel industry as a whole, may cause steel-using plants in large numbers to close down or go on short time.

[14] Sometimes the man-hours directly lost in strikes would have been lost, at least in part, anyway because of part-time employment. John L. Lewis has contended that this is true of the strikes in the bituminous coal industry. "In the coal industry all that strikes have ever done—and there have been many of them—is to concentrate the idle time." *Taft-Hartley Revisions,* Part 4, p. 1923. Hearings, Committee on Labor and Public Welfare, United States Senate, 83rd Cong., 1st Sess. (April, 1953).

Taking everything into account it seems true beyond question that the national output is harmed by strikes. Whatever truth there may have been in Gompers' statement when it was made, and even with respect to that time its validity is open to question, it would be incorrect today. Strikes, on the whole, reduce the total output of the nation and hence its total income.

Subjective Aspects of Strikes. In our discussion of the causes of strikes we noted the importance of psychological factors. At this point we should again point out the significance of these factors.

Supporters of the doctrine of the class struggle are inclined to look upon all strikes, whether the workers win them or lose them, as successful. Strikes engender class consciousness, thus helping to create the proper mental atmosphere for the breakdown of the capitalistic system. But one need not subscribe to the class struggle notion to detect psychological values inherent in some strikes. They may give the workers an outlet for pent-up feelings; the opportunity for united, and possibly satisfaction-yielding, action; and relief from the drabness and monotony of their daily tasks. Finally, strikes may give workers some control over the conditions under which they work. If strikes were not permitted, such psychological needs would go unsatisfied, unless, of course, other steps were taken to meet them. Should these needs go unsatisfied, the consequent unrest would manifest itself in such forms as excessive labor turnover, ca' canny, and poor morale.

But this argument must not be misinterpreted. It does not imply that all strikes yield psychological advantages to those who engage in them, nor does it suggest that no steps should be taken to prevent strikes. All that it means is that under the existing conditions in industrial relations, and with human nature as it is, strikes may aid in satisfying certain deep-seated psychological wants of the workers. To have these wants satisfied in more peaceful ways is one of the great tasks confronting present-day business management and society at large.

Picketing

Though picketing may be used for various nonlabor purposes, as when persons with placards march up and down in front of the White House, the practice is essentially a union device or weapon.

Types of Labor Picketing. The first and most important type of labor picketing is that associated with strikes. As an accompaniment of a strike, picketing makes it difficult, if not impossible, for the employer to make use of strikebreakers. It generally aids in preserving, and possibly increasing, the morale of the strikers. Picketing, moreover, is an avenue of communication for the strikers, through which they can request the public, by withdrawing its patronage, to aid them in remedying a situation that they believe should be remedied. In larger plants or enterprises picketing is a means of conveying information not only to the public but to the workers themselves. More of the workers may go on strike as a result of it. Picketing, furthermore, serves to inform other unionists that a strike is on.

Picketing may have a number of other objectives in addition to the furtherance of a strike. A union may picket an employer because of his buying policies (i.e., his buying from another employer who is supposed to be "unfair"). Such a practice is sometimes called secondary picketing and is equivalent to a secondary boycott.

Picketing may also arise out of jurisdictional disputes. Two unions may both claim the right to perform the same piece of work or may both be engaged in organizing the same workers. In the struggle between the two unions over jurisdiction, particularly over membership jurisdiction, the minority or losing union may resort to picketing.

Picketing may also be resorted to by one union in order to get another union to change its employment policy, or to obtain assistance from it. It may be used to force members to pay their dues. It may also be used to show displeasure with items appearing in the press.[15]

Picketing Methods and Techniques. Various methods and techniques are used in picketing. One is mass picketing. This picketing is similar to what is sometimes called "chain" picketing; and if it is carried on around the whole plant it is sometimes labeled "circular" picketing. Mass picketing makes a more impressive showing than picketing done by a few persons; it helps to preserve solidarity among the strikers; it may also make it easier, sometimes, for union leaders to control the strikers. But mass picketing, because of the very enthusiasm it creates, may easily lead to violence. It is not surprising, therefore, that its use is often banned or restricted, either

[15] For examples of picketing, see the author's *Contemporary Unionism in the United States,* pp. 413-414. New York: Prentice-Hall, Inc., 1948.

by definite legal statutes or by court, labor board, or labor commission decisions.

The pickets are usually members of the union that is on strike; and if strike benefits are paid, service on the picket line may be a condition of receiving such benefits. Sometimes, however, the union may elicit, or at least accept, the aid of nonmembers and of nonunionists. And sometimes professional pickets are employed. Like professional mourners they may not know much about the subject around which their activities center, but they are able to perform their task effectively. It would be a great error to omit mentioning here the crowning of "Miss Picket of 1946," in Cleveland.

Where pickets are few in number, they usually carry placards or signs. Even in mass picketing a certain number of signs may be used. The pickets may also convey messages orally, which, if directed toward strikebreakers, are likely to be decidedly uncomplimentary.

On occasion unions use the "flying squadron" technique. Groups of unionists move from plant to plant, and possibly from town to town, extending aid to weaker groups who are engaged in organizing work or in carrying on strikes. Sometimes actual "flying squadrons" involving the use of airplanes are used, as in a strike against two hotels in the Catskill Mountains during the summer of 1953. Ingenuity in picketing methods seems to have no bounds!

Legal Aspects of Picketing. There appears to be only one generalization concerning the legal status of picketing: that in order to be lawful, picketing must be peaceful and, presumably, must be carried on in pursuance of a lawful objective. In other words, both means and ends must be "proper." But at this point simplicity and clarity end, and complexity and confusion begin. What constitutes "peaceful" picketing, and what is a "lawful" objective? There is disagreement on these two points from one state to another and from one court to another.

In 1940 the United States Supreme Court handed down a famous decision in the case of Thornhill *v.* Alabama, in which picketing was liberally interpreted as being a form of free speech. After World War II, however, many courts began to tighten up in their attitude toward picketing; and picketing rights became narrower than they had been during the years immediately following the Thornhill decision.

One or two limitations on picketing, under the Labor Management Relations Act, are especially worthy of note. Though peaceful picketing is generally looked upon as legal, if the object of the picketing is in contravention of the act (e.g., coercive statements or actions in an attempt to prevent members of other unions from crossing the picket line) the picketing is illegal. Moreover, picketing that is *inseparably* associated with secondary boycotts would appear to be illegal.[16] Numerous states also ban secondary picketing.

The Boycott

The boycott and the strike are both directed toward the same end—the winning of concessions for a group of workers from an unwilling employer. They involve, however, the use of different means. A strike involves a withholding of labor from an employer, whereas a boycott involves, or represents, a withholding of patronage from him.

Classification of Boycotts. A *primary boycott* is one in which a group of workers, either with or without the voluntary cooperation of their friends, abstains from the purchase of the products of their employer. The "friends" may be other unionists and nonunionists whose support has been obtained without coercion.

A *secondary boycott* is one in which third or outside parties are involved. The third party may be a company that supplies raw materials or finished goods to the unfair employer; it may be an employer who has dealings with a competing union; it may be members of the public who, as a result of external pressure, abstain from buying the products of a boycotted producer. In these instances the third party has no *direct* concern in the controversy that produces the boycott, and in all instances the third party is injured or victimized for something for which it is not, in any significant manner, to blame.

There would seem to be a clear line of demarcation between primary and secondary boycotts; but, in actual practice, the placing of the line has been somewhat arbitrary, and all the authorities would not agree on the correct location.

Another classification of boycotts, based on the status of the boycotters, may also be used: the two types included are the "consumers'

[16] On these points see the Prentice-Hall *Labor Course,* 1953, paragraphs 4374, 4436. See also paragraphs 11,165 and 11,166 for other information concerning the legal aspects of picketing, especially relative to the states.

boycott" and the "workers' boycott." This differentiation has been made by Professor Edwin E. Witte, who describes the former as "a collective refusal to purchase boycotted commodities," and the latter as a refusal "to work upon or with boycotted materials." [17] This distinction is a useful one, although the workers' boycott is, in the final analysis, an attempt to force the users of the materials to stop buying them.

The primary boycott is a weak weapon in the hands of labor. Such a boycott stands little chance of success, since the percentage of a producer's output bought by the producer's own employees and their friends is ordinarily a small part of his total output. Extensive cooperation from friends is necessary if the boycott is to succeed, and this cooperation is not easy to obtain. The secondary boycott, in its diverse forms, is a much more effective weapon, but it is also much more vulnerable from a legal point of view. Although the primary boycott is generally looked upon as being within the law, the secondary boycott, in most jurisdictions, is regarded as illegal.

Legal Aspects of the Boycott. The use of the boycott by American workers goes back more than one hundred years, but it was not until the 1880's that the weapon came to be extensively employed. "Almost without warning," Professor Leo Wolman points out, "the boycott suddenly emerged in 1880 to become for the next ten or fifteen years the most effective weapon of unionism." [18] The use of the weapon continued on into the present century, but as time went on its legality came to be seriously questioned.

The most outstanding of several Supreme Court boycott cases was the so-called Danbury Hatters' case, in which the Hatters' union was successfully sued for triple damages under the Sherman Anti-Trust Act. The Supreme Court upheld (in 1908) the applicability of the Sherman Act to labor unions and (in 1915) approved the levy of $252,000 imposed against the members of the Hatters' union. Confronted with the first of these decisions, the AFL set out to gain immunity for labor under the Sherman Act. It appeared that the union objective had been achieved by the passing of the Clayton Act in

[17] *The Government in Labor Disputes,* p. 38. New York: The McGraw-Hill Book Co., 1932.

[18] *The Boycott in American Trade Unionism,* p. 26. Baltimore: The Johns Hopkins Press, 1916. Detailed information concerning the earlier history of the boycott will be found in this book and also in Harry W. Laidler, *Boycotts and the Labor Struggle.* New York: John Lane Co., 1913.

1914. But union hopes turned out to be ill-founded. This fact was clearly demonstrated in 1921 by an adverse Supreme Court verdict in the Duplex Printing Co. case, which involved a secondary boycott.

Any doubt that may have lingered over the years concerning the legal status of the secondary boycott in industries of an interstate character was removed with the passing of the Labor Management Relations Act. Under this act it is an unfair labor practice for a union "to engage in, or to induce or encourage the employees of any employer to engage in a strike or a concerted refusal in the course of their employment to use, manufacture, process, transport, or otherwise handle or work on any goods, articles, materials, or commodities or to perform any services," if the purpose of these acts is to force "any employer or other person to cease using, selling, handling, transporting, or otherwise dealing in the products of any producer, processor, or manufacturer, or cease doing business with any other person."

In the case of this particular unfair labor practice, which includes jurisdictional strikes as well, the National Labor Relations Board is obliged to obtain a five-day restraining order without notice if it finds that the employer will suffer "substantial and irreparable injury." Moreover, an employer who is injured by a secondary boycott or a jurisdictional strike has the right to sue the union for damages sustained and the cost of the suit.

18

THE CONTROL AND SETTLEMENT OF INDUSTRIAL DISPUTES

Disputes between unions and employers appear to be more or less inevitable; in fact if complete harmony existed one might suspect that there was something wrong. Because of the nature of the employment relationship differences of opinion are bound to arise. Fortunately, however, most of these differences and disputes never lead to actual conflict. They are settled peacefully, through the process of collective negotiation and collective bargaining, without eventuating in strikes or lockouts.

Since both the unions and the employers are desirous that their disputes should be settled, over a wide range of American industry both have agreed to the use of policies and techniques that facilitate effective settlement. Often this approach to the problem involves the use of outside talent furnished by either governmental or private agencies. Sometimes, however, the parties to a dispute are under legal compulsion to bring it before a governmental body.[1]

In the present chapter we shall devote most of our attention to the more important of the techniques that are used in the attempt to prevent differences between unions and employers from breaking out into open warfare. First, however, we shall note certain restrictions on work stoppages that are either self-imposed by the unions or are agreed to jointly by the unions and employers and em-

[1] In 1950 governmental agencies aided in the settlement of 26 per cent of the *actual* work stoppages that ended during the year. These stoppages were responsible for 85 per cent of the man-days of idleness. *Analysis of Work Stoppages During 1950*, p. 15, Bureau of Labor Statistics, United States Department of Labor.

bodied in their collective bargaining agreements. We shall also point out certain restrictions that are placed on strikes by the government.

Strike Restrictions

Union rules concerning the taking of strike votes and the granting of approval of strike action by union leaders constitute definite restrictions on work stoppages. But some unions go still further in their strike-control policies. A number of unions very intimately associated with the public welfare prohibit strikes completely. Most organizations of public service employees have in their constitutions provisions that rule out strikes: thus the constitution of the National Federation of Federal Employees states that "under no circumstances shall this Federation engage in or support strikes against the United States Government." The AFL will not issue a charter to any union of public employees unless the union's constitution has a no-strike clause in it. The inclusion of such a clause in a union's constitution is not an absolute guarantee against the occurrence of strikes, but stoppages will probably not occur unless employment conditions become extremely unfavorable.

Under the Taft-Hartley Act strikes by federal government employees are definitely ruled out. Employees of state and municipal governments are not subject to such rigid control, though their freedom of action may be somewhat limited. The whole question of strikes in the public service is an involved and controversial one: on the one hand, the employees are "servants" of the people, and very often servants whose work is of the utmost significance; on the other hand, they may be servants who are not well treated.[2]

Turning to private employees and employers it should be noted, first, that there are various kinds of strike-restriction provisions included in collective bargaining agreements.[3] Many agreements contain provisions that specifically prohibit strikes and lockouts for the duration of the agreement, and some also extend this prohibition to the period during which a new agreement is being negotiated. Some agreements that contain a provision prohibiting strikes recog-

[2] The question is taken up in *Employee Relations in the Public Service.* Chicago: Civil Service Assembly of the United States and Canada, 1942.

[3] For an extensive treatment of such provisions see *Collective Bargaining Provisions,* Bulletin No. 908-13, Bureau of Labor Statistics, United States Department of Labor.

nize, however, certain circumstances under which work stoppages are permissible, such as failure by the employer to live up to an agreement, or failure on his part to abide by the decision of a duly appointed arbitrator.

A collective bargaining agreement may include provisions relating to the matter of strike votes and approval of contemplated strikes by representatives of the parent union. It may also provide for giving the employer advance notice of strikes.

Penalty clauses for contract violations are frequently included in agreements. Individual workers participating in unauthorized strikes may be subject to discharge, suspension, or monetary punishment. The union itself may be required to take certain action concerning unauthorized strikes. Some agreements provide for an imposition of fines on the union, though it has become rather common for unions to insist on financial safeguards of one sort or another, including freedom from all financial liability, in agreements. Employers who are responsible for illegal stoppages of work may also be punished.

Collective agreements may place restrictions on sympathetic strikes. Furthermore, they may restrict strikes connected with secondary boycotts and job jurisdictional strikes—both of which are ruled out under the Taft-Hartley Act. In many agreements, however, unions are given the right to refuse to have anything to do with goods from companies whose workers are on strike or are unorganized, or from companies that are "unfair." Agreements may also contain provisions setting forth the circumstances under which workers may refuse to cross picket lines.

Finally, some agreements provide that disputed issues that have resulted in a strike or lockout will not be taken up until the workers are back on the job.

The provisions in collective bargaining agreements imposing restrictions on strikes and lockouts unquestionably help to reduce disputes and stoppages. But alone they are not enough; other "approaches" must be used. To these we shall now direct our attention, beginning with conciliation and mediation.

Conciliation and Mediation

In discussions of industrial disputes the terms "conciliation" and "mediation" are sometimes used interchangeably, and ordinarily not much harm is done by using them in this fashion. But there is some merit in making a distinction between the terms, particularly in view of the strong opinions held on the matter by some of the experts in the field.

Both conciliation and mediation, regardless of the flexibility with which they are defined, involve the use of outsiders. These outsiders try to aid in bringing about a settlement of the disputes, but they do not hand down any verdicts or awards. Under conciliation the outsider acts as a go-between, meeting with the two parties separately, bringing them together, and in general trying to aid them in coming to an understanding. His chief job is, in Professor George W. Taylor's words, "to keep negotiations going." [4] The conciliator does not offer a solution to any particular issue, though in an attempt to "get them talking again" and for other purposes he may suggest alternative solutions.[5]

In mediation the outsider does propose specific solutions; he acts positively. But he does not hand down any decisions—that is, he does not act as an arbitrator. The mediator can exert a definite influence on the course of collective bargaining and on the nature of the employment relationship, particularly if the mediator is a governmental appointee and if his suggestions are based on the results of an official fact-finding survey.

Appraisal. The use of conciliation and mediation in industrial disputes is on the whole very desirable. The help that an impartial outsider, or committee of outsiders, can render in bringing labor and management together may be of great value. The two parties to a dispute may get so aroused over their differences that they cannot act with due intelligence and negotiations between them may break down. The presence of a fair-minded, dispassionate, tactful outsider can do much to ease the tension and promote the continuance of negotiations.

If the impartial outsider makes definite suggestions, thus acting as a mediator, there is an element of danger present, however; the

4 *Government Regulation of Industrial Relations,* p. 102. New York: Prentice-Hall, Inc., 1948. Professor Taylor, one of the country's outstanding "triple threats" to industrial strife (as conciliator, mediator, and arbitrator), believes that a distinction should be made between conciliation and mediation.

5 A detailed presentation of the procedural steps involved in conciliation, and of other aspects of the conciliation process, will be found in an article by W. E. Chalmers in the *Industrial and Labor Relations Review,* April, 1948.

same danger that occurs under arbitration. The parties to the dispute may resort to mediation too readily; they themselves may not try hard enough to settle their differences. Such facile mediation was common under the operation of the National Defense Mediation Board early in World War II. It has also been happening under the operation of the National Mediation Board in the railroad industry.[6] Mediation is unquestionably a very desirable policy in industrial disputes, but only after the parties to the disputes have made a genuine effort themselves to iron out their differences.

If resort to mediation is sometimes excessively fast, it is also on occasion excessively slow: use of the process may be delayed until there is a very serious deadlock and a strike is under way. It has been said that "the true test of the mediators' mettle is not how many strikes they have 'settled' but how many they have averted." [7] To meet this test the mediators must come into the picture at the proper point of time—not too soon and not too late.

Conciliation and Mediation Agencies. In this country we have a variety of bodies that furnish conciliators and mediators in industrial disputes. Probably the most important one is the Federal Mediation and Conciliation Service, which employs more than 200 mediators and conciliators, almost all of whom are scattered around the country in the twelve regions under the Service. Most of the disputes dealt with by the Service come to its attention by means of "dispute notices." The Taft-Hartley Act provides that when either the employer or union wants to modify or end an existing contract the party seeking the change must notify the other 60 days before the proposed modification or expiration date, and that if no settlement has been arrived at 30 days before this date the Federal Mediation and Conciliation Service, and any state or territorial mediation body that exists, in the state or territory involved, must be notified that a dispute is present.

During the fiscal year 1952 the Service had 15,468 mediation assignments. Of these, 13,323 came to it in the form of "dispute notices." The Service also receives a certain number of requests from unions or employers, or from both, for mediation aid; these numbered 1,928 in 1952. Finally, in disputes that threaten the public in-

[6] Taylor, *op. cit.*, p. 109. *Sixteenth Annual Report of the National Mediation Board*, 1950, p. 34.

[7] Editorial, *The New York Times*, December 12, 1951.

terest, the Service may directly intercede; in 1952 there were 217 such instances of direct intercession. The Service does not play an active role in all the cases over which it accepts jurisdiction. In many of them (slightly over half in 1952) it acts in a stand-by capacity; and in some it is simply a consultant. In 1952 it participated actively in 42 yer cent of the cases.[8]

One aspect of the work of the Federal Mediation and Conciliation Service that deserves special mention is its efforts at "preventive mediation"—a type of activity that is aimed at improving the "day-to-day relations between labor and management."

Under the Railway Labor Act provision is made for conciliation and mediation procedures as well as for voluntary arbitration and fact-finding. This law establishes a National Mediation Board and a Railroad Adjustment Board. The former, which is composed of three nonpartisan members, has two chief functions to perform: the mediation of disputes relating to rates of pay, rules, and working conditions, and the determination of official bargaining agents. Its work is limited to railroads and airlines. If the National Mediation Board cannot bring about a settlement of a dispute by mediation, it has the duty of trying to get the parties to agree to arbitration, with the board standing ready to help in the arbitration proceedings. If a dispute cannot be settled by the parties themselves or with the mediation aid of the board, and if the board thinks the dispute will substantially interfere with interstate commerce, it must notify the President, who may set up an emergency fact-finding board. We shall say more about fact-finding on the railroads shortly.

The Railroad Adjustment Board, the second of the agencies provided under the Railway Labor Act, deals with disputes over the application and interpretation of collective bargaining agreements already in force. Its work is more detailed than that of the National Mediation Board, which has to do only with disputes over terms of new agreements. The Railroad Adjustment Board is divided into four divisions, each with equal representation of employers and employees. The first division, which handles the largest number of cases, has jurisdiction over disputes relating to such important occu-

[8] *5th Annual Report,* Federal Mediation and Conciliation Service, Fiscal Year 1952, pp. 33, 34, 36, 39. Of the 15,468 cases the Service declined to act in 1,905 because of "jurisdictional reasons"—especially because the cases involved intrastate commerce.

pational groups as engineers, firemen, conductors, and trainmen. The railway unions are not compelled to bring their disputes to the adjustment boards; such a step is permissive. Unfortunately, there has grown up a tendency to avoid consulting the adjustment boards and to resort to belligerent methods instead.[9] The unions that come under Adjustment Board Number 1 complain that it is too slow in processing the cases before it, and as a consequence they sometimes bypass it. By setting a strike date over an issue that should be settled by the adjustment board, they create an "emergency," and set in motion the elaborate machinery (mentioned in the previous paragraph) designed to handle serious issues.

The labor departments of the various states provide conciliators and mediators for industrial disputes, and a number of cities have established bodies to carry on activities in these fields. The work of the Toledo Labor-Management Citizens Committee is especially notable.[10] There may also be "private" mediation and conciliation. For example, the so-called impartial chairmen that are found in a considerable number of American enterprises or groups of enterprises sometimes mediate disputes as well as arbitrate them.[11]

One other agency may be mentioned, namely the Anthracite Board of Conciliation. This board has had outstanding success in settling, by conciliation and arbitration, disputes that have arisen in the anthracite coal industry over the interpretation of collective bargaining agreements. In 1953 the board observed its fiftieth anniversary.

Voluntary Arbitration

The Nature of Arbitration. The essence of arbitration in industrial relations is the handing down of a decision by an outside person or board on an issue, or issues, that cannot be settled directly by the parties involved. If both labor and management agree to the use of this procedure, the technique is called voluntary arbitration. If

9 *The New York Times,* May 14, 1950.

10 A description of the Toledo plan and of the plans of a number of other cities, by Victor H. Rosenbloom, will be found in the *Labor Law Journal,* October, 1952.

11 A good illustration of this "dualism" is found in the impartial chairmanship in the full-fashioned hosiery industry. See Thomas Kennedy, *Effective Labor Arbitration,* pp. 1, 57-58, 218. Philadelphia: University of Pennsylvania Press, 1948.

it is imposed upon them by the government, the technique is known as compulsory arbitration.

These two types of arbitration could be further broken down on the basis of how the award is accepted. Thus voluntary (agreed-upon) arbitration could have either voluntary or compulsory acceptance of the award; and the same could be true of compulsory arbitration. We shall assume, however, that voluntary arbitration is voluntary with respect to both initiation and acceptance of decisions, and that compulsory arbitration is compulsory in both respects. This assumption is not far from the facts, at least in this country.

Voluntary arbitration is very widespread. In thousands of collective bargaining agreements it is the final step in the grievance-handling procedure. Indeed, the use of this technique in connection with unsolved grievances is generally looked upon as a very desirable if not indispensable characteristic of good industrial relations. The suggestion has been made, in fact, that legislation should be passed requiring employers and unions to submit unsettled disputes over the *interpretation* and *application* of existing agreements to the process of arbitration. Though this would mean the adoption of a type of compulsory arbitration, it must be noted that the kind of disputes that would be covered would for the most part relate to minor matters. Disputes concerning *new* agreements would not be subject to the process.

But one can argue, apropos of the latter point, that there is no good reason why the use of the arbitration technique should not be used, as a last resort and *voluntarily,* in connection with new agreement disputes. It must be admitted that this is a controversial issue, though it should be pointed out that quite often arbitration is used in connection with such disputes.[12]

There is considerable variation in the scope of the issues that may come under an arbitrator's jurisdiction. In the case of grievances arising under collective bargaining agreements, the scope is conditioned in part by the range of provisions found in the agreements. But it may also be conditioned by specific statements on the

[12] There is rather strong support for this practice among union and management (small firms) representatives and arbitrators. For the results of a survey on this question and on other matters relating to the general question of arbitration, see the highly informative article by Edgar L. Warren and Irving Bernstein in the *Industrial and Labor Relations Review,* January, 1951.

matter of arbitrable issues, or by a listing either of the nonarbitrable issues or of those that are arbitrable. Although, in general, only disputes that involve the interpretation or application of the actual provisions of agreements are within the jurisdiction of the arbitrator, some agreements provide that any disputes that arise during the time an agreement is in force may be brought to arbitration. Issues that are frequently outside the arbitrator's jurisdiction are such matters as general wage changes, management prerogatives, and production standards.[13]

Should the arbitrator act as a mediator if a suitable occasion arises? As we have already noted, the impartial chairmen in some American industries perform this double role. Moreover, if arbitration is performed by a tripartite board, instead of by a single arbitrator, the mediation function, as Professor Taylor points out, is inherent in it.[14] It would seem that the arbitrator should not shun the role of mediator if that role seems to him a reasonable one.

The Arbitrator. Various terms are used to describe arbitrators. In the men's and women's clothing industries the term "impartial chairman" is used. In some companies in the automobile, rubber, and shipbuilding industries the term employed is "umpire." The most common term is simply "arbitrator."

In performing his duties the arbitrator (whatever term is applied to him) is supposed to act impartially, deciding each issue on its merits rather than on the basis of any predilections of his own. He listens to the two sides of the issue and gives attention to any written testimony that may be submitted. Then, acting in a judicial capacity, he makes an award. In addition to being impartial the arbitrator, according to an authoritative pronouncement on the subject, [15] should also be intelligent, of sound judgment, immune to pressure, and well acquainted with general labor relations. Moreover, he should have

[13] More detailed information on the scope of the arbitrator's work will be found in *Collective Bargaining Agreements,* Bulletin No. 908-16, pp. 87-96, Bureau of Labor Statistics, United States Department of Labor.

[14] It might also be added, as Professor Taylor further declares, that tripartite arbitration has a kinship to collective bargaining. The neutral member of the board and *either* of the other members can reach an agreement as conclusive as one reached by labor and management representatives themselves. See *Government Regulation of Industrial Relations,* pp. 136-137, 367. New York: Prentice-Hall, Inc., 1948.

[15] *Arbitration of Grievances,* Bulletin No. 82, p. 13, United States Department of Labor, Division of Labor Standards.

some experience in the industry in which he is acting and be acquainted with "job evaluation and incentive wage-payment plans." The arbitrator must indeed be an uncommon man!

The arbitrator may be either temporary or permanent; that is, he may act on a single case—with possible re-appointment, however, for later cases—or he may serve for a given period of time, perhaps for the duration of the agreement. A permanent arbitrator need not be on a full-time basis, of course. The impartial chairmen in the clothing industries are permanent; some of the umpires in the three industries mentioned a few paragraphs back are permanent but some are temporary. The simple term "arbitrator" generally covers temporary appointments.

Numerous agencies or institutions in this country furnish arbitrators to American industry. The Federal Mediation and Conciliation Service keeps a file of arbitrators and will suggest a panel from which the actual arbitrator can be chosen, or it will itself select the arbitrator if the two parties cannot agree. The Railway Mediation Board will serve in the capacity of arbitrator. State Labor Departments will also furnish arbitrators. Of outstanding significance in the field is the American Arbitration Association, an organization with thousands of names on its lists of arbitrators.

Individual Versus Board Arbitration. Arbitration may be carried on by single persons or by boards, especially by tripartite boards. On these boards there is at least one representative of each of the parties as well as an outsider who acts as chairman. Arbitration boards may also be composed wholly of outsiders, though in ordinary disputes there appears to be real value in having employers and employees directly represented.

No one arbitration system is best for all companies and all industries, since each case has its own particular conditions.[16] It appears, however, that the tripartite arrangement has special merit in disputes over the negotiation of new agreements. Information supplied by the representatives of labor and management is often vital to the settlement of such disputes. In disputes over the application of existing agreements the tripartite plan is of questionable value. In the

16 Further information on "systems" and "terms" used in arbitration will be found in the bulletin mentioned in the previous footnote, pp. 4-10; and in *How to Arbitrate a Labor Dispute,* by Theodore W. Kheel, pp. 9-11, pamphlet published by Prentice-Hall, Inc., 1946.

former disputes the issue is one of "interest"; in the latter it is one of "rights." Biased persons, who have a definite stake in the outcome of a decision, are not the best qualified to pass on the question of rights. "Whatever may be said in favor of the tripartite boards in the arbitration of interests," one experienced arbitrator has declared, "it seems to me that there is no good reason whatever for tripartite boards in the arbitration of rights." [17]

Appraisal. Voluntary arbitration is an excellent technique for handling disputes that cannot be solved by management and labor through direct negotiation. The voluntary aspect of the technique makes it especially desirable. It is a notable achievement when management and labor agree to submit an unsolved issue to an outside person or board for decision, instead of leaving the issue unsettled and a potential cause of unrest. But, as with most good things, excess should be avoided. The arbitration technique should not be used as a substitute for collective bargaining and collective dealing. Labor and management themselves should try diligently to solve their own problems without having recourse to the services of outsiders. Only in case of necessity should they seek the aid of arbitrators.[18]

Compulsory Arbitration

Proposals for the use of compulsory arbitration generally arise in connection with disputes in industries on which the public is vitally dependent. If work stoppages occur in such industries, not only may the public be seriously inconvenienced but the public health and welfare may be endangered. Such stoppages, it can be argued, should be declared illegal; the government should force the two parties to submit their disputes to arbitration; and the verdict of the arbitrators should be legally binding. This, in essence, is the case for compulsory arbitration.

On the surface such a plan seems to have much to commend it, but further analysis reveals a number of weaknesses, some extremely serious. In the first place, it is not easy to state precisely what disputes are of a public emergency character. For example, is a strike

[17] Professor Emanuel Stein, in *Proceedings* of New York University's Third Annual Conference on Labor, p. 176. Albany: Matthew Bender & Co., 1950.

[18] For a detailed discussion of this question see Harold W. Davey, "Hazards in Labor Arbitration," *Industrial and Labor Relations Review*, April, 1948, pp. 386-405; see also Professor Stein's contribution in the publication cited in the previous footnote.

of telephone workers a public emergency strike? The Attorney General of New Jersey has given an affirmative answer to the question, whereas a labor-management committee in Massachusetts has replied negatively.[19] The supporters of compulsory arbitration may, in the interests of "making sure," bring under such arbitration disputes that should be left in the hands of the parties themselves for voluntary settlement.

A second possible weakness of compulsory arbitration relates to politics and government. Political considerations may enter into the administration of such arbitration, and the principle itself may become a political issue. Moreover, there is a tendency under compulsory arbitration for the government to move into the area of price control as well as that of wage control. One aspect of this problem arises when a public utility commission has to decide whether or not a wage increase granted by compulsory arbitration should be taken into account when it sets rates.[20]

Another weakness of compulsory arbitration, especially with respect to wages, is the absence of satisfactory criteria for use by the arbitrators in making their decisions. In disputes relating to wages the arbitrators should award wages that are fair. But what are "fair" wages? Opinions differ. In the absence of clear-cut wage criteria the arbitrators may simply resort to compromise, which may ultimately lead to a deterioriation of labor-management relations.

Possibly the greatest weakness of compulsory arbitration is its tendency to undermine collective bargaining. The parties to a dispute "regard themselves as divested of responsibility for settling the case themselves," as Cyrus Ching, the first chairman of the Federal Mediation and Conciliation Service, points out.[21] "Bargaining becomes a sham. When either side feels that it may get a better deal from the compulsory action of government than by responsible negotiation, it maneuvers to force government intervention." This

19 *Proceedings* of Annual Meeting, 1949, Industrial Relations Research Association, pp. 16-17. Professor Thomas Kennedy has a good article in this issue on "The Handling of Emergency Disputes," with special reference to the compulsory arbitration law of New Jersey.

20 On the question of compulsory arbitration and price control see Professor Daugherty's remarks in the publication cited in the previous footnote, p. 44; see also Professor Kennedy's remarks on pp. 25-26.

21 *3rd Annual Report,* Federal Mediation and Conciliation Service, p. 3. Specific ways in which collective bargaining may be weakened are treated briefly by Professor Kennedy in the article referred to in footnote 19.

weakness of compulsory arbitration is not mere hearsay. It has expressed itself in actual practice in New Zealand, for example; and, closer to home, in the public utility field in New Jersey.

Finally, compulsory arbitration is not an absolute preventive of strikes. It makes strikes illegal in the branches of industry to which it applies, but it cannot prevent their occurrence. The workers may leave their jobs because of their dissatisfaction with an arbitration award. Thus there arises another problem, namely that of punishment or sanctions. It is an easy matter to insert penalties in a law, but it is not always easy nor practicable to apply them.

Any extensive adoption of the principle of compulsory arbitration in this country seems out of the realm of possibility. There is strong opposition, especially on the part of organized labor, to the use of the principle. A notable exception among union leaders who have spoken on the matter is President Hayes of the Machinists' union. In 1953 Mr. Hayes spoke in favor of compulsory arbitration of disputes that *really* threaten "our national security or welfare." [22] Despite the opposition, however, about ten states have laws that provide for compulsory arbitration of disputes in public utilities.

Fact-Finding—Emergency Boards

The policy of establishing emergency boards to obtain the facts in serious industrial disputes has become increasingly common in this country. Under such an arrangement boards are set up to investigate disputes and to report their findings. During the time the boards are making their investigations, and perhaps for a certain number of days after they issue their report, no work stoppages are permitted. But after this cooling-off period has elapsed strikes are permissible.

Fact-finding of this type is more severe than voluntary arbitration in that it has a number of compulsory features. Investigatory boards must be set up, if the conditions warrant the step, and strikes are ruled out for a certain period of time. Fact-finding is less severe than compulsory arbitration, since it does not involve the submis-

[22] Details of Mr. Hayes' plan will be found in *Labor Management Relations,* Part 5, pp. 1611 ff., Hearings, Committee on Education and Labor, House of Representatives, 83rd Cong., 1st Sess., H. Res. 115. For the results of a survey among management and union representatives and arbitrators, on the question of compulsory arbitration, see the article by Warren and Bernstein referred to in footnote 12.

sion of an award that must be accepted or an absolute prohibition of strikes. Fact-finding may thus be looked upon as a middle-of-the-road approach to labor disputes in essential industries.

Appraisal. The fact-finding method of approach, with its accompanying cooling-off period aspect, has two possible merits. In the first place the public can obtain a more accurate picture of the issues involved in a dispute and hence be in a position to exercise its influence more intelligently. For this potential benefit to be effective, however, the members of the public (or a sizable portion of them) must become acquainted with the facts that have been found, and their judgment must be influenced by the facts. It would seem that at best this benefit can be only partly achieved.

The second possible benefit of fact-finding is that during the cooling-off period the two parties directly involved have a chance to view the issues on which they disagree in a more sober frame of mind. When they are able to give a second, and a third, thought to these issues, they are more likely to reach an agreement. It must be recognized, however, that a period of enforced peace may sometimes raise the emotional temperature of the disputants, particularly on the labor side, rather than lower it. If the postponing of a strike is likely to lessen the chances of its success, labor is not likely to view the delay in a quiet, contemplative mood.

On balance the principle of compulsory fact-finding in connection with disputes in vital industries is desirable, though in extreme situations it is well to supplement it by some other policy. A crippling strike in these industries should not be permitted to go on endlessly. The experience of this country in the use of the fact-finding policy has not been too successful—how successful it has been is a matter of controversy—but in general it appears to have yielded positive results.

Examples of Fact-Finding. The fact-finding technique has been used for quite some time in the railroad industry. In the early part of the present chapter we noted briefly that if the National Mediation Board cannot bring about a settlement of a dispute, and if it is of the opinion that the dispute will substantially interfere with interstate commerce, it must notify the President, who may establish an emergency fact-finding board. If the President decides to set up such a board, the board has 30 days in which to make its investigation of the dispute and issue its report. During this period, and for an additional 30 days after the submission of the report, "no change, except by agreement, may be made by the parties to the controversy in the conditions out of which the dispute arose." This implies that no strike may take place during the specified period.

The Railway Labor Act, with its National Mediation Board and its Adjustment Board, has been referred to in times past as a "model" labor law; but doubts have been expressed concerning the appropriateness of that designation. The emergency-board procedure has been criticized on the grounds that instead of being an important device for promoting peace it has held back (or at least has *probably* held back) collective bargaining and voluntary arbitration.[23] It has been said that except in rare instances "there is no bargaining under the Railway Labor Act in many cases"; the parties merely act in a perfunctory manner until an emergency board is established. The National Mediation Board itself has expressed concern over this sidestepping of genuine collective bargaining "in national cases." [24] When the Act was passed in 1926 the general feeling was that emergency boards would be used only in the event of truly major disputes. But numerous boards have been set up to deal with minor disagreements of a sort that should be settled by the parties themselves, with mediation and voluntary arbitration if necessary.

The emergency-board procedure has not led to peace in the railway industry. The findings of the board have been frequently rejected. Between 1941 and 1950 the unions refused to accept the emergency boards' recommendations in five out of seven important disputes, with the result that the government had to take over the railways temporarily in three of them. In all of these disputes labor ultimately won more than the fact-finding boards recommended. Hence the charge has been made that labor looks upon the recommendations of these boards "as only a spring board upon which to predicate additional demands." [25]

Clearly the record of the Railway Labor Act in bringing about amicable settlements could be much better. Though neither the unions nor the employers are under any legal obligation to accept the

[23] Herbert Northrup in *Proceedings* of the Annual Meeting of the Industrial Relations Research Association, 1948, p. 87. See also p. 85.

[24] *Annual Report* of the National Mediation Service, 1950, pp. 7, 25, 34.

[25] *Hearings*, Subcommittee on Railway Labor Act Amendments of the Committee on Labor and Public Welfare, U. S. Senate, 81st Cong., 2nd Sess., S. 3463, p. 16; testimony of Walter S. Franklin, President of the Pennsylvania Railroad Co.

recommendations of the fact-finding bodies, one would expect, or at least hope for, a larger measure of compliance than there has been. It has been this noncompliance that has been to no small degree responsible for criticism of the Act and for the demand that compulsory arbitration be introduced into the industry. In 1950 a bill (S. 3463) to provide for such arbitration was introduced in the Senate. Hearings were held on the proposed measure but no action was taken.

The technique of fact-finding came into special prominence with the passing of the Taft-Hartley Act. Under this law a complicated plan for coping with national emergency strikes was set forth. The various procedural steps follow.

(a) If the President thinks that an actual or threatened strike covering a whole industry or a substantial part of it imperils or would imperil the health and safety of the nation, he has the right to appoint a board of inquiry. This board makes an investigation of the strike and submits a report within such time as the President shall prescribe. The report, which does not contain any recommendations, is filed with the Mediation Service, and its contents are also made public.

(b) When he receives the report from the board of inquiry, the President may direct the Attorney General to petition the district court for an injunction to prevent the strike from taking place or continuing. The court is to issue the injunction only if it finds that the strike affects all or a substantial part of an interstate industry and that "if permitted to occur or continue," it would imperil the health or safety of the nation.

(c) After the injunction has been issued, the parties to the dispute are compelled to "make every effort to adjust and settle their differences, with the assistance of the Service created by this Act." The President shall also reconvene the board of inquiry upon the issuance of the injunction, and at the end of 60 days, if the dispute is still not settled, the board shall again report to the President. Included in its report, which is made public, is the last offer made by the employer for the settlement of the dispute.

(d) During the 15 days following the presentation of this report the National Labor Relations Board takes "a secret ballot of the employees of each employer involved in the dispute on the question of whether they wish to accept the final offer of settlement made by their employer." Within five days after the voting the NLRB notifies the Attorney General of the result.

(e) Upon having the results of the balloting certified to him (or upon settlement of the dispute, whichever is sooner) the Attorney General requests the court to discharge the injunction, which it is directed to do.

(f) Then the President reports on the whole matter to Congress, "with such recommendations as he may see fit to make for consideration and appropriate action."

It is clear that the Labor Management Relations Act does not ban strikes in vitally necessary industries. It does not provide for compulsory arbitration. It does provide, however, for a cooling-off period, which may run as long as 80 days, instituted through the issuance of an injunction. During this period strikes and lockouts are illegal.

It should be noted that the law clearly states that the government cannot force a person to work nor prevent any individual worker from quitting his job. It also states than an employee or group of employees who leave their jobs because of "abnormally dangerous conditions of work" are not guilty of a strike under the act.

Between 1947 and 1953 the procedure just described was invoked 12 times, including three times in the bituminous industry. During this period the feeling that the Taft-Hartley plan for dealing with national emergency disputes was not satisfactory became more and more widespread, and indications pointed to its early alteration. The plan is too complex, and there is good reason for believing that it has been applied in situations that did not warrant its use.

Plant Seizure

Plant seizure by the government as a means of preventing very serious work stoppages has been used to some extent in this country. Under such a policy the government does not actually operate the plant or industry in a technical or business sense. The regular personnel continues to function as before, though the government is nominally in charge. With the plant or industry in the hands of the government, the workers are not supposed to go on strike. If they stop work, they are striking against the government, i.e., breaking the law.

Under the seizure policy the profits ordinarily go to the employer, as usual. The suggestion has been made that they should go to the government instead. This would be a rather extreme—and possibly unconstitutional—step to take. A compromise might be worked out under which a certain percentage of profits would be paid to the employer, with the government being the "residuary legatee." An example of this arrangement is found in Virginia, except that the government's percentage is specified. Under the Public Utilities Act of that state, the state government receives 15 per cent of the net income of a seized enterprise. It would also seem proper, under the seizure policy, to withhold further concessions to labor until ownership is back in the hands of the private employers (this is done under the Virginia act.) It has been suggested that plant seizure "might well be made as *unpleasant* as possible" to the employer and workers, [26] in order to give a greater incentive to the two parties to settle their dispute before the seizure stage is reached.

The seizure policy generally, but not invariably, prevents strikes. But by itself it does not settle them. An agreement between the two contestants must ultimately be worked out, possibly with the aid of government mediators. The policy itself, therefore, is no final solution to labor-management disputes, and it should be used only when the need is truly great, when there is a genuine emergency.

National Emergency Disputes and Discretionary Policy

A discretionary approach to the problem of national emergency disputes is advocated by some experts. Various lines of action—fact-finding, seizure, issuance of an injunction—might be taken, but the parties to any particular dispute would be left in the dark concerning the specific policy to be adopted. In his 1953 testimony on revision of the Taft-Hartley Act, Walter Reuther advocated this approach, pointing out that under the uncertainty feature neither party would be able "to calculate that its own interests would be better served by governmental intervention than by negotiation." This approach has also been advocated by others.[27]

[26] J. L. Miller, in *Proceedings* of the Industrial Relations Research Association, 1948, pp. 96, 97.

[27] Professor Archibald Cox, who also favors giving the President "the widest possible discretion in deciding . . . whether to intervene in a dispute," argues that the soundness of the discretionary policy is demonstrated by "both experience and analysis." *Proceedings of the Fifth Annual Conference on Industrial Rela-*

The National Association of Manufacturers, however, has spoken out against the discretionary policy, asserting that the national emergency strike provisions in the Taft-Hartley Act have worked out well and should be retained.[28] Other opponents of the measure argue that what we need is a *definite* policy, one embodied in a law and not one to be decided upon by the President or any other governmental group. The discretionary policy is not without its weaknesses, but on the whole it appears to be a desirable approach.

Preventive Action

As a concluding point in our discussion of means for coping with industrial disputes it might be pointed out that action could be taken to prevent disputes from arising in the first place or at least from assuming serious proportions.

Action of this type could take two chief forms. First it could involve the passing of legislation aimed at the elimination of certain policies or arrangements that appear to foment industrial strife or make it more serious. It has been suggested, for example, that industry-wide collective bargaining and also industry-wide unions should be ruled out. The feasibility of such a move is open to very serious question.

The second form of preventive action relates to the cultivation of certain habits of mind—enlightenment, tactfulness, broadmindedness, nondogmatism—on the part of labor and management, and the establishment of adequate means for handling industrial differences when they arise. Numerous suggestions along these lines can be found in the notable collection of monographs published by the National Planning Association under the general title, *The Causes of Peace Under Collective Bargaining*. These monographs are actual case studies and represent a valuable contribution to industrial relations writing.

---

tions, 1953, pp. 24-26; Department of Industrial Relations, School of Business Administration, University of Buffalo.

28 *Taft-Hartley Act Revisions*, Part 1, p. 271, Hearings, Committee on Labor and Public Welfare, United States Senate, 83rd Cong., 1st Sess. On p. 37 of the publication quoted in the preceding footnote H. C. Winch states, in opposition to the discretionary policy with respect to dispute procedures, that "We must have a government of laws, not of men."

19

UNIONS AND THE CONTROL OF INDUSTRY

According to an early American economist, "The capitalist is the captain of industry, who takes the unorganized mob of men, drills it into a disciplined army, supplies them with weapons, ammunition and a commissariat, and leads them to industrial conquests." [1] This picture is overdrawn but it brings out in a general way the traditional view of the capitalist, or, to use a more appropriate term, the capitalist-employer, under the free enterprise system. The capitalist-employer has long been looked upon as a captain or order giver exercising extensive control over men and things.

But the captain's authority has not been exercised without protest from the troops. Over the years there have been numerous critics of his power. Some of the critics have advocated the complete elimination of the captain; others, with more moderate aims, have pressed for a curtailment of his authority, and a corresponding increase in the authority of other groups, particularly organized labor.

Descending from the lofty verbal eminence to which our early American economist has taken us, let us classify the critics of capitalist-employer power into a number of categories. In the first category are the radical social reformers, who have sought the withdrawal of all power from the private capitalist-employers and the transference of this power to new employers, namely the public. In this category are the socialists and communists.

In the second category are the reformers of a less extreme turn of mind, who have argued not for the replacement of the present

[1] Robert E. Thompson, *Political Economy*, p. 135. Philadelphia: Porter & Coates, 1882.

system but for the establishment of working alliances between the employers and the workers, or at least the setting up of arrangements that would bring employers and workers more closely together.

In the third category are the reformers who have limited their aims to a simple, and often very moderate, reduction in the scope of the control exercised by the employer and an increase in the degree of control exercised by labor, by *organized* labor. These reformers are the ordinary union members and union leaders, who, without any interest in transforming the industrial organization of society or in establishing "Murray Plans," are nevertheless very desirous of reducing the power of employers. This desire finds expression in many ways, and efforts to achieve it have created one of the most important problems in present-day labor relations, namely the problem of management prerogatives.

We are now prepared to examine in some detail the question of control in industry. Our approach to the question will be in terms of the three categories we have just defined.

Radical Plans of Industrial Control

There have always been some persons who have believed, with G. D. H. Cole, [2] that what the present economic order needs is not mending but ending. They have therefore advocated the replacement of capitalism by some other type of "ism," usually socialism. Since socialism, both in theory and in fact, has been of different varieties, we shall note the essential characteristics of industrial control under a number of these varieties.

Democratic Socialism. Under democratic socialism the major industries of the economy are publicly owned, and the control of these industries is supposed to reside ultimately in the hands of the owners. This system resembles capitalism, then, except that the owners are different. Since the members of the public obviously cannot directly manage the socialized industries, a nice problem arises concerning the form that management should take.

This issue is a large one and we shall consider only a single aspect of it, but this aspect is very important. What should be the relationship between the unions and management? Should the unions as such be directly represented on the board that manages the plant or industry, or should this board be composed of persons appointed by

[2] *Labor in the Commonwealth,* p. 138. New York: B. W. Huebsch, Inc., 1920.

the democratically elected government, persons who in numerous cases would be unionists but who would not officially represent the unions?

This question has come to the forefront in Great Britain, and there opinion is divided. Within the Trade Union Congress, for example, one group believes in the principle of direct union representation on the management boards of industry; another group thinks that the unions involved should be consulted but not represented as such.[3] The latter view has prevailed in the TUC. It should be added, however, that the organization strongly favors union (or joint) consultative machinery at the various levels of industry, including the factory level. Those who oppose direct union representation on the control boards of industry believe that the unions should retain their independence,[4] that by being independent the unions are in a better position to look after the interests of their members. If unions were officially represented on the governing body of a plant or industry, the welfare of the members of the union might be sacrificed unduly to the welfare of society as a whole. As one writer has put the issue, though the British unions should do their utmost to increase production, "they must neither be, nor appear to be, the Government's subordinate agents in putting across its economic policy." They must not accept responsibility for the successful operation of industry nor for exercising discipline over their members.[5]

Guild Socialism. Several decades before the outstanding victory of the British Labor Party at the polls in 1946, a different type of socialism received considerable attention in Britain. This was guild socialism.[6] Under this type two principles were emphasized, namely functional democracy (or political pluralism) and self-government in industry. Under the latter the syndicalist notion of control by the workers, both manual and brain workers, in each industry was emphasized. It was felt that the various industries should be administered in this way rather than by departments of the government.

[3] See *Monthly Labor Review*, October, 1948, pp. 368-369.

[4] For discussions of this issue see Hugh Dalton, *Practical Socialism for Britain*, pp. 161-164. London: George Routledge & Sons, Ltd., 1936; *Political Quarterly*, January-March, 1949, article by G. D. H. Cole, especially p. 25; J. T. Murphy, *Modern Trade Unions*, pp. 182-196. London: George Routledge & Sons, Ltd., 1935.

[5] *The New Statesman and Nation*, November 27, 1948, p. 455.

[6] Good descriptions of guild socialism, and also of syndicalism, will be found in *The Encyclopedia of the Social Sciences.*

Over all these industrial units there would be an Industrial Guilds Congress. There would also be a separate body to look after the interests of the consumers.

An attempt was made to apply the guild principle in the building industry, but with little success. By the middle of the 1920's the guild socialistic movement was largely a thing of the past. It deserves mention here because of its principle of industrial self-government, a principle that has influenced the general socialistic movement in Britain and possibly elsewhere. The principle is still a rather vague one, however, and there is some difference of opinion on what it really implies. In general, it is clear that the guildsmen wanted to avoid, on the one hand, the tendency toward centralization that ordinary socialism seems to imply, and on the other, the decentralization of self-seeking individualism.[7]

Syndicalism. A few words should be said about syndicalism since it bears a rather close resemblance to guild socialism. Under syndicalism each industry, which would be socially owned, would be managed by independent syndicates of workers. These syndicates, however, would be joined together loosely into a national organization.

The syndicalist philosophy has been an element in the labor movement of a number of countries, especially France. The notion of each industry being solely under the control of the manual and brain workers of that industry has not met with widespread acceptance, however, though elements of the notion were applied in the fascistic structure of Italy, and some writers, like Professor Henry C. Simons, [8] fear that unions in this country, especially when they engage in industry-wide bargaining, have within them the seeds of syndicalism. The communists have been sympathetic to certain syndicalist ideas, but communism in action—as we see it in Russia—represents the very antithesis of the syndicalist philosophy of decentralized industrial control.

Communism. Though Russian leaders say their economy is a socialistic one and that communism is still to be achieved, the latter

[7] An excellent appraisal of guild socialism will be found in Adam B. Ulam, *Philosophical Foundations of English Socialism,* pp. 86-95. Cambridge: Harvard University Press, 1951.

[8] See "Some Reflections on Syndicalism," *The Journal of Political Economy,* March, 1944; reprinted in Henry C. Simons, *Economic Policy for a Free Society.* Chicago: The University of Chicago Press, 1948.

term is the one more commonly used in this country with reference to Russia, and we shall use it here.

Under communism, or any authoritarian economic system, the degree of control exercised over industry by the workers and their unions must of necessity be limited. The experience of Soviet Russia proves this point, though the Soviet leaders and theorists would perhaps deny the conclusion. Russia is a highly planned economy and one in which there is great centralization of control. Though the unions have a variety of functions to perform, such as administering the social security system, arranging recreational and educational activities for the workers, checking on safety measures, engaging in limited collective bargaining, and—especially—promoting production, they do not control the actual operations of industry. They do not determine what should be produced, how much should be produced, where it should be sold, whether an extension should be built to the plant, or how long the standard work week should be. These vital questions are decided by the higher-ups. If the separate unions in Russia had such control powers, the nice coordination that comprehensive planning requires would never be achieved. In so far as the Russian unions exercise influence in the determination of the over-all policies of the economy, they may be said to possess some degree of control over industry. But this influence is quite small.

In general it may be said that the Russian unions instead of controlling are controlled. As time goes on they may gain more power; but in any centrally planned, authoritarian economy the amount of real power that can be entrusted to the unions cannot be large.

The "plans" for altering the balance of industrial control that we have just been examining all involve the displacement, completely or substantially, of private enterprise. We shall now survey a number of more moderate plans.

More Moderate Reform Plans

Industry Council Plans.[9] In the early part of the World War II period the CIO, which had already evinced interest in the general

[9] Industry council plans resemble the codetermination system in Western Germany, about which much has been said, and done, during the last few years. For informative discussions of this system see Paul Fisher, "Labor Co-determination in Germany," *Social Research,* December, 1951; and William H. McPherson, "Co-determination: Germany's Move Toward a New Economy," *Industrial and Labor Relations Review,* October, 1951.

matter of planning, suggested a plan the immediate object of which was to "win the war." The plan involved the establishment of industry councils in the major industries, each council to contain representatives of labor, business, and the government. (Later it was suggested that consumers be included "where possible.") The tasks of these councils were, in Philip Murray's words, "to prepare the production schedules of the given industry for war purposes, to provide the means whereby expansion could be made, to increase the production of essential war goods, to establish and build plants in communities where the need for them was evident." [10] In addition to the industry councils the Murray Plan provided for the setting up of a National Production Council (or Board) to serve as a coordinating agency for the industry councils. Originally it was proposed that this council be composed of representatives of labor, management, and the government, with the President of the United States acting as its chairman. Later it was suggested by the CIO that agriculture be represented as well. The suggestion was also made that consumers too be given representation.

Although the Murray Plan was not adopted during the war period, it and the other CIO plans probably had some effect in bringing about the establishment of the labor-management production committees that were quite common at the time. They also probably influenced general governmental policy with respect to production organization.

Interest in the Murray Plan did not end with the war years. Mr. Murray claimed that the plan was just as essential in peacetime as in times of war, and the CIO has passed convention resolutions maintaining its peacetime applicability. In 1951 the CIO Resolutions Committee expressed the hope that through "an interchange of ideas and decisions between the Industry Councils and the National Production Board" a "general national plan may be evolved by democratic methods, and adjusted and perfected constantly through the years." At the same convention President Murray likened the plan to the codetermination scheme in Western Germany and stated that if society accepted it, it would be a "far cry from Socialism." [11]

[10] *The Nation,* November 4, 1944, p. 554.

[11] Convention *Proceedings,* pp. 251-254. How serious is the union advocacy of the industrial council plan is a matter of dispute. Daniel Bell's statement in

Another plan relating to the control of industry, and to the whole problem of industrial relations, is that advanced by leaders and scholars of the Catholic Church. The Catholic Plan, which involves a type of industrial order somewhere between socialism and capitalistic individualism, provides for cooperative action on the part of unions and employers at various levels.

In his notable encyclical *Quadragisimo Anno* (1930), Pope Pius XI declared that as far as possible it is advisable that "the work contract be somewhat modified by a partnership contract," and went on to state that "workers and others thus become sharers in ownership or management or participate in some fashion in the profits received." [12] This philosophy was restated by Pius XII in 1950, together with certain observations concerning labor's rights that at the time led to considerable discussion.[13]

Briefly, the Catholic Plan (expanded since the encyclical *Quadragisimo Anno*) provides for the establishment of quasipublic cooperative bodies of employees and employers. These bodies, which would supplement unions and employer organizations and not supplant them, would exist at various levels. From the single enterprise, or single trade, they would extend all the way up to industry-wide councils and to an over-all national council. Not only manufacturing, but agriculture, finance, and other "industries" might be covered as well. Moreover, the planning structure might provide for international cooperation.

The partnership idea has appealed to others besides Catholic theologians and scholars. More than a century ago John Stuart Mill, who stated that the subject of "healing the widening breach between those who toil and those who live on the produce of toil" is one "on which almost every thinker has his Utopia," advanced the idea. Mill wanted to see the worker elevated from a mere "receiver

---

Fortune (April, 1953, p. 123) that the "occasional" demands for such councils or for codetermination, are "merely rhetorical flourishes of convention speechmaking" seems extreme.

[12] *Quadragisimo Anno,* and also the famous encyclical *Rerum Novarum* (of Pope Leo XIII), are reprinted and extensively interpreted in J. Husslein, *The Christian Social Manifesto.* Milwaukee: The Bruce Publishing Co., 1931. For a more recent discussion of the general subject treated above, with special reference to the United States, see John F. Cronin, *Catholic Social Principles,* Chap. VII. Milwaukee: The Bruce Publishing Co., 1950.

[13] See *America,* July 15, 1950, p. 395; August 5, 1950, pp. 459, 461-466.

of hire" to some sort of partnership in industry.[14] More recently the idea has been associated, at least to some extent, with what is ordinarily called union-management cooperation, a type of "partnership" arrangement (of limited scope) that we shall discuss shortly. The vision of capital and labor working together as partners, rather than as class antagonists, is one that has definite appeal. The great problem is to devise effective means for bringing the vision closer to reality.

In concluding our discussion of industry councils a few words should be said by way of appraisal. The acceptance of the council plan would involve an important change in the general nature of industrial control and in the philosophy of industrial relations. It would mean the introduction of functional, or pluralistic, government into industry. Such an arrangement would not meet with ready acceptance by management, with its strong desire to retain its old prerogatives. It would also meet with opposition from highly class-conscious unionists.

The industry council idea would involve a more extensive use of the planning principle in American industrial life. "The heart of the Industry Council Program," one of the CIO leaders has declared, "is the idea of national economic planning." [15] How much planning, one might well ask, would such a program involve? And how much planning do we want?

Moreover, when unions and management cooperate on an industry level there is danger that the two parties will—"in the interests of achieving stability"—restrict production rather than increase it. The existence of a *national* council, and the representation on it and also on the industry councils of consumers, might prevent restrictive policies; but one cannot be absolutely certain of this result. Should restrictionism arise it may be necessary to exert extensive governmental control.

The possibility of restrictionism, and of other undesirable con-

[14] *Dissertations and Discussions,* Vol. II, p. 289. Boston: William V. Spencer, 1865. See also Mill's *Principles of Political Economy,* Ashley ed., Book IV, Chap. VII. London: Longmans Green & Co., 1926. From the latter source we learn that Mill believed that "if mankind continues to improve" the kind of association that would finally predominate would be associations of the workers themselves (rather than workers in partnership with capitalists) who would select their managers.

[15] Mr. Brophy describes and argues for the industry council plan in *The Commonweal,* November 12, 1948, pp. 110-112.

sequences, is tied up with the moral quality of the persons, both employers and unionists, under the plans. Are they likely to act "properly"? It should be noted that the Catholic plan calls for a change not only in industrial government but also in "individual" government. "All that We have taught about reconstructing and perfecting the social order," said Pius XI, "will be of no avail without a reform of morals" (a sentiment that undoubtedly would have been shared by Carlyle, who believed that the greatest Reform Bill is that which is passed in the human breast).

One final observation should be made about industry council plans. In terms of structure, and assuming only workers and employers would be represented on the various councils, there is a high degree of similarity between such plans and the defunct Fascist set-up, with its employer and employee syndicates, that was found in Italy. Of course, the proposed industry councils in this country would not be under the domination of an all-powerful state. At least one hopes not.

In view of the limitations and dangers we have just suggested, does the industry council idea have anything to commend it? Should it be applied? A recent writer on the subject suggests that there should be "modest and tentative experimentation with it." [16] To establish any type of industry council plan on a large scale at the present time would seem to be undesirable.

Union-Management Cooperation. Another moderate reform plan that would give unions some measure of control power is union-management cooperation. Under this arrangement the union cooperates with management in the discovery and application of new ideas for increasing output. Cooperation of this sort involves *participation* by the union in functions that are generally performed by management alone; and the term "participation" has come into widespread use as a substitute for the older expression.[17]

[16] Howard B. Bowen, *Social Responsibilities of the Businessman,* p. 174. New York: Harper & Bros., 1953. Professor Bowen's book, which is one in a series on "Ethics and Economic Life" produced by a study committee of the Federal Council of Churches, contains a useful chapter entitled "The Industry Council Plan."

[17] The term "participation" is applied to, or at least associated with, other arrangements in addition to union-management cooperation. These include "multiple management," "consultative supervision," and "bottom-up management." See the discussion by Douglas McGregor in *Management Record,* September, 1950.

Union-management cooperation first came into prominence in this country in the early 1920's, though it had received a certain amount of attention during World War I.[18] The Baltimore and Ohio railroad applied the plan with considerable success (a term commonly used at the time was the "B & O Plan"). In Canada the Canadian National Railways also made successful use of the plan. These companies still carry on with the cooperative scheme. On other railways the plan failed.

Union-management cooperation on the B & O and the CNR has been of the "committee" type, with joint committees of management and labor at a number of levels. But other kinds of cooperative arrangements have also been put into operation. Unions have acted jointly with management in matters of research; they have tried to stimulate sales; they have supplied management with technical aid (the Printing Pressmen's Union is an outstanding example); they have aided in the promotion of general efficiency, including, in the ladies' garment industry, management efficiency!

The committee type of union-management cooperation is the kind with which we are here most concerned. During World War II this type of union-management cooperation (labor-management cooperation, to use the more accurate term) was greatly emphasized. More than 5,000 committees were set up. Many of these committees were of little or no consequence, but the number of successful ones was large enough to make the experiment definitely worth while. Production during the war period was unquestionably increased as a result of their work. After the war was over most of the committees unfortunately went out of existence, but a few hundred survived.[19]

Since the end of World War II much less has been heard of union-management cooperation, at least in the United States; but a considerable number of cooperative ventures are being carried on, some with marked success. A new kind of cooperation, sometimes referred to as the Scanlon Plan (its author, Joseph N. Scanlon, is on the staff of the Massachusetts Institute of Technology and is a former officer of the Steel Workers' union) has aroused consid-

[18] For a brief account of the historical background of union-management cooperation, especially during World War II, and for an analysis of such cooperation, see the author's *Contemporary Unionism in the United States,* Chapter 26. New York: Prentice-Hall, Inc., 1948.

[19] *Monthly Labor Review,* August, 1948, pp. 123-126.

erable interest and gives promise of continued growth.[20] The Scanlon Plan, which in truth is not a definite plan or arrangement, involves participation by the workers in the process of improving methods of production, and the receipt by the workers of "productivity bonuses."

Union-management cooperation, or "participation," represents the attainment of an advanced stage in union-management relations. Where such participation is carefully introduced and carefully operated, a number of important results may be achieved, results that will be of benefit to the employer, to the workers, and to society at large.

From the standpoint of the employers the following are some of the potential benefits. (a) For one thing the employer will probably have a more competent working force. This is due not only to the greater opportunity the workers have for giving expression to their ability and ingenuity but also to the improvement in the general psychological atmosphere of the plant or enterprise. An atmosphere of mutual trust and respect, of good will and cooperativeness, is more conducive to high productivity than one of mutual dislike and fear. With higher morale, and using better methods, the workers will turn out not only more goods but better goods. The experience of the joint committees during World War II bears out the truth of this statement, as does the prewar experience.

(b) Production is also increased as a result of the suggestions the workers make and the ideas that emanate from joint consultation between union and management representatives.

(c) The amount of supervision required may be much less, and costs should be reduced as a consequence; accidents may be cut down, and compensation expenses reduced; absenteeism and labor turnover, two things that may be very costly, may be less; materials may be saved; and tools and equipment may, through better use, last longer.

(d) Union-management cooperation promotes efficiency not only on the part of the workers but also on the part of management. By stimulating management into making a more careful study of pro-

[20] For a discussion of the Scanlon Plan by George P. Schultz, one of Scanlon's colleagues, see *Frontiers of Personnel Administration,* pp. 77-87. New York: Department of Industrial Administration, Columbia University, 1951.

duction problems, it leads to improvements that would not otherwise be made.

(e) Management may assume a broader point of view concerning the underlying purpose of industry and even of life in general. Stimulated by cooperation with the union, management may become more interested in making goods and less interested in making money, although its ability to make money should be increased (for reasons just mentioned). It should be pointed out, however, that although union-management cooperation may encourage the development of this broader vision on the part of management and also on the part of labor, breadth of vision is essential to the success of union-management cooperation.

The gains to the workers and to society at large from union-management cooperation can to some extent be gathered from the list of potential results just presented. In brief, the workers benefit in both economic and noneconomic ways. The noneconomic benefits, which involve such intangibles as the opportunity of "doing," the feeling of individual worth, and the achievement of a higher level of industrial democracy, are to be especially emphasized. These values, as well as the value of a higher standard of living, are of great significance to the individual worker as well as to society.

Union-management cooperation does not succeed automatically. Certain conditions are necessary before it can succeed, and a nice problem for the student of labor is to figure out what these conditions are.

Labor Representation on the Board of Directors. Under the capitalistic form of industry the directors of business organizations represent the owners, i.e., the stockholders. The owners may sometimes be employees, and very often they may be consumers of the products their particular business turns out; but the directors represent them solely in their capacity as capital suppliers, not as labor suppliers or as consumers. This type of arrangement is so common that we generally take it for granted. It would be possible, however, to have a different kind of structural set-up for business directorates, and a number of proposals to that end have been made.

During the 19th century there was considerable discussion of what was called copartnership in industry. This involved employee stock ownership and was connected with the principle of profit sharing. Under the copartnership plan employee-owners elect a number of directors from their own ranks to act with the other directors. Though the plan was tried out in a number of companies in Great Britain and on the continent (the Godin plan has long attracted attention), it was not widely adopted; and today one hears little about it. Though there are thousands of employee-owners in some of our large enterprises, the idea of separate employee-directors meets with little support. As the number of such owners increases, and particularly as the volume of stock held by them becomes larger, this plan may receive more attention; whether or not it does remains to be seen.

Another plan involving the idea of employee-directors provides for union representation on the board. These directors would not represent the employees as owners but as union members. This type of arrangement is sometimes discussed, though interest in the plan is not widespread. (An attempt has been made to place two union representatives on the board of the American Telephone and Telegraph Company, but without success.)

The policy of the union, or unions, in an enterprise having representation on the board of directors might produce certain worth-while results. Such representation could improve the lines of communication between the ordinary employees and the directors; it might promote the making of useful suggestions by the employee-directors for improving production methods and general employee relations; it might lead to a more moderate policy in labor matters on the part of both union and management. However, this type of pluralistic industrial government does not seem very practicable at the present time. The presence of one or two union men on the board of directors might lessen the aggressiveness of the union to such an extent as to arouse extreme dissatisfaction among the workers. They might fear that they were being sold out. On the other hand, the union directors might, in the interests of currying favor with their fellow unionists, engage in stalling tactics on the board. Again, the other directors would probably feel that it was a nuisance having union members on the board. Furthermore, it is possible that the directors' meetings might degenerate into rather inconsequential gatherings, with the important issues being handled on the outside.[21] Finally, if the union representatives serving as directors

[21] For further discussion see Sam A. Lewisohn, *Human Leadership in Industry,* pp. 3-7. New York: Harper & Bros., 1945.

were officials of the parent union, it is possible that there might be "interlocking directorates," with the union men acting on the boards of a number of competing enterprises. This, as J. M. Clark points out,[22] might lead to the settlement of differences through the adoption of restrictive policies. Such settlements would be at the expense of the public.

In view of the various considerations we have noted, it is not surprising that the plan for union representation on the directorates of American enterprise has met with little support. The outlook for this type of moderate reform plan does not seem too promising.

Management Prerogatives

Walter Reuther has declared that "you can't have free labor without free management." [23] In a basic sense, and the sense in which Mr. Reuther was speaking, this is correct, as the experience of Russia and Nazi Germany indicates. However, looking at the matter from another point of view it can be said that management cannot be free if labor is free. The possession of freedom by the workers implies that they have the right to form unions; and the establishment of unions involves a definite curtailment of management's freedom.

In Chapter 14 the point was made that collective bargaining, which is the chief method used by unions in seeking their objectives, represents a change in the form of industrial government, namely a shift from the principle of unilateralism to that of bilateralism. This shift means that the unions now participate in the control of industry. Even though they may not look upon their demands for such things as seniority rights, vacations with pay, and the union shop as a struggle for control, that is what these demands represent. In fact we may go so far as to say that unionism by its very nature involves the question of control. Parenthetically, we may say too that the presence of unions in an enterprise introduces a new type of gap between control and ownership (the old gap being caused by the wide dissemination of stock ownership, the issuance of nonvoting stock, and so on).

[22] *Guideposts in Time of Change,* p. 185. New York: Harper & Bros., 1949.

[23] *The Economics of Collective Bargaining,* p. 4; pamphlet, Institute of Industrial Relations, University of California. Mr. Reuther also affirmed that there cannot be free management without free labor.

During recent years the "control" aspect of unionism has come into more prominence. The unions have greatly increased the variety of their demands, going beyond the old triumvirate of high wages, shorter hours, and better working conditions. And as they have expanded their demands they have cut deeper and deeper into the territory management has traditionally guarded as its own. Hence there has arisen in dramatic form the question of where "The Frontier of Control" [24] should be located. Or, to state the issue in other words, there has come into the forefront the question of "management prerogatives."

As one would expect, there has been an immense amount of disagreement between unions and management over the scope of these prerogatives. This disagreement was well brought out in the National Labor-Management Conference, called by President Truman and held in November, 1945.[25] Committee II of the Conference, the Committee on Management's Right to Manage, found it impossible to submit a joint report. The labor members of the committee, though believing that "the functions and responsibilities of management must be preserved if business and industry are to be efficient, progressive, and provide more jobs," were opposed to spelling out the specific functions of management, a procedure that the management representatives favored and that, in their separate report, they partially followed. The management men concluded from labor's opposition to the listing policy that the unions would "continue to expand into the field of management," a conclusion that was clearly correct. This philosophy of expansion would lead to joint management, something that the management representatives opposed.

The unions have repeatedly stated that they do not want to run industry. Nevertheless nearly all of their policies restrict or interfere with management's performance of this function. Ordinary demands for wage increases represent interference with management's prerogatives, though they may not be viewed in this light by either management or the union. A demand for the use of the seniority principle in layoffs and promotions, or for union par-

[24] This is the title of a book written by Carter L. Goodrich, and published by Harcourt, Brace & Howe, in 1920. Dealing with British unionism, the book is a pioneer contribution in the field of "management prerogatives."

[25] See Bulletin No. 77, United States Department of Labor, Division of Labor Standards.

ticipation in decisions concerning technological improvements, or for the abolition of contract work done by outsiders—these demands not only represent interference but are likely to be looked upon as doing so.

That unions have been trespassing more and more on the preserves of management is generally recognized, and sometimes deplored. Professor Neil Chamberlain, who has made an extensive study of the subject, has stated that of the "broad areas of management responsibilities there is not one in which labor unions have not at some time intervened"; [26] and the extent of the intervention is increasing.

In view of the legal responsibility of the managers to the owners, the traditional and firmly established view concerning the place and functions of management in industry, and the power-consciousness of the managers, it is not surprising that the inroads that labor has been making into management territory have been strongly opposed. Nor is it surprising that management, following the precedent established by the unions, has come out more and more for "management security."

In their approach to the difficult and explosive problem of rights or prerogatives, management may use either of two points of departure. It, and the union too, may think of the problem in general, more or less abstract terms; or it may think of it in terms of specific situations or cases. The former approach, though it may give rise to an interesting intellectual exercise, can, when used by the men on the ground (and not in the classroom), lead to a great deal of emotional heat. The latter approach, which involves taking up each case on its own merits without talking vaguely about management's rights or labor's rights, is likely to lead to better solutions and more amicable industrial relations. The "problem-centered" approach, rather than the "principal-centered" one seems to be one of the fruitful "causes of industrial peace." [27] It gives the collective

[26] *The Journal of Political Economy,* March, 1944, p. 103. Professor Chamberlain's views are set forth at length in *The Union Challenge to Management Control.* New York: Harper & Bros., 1948. Arthur M. Ross takes a position somewhat opposite to Chamberlain's. He argues that the "erosion of managerial authority" is not as great as is sometimes alleged. See *Labor Law Journal,* June, 1951, p. 437.

[27] See, for example, Case Study No. 7 in the series, *Causes of Industrial Peace Under Collective Bargaining,* p. 71, by Charles A. Myers and George P. Shultz. Washington: National Planning Association, 1950.

bargaining process a degree of flexibility that is often extremely valuable. At the same time, however, it leads to a situation of uncertainty, a situation that management and also the union may well want to avoid. In many collective bargaining agreements there are provisions of one sort or another, therefore, relating to the rights and responsibilities of management and the unions.[28]

Some employers believe that the specific rights of management should be set forth in agreements in order to avoid confusion on what is, and what is not, subject to the collective bargaining process. Other employers are opposed to this policy. They feel that such a listing may be incomplete and that the unions may get the impression that anything not specified may be bargained over. A "saving clause" may obviate such a difficulty, of course; and sometimes such a clause is inserted in the agreements.

In the agreements in which the rights of management are specified, the individual rights are usually of two broad types: those that have to do with "the tangible aspects of the business," such as location of plants, technological methods, and business practices; and those relating to employer-employee relations, such as hiring, promotion, and discipline. In the other type of agreements there may be only a very general statement concerning management rights, such as "The union recognizes that the management and operation of the company's business is vested solely in the company." In some agreements in which the specific rights of management are listed, there may be a provision to the effect that in practice these rights are subject to the other contract provisions. And even where a provision of this character is not found, such a limitation on the specific rights is generally implied.

In addition to setting forth the rights of management, collective bargaining agreements may list the rights of the union. Such a list may include specifications on the presence on company property of outside representatives of the union, the examination of company records, and the use of bulletin boards.

There is occurring before our eyes an unmistakable realignment of the frontier of control in industry; and a problem arises concerning the extent to which this realignment should go. The ques-

[28] Bulletin 908-12 of the United States Department of Labor, Bureau of Labor Statistics, deals extensively with the subject.

tion is a difficult one; it is clear that it cannot be settled in terms of "what has been." The fact that management has exclusively performed certain functions in the past is no justification in itself for the continuance of the practice. The dictum that "Whatever is, is best" is not true in industrial relations, or in anything else. On the other hand, no change in past procedures can be justified on the basis of "a change for the sake of change." The issue is one that must be considered in the light of two basic criteria (assuming that the process of realignment does not go beyond the ordinary legal limitations imposed by property rights). The first is the output of industry, which in turn is tied up with productive efficiency. The second is what might be called democracy in industry. The former, which is of special interest to management and should be of greater interest to the unions, relates to the *product* of industry. The latter, which is of particular concern to the unions and should be of greater concern to management, relates to the *processes* of industry. Without belittling the contribution that large industrial output makes to the wealth and welfare of the nation, it is still possible for one to say that some loss in productive efficiency might be sacrificed in the interest of greater union participation in industrial control. But there is a danger that if management is greatly restricted in the performance of its traditional functions, efficiency and output may be seriously impaired. This would be harmful to the workers, to management, and to the populace at large.

No precise statement can be made concerning the proper distribution of power between management and unions. The line of demarcation would vary from place to place and from time to time. If the "product-process" ends of industry are given careful thought by both parties; if a flexible, nondogmatic attitude is assumed by both; and if the "problem approach" is used, solutions to the issue should ordinarily be within reach. The issue is indeed a thorny one, but if it is properly handled it should not lead to industrial strife.[29]

[29] For discussions of possible techniques that could be used in handling the issue, see *Partners in Production,* pp. 103-112. New York: The Twentieth Century Fund, 1949; also Chamberlain, *op. cit.,* Chapters 10-12. Chamberlain's proposal is for a system of "functional integration," within each enterprise, of the union or unions and management.

Industrial Control and the Government

For a long time industrial control was almost wholly in the hands of the employer. With the growth of unions the employer has had to share this control; as we noted earlier, a system of bilateral government in industry has to an increasing extent been substituted for a unilateral type. In reality, however, the new system is more accurately described as a trilateral one. Over the years, and especially since the middle of the 1930's, the government has intervened increasingly in industrial affairs. Congress has passed wage and hour laws, industrial relations acts, and social security measures. The state governments have passed legislation of a similar character. In addition there has existed for many years legislation relating to such matters as workmen's compensation, factory conditions, and wage payments.

All of this legislation represents, either directly or indirectly, interference in the control of industry. It curtails the freedom with which the employers operate their businesses. Though the employers exercise the major portion of industrial control, and will continue to do so as long as the system of free enterprise exists, it is important to bear in mind that the government and the unions both share in the control.

There is widespread agreement among students of labor that apart from governmental interference in such matters as workmen's compensation, minimum wages, and child labor, there should be for the most part freedom of action for management and unions to work out by themselves the solutions to industrial relations problems. In other words there should be, in peacetime at least, free collective bargaining, subject to such controls as will prevent the grosser abuses that may arise under such bargaining.

A certain amount of government intervention is necessary if adequate balance is to be preserved in the matter of industrial relations. The extent of the intervention is, and should be, subject to change, however. It should change with variations in the atmosphere of public opinion. But wise public policy in this field is not easily achieved. There is likely to be a lag between changes in public thinking and the adoption of appropriate legislation; laws may be unduly inflexible and not make proper allowance for exceptional, and sometimes highly important, situations; on occasion the legislation may achieve a result opposite to that anticipated. Greater enlightenment on the part of our legislators and improved administrative procedures are probably necessary before we can produce policies that are "informed and appropriate to the ends sought." [30]

[30] For a fine discussion of the topic touched on above see Murray Edelman, "Government's Balance of Power in Labor-Management Relations," *Labor Law Journal,* January, 1951, pp. 31-35.

20

UNIONS, THE STATE, AND SOCIETY

In the preceding chapters we have examined rather minutely many of the practical, down-to-earth aspects of American unionism and American industrial relations. Now we must lift up our eyes and look at some of the larger issues that stand out on the horizon of our study. The particular issues that we shall deal with at the present point center around the relationship of unions, the state, and society. This relationship constitutes an extremely important issue in the general field of labor, and it is desirable for us to study it with care.

State and Society

After the long analysis contained in the last ten chapters we should be reasonably well acquainted with the nature of a union. But what is a "state"? And what is "society"? These terms must be analysed before we can proceed with our discussion.

The state may be looked upon as that organization or institution within society that possesses the legal and constitutional power to enforce commands. The particular agency that enforces these commands is the "government"; in our discussion we will use the terms "state" and "government" interchangeably.

Society, as the preceding definition implies, is more comprehensive than the state. It includes the state but it includes many other institutions as well, institutions of a noncoercive nature such as churches, unions, business organizations, bridge clubs, and sewing circles. Society is thus a social unit of a diverse and comprehensive nature. It is a community made up of individuals who are members of the state, but who at the same time are usually members, *voluntary* members, of numerous other bodies. We may think of society, therefore, as being composed of individuals who are bound to one another not by one relationship but by what Professor Robert M. MacIver has aptly called a "web of relationships." [1]

The community to which the term "society" refers may vary greatly in the diversity of its activities and organizations. It may also vary in its geographical extent. It is possible to think of a local society, or of a national society, or even of an international (world) society. In the present discussion we shall give attention to all three of these, concentrating for the most part however on the first two.

The difference between the state and society and the relationship of unions to both can be well expressed diagrammatically. Figure 2 relates to a free society, such as we have in the United States; Figure 3 relates to an unfree, authoritarian society such as Russia.

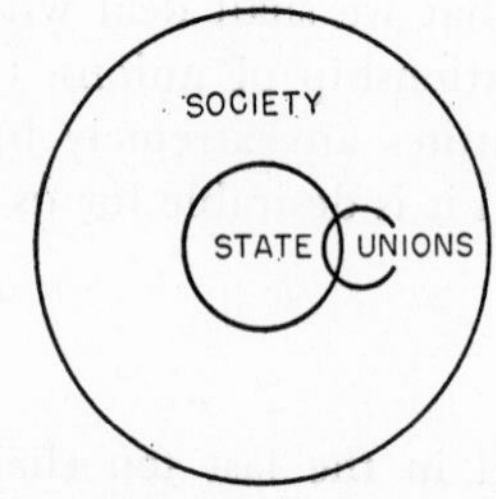

Fig. 2. Unions, state, and society in a free economy.

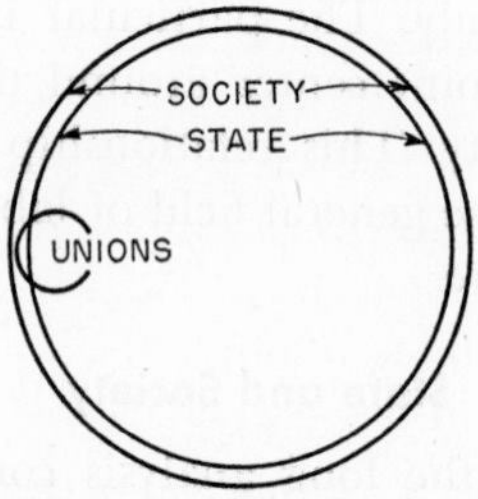

Fig. 3. Unions, state, and society in an authoritarian economy.

In an authoritarian society the state bulks large. It exercises control over a large part of society; even the painting of pictures and the composing of music may be subject to its coercive influence. Labor organizations are dominated by the state and possess little real freedom; as Figure 3 shows they are largely "within" the state. In Russia, for example, the unions are not independent bodies but, as the AFL has long declared, company unions. The company in Russia is the state and, like many companies in this country in the era before the Wagner Act, it controls the unions.

In a free society the state is small in comparison with society. In fact, in a totally free society, such as that envisaged by the an-

[1] *The Web of Government.* New York: The Macmillan Co., 1947.

archists, there would be no state whatsoever. All of one's allegiances would be of a voluntary character; complete laissez-faire would prevail. In the actual free societies, if we may still use the term, there is a coercive state but its functions are limited. However, as we are all well aware, the influence of the state has been growing greater and greater. To some extent this has been inevitable. In any society that becomes increasingly industrialized and more and more complex and interdependent the powers of the state must expand. But, one may well ask, how far should they expand? How "positive," to use Harold Laski's term, should the state become? This is a question that we may well ask but that we cannot take the time to discuss.[2] The particular issue to which we must direct our attention at this point is the interrelationship of the state and the unions.

Unions and the State

Before discussing the interrelationship between unions and the state, we should first examine two political characteristics of unions. The first of these is the parallelism, in both structure and function, between the typical union and the state.

Unions as Private Governments. The national and international unions, which, it will be recalled, are the most powerful units in the general union structure, resemble the national state. The fact that the majority of these labor organizations have members in Canada lessens somewhat the degree of resemblance, but by no means destroys it. The local units that make up the nationals and internationals may be compared to the local or municipal governments. And the organizations between the locals and the parent union bodies resemble the state governments.

A second type of structural parallelism between unions and the state is also worthy of notice. This involves the two labor federations, the AFL and CIO. The central organizations of these bodies resemble the national government; the state federations and state industrial union councils resemble the state governments; and the city central bodies and local industrial union councils resemble the municipal governments. Though there is a higher degree of

[2] Further discussion of the relationship between the state and society will be found in Robert Warren *et al.*, *The State in Society*. New York: Oxford University Press, 1940; Felix Morley, *The Power of the People*, Chapter 5. New York: D. Van Nostrand Co., 1949; and Ernest Barker, *Principles of Political and Social Theory*. Oxford: Clarendon Press, 1952.

structural similarity between the union organizations and the parallel government bodies in this breakdown than in the first, the first is the more significant because the union units in it more closely resemble the parallel government units in terms of power and functions.

A national or international union is a sovereign body, like the national state. It passes laws, levies "taxes," and on occasion engages in "war." Like the national state such a union organization may be bureaucratic, may be exposed to graft, and may come under the control of dictatorial leadership. Like the state, too, it may join other unions in alliances, such as the AFL, the CIO, and the International Trade Secretariats. Where the union shop exists, membership in the union is compulsory, just as membership in the state is compulsory.

Because of these points of similarity between unions and the state it is not surprising to find the former sometimes referred to as "private governments." This is, indeed, what they are. There are other private governments as well, such as those among business and farm groups; and the number of these "governmental" bodies has been increasing.[3]

The parallelism between unions and the political state weakens, however, when unions are viewed in terms of their external operations, especially those relating to collective bargaining. No longer are they sovereign bodies passing legislation independently. Their powers of government are shared with business; or, to state the matter more accurately, and in a manner suggestive of historical sequence, the unions share with business the powers of governing industry. As we noted in Chapter 14 there is a bilateral determination of the labor "laws" under which business is to operate. In the political sphere there is nothing exactly comparable to this. However, it is still proper, and also very meaningful, to refer to the process of collective bargaining as legislative in character.

Unions as Political Institutions. Unions have been referred to not only as private governments but also as political institutions.

[3] Professor Charles E. Merriam spoke of "the vast proliferation of what might be called private governments within the general framework of the political state." See *Public and Private Government,* p. 7. New Haven: Yale University Press, 1944. Further discussion of the "private government" concept will be found in Beardsly Ruml, *Tomorrow's Business,* especially Chapter 3. New York: Farrar & Rinehart, Inc., 1945.

The term "political" as it is used here refers not to the participation of unions in national, state, and municipal politics, but to the internal operations of the unions, and especially to the operations centering around the union leaders. Like any political unit or organization a union is interested in its own preservation and in attaining greater influence. Its officers, like political leaders, are interested in retaining power; and to this end they must constantly seek to "deliver the goods." [4]

It might be pointed out, incidentally, that it is especially desirable that management understand the political nature of unionism, since such an understanding can contribute significantly to amicable industrial relations.

The Interrelationship of the Unions and the State. In terms of its relationship to the state, a union—all unions, in fact—may be thought of as an *imperium in imperio.* Our problem now is to discuss the interrelationship of the *imperium* and the *imperio.*

To begin with, to what extent does the *imperium* exercise control over the *imperio*? To an excessive extent, antiunionists would declare. To an inadequate extent, unionists would respond. The exact influence that American unions exert over the state is difficult to gauge. Moreover, the degree of influence varies considerably from time to time. Of one thing we may be certain, however, and that is that over the last few decades the power of unions in the affairs of the state has grown considerably. With the large increase that has taken place in union membership, and with the expansion of union political activities, organized labor has become a political force to be reckoned with.

As the numerical strength of the unions continues to grow, the influence of unions in the political state will increase. It is conceivable that in time the state will come under the domination of the unions, which is a condition that some persons, such as the late Harold Laski, [5] strongly favor. As far as the United States is concerned, however, this domination is not likely to be achieved very soon. The

[4] For a discussion of the "political institution" idea, see Arthur M. Ross, *Trade Union Wage Policy,* pp. 13-16, 37-43, 63-64. Berkeley and Los Angeles: University of California Press, 1948.

[5] See *The American Democracy,* Chapter VI. New York: The Viking Press, 1948. Laski contends that the establishment of a labor party in the United States is indispensable to the attainment of the objectives of the American labor movement. *Ibid.,* pp. 247, 255.

attainment of such a condition would involve the establishment of a labor party, and for a number of reasons (see Chapter 12) the setting up of such a party does not seem to be imminent.

Turning now to the influence of the state over the unions, we should refer again to Figures 2 and 3. In a free society unions, like other social organizations, carry on their activities largely outside of any *direct* controls imposed by the state. It is asumed that these organizations in seeking their own good are generally led "as by an invisible hand" to promote the good of everybody, or at least not to harm the good of everybody. This harmony-of-interests doctrine, it is interesting to observe, is reversed under an authoritarian system. There each social organization in seeking, probably under compulsion, the good of everybody is supposed to promote its own good.[6]

With the growth of large social units, such as "big labor" and big business, the likelihood of diverging interests between society and its constituent units increases. Thus there arises a growing need for state intervention, to the end that a large degree of harmony of interests may be achieved.

The imposition of state controls is usually fraught with danger, however, and such controls should not be adopted if there are other means that can be used. To some extent there *are* other means. A more highly developed social consciousness on the part of the economic and social groups in society would obviously help. To some extent such a consciousness has been developing in American society; it is still a rather slender reed, however, though probably not as slender as some persons believe.[7]

Another way in which the general good can be protected is to have the groups act as checks on one another. Thus big labor may serve to counterbalance big business, and vice versa. The "conflict of opposites" may, in Hegelian fashion, result in a compromise or synthesis that is conducive to the general good, at least as conducive

[6] It makes a vast difference whether the quest for the general good is undertaken voluntarily or involuntarily.

[7] Professor Clair Wilcox has said that "To expect the leaders of pressure groups"—in which unions are included—"to become farsighted, to embrace altruism, or to be guided by the precept of the Golden Rule is to expect the leopard to change his spots." *The Harvard Business Review,* November, 1950, p. 59. In contrast to Wilcox's opinion is the view that "simple morality" is at the bottom of the "transformation of American capitalism." *Fortune,* February, 1951, pp. 79, 158. The truth is probably located somewhere between these two extremes.

to the general good as can be expected. However, if the "opposites" should join forces and cooperate in restricting production and raising prices, the general good will clearly not be promoted to the extent that it should be.

The state must stand in readiness, therefore, to prevent self-seeking groups, acting individually or cooperatively, from doing things that are either socially harmful or, as is more likely, that do not contribute to the social good as much as they should contribute.

Unions and Society

The Changing Status of Unions. One of the most important developments in American society during recent decades has been the change that has taken place in the position and power of unions. Unions have long existed in this country; and in certain industries and certain communities they have been firmly entrenched and highly influential. But looking at industry in general, and at society as a whole, the fact remains that in times past labor organizations to a large extent have been peripheral institutions. Beginning in the middle of the 1930's, however, this condition began to undergo a profound change. Unions started to grow at great speed and soon moved into a more central and more strategic position in both industry and society. Today their position is one of prominence and power. It is true, of course, that there are industries and communities in which labor organizations still count for little; but the number of these is becoming smaller. The likelihood is that during the years ahead union growth will continue, though at a slow rate, and union influence will expand. As social institutions the unions will become increasingly important.

The change that has taken place in the position of unions in society is reflected in many ways. To begin with, it is clearly seen in the vast amount of attention that is now given by the public at large to union affairs and activities. Our daily papers contain a great deal of news concerning unions, especially when they go on strike or do other things that are supposed to be harmful to society. Some papers have special labor experts on their staff. When more than 200 reporters are on hand at a union convention—specifically, at a recent CIO convention—it is unquestionable proof that unions play a key role in the affairs of society. Not only do our newspapers devote a large amount of space to union news but many of our magazines do likewise. Some of the latter have special labor departments or sections. In addition, union news is disseminated in large quantities over the radio.

The changing place of unions in society is also reflected in the increasing public recognition given to unions and union leaders. Union representatives are asked to serve on a wide range of governmental bodies; this practice is not new, but it has become more and more common. Particularly significant is the appointment of union men to offices in the field of international relations. Thus, for example, 31 union leaders aided in the labor program of the Economic Cooperation Administration, and others have been appointed by the State Department as labor attachés.[8] No union leaders have been appointed as yet to ambassadorial posts, but that step is just a question of time. It might be mentioned that an American union leader, John L. Lewis, found a niche in a book entitled *The 100 Most Important People in the World Today,* published in the early 1950's.

At the same time that union leaders are being called upon increasingly to serve in posts of an international nature, the unions are taking an added interest in international affairs. This interest is clearly manifested in the active participation of both the AFL and the CIO (and also the United Mine Workers) in the International Confederation of Free Trade Unions; in the granting of financial aid to foreign unions; [9] in the large amount of attention given to international affairs at the annual conventions of the two federations; and in other ways.

In local communities unions are receiving an increasing amount of recognition—quite often, however, as a result of their own initiative. Union members are found on school boards, on community chests (in 1952 it was reported that 50,000 members of the AFL and CIO were serving on community chests and councils and affiliated bodies), [10] and on other community organizations. In 1950 the City of Brotherly Love even went so far as to pick a unionist as "Man of the Year." Occasionally an institution of higher learning confers an

[8] *Fortune,* October, 1951, p. 115.

[9] CIO unions, for instance, gave over $15,000,000 to the trade union movements of other countries during the decade ending in 1951. *The CIO News,* October 1, 1951, p. 6.

[10] For a description of the community service activities of the CIO and the AFL see *The House of Labor,* ed. by J. B. S. Hardman and M. F. Neufeld, Chapters 29, 30. New York: Prentice-Hall, Inc., 1951.

honorary degree on a union leader (Walter Reuther and David Dubinsky, for example, are both LL.D.'s), but such an act is still a deed of considerable daring.

The greatest piece of evidence indicating the changing status of unions in society is furnished, of course, by industry. As we indicated in Chapter 14, the government of our business units is to an increasing extent being changed from unilateralism to bilateralism. Through collective bargaining unions are participating more and more in the formulation of the private laws under which industry is governed. This change is one of immense significance, from the standpoint of both industry and society. Indeed it represents in both spheres a veritable revolution.

The increasing political strength of labor is also indicative of the new place occupied by unions in society. Though this strength is by no means completely unified, it is nevertheless of great influence. The political power of the unions is widely recognized by the populace at large. It is also widely recognized by candidates for political office.

What is Emerging? Professor Slichter has advanced the notion that we are changing from a capitalistic to a "laboristic" society. With more than three out of every four persons working for a living in the United States now having the status of *employees*—a condition very different from that of a century ago—Professor Slichter believes that "employees and their representatives are coming to replace businessmen as the most important single influence in the community." [11]

Professor Slichter's thesis is contrary to that of James Burnham, who, in his *Managerial Revolution,* argues that the key men in society are now the managers (not the capitalists). It is also somewhat contrary to the contention of Thorstein Veblen, who, in *The Engineers and the Price System* and in other writings, emphasized (as did the technocrats) the great importance of the technologists.

What type of society, one may well ask, do we *really* have? Is it essentially capitalistic, or laboristic, or managerial, or technological? This is a difficult question and one on which, in Edmund Burke's

[11] *The Harvard Business Review,* May, 1949, p. 49. See also *What's Ahead For American Business?* pp. 25-26, 191-192. Boston: Little, Brown & Co., 1951. Professor Edwin E. Witte has argued against the laboristic theory, maintaining that (at the present time) our society is far more managerial than laboristic. See his article in the *Industrial and Labor Relations Review,* October, 1950.

fine language, "an appeal to the authorities only thickens the confusion." All the characteristics suggested by these terms are associated with present-day society; and furthermore all the characteristics are highly important. It seems to the present writer, however, that the laboristic feature has become, and will continue to become, increasingly significant. The grounds for this belief are the continuing large number of persons with the status of employees, the increasing development of unions, and the constant raising of the educational levels of the masses.

It is not to be inferred that the employees are going to control completely the capitalists and the managers and the technologists; but it does seem likely that the employees are going to exercise a much larger measure of control in the future than they have in the past. And what is more, employee interests and employee values are going to be reflected more and more in the standards and practices of society. The "probable future of the working classes" is one of greater power and influence.[12]

In the course of time, as real wages go up, an increasingly large number of employees will become part owners of industry through the purchase of stock. This development will have a definite effect on society. It seems likely, however, that for many years the employee point of view among the bulk of the populace will prevail over the owner point of view. This is as far as we shall carry our speculation.

That unions are now highly important institutions in American society is beyond dispute. Let us examine now the general effects of the unions on the well-being of society. Do unions promote the welfare of society or do they harm it?

The Welfare of Society. In considering the question of unionism in its relationship to social welfare, it must be admitted at the very outset that we cannot reach any quantitative conclusions, since neither the various effects of unionism nor human welfare can be accurately measured.

Social welfare is what one might call a multidimensional magni-

[12] The student of labor will find the discussions of the "probable future of the working classes" in the following three sources of definite interest. John Stuart Mill, *Principles of Political Economy,* Ashley ed., Book IV, Chap. VII. London: Longmans Green & Co., 1926. Arnold Toynbee, *Lectures on the Industrial Revolution,* New ed., Chap. IV. London: Longman's Green & Co., 1908. *Memorials of Alfred Marshall,* ed. by A.C. Pigou, pp. 101-118. London: Macmillan & Co., 1925.

tude; to state the notion in different terms, it is a magnitude with many elements or parts. Fortunately it is possible for our present purpose to place all of these parts into two categories, which we can label "economic" and "noneconomic." Social welfare, therefore, may be thought of as containing two subdivisions, namely economic welfare and noneconomic welfare. The difference between the two is easy to comprehend: the former can be measured, at least approximately, in money terms; the latter cannot.

The economic welfare of American society may be best measured in terms of the national income or, what is the same thing, in terms of the national output. If the national output is increased, population remaining the same or not increasing proportionately, economic welfare is increased. It must be assumed, of course, that there is no increase in the general price level and that the pattern of income distribution remains the same.[13] If the national output is decreased, economic welfare is diminished.

It does not follow, however, that changes in economic welfare always bring about similar changes in total social welfare, either in direction or in degree.[14] But generally speaking an increase in the national output and in economic welfare brings about *some* increase in total welfare, and a decrease in the former is likely to cause a decrease in the latter.

In dealing with the influence of unions on the general welfare of society, it is necessary to give attention to the effects unions have on production. But it is also necessary to consider the effect they have on the noneconomic welfare of society—on such things as the feeling of worth and dignity on the part of the individual members of society, their active participation in political and industrial affairs, and their possession of free speech, good health, and trustworthy friends. Such things cannot be measured in money terms, but are of great concern to the welfare of the individual and of society at large.

[13] It is conceivable that if the enlarged national output were more unequally divided than the original output, the economic welfare of society under the greater output might be less than under the smaller output. Stating the same point in a somewhat different way, an increase in per capita output (or income) does not *necessarily* mean an increase in economic welfare.

[14] This whole question is discussed at length in Professor A. C. Pigou, *The Economics of Welfare,* 2nd ed., Chapter 1. London: Macmillan & Co., 1924.

Unions and Economic Welfare. In Chapter 23 we shall discuss at length the effect of union action on the size of the national output and on average real wages. Here we shall simply state the conclusion we shall reach in that discussion: the over-all effect of union action on production appears to be favorable. However, even if unions have an adverse effect on production, they are still desirable in any society of a democratic nature. Unions are not merely economic institutions, and must not be appraised solely in economic terms. They confer upon the workers individually and upon society as a whole benefits that cannot be measured in terms of dollars and cents. It is to these noneconomic benefits that we shall at the present point direct our attention.

Unions and Noneconomic Welfare. In the discussion that follows we shall not attempt to deal with all the ways in which unions contribute to the noneconomic welfare of their members, of nonunionists, and of society. Rather, we shall concentrate on a few of the more outstanding ones, particularly the contribution unions make to the functioning of a democratic society.

(1) Unions help to give greater meaning to the lives of their members, which is assuredly an important element in the welfare of society. Under mechanized production work tends to become monotonous and unpleasant. The individual worker loses much of his individuality; he often becomes a mere hand—a cog, and a little one at that, in the machine. Unions help to remedy this condition. They give the worker a feeling of individual worth; they increase his self-respect, at the same time that they decrease his feeling of dependence on the employer. They give him a sense of "belonging," and enhance his stature both as a worker and as a citizen. It may be that in some instances they have "warped him, weakened his courage and self-reliance, dimmed his hope of the future, made him bitter, envious and discontented." [15] On the whole, however, there can be no doubt that unions do a great deal to make the outlook of the worker broader and his life more interesting.

Professor Frank Tannenbaum goes so far as to say that unions concern themselves with "the whole man," and have as their ends

[15] The writer of the above words thinks it is questionable if unions have done as much good as of harm to the American worker. See Bulletin No. 122, Personnel Service, American Management Association, p. 34.

"the good life." [16] As a statement of "what is" this seems exaggerated, certainly as applied to the actual functioning of most American unions. As a statement of "what ought to be," the view is subject to controversy.[17] The point should be emphasized, however, that to an increasing extent unions in this country are concerning themselves with matters of a noneconomic nature.

(2) The pressure that unions have long exerted for better and more extensive educational facilities has been an important factor in the educational progress of the nation. The building up of our public school system has been in part a response to union influence. The more recent ventures of unions into the field of workers' education, although limited to union members, have also contributed to general educational progress. Moreover, the opportunities that unions give their members to participate actively in organized effort and to become leaders in their organizations are by no means devoid of educational content.

(3) The union struggle for higher wages, shorter hours, and improved working conditions has contributed to the better health of the workers and to that of the nation as a whole. To some degree this improvement has been an economic achievement: it has been a factor in bringing about greater production. But better health contributes to noneconomic welfare as well. It has psychological benefits that cannot be measured in terms of dollars and cents. The success achieved by the Amalgamated Clothing Workers in curbing sweatshops in the men's clothing industry, for example, represents both an economic and a noneconomic victory, not only for the union but for society at large.

(4) Any discussion of unionism and the welfare of society would be incomplete without some consideration of the relationship between unions and democracy. Since, in contrast to many of the other topics already mentioned in the present chapter, it has not been

[16] *A Philosophy of Labor,* pp. 10-11, 162-163, 198-199. New York: Alfred A. Knopf, 1951.

[17] A nice problem exists concerning the extent to which unions should cater to the varied interests of their members and increase their union- and labor-consciousness. Should unionism be "limited" or "total" in character, to use Will Herberg's terminology? See *Labor and Nation,* April-May, 1946. Herbert Northrup, agreeing with Herberg's point of view, declares that democracy in this country is fortified rather than imperiled by the absence of "a cohesive, class-conscious organization which is essentially interested in all aspects of workers' lives." *Labor and Nation,* May-June, 1949, p. 36.

previously discussed, it will be given extended treatment at this point.

Unions and Democracy

Speaking at the 1940 convention of the AFL, Sir Walter Citrine, Secretary of the British Trades' Union Congress, declared that "Trade unionism is both a cause and a product of democracy." That unionism is a product of democracy is a fact that cannot very well be denied. Unionism, in the sense of free, autonomous labor organizations, cannot exist under a system of political dictatorship. But is unionism a cause of democracy, as Sir Walter further stated? Does it promote acceptance of the democratic ideal? Does it extend the application of democratic processes and ends? Let us "look at the record."

Nondemocratic Practices. It is very easy to point to union policies and practices that are definitely undemocratic in nature. The treatment meted out to Negroes by some unions is an example. A considerable number of unions either exclude Negroes from membership or give them a subservient status. Such practices are not those of a government of the people, by the people, and for the people.

Another debit item in the record is the presence in some unions of dictatorial leaders. If there is any one thing which, above all others, characterizes a democratic organization, it is the free, unfettered election of its leaders. Unless its leaders are elected by the membership, no organization can be called democratic. Democracy is a process, and free elections are the most important part of the process. Self-imposed and self-perpetuating leadership, no matter how successful it is in winning gains for its constituents, is incompatible with real democracy. It is impossible to say how extensive dictatorship is in union organizations. The more outstanding dictators, particularly those who are racketeers at the same time, generally receive a great deal of publicity. But the little dictators are ordinarily unknown to the public, and the scope of their work or control cannot be ascertained. It is probably considerable.[18]

[18] A good statement on the "democratic rights of union members," which covers the two points raised above as well as others—particularly the matter of disciplinary action against union members for misconduct—will be found in the CIO's Convention *Proceedings,* 1952, pp. 292-294. See also the discussion of union

Another nondemocratic feature of unionism is the long tenure of office found in numerous labor organizations. Despite free elections the same men stay in office year after year. The problem involved here is not an easy one, as we noted in our discussion of union government; but there is a strong likelihood that the quality of democracy in many unions would be improved if the tenure of office were reduced in length, or at least in continuity. Such a reduction could be achieved by opening up the columns of the union paper to persons or groups opposing "the administration," which is seldom done; by establishing, where possible, the party system in union government; or by placing limitations on continuous years in office.

Certain union policies in the field of collective bargaining are nondemocratic, in the sense that they prohibit or restrict freedom of action on the part of the individual unionist and perhaps of the individual worker. The chief argument against the union shop and the closed shop, for example, is that they are undemocratic; they are un-American; they abridge the individual's right to work (without belonging to the union). It must be confessed that such shops have a nondemocratic tinge in that they force some workers to become unionists against their will. However, as we noted in Chapter 15, there are arguments on both sides of the issue, and one cannot reach a conclusion on it simply by referring to one argument, especially when that argument itself may be called into question.[19]

Democratic Practices. If the record relating to unionism and democracy contains debit entries, it also contains credit entries. In the first place, although many union groups are run in a dictatorial fashion, many are conducted on a democratic basis, with the rank-and-file members having the opportunity not only to express their views and influence action but also to rise to positions of leadership.

---

discipline in Chapter 11. It should be pointed out that in the absence of unions the number of dictators on the side of management would be much larger. Clyde Sommers, in a discussion entitled "Union Powers and Workers' Rights" (in which he emphasizes the power exercised by unions over individual workers), well observes that "the economic soil from which unions spring has been almost barren of democratic practices." *Michigan Law Review,* Vol. 49, 1951, p. 817. (Reprint Series, Department of Industrial Relations, School of Business Administration, University of Buffalo.)

19 It can be argued that union-security shops *are* democratic when the majority of the workers want them. Of course, if such shops are imposed on the workers and on management by dictatorial union leaders, they do not represent the will of the majority and are obviously nondemocratic.

The opportunity thus afforded by the unions—the local unions—for debate and for active participation in a wide range of activities is in keeping with the democratic tradition.

The fact must be recognized, however, that in many union groups the degree of *active* democracy is limited.[20] Attendance at meetings of local unions is often very small, with most of the union members assuming an attitude of complacency or indifference toward union affairs. There are occasions, to be sure, when interest rises to a high level; but in day-to-day affairs the rank-and-file members of many unions, particularly the more sizable ones, exhibit little interest. This problem has recently attracted the interest of labor students, and much has been written on the subject.[21]

In any organization founded on democratic principles there is a real danger that the early enthusiasm for democratic procedures will weaken as the organization becomes well established. As long as it has to struggle for existence its members display a keen interest in how it functions, but when once the organization becomes accepted, when once it has "arrived," the interest is apt to drop off. This happens in some unions, but it need not invariably happen if the unions take definite steps to overcome the tendency. And, as a matter of fact, some unions are already taking steps to increase membership interest in union affairs. Democracy in unions, like democracy in the political state, is something that must be nurtured.

The government of the parent unions represents democracy to some degree, especially where the referendum is used. As we noted in Chapter 11, the referendum may be rather cumbersome, but it is unquestionably democratic. One cannot speak with the same degree of enthusiasm about the conventions of the parent organizations.[22] The delegates to these gatherings are generally "professionals"—not ordinary rank-and-file members. Some of the delegates attend with excessive frequency. Sometimes delegates find it difficult, if not im-

[20] The degree of activity, in local unions, tends to vary inversely with the size of the local. A fine discussion of the point will be found in Joel Seidman, "Democracy in Labor Unions," *The Journal of Political Economy*, June, 1953.

[21] The most extensive study is George Strauss and Leonard R. Sayles, *The Local Union: Its Place in Industrial Government*. New York: Harper & Bros., 1953. See also Joel Seidman's article referred to in the previous footnote, and Kermit Eby, "The 'Drip' Theory of Labor Unions," *The Antioch Review*, Spring, 1953.

[22] For discussions of this issue see the articles by Seidman and Eby cited in the previous footnote.

possible, to get a hearing on the convention floor. Sometimes important matters are dealt with in a rather careless way. The president of the union, who is chairman of the convention, frequently wields extensive power over committee appointments. The conventions, obviously, do not provide an example of democracy at its best; and yet, with all their weaknesses, they are by no means wholly undemocratic. They represent a few drops—more than a few drops, indeed—in the democratic bucket. It is well to point out, however, that they would make a greater contribution if the differences in union policy were organized more or less on party lines, as in the International Typographical Union, and if union policy reflected more discussion by the rank and file.[23]

Another democratic practice in unionism, and one of immense significance, is the grievance machinery provided for in collective bargaining agreements. The settlement of grievances no longer resides solely in the hands of management. Unions now participate actively in the work along with representatives of management. The establishment of grievance procedures gives thousands of workers experience in applied democracy, a type of experience they would probably not get anywhere else.[24]

The whole process of collective bargaining may be viewed as an achievement in democracy. Indeed it is sometimes referred to as "industrial democracy." Unionism represents an attempt to replace autocratic processes in industry by democratic ones, although quite often, unfortunately, it merely substitutes other forms of autocracy. But looking at unionism as a whole it can be said that in the work of collective bargaining and in the performance of other union activities a great many workers are given the opportunity of participating in meaningful undertakings. Possibly 3,000,000 persons are engaged actively in union "work." [25] This participation certainly contributes to the development of a democratic society.

[23] On this point see Eby's article. Joel Seidman aptly describes the ITU as the "Great Britain of unionism," and states that "compared to the ITU, most unions are in the Latin-American stage of political development." *Ibid.*, p. 229. An extensive analytical description of the ITU, by Seymour M. Lipset, will be found in *The British Journal of Sociology,* March, 1952. (Issued also as Reprint No. 42 by the Institute of Industrial Relations, University of California.)

[24] In the Steelworkers' union alone about 25,000 workers are engaged in grievance work, at various levels. *Steel Labor,* June, 1952, p. 15.

[25] "About 3,000,000" is suggested by J. B. S. Hardman in the *Harvard Business Review,* January-February, 1953, p. 45. The figure appears to be a little high.

Unions contribute to the dignity and self-esteem of the worker and in this way help to strengthen the foundation on which democracy is built. Without unions the worker is definitely subservient to his employer. He must do what the employer orders or run the risk of being discharged. The only defense he has is his right to quit his job, and the exercise of that right is not always pleasant. The employer may, of course, be benevolent and grant his workers concessions far beyond those that a union could win for them. But that is paternalism, and paternalism is fraught with danger, not only because it may be withdrawn at any time but also because it may debase those who profit from it.

Besides contributing to the development of the worker as a member of industrial society, the unions also contribute to his development as a citizen. They encourage their members to vote on election day, and discuss in their journals and other publications many of the issues that confront the electorate. Their members frequently serve on educational and other civic bodies. Activities along these lines, regardless of the impelling motive behind them, make the union members better citizens.

Conclusions. An examination of the record, only part of which we have actually passed in review, offers convincing evidence that unions are not only a result of democracy but also, on the whole, a cause of democracy. Not only do they aid in the application of the democratic ideal in the field of politics, but also they extend the ideal to another segment of human affairs, namely industry. The cause of democracy in this country would suffer if unions were nonexistent.

But, as is clear from our previous discussion, unions are not democratic institutions *par excellence.* Neither are cooperative societies, churches, or the political state. In appraising unions, therefore, both as democratic institutions and in terms of their contribution to a democratic society, it is not fair to judge them in terms of a perfect, and unattainable, ideal. It is still legitimate, however, and also highly desirable, to try to devise means both private and public that will enable them to come closer to the ideal.

Further Considerations. Any democratic nation engaged in war must submit to a large degree of centralized, authoritarian control. In the interests of national safety the democratic process must be set aside in many activities. This fact should suggest why unions have had difficulty in adhering closely to the democratic ideal. Whereas nations have been engaged in wars only intermittently, unions have been engaged in them frequently and, as a consequence, have had to depart from strict adherence to democratic principles and procedures.

Unions, in a sense, have been "fighting democracies," out of choice or necessity. Some years ago A. J. Muste pointed out that unions try to embody within themselves two very different types of social structure: that of the army on the one hand, and that of the democratic town meeting on the other.[26] In seeking to do this they are confronted with a difficult problem, since in a town meeting authority is derived from below, whereas in an army authority is derived from above.

As the fighting stage in union-management relations declines, and there is some reason for believing that this is the trend, unions will be able to make a more extensive use of the democratic process, just as a nation in time of peace can make a more extensive use of it. Democracy in unions, then, will tend to grow as employer opposition to unions diminishes.

Finally, there is the general problem of democracy and efficiency. In democratic political states and in unions the fundamental problem, as the Webbs long ago pointed out in their *Industrial Democracy,* is "how to combine administrative efficiency with popular control." It is interesting to observe that in both unions and political democracies it has been found necessary, in the interests of administrative efficiency, for the electorate to submit to an increasingly large amount of centralized control. Self-government has had to suffer more and more in the interests of good government.[27]

The trend toward centralization is not without its dangers. It may lead to a great deal of bureaucracy and to a weakening of the initiative of the persons whom the bureaucrats are serving. When this happens the very foundation of democracy itself is endangered. Although democracy, like any other form of government, must yield tolerably satisfactory results and must be tolerably efficient, it must

[26] J. B. S. Hardman and Associates, *American Labor Dynamics,* p. 332. New York: Harcourt, Brace & Co., 1928.

[27] "Self government," said Sir Henry Campbell-Bannerman, "is better than good government." Although this paradoxical statement contains a fundamental truth, the statement is misleading. It wrongly suggests that self-government and good government are incompatible.

be remembered that democracy is a process and not a product. As applied to unions democracy is not to be thought of in terms of fat pay envelopes, short hours, and improved conditions. Rather it is to be thought of as the means, or the process, whereby these worthy objectives are attained. To protect and preserve the process is a task for the union members, just as, on a larger plane, it is a task for citizens in general.

The Social Control of Unionism

Since society as a whole is in every way greater than any of its parts, and hence deserves more consideration, it follows that whenever the welfare of the whole is in conflict with the welfare of a part the former should have precedence over the latter. In other words, the interests of the many should always stand above the interests of the few. Such a consummation is indeed one devoutly to be wished; but how is it to be achieved? Primarily, it would seem, through social control, particularly governmental social control.

As applied to unions, social control involves the passing of such laws as will either prohibit unions and unionists from doing things harmful to society or, to a more limited degree, force them to do things that are good for society. Social control, in other words, is aimed at sins of commission as well as at sins of omission.

We should not overestimate the effectiveness of legislation in promoting good industrial relations. Many years ago Dr. Johnson declared that

> Of all the ills that human hearts endure,
> How small the part that laws can cause or cure.

Today most people would not go as far as Dr. Johnson. They would maintain that to a very considerable extent laws *can* cause human ills as well as cure them. But the fact remains that most of the ills of industry, at least in so far as labor-management relations are involved, are caused by weaknesses that have developed within industry and must be cured by methods applied by industry itself—specifically by employers and unions.

A second observation is that the merit of any law is determined in part by its administrative feasibility. When considered in the abstract a particular piece of legislation may seem very desirable, but such legislation may be so difficult or costly to administer that it is of doubtful value. A good illustration of this point was the provision in the Taft-Hartley Act relating to the necessity of holding elections on the union shop. As applied to the building and construction industry the provision was unfeasible from an administrative standpoint and was largely disregarded. For industry in general it was a costly provision to administer. In view of these facts, and the further fact that the results of the elections were of a decidedly affirmative nature, it is not surprising that the provision was finally eliminated almost wholly.

A concluding point to be emphasized is that though the welfare of society as a whole should take precedence over the welfare of any group in society, society as a whole should guard against the very real danger of exercising excessive control over its constituent groups. We do not want to establish, in the interests of the general welfare, an omnicompetent state, a state that overemphasizes the principle of conformity. The interests of minority groups should not be sacrificed unduly.

Part III

▼

WAGES AND HOURS

21

WAGE DOCTRINES AND WAGE THEORIES

In the present chapter and the ones that immediately follow we shall use the words "theory," "doctrine," and "policy" a great deal, with specific reference to the question of wages. As an introduction to the discussion in these chapters we shall pause briefly at this point to consider the meaning of the three words as we shall employ them.

A wage theory is a generalization concerning wages stated either in terms of a cause-and-effect relationship or in terms of equivalence. Such a theory says that wages are "determined by" this or that force or are "equal to" this or that magnitude. Over the years economists, with their keen interest in discovering and setting forth the laws or principles according to which the economy operates, have enunciated a number of these generalizations.

A wage theory, even though it may involve numerous assumptions, relates to "what is"; [1] it has to do basically with the world of reality. A wage doctrine, on the other hand, relates to "what ought to be"; it has to do with the world of the heart's desire. To borrow a few words from Webster, a wage doctrine is something that is taught, a position, a tenet, a dogma, or a principle of faith. The notion of a just wage, for example, is a wage doctrine and not a wage theory; it points to a condition that is wanted, not to one that necessarily ex-

[1] Sometimes exaggerated opinions are held concerning the degree to which a wage theory describes "what is." A good example is the following statement of Henry Fawcett's: "... the wages paid in any industry are not the result either of caprice or change, but are regulated by principles, which are as certain in their operation as are the physical forces from which all natural phenomena result." *The Economic Position of British Labor,* p. 130; see also pp. 119-120. Cambridge and London: Macmillan and Co., 1865.

ists. If a wage theory is looked upon not only as an explanation of reality but as a statement of what ought to be, it may also be viewed as a wage doctrine. But all wage theories should not be thus regarded: the subsistence theory, to cite one example, could hardly be looked upon as a proper goal for national policy.

A wage policy, the last term in our list, is a plan aimed at achieving the purpose implied in a given wage doctrine. Thus a minimum wage law, or a scheme for adjusting wages to changes in the cost of living, may be looked upon as a policy aimed at achieving a just wage. In the chapters to come we shall have occasion to study a wide variety of wage policies designed to attain a wide variety of ends.

In the present chapter, however, we shall devote our attention to doctrines and theories. First we shall examine three wage doctrines which, though rather old in origin, are by no means devoid of present-day significance. Then we shall take up, for the most part in chronological order, a number of wage theories, giving special attention to the important "marginal productivity theory," a theory which of necessity must come well within the intellectual horizon of every student of labor.

The Just Wage

The notion of a just wage often enters into discussions of wage questions and sometimes plays a part in actual wage policy. The word "just" is ethical in nature and suggests the idea of fairness. Like many other ethical terms it does not lend itself to precise definition, and disputes may easily arise over its exact interpretation.

The doctrine of a just wage was highly important in Europe during the Middle Ages, when the influence of the church was at a very high level. At that time economic ideas and policies were largely subordinated to ethical principles; the ethical man, not the economic man, was the central character in thinking and writing. The just wage, which constituted part of the larger doctrine of the just price, was taken to mean a wage that would make it possible for the worker and his dependents to live decently in whatever social category they were placed.[2] It will be noted that "decency" was related to one's po-

[2] Alexander Gray, *The Development of Economic Doctrine,* p. 53. New York: Longmans, Green and Co., 1931. See also George O'Brien, *An Essay on Medieval Economic Teaching,* pp. 120-123, 126, 127. London: Longmans, Green and Co., 1920.

sition in life, a good indication of the key importance of status in the medieval period.

At the present time the idea of a just wage has numerous, if partial, applications. It is used in our state minimum wage laws and the wage laws of the federal government. Indeed, our most important wage measure, the Fair Labor Standards Act, has an ethical adjective in its title. Considerations of fairness and reasonableness enter into wage discussions between unions and employers and into actual wage policy. The common union argument that wages should go up when profits go up has not only an economic basis but an ethical one. The idea of a just wage may influence individual employers to pay their workers voluntarily a wage higher than the one the market forces call for.[3]

The just-wage principle finds clear expression in the slogan "From each according to his ability, to each according to his needs." Distribution of income according to need—which the Russians claim as their ultimate goal—is based on an ethical foundation. In this country we have not made extensive use of the need principle in our regular wage system, but it is given recognition in another way. In addition to the wage that workers receive directly, an extra payment, sometimes referred to as a "social wage," comes to the workers in such forms as old-age pensions and unemployment insurance. In old-age assistance, in particular, the element of need is clearly taken into account.

What, specifically, is a just wage? Is it simply one that makes possible decent living standards? If so, what constitutes decent living standards? Is it a wage that keeps abreast of increases in the productivity of the plant—or of the industry, or of the economy as a whole? There will probably be general agreement that no wage should be below the minimum requirements of physical subsistence; but how far above that level wages should go, in order to be "just," is a matter that cannot be definitely settled (though approximations of a sort can be reached).

One thing at least can be stated definitely: a wage based on marginal productivity (that is, a wage based on the "economic worth" of

[3] Note the remarks of Professor Lester in *Insights into Labor Issues,* ed. by Richard A. Lester and Joseph Shister, pp. 202, 211. New York: The Macmillan Co., 1948.

the worker) is not necessarily a just wage. There has been some tendency in times past to look upon such a wage as just.[4]

The Doctrine of the Utility of Poverty

The doctrine of the utility of poverty was widely held in England during the 17th and 18th centuries and, in a somewhat modified form, on into the 19th century. Its foundation was economic in character. Low wages were advocated as tending to make workers more industrious, more willing to work longer hours. Such an increase in work would increase the output of the nation and its ability to compete with other nations in foreign trade. The period during which this doctrine held sway was the period of Mercantilism, and at that time the importance of selling goods abroad in exchange for the precious metals was strongly emphasized.

The doctrine of the utility of poverty was based on the assumption that the workers, or certainly many of them, were lazy and satisfied with low living standards. It was felt that if wages were at a high level they would not work a full week; they would resort to absenteeism. In the more sophisticated language of modern economics, the doctrine embodied the belief that the short-run supply curve of labor, expressed in terms of man-hours, bent back to the left (and at a rather low wage rate).

Numerous statements of this doctrine can be found in the writings of the time, but probably the most striking assertion of the principle is that of one of the later writers of the period, Arthur Young: "Every one but an idiot knows that the lower classes must be kept poor or they will never be industrious." [5] Young was of the opinion that wages in England were too high, though he said he could not specify what they should be; he admitted, moreover, that wages could be too low as well as too high.

Most of those who supported the doctrine of the utility of pov-

[4] J. B. Clark, one of the formulators of the marginal productivity theory, held this view. In justice to Clark it should be said that in his view adherence to the marginal productivity principle would bring equilibrium to the economic system—with full employment. A situation of this sort might be interpreted as one which has considerable ethical "content."

[5] For a long discussion of the doctrine, with numerous statements of it, see Edgar S. Furniss, *The Position of the Laborer in a System of Nationalism,* Chap. VI. Boston: Houghton Mifflin Co., 1920. See also Michael T. Wermel, *The Evolution of the Classical Wage Theory,* Chap. 1. New York: Columbia University Press, 1939.

erty advocated not a direct lowering of money wages but rather an increase in prices. This change would result in lower real wages (per hour) and hence make the workers more willing to work longer hours.

It is difficult to say exactly how valid the doctrine was during the time it held sway—it probably possessed a large measure of truth. Brentano believed that as applied to the English workers of the 17th century and the first part of the 18th it was "quite sound . . . just as a similar view still is for the workmen of the East or of our own backward country districts." [6] Today we no longer believe in the beneficent effects of low wages, although a reduction of wages in the low-wage range may bring about an increase in the number of man-hours offered in the labor market (see p. 38).

Another wage doctrine, related to the old notion of the utility of poverty, is that low prices are a result of low wages—not necessarily poverty wages, however. This idea is unquestionably true in some instances, but it does not possess general validity. We know now that high wages do not of necessity mean high labor costs per unit of output and hence high prices. High wages and low labor costs may go hand in hand; whether they do or not depends on the productivity of labor, which may itself be partly determined by the wage rate.

The Economy of High Wages

In his *Wealth of Nations,* which contains many wage ideas, Adam Smith declared that "The liberal reward of labor as it encourages the propagation so it encourages the industry of the common people." This statement is both an endorsement of the Malthusian principle and a denial of the doctrine of the utility of poverty. "Where wages are high," Smith goes on to say, "we shall always find the workmen more active, diligent, and expeditious than where they are low." He admitted that some workers would be idle for three days a week if they could earn enough in four days to keep them for seven, but maintained that such a situation was "by no means the case with the greater part." [7]

That workers may be made stronger and more industrious by

[6] *Hours, Wages in Relation to Production,* p. 39. London: Swan Sonnenschein & Co., 1894.

[7] Everyman's Edition, Vol. I, p. 73. Smith points out that high wages may cause some persons to overwork rather than underwork.

high wages is a definite possibility. The physical energy of the worker may be sapped if his wages are low, and he may be disgruntled and discouraged. In such a condition he would obviously be an inefficient worker. However, one must not push this idea too far. There is obviously a limit to the degree to which high wages can increase individual productivity, a limit governed by such things as the method of wage payment used, the psychological attitude of the worker, and the use made of the increased earnings.[8]

A second version of the doctrine of the economy of high wages presupposes that the employer is compelled to pay higher wages as a result of governmental action, union pressure, or competition in the labor market. Faced with the necessity of paying high wages the employer, it is argued, will introduce various improvements of a cost-reducing nature.

That high wages, arbitrarily imposed, may lead to improvements in methods and machines is a fact that has long been recognized (we shall take up this point in Chapter 23). But the necessity of paying high wages may also lead to curtailed output and unemployment, and possibly to bankruptcy. And even if the employer should introduce improvements, there is a definite limit to the extent that the "shock" is operative.

A third version of the doctrine we are now considering, and one that has been particularly popular during the last three decades, is the purchasing-power notion. According to this doctrine, to keep the economy stable and operating at a high level, wages should also be kept high. "The surest support of the 'economy of high wages,'" John A. Hobson affirms, "is the conviction that it will operate as a stimulus to industry through increased consumption." [9] This belief, which is very widespread especially in union circles, is partly valid, but the degree of its validity can be greatly exaggerated.

The Subsistence Theory of Wages

The first wage theory, though not the first wage idea, to come into prominence was the subsistence theory. During the latter part of the 18th century and the first part of the 19th this theory reigned su-

[8] A. G. Pool, *Wage Policy in Relation to Industrial Fluctuations,* pp. 17-18. London: Macmillan & Co., 1938.

[9] *The Evolution of Modern Capitalism,* p. 284. New York: Charles Scribner's Sons, 1896.

preme. At that time the workers in France and in England were very poor; their real income was low, just sufficient to enable them to keep body and soul together. Under these conditions it is not surprising that members of the physiocratic school of economists in France and of the classical school in England should have reached the conclusion, and have formulated it as an economic law, that wages tend to equal the means of subsistence. Such a theory appeared to be definitely in accordance with the facts.[10]

An extreme statement of the theory was set forth by Turgot. "In every sort of occupation it must come to pass, and in fact does come to pass, that the wages of the artisan are limited to that which is necessary to procure him a subsistence. . . . He earns no more than his living." [11] Turgot admitted, in response to a criticism of the theory, that for biological reasons it was fully applicable only in long periods, not in short ones. This is a point that should be remembered about the subsistence theory. For biological reasons the theory was definitely of a long-run nature. In this respect it differed from the wage-fund theory (shortly to be discussed) which was of a short-run character.

The subsistence theory, which in its extreme form was called the iron law of wages, was indeed a hard, harsh theory. Later writers softened it up somewhat by including in the term "subsistence" comforts of life as well as necessities.

David Ricardo adhered to the softer version. "The natural price of labor," said Ricardo in a well known statement, "is that price which is necessary to enable the laborers, one with another, to subsist and to perpetuate their race, without either increase or diminution" (that is, as Professor E. C. K. Gonner points out, to maintain the workers "in the same position of life or comfort"). Ricardo goes on to make it plain that the wages he has in mind will enable the worker to purchase 'the quantity of food, necessaries, and conveniences become essential to him from habit." And he goes still further. He

[10] Professor D. H. MacGregor has pointed to the importance of the anti-combination laws of 1749, the later destruction of the power of the justices of the peace to fix certain wages, and the removal of apprenticeship regulations as factors in the wage situation in England. "The 'iron law' of wages," says MacGregor, "was both the teaching of the time and the only possible effect of the legal system." *The Evolution of Industry*, pp. 65, 66. New York: Henry Holt & Co., 1912.

[11] Quoted by Alfred Marshall, *Principles of Economics*, 8th ed., pp. 505-506. London: Macmillan & Co., 1925.

points out that the "natural price of labor, estimated even in food and necessaries," is not to be interpreted as being "absolutely fixed and constant." It differs from place to place, and from time to time, depending essentially "on the habits and customs of the people." [12]

Ricardo's view of subsistence was thus quite flexible. Moreover, he pointed out that in an improving society the actual wages paid to the workers could be above the so-called natural wages both indefinitely and constantly. He was of the opinion, however, that after all the good land of a nation had been put into use, real wages would come down—as rents increased. On the whole, Ricardo's theory certainly did not picture the workers living at a crude physical subsistence.

The subsistence theory, whether it was stated in the extreme form of Turgot or in the moderate form of Ricardo, was based on the "principle of population," and not, as Davidson makes clear, on the rapacity of the employer.[13] If wages rose above subsistence, population was supposed to increase, pulling down wages. If wages fell below subsistence, the opposite was supposed to happen.

With the passing of time, and as applied to Western nations, the subsistence theory has lost most of whatever validity it possessed. The theory is still largely applicable to certain Eastern nations, however, where population growth has kept pace with the growth of industrial and agricultural output. But even where it is applicable the theory must be stated in a form to admit of exceptions with respect to both individuals and occupations.[14]

The Wage Fund Theory

The wage fund theory (or the wages fund theory, as it has often been called) was a commonly held wage theory in England in the middle part of the 19th century. Its most outstanding exponent was the English economist and social philosopher John Stuart Mill.

A supply-and-demand explanation of wages, this theory related

[12] See Ricardo's *Principles of Political Economy and Taxation,* Gonner ed., Chapter V. London: G. Bell & Sons, Ltd., 1929.

[13] John Davidson, *The Bargain Theory of Wages,* p. 9. New York: J. P. Putnam's Sons, 1898.

[14] T. E. Cliffe Leslie early criticized the subsistence theory of Ricardo on the grounds that if the theory held, the rate of wages in different occupations could not vary in accordance with the nature of the work. *Essays in Political and Moral Philosophy,* p. 192. Dublin: Hodges, Figgis & Co., 1888.

not to the wages of specific individuals but to the general or average level of wages. The supply element was made up of the workers—"those who worked for hire," as Mill stated it. The demand element was the so-called wage fund, composed (principally) of that part of circulating capital "which is expended in the direct purchase of labor." The average wage was determined by the relationship between these two magnitudes. Or, stating the principle arithmetically, the average wage was the quotient resulting from dividing the wage fund by the number of the workers.

The wage fund theory was a simple one, but it was not without its dangerous implications. It suggested that if some workers, through collective action, succeeding in forcing their employers to pay them higher wages, other workers would suffer as a consequence. Little wonder that the unions were critical of the doctrine!

But other persons besides unionists criticized the theory. A number of Mill's fellow economists, such as Cliffe Leslie, Longe, and Thornton found fault with it; and in 1869 Mill, in reviewing a book by Thornton, renounced the theory.[15] Mill's renunciation was based on his conversion to the belief that there was in reality no definitely fixed wage fund at any given time. "Exists there any fixed amount which, and neither more nor less than which, is destined to be expended in wages?" Mill asked himself in his review article; and he concluded that there was not. He concluded that the wage fund possessed flexibility in that the workers could cut into the share of the employers.

Some economists have felt that Mill made a mistake in giving up his theory, or at least in conceding as much as he did. Professor Frank W. Taussig was of this view. In a study first published in 1896, [16] Taussig attempted to state the wage fund theory in an acceptable form. He emphasized the idea of real wages, rather than money wages. This version of the doctrine was by no means unfamiliar to the older economists; in fact, as Taussig points out, Ri-

15 Mill's renunciation was published in the *Fortnightly Review*, May, 1869. Key excerpts from the article can be found in the bibliographical appendix to the Ashley edition of Mill's *Principles of Political Economy*, pp. 992-993. London: Longmans, Green & Co., 1926. The view of a recent writer, Professor Samuelson, that the wage fund controversy was "largely over empty words," seems rather extreme. *Impact of the Union*, ed. by David McCord Wright, pp. 316-317. New York: Harcourt, Brace & Co., 1951.

16 *Wages and Capital*. New York: D. Appleton & Co., 1900.

cardo and the abler of his followers usually adhered to it. However, in much of the discussion of the theory it was not clearly stated which version was being used. Mill certainly emphasized the money wage approach.

Thinking in terms of real wages Taussig introduced the notion of a wage flow rather than a wage fund, thereby suggesting the idea of wages coming not from a pool but from a stream, a stream that is subject to some change in volume. If the doctrine is interpreted in this way, it has distinct merit. It indicates the highly important fact that the average real wage in a country is subject to some change, even in the short run, but not to changes of great size. The real-wage flow in a country depends on the output of the elements that make up real wages—automobiles, food, clothing, movies, and the like—and the quantity of these items usually changes slowly. Average *money* wages in a country can be increased very rapidly through the use of inflationary methods; but increases in *real* wages cannot be achieved in this way, though there are times when moderate monetary stimulants may aid production.

Though little is heard today about the wage fund in free economics, it is interesting to note that the concept is used in highly planned societies. In fact such societies must in their planning think in terms of a wage fund, in both a monetary and a real sense. In Russia, for example, the planned monetary wage fund for 1950 was 252 billion rubles.

The Marginal Productivity Theory of Wages

The theory of wages that has commanded most attention and respect from economists during the last half century has been the marginal productivity theory. This theory, which constitutes part of a general theory of income distribution, is usually looked upon as the "orthodox" explanation of wages. Like certain other orthodox economic ideas it has been subject to criticism, particularly during recent years; one critic has gone so far as to state that "we can hardly claim to have a theory at all." [17] The theory is still widely held, however, though probably in a less absolute form than previously; hence it merits our careful attention.

According to the theory wages tend to equal (or measure, or

[17] Arthur M. Ross, *Trade Union Wage Policy*, p. 1. Berkeley: University of California Press, 1948.

express) the marginal productivity of labor. It will be observed that the theory does not say or imply that in the real world wages invariably and exactly equal marginal productivity, but that they *tend* to equal it. It will be noted too that the theory does not state that wages are *determined by* marginal productivity. To interpret the theory solely in terms of a cause-and-effect relationship is wrong, if one is thinking of a dynamic economy.[18] To be sure, changes in marginal productivity do lead to changes in wages; but frequently the very reverse is true. With the spread of unionism and the divergence of the wage market and the job market (consequent upon the enlargement of the wage market) this has become increasingly true. However, the theory merely states that wages tend to be equal to marginal productivity or, as Professor D. H. Robertson puts it,[19] they tend to *measure* marginal productivity.

The Marginal Productivity of Labor. The expression "marginal productivity" is a rather technical one and requires some analysis. Perhaps the easiest way to begin the analysis is to imagine a factory with, say, 100 workers in it, all of the workers being of exactly the same type or quality—that is, possessing the same ability and initiative.[20] Now let us assume that one of the workers is removed from the group, and that no corresponding change is made in the volume of capital in the plant or in the "arts of production." The total

18 Professor J. B. Clark asserted that in a state of pure competition this cause-and-effect relationship existed, i.e., that wages are determined by marginal or final productivity. As Professor Robbins has pointed out, this view was justified in the static state—and with a given labor supply—assumed by Clark. See *The Economic Journal,* June, 1930, p. 209. Clark's cause-and-effect relationship is also applicable if one applies the marginal productivity theory to society as a whole, as Clark did, and thinks in terms of average real wages in the economy.

19 *Economic Fragments,* pp. 42, 43. London: P. S. King & Son, Ltd., 1931. Professor Robertson discusses, on pp. 42-57 of this book, some of the criticisms that have been leveled at the marginal productivity theory of wages.

20 The units of labor may be thought of as workers of the same type—a homogeneous labor supply, in other words. They may also be thought of in terms of labor units, not as worker units. One worker, a highly skilled worker or very diligent worker, may represent two or three labor units or more. This device is used by Frederick B. Garver and Alvin H. Hansen, *Principles of Economics,* p. 411. Boston: Ginn & Co., 1928. J. B. Clark (*Essentials of Economic Theory,* p. 141. New York: The Macmillan Co., 1907) thought of the units as "detachments," each unit being composed of a given complement of workers—in a shoe factory it would be necessary to "add lasters, welters, sewers of uppers, etc., in a certain proportionate way." All three of the methods we have noted are abstract, but the one used in the text seems preferable.

product of the factory will be less with 99 workers than with 100. The difference in the total product or output, consequent upon the removal of one worker, is the marginal product of the group. Thus in the hypothetical illustration we have used the loss in product per day may have been $5. This is the decline in the total value of the product resulting from the removal of one worker from the group of 100. Since, by assumption, the workers in the plant are all of the same kind the removal of any one of the workers would have brought about a decline in value product of $5 per day. Conversely, if the number of workers in the plant had been increased from 99 to 100, the hundredth worker would have added output worth $5 per day.

If a further worker (the 101st) had been added, the addition to the total value output would probably have been something less than $5; and if still another worker had been added, the size of the new addition would have been still less. In other words, the addition to the total product declines, at least after a certain point is reached, with the addition of successive workers.

In the illustration we have used (we shall assume that it relates to a competitive labor market) the wages of each of the 100 workers, according to the theory we are now discussing, would have tended to equal $5 a day. If instead of 100 workers there had been 200 workers in the plant, the marginal productivity of the group would have been less than $5, and wages also would have been less. On the other hand, if there had been 50 workers, both marginal productivity and wages would have been more than $5.

This situation may be depicted on the traditional graph used in economics, with marginal productivity (and wages) represented on the vertical axis and number of workers on the horizontal axis. The curve of marginal productivity slopes downward to the right, except at the beginning.[21]

To carry our analysis a step farther, let us imagine not one plant

[21] J. B. Clark shows the curve declining from the very beginning. Clark's view is that two units of labor produce less than double the amount of one because the *amount* of (money) capital per unit of labor is less with two units than with one, though the *form* of the capital will be different. See *Essentials of Economic Theory*, pp. 135-136. New York: The Macmillan Co., 1907. This does not seem to give adequate weight to the advantages of specialization and cooperation in the use of labor, or to situations where a change in the form of capital, even though the amount of it remains constant, can lead to larger marginal products.

in the community but a number. For each one it is permissible to think of a marginal productivity curve, showing the decline (after a certain point) of the product additions or increments that *would* result from the use of additional workers. These curves need not, and probably would not, all occupy the same positions on their respective graphs, for reasons that will soon be apparent. However, if the plants all used the same kind of labor, if the nonincome aspects of the employment situation in the plants (such as ventilation, affability of bosses, and nature of the work) were the same, and if the workers were adequately mobile, the *actual* marginal productivity of labor in the various plants would tend to be the same and so would wages. This would be in keeping with the principle of opportunity cost. The wage established, which would be the "going rate of wages," thus would reflect, or be equivalent to, the common margin throughout *all* the plants. And each plant, viewed singly, would have to pay a wage equal to the going rate.

In practice the noneconomic aspects of employment, for a given type of labor, are not always the same. Hence there may well be differences in the actual marginal productivity of labor from one plant to another, and consequently differences in wages from plant to plant. Moreover, there are obstacles in the way of labor mobility, such as home ties, presence of friends, inconvenience of moving, and sheer inertia, that may prevent an equalization of marginal products.[22]

However, equality of wages for labor of a given type in a given labor market is not an absolutely necessary condition for the operation of the marginal productivity theory of wages. In plants with wage differences, wages could still tend to equal marginal productivity, the latter varying from plant to plant owing to the operation of forces shortly to be examined. Statistics showing the existence of wage differences in a labor market for the same kind of labor do not necessarily indicate any divergence between wages and marginal productivity. They may simply mean that the same type of workers, even working with the same degree of intensity, may produce different outputs—the difference depending on the other factors of production with which the labor works.

22 A detailed discussion of obstacles in the way of mobility will be found in Lloyd G. Reynolds, *Labor Economics and Labor Relations,* pp. 344-350. New York: Prentice-Hall, Inc., 1949.

On the specific matter of labor immobility mentioned above, it should be pointed out that to establish equality of labor productivity at the various margins of use it is not necessary that all workers be able to move, that they all be "organized like a Tartar tribe, packed and saddled ready for flight" (to use Francis A. Walker's expression).[23] Possibly only 10 or 15 per cent, or even less, of the work force must be mobile.[24]

Determinants of Marginal Productivity. What the actual marginal productivity of labor is in any plant depends on the position of the marginal productivity curve and on the number of workers who are employed in the plant. The latter factor we may set aside, since its influence is obvious; but the former factor definitely calls for further study.

The marginal productivity curve, which shows the increments of output attributable to successive workers, is influenced in part by the quality of the worker. The curve for skilled workers is higher on the graph than the curve for unskilled workers; the curve for diligent unskilled workers is higher than that for lazy unskilled workers. The position of the curve is greatly affected by the quantity and quality of the factors of production that labor works with. The marginal productivity of, say, 100 workers is larger if the workers have a great deal of capital, in the form of machines, to work with than if they have very little. It is larger if they have a large (but not too large) group of foremen and other management representatives to guide them than if they have a very small group. The quality of the machinery, of management, and of techniques is also important.

The marginal productivity of labor in this country has been high, and wages on the whole have been high, not simply because we have a lot of industrious and skilled workers, but because we have a large quantity of good machinery and other capital goods and also a large supply of good managers and management representatives.

The marginal productivity of labor can be thought of solely

[23] *The Wages Question,* p. 180. New York: Henry Holt & Co., 1876.

[24] In view of this fact criticism of the notion of workers seeking jobs in terms of the "net-economic advantages" associated with them loses some of its force; that is, as far as the criticism is associated with wage theory. For a criticism of the "net-economic advantage" idea, see Joseph Shister, *Economics of the Labor Market,* pp. 391-398. Philadelphia: J. B. Lippincott Co., 1949.

in *physical* terms, such as number of chairs or number of hats. But in discussions of wages, productivity must be interpreted in value or *pecuniary* terms. And the position of the pecuniary marginal productivity curve is a function not only of labor, capital, and management factors but also of the price that is obtained for the physical product. This price, in turn, is affected by such influences as demand intensity for the product and degree of competition in the industry. It is also affected by changes in the general price level.

Physical and Pecuniary Marginal Productivity. In dealing with the productivity of labor and problems relating to it, it is frequently desirable and also necessary to distinguish between physical and pecuniary aspects. The two are closely connected but do not need to change in exactly the same way. One or two examples will illustrate this point. During the time of inflation the pecuniary marginal productivity of labor in various employments may increase very sharply. The pecuniary marginal productivity curves—if we may think in terms of graphs—will shift upwards. But there may be no change whatever in the physical marginal productivity of labor. Again, a single producer in a monopolistic position may increase the pecuniary marginal productivity of labor in his plant by raising the price of his product, without any change in the physical output of his workers. For single producers who are *not* operating under conditions of perfect competition, pecuniary marginal productivity always declines more markedly as successive workers are added than does physical marginal productivity. This difference in decline is due to the fact that, whereas pecuniary marginal productivity reflects changes in physical marginal productivity, it also reflects (in keeping with the law of demand) the drop in the product price necessitated by the placing of more units of output on the market.

It is evident that the marginal productivity that measures or equals the money wages of any particular group of workers is a resultant of both physical and monetary influences. It should be noted, however, that when one is thinking of real wages, particularly the real wages of the workers as a whole, the significant factor is physical marginal productivity and not pecuniary productivity. For specific groups of workers, say in a monopolistic industry, real wages may be high even though physical productivity is rather low; but such a condition is not possible for workers in the aggregate.

Criticisms and Refinements. The marginal productivity theory of wages has been subject to a variety of criticisms, some of which we shall now examine.

(1) One criticism is to the effect that the employer does not know what the marginal productivity of labor is. He does not know what the "last" worker adds to the total product, nor do the workers themselves know. To some extent this is a valid criticism. The employer cannot experiment as easily with various "inputs" of a factor of production as the professor can (imaginatively) in the classroom. Nevertheless, it would be unreasonable to say that the employer has no idea whatever concerning the effects on production of additional units of labor. He probably has never heard of the term "marginal productivity," but he is definitely aware of the term's meaning. If we use the word "tendency" in our definition of the marginal productivity theory with some degree of flexibility, the lack of *precise* knowledge on the part of the employer concerning the marginal productivity of labor would not seem to be a very serious criticism of the theory.

(2) It may be argued, however, that even though the employer has some idea of what the marginal productivity of his labor is, he may pay a wage that is higher than the productivity level. He may be a benevolent employer, willing to sacrifice some of his profits in the interests of his workers, or he may be desirous of making a favorable impression on the public. There is good reason for believing that employers sometimes pay their workers a wage that is higher than the one indicated by productivity. But the extent of this policy does not seem to be widespread enough to warrant the entire rejection of the marginal productivity theory. The existence of benevolence in business does suggest, however, the desirability of using the theory with some discretion.

(3) It may be argued that sometimes the employer does not need to pay a wage equal to the marginal productivity of his labor. Thus if there is a single, profit-making employer of labor in a given community (a monopsonist), and if the supply curve of labor is completely or highly inelastic where it crosses the marginal productivity curve, as it may well be, the actual wage may be less than the marginal productivity wage. Under these circumstances the employer cannot obey the "general rule of policy" involving the hiring of workers to the point where wages and marginal productivity are

equal; more workers are not forthcoming at higher wages. To those he has in his employment he can pay a wage less than their marginal productivity because they will not leave him.

Much the same general situation could exist if a number of employers acted in collusion in hiring labor (oligopsony), each refraining from bidding labor away from the others by paying the wage equal to marginal productivity.[25]

(4) The existence of unions and collective bargaining should not be looked upon as being inconsistent with the marginal productivity theory. In some cases unions may bring wages closer in line with marginal productivity. It would seem, however, that in more instances the unions push wages *above* marginal productivity, forcing the employer to take steps to increase the latter—either by price changes, by changes in the methods of production, or by reducing the size of his work force. The result of each of these methods is a drawing together again of wages and marginal productivity, a tendency toward their equalization.

It may be argued, however, that the employer may have difficulty in making some of the adjustments that we have just referred to, adjustments necessitated by the higher wages forced upon him by unions. For example, he may not be able easily to substitute capital for labor. Moreover, he may find seniority rules troublesome in adjusting his work force.[26] Although such difficulties often do prevent a nice balance between wages and marginal productivity, their long-run magnitude must not be exaggerated.

(5) In some situations it is difficult, if not impossible, to apply the marginal productivity theory in a meaningful way. For example, to think of added "inputs" of opera singers, movie stars, or college professors, and of the resultant increase in value product, is rather unreal (thinking in terms of man-hours does not entirely save the situation). For such special cases it would seem preferable to use

25 A more extended discussion of monopsonistic and oligopsonistic situations in the labor market will be found in Mary J. Bowman and George L. Bach, *Economic Analysis and Public Policy,* 2nd ed., pp. 509-511. New York: Prentice-Hall, Inc., 1949.

26 An extensive discussion of restrictions and limitations on management in making adjustments will be found in a chapter on "Unionism and the Marginal Productivity Theory," by Nathan Belfer and Gordon F. Bloom, in *Insights into Labor Issues,* ed. by Richard A. Lester and Joseph Shister. New York: The Macmillan Co., 1948.

an ordinary supply-and-demand explanation of income. Remember, however, that the marginal productivity theory is not inconsistent with the supply-and-demand theory. In reality it is a refinement of it.

(6) A final criticism is that the marginal productivity theory does not jibe with the facts. Undoubtedly a discrepancy between theory and fact often exists. The widespread advocacy of "equal pay for equal work" suggests that the marginal productivity theory is not wholly operative. More definite evidence, in the form of statistics, has been presented to prove the point. Professor Lester has submitted figures which, he believes, show that wage determination does not work out in the precise manner suggested by the marginal productivity theory, and he has discussed at length the weaknesses of the marginal explanation.[27] The existence of exceptions to the theory cannot very well be denied; on the question of how numerous and how significant the exceptions are there is difference of opinion.

In view of all the criticisms that have been noted in the previous paragraphs, and the concessions made, one might ask if the marginal productivity theory has any validity at all. Does it throw revealing light on wages—their levels,[28] their variations, their long-time growth? Does it help one to understand the processes of industry and the general functioning of the economy? The proper answer to these questions is, in the estimation of the present writer, yes. But, as was pointed out earlier, the theory must not be applied too rigidly to actual situations. The conclusions of the theory must be modified, in individual cases, to the extent that the assumptions at the basis of it are not found in practice. This is true of any scientific law, including the law of gravity.

[27] For a discussion of marginalism by Lester, Machlup, and Stigler, see the references noted in footnote 24 in Chapter 22.

[28] If one is willing to use his imagination and apply the theory to all of society, as J. B. Clark did, he can see additional value in it. The labor "detachments" or units in this case would be very large and very inclusive—shoemakers, cotton spinners, builders, and others mentioned by Clark. The real wage in society would depend on the magnitude of the product (physical) of the final unit of labor, each and all units getting a wage equal to the marginal product. This is in reality another way of saying that the average real wages of a nation are dependent on the physical output of the nation, a simple point to be sure, but one that is easily forgotten. For a good discussion of the average real-wage level for the economy as a whole, a discussion that gives attention to Clark's ideas, see Lloyd G. Reynolds, *Labor Economics and Labor Relations*, pp. 431-439. New York: Prentice-Hall, Inc., 1949.

Range Theories

Dissatisfaction with the marginal productivity theory of wages has led to the formulation in recent years of a number of "range" theories. These theories (if we may call them such) specify upper and lower limits within which wages may be placed depending on a variety of circumstances. This approach to the wage theory problem is not entirely new, however, since it was used in the so-called bargain theory of wages, set forth by John Davidson more than half a century ago.[29]

According to Davidson's theory the lower wage limit is set by the worker and represents the minimum wage he is willing to accept. The position of this minimum is determined by the utility of the money wage to the worker and the disutility of the work. The employer will not have an easy time trying to compel the worker to work for less than this minimum. The upper limit is established by the employer and indicates the most he is willing to pay. This maximum is based on the "discounted value of the product created by the laborer's exertions," and the employer can be forced to go beyond it "only with the greatest of difficulty." If wages are forced above this limit, the other claimants to the product would object; and the employer would "have to face the necessity of establishing a new balance unless he is content to see his own share shrink without protest."

The actual point at which wages are established between the two limits described depends on the bargaining strength of the two parties. If labor is strong and the employer weak, wages will move toward the upper limit, and vice versa. They will usually not be exactly at either the lower limit or the upper one.

The position of labor within the limits may change from time to time, and the limits themselves probably shift upwards from year to year, Davidson stated. He also declared that the limits were not "absolutely fixed."

Professor Shister has recently set forth a theory of wages (relating to the individual firm) in which he uses the upper and lower limit analysis.[30] In Shister's theory the lower limit is determined

[29] *Op. cit.,* Chap. IV.

[30] *Economics of the Labor Market,* Chap. 15. Philadelphia. J. B. Lippincott Co., 1949.

by what the employer must pay "to attract and retain the necessary amount of labor." The upper limit is determined by the "profitability" of the business. The actual wage is somewhere between these limits, its exact position being governed by the influence of three sets of factors: (1) objectives of management; (2) presence or absence of a union; (3) influence of the government.

Professor Reynolds also uses the device of an upper and a lower limit in his explanation of how wages are determined in a nonunion plant.[31] The upper limit is a maximum beyond which the employer "could not go for budgetary reasons"; the lower limit is a minimum below which the employer "could not hold enough labor to meet production schedules." These two limits, it will be noted, are essentially the same as those used by Shister.

The positions assumed by the two limits mentioned by Reynolds are subject to some variation. They change according to the time period involved—over a short period of time, for example, an employer may be able to benefit from a very low minimum limit. The upper limit varies from firm to firm, owing to the nature of the product market and the internal efficiency of the plant.

The actual wages paid in various plants in a given community for a given type of labor may vary widely, says Reynolds, depending in the main on differences in degree of competition in the various industries represented by the plants, differences in individual plant efficiency within each industry, and management policies (in terms of generosity or niggardliness) with respect to wages.

The theories of Shister and Reynolds, and to some extent the theory of Davidson, add a certain amount of "realism" to wage discussions. They point to specific wage-influencing factors that the pure marginalist may easily neglect. However, it should not be assumed that the range theories are incompatible with the marginal productivity theory. The latter theory, correctly interpreted, makes due allowance for the effect of the various influences which, in Shister's and Reynolds's theories, determine the location of the actual wage between the upper and lower limits.

[31] *Labor Economics and Labor Relations*, pp. 352-358. New York: Prentice-Hall, Inc., 1949.

22

UNIONS AND WAGES

One of the most important and involved questions in the field of labor is the effect of unions on wages. The question has numerous aspects, some of which call for careful analysis. Before embarking on this analysis, however, we shall examine the specific objectives of union wage policy and certain wage doctrines and wage ideas that unions support.

Objectives of Union Wage Policy

Union wage policy is aimed not at one objective but at a considerable number. To assume that unions, and union leaders, are solely interested in fatter pay envelopes is an unwarranted simplification; in fact, it is an absolute error.

Whatever the specific objectives of union wage policy may be, the union leaders play a key role in their determination. The contention of Professor Arthur M. Ross that the wage policy of unions "is inevitably a leadership function,"[1] seems sound, certainly if broadly interpreted. Union leaders, of course, cannot disregard the wage interests of their constituents; but the leadership ordinarily must take the initiative in formulating wage plans and in trying to have them accepted by management.

The major aim of union wage policy is "more and more"—not that union leaders and union members are constantly and consciously seeking to maximize the income of those in the union,[2] but

[1] *Trade Union Wage Policy,* p. 39. Berkeley: University of California Press, 1948.

[2] Professor John T. Dunlop believes that the maximization of the wage income for all the members of the union is probably "the most suitable generalized model of the trade union for analytical purposes." See *Wage Determination Under Trade Unions,* pp. 32-44. New York: The Macmillan Co.,

simply that they usually want wages to keep on going up. The "more and more" principle, it should be pointed out, can be applied not only to wages but to leisure and to many of the "control" objectives of unions as well.

Union wage policy also reflects the "political" interest or concern of union leaders. Wage increases, says Professor E. Wight Bakke, "become a political symbol of political service." [3] And Professor Clark Kerr, after stating that unions are primarily political organizations and not economic monopolies, goes on to declare that "The political test of meeting workers' notions of equity has more of an impact on wage policy than the economic test of income maximization." [4] It is possible that the political aspect of unionism has been exaggerated, but it cannot be denied that political considerations play a very significant part in union wage policy.

Another objective of union wage policy is to win the allegiance of nonunionists. Abstract arguments about labor solidarity are much less likely to bring nonunionists into the union fold than promises that their wages will be higher if they join the union. Once they are in the fold, the union is under some obligation to carry out its promises. Incidentally, it should be pointed out that employers may fashion *their* wage policy in such a way as to discourage workers from entering the union fold.

Union wage policy is also used to bring about a more equitable sharing of work and the hiring of more workers. At least these results tend to follow when unions insist upon the payment of higher rates for overtime.

The wage policy of unions is also used to bring about improvements in certain management practices, as when unions demand minimum call pay, or higher rates for work done at unsatisfactory times such as Sundays or holidays. Sometimes wage policy (specifically, a dismissal-wage plan) may be aimed at preventing the employer practice, common in the clothing industry, of going out of business.[5]

1944. For a criticism of the maximization principle, see Ross, *op. cit.*, pp. 7, 8, 22, 48.

[3] *Wage Determination and the Economics of Liberalism,* p. 88. Washington: Chamber of Commerce of the United States, 1947.

[4] Industrial Relations Research Association, *Proceedings,* 1949, p. 79.

[5] At its convention in 1950 the International Ladies Garment Workers' Union authorized its officers to seek in all future collective bargaining agree-

Another objective of union wage policy may be the achievement of a higher social status for the workers, as when unions seek vacations with pay as an alternative to further increases in the basic wage rates.

But the wage policies of unions may involve concessions as well as demands. Thus a union may permit the payment of substandard wages as a means of meeting the competition of machinery, or for the purpose of encouraging the training and use of apprentices and the employment of aged and handicapped persons. Sometimes a union seeking a wage increase will temper its demands in the interests of maintaining a cooperative working basis with management. In fact it may even temporarily forego wages completely in an effort to keep an employer in business, as a union did in a Detroit firm in 1951, amid considerable newspaper publicity. In such a case union wage policy may be viewed as a form of mutual aid, to use Professor Ross's terminology. Possibly, too, as Professor Ross states, wage policy may be influenced by considerations of public reaction.[6]

Union Wage Doctrines

In the preceding section we discussed various objectives of union wage policy. Now we shall turn to a survey of a number of union wage doctrines. These doctrines, which may be looked upon as constituting the wage philosophy of unions, are closely related to some of the objectives. They serve as a logical (sometimes an illogical) foundation for them.

The unions use their wage doctrines with no small amount of flexibility. A particular doctrine may be greatly emphasized at one time, when it seems especially pertinent, and set aside at another time. Union leaders are aware that objective circumstances have a great deal to do with the effectiveness of any idea or doctrine, as John Stuart Mill pointed out a century ago.

---

ments a provision setting up a fund to be used for this purpose. "I am interested in the employer having no inducement for going out of business," President Dubinsky stated. *The New York Times,* June 2, 1950.

6 For a more extensive discussion of the nonincome objectives of union wage policy see Professor Dunlop's article in *The American Economic Review,* Supplement, March, 1942, especially pp. 291-294. Also see his book, *Wage Determination Under Unionism.* New York: The Macmillan Co., 1944.

The "More and More" Doctrine. The major objective of union wage policy, as we noted earlier, is "more and more." This objective may also be looked upon as a union wage doctrine, and we shall so view it. The "more and more" idea that was to Samuel Gompers a very important article of faith has become well embedded in the wage philosophy of American unionists.

It is true, as we have already pointed out, that there are times when a union will refrain from pressing for a wage increase and will even accept a wage cut; but the more or less constant quest of unions is for higher and higher wages. For the unions there is no final wage goal, no goal, which, once achieved, will produce a period of permanent quiet on the labor front.

The "more and more" doctrine must be viewed in both an absolute and a relative sense. The unions naturally want higher money wages and higher real wages—in view of the increase in the productivity of industry such a desire is to be expected. But the unions, or at least many of the union leaders, also think in relative terms: they want the union members to receive an increasingly large share of the national income. Like Francis Bacon, they believe that "money is like muck, not good unless it be spread." Whether or not it is possible for unions, through the process of collective bargaining, to cut appreciably into the other distributive shares is a nice question, one we shall discuss later in the chapter.

The Purchasing-Power Doctrine. Since the middle of the 1920's, when a wave of interest in technological change and technological unemployment began to engulf the nation, the unions have used the purchasing-power doctrine a great deal in their discussions of wages. This doctrine was given special recognition at the time of the 1925 AFL convention, when the Federation based its demand for what it called a higher "social wage" on the purchasing-power notion. With the national output increasing, said the AFL, wages should go up proportionately; otherwise production will outrun consumption. "Stocks accumulate. They grow and grow. Industrial instability arises, industrial instability turns to depression and depression to crises." [7]

During the middle of the 1940's another version of the purchasing-power doctrine came into the picture. Unionists began to

[7] *The American Federationist,* August, 1927, p. 923.

argue in terms of the relative aspect of the "more and more" doctrine. "The new conception demands," said Solomon Barkin, Research Director of the Textile Workers' Union, "that labor share not only in the increase in national productivity but also enlarge its share of the national income." If labor's share is increased, "a more adequately balanced economy, one in which a more equitable distribution of income prevents quick accumulation of idle capital," will be achieved.[8]

In the past the purchasing-power doctrine did not meet with much favor among economists. But during recent years, and under the influence of J. M. Keynes, there appears to be a growing feeling among economists that the argument has something in it.

The Ability-to-Pay Doctrine. In their thinking on wage matters unionists often give attention to profits. This practice became particularly widespread during the period following World War II, an outstanding episode in the development being the 1945-1946 dispute between the Automobile Workers' union and General Motors. Since that time the ability-to-pay doctrine has been widely discussed.

From the standpoint of the union the doctrine serves as a very good talking point when profits are high. When profits are low or nonexistent, however, the doctrine must be carefully kept out of sight. During prosperous times there arises the question of to what extent the ability-to-pay principle should interfere with the standard-rate principle. Also, what will be the effect of payments based on ability to pay, upon the allocation of productive factors? If profits (assuming them to be large) are cut into deeply by especially high wages, resources may not enter the industry in proper volume.

Speaking generally there seems to be little likelihood that the unions can compel any *extensive* adherence to the ability-to-pay principle. During the wage controversies that occurred after World War II the unions argued that higher wages could be paid without increasing prices if the increment were to come out of profits. But each "round" of wage increases was followed by higher prices. Profits were well protected.

The Productivity Doctrine. During the early 1950's the productivity doctrine, which is implied in the "more and more" principle, came to occupy, as a separate notion, a very outstanding place in

[8] *Labor and Nation,* February-March, 1946, pp. 8, 10.

wage discussions. Under the productivity doctrine wages are supposed to reflect changes in labor productivity; they are increased on the basis of an "annual improvement factor" relating to productivity.

The doctrine was given tangible expression in the 1948 and 1950 contracts between the UAW and General Motors. (The same contracts, it should be pointed out, also embodied a cost-of-living formula for wage changes.) The policy of linking wages to productivity changes represents a highly significant development, which we shall examine in detail in the next chapter.

The Cost-of-Living Doctrine. The principle of adjusting wages to changes in the cost of living has on occasion met with union approval. Ordinarily the unions would oppose this principle as the sole criterion for changing wages, since it would mean a freezing of real income. In a time of declining prices it would mean wage cuts, which unions would obviously dislike.

The cost-of-living principle was adopted on a large scale during the early 1950's, in the form of "escalator" clauses in union agreements. It will be recalled that during these years prices were on the upgrade.

The Effect of Unions on Wages

Some years ago the CIO's official paper carried the following announcement: "Five Billion Wage Increase, Vacations and Security Won by CIO for Members." Similar though less sweeping declarations could be quoted from other labor periodicals. In the opinion of the editors of these journals, and also in the estimation of the leaders and rank-and-file members of the unions, there is no doubt whatever about the possibility of workers winning higher wages through the process of collective bargaining, and they could cite thousands of "case histories" that would seem to prove the point.

In the light of this situation it might seem foolish to enter into a detailed discussion of the relationship between collective bargaining and wages. Such a discussion is necessary, however, and for two reasons. In the first place, the question is often considered from such a narrow point of view that only part of the story is told. Secondly, the question is so highly involved that simple treatments of it are almost certain to be inadequate.

Methods of Approach to the Problem. The relationship between collective bargaining and wages may be studied in terms of money wages or real wages; from a short-run or a long-run point of view; or from the standpoint of various groups. The "wages" in question may be the total wages of the group (say, a local union) that does the bargaining; the wages of the members of the parent union with which the bargaining unit is affiliated; or the wages of all workers, both union and nonunion. No satisfactory discussion of the relationship between collective bargaining and wages is possible unless all the points of view are considered.

In taking up the question before us we shall start with a simple illustration. Let us assume that a union is established among the workers of the Acme Manufacturing Company, and that one of the first acts of the union is to force the company to raise wages by 15 per cent. Here, right at the very beginning of our discussion, we come to the first of our conclusions or generalizations. A union group, such as the local in the Acme plant, has the power to raise the money wages of its members. Wage increases of this character are very common. They are the type that union journals generally publicize.

In addition to being able to raise their money wages through collective action, the Acme workers are able to raise their real wages as well. But the increase in the latter may be much less than in the former.

A very important question now arises, and in attempting to answer it we shall be forced to consider some of the main aspects of our problem. Where is the money coming from with which to pay the higher wages to the Acme workers? It may come from three main sources, and to these we shall now turn our attention.

Profits as a Source of Higher Wages

The "extra" wages paid to the Acme workers may come, at least in part, out of profits. Profits are widely looked upon by unionists as a fruitful source of wage increases, and a very common union claim is that increased wages can be paid out of profits with no necessary increase in prices.

Why Profits May Be a Source of Higher Wages. Profits may, within limits, constitute a source of higher wages. In the first place, unions, by forcing an employer to pay a wage more closely in line with the marginal productivity of the workers, may cut into the abnormal profits that the employer had been making when wages and productivity were not equal.[9] Such a wage increase need not lead to any reduction in the work force. This could be the case where there is only one buyer of labor in the market (simple monopsony); or where there are two or more buyers acting in collusion (oligopsony) and, in the absence of a union, keeping wages below marginal productivity. Again, a company that enjoys monopolistic advantages in the *product* market may, at least for the time being, absorb an enforced wage increase by reconciling itself to lower profits. For a number of reasons, including possible public disapproval, it may hesitate to pass on the increased wages in the form of higher prices.

Even if the company decides to protect its profits by substituting cheaper factors of production, namely additonal capital goods, for some of the more expensive labor, it may not be able to make the adjustment at once. Its investment is "sunk," and rapid changes in the capital-labor mix may not be easy to make. In time, of course, the adjustments can be made and labor can be economized. In the parlance of economics this means that although the demand for labor from a short-run point of view may be highly inelastic, judged from a long-run point of view it may be elastic.

If a profit-making producer is benevolent in nature, he may be willing to have wages cut into his profits. This point is emphasized in some of the newer wage theories, as we noted in the previous chapter.

It is not always benevolence that makes possible the cut into profits. In a business in which there is a wide divergence between ownership and management, especially high wages may be granted by managers who are more interested in bringing about a smooth-running, reputable organization than in making still higher profits for the owners. When this policy is pushed far in any business, the

[9] Under the conditions of (a) full comprehension on the part of the employer of what the marginal productivity of labor actually is; (b) competition among employers in the labor market; (c) adequate labor mobility; and (d) the nonexistence of technical obstacles in the way of varying the proportions between labor and the other factors of production—under these conditions there would be exact equivalence between the marginal productivity of labor and wages, for the simple reason that the employer would add units of labor to his plant until such equality was established. Since these assumptions are not always found in practice, the possibility that profits may be cut into by union action must be recognized.

enterprise in a sense—and in J. M. Keynes' terminology [10]—is socializing itself.

Finally, an employer interested in avoiding unions may pay his nonunion workers a high wage in order to keep them uninterested in labor organizations. He may be willing to pay the extra wage out of profits. Sometimes management personnel receive higher wages as a result of union action among the production workers. In a study of three plants made a few years ago, all management men received an unannounced salary increase shortly after the workers received an enforced wage increase, and "many of the managers revealed sentiments of indebtedness toward the unions" for their salary raises.[11] Here, too, profits may have been a source for the higher incomes.

Profits Are a Very Limited Source of Higher Wages. Although profits, and one might also include interest and rent, constitute a possible source of the higher wages won by union groups, the importance of this source should not be overstated. There is good reason for believing that only to a very limited extent do wage increases actually come from profits.

Over the years, and despite the increasing unionization of workers, the percentage of the national income going to wage earners has shown only moderate changes.[12] Apparently, there are various protective measures, such as raising prices, that employers may adopt to maintain their share of the national income.

On the whole, then, union-obtained wage increases do not come from the profit pool. This condition has been referred to by R. G. Hawtrey as an "iron law of wages," [13] and the term is not altogether inappropriate. Unions will undoubtedly continue to look upon profits, however, as a fruitful source of the higher wages they expect to achieve through collective bargaining.

The Indirect Approach. If unions cannot win any sizable slice of the profit share through collective bargaining, they may be able

[10] *The End of Laissez Faire,* pp. 42-44. London: Hogarth Press, 1926.

[11] Melville Dalton in *American Sociological Review,* October, 1950, p. 616.

[12] On this general point see Joan Robinson, *An Essay in Marxian Economics,* pp. 97, 98. London: Macmillan & Co., 1942. J. M. Clark suggests that possibly the clue to this stability is found in the operation of forces that keep the "profit" share constant. See *Guideposts in Time of Change,* p. 162. New York: Harper & Bros., 1949.

[13] *Economic Rebirth,* p. 69. London: Longmans, Green & Co., 1946.

to obtain a good piece of it by political means. In other words, a more effective way of redistributing the national income, of enabling labor to cut into the other distributive shares, is through the use of appropriate tax and expenditure policies. This approach has been supported by such men as Keynes, Robertson, and Hansen.[14]

The use of fiscal means for redistributing the total income of the nation (for the workers total income includes both their individual wage and their "social wage," in the form of old-age pensions and the like) does not mean that the unions should refrain from the policy of pressing directly for higher wages. In view of the psychological and political problems that would be involved in attempts to get such policy into operation, it would be ridiculous to make such a suggestion. And what is more, the direct pressure exerted by unions for higher wages may possibly increase the size of the national income and the income of labor. This part of our problem, however, we shall deal with later.

Dangers. In attempting to redistribute the national income, by whatever method, there is a danger that profits will be cut into too deeply. In a free-enterprise economy the prospect of private profits is the great driving force in industry. Moreover, profits are an extremely valuable source of savings. If large inroads are made into profits, the economy as a whole may be harmed. Labor too will feel the effects.

The unions, of course, grant that profits are legitimate, but they must be "reasonable"—so far no generally acceptable definition of reasonableness has been formulated. One can hazard the guess, however, that if by "reasonable" we mean the level of profits that is best in terms of economic stability, real income, and economic growth, the definition would embody a profit figure somewhere between the union estimate and the employer estimate.

Another point should be mentioned concerning unions and profits. If in a given instance—we are not in the present case referring to industry and unions as totalities—profits are deeply cut into, the allocation of productive factors will be interfered with.

[14] *The Political Quarterly,* January, 1930, pp. 119-124. D. H. Robertson, *Economic Fragments,* p. 57. London: P. S. King & Son, Ltd., 1931. A. G. Hansen, *Economic Policy and Full Employment,* p. 50. New York: McGraw-Hill Book Co., 1947.

If the high profits are taken by the unions, there will be little incentive for resources to flow into the industry, and the general pattern of production will be distorted.[15] It must be borne in mind, however, that entry into some industries is not easy: it is not a simple matter to start a new automobile company or a new steel company, for example. This argument should not be overemphasized, therefore.

One final danger should be noted. In so far as profits are cut into by union-enforced wage increases, the burden is shifted in part to the government in the form of lower tax revenues.[16] The ultimate incidence of the extra wage cost is not easy to trace, but part of the load may well be on the public at large.

Before passing on to a consideration of the next source of higher wages, it is pertinent to observe that recent union policy in connection with collective bargaining has made it increasingly difficult for higher wages to come out of profits. Both industry-wide bargaining and pattern bargaining have increased the likelihood that wage gains will reflect themselves in higher prices rather than lower profits, for a reason that we shall note shortly.

Higher Prices as a Source of Higher Wages

The higher wages that the workers of the Acme Company received may, in the second place, come out of prices. That is, the higher wages received by the Acme workers may be passed on to the consumers, at least in part, in the form of a higher price on the product the company sells. But here we must move very cautiously in our analysis. If the Acme Company is in an industry that is perfectly competitive (that is, the demand for the *company's* product is infinitely elastic), the price could not be raised. If the company did raise the price, its sales would sink to zero, and employment

[15] Further discussion of this point will be found in Henry C. Simons, *Economic Policy For a Free Society,* Chap. VI. Chicago: The University of Chicago Press, 1948. See also Fritz Machlup's remarks in *Wage Determination and the Economics of Liberalism,* p. 64. Washington: Chamber of Commerce of the United States, 1947.

[16] At the time of the famous steel dispute in early 1952, Benjamin Fairless expressed the opinion that if the wage increase sought by the union was granted without a price increase, 79 per cent of the cost would come out of federal income (corporate) revenues, 2 per cent out of state and local tax revenue, and 19 per cent out of corporate profits after taxes. *The New York Times,* April 18, 1952.

and wages would also fall to that level. Perfect competition, however, is for the most part an assumption rather than a fact, so some price rise is likely to be possible.

Demand and Displacement. Now another problem appears. Consumers ordinarily buy fewer units of an article at a higher price than at a lower price. Thus if the employer raises his price his sales will decline, the amount of the decline depending on the degree of elasticity of demand. If the sales fall off very little, that is, if the demand is inelastic, the price may be increased without any large decline in the labor force. If, on the other hand, the demand is very elastic, the increased price may lead to a large curtailment of the labor force, possibly so large that the total earnings of the workers will be less than previously. The *employed* workers are receiving higher wages than they did before, but their gains have been more than offset by the wage loss of the displaced workers.

The nature of the demand for an article, or articles, produced by unionists is of immense importance in determining the extent to which higher wages can be passed on in the form of higher prices. The matter, therefore, deserves further consideration.

The conditions under which an article is made help to determine the demand elasticity of the article. As we have already noted, under perfect competition the demand for the output of a single producer is infinitely elastic, and such a producer could not raise his price as a means of passing on a wage increase. If, however, the producer is a monopolist, with complete control over the supply of the article, the demand is much less elastic and a price increase, without a complete loss of sales, is possible. If the producer is operating under conditions of monopolistic competition, the demand for his article is more elastic (or less inelastic) than if he were operating under pure monopoly, but some price rise is also possible here. As a broad generalization, one can say that the possibility of passing on a wage and price increase, without serious curtailment of the work force involved, varies inversely with the degree of competition (in the product market) to which the company is exposed.

This leads us to a second, and closely related, consideration. As we have emphasized, the demand for the output of a producer under perfect competition is infinitely elastic. Now, the larger the number of producers covered by a given wage increase, the less elastic the market demand for their product, and hence the greater the possibility of passing on a wage increase in the form of higher prices. Thus the demand for the output of an *industry* (which, it should be noted, is the same as the demand for the output of a pure monopolist) is less elastic than the demand for the output of one *plant* or *company* in the industry. This fact suggests the idea that under industry-wide collective bargaining enforced wage gains may be reflected in higher prices.

To carry the analysis one step farther, the demand for the output of *all industries* is still less elastic than the demand for the output of one industry. In fact, the demand for the products of all industries and businesses (these may be viewed as one huge monopoly) may be considered almost infinitely inelastic if not completely so, especially if the supply of money and credit increases "adequately" as general wage pressure becomes effective. Under such circumstances (and these circumstances are by no means imaginary) the wage gains could be very easily passed on in the form of higher prices. This suggests another point, namely that pattern bargaining, or follow-the-leader bargaining, which covers employers not merely in one industry but in numerous industries, can lead to substantial price increases (as it did in the late 1940's and early 1950's). The period of the various "rounds" of wage increases was a period in which the price level ascended correspondingly. As we shall point out in the next chapter, however, union pressure was not the only, perhaps not even the chief, factor in accounting for higher prices at that time.

The more extensive, then, is the "area" covered by a given wage increase, the easier it is to pass on the increase to the consumers, including labor itself, in higher prices.

If higher wages in general are followed by higher prices in general, the real wages of the workers may be increased very little. But very often under collective bargaining the real wages of particular groups of workers are increased. In this connection let us consider the Acme workers again.

Concentrated Gains and Diffused Losses. If the union forces the Acme Company to pay higher wages, the company may be able to raise its prices. This price rise will result in some decrease in sales and probably some decline in employment in the plant. Setting aside the employment effect for the moment, let us give attention to the price effect.

The consumers now have to pay a higher price for the product of the Acme plant. Among the consumers are the Acme workers. Since these workers spend only a small fraction of their income on the product their company turns out, the higher price affects them very little. In other words, the real income of these workers increases along with their money income, although not quite to the same degree. If there has been no increase in the physical output of the company consequent upon the wage boost, the increase in the real wages of the Acme workers has been at the expense of other groups in society, namely the consumers.

But now we must look beyond the Acme Company and think of the many other enterprises in which unions are carrying on their bargaining activities. Let us assume that all of these enterprises are forced to pay higher wages. If we further assume that the higher wages are for the most part passed on to the consumers—and this assumption, in the absence of an increase in the physical productivity of the workers receiving the higher wages, appears to be warranted—the higher wages are paid largely by the workers themselves in the form of higher prices.

Narrowing down our analysis once more to the Acme workers, we see that they pay a higher price not only for the article they themselves make but for the many other things made by union, and nonunion, labor. Viewing, now, the field as a whole, we find that money wages in general have gone up but, since prices have risen, the purchasing power of the money wages has either remained the same or has changed only slightly.

That this is not merely a possible result of collective bargaining, and of unionism in general, but the actual result is a view that appears to be widely held among economists. Some years ago Professor F. W. Taussig declared that he quite agreed "with those who contend that the mere matter of wages is not likely to be affected one way or the other by the presence or absence of unions." [17] Taussig, however, recognized the noneconomic value of unions. Even such a sympathetic student of unionism as Professor R. F. Hoxie admitted that economists are right when they say that unions cannot raise the

[17] *Wertheim Lectures in Industrial Relations,* p. 222. Cambridge: Harvard University Press, 1929. Professor Gottfried Haberler, however, refers to the claim that unions cannot influence the real wage level as "an old classical tenet" that has either been largely given up or severely changed by many neoclassical economists." *Impact of the Union,* ed. by David McCord Wright, p. 35. New York: Harcourt, Brace & Co., 1951.

general wage level, although he points out that union wage methods and theories are not necessarily fallacious. More recently, Professor John J. Dunlop, in speaking of the rising wage level during the period from 1820 to 1945, stated that the role of the unions was "probably relatively minor." [18] The prevailing view among orthodox economists seems to be that unions do not have much effect on the average real wage of the workers—of *all* workers, not just union workers. This contention may be supported or denied; it cannot be scientifically proved or disproved.

The contention raises a very important question: What is the effect of unions on production? Implied in this question is another one: Is greater production a possible source of union-enforced wage increases? Before taking up these issues we shall digress a little and consider the employment effects of union wage action.

Employment Effects

The possibility that enforced wage increases will lead to unemployment must be recognized. The curtailment of the work force in the plants where the wage increase has been made may not occur directly. It may be brought about indirectly by the employers holding down the hiring rate in their enterprises, while the separation rate (covering layoffs, quits, and discharges) remains at the old level.

How much thought do unions give to the specific unemployment effects of their wage demands? Probably not a great deal. Ross argues that "the typical wage bargain (with certain significant exceptions) is necessarily made without consideration of its employment effect." [19] Lindblom declares that unemployment is not an adequate restraint on union monopoly, except in some instances and in the long run.[20]

There are various reasons why union leaders may give little consideration to the employment effects of their wage policies. For one thing they may not be in a position to figure out what these effects will be. The effect on employment in any specific case will depend on such things as the percentage that labor costs constitute of total

[18] *Wage Determination and the Economics of Liberalism,* p. 37. Washington: Chamber of Commerce of the United States, 1947.

[19] Arthur M. Ross, *Trade Union Wage Policy,* p. 14. Berkeley: University of California Press, 1948.

[20] Charles E. Lindblom, *Unions and Capitalism,* pp. 75, 78, 89. New Haven: Yale University Press, 1949.

costs,[21] the nature of the demand for the article, and general business conditions. It will also depend on the willingness of the employer to absorb, at least for the time being, part of the increased wage cost; and on the speed with which capital can be substituted for labor. Any conclusions reached concerning the employment effect would usually be very indefinite; and even if the union leaders could tell with any degree of precision what the effect will be, it does not follow that they would regulate their wage policy in accordance with the anticipated effect.[22]

Extremism on this controversial matter should be avoided, however. In some cases union leaders *do* give thought to the potential employment effects of their wage demands; in fact, they do so rather often, according to George P. Schultz and Charles A. Myers in their criticism of the point of view expressed by Ross.[23]

Let us look at the matter now from the standpoint of management. It is not to be assumed that employers, when confronted with an enforced wage increase, that shifts wages above the marginal productivity of labor, make instantaneous and mathematically precise adjustments, including adjustments in the amount of labor they use, to the new situation. Here, too, there are obstacles in the way. The typical employer does not know accurately what the marginal productivity is of any specific group of workers in his plant, particularly in plants with a variety of products. Moreover, there may be technical and economic difficulties in the way of changing at once the capital-labor mix in the plant. For these and other reasons employment adjustments may be delayed, and when they are made they may not be of a nicely balanced nature.[24] But it is true that in time some adjust-

[21] Professor Milton Friedman has a good discussion of the demand for labor in terms of the Marshallian joint-demand analysis, in *The Impact of the Union*, ed. by David McCord Wright, pp. 207-212. New York: Harcourt, Brace & Co., 1951.

[22] Further discussion of the obstacles in the way of ascertaining the employment effect of union wage policy will be found in Fritz Machlup's article in *Wage Determination and the Economics of Liberalism*, pp. 51-54. Washington: Chamber of Commerce of the United States, 1947. The same topic is discussed in J. R. Hicks, *The Theory of Wages*, Chapter X. London: The Macmillan Co., 1932.

[23] *The American Economic Review*, June, 1950, pp. 362-380.

[24] For a more detailed treatment of this point see Professor Lester's contribution to *Insights into Labor Issues*, ed. by Richard A. Lester and Joseph Shister, pp. 218-220. New York: The Macmillan Co., 1948. The question we have been discussing above is part of the larger issue centering around the validity of the marginal approach in wage analysis. In recent years the issue has been debated

ments will generally be made, and these adjustments may be in employment.

The employment-effect question is one that will continue to be debated. All that is known for certain now is that union leaders do give some thought to the matter, and that employers do make some adjustments in employment as a consequence of enforced wage advances. We can be reasonably certain in the matter of "direction" of thought or adjustment, but not in the matter of "degree."

Returning again to our illustration, let us assume that the Acme company adjusts itself to the wage increase by reducing either directly or indirectly the size of its work force. The *employed* workers have obtained higher wages, both money and real. But these gains have been made at the expense of other workers, who are now out of jobs.

Some of these workers may have difficulty in obtaining employment, but in an economy as dynamic as ours it is likely that all of them, or most of them, will in time succeed in getting new jobs. But now we see another angle to our problem.

The competition of the excluded workers in the labor market will tend to reduce wages in the occupations to which these workers turn. In the terminology of economics, there will be a movement downwards on the marginal productivity curve. Thus the high wages of the "favored ones" in the Acme Company have resulted in lower wages for the less fortunate workers on the outside. The *total* wages received by the two groups may be the same, or more, or less than previously, depending on the nature of the demand for the workers in the two groups, the number of workers in the two groups, and the wage levels in the two groups.[25]

During a time of economic expansion the adverse wage effect outside the bargaining group may not be apparent. But it may be present nevertheless. It may involve a less rapid increase in the wages of those outside the group, rather than an actual wage decline.

On the whole, the analysis so far seems to indicate that whereas union groups considered separately may raise both the money wages

---

by Lester, Machlup, and others. Contributions to the discussion will be found in *The American Economic Review,* March, 1946, pp. 63-82; September, 1946, pp. 519-554; and March, 1947, pp. 135-156.

[25] A brief discussion of this matter will be found in Sumner H. Slichter, *Modern Economic Society,* pp. 636-638. New York: Henry Holt & Co., 1931.

and the real wages of their members (their employed members), the general effect of union action on the average real wages of all workers would seem to be small. But this result is based on the supposition that unions as such have little or no effect on the volume of production. Is this true?

Greater Production as a Source of Higher Wages

If we may return once again to our illustration, we may say that the higher wages obtained by the workers in the Acme plant may have come not out of profits or from higher prices but out of greater production. That is to say, the higher wages may have led, directly or indirectly, to greater worker productivity. The marginal productivity curve for labor, and hence the demand curve for labor (the two are the same), may have been raised. Under such conditions the source of the higher money wages and the higher real wages of the Acme workers is enlarged, and there is no necessary drain of money or real income from the profit receivers, the consumers in general, or other workers.

If a given group of workers wins higher money wages and there is no commensurate increase in its productivity (expressed in physical terms), some other group is going to suffer. This suffering group may be the profit receivers, but it is much more likely to be the consumers, especially as the size of the bargaining group increases. If all workers win higher money wages and there is no increase in the physical output of industry, then all the workers largely pay the bill—in their capacity as consumers.

Is production in the Acme plant greater with the union there than it would be if the union were absent? Or, to state the question in a form that gives it general applicability, is the aggregate production in all industries, or in the country as a whole, greater than it would be if unions were nonexistent? We are considering now not only union wage policies but the whole gamut of union policies and activities.

Economists have not given this question very careful attention except for a certain amount of piecemeal discussion.[26] However,

[26] Professor Slichter is an exception. See his book, *Modern Economic Society,* pp. 640, 646. New York: Henry Holt & Co., 1931. See also his contributions in *Explorations in Economics,* Notes and Essays Contributed in Honor of F. W. Taussig. New York: McGraw-Hill Book Co., 1936; and *Collective Bargaining Contracts.* Washington: The Bureau of National Affairs, Inc., 1941.

there seems to be a rather widespread assumption among them that unions either decrease the size of the national output, or leave it about the same—that is, that unions have little or no effect on the average real wage of all workers.

The question we have just raised is a highly important one and we shall give it extended treatment in the next chapter.

23

UNIONS, WAGES, AND NATIONAL WAGE POLICY

We know approximately what the size of the national output is with unions in existence. We do not know what it would be if unions did not exist. Although a verifiable conclusion on the question of the effect of unions on production is thus ruled out, we can at least work toward what we might call an intelligent guess.

In discussing the effect of union action on the output of the nation, we shall first give attention to specific ways in which unions (a) hinder production, and (b) further production. Then we shall turn to four aspects of the question that are more general in nature but that have a very close bearing on the issue before us.

Union Policies and the National Output

In taking up specific union policies and their effect on production we shall limit ourselves to a number that are either especially significant or good for illustrative purposes.

How Unions Hinder Production. (1) One way in which unions impede production is through the adoption of various restrictive practices. Bricklayers may insist that a hod rather than a wheelbarrow be used in bringing mortar to the wall. Granite cutters may rule that brooms rather than compressed air be used in removing dust. Electricians may require that piping be cut, bent, and assembled where it is used.[1] It is impossible to say how widespread such make-

[1] These examples are taken from an article by Corwin D. Edwards in *The American Economic Review,* Papers and Proceedings, March, 1942, pp. 439-442. Mr. Edwards, it should be pointed out, distinguishes between "reasonable" and "unreasonable" restraints.

work rules are among American unions. That they are sufficiently extensive to constitute at least a minor social evil seems indisputable.

In giving attention to the restrictive policies of unions a number of considerations must be borne in mind. In the first place unionists are not the only persons in society who limit production. Employers may consciously limit production when they think it pays, or they may limit it more or less unconsciously by inefficient methods. Farmers also limit production when they feel that it is to their economic interest to do so. Two (or three, or four) wrongs never make a right, however, and the fact that other groups in society do what amounts to the same thing that the unions are doing is no justification for unionists holding back production. From the social point of view output restriction is bad no matter what group does it.

Another point to be noted is that output restriction among workers is not limited to unionists. Nonunionists, although they cannot act as a group, sometimes use restrictive practices also; and these practices, though not usually the same as those used by the unions, are by no means of little consequence.[2]

It should be noted, furthermore, that the restrictive practices of unions (and of other organizations) may not always be completely antisocial or unreasonable. Union opposition to new machines, for example, may, to some extent at least, be justified when such machines imperil health, are dangerous to operate, or involve a great deal of labor displacement.

Finally, it should be observed that restriction of output by labor results to no small extent from fear of unemployment. This fear is partly groundless, but not completely so. If workers felt that there would always be adequate employment opportunities open for them, they would be much less interested in "making the job last."

(2) The effect of strikes on production cannot be measured with any degree of accuracy. Some of the output lost while strikes are in progress is made up after the stoppages are settled. Part of it, indeed, may be "made up" (by extra production) even before the stoppages begin. Moreover, the loss in output experienced by the company whose workers are on strike may be compensated for by an increase in production in competitors' plants.

2 On the general question of output restriction by nonunionists, see S. B. Mathewson, *Restriction of Output Among Unorganized Workers.* New York: The Viking Press, 1931.

It seems too optimistic, however, to conclude that strikes have no appreciable effect on the total output of the nation. Not all the time lost in strikes is made up. Time-and-a-half rates may keep the employer from working his men overtime. Nor does it always happen that what one company loses in production, as a result of a strike, other companies gain. If a strike is industry-wide, such offsetting gains, of course, are ruled out. To these unregained direct losses involved in strikes must be added the unregained indirect losses. Many strikes at the present time lead to serious idleness in other industries, in which (in turn) the production losses are by no means made up.

There is every reason for believing, therefore, that strikes—most of which involve unions—are on the whole harmful to the national output. It must not be forgotten, however, that strikes are an outlet, and possibly a cure, for grievances which, if not given an outlet, may lead to more or less permanent bitterness and dissatisfaction, which in turn are harmful to production.

(3) Some union rules definitely curb management initiative. Although such curbs are socially desirable when the initiative expresses itself in the wrong direction, there is a danger that obstacles will be placed in the way of managerial efficiency. For example, union control over hiring may make it difficult for the employer to obtain the best men available, just as control by the union over discharges may make it inconvenient at times to get rid of incompetent workers. Moreover, union control (based on the seniority principle) over layoffs and promotions may be harmful to efficiency (see Chapter 15).

(4) Union opposition to incentive methods of wage payment is another obstacle in the way of larger output. Although not all unions are opposed to these methods, opposition to them is extensive and production is probably harmed as a consequence.

How Unions Promote Production. The ways in which unions may aid or stimulate production are not as obvious as the ways in which they may harm production, since most of the favorable influencing factors operate indirectly and are not aimed specifically at greater production.

(1) Adequate response to the common union demand for improved physical conditions of work—better sanitation, ventilation, lighting, and the like—improves the health of the workers and thus makes them more productive. To the individual employer, who ordinarily does not look upon his workers as part of his *permanent* in-

vestment, the cost of making these changes may be greater than the gains. But from the standpoint of society (which is interested not only in the weekly or yearly output of the worker but also in his lifetime output) the gain may be appreciable.

(2) The impetus given to industrial mechanization, and hence to cheaper and greater production, by enforced higher wages and shorter hours and by the threat of strikes, has long been recognized. Early in the last century Ricardo pointed out that "Machinery and labor are in constant competition and the former can frequently not be employed until labor rises." The forceful reduction of hours has been viewed in the same light. Ira Steward in this country based his "Golden Law of Wages" on the belief that a compulsory reduction of hours (in this case by legislation) would lead to increased mechanization. On the matter of strikes and mechanization one can cite the authority of Karl Marx. In his *Capital* Marx declares that machinery constitutes "the most powerful weapon" used by the capitalist-employer "for repressing strikes."

To the opinions expressed on this question one can add the weight of concrete historical evidence. For example, the high wages resulting from the scarcity of farm labor during the Civil War were a very important factor in bringing about the marked increase in the use of agricultural machinery that occurred at that time.[3]

If necessity is the mother of invention—a distinction and a responsibility which, in truth, necessity must share with others—unions, as a result of their demands for higher wages and shorter hours and their threats to strike if their demands are not granted, have a legitimate claim to being the grandmother, or grandfather, of invention. Unions certainly help to create necessity. To some extent unions have been of indirect influence in the original making of mechanical inventions. Most of their influence, however, has probably been reflected in the more extensive use of already existing inventions.

(3) Output is increased when there is union-management cooperation. Since the central aim of this cooperation is to improve production methods, the total output of the nation is certain to be increased. The specific ways in which union-management cooperation promotes production were dealt with in Chapter 19.

[3] See Holland Thompson, *The Age of Invention*, pp. 126-127. New Haven: Yale University Press, 1921.

(4) The control exercised by unions over management prerogatives may, in some instances, have a favorable effect on production. For example, take the matter of union control over the firing policies of management. To an increasing extent unions have won the right to review discharge cases. This right, if exercised extensively, may be bothersome to the employer and may sometimes contribute to productive inefficiency, as we noted earlier; however, it may in some instances have the opposite effect. Thus, it may induce the employer to be particularly careful in his selection of workers as well as in their placement, so that the number of discharges will be kept down to a minimum.

In contrast to the unions of Soviet Russia, American labor organizations do not have as their primary purpose the increase of productive efficiency and the enlargement of the national output. American unionists, like their employers, are more interested in making money than they are in making goods (not that the two are incompatible). Nevertheless, to some extent they take a direct and active interest in improving production, and many of their specific policies indirectly, and generally unintentionally, contribute to that end. There are still other general aspects of the problem, however, that must be considered, and to these we shall now give attention.

Unions and the Allocation of Productive Factors

Considerable discussion has taken place concerning the effect of unionism on the allocation of the factors of production. The question is of definite importance because the size of the national output and of average real wages is governed, in part, by the effectiveness of the allocation process. If the allocation is "good," the industrial output is enhanced; if it is "bad," the output is diminished.

Interpretation of Allocation. But what is meant by good allocation? Or, to state the question in absolute terms, what is meant by ideal or perfect allocation? The factors of production are allocated in a perfect manner when production is maximized, i.e., when the productive factors, including labor, are distributed (allocated) in such a way that any shift from their pattern of distribution would pull down aggregate production. Speaking of labor, and using the terminology of economics, allocation is at its best when the marginal productivity of labor, of a given type, is the same in all of its uses; that is, when there is "equality at the margins."

The marginal productivity here referred to is not physical marginal productivity—one cannot compare incomparables like roller skates and lead pencils—but pecuniary or value marginal productivity. The latter is in terms of dollars and cents and is thus quite comparable.

It is highly important to note, however, that pecuniary productivity reflects the price of the product and that this price reflects the pattern of consumer demand—which, in turn, is partially based on the way wealth is divided. When we speak of equalizing marginal products, therefore, we must think in terms of a given distribution of wealth. This suggests that the "best" allocation is not necessarily the best! It is only the best with reference to a particular distribution of wealth. This is a significant consideration, but from the standpoint of systematic analysis the assumption of a given distribution of wealth—the present distribution, in fact—must be made.

Union Influence on Allocation. Recognizing this limitation to our analysis, let us now turn to our central problem. Do unions distort the allocation pattern? Some union practices undoubtedly have that effect.

(1) Restrictions on free entry to unions, by such means as high initiation fees and discriminatory policies, tend to keep workers out of employments or jobs into which they would like to move, and into which society, expressing its wishes through the price mechanism, wants them to move. These workers must turn to other kinds of employment, employment for which they may not be well fitted or in which they are not much interested. In general it can be said that the larger the market in which individual workers may offer their "wares," the better the allocation. Anything that segments or Balkanizes the market, and some union policies have such an effect, harms allocation. But labor markets may be narrowed in other ways.

(2) High wages obtained in a given company or industry through union pressure may bring about some economy in the use of labor. The workers who are squeezed out of their jobs will obtain employment elsewhere, probably at wages lower than those their retained colleagues are receiving. Allocation here will be harmed. The degree of harm, however, will depend on two things: (a) the number of workers who are forced to look elsewhere for jobs, and (b) the effect of the given wage increase on the general wage pattern. These two, of course, are closely related.

The employment effect question, as we noted in the preceding chapter, is a matter of debate. So too, we may now add, is the wage distortion question. Some writers, including Kerr and Dunlop, believe that unions have not had highly important effects on interindustry wage differentials. Kerr declares that whereas institutional controls in the labor market are conducive to single rates in definite crafts and industries, "the best, although not thoroughly convincing, evidence now indicates they have surprisingly little effect, however, on inter-industry differentials." [4] Dunlop says that there is considerable evidence to test the truth of the contention that unionism has "distorted" the wage structure and caused unemployment; he even politely asks his colleagues to "'put up or shut up' on the consequences of unionism *to date* for the structure of wage rates in this country." [5] Although denying the presence of significant wage distortion by unions at the present time, Dunlop does, however, admit the possibility of distortion in the future.

The issue here is a debatable one and the authorities are not agreed. As so often happens, the truth is probably somewhere between the extremes.

It is pertinent to note at this point that the larger the collective bargaining unit, the less adverse the effect on allocation. Dunlop ventures the opinion that "on balance" larger collective bargaining units adopt wage policies that are more favorable to "larger outputs and better allocation" than those of smaller units.[6]

(3) Another angle to the allocation problem has to do with the way in which the economic gains resulting from technological improvements are distributed. These gains can go to the consumers in the form of lower prices, to the workers in higher wages, and to the employers in higher profits. In general, it seems desirable that most of the benefits should go to the consumers (including the workers). Where the unions are strong, however, it is likely that technological benefits will be absorbed to a very substantial degree by higher wages.

[4] Industrial Relations Research Association, *Proceedings*, 1949, p. 78.

[5] *The American Economic Review*, June 1950, p. 465. Professor Friedman, who may be linked with Kerr and Dunlop on the issue, argues that the effect of unions on wage structure is exaggerated. See *The Impact of the Union*, ed. by David McCord Wright, pp. 215-226. New York: Harcourt, Brace & Co., 1951.

[6] *Wage Determination Under Trade Unions*, p. 226. New York: The Macmillan Co., 1944. The point made by Dunlop is not inconsistent with the one presented at the end of section (1) on p. 447.

If consumers receive the gains in the form of lower prices, more units of the goods are demanded and produced, and productive resources are drawn into the industry turning out the goods. If the gains go to the wage earners, the industries that expand are those into which the workers direct their expenditures. There is good reason for believing that the allocation pattern in the first case is superior to that in the second.

The extent to which prices are reduced following a technological improvement depends not only on the presence or absence of unions but on the degree of competition that exists in the industry. If the industry is highly competitive, high profits made by any unit in the industry will not be "impounded" very long. Other producers will enter the field and those already in it will introduce the improvement, and prices will fall. If the industry is a monopolistic one, however, the high profits may be retained for a long time, without any resources being drawn into the industry. A union here has a good chance of cutting into the enlarged profits, but there is a possibility that the output of the industry and the resources in it may be restricted more than ever.[7]

(4) The question of allocation inevitably brings up the problem of monopoly. The case against ordinary industrial monopoly rests primarily on its effect on the allocation of productive resources. By keeping his price high (thus limiting sales and output) or by controlling his output (thus keeping up price) the monopolist hinders the entry of resources into his field. The resources thus excluded must seek employment elsewhere—in fields that from a social standpoint are less advantageous. As a consequence the total output of society is harmed.

In recent years the charge has been made that unions are monopolies. The unions have denied the appropriateness of the appellation,[8] and a great deal of discussion has taken place over the issue.

[7] See Fritz Machlup's argument on this point in *Wage Determination and the Economics of Liberalism,* pp. 62-65. Washington: Chamber of Commerce of the United States, 1947. The contention above would be true only if one assumes that as a result of union influence prices stay up longer than they otherwise would have. This assumption is likely to be correct.

[8] See the CIO's *Economic Outlook,* April, 1950. This issue is entitled "'Labor Monopoly'—a Phony Issue." See also "The Myth of Labor Monopoly," in the AFL publication *The American Federationist,* February, 1950.

Unions as Monopolies. The charge that unions are monopolies has arisen particularly in connection with industry-wide collective bargaining. In 1947 an attempt was made to pass federal legislation limiting the size of the bargaining unit; and off and on suggestions are made that unions should be brought under the anti-trust laws, presumably in order to prevent industry-wide bargaining.

The term "monopoly," as it is usually understood, is a very uncomplimentary epithet, and it is not surprising that the unions should resent its application to them. It is true, nevertheless, that unions are monopolistic in nature. To be sure, unions oppose monopolistic totalitarianism (i.e., communism) on the one hand and business monopoly on the other; and through the "countervailing power" they exercise,[9] on both a national and an international plane, they confer real benefits upon society. In characterizing unions as monopolies it should be understood that there are differences between industrial monopolies and labor monopolies, and that the degree of labor monopoly varies a great deal from one organization to another.

The monopolistic feature contained in unionism is found in the power of unions over the sale of their "product." This power may be expressed in various union practices that directly limit the number of workers employed; or, as is much more likely, it may express itself in wage policy that indirectly restricts employment.[10] In whichever way it expresses itself it may lead to a misallocation of labor.

However, the social loss resulting from this misallocation is likely to be less serious than the loss resulting from the misallocation accompanying industrial monopoly. In the first place, the beneficiaries of union monopoly "profits" are likely to be more numerous than those of industrial monopoly profits. In the second place, when arbitrarily high wages are forced on employers, they may be induced to take steps that will eventually lead to more production and possibly lower prices and more employment; no parallel process takes

[9] For a stimulating discussion of the countervailing-power thesis, including reference to unions, see J. K. Galbraith, *American Capitalism*. Boston: Houghton, Mifflin Co., 1952.

[10] Professor Chamberlain emphasizes that the monopolist—labor or other—does not literally restrict supply. That is done by "the market," reacting to the higher price or wage. *The Impact of the Union*, ed. by David McCord Wright, pp. 172-173. New York: Harcourt, Brace & Co., 1951. In this book Professor Chamberlain discusses at some length "The Monopoly Power of Labor."

place where there is product monopoly. Again, the extent to which monopolistic unions actually change wage differentials and allocation seems often to be exaggerated.[11]

Considering from various angles the general question that is before us, as we have attempted to do in the preceding discussion, it would seem that the over-all effect of unions on the allocation of resources is unfavorable.

Unions and Economic Stability

It is desirable to have the factors of production well allocated, but it is also desirable to have them steadily employed. What is the effect of union action on steadiness of employment, particularly of labor? In given instances there can be no doubt that union action leads to unemployment. But does unionism in general increase the amount of unemployment in the economy as a whole? This is indeed a difficult question to answer. Unions introduce certain rigidities into the system which, if considered by themselves, make the system less flexible and more susceptible to unemployment. But unions operate in an environment in which there are other large units and blocs, notably in business and agriculture. And there is some reason for believing that the rigidities introduced by the unions may help to offset or balance the rigidities introduced by these other units into the economy.

If unions, and large and interdependent business and agricultural units, were nonexistent—if, in other words, we had the type of atomistic competition envisaged by the early economists—the business cycle would be much less serious. The economy would be highly flexible, and dislocations and imbalance would soon be corrected. If, however, only the unions were nonexistent, the degree of instability might not be reduced at all. In fact it might be increased.

Turning to the specific question of union wage policy and economic stability, it should be noted that union opposition to wage cuts during a depression may well reduce the severity of the depression.[12] Consumer spending may be maintained at a level high

[11] For a discussion of this general theme, see Professor Friedman's paper in *The Impact of the Union*, ed. by David McCord Wright, pp. 204-234. New York: Harcourt, Brace & Co., 1951. See also the section on employment effects in the preceding chapter.

[12] Some economists believe the reverse. See, for example, Professor Viner's statement on p. 32 of *Wage Determination and the Economics of Liberalism.*

enough to direct resources that might have been idle (not used for investment) into consumer goods industries. Approaching the problem from a different angle, the Subcommittee on Economic Stability of the American Economic Association believes that the growing power of unions "has much reduced the danger that future business contraction will be intensified by deflationary price spirals, such as occurred in the early 'thirties." [13] If such spirals are reduced, the degree of instability should also be reduced. It would seem that most economists, however, feel that a policy of "selective" wage cuts during a depression is helpful to employment.

During the prosperity phase of the cycle union wage policy, aimed in the first instance at directing more of the income stream of society into wages (and hence increasing the demand for consumer goods, and also the demand for factors of production in the consumer-goods industries), may prolong prosperity and in the long run promote total production and total savings and investment.

The relationship between union wage policy, which is characterized by downward rigidity and upward flexibility, and the business cycle is very obscure, and business cycle theorists have done little in recent years to dissipate the obscurity.[14]

Unions and the Volume of Capital

Average real wages are closely tied up with the amount of capital used in industry. The more capital per worker—capital embodied in such things as dynamos, punch presses, and jigs—the higher the level of real wages. In other words, the more "roundabout" or "capitalistic" the method of production, the higher the material standards of living.

The roundabout method of production, when it is highly developed, involves the creation of a large supply of capital goods, which, in turn, involves saving. Let us examine the effect of unions on the volume of savings and on the growth of capital goods.

Washington: Chamber of Commerce of the United States, 1947. Professor Viner's statement is somewhat conditional, and the policy (of lower wages) is admitted to be politically impracticable and undesirable.

[13] *The American Economic Review,* September, 1950, p. 537.

[14] See Gottfried Haberler's remarks in *The Impact of the Union,* ed. by David McCord Wright, p. 37. New York: Harcourt, Brace & Co., 1951.

Broadly speaking, the volume of saving in any country is connected with the absolute size of the national income and the percentage of the national income that is saved. These two factors, of course, are closely connected. The size of the national income is to be thought of not in terms of one year (which may be a year of depression or a year of prosperity) but over a period of, say, one or two decades.

Do unions have a favorable effect on the size of the national income over such a period? This question involves giving attention to the specific ways that unions aid or harm production, to the effect of unions on the allocation of productive resources, and to their effect on economic stability. Whereas it is impossible to venture a final, authoritative answer on the point, the writer would hazard the guess (though such an act is most unscientific!) that the national income is perhaps larger with unions than it would be without them.

There is reason for believing, however, that unions *decrease* the percentage of the national income that is saved. The amount of savings may be reduced a little as a result of a cut in profits, following union wage pressure—even though such a cut is not likely to be very deep, as we have already noted. If we take into account, as we should, union political pressure exerted in behalf of high taxes on large incomes, there is greater reason for believing that unions reduce the amount of saving.

The question we have raised is a highly complex one and it is impossible for us to give a dogmatic answer to it. Professor Slichter, who has examined the problem from a monetary standpoint (and in terms of collective bargaining, not in terms of all union activities) reaches an indefinite conclusion. But it is Slichter's contention that whereas "the effect of collective bargaining upon the rate at which the *quantity* of capital increases is uncertain, its effect upon the rate at which the *quality* of capital improves is certain." [15] The improvement of the quality of capital is achieved through the stimulus given to technological research by union pressure for higher wages. In Professor Slichter's opinion, this particular effect of collective bargaining gives greater promise of helping to raise living standards than any other effect.

[15] *The Economics of Collective Bargaining,* pp. 40-45. Berkeley and Los Angeles: University of California, the Institute of Industrial Relations, 1950.

Unions and Economic Growth

A final question in the present discussion is the relationship between unions and economic growth. Much of what has already been said has a bearing on this point, but the issue, as a separate problem, has not been raised.

In considering the economic well-being of a nation the matter of growth is of immense importance, unless the people of the nation are close to the saturation point with respect to commodities, services, and leisure—that is, unless they are just about satisfied with the economic *status quo*. Since no nation is in such a position, the question of economic growth, particularly in relationship to unionism, is a significant one.

Do unions promote or retard economic growth? It is not difficult to point to union policies that seem to be obstacles in the way of growth. The seniority policy (for which unions are largely responsible), standardization practices of one type and another, and union control over management initiative may be mentioned as examples.[16] On the other hand, some union policies stimulate growth: for example, the constant "needling" of unions for better pay may stimulate improvements, as may union-induced changes in the conditions of work and direct union aid in the solution of production problems.

The chances are that the net effect of union action on economic growth is not much one way or the other. It would be well, however, for the unions, in their own interest, to give more thought to the general problem of economic growth in the economy and to means in their power for promoting it. A greater willingness is necessary on the unions' part to witness and experience change, the inevitable accompaniment of growth. There is, as the title of an excellent book (by A. G. B. Fisher) informs us, a "clash between security and progress," and there is a danger that unions in their attempts to achieve security will unduly check progress. An optimum balance between

[16] Professor David McCord Wright, who has given special attention to the question of economic growth, seems to take a rather dismal view of the relationship between unions and economic growth. See *The Impact of the Union,* ed. by Professor Wright, Chapter XII. New York: Harcourt, Brace & Co., 1951. Professor Wright has a fine discussion of the general problem of economic growth with reference to planned and unplanned societies (including unions) in his book *Capitalism.* New York: McGraw-Hill Book Co., 1951.

the two must be found—a balance, moreover, that involves the provision of aid to the victims of progress.

Conclusion

After this long discussion it would be comforting if we could state precisely and categorically what the effect of union action is on the size of the national income and on average real wages. Unfortunately we cannot. We know that specific union groups can raise both their money wages and their real wages, and that all union groups considered as a totality can also raise their money wages and real wages. But does the action of all unions raise the real wages of *all* workers, union and nonunion? To this question we cannot give a positive, verifiable answer. The author would guess that the national income and average real wages are somewhat higher with unions than they would be without unions. He would point out, however, that the real wages of some groups may be lower than they otherwise would be because of the presence of unions in our midst. College professors are perhaps a case in point!

The question of unions and average real wages is of great importance, but the case for, or against, unions does not rest entirely upon it. Even if unions adversely affect the real income of the nation and the average real income of *all* workers (but increase their own real income), other factors enter into the "union question." Unions are not solely economic institutions and, as we stated in Chapter 20, they must not be appraised only in economic terms.

National Wage Policy

The idea of a national wage policy is based on the belief that there are times when the wages established in the market by demand and supply forces (including union pressure) are not at levels conducive to the general welfare. Hence, it is felt, wages in such times should be subject to some degree of control, of either a voluntary or a compulsory character.

National wage policy relates to the control of wage levels particularly during periods of depression and periods of prosperity. In Chapter 6 we examined wage policy during depressions, pointing out the danger that at such times wages might go too low. At this point we shall discuss wage policy during periods of prosperity, when the danger is that wages will go too high. The latter aspect of the problem received widespread attention during the late 1940's and early 1950's, and will undoubtedly give rise to extensive discussion in the future. First we shall consider wage policy during war periods, which are marked by great industrial activity if not by prosperity.

Wage Policy During War. The necessity of establishing wage ceilings during war periods has been very apparent; during both World War I and World War II wages, along with prices, were subject to extensive controls. The chief reason for placing limits on wages during a war period is fairly obvious. At such a time the resources of the nation, including its manpower, are directed in substantial measure into the production of war goods. The volume of consumer goods is either decreased or kept from increasing. The size of the work force, including those in the armed service, is abnormally large. Under these conditions the amount paid out in wages is large, owing not only to the increase in the size of the work force, and to longer hours, but to the strong tendency for wages to rise in a tight labor market.

Unless controls are imposed, the volume of monetary purchasing power flowing into the hands of the workers, and mostly designed for spending, will be much larger than the value of the consumer goods (in terms of the prevailing prices) that are entering the market. The inevitable result will be inflation and a disruption of the war effort. The government is therefore forced to institute wage and price controls. It adopts, as a temporary expedient, the sort of policy that is in permanent use in Russia; except that in Russia another highly effective mechanism for mopping up excess monetary purchasing power, and for forcing the workers to save, is in use, namely the turnover tax.

Wage Policy During Peace. During a time of great national emergency there is little objection in this country to the introduction of a national wage policy, accompanied by price controls. But during peacetime opposition to such a step is very strong. Yet there has been developing in this country, at least among economists, a feeling that even in times of peace some sort of national wage control may be desirable. This feeling has been an outgrowth of two developments in the economy: the growth of "big unionism" and the attainment, during and following World War II, of full employment.

As we noted in the previous chapter, the upward pressure that unions are now exerting on the general wage level is very strong, much stronger than when unions were less numerous and had fewer members, when industry-wide and pattern bargaining were less extensive, and when the pressure on union leaders to deliver the goods, and keep on delivering them, was not so great. Because of these factors, and because of strong employer competition for workers (as under full employment),[17] it is almost inevitable that money-wage increases will outrun the increase in the physical output of goods.

If this happens, and if the wage earners do not save the "proper" proportion of their enlarged money incomes, prices must go up. Inflation is in the saddle and it will ride mankind unless control measures of some sort are adopted.[18]

The excess monetary purchasing power could be mopped up by higher income taxes on the wage recipients; but for a number of reasons, including political unfeasibility, this device is not likely to be used to the extent necessary for the purpose in hand. The problem could be attacked by more rigid controls over the total money supply, but the likelihood of this being done on an adequate scale is not great. Another control policy is to set limitations on wage increases. This brings us to the question of national wage policy.

Characteristics of a National Wage Policy. The aim of a national wage policy might be full employment; it might be general economic stability, presumably at or near the full employment level; it might be a stable price level. These aims are not mutually exclusive, but one—say, a stable price level—could be given paramount consideration.

To achieve a stable price level, and assuming no change in the relative shares of the national income going to labor and to the other productive factors, money wages in general (expressed, probably, in terms of average hourly wages) should not advance more rapidly than the increase in the physical output of industry (on a general, man-hour basis). The latter increase is somewhere around 2 per cent per annum—there is some difference of opinion concerning the exact

[17] There has been considerable discussion among economists as to whether big unionism or full employment has been chiefly responsible for the postwar inflation. Professor W. A. Morton has been an outstanding supporter of the full-employment explanation. See *The American Economic Review,* March, 1950. For replies to the Morton argument see *ibid.,* September, 1950.

[18] A more optimistic view on the relationship between union wage pressure and inflation is presented by Arthur Ross in *The Labor Law Journal,* June, 1951, p. 440.

figure.[19] In specific industries, and with reference to particular groups of workers, the increase in productivity may be much more than 2 per cent; just as in other cases it may be, and is, much less.

A wage policy geared to a general equivalence between the rates of increase in money wages and in physical productivity does not imply that *all* money wages should go up at the same rate. On the other hand, such a policy does not mean that there should be complete equivalence, in *each and every* case, between individual productivity increases and wage increases. The latter policy would be, in Fritz Machlup's picturesque language, economically foolish, ethically undesirable, and politically impossible.[20] The *average* wage increase, however, should be about 2 per cent a year; that should be the goal for society.

Union and a National Wage Policy. But, it may be asked, how will wages, on the average, be kept to an annual increase of 2 per cent? It seems rather doubtful, as far as the immediate future is concerned, that individual unions will voluntarily limit their wage demands to such a figure. For one thing the unions are desirous of increasing their *share* of the total national income, and hence they seek wage advances larger than the percentage by which the total output of the nation is increased. In the second place, union leaders are under enormous pressure to keep on winning wage increases, in order that the union may survive and the leaders may retain their jobs. Union leaders will not easily become reconciled to limiting their wage demands to any productivity standard.

Despite the difficulties in the way, some students of the problem endorse the idea of a voluntary approach to the matter of a wage policy. Sir William Beveridge, after pointing out the inflationary danger of sectional or diffused wage bargaining by unions, makes two suggestions. The first is that the central labor organization (the Trade Union Congress in Great Britain) attempt to achieve "a unified wage policy which ensures that the demands of individual un-

[19] For a number of estimates, see J. Frederic Dewhurst and Associates, *America's Needs and Resources,* p. 27. New York: The Twentieth Century Fund, 1947.

[20] *Wage Determination and the Economics of Liberalism,* p. 65. Washington: Chamber of Commerce of the United States, 1947. Further discussion of this general point will be found in J. M. Clark, *Guideposts in Time of Change,* pp. 175-177. New York: Harper & Bros., 1949. See also Clark's remarks in *The Impact of the Union,* ed. by David McCord Wright, pp. 13-19, 28-29. New York: Harcourt, Brace & Co., 1951.

ions will be judged with reference to the economic situation as a whole." [21] Sir William, it should be added, also advocates the adoption of a price policy aimed directly toward stability in the price level. His second suggestion is that voluntary arbitration be used in cases where unions and employers cannot agree on wage terms.

A comprehensive labor group or federation, if it could impose its wishes on its constituent units, could undoubtedly do much to check wage-pressure inflation.[22] But such a group is not likely to be able to impose its will, certainly in the United States. In this country the doctrine of voluntarism, with its great emphasis on home rule, is strongly entrenched in the AFL and also in the CIO (except on matters of ideology). This obstacle, and the others we noted at the beginning of the present section, will not be easily overcome. But until they are, hopes for a unified, inflation-proof wage policy sponsored by the unions must go unrealized.

There are certain developments, however, that might well hasten the achievement of such a wage policy. If the union movement continues to grow, it will bring within its ranks not only more workers but more consumers. As a result, the consumer interest in society (which is especially concerned with inflation) will be more strongly represented in the labor organizations, and might have a moderating effect on union wage policies. Relatively more emphasis would be given to the workers as consumers, and relatively less emphasis would be placed on them as producers.

Increased knowledge on the part of union members and union leaders concerning the actual functioning of our free enterprise market economy would contribute to the end sought. Such knowledge would involve, among other things, a wider realization of the fact that higher wages—higher *real* wages—must for the most part be sought in greater production.[23] It should be added (by way of bal-

[21] *Full Employment in a Free Society,* pp. 199-200. New York: W. W. Norton & Co., 1945.

[22] Professor J. M. Clark takes up the issue of voluntary union control over wages in *Guideposts in Time of Change,* pp. 182-184. New York: Harper & Bros., 1949; and *The Impact of the Union,* ed. by David McCord Wright, pp. 27-31. New York: Harcourt, Brace & Co., 1951.

[23] It is assumed that the greater production—or, rather, the greater productivity—will result in lower prices. If, at a time of full employment, the greater productivity simply results in higher wages (or higher profits), it does not aid greatly in the solution of the inflation problem. Apart from the amount that is taken in taxation or is saved, monetary purchasing power goes up, with the

ance) that management too should increase its knowledge concerning the operation of the free enterprise system, with special emphasis on the prerequisites for balance in the system.

A willingness on the part of employers to reveal more of the facts about operating costs, prices, and profits would contribute to the adoption of a less inflation-producing wage policy on the part of the unions. If an employer is secretive about these matters, the union will be inclined to assume that he can give a wage increase much larger than he is willing to admit, and will accordingly press for such an increase, possibly using all the weapons in its armory to gain its ends. The beneficent influence of a straightforward presentation of the facts by management cannot be denied.

There is some hope that union wage policy, in so far as it relates to the inflation problem, will improve in the years ahead; but a unified wage policy still seems to be a long way off and the threat of serious inflation during periods of high employment a real danger.

The policy of voluntary arbitration in cases of inability of employers and unions to agree on wage terms is indeed a commendable one, and is already used to some extent in this country. To be of real use against inflation, however, the policy would have to be used by all the chief segments of the economy, and the arbitrators would have to give consideration to the effect of given wage changes not only on the employer and the workers in question but on the economy at large. In this case the effect of the wage changes on the general price level would be of paramount importance.

A policy of this character might in time be adopted on a sufficiently large scale to act as a preventive of *extreme* inflation. But as long as it remained on a voluntary basis many union groups and many employers would not adopt it.

The Government and a National Wage Policy. It would seem that a compulsory national wage policy is the only one that would yield immediate results. Such a policy is not an appealing prospect. If wage levels are to be under government control, will it not be necessary to subject profits and prices to government control? And if all these controls are introduced, a long step will have been taken

---

resultant pressure on prices. For a discussion of this point see J. K. Galbraith, *American Capitalism,* pp. 204-205. Boston: Houghton Mifflin Co., 1952.

in the direction of an authoritarian, planned economy. The market or price-guided economy will have been seriously undermined.[24]

A different type of approach to the general problem we have been discussing has been suggested by G. Rehn, a labor economist employed by the Swedish TUC.[25] Mr. Rehn's plan has two basic characteristics: a limitation on profits and a mopping up of monetary purchasing power. He feels that profits in general should be "so small that any exaggerated wage competition between firms is checked." Where low profits discourage private initiative from providing adequate jobs for the available workers, the state should step in with measures to prevent any unemployment that may occur. These measures include the establishment of a well organized labor market and control over the location of industry. The second characteristic of Mr. Rehn's proposal is perhaps the more radical one, since it involves the imposition of high *indirect* taxes as a means of cutting down purchasing power. Under this arrangement there would be a great deal of "collective" saving. Mr. Rehn's plan is an interesting one; it involves an attack on the two main inflation "fronts." But however feasible it might be for Sweden, it is out of the question for the United States—we are too far from the "middle way."

It is obvious that we are confronted with a very serious problem. Can large-scale unionism, full employment, and a free enterprise economy coexist? Some students of the matter, including Lindblom, think they cannot. The issue is debatable. But it seems clear that if we are to have full employment as a more or less permanent situation some changes will have to be made in our wage policies. This does not rule out, of course, changes in our monetary and fiscal policies, directed toward inflation control.[26]

[24] An extensive discussion of various policies for coping with the inflationary danger, ending on a note of optimism (and involving a considerable amount of government control), will be found in Eugene Forsey's contribution to *Insights into Labor Issues*, ed. by Richard A. Lester and Joseph Shister. New York: The Macmillan Co., 1948.

[25] A good discussion of Rehn's proposal will be found in *Wages Policy Under Full Employment*, ed. by Ralph Turvey, especially Chapters 3, 4, and 6. London: William Hodge & Co., 1952. This little book by a group of Swedish writers deals in a stimulating fashion with the problem suggested by its title.

[26] Some economists have considerable faith in monetary and fiscal policies as means of preventing a continuing wage-price spiral. See, for example, Professor Haberler's remarks in *The Impact of the Union*, ed. by David McCord Wright, pp. 39, 42, 58. New York: Harcourt, Brace & Co., 1951.

24

LEGISLATIVE WAGE CONTROL

In most countries the labor market is not "free." The selling of labor is not under the complete control of the individual worker, nor is the buying of labor under the complete control of the individual employer—one of many in the labor market. Three developments have substantially destroyed the free labor market and brought into being a more or less controlled market: these are the growth of large employer units, the extension of collective bargaining, and the enactment of wage (and hour) laws. We shall examine all of these developments, concentrating first on wage laws.

Government regulation of wages is not new.[1] In 1351 the English Parliament passed the Statute of Laborers, a measure that involved wage control in a number of crafts and industries. It is interesting to note, however, that this law, unlike later wage legislation, imposed maximum rather than minimum rates. As the Industrial Revolution got under way a new demand for wage regulation arose, but this time it came from the workers and others (including some employers) who sought the establishment of minimum rates.

Although various labor laws were passed in Britain during the 19th century, it was not until the Trade Boards Act of 1909 that the principle of the minimum wage was embodied in legislation. The view that David Ricardo had expressed—"wages should be left to the fair and free competition of the market, and should never be controlled by the interference of the legislature"—had long remained the accepted, or at least the controlling, doctrine.

Previous to 1909, however, wage legislation had been passed in

[1] An historical account of wage regulation, with special reference to Great Britain, will be found in Dorothy Sell, *British Wage Boards,* Chapter 1. Washington: The Brookings Institution, 1939.

Australia; the initial law was the Factory and Shop Act of Victoria, adopted in 1896, though the New Zealand Industrial Conciliation and Arbitration Act of 1894 was in a sense a minimum wage law. Other minimum wage laws were passed in Australia, and when our first minimum wage laws in this country were passed, beginning with the Massachusetts law of 1912, the measures passed by New Zealand and Australia served as useful guides.[2]

Today the United States has a variety of wage laws, and the general principle of minimum wage legislation is widely accepted throughout the world.

State Minimum Wage Laws

As we have just noted, Massachusetts in 1912 enacted the first state minimum wage law in the United States. In the following year eight other states followed suit. Then progress in the field slowed down greatly. However, by 1923 fifteen states and the District of Columbia had passed minimum wage legislation—though not all the laws were operative.[3]

Many attempts were made to have state minimum wage laws thrown out on the grounds of unconstitutionality. In 1917 the Supreme Court of the United States upheld the Oregon law (Stettler *v.* O'Hara) in a very close decision. In 1923, however, the court, with some change in its personnel, held the District of Columbia law to be unconstitutional (Adkins *v.* Children's Hospital). This was a serious blow to the cause of minimum wage legislation; six other laws were held to be unconstitutional on the basis of the District of Columbia verdict. The fact that the Massachusetts law was upheld was not of great comfort, since that law was nonmandatory in character, depending for its application on the force of public opinion.

From 1923 until 1937 minimum wage legislation in the United States was of little significance. Then the tide turned. In 1937 the Supreme Court upheld the state of Washington minimum wage law for women (West Coast Hotel Company *v.* Parrish), overruling the District of Columbia decision of 1923. The court took the position

[2] An extensive study of the early minimum wage laws in this country, including some historical background, will be found in Bulletin No. 61 of the Women's Bureau, United States Department of Labor, *The Development of Minimum Wage Laws in the United States, 1912 to 1927.*

[3] Don D. Lescohier and Elizabeth Brandeis, *History of Labor in the United States,* 1896-1932, Vol. III, p. 504. New York: The Macmillan Co., 1935.

that such legislation did not contravene the due process clause of the federal constitution. Following this decision the federal government passed the Fair Labor Standards Act in 1938, the most important piece of wage legislation in the country, and the states began to show renewed interest in the minimum wage principle. By 1941 more than 25 states and territories had minimum wage laws on their statute books.

State minimum wage laws have been for the special benefit of women workers and minors. There has been a slight trend in the direction of broadening their coverage, however, to include adult male workers. By 1952 five states—Connecticut, Massachusetts, New Hampshire, New York, and Rhode Island—had laws applicable (or partially applicable) to adult males.

Most of the state minimum wage laws provide for what is known as wage board procedure. The laws do not specify a minimum wage. Rather they provide for an establishment of agencies—wage boards—which, after study, prescribe an appropriate minimum wage for each occupation or industry concerned. It is common, in setting wage rates, to make a distinction between experienced and inexperienced workers, and sometimes between adult workers and minors.[4] In Arkansas, Nevada, South Dakota, Massachusetts, and New Hampshire the minimum wage rates are specified in the law; in the last two states, however, the wage board procedure is also used. It is common practice for state minimum wage orders to provide for the payment of overtime rates.

The Fair Labor Standards Act

The Fair Labor Standards Act or, as it is commonly called, the Wage and Hour Law, was passed in 1938 and substantially revised in 1949. In addition to placing a floor under wages and a ceiling over hours, the law contains provisions relating to the employment of child labor.[5]

The standard work week during the first year of the law's operation (beginning on October 25, 1938) was set at 44 hours. The next

[4] A convenient summary of some of the chief provisions in the various state minimum wage laws will be found in *State Minimum Wage Laws and Orders*, Bulletin No. 227, Women's Bureau, United States Department of Labor.

[5] A detailed description of the Fair Labor Standards Act, as well as the actual text of the law, will be found in the Prentice-Hall *Labor Course*, published annually.

year it dropped to 42 hours; and at the beginning of the third year it fell to 40 hours. This is the standard that exists at the present time. Work in excess of 40 hours constitutes overtime, and for such work at least time-and-a-half must be paid. To this rule there are some exceptions, however, as we shall see in Chapter 27. At the time the act was passed there was a considerable amount of unemployment, and it was hoped that the time-and-a-half rule would help to create jobs, through the process of spreading work.

During the first year of the act's operation the minimum wage was 25 cents an hour. Then the standard became 30 cents for the next five years. On October 25, 1945, the general standard was to become 40 cents. The law provided a means whereby, in appropriate cases, the minimum standard could be raised more rapidly toward, or to, the 40-cent standard. Specifically it arranged for the establishment of "industry committees" of an *ad hoc,* tripartite character. These committees, after hearings and study, could recommend wages higher than the prevailing minimum, but not higher than 40 cents. If, after further hearings, the administrator of the law so desired, he could order the payment of the higher minimum. From 1939 to 1943 a total of 71 industry committees had convened; the hourly wage rates they recommended ranged from 32½ cents to 40 cents.[6] By July, 1944 (more than a year before the outside date specified in the law) the 40-cent minimum had been established throughout all the industries covered.

With the rapid increase in wages that resulted from the defense and war program in the early 1940's, the 40-cent minimum became largely meaningless. Most workers, at least those engaged in interstate commerce, were then receiving wages considerably above 40 cents an hour. A higher minimum therefore seemed desirable. After considerable discussion the law was finally altered in 1949 to provide, among other things, a new minimum of 75 cents an hour.

This increase from 40 cents to 75 cents did not affect as many workers as one might expect. Secretary of Labor Tobin estimated that of the 22 million workers covered by the law, 1½ million obtained wage increases.[7] This figure relates only to direct wage in-

[6] A description of the work of these committees will be found in the *First Annual Report* of the Administrator of the Wage and Hour Division of the United States Department of Labor, pp. 72-90.

[7] *Labor Information Bulletin,* January, 1950, p. 1.

creases; how many wage earners who were already receiving at least 75 cents an hour benefited as a result of the upping of the minimum it is impossible to say.

Under the amended law, as under the original measure, wages less than the minimum may be paid to certain workers—learners, apprentices, and handicapped persons—if a certificate of permission is duly obtained. These certificates are issued, however, "only to the extent necessary to prevent curtailment of employment opportunities."

The Walsh-Healey Act and the Davis-Bacon Act

The Walsh-Healey Act (Public Contracts Act) was passed in 1936 and has been amended a number of times. The act establishes certain basic labor standards that must be observed by employers who have contracts from the federal government relating to materials, equipment, and such and amounting to more than $10,000. Subcontractors (i.e., contractors who merely, and normally, supply parts to the industry involved) are not covered by the law; but "substitute" contractors are covered. Some contracts—advertising, for example—are not covered by the law.[8]

The theory underlying the law is that "the Government should not permit firms bidding for a Government contract to undercut one another's bids through either wage reductions, child labor, prison labor, or bad safety-and-health conditions." [9]

In addition to its provisions concerning child labor, prison labor, and safety and health conditions, the law sets forth certain minimum wage and maximum hour standards. In contrast to the Fair Labor Standards Act, the law does not specify a definite minimum wage. Instead, after hearings have been held, the Secretary of Labor authorizes the issuance of special minimum wage orders. The wage established may vary from state to state in the same industry, and from industry to industry in the same state, since minimum wages are determined by both state and industry standards. In most of the minimum "wage determinations" in given industries, however, the figure is uniform for all states.

[8] See Prentice-Hall *Labor Service* for details on this and other points connected with the law.

[9] *Annual Report,* 1949, Wage and Hour and Public Contracts Division, United States Department of Labor, p. 17.

Overtime under the Walsh-Healey Act must not be less than time-and-a-half, and is, in contrast to the Fair Labor Standards Act, calculated on a double standard: overtime must be paid for work in excess of 40 hours a week *or* 8 hours a day, whichever results in the larger amount of earnings for the worker.

Between 1937 and 1951 more than 625,000 contracts (totaling over $138 billion) awarded by the federal government were subject to the provisions of the Walsh-Healey Act.

The Davis-Bacon Act, or Prevailing Wage Law as it is sometimes called, was passed in 1931, and it too has been amended a number of times. This law provides that "prevailing wage rates" in the locality be paid for construction work done for the federal government. The law is applicable only if the contract, or subcontract, amounts to more than $2,000. The Davis-Bacon Act covers not only construction work undertaken directly for the federal government, such as the building of post offices, but also work done for other agencies that receive federal financial assistance. For example, airports built by local governments, under a grants-in-aid program, are covered by the law. It should be pointed out that the "prevailing wages" paid under the Davis-Bacon Act are not minimum wages in the ordinary sense. In this respect the act differs from the Fair Labor Standards Act and the Walsh-Healey Act.

Issues in Minimum Wage Laws

In formulating minimum wage laws governments must give attention to a number of important problems. One problem is to determine on what particular basis, or bases, the minimum wage is to be established. At least three bases could be used.[10] First there is the cost-of-living basis—the minimum wage may be a "living wage." In determining what this wage is, budget studies are frequently made. In a considerable number of the state minimum wage laws of this country a cost-of-living standard is used.

A second basis is that of "fairness," a criterion that is associated with the value of the work performed. In some state laws provision is made for establishing wages "fairly and reasonably commensurate with the value of the services rendered" in cases where actual wages

[10] Lengthy discussions of possible criteria will be found in E. M. Burns, *Wages and the State*. London: P. S. King & Son, Ltd., 1926; and J. H. Richardson, *A Study on the Minimum Wage*. New York: Adelphi Co., 1927.

are considered to be less than fair and less than enough to maintain a healthful standard of living. Sometimes "fairness" may be determined by comparison with wages paid for like work and for like skill. Under the Walsh-Healey Act the notion of fairness in this sense is clearly reflected.

Finally, ability to pay may be used as a basis for the minimum wage. At least one state uses this as a standard (not the sole standard, however); and the principle was given definite though partial recognition in the original Fair Labor Standards Act. Under that Act, with its industry committee procedure, wages higher than the statutory minimum, but not higher than 40 cents an hour, could be established if conditions in the industry (not in the separate plants in the industry) warranted it.

Because minimum wage laws often provide for the use of more than one of these bases, difficulties can easily arise; the cost-of-living criterion, for example, may not be quite consistent with the ability-to-pay principle. Moreover, problems can arise when only one basis is used. If the cost-of-living principle is used, how high should the standard of living, on which the minimum wage is to be based, be set? How large should the worker unit be? How frequently should adjustments be made to changes in the cost of living?

A second problem associated with minimum wage laws is that of exemptions. Certain workers are not "worth" the minimum wage the employer is compelled to pay. Their defects may be mental or physical deficiencies, lack of training, or inefficiency caused by old age. Unless the employer is permitted to pay these workers a wage less than the minimum he may not retain them in his service, or he may not hire them in the first place.

In view of this situation minimum wage laws commonly have exception provisions. Employers may be given permission to pay learners or apprentices a wage less than the minimum for a given period of time, or to employ handicapped workers at a subminimum wage. In all cases, however, the employer must receive proper authorization before he has the right to pay less than the minimum rate.

The recognition of exceptions is clearly desirable, but it is possible for the privilege to be abused. The limitation of the period during which substandard wages may be paid to learners is an attempt to prevent a possible abuse. An employer may be tempted, however, to discharge workers who are about to be entitled to the minimum and hire a new crop of employees. Another type of safeguard is to limit the relative number of persons who may be hired at wages less than the minimum.

A third problem relating to minimum wages has to do with the machinery to be used in establishing the rates. There are two chief means. First, the minimum may be specified in the law. This policy is followed under the Fair Labor Standards Act and also under a small number of the state minimum wage laws. Secondly, the minimum, or rather the minimums, may be established by special agencies set up for the purpose. These agencies, ordinarily called wage boards, are composed of representatives of employers, employees, and the public. These boards, probably after a preliminary investigation by the "commissioner of labor" or some other permanent governmental agency, make a study of the industry or occupation for which a minimum wage is being considered. Using one or more of the bases dealt with above they recommend a certain wage. This technique is widely used under the state minimum wage laws, and also under the Walsh-Healey Act. It is also used extensively in other countries. Sometimes the two techniques may be combined. Minimum wages may also be fixed by the permanent labor commissions of the government or by arbitration courts.

Economic and Social Aspects of Minimum Wages

The question of establishing minimum wages by law has long been debated. Various arguments on both sides of the issue have been advanced.

The Case for Minimum Wage Laws. (1) Supporters of such legislation have argued that the establishment of minimum wage levels protects the "fair" employer against competition from "unfair" ones. The latter cannot use unduly low wages as a means of undercutting the former; hence competition is placed on a superior level. Other means besides wage cutting will have to be used to gain competitive advantages.

This argument definitely has merit, although it must be recognized that high-wage employers are not necessarily at a disadvantage compared to low-wage employers. Employers who pay high wages may be able to attract a better quality of labor; and, what is more, the higher wages they pay may simply reflect the better methods and techniques they are using in their plants.

(2) A second argument in favor of minimum wages, and one that is a little inconsistent with the argument just noted, is that such wages act as an incentive to the low-wage employers to improve methods in their plants. Confronted with the necessity of paying higher wages, possibly wages higher than the marginal productivity of the workers, low-wage employers will introduce technological improvements and change their plant organization in an attempt to make the workers worth the new wages they are receiving.

Putting this argument in a more theoretical form we can say, with Professor Pigou,[11] that the actual demand schedule for labor is not the same as the schedule usually drawn in elementary diagrams—that is, something independent of labor's supply price—but "is liable itself to be raised when the price is raised." And this possibility, Professor Pigou asserts with reference to English experience, is not confined to "sweated industries such as the Trade Boards originally covered." If the demand curve for labor, which is also the productivity curve for labor, is raised, higher wages can be paid without bankrupting the firm or forcing it to curtail the size of its work force. It is possible, however, that some change may occur in the personnel of the work force because of the necessity of using new types of labor.

The argument that we have just been describing should not be overemphasized. The fact must be recognized that employers, with their interest in making large profits, have a strong inducement to introduce improvements without the stimulus of a higher minimum wage, especially if they are engaged in highly competitive industries. The "shock theory" should therefore not be pushed too far.[12]

(3) Another argument is that minimum wage laws give the workers a better standard of living—a health and decency standard. They are less likely to be sick and less prone to accidents. Their morale

[11] A. C. Pigou, *Wage Statistics and Wage Policies*, pp. 27-28. London: Oxford University Press, 1949. Additional support for Pigou's contention will be found in Dorothy Sells, *British Trade Boards*, pp. 325-330. Washington: The Brookings Institution, 1939. In accounting for the absorption and enforcement of the English minimum wage regulations, Miss Sells emphasizes the manner in which the regulations were adopted and the cooperative attitude of most employers in applying the regulations.

[12] A hostile criticism of the "shock theory," by George J. Stigler, will be found in *The American Economic Review*, June 1946, pp. 359-360.

is improved. All of these factors make them more efficient workers and worth the higher wages now being paid to them. This is a version of the old doctrine of the "economy of high wages," noted in an earlier chapter. There is truth in this argument, but the degree of truth depends on the wage levels before and after the laws are passed.

(4) A further argument, one that is applicable to a national minimum wage, relates to economic stability. It is contended that the establishment of minimum wage levels helps to provide the purchasing power necessary to take all the goods off the market. Assuming a competitive economy and the full utilization of resources, it is very easy to show the unsoundness of the argument. Under conditions as they actually exist, however, it is possible that the establishment of a national minimum wage, or the raising of the level of the prevailing minimum, may contribute to economic stability. A better balance between consumption expenditures and savings (and investment) may be reached. But too much confidence should not be placed in the argument. A minimum wage need not necessarily lead to more purchasing power and a more stable economy.

(5) It may be contended that minimum wage laws reduce dissatisfaction in industry and thus reduce the amount of labor friction and strife. This, in turn, promotes industrial output. The English experience, for example, seems to bear out this claim.

(6) It may be argued, further, and with some reason, that minimum wage laws that involve wage board procedure represent a contribution to industrial democracy. Workers and their representatives have an opportunity to play some part in influencing the wage level. Wages are to a degree directly made by the workers themselves and not simply for them.[13] This argument for minimum wages is not particularly strong. Because of the effect of the supply of labor on wages, it can be said that wages are always made in part *by* the workers. Moreover, as applied to the present time, the argument loses much of its significance because of the widespread existence of unions.

(7) A final argument in favor of minimum wages is that such

[13] It is interesting to note that Dorothy Sells, who emphasizes the contribution of wage board procedure to "industrial self-determination," gives her book *British Wage Boards* the subtitle "A Study in Industrial Democracy."

wages are a boon to the unorganized workers. In unionized occupations and industries most of the workers receive a wage that guarantees them a tolerably satisfactory standard of living. The unions see to that. But the same cannot be said of nonunion groups. They have no institution to advance their cause except the "market," and it may use them rather shabbily.

Without question, minimum wage laws are of special benefit to unorganized workers. It may well be that some of the gains achieved by these workers are at the expense of organized workers, especially if the size of the national "pie" is not increased as a result of the establishment of minimum wages and if prices go up as a consequence. On the other hand, however, unionized establishments and their workers may be exposed to less severe competition from nonunionized plants if there is a minimum wage law.

The attitude of organized labor toward minimum wage laws is one of approval. Both the AFL and the CIO have been strong supporters of the Fair Labor Standards Act and have advocated the raising of the minimum wage level under the law.

The Case against Minimum Wage Laws. The case for minimum wages, established by law, is indeed a formidable one; but there are arguments on the other side too. Possibly few economists would go so far as Professor Willford I. King, who holds that minimum wage laws of any kind are antisocial,[14] but a considerable number would probably give only slight support to them.

(1) One of the outstanding arguments against minimum wages is that they lead to unemployment. Professor King has declared that "it is clear that the immediate effect of the enactment and enforcement of any minimum wage law is to throw out of employment all persons whose qualifications are not such as to enable them to earn more than the legal minimum." This is a sweeping statement, but it possesses an element of truth. If wages are arbitrarily forced up to a point higher than what the workers are economically worth, some of the workers, particularly the poorer ones, may be let out. Such a result is not, of course, inevitable.

For one thing employers may take other steps to cope with the

[14] *Amendments to the Fair Labor Standards Act of 1938,* Hearings before the Committee on Education and Labor, House of Representatives, 81st Cong., 1st Sess., on H. Res. 2033, Vol. I, p. 758. Professor King presents, in orthodox fashion, the case against minimum wage laws.

situation. As we have already noted, they may improve their methods of production, thus increasing the productivity of the workers. The workers themselves may become more efficient. The employer, moreover, may be willing to take a cut in profits, at least for the time being. And what is more, minimum wage laws usually have certain safeguards against possible labor displacement. As we observed earlier, exemptions may be made for learners, for handicapped persons, and for older workers.

In this same general connection it is interesting to note that under the original Fair Labor Standards Act the industry committees were charged with the task of recommending to the administrator of the law "the highest minimum wage rates for the industry which it determines, having due regard to economic and competitive conditions," to the end that such wage rates "will not substantially curtail employment in the industry."

The extent to which minimum wage laws lead to unemployment depends in part on the size of the wage jumps provided by the laws. It also depends on the nature of the laws. A minimum wage measure that sets a flat rate for all industries is likely to cause relatively more unemployment than a law that provides for wage boards and separate minimums for different industries and occupations.

It might be argued that unemployment for a small number of persons is a lesser evil than low wages for a large number. This argument gains weight if there is an unemployment insurance scheme, if there is a vocational retraining program in operation, and if there is a good system of labor placement bureaus. Under these conditions the lot of the unemployed worker is definitely eased and the chance of his re-employment increased.

(2) It may well be true that in some instances minimum wage laws, as Professor King avers, not only throw people out of work but "pauperize them, destroy their self respect, and make them miserable." But it seems clear that in more instances such laws increase the income of the workers, improve their morale, and add to their happiness.

(3) Professor King, in urging the repeal "of all federal wage-fixing laws now on the statute books and the enactment of no new ones to take their places," declares that "minimum wage laws help to bring on depressions and thus impoverish the nation." Professor King strongly emphasizes the desirability of wage flexibility, going

so far as to say that the Great Depression of the 1930's would not have taken place if, in 1929, wage rates had fallen commensurately with the decline in "spending power"—with the drop in demand. (Professor King is obviously not a Keynesian!)

The extent to which minimum wage laws contribute to the occurrence of depressions seems to be extremely limited. If wage inflexibility aids in bringing on, and perpetuating, depressions, the inflexibility produced by union action—at levels considerably higher than the minimum wage floors—is of much greater significance than the inflexibility resulting from minimum wage laws. The disinclination of many employers to cut wages when demand falls off should also be mentioned. Moreover, one might well argue that wage inflexibility rather than helping to produce depressions helps to avoid them (this point was discussed in Chapter 6). At any rate the elimination of minimum wage laws as a means for helping us to overcome depressions cannot be seriously considered.

(4) Another argument against minimum wage laws is that such laws "take away from the individual that liberty which our Nation was founded to protect." Professor King believes that "any law limiting a man's rights to dispose of his labor on such terms as he sees fit constitutes a serious infringement on his liberty." Minimum wage laws do indeed represent some infringement on a worker's liberty, especially when the impossibility of working for a low wage may result in his becoming unemployed. But, although individual persons may be victimized by such laws, the total situation must be taken into account. If some persons suffer as a result of minimum wage laws—and it will be recalled that the laws ordinarily contain provisions that attempt to reduce the number of such persons—many others benefit from them. On balance the gains seem definitely to outweigh the losses.

(5) The old argument that the minimum wage will tend to become the maximum seems to be without any substantial basis. If there is any sizable amount of competition in the labor market, the wages of many of the workers should be well above the minimum. When a minimum wage is established, the higher-paid workers as well as the lower-paid ones tend to receive a wage increase, though the increase for the former is relatively less than that received by the latter.

There is a final consideration to be noted in connection with the minimum-wage question. If the money (and real) wages of any group of workers are arbitrarily increased and if there is no increase in the physical productivity of these workers, then the higher wages of the group in question are at the expense of other persons in society. The profit receivers or the consumers will foot the bill. A shift in real purchasing power from higher-paid persons to lower-paid ones may be sound both ethically and economically, but there is a limit to the extent to which such a shift can be socially advantageous. In fact, if it is carried too far it can be positively harmful. Care must be exercised, therefore, in establishing minimum wage levels. They should not be too high.

But there is good reason for believing that minimum wage laws usually bring about more than a mere redistribution of the total income of the state or nation. They probably aid, indirectly, in increasing the size of the income.

The case for the minimum wage is much stronger than the case against it. The important issue involved in minimum wage legislation is really not the principle of such a wage, but the level at which the wage should be established.

Family Allowances

A family-allowance scheme is an arrangement under which the wage earner, in addition to receiving his regular pay, which tends to approximate the value of his services, receives a further amount based on the size of his family. The setting up of a family-allowance plan thus represents a combination of the productivity and the need principles of income distribution.

The case for family allowance rests on two main facts. In the first place, and despite a common statement to the contrary, two persons cannot live more cheaply than one—nor can three live more cheaply than two, nor four than three. The economic needs of a family do not vary in inverse proportion to its numbers. In the second place, over a very wide range of employments no consideration is given to family size in the determination of wages. This is true when wages are determined either individually or collectively. There are exceptions, to be sure, but for the most part the size of a worker's family is not a factor in the determination of his wage.

Family allowances help the low-income worker who has dependent children to meet the situation that arises from these two basic facts. Such allowances, however, may be supported on more specific grounds. They contribute to the health of the worker and his family, thus improving the physical quality of the populace. It has been said that "the desire to improve the physical circumstances in which children are raised, as well as to strengthen the family environment in which they live, has undoubtedly accounted for much of the spread of schemes of family allowances during the past two decades." [15] By providing a better family environment, family allowances may contribute to a decrease in juvenile delinquency—as has happened in Canada [16]—and to other desirable ends.

Family allowances improve (or can be geared to improve) the educational standards of the members of the lower-income groups. Family allowances, furthermore, introduce an element of stability in the economy; this objective figures in the Canadian scheme, for example. And, especially if designed in a certain way, family allowances can be used to promote population growth. This seems to be an objective in the plans of such countries as France, Spain, and Russia.

It may be argued, on the other hand, that family allowances promote laziness; possibly lead to excessive population growth, especially on the part of the lower-income groups; and, particularly in the United States, are really not necessary.

Despite any objections that may be raised, however, the principle of family allowances has met with widespread support throughout the world. In 1947 more than 25 countries, including most European nations, had family-allowance schemes; and the number has increased since then.[17]

The idea of passing family-allowance legislation has never met with extensive support in the United States, which is one of the few nations without such a law on its statute books. Some recognition is given to the principle, however, and in a number of ways. Payment in the armed services is based in part on number of children; in some cities the salaries of school teachers depend on the size of their families; under our Old-Age and Survivors' Insurance law pension payments are supplemented by payments for depend-

[15] *International Labor Review,* April, 1948, p. 322.

[16] *Labor,* April 26, 1952, p. 2.

[17] An informative and useful article dealing with family-allowance schemes (as of 1947) throughout the world will be found in *International Labor Review,* April and May, 1948.

ent children, and in addition we have a special "assistance" program for dependent children who do not have support from their parents; in our income tax laws credits are allowed for children; and, finally, in private employments the principle is sometimes recognized.

To see how a family-allowance plan may be arranged we will note, in general terms, a few of the features of the Canadian law, pointing out some of the contrasts between its features and the features of other laws. Canada passed a Family Allowance Act in 1944, which became operative on July 1, 1945. Under the Canadian measure, sometimes referred to as the "Baby Bonus," payments are tied up closely with the number of children in a family and the age of the children. As in the majority of other countries, payments begin with the first child.

The Canadian law states that the benefits must be directed "exclusively toward the maintenance, care, training, education, and advancement of the child." Since the allowances are not paid if the child is not in school (or receiving an equivalent education) it is not surprising that one of the early results of the law was a considerable increase in school attendance,[18] a possible gain from family allowances that we noted earlier. Another result of the measure was a marked increase in milk consumption, which unquestionably contributes to better health. In Britain the payments are not for the exclusive benefit of the children but for the benefit of the family as a whole.

Under the Canadian law the moneys used for family allowances come from the general revenues of the country. A number of other countries also use this plan for financing the allowances. But three other arrangements are in use: special income taxes for the purpose, as in Australia and New Zealand; employer contributions, as in France and Rumania; and joint contributions from employer and worker, as in Spain and Chile. Most plans are financed wholly by the state or by the employer. The Canadian family-allowance scheme is administered exclusively by the state, as are about half the other national family-allowance plans.

Equal Pay For Equal Work

If the marginal productivity theory of wages worked out with precision, women doing exactly the same amount of work as men

[18] *Newsweek*, July 8, 1946, p. 45.

would be paid the same wages as men. But in many instances women are discriminated against in the matter of wages. As a result of this discrimination there is a widespread feeling that legislation should be passed preventing employers from paying less to women than to men—for equal work.

The equal-pay principle is not new in this country. It was supported by the old Knights of Labor, and it has figured in AFL discussions for more than half a century. It was supported by War Labor Boards in World War I and World War II,[19] and in more recent years by the Wage Stabilization Board. The principle has been embodied in numerous collective bargaining agreements, and has been adopted by various public agencies and by some private employers. In addition it had found expression by 1952 in 13 state laws.[20]

Michigan and Montana were the pioneer states in this field, having passed their equal-pay laws in 1919, more than twenty years before any other state acted. Up to the present time no federal law relating to nongovernmental employees has been passed on the matter, though a number of attempts have been made. It might be pointed out that in a considerable number of other countries the principle of equal pay has been given legislative or constitutional recognition. These include Mexico, Brazil, France, Russia, and Yugoslavia. Moreover, the International Labor Organization has adopted a "Convention" (operative in 1953) on the principle.

Various arguments have been used in support of the equal-pay idea. It has been defended in terms of justice—justice to women workers. If women do as much work as men, it would seem only fair that they should get as much pay. Any argument to the contrary based on relative needs does not have much relevance, especially when it is borne in mind that some women workers have greater family responsibilities than many men workers. Moreover, any argument to the effect that women are poorer "pleasure machines" than

[19] For a brief historical account see Dorothy S. Brady's article "Equal Pay for Women Workers," in *The Annals of the American Academy of Political and Social Science*, May, 1947, pp. 53-60.

[20] The key features of the laws for the various states (as of 1950) will be found in *Hearings* on Equal Pay for Equal Work for Women (H.R. 1584 and H. Res. 2438) before a Special Subcommittee of the Committee on Education and Labor, House of Representatives, 81st Cong., 2nd Sess., 1950, pp. 98-103.

men [21]—a notion expressed by the English economist, Edgeworth—is also of little relevance to the issue, since the argument itself seems invalid.

The justice argument is therefore a very powerful one. In terms of work and wages it is as unjust (if we may borrow a principle from Aristotle) to pay unequal wages for equal work as it is to pay equal wages for unequal work.

Another point raised in favor of the equal-pay idea is that it helps to prevent the undercutting of men's pay. There can be little doubt that if employers can hire women workers more cheaply than men, they will often try to force down men's wages.

A still further argument relates to purchasing power. Adoption of the equal-pay principle will increase the purchasing power of the consumers, with the various benefits that follow from such a gain. This argument may have some merit but its significance can easily be exaggerated. Attempts to increase the "purchasing power" of specific groups, when there is no commensurate increase in their physical productivity, may lead to certain undesirable results for some workers, and may even harm the intended beneficiaries. Unemployment may result and prices may go up. However, there is some reason for believing that raising the pay of women workers up to the level of men workers would not have such dire results.

It has also been argued that equal pay for equal work promotes labor mobility and increases the efficiency with which labor is used. This contention may be true, certainly when male workers build up a distinction between "men's" jobs and "women's" jobs when such a distinction is not really present, and thus try to maintain their wages at a level higher than is justified. In such instances adherence to the equal-pay principle unquestionably facilitates "the distribution of the labor supply according to the capacities and abilities of the workers" and promotes "labor mobility in the interests of production." [22]

A final argument is that the equal-pay principle, if embodied in legislation, will protect the fair employers (who use the principle) against the competition of unfair employers. This argument is sound.

[21] Wesley C. Mitchell, *Lecture Notes on Types of Economic Theory,* Vol. I, pp. 110-111. New York: August M. Kelly, 1949.

[22] International Labor Office, *Equal Remuneration For Men and Women Workers For Work of Equal Value,* International Labor Conference, 33rd Sess., 1950, Report V (1), pp. 2, 7.

In view of the strong case that can be made out for the principle of equal pay for equal work, one may wonder why it has not met with wider legislative support in this country; why, for example, the federal government has not passed an equal-pay law. There has been extensive support for such a law, but also strong opposition to it. Both the National Association of Manufacturers and the United States Chamber of Commerce oppose such federal legislation. These bodies are not against the principle of equal pay—they favor it—but are opposed to the federal government passing a law to enforce it. The NAM has maintained that certain developments make a federal equal-pay law "of dubious value." These developments include the "general acceptance" of the principle by employers; collective bargaining agreements; and the "tremendous increase in the establishment of job-evaluation systems under which pay differentials based on sex are automatically abolished." The NAM believes that "through channels already established" the limited problem that remains can be handled "without the need for another federal law and all the machinery, the expenditures and the governmental interference that such a law would entail." [23]

The equal-pay principle is indubitably sound, both economically and ethically. Whether or not it should be embodied in legislation is clearly controversial. The present writer would cast his ballot, somewhat hesitatingly, for federal legislation on the matter; but less hesitatingly for additional state legislation. The fact should be recognized, however, that such legislation might increase the pressure for laws establishing family allowances.[24]

A nice point in any law concerning equal pay has to do with the meaning of terms. What does "equal pay for equal work" mean? The expression is subject to three general types of interpretation. First, it may be thought of in terms of "relative job performance of men and women on work of comparable character." Such relative job performance is not easy to measure, nor is it easy to define what is meant by "work of comparable character." Second, the expression may be thought of "with reference to costs of production or over-all value to the employers." This approach involves consideration of special costs

[23] See *Hearings* mentioned in footnote 20, pp. 56, 62.

[24] *The Economist* (June 30, 1951, p. 1550) in writing about the equal-pay principle in England expresses the belief that the adoption of the principle would lead to very strong pressure for *higher* family allowances.

that may be involved in employing women, such as additional supervision and higher absenteeism. Third, the expression may be interpreted in terms of "job content without regard to sex." [25] Jobs are evaluated and classified in terms of their content and rates are determined for them. Workers, whether they be men or women, are then paid on the basis of the job they perform.

Examples of the use of all three interpretations may be found in the history of the equal-pay principle. The International Labor Office has expressed its preference for the third interpretation, and so have a number of private employers in the United States. Considerable variation remains, however, in the matter of definition. Some collective bargaining agreements, for example, use the second definition.[26]

[25] See ILO publication mentioned in footnote 22, pp. 19-51.

[26] A description of the equal-pay principle, including its application in collective bargaining agreements, will be found in the *Monthly Labor Review*, January, 1952, pp. 41-45.

25

WAGES AND OTHER INCENTIVES

The old socialistic slogan, "From each according to his ability, to each according to his needs," is an admirable one; a loftier ideal could hardly be imagined. But the trouble with the slogan is that it does not seem to work. It is difficult enough to measure the needs of the populace, particularly in a society in which living standards are above the subsistence level; but this difficulty is small compared with the one involved in getting people to work according to their ability when they are paid according to their needs. With *homo sapiens* in his present state, the second difficulty seems to be beyond solution. Soviet Russia, however, expects to overcome the difficulty![1]

Quite apart from the practicability of the socialistic slogan, there is the problem of trying to get people to work closer to, if not according to, their ability. Various incentives may be used, and in the present chapter we shall examine some of them.

The question of incentives is a very important one, especially in an industrialized society. The economic and political well-being of a nation and the material living standards of its members are both intimately associated with the effectiveness of its incentives to productive effort. This is true whether the nation is capitalistic, socialistic, or communistic.

As we noted in Chapter 1, there is good reason for nearly all of us to work. Our individual survival is dependent upon our labor. But the question of incentives has to do for the most part with work that

[1] Stalin, in making a distinction between socialism and communism, says that under the latter "each works according to his abilities and receives articles of consumption, not according to the work he performs, but according to his needs as a culturally developed individual." *Leninism,* p. 548. London: George Allen & Unwin Ltd., 1940. It appears that the establishment of real communism in Russia is a long way off.

is beyond this "irreducible minimum," work that we are capable of doing but which, for various reasons, we may not be willing to do.

Incentives, as we are using the term, are aimed at getting workers to produce more. A given worker may increase his output by working longer hours (assuming his present work week is not beyond the "output optimum") or by working harder. As Professor Pigou has said,[2] work "is not a one-dimensional entity"; it is two-dimensional, having both duration and intensity. In the discussion that follows we shall give chief emphasis to the intensity dimension.

Classification of Incentives

Incentives may be classified in at least three different ways. To a considerable extent these classifications overlap, but their coverage is not wholly the same.

Negative and Positive Incentives. Negative incentives are punitive in character. They take the form of punishment that is meted out to persons whose work is unsatisfactory, either quantitatively or qualitatively. The most common negative incentive is discharge.

The possibility of losing one's job is a strong incentive to effort. Its effectiveness, however, varies according to a number of factors. If management is lax in its supervision, workers may work far below their capacity and yet retain their jobs. In many workers the "instinct of workmanship" is not strongly enough established to induce them voluntarily to do a good day's work. Moreover, the physical conditions of work may make for inefficiency. Again, if other jobs are available, the possibility of being discharged may not be greatly feared by the workers. This is one of the serious problems found under full employment, and it points to the need of developing new types of incentives.

Demotion to a lower job category and wage reductions are other types of negative incentives. In Russia still other kinds have been used, certainly for "workers" in the upper categories. Prison terms, possibly in Siberia, may be imposed for gross incompetency. In this country, however, no plant manager or worker is ever sent to jail in northern New Hampshire or northern Minnesota because he has failed in his job.

Positive incentives take the form of rewards for work well done,

[2] *Socialism Versus Capitalism,* p. 94. London: Macmillan & Co., 1937. Chapter VI of this book is entitled "The Problem of Incentive."

or (in our elastic use of the term) of conditions conducive to good work. Positive incentives are much more effective than negative ones. Instead of trying to force a person to work well they are directed toward eliciting from him a good day's work on a voluntary basis.

Pecuniary and Nonpecuniary Incentives. Pecuniary incentives take the form of money rewards. They have long been used and are effective, within limits, in achieving the goal of increased effort.

Nonpecuniary incentives are rewards that are not expressed in terms of dollars and cents. They involve a nonmonetary type of recognition (or condition) and are based on the supposition, which is undeniably correct, that the worker is not a mere economic man interested only in maximizing his income.

Individual and Group Incentives. Under the plan of individual incentives the worker is the recipient of rewards for his individual achievements. These achievements can ordinarily be identified and measured. Sometimes, however, a number of workers cooperate very closely in a given production process and the contribution of each cannot be accurately gauged. In such a case the group as a whole may be rewarded. The reward may be of a pecuniary nature, or, as in the case of plant achievement flags during World War II, it may be nonpecuniary.

In the discussion that follows we shall concentrate on the second classification, the one relating to pecuniary and nonpecuniary incentives.

Pecuniary Incentives

The assumption on which pecuniary incentives are based is that if a person is paid more, or if he has a prospect of receiving more, he will work harder. The inducement to effort is monetary gain. It must be emphasized, however, though the point is rather obvious, that it is usually not monetary gain as such that the worker is interested in but the things he can buy with his money. His "love of money," in other words, is really a love for a wide variety of commodities and services.[3] If these are limited in quantity, monetary incentives may be seriously weakened.

[3] A good discussion of this point will be found in T. E. Cliffe Leslie, *Essays in Moral and Political Philosophy,* Chapter 1. Dublin: Hodges, Figgis & Co., 1888. Sargent Florence uses the term "transpecuniary incentive" when workers think in terms of the things their money wages will buy. See *The Political Quarterly,* October-December, 1947, p. 284.

Monetary rewards for greater effort may be tied directly to the results of the effort (piece-rate payment) or they may be associated with it indirectly (day-rate payment). Under the day-rate method the worker hopes that if he works diligently he will be promoted to a job with a higher rate of pay, or that he will receive a higher rate in his present job. Under the piece-rate method wages are calculated in terms of output units. Under the day-rate (or time-rate) method some unit of time—anything from an hour to a year—is used for figuring out the wage.

The piece-rate method of wage payment has long been in use and at present is rather widely employed. It is interesting to note that Russia uses the method more extensively than any other country in the world; over 75 per cent of Russian workers are paid on the piece basis. This seems rather paradoxical in the light of Marx's statement that "piece-wages are the form of wages most suitable to the capitalist method of production." [4] However, Russia has been quite willing to revise Marx whenever necessary, though in the matter of wages it is her ultimate aim to discard the piece-rate method and, as we have already pointed out, pay everyone on the basis of need. In Great Britain incentive methods of wage payment covered about 28 per cent of the workers in the late 1940's; [5] and in the United States about 30 per cent of the workers in manufacturing industry are on an incentive wage basis.[6]

The effectiveness of incentive wages as a factor in increasing output appears to be significantly related to the social background of the workers. There is some evidence to show that the effectiveness varies directly (though within limits) with educational levels, degree of economic security, extent of adherence to a laissez-faire point of view, and the strength of individualistic ideas.[7]

The incentive method of wage payment ties wages to worker output; the method is based on results, or productivity, and thus exemplifies the use of the productivity principle of income distribution. In this respect it differs from the need principle and the equality

[4] *Capital,* Everyman's ed., Vol. 2, p. 607. London: J. M. Dent & Sons, 1930.

[5] *The Economist,* May 18, 1948, p. 809.

[6] This figure is based on an extensive study made by the United States Bureau of Labor Statistics in 1945 and 1946. The percentage has changed little over the recent past. *Monthly Labor Review,* November, 1947, p. 535.

[7] See Melville Dalton, "Worker Response and Social Background," *The Journal of Political Economy,* August, 1947.

principle. The great merit of the productivity principle is the stimulus it affords to exertion, just as the great weakness of the other two principles is the discouragement they give to exertion. The productivity principle, because of the inequality that arises from its operation, is also conducive to saving—at least in the short run. However, this very inequality seems to be a factor in cyclical instability, which is harmful to production and to the saving process.

We cannot discuss at greater length the pros and cons of these various methods of income distribution, but it seems clear that for a long time to come the productivity principle will be the prevailing one. To an increasing extent, however, it will probably be modified by the need principle. This modification is already apparent, as we noted earlier, in such measures as our minimum wage laws, our social security program, and our income tax policies.

Types of Incentive Wage Plans

Most incentive wage plans in the United States are of a piece-rate character and operate on an individual rather than a group basis. Bonus plans are more likely to be of a group nature, though the individual bonus plans still predominate. The figures in Table 16, were compiled by the Bureau of Labor Statistics after an extensive study of 56 manufacturing and 8 nonmanufacturing industries.

Table 16

Types of Incentive Plans in American Industries, 1945–46 *

Plants with incentive plans	34%
Predominantly piece-rate	29
Individual	28
Group	1
Predominantly bonus	5
Individual	3
Group	2
Plants without incentive plans	66

* *Monthly Labor Review*, November, 1947, p. 536.

Individual Piece-Rate Plans. Individual piece-rate plans are of numerous types. No small amount of ingenuity has been exercised in devising new varieties, and the outside observer can only hope that some of the complexity achieved is merited by the results obtained. We shall examine only the three main types, classified by Sargent Florence as straight, progressive, and degressive.

Straight piecework is the simplest type. Under this arrangement earnings are geared directly and proportionately to output. If the output of a worker increases from 100 units per hour to 110 units, an advance of 10 per cent, his earnings for the hour will go up 10 per cent. This type is easy to understand and relatively easy to administer. It should be pointed out that a "floor" may be established so that earnings will not fall below a given level.

A somewhat more complicated type is the so-called differential (or progressive) piece-rate plan, often linked with the name of F. W. Taylor, the "Father of Scientific Management." Under this plan a given piece rate applies to an output of a certain magnitude (within a definite time period), and a higher rate applies to all output above the figure specified. Thus, a worker may be paid $1 a hundred for all units of output up to 500 (per day) and $1.25 for all output in excess of 500. This plan, which offers a strong inducement to the worker to reach the "plateau," is widely used in Russia, [8] where the drive to increase production is particularly strong.

The degressive principle is found in the Halsey plan of wage payment.[9] This plan involves the use of an hourly (or weekly) wage rate and also a premium piece rate, the latter becoming applicable if output surpasses the standard established. The piece-rate premium is geared to the amount of time saved. Suppose, for example, that a worker receives $1 an hour for a 40-hour week, that the standard output for the week is 60 units, and that the piece-rate premium is 50 per cent of the day rate for the time saved. If the worker produces not 60 units a week but 90, he saves half the time, or 20 hours. Thus his wage for the week would be 40 × $1 (i.e., 40 hours of work at $1 an hour) plus 50 per cent of 20 × $1. The total comes to $50 for the

[8] It has been estimated that in 1938, 32 per cent of the workers in large-scale industry in Russia were under progressive piece-rate plans; and 43 per cent were under proportional plans. Abram Bergson, *The Structure of Soviet Wages,* pp. 160-161. Cambridge: Harvard University Press, 1944.

[9] Arithmetic illustrations of the Halsey Plan and of various others will be found in Dale Yoder, *Personnel Management and Industrial Relations,* Chap. 13. New York: Prentice-Hall, Inc., 1942. This chapter includes a general discussion of a considerable number of wage plans.

week. It will be seen that the increase in earnings for the week is somewhat less than proportional to the increase in output.

Group Incentive Plans. Under group piecework an increase in output achieved by a given group of workers results in higher wages for the members of the group. Each member usually has a base rate, which is guaranteed. The "extra" pay he receives is determined by the extent to which the standard group output is increased. If the output is increased 25 per cent, the earnings of the group are increased 25 per cent, each person getting his due share. Under the group bonus plan, on the other hand, the extra pay for greater output may not be proportional to the output increase.

Though group incentive plans are much less common than individual plans, there is something to be said in their favor.[10] In some cases a group plan is the only feasible plan—for example, where there is such close cooperation between the individual members of a work group that the product of each worker is not clearly distinguishable. Group incentive plans lessen the amount of supervision that is necessary, since the members of the group can act, at least to some extent, as their own supervisors. Such plans, moreover, lead to a certain amount of mutual assistance among the workers and also promote flexibility in the work force. They also stimulate a feeling of solidarity among the group members (a factor that is probably of some significance in accounting for the extensive use of group incentives in Russia). Group incentive plans, moreover, may lessen the amount of inspection and clerical work, since the workers themselves may be more concerned with the quality of their work. Moreover, the amount of working capital tied up in output waiting inspection may be decreased.

Though much can be said in support of group incentives, the question is not wholly one-sided. Especially good workers may dislike group incentive plans because their earnings may be less than they would be under individual plans. Moreover, difficulties arise when the personnel of the group changes (probably involving some alterations in base rates) and when the size of the group fluctuates. To some extent these disadvantages are governed by the size of the group; the larger the group, the more intense the disadvantages. In

[10] For an extensive discussion of the advantages and disadvantages of group wage incentives, see Z. Clark Dickinson, *Compensating Industrial Effort,* Chap. 14. New York: The Ronald Press Co., 1937.

many cases twenty would appear to be about the maximum number that should be in a group.

The Pros and Cons of Incentive Wage Plans

The greatest advantage of incentive wage plans is the stimulus they give to greater production. When the wages of a worker are tied up directly to his output he has a strong inducement to work harder. This is beneficial to him, since it ordinarily increases his wages; it is advantageous to the employer, since it enables him, by spreading his overhead more thinly, to cut his costs; and it is helpful to society, since it increases the size of the national output.

The use of incentive wage plans seems to be fairer to the worker than the use of the ordinary day-rate plan. If worker *A* works more diligently than worker *B,* it is only right that he should receive more pay. Incentive wage plans appear to be a good means for achieving this result.

But these plans are not without their adverse results. For one thing they tend to lead to poor workmanship; quantity is attained at the cost of quality. An increase in the pace at which the worker operates greatly increases the likelihood of his being slipshod in his work, possibly damaging the product and perhaps the machine as well. Poor workmanship is costly to the employer and to society; to prevent it the employer may have to hire more inspectors, whose salaries may offset any gains he may have made in lower supervisory costs.

Incentive methods of wage payment may also lead to excessive strain on the workers. Many years ago Adam Smith said that when workers "are liberally paid by the piece" they "are very apt to overwork themselves, and to ruin their health and constitution in a few years." The employer, and even the worker himself, may not be too concerned with this outcome (exaggerated, to be sure, as applied to the present day), since their point of view is typically of a short-run character. But society is interested in the long run, as well as in the short run; it is interested in the *lifetime* output of the worker, not simply his output for a given year or for the period he is employed by a given company.

It should be added that incentive wage plans may be costly to install and administer. Careful and extensive job evaluation studies may be involved. The amount of record-keeping is of necessity increased, and the calculation of payrolls is rendered more difficult.

Such plans, furthermore, may lead to worker discontent, owing to the difficulty of understanding the particular plan that has been introduced, and to the pace under which it may force the workers to work. If the employer should resort to rate-cutting, a policy that has been fairly common, worker resentment may be very high.

In addition to leading to resentment on the part of the individual worker, incentive wage plans may provoke resentment on the part of the unions. But this is a topic to which we shall give separate attention.

Unions and Incentive Wage Plans

Unions are keenly interested in the type of wage payment plan the employer adopts. Contrary to a rather widespread notion they do not invariably favor time work. Some unions strongly prefer piecework, and some have even fought to force employers to adopt the piece-rate method of wage payment. Other unions, however, are strongly opposed to piece wages for a number of reasons.

Interestingly enough, the attitude of the union toward the two basic plans of wage payment very often reflects the attitude of the employer toward them. There are certain underlying conditions essential to the successful operation of each of the plans, and neither the union nor the employer will press for the adoption of the plan that the conditions do not warrant. Thus if each unit of production is complex and cannot be clearly defined, if the character of the unit changes frequently, and if the conditions under which the work is done are subject to wide variation, both the union and the employer will probably prefer the day-rate system to its alternative. There are numerous instances, however, in which either system or plan could be used; in such instances the union may prefer one plan, probably day work, and the employer the other.[11]

Opposition to Piecework. Union opposition to the piece-rate method of wage payment is based not on abstract argument but on practical, and often painful, experience.

(1) After definite piece rates have been established, and after the

[11] For further discussion of the subject treated in this section see "Industrial Wage Plans and Collective Bargaining," *Monthly Labor Review*, July, 1942; also Sumner H. Slichter, *Union Policies and Industrial Management*, Chapters X and XI. Washington: The Brookings Institution, 1941. Another good source of information is Van Dusen Kennedy, *Union Policy and Incentive Wage Methods*, Chapter III. New York: Columbia University Press, 1945.

workers have shown their ability to increase their output and their earnings, employers have sometimes reduced the rates. This policy naturally offends the workers, for it means that they are compelled to work still harder if they are to maintain their earnings. Sometimes rate-cutting may be justified, as when the employer introduces improvements that enable the workers to increase their output with no extra effort (even here the workers are entitled to some share in the resulting gains), but much rate-cutting has been done when no such improvements have been made.

(2) Unions often oppose piecework because they believe it will lead to excessive speeding on the part of the workers. This may result from rate-cutting or, especially in industries where work is scarce, it may be due to the desire of the individual worker to maintain or increase his earnings.

(3) Some opposition to piecework grows out of the union fear of unemployment. With production speeded up, less time is required to produce a given output; hence the job will not last as long as it otherwise would. The economist can easily show that from a long-run point of view, and in terms of all industry, this fear is without a solid foundation; but the union is not likely to consider the matter in terms of the long run and from the standpoint of industry in general.

(4) The piece-rate method of wage payment tends to promote competition among workers, and thus to lessen the degree of labor solidarity. Some union members will earn much more than others, and jealousy may arise as a consequence. Even where there are group incentive plans in operation, friction and ill feeling may develop. The self-supervision that such plans are supposed to involve may lead to discord. Labor solidarity may be weakened further if the employer shows favoritism in allocating the "plums" (jobs in which earnings can be especially high).

(5) In the establishment of incentive wage plans time and motion study techniques are commonly used. Jobs are studied in an effort to reduce the motions (or "therbligs") involved to a minimum; and the stop watch is used to time the various motions in the total operation. There has been a long history of union opposition to these scientific-management methods, and it is not surprising that some of the union opposition to incentive wages should grow out of the means used in setting up such wage systems.

A similar consideration grows out of the belief that under the piece-rate system employers sometimes become satisfied with inefficient managerial polices. When wages are on the piece basis, all or part of the cost of such inefficiency is borne by the workers.

(6) Since incentive wage systems must frequently be changed, friction can easily arise over the nature of the changes made. For this and other reasons such systems are a fruitful source of grievances. The handling of such grievances may take up a lot of the time of union shop stewards or officers.

(7) When, instead of using the straight piece-rate method, the employer uses a complex form, the union may object because of the difficulty the workers have in understanding the system. Some systems are based not on the number of units of output produced but on other criteria ("manits," for example), and the workers have no little difficulty in trying to understand and check the relationship between what they do and what they get.

Partiality Toward Piecework. The preceding list of union objections to the piece-rate method of wage payment is a formidable one. There are reasons, however, why unions sometimes prefer this method to ordinary time work. If the unit of output can be definitely and easily measured, and if working conditions remain essentially the same, the members of the union may be able to derive distinct benefits from piecework. It may strengthen the union's bargaining position; it fits in better with collective bargaining of wide geographical scope; it may give the union and the employer greater protection against nonunion competition; it enables the union members to obtain higher earnings without forcing higher labor costs on the employer. For these, and a few other subordinate reasons, some unions are partial toward the piece-rate method, but such unions are still in the minority.[12]

Union Control Over Piecework. Where piecework (including all incentive methods) is introduced it is very common for the unions to exercise control over its application. This control, which protects the workers from the abuses that may arise under the system, takes a number of forms. Sometimes specific guarantees and prohibitions are embodied in the collective bargaining agreements. Thus there may

[12] For a more extensive treatment of this phase of the question, see Slichter, *op. cit.*, pp. 287-296. Professor Kennedy is of the opinion that organized labor is less favorably inclined to incentive wages than Professor Slichter's analysis would seem to indicate. See Kennedy, *op. cit.*, p. 51.

be a provision to the effect that the piece rates will not be tampered with during the life of the agreement unless (and this feature is usually added) the employer introduces improvements. Sometimes a minimum hourly, daily, or weekly wage is agreed upon. Frequently it is provided that the workers are to be paid if they lose time as a result of employer negligence or because of factors beyond their control. Secret time studies and other unfair practices may be prohibited.

A second type of control involves the active participation of the union in establishing the piece rates and the job standards. Unions often set up price committees that must give their approval before the piece rates can be applied. This policy is widespread in the clothing industry, in which there are frequent changes in style, necessitating a more or less continuous adjustment in the piece rates and job standards. Unions have become increasingly interested in the time-study method as a basis for determining piece rates, and a few of them attempt to regulate its use. The International Ladies Garment Workers' Union even has its own time-study experts.

In still another way the unions attempt to control the use of piecework. They insist on the right of appeal in the event of dissatisfaction with the rates established or with the way in which they have been established. Generally the ordinary grievance machinery provided in the collective bargaining agreements is used for this purpose.[13]

Nonpecuniary Incentives

Incentives of a nonmonetary character sometimes seem to be much more influential than the incentive provided by monetary rewards.

In the present part of our discussion we shall use the term "incentive" in a comprehensive manner to include all factors that either directly or indirectly elicit extra effort on the part of workers. Some of the factors to which we shall give attention are "conducives" (to use Sargent Florence's term) rather than incentives in the narrow sense, but we shall include them in our analysis. Both conducives

[13] For a description, with examples, of control features over incentive wages, see Bulletin No. 908-3, *Collective Bargaining Provisions: Incentive Wage Provisions; Time Studies and Standards of Production.* Bureau of Labor Statistics, United States Department of Labor, 1948.

and incentives can be viewed in terms of worker morale, the basic quality to which they contribute and, in turn, the fundamental factor in work effort.[14] Let us now examine some of the specific non-economic influences that stimulate work effort.

(1) *Physical Plant Environment.* One influence that promotes effort on the part of workers is a favorable plant environment. That a clean, airy plant is conducive to good work is becoming more and more widely recognized. Factory design and construction have been undergoing change and in numerous instances our factories now approach, if not equal, the type of establishment envisaged by William Morris in his delightful and provocative essay "A Factory As it Might Be."

In some instances the work environment is improved by the use of color combinations. Care must be exercised here, of course; otherwise the worker might be quite confused in his toil by clashing and riotous color combinations. But a new science, centering around the industrial use of color, has been developed.

In some plants the general work environment is improved, and the output increased, through the use of music. Here too care must be exercised; the music must be fitted to the type of work performed. Irreparable damage might be done in some jobs if the workers had to listen to boogie-woogie music, for instance, or to some of the newer products of man's inventive genius.

Psychological Plant Environment. A highly important part of the working environment is the psychological atmosphere that permeates it. If this atmosphere is of the improper kind, its influence may offset the good effect produced by a fine physical environment.

The psychological atmosphere in a plant is largely the responsibility of management, and a variety of factors contribute to its quality.[15] Fairness in employee relations is one of the most important. The employer must not play favorites; he must be willing to give

[14] C. A. Mace declares that "The problem of incentives *is* the problem of morale, and morale is the summation of many effects." *The Nineteenth Century* (now *The Twentieth Century*), December, 1948, pp. 326-327. This view is somewhat similar to the opinion expressed by Max Weber some decades ago that the "total feeling" of workers has an effect on their production. See Melville Dalton's article in *The Journal of Political Economy,* August, 1947, p. 323.

[15] A useful discussion by Daniel Katz of a theme closely related to the above question will be found in *Current Trends in Industrial Psychology* by Wayne Dennis *et al.* Pittsburgh: University of Pittsburgh Press, 1949. Mr. Katz's contribution is entitled "Morale and Motivation in Industry."

careful attention to grievances; he must be reasonable in his policies and expectations.

The psychological atmosphere in a plant is also determined in part by the care with which workers and jobs are adjusted. Usually the adjustment has had to be on the side of the worker, but there appears to be a growing recognition that jobs should also be adjusted to the worker.

Finally, the presence of friendly work groups in the plant should be emphasized as a factor influencing the psychological atmosphere. The importance, to the worker, of acceptance into the group has been stressed by Elton Mayo in his outstanding discussion of the significance of groups in modern industry.[16] Mayo discards "the rabble hypothesis," which pictures humanity "as a horde of individuals, each actuated by self-interest, each fighting his neighbor for the scarce material of survival," and plays up the "working-team" concept. The former stresses financial incentives "as the only effective human motive," as a powerful, if not the most powerful, characteristic of human beings. The latter stresses team membership in work.

It is possible that Mayo overemphasized the significance of the working-team idea, but that it is a very important concept cannot be denied. A worker who is an accepted member of a group—of which there may be many in a factory—will be happier and probably more productive than if he is rejected and carries on alone. It behooves management, therefore, to do all it can to promote group acceptance of the individual workers and to recognize the importance of the group as a factor in employee relations.

The "System" Environment. So far in our discussion of environment as an incentive factor we have limited ourselves to the plant level. But the problem is one that extends much beyond the individual factory. It can be thought of with reference to the whole economic system.

Socialists have argued that under the capitalistic system workers will not render services equal to their ability. Thus R. H. Tawney declares that "it is idle to expect that men will do their best under a system which they do not trust," and it is also idle to expect "that they will trust any system in the control of which they do not

[16] *The Social Problems of an Industrial Civilization,* especially pp. 59, 76, 83, 111. Boston: Division of Research, Graduate School of Business Administration, Harvard University, 1945.

share." [17] Is Tawney correct? Is it true that a socialistic, or communistic, system provides a greater incentive to individual effort than a competitive private enterprise system?

Stalin has affirmed that under the Soviet system the working man "works not for the exploiters, but for himself, for his class, for society." [18] He is "a public figure in a way," and Stalin has no doubt that he will turn out to be a more productive worker than the worker under capitalism. But does the typical worker under a socialistic type of society feel that he is part owner of the "great enterprise" for which he works? Does he feel that he is "a public figure in a way," and does he, in keeping with such figures (the better ones, it should be added) in other countries, work diligently for the common good? [19]

These questions raise the whole issue of private enterprise economies versus highly planned economies, with special reference to incentives to work. This is a fascinating issue, but unfortunately we cannot take the time to delve into it. Each of us, however, should try to reach a conclusion on the point.

Miscellaneous Incentives. Workers who do good work, in terms of either quantity or quality, are ordinarily rewarded by higher pay. But, in addition, they may receive "recognition" of other types. For example, the boss may commend them for their achievements—a very economical type of recognition, but one that may be quite effective. In times of war workers who make useful suggestions for improving plant methods may receive not only monetary rewards and plant recognition but also government certificates or citations. During World War II in this country plants as entities were also honored for production achievements by being given the right to fly a special flag. In peacetime, however, public recognition is not given to workers or plants for notable accomplishments in the matter of production.

This policy, it is interesting to note, is in constant use in Russia. The Soviet government has a series of honors that it confers on workers and others for outstanding achievements. The title "Hero of Socialist Labor," which automatically enrolls its possessor in the Order

[17] *The Acquisitive Society,* p. 151. New York: Harcourt, Brace & Co., 1920.

[18] *Op. cit.,* pp. 553, 547.

[19] In this connection one might cite a meaningful statement made by C. A. Mace that "the effectiveness of a target depends on the degree to which it is personal, proximate, and precise." *The Nineteenth Century* (now *The Twentieth Century*), December, 1948, p. 322.

of Lenin and entitles him to wear "a gold medal which is a five-pointed star bearing the hammer and sickle," is the chief award in the country.[20] Stalin was the first one to "make the grade" and receive the honor. Recognition is also given to deserving Russian workers by means of publicity. The names of meritorious workers are given national prominence and their pictures are commonly inserted in the press. Sometimes workers are made national heroes. This was true of the miner Aleksei Stakhanov, who applied the principle of specialization to the mining of coal with very successful results. Recognition and publicity of this sort may backfire, however, as it did with Adolf Henneke in Eastern Germany. Henneke, the "superminer," became the butt of numerous jokes.[21]

In the United States workers are not given medals for outstanding performance. They are not made members of any select order, nor are their names and their pictures brought to the attention of the public. Policies of this sort would seem rather fantastic to us and their feasibility is open to very serious doubt.

During a time when the national welfare is endangered the workers have a strong nonmonetary inducement to work hard. War, or the threat of war, is a strong stimulus to industrial effort. It is interesting to observe that even in times of peace Russia attempts to create a sort of war psychology with reference to work. Various terms that are used suggest that the workers are engaged in a battle. Thus in Molotov's pamphlet on the *Stakhanov Movement* we find such words and expressions as "new warriors," "front," "fight," "standardbearers," and "army of fighters for high productivity."

How effective such terms are in encouraging workers to work harder, it is impossible to say. There is good reason for believing, however, that they have more effect in Russia than they would have in this country. A proclamation urging American workers to wage a "fight" on the production "front" in the interests of higher living standards and greater national strength would probably elicit little enthusiasm. For the most part, our nonmonetary incentives must be of a different type.

20 *U.S.S.R. Information Bulletin,* January 14, 1949, p. 8.

21 For examples see *The New York Times,* Magazine Section, March 6, 1949, p. 16.

26

NONWAGE INCOME AND ECONOMIC INEQUALITY

Most of the income received by workers comes to them in the form of wages. These wages are usually paid at regular intervals of a week or two and are calculated on a time or piece basis. There may be supplements to these wages, however, which either directly or indirectly add to the workers' incomes. In the first part of the present chapter we shall discuss the more important of these supplements, considering them not merely as means for increasing incomes but as devices for improving labor-management relations.

Profit Sharing

Profit sharing is not of recent origin. The first application of the principle in this country goes back more than 80 years, to the 1860's. In fact, it has been stated that the first plan in this coutry was set up by Albert Gallatin in 1794, but this contention seems questionable. In France, a country especially well known for its ventures in profit sharing, the principle was put into operation at least as early as 1820. Profit-sharing plans have thus been tried for a long time, and in many cases found wanting. Despite the rather high mortality rate among such plans a considerable number are in use at the present time, not only in the United States but in other countries; and interest in the profit-sharing principle is at a relatively high level.[1]

[1] Much has been written over the years about the principle of profit sharing. An extensive bibliography of earlier discussions of the subject will be found in *Profit Sharing in the United States,* by Boris Emmett, Bulletin No. 208, Bureau of Labor Statistics, U. S. Department of Labor. A review article on profit sharing by P. S. Narasimhan, in which reference is made to some of the more outstanding recent writings on the subject, is contained in the *International Labor Review,*

In its broadest sense profit sharing is simply the sharing of profits by an employer with his employees. In the discussion that follows we shall use the term in this fashion, though a strong case can be made out for a narrower definition—one that might, for example, limit the term to schemes under which the share of profits going to the workers is prearranged.[2]

Though the principle of profit sharing is quite simple, profit-sharing systems vary. Thus in 1949 it was reported that there were about 85 different types of plans used by the members of the Council of Profit-Sharing Industries, a nationwide organization devoted to the furtherance of the profit-sharing idea. And these types do not represent all the conceivable ones that could be used, as the following classification will suggest.

Classification. On the basis of methods of introduction, profit-sharing plans may be divided into four categories. First are the plans introduced voluntarily by management acting alone. Most of the plans in the United States are of this kind; the employers institute them without coercion from the government or from labor organizations, and without the cooperation of the workers. In the second category are the jointly initiated plans. Here the employer and the employees (and particularly the unions) jointly work out the profit-sharing scheme to be used and jointly administer it. In the third category are the profit-sharing plans established by law. Plans of this character are not found in the United States, but in some of the South American republics and in a number of iron curtain countries in Europe, including Russia, such plans exist.[3] In the final category are the plans prescribed, compulsorily, by arbitration tribunals. Plans of this type are apparently nonexistent in the United States, but a few examples are found in India.

Chief Features. The details of profit-sharing plans in this country cannot be examined in the present analysis, but a few of their chief features should be noted. With respect to the question of payment, the plans are of two kinds: in some, payments are made periodically

---

December, 1950. The subject is discussed comprehensively in Kenneth M. Thompson, *Profit Sharing*. New York: Harper & Bros., 1949.

2 A discussion of definitions will be found in Thompson, *op. cit.*, pp. 16-19.

3 A description of these plans, and also of the other plans mentioned, will be found in P. S. Narasimhan's article noted in footnote 1.

in cash; in others, payments are deferred and the sums are accumulated in a reserve until they are handed over to the employee at some specified time, as when he retires. Should he be dismissed for "cause," the payment to the employee will probably be only a fraction of the amount in reserve. Both of these methods of payment have their advantages and disadvantages, and a case can be made out for each, as well as for a combination of the two.[4]

Under most profit-sharing schemes in this country the percentage of profits to be distributed among the employees is specifically stated in advance. On the matter of amount there is a great deal of variation. The formula used may be quite simple, such as "20 per cent of profits before taxes"; or it may be complex, involving, for example, different percentages depending on the amount of profits.

Another feature of profit sharing relates to eligibility. In some cases all employees are covered, but in most instances a definite "probationary period" must first be served. The amount that each employee receives is usually tied up with his earnings, a pro rata basis being commonly employed.[5]

Benefits and Weaknesses. Various benefits have been claimed by the proponents of profit sharing. For one thing it is said that profit sharing promotes industrial peace, a contention that on the whole would seem to be valid. Workers who have a stake in the profits of the company are less likely to go on strike than workers whose total income comes to them in the form of wages. There may be dissatisfaction, however, if no profits are made, though actual industrial disputes may not follow as a consequence.

Another alleged benefit of profit sharing is greater production. This result is a definite possibility. The prospect of sharing in the profits of the employer should decrease labor turnover, act as an incentive to effort, and serve as a stimulus to the discovery of improved methods. The workers, one employer has stated,[6] "are quick to tell management if there is some improvement that can be made to speed

[4] A discussion of the relative merits of profit-sharing "plans" and profit-sharing "trusts," by Gustave Simons, will be found in the *Industrial and Labor Relations Review,* October, 1948, pp. 79-83.

[5] A useful exhibit of the key features of a list of representative profit-sharing plans in the United States will be found in an article by Robert L. Rowe in the *Harvard Business Review,* September, 1949.

[6] *The New York Times,* November 9, 1948.

production." A profit-sharing scheme, however, does not have in large degree the "personal, proximate, and precise" characteristics which, as we noted in the previous chapter, are so important in incentive plans.

A further benefit claim for profit sharing is that it increases purchasing power without resulting in higher prices. There is some truth in this argument. However, it is possible that employers in industries that are not highly competitive may charge higher prices than they would otherwise charge, so that funds will be available to pay profits to employees. In such a case purchasing power would be merely redistributed.

Other motives—other "benefits"—may also impel employers to go in for profit sharing. They may want to lessen the interest their workers have, or may have, in unionization. They may also try to use profit sharing as a means of avoiding increases in basic wage rates. An employer who can do this may make easier adjustments to the vicissitudes of business, but his program is not likely to arouse any enthusiasm on the part of the workers, especially if they are unionized.

The possible benefits of profit sharing, both to the employer and to the worker, seem substantial; but the fact remains that many profit-sharing schemes have failed. Their failure has been due partly to the external factor of unfavorable business conditions in the economy as a whole and partly to internal weaknesses in the enterprises themselves. The lack of a satisfactory over-all plan of labor relations has probably been a significant element in the disappearance of many of the plans. Profit sharing itself is not a clue to good labor-management relations, but along with other enlightened policies it may lead to worth-while results, from the standpoint of both the employer and the employee.

Unions and Profit Sharing. For the most part the unions have been either lukewarm or definitely hostile to profit-sharing schemes. They are fearful that such plans when initiated solely by management may divert the interest of the workers from unionization and collective bargaining; that they lead to monetary gains that are uncertain and changing as contrasted with the steadily rising gains that can be made through direct wage increases achieved by collective bargaining; and that such plans will delude the workers into believing that they are partners with the employer, when there is no sound basis for such a belief (most profit-sharing plans provide for administration solely by management).[7]

The AFL has declared that it is not opposed to profit-sharing plans if they are arranged through the process of collective bargaining and if, furthermore, they meet certain other requirements: that they "do no interfere with normal wage increases, and that workers are given adequate facts on company earnings and share equally in administering the plan." These conditions are not always readily granted, and it is not surprising that the unions, on the whole, prefer to better the economic position of their members through the winning of higher wages rather than through acquiring a share of profits. Moreover, the AFL has contended, in contrast to the view of some employers, that collective bargaining is the only foundation for true industrial partnership, since it places management and labor on an equal footing in the determination of questions that relate to them.

Profit-sharing plans in unionized plants are not an impossibility, however.[8] But before they can be successful a number of conditions or requirements, suggested by the previous discussion, seem to be essential. The plans, even if not initiated on a bilateral basis, must be administered bilaterally, with the unions in possession of adequate facts concerning company operations. The plans must be geared into a broader program of industrial relations. They must not be used as a means to undermine the confidence of the workers in their union.

Profit sharing, as it appears at the present time, does not offer the social reform possibilities that some of the earlier exponents of the principle envisaged. However, it can still serve a useful purpose in individual enterprises.

Profit Sharing and Copartnership. A few words should be added about the earlier attitude toward profit sharing, especially in rela-

[7] See "Statement of the American Federation of Labor on Profit Sharing," in *Hearings* before the Joint Committee on the Economic Report, 81st Cong., 2nd Sess., January, 1950, pp. 274-275. See also *The American Federationist,* August, 1950, pp. 13-16.

[8] Joseph N. Scanlon presents three "case studies" of profit sharing in unionized plants (two failures and one success) in *Industrial and Labor Relations Review,* October, 1948, pp. 58-75. Mr. Scanlon declares that "a sense of participation and partnership is the fundamental prerequisite" in profit-sharing plans, and that the type of the plan is of secondary importance.

tionship to what was known as copartnership in industry. Late in the 19th century and early in the 20th, the principle of copartnership was widely advocated as a new basis for industrial organization.

In its strict and somewhat narrow sense copartnership differed from both profit sharing and employee stock ownership, yet it involved both. The employees came into possession of stock but the funds for buying the stock did not come wholly out of wages, as they have in the more recent experiments in employee stock ownership; they came, at least in part, from profits distributed to the workers.[9] Today, under the prevailing profit-sharing schemes, the share of profits paid to workers is ordinarily in the form of cash payments (immediate or deferred) and does not take the form of stock. Thus the workers do not become part owners of the companies for which they work, as under copartnership.

Copartnership, which in its perfect form was to bring in consumers as owners as well as workers, was supposed to take the best elements from socialism, syndicalism, voluntary associationism, and capitalism and try "to conserve and to harmonize them in the common interest of all." [10] This vision was indeed an attractive one, but like many other visions it has not been realized. Today little is heard about copartnership.

An approach to the copartnership principle, it might be noted, is found in the joint plan of profit sharing and multiple management in the enterprises of Eric Johnson. Each company in the Johnson group has a junior board of directors, composed of seven employee representatives. This double plan serves to give the workers "a stake in capitalism," something Mr. Johnson definitely favors. The stake is not as large, however, as the older supporters of copartnership desired.

Employee Stock Ownership

Development, Decline, and Revival. The practice of selling stock to employees first came into prominence in this country during the 1920's. It is true that some companies had adopted the policy earlier, but it was not until the 1920's that the number of such companies

[9] See Aneurin Williams, *Co-Partnership and Profit Sharing,* pp. 17-19. New York: Henry Holt & Co., 1913 (Home University Library).

[10] Williams, *op. cit.,* pp. 244, 246.

grew to any magnitude and public interest in the matter became widespread.[11]

The period of the 1920's was one in which the growing financial power of labor impressed numerous observers, including certain union leaders. This power was evidenced by the expansion of workers' accounts in savings banks, by the establishment of labor banks, and by the purchase of corporate securities by employees. One writer, Professor T. N. Carver, spoke of these developments as "the present economic revolution in the United States" and wrote a book with that title; [12] and others wrote articles with such titles as "Every Man His Own Capitalist" and "Making Workmen Capitalists."

Along with the increasing ability of workers to invest in securities there seems to have been a preference on the part of some employers for employee stock ownership over profit sharing. Stock ownership was usually much less costly than profit sharing, and it did not possess the characteristic of philanthropy.

The growth of employee stock ownership during the 1920's represented an interesting venture in the field of labor-management relations. The motives that prompted employers to establish plans of stock ownership for their employees were varied. In some instances they were moved by a desire to ward off the unionization of their workers, a desire that organized labor clearly recognized and strongly resented. In numerous other cases, however, employee stock ownership was looked upon as an enlightened method of improving employee morale, reducing labor turnover, and in general arousing greater interest on the part of workers in the enterprises with which they were connected. All of these objectives (and others) were, and still are, possible results of employee stock ownership.

The AFL recognized the fact that some of the plans were not antiunion in character, but on the whole it regarded employee stock ownership with suspicion and assumed an attitude of opposition to

[11] A detailed account of employee stock ownership plans, entitled *Employee Stock Purchase Plans in the United States,* was published by the National Industrial Conference Board in 1928.

[12] Boston: Little, Brown & Co., 1925. For an extensive bibliography of articles on employee stock ownership see *Monthly Labor Review,* June, 1927, pp. 214-223. See also the section (pp. 107-119) on "Major Findings of Former Studies of Employee Stock Ownership" in Bryce M. Stewart and Walter J. Couper, *Profit Sharing and Stock Ownership for Wage Earners and Executives.* New York: Industrial Relations Counselors, 1945.

it. At the 1925 convention of the Federation the resolutions committee declared that the purpose of employee stock ownership "is of the same genus as company unionism—an attempt to forestall [a] virile trade union movement." At the 1926 convention the executive council of the AFL expressed a similar view and went on to declare that the hope that such a policy would ultimately lead "to the democratization of industry" was fallacious because usually the stock sold to workers was of the nonvoting type. But the council did recognize the existence of "good" employee stock ownership plans and suggested the exercise of "the utmost discriminating care" in judging individual examples.

The "examples" increased in number until the end of the 1920's; then, with the coming of the Great Depression, the employee stock ownership plans fell upon evil days. Employers adopted a variety of techniques to cushion the impact of the depression on employee stock owners. One method was to refund the amounts that had been subscribed.

The Great Depression resulted in the discontinuance of many of the plans, but it did not destroy the movement. Some of the plans survived and have continued down to the present. New plans have been set up—even during the years of depression a number of employers initiated plans. However, the policy of having employees buy stock is not as important today as it was in the middle and latter part of the 1920's. According to a study published by the Brookings Institution in the early 1950's (see next section) the number of employee stockholders in six industrial classifications was somewhat less than 800,000. In terms of percentage of employees owning stock, the public utility industry was in first place, with almost 16 per cent. Manufacturing was at the bottom of the list with 1.4 per cent. The average for the six classifications was 3.2 per cent.

Employee stock ownership, which has been distinctly an American phenomenon,[13] cannot be looked upon as a significant success. Although some companies and some workers have undoubtedly ben-

[13] In a sense employee stock ownership is more a Russian phenomenon than an American. In Russia the owners of industry are, at least in theory, the citizens of the country, including the workers. The "stock certificates" are of a decidedly abstract nature—they do not really exist—and are very largely of the nonvoting type! Ownership and management are widely divergent. Is it possible for them to come close together in Russia, or in any socialistic economy? This is a nice question for students of labor.

efited from it, on the whole the record has not been impressive. Numerous plans have been discontinued—the mortality rate among employee stock ownership plans has been greater than among profit-sharing schemes—and many workers have been disillusioned. It is hazardous for workers to tie up any large percentage of their savings in the company that employs them. The trend toward limiting employee participation in stock ownership, a trend noted by Stewart and Couper, thus seems desirable. This leads us to a brief consideration of a still broader aspect of our problem.

General Ownership of Stock by Workers. In addition to owning stock in the company that employs them, workers may hold stock in other corporations. Previous to 1952 information on the extent of stock ownership by the American public, including the workers, was very sparse. Estimates (of a "responsible" character) placed the number of stockholders as high as 15 million. An extensive study carried out by the Brookings Institution and published in 1952 [14] revealed that the number is much less than 15 million. According to the Brookings estimates there are 6,439,000 persons who own shares in companies whose stock is publicly held. In addition 3,000,000 persons have stock ownership rights in enterprises whose stock is privately held. Many of the latter hold shares of the first type; hence the two figures must not be added together.

Although some of our corporations have hundreds of thousands of stockholders, including a sizable number of employees, it is clear that the bulk of the workers in this country do not own stock. A great many of them have life insurance policies, savings accounts, and government bonds, as the Brookings study reveals, but not many have direct (or even indirect) ownership rights in American industry and business.

Welfare Plans

Employer-financed welfare plans have long existed in American industry. Under their industrial relations programs numerous employers have introduced such welfare undertakings as pension plans,

[14] Lewis H. Kimmel, *Share Ownership in the United States.* Washington: The Brookings Institution, 1952. An interesting table showing the extent of stock ownership among the various "spending units" in the country, classified according to income, will be found in *The Economic Report of the President* (Council of Economic Advisers), January, 1951, p. 228. See also p. 97 of the Brookings study.

An examination of the figures in the preceding table clearly reveals that there are still many small-income families in this country. Poverty is still with us. The figures should also reveal, or at least suggest, that the incomes of the families in the lower categories cannot be raised to any large extent by reducing (through tax measures) the incomes of the much smaller number of families in the higher categories. Moreover, we are already close to the "saturation point" in the taxing of the especially high incomes.

In this general connection reference should be made to the phenomenal change that has taken place during the last two decades in the *net* incomes of the high-income receivers. In 1929 the top 5 per cent of the income receivers in this country obtained 34 per cent of the total "disposable income" (personal income, plus capital gains, minus federal income taxes). In 1939 the percentage stood at 27 and in 1946 at 18, which is the approximate figure for the present time. During this period the share of the highest category of income receivers fell 16 points, out of a maximum drop (involving complete equality of incomes) of 29 points. If undistributed profits are taken into account, the drop would have been 14 points. The change that has taken place in the pattern of income distribution during the last two decades has been aptly described by Arthur F. Burns as "one of the great social revolutions of history." [19]

The limited extent to which the incomes of the poor can be increased by taxing the very rich should be evident from the figures we have just presented. The not-so-rich (which would include some of the higher paid skilled workers) might be taxed still more heavily, in the interests of the poor. But if the living standards of the latter are to be raised to any significant degree other methods will have to be used.

Effects of Inequality

Favorable Effects. Inequality in incomes has various effects, some of which are good but many of which are bad. There can be little doubt that inequality has contributed to capital accumulation, a factor that has been of the utmost importance in the growth of material living standards. Capital accumulation involves savings,

[19] The above figures, which are based on studies by Simon Kuznets, are taken from Professor Burns' introduction to the 31st *Annual Report* of the National Bureau of Economic Research, May, 1951, p. 4.

and most saving has been done by the receivers of the larger incomes. But this point must not be pressed too far. Inequality in incomes has probably been a factor in causing economic fluctuations and the accompanying business slumps, a contention that John A. Hobson vigorously advanced and J. M. Keynes later supported. It is possible, therefore, that if the degree of inequality had been reduced, the *absolute* volume of saving in the long run might have been larger, even though the relative volume (percentage of national income saved) during the prosperous years had been less. This is a possible result, but not a probable one.

Very closely related to the preceding point is the effect of inequality on investments. The possibility of reaping, and retaining, substantial gains is unquestionably a strong inducement to invest. If a ceiling were placed on the amount of income one could receive from investments, there can be little doubt that many people would limit the investment of their savings, and probably restrict their savings as well.

Inequality in incomes has served as a strong incentive to effort. It is not clear how much income inequality is necessary to evoke the greatest amount of effort; but obviously the degree of inequality in this country in times past was, in general, greater than was necessary to call forth the actual amount of effort realized. This situation has been largely corrected now through the imposition of progressive income taxes.

It should be noted that large incomes from inherited wealth or from nepotist-bestowed jobs may impel one to laziness rather than to effort.

Unfavorable Effects. In Chapter 3 we observed the bad effects inequality has on the pattern of production. When the price mechanism guides production, goods are produced in response to effective demand. Since the effective demand of a person is determined by the money he has to spend, a large-income receiver can exert much more influence on the course of production than a small-income receiver. In this way the production pattern can be distorted until it does not accurately reflect the need pattern.

As we pointed out a moment ago inequality in incomes is a factor in cyclical instability, though there is no reason whatever for believing that the business cycle would disappear if we had complete income equality. However, a marked reduction in the degree of inequality would probably reduce the amplitude of the cyclical swings in business activity and consequently reduce the volume of cyclical unemployment. But here the two points we made earlier should be recalled. If the lessening of inequality resulted in a serious drop in capital accumulation and a weakening of incentive, the stability achieved might be at an undesirably low level.

Inequality leads to dissatisfaction on the part of the lower-income receivers, not because they are necessarily in penury but because their incomes are small relative to the incomes of certain other persons. Envy is especially rife when those with the larger incomes engage in what Thorstein Veblen called "conspicuous consumption."

Inequality has been and to some extent still is a factor in political power. Although it is foolish to talk of "Wall Street" as running the country, it is not so foolish to say that wealthy persons can influence the election of candidates and the course of legislation by extending financial aid. But this particular factor is not as important now as it once was, not with organized labor raising funds for political purposes.

A final weakness of economic inequality is the obstacle it places in the way of genuine democracy. A democratic society does not necessarily involve complete equality in incomes, to be sure; but democracy cannot easily function in a society in which there are very sharp differences in income. Such differences lead to inequalities in social prestige (under the prevailing standards of social appraisal), in political power, and in manner of living and thinking. These results, in turn, constitute poor soil for the flower of democracy.[20]

Coping with Inequality and Poverty

The problem of inequality and the problem of poverty, though intimately related, are by no means the same. And not being the same they cannot be dealt with in exactly the same way. We have already made notable progress in reducing the degree of inequality, particularly by the use of governmental means—progressive income taxes, inheritance taxes, social security programs, educational programs, and vocational guidance.

[20] A long discussion of the general theme of the above paragraph will be found in Harold J. Laski, *Liberty in the Modern State,* Chapter III. New York: Harper & Bros., 1930. (New York: The Viking Press, 1949. Also Penguin Books, 1937.)

The problem of poverty can be partly solved by the use of the above-mentioned means, but it must also be approached from another angle, namely that of greater production. The total output of the nation (which is also its total income) must be increased if we are to "abolish" poverty and raise substantially the incomes of the low-income groups. And what is more, the output of low-income families and individuals must also be increased—such an increase will reduce inequality at the same time that it cuts down the amount of poverty. In approaching the question of low incomes and poverty we must give up the oft-reiterated but utterly fallacious notion that we have "solved the problem of production." With possibly 15 million families having an annual income of less than $3,000, and with additional effort at *redistributing* the present income of the nation of very little effectiveness, the problem of production is far from solved. We still have to discover additional ways to increase the output of the nation.

27

SHORTER HOURS—IN FACT AND FANCY

One of the most important economic and social changes of recent decades has been the remarkable decrease that has taken place in the length of the work day. No longer is it necessary for one to ask, with the English political philosopher William Godwin, "Is there not a state of society practicable, in which leisure shall be made the inheritance of every one of its members?" Such a state of society is already in existence, not only in the United States but in many other countries. Leisure is now our inheritance, and there is every likelihood that in the years ahead the size of the inheritance will be greater than it is today.

The achievement of the age of leisure was not a sudden event.[1] It was a gradual process, an evolutionary development. A variety of influences operated to bring it about and a variety of results, some of them of immense significance, have followed from it.

Changes in the Length of the Work Day

During the period of this country's existence the length of the work day—to be more exact we should really speak in terms of the work week or even the work year—has been cut approximately in half. Information relating to hours of work is fragmentary for the early years, but coming down to 1830 we find the United States census of that year presenting statistics on the subject. According to the census 81.1 per cent of those who were in receipt of regular

[1] In speaking of the age of leisure we are referring to the modern period and to industrialized societies. In earlier periods leisure was by no means unknown; nor is it unknown in nonindustrialized societies today.

wages worked more than 10 hours a day, and 13.5 per cent had a work day of more than 13 hours.[2] Ten years later, in 1840, the average work week, as estimated by the statistician Mulhall (in his *Dictionary of Statistics*) was 78 hours, which, with Sundays excluded, would be equivalent to a 13-hour day. This estimate would seem to be high.

Obviously one cannot say *precisely* what the average length of the work day or work week was in 1790 or in 1830 or in 1850, or even what it is today; and for our present purpose mathematical exactness is not necessary. We can feel reasonably sure, however, that during the first part of the last century the average worker in industry put in almost twice as many hours a week as the worker today. It was clearly not possible for him, as it was for Thoreau's "really efficient laborer," to "saunter to his task surrounded by a wide halo of ease and leisure." Even the factory girls of the progressive and publicized city of Lowell had in the 1830's a 78-hour week.

During the past hundred years the length of the work week has been reduced by a series of irregular jumps, ordinarily in response to pressure from the unions. Notable changes included the achievement of the 10-hour day and, later, the five-day week. Today the standard work week in American industry is 40 hours. When workers work more than 40 hours, the extra hours are compensable at time-and-a-half or more. In some industries both the standard and the actual work week is less than 40 hours, but the number of such industries is not large.

In addition to the decrease in the length of the regular work day and work week there has been, especially in recent years, a marked drop in the number of work days per year in American industry. This drop has been brought about very largely by the adoption of paid vacations. The widespread introduction of this policy is one of the most outstanding recent developments in industrial relations and in the general field of social progress. Not so long ago vacations were limited very largely to office employees. Now they are enjoyed by millions of factory employees as well.

To no small extent the rapid growth of paid vacations has been due, in the first instance, to pressure from unions, the vacation

[2] See David A. Wells, *Recent Economic Changes*, p. 415. New York: D. Appleton & Co., 1899.

privilege having become one of the leading demands of the union organizations. The rapid spread of the vacation privilege during the early 1940's was partly due, however, to the policy of the National War Labor Board in permitting vacations with pay, and certain other fringe benefits, in place of direct wage increases. But it should be pointed out that there were at that time, and have been since, more fundamental factors involved in the achievement of vacations, factors that we shall discuss in the last part of this chapter.

Between 1940 and 1944 the number of workers under collective bargaining agreements who were covered by vacation plans increased from about 2 million to 11½ million, a truly phenomenal rate of growth. In 1944, 82 per cent of the plant workers in private industry (manufacturing and nonmanufacturing) were covered by vacation plans. The percentage for all employees, both plant and office, was 86.[3] Today the proportion of employees having vacations with pay is still larger. In almost all unionized plants paid vacations are now the rule—the construction industry, with its high degree of seasonality, is a notable exception. And in nonunionized plants vacations, if not the general rule, are at least very common.

The general trend has been in the direction of longer vacations. In 1943, for example, the most common vacation period (maximum) provided for in union agreements in manufacturing industry was one week. By 1944 it was two weeks. Two-week vacations are still the most common, but now there are numerous instances in which the vacation period extends beyond two weeks.

Utopian Standards

Over the years numerous estimates have been made concerning how short a work day would be possible if certain developments took place or if certain changes were made in the institutional framework of society. Back in the early part of the 16th century Sir Thomas More thought in terms of the six-hour day, and that was the standard he set up, imaginatively, for the subjects of King Utopus. Such a short work day was achieved not through extensive mechanization or by the use of Stakhanovite methods, but my making labor compulsory and by exercising some guidance over pro-

[3] See *Paid Vacations in American Industry, 1943 and 1944,* Bulletin No. 811, Bureau of Labor Statistics, U. S. Department of Labor.

duction. Almost everyone, women as well as men, had to work; and their efforts were directed wholly to the making of necessities.

In the City of the Sun the heroic Tommaso Campanella (1568-1639) established a work day of about four hours. Here again labor was compulsory. As Campanella expressed it, "While duty and work is distributed among all, it only falls to each one to work about four hours a day." Johann Andreae, who lived about the same time as Campanella, set up a work day of about six hours for Christianopolis.

Coming down several centuries we find that Benjamin Franklin too thought in terms of the four-hour day. In a letter to Benjamin Vaughan in 1784 Franklin ascribed the presence of so much want and misery in the world at that time to the employment of men and women at work that did not result in the production of articles really essential to existence and to the fact that these men and women, along with those who did nothing, consumed "the Necessaries raised by the Laborious." Franklin mentioned the computation made by a Political Arithmetician who had estimated that if every man and woman would work on something useful for four hours each day, enough would be produced to ensure the necessities and comforts of life. "Want and Misery would be banished out of the World, and the rest of the 24 hours might be Leisure and Pleasure." William Morris was another exponent of the four-hour day. In his essay "A Factory As it Might Be" he spoke of a work period of "say, to be within the mark, four hours a day."

The four-hour day has been a favorite one with writers of the past. But some students of the subject, especially in more recent times, believe that the four-hour day, as a future possibility, is much too long. Some years ago Dr. C. C. Furnas wrote a book that took him, in his own words, on "an informal excursion into the era of the two-hour working-day." Such a work day was considered to be a possibility long before Dr. Furnas took his excursion, however. William Godwin spoke of the two-hour day in his book *The Enquirer,* published in 1798. And what is even more startling, Godwin in his monumental *Enquiry Concerning Political Justice,* published a short time before *The Enquirer,* had given attention to the half-hour day! He thought that if property were equally divided, and if everyone had to work, a half-hour work day devoted to serious manual labor would be enough to supply the people with the essentials of life.

Other estimates of the possible length of the work day could be cited, estimates made by both utopian and nonutopian writers. Only one more will be noted, however. According to a newspaper report of October, 1949, Professor Clark Kerr stated that by 1990 laboring men would have a 20-hour week, and by 2050 a 10-hour week!

It is a common occurrence for the dreams and fancies of one day to become the realities of the next. The 10-hour day and the eight-hour day once existed largely in the imagination. But gradually they took on the solid form of reality, first the one and then the other. Now we are moving from the eight-hour day (or forty-hour week) toward other standards. That we shall achieve the utopian six-hour day of Sir Thomas Moore seems beyond question. We shall probably achieve the four-hour standard that Campanella and Andreae and Morris and others had in mind. In time we may actually have the two-hour day of Godwin, Furnas, and Kerr. But we must draw the line there. We cannot (at present) ever think of the half-hour day!

The shorter day of the future will be achieved not by forcing everybody to work or by confining production to the making of necessities, two popular means suggested by earlier writers. Future reductions in work hours, just as past reductions, will be the result of continued technological improvements, now including the industrial use of atomic energy. The economic issues involved in these reductions will be formidable enough, but they are small compared with the noneconomic problems to which this "super-leisure era" will give rise.

Arguments Used by Labor for Shorter Hours

The progressive reduction in the length of the work day has been accomplished by a large amount of verbal advocacy of the reduction. Various arguments have been advanced, particularly by organized labor, to show the "reasonableness" of shorter hours, and these arguments have undoubtedly been of considerable influence in bringing about the change that has taken place.

The nature of the argument or arguments advanced at any particular time in favor of shorter hours usually bears a close relationship to the objective conditions prevailing at the time. That is to say, a decrease in the length of the work day is supported not so much in terms of abstract principles as in terms of specific situations to be corrected or specific problems to be solved. As a result the types of arguments used by labor in its struggle for shorter hours have changed from time to time, as has the emphasis placed on the various arguments.

The Citizenship Argument. Perhaps the earliest argument used by labor for shorter hours was that based upon the need of leisure as a means for promoting good citizenship. If a worker had to be at his job from sunrise to sunset, as he had to be well into the last century, he had little time to give attention to public issues. Consequently his status as a citizen was certain to be inferior. This argument came into prominence during the latter part of the 1820's in the campaign for the 10-hour day.

During the years that followed some use was made of the citizenship argument, but other reasons for shorter hours came to be advanced and the old argument faded somewhat into the background. Today it is relatively unimportant, although it has not disappeared. George Meany of the AFL made some use of a modernized version of it a few years ago when he declared that in any occupation in which effort is "intensive, monotonous, repetitive, and fatiguing," a shorter work week, now more than ever before, would "serve to raise the cultural and spiritual level of our life and make us better people." In some occupations Mr. Meany declared (quite correctly), "the time away from the job is the only time the worker has to really live, to live as an individual, as a member of his family, and as a member of his community."

The Health Argument. The health argument for shorter hours came into prominence with the development of the factory system. As long as industry was on a small scale, with little machinery in use, and as long as the principle of specialization was not extensively applied, long hours did not necessarily undermine the health of the worker, although they may have curbed his spirit and intellect. But the growth of factories, with the conditions that accompanied them, definitely created a health hazard.

The health argument has been one of the most reasonable and one of the most effective arguments used in support of shorter hours. Because of the great reduction that has taken place in the length of the work day the truth behind this argument is not as substantial today as it used to be. It is still possible, however, for a worker's health to be undermined in his occupation, even though he is employed only six or seven hours a day—especially in occupations where speed is emphasized and where the physical conditions of work are unsanitary and dangerous. Workers in such occupations need a large margin of leisure in which to regain their strength and enthusiasm for the next day's work.

The Greater-Pay Argument. During the latter part of the 1860's a vigorous campaign for the eight-hour day was carried on under the leadership of Ira Steward. Steward's wife gave poetic expression to the argument in a verse that was once popular in union circles:

> Whether you work by the piece
>   Or work by the day,
> Decreasing the hours
>   Increases the pay.

According to this argument a reduction in hours is desirable because it will lead to higher wages or pay, not simply higher wages per hour but higher wages per day or per week. This is a very optimistic notion, and the descriptive expression "Golden Law of Wages," which has been applied to it, is not inappropriate. The doctrine stood in direct contrast to the old Iron Law of Wages, which asserted or implied that wages tend to fall to the subsistence level.

The type of reasoning used by Steward and his associates was as follows. If the length of the work day were reduced, the wants of the workers would become greater. With this increase in their wants many of the workers would demand higher hourly rates of pay. ("My theory is, first, that more leisure will create motives and temptations for the common people to ask for more wages," said Steward.) Confronted with the demand for higher wages, and being forced, at least in many instances, to accede to them, the employers would be saddled with higher labor costs. But, according to the argument, the employers would meet these higher costs by introducing more machinery, which, in turn, would lead to an increase in the output of industry and in real wages. Thus all things would work together for the good of the workers.

Steward's doctrine has not survived in its complete form, but parts of it are still in use.[4] It is sometimes argued, for example, that additional leisure more or less directly contributes to greater production and greater business. "Shorter hours mean more leisure, more leisure means more consumption and more business. Don't you eat more, drink more and raise more cain when you are on a holiday, on a vacation, or when just plain loafing? Don't you start to make whoopee the moment you are out of the slave pen?" [5]

The reply of the economist to this kind of reasoning is that unless the increased leisure makes for greater efficiency on the part of the worker it will not lead to greater production and greater consumption. Leisure may increase people's wants, but unless it in one way or another promotes production it cannot increase their ability to satisfy their wants.

It is true that people usually get more satisfaction out of their income, especially when it is spent on such things as automobiles, radios, and picture shows, if they have more time in which to consume it. It would be much more logical, therefore, although not necessarily more effective, for the workers to argue for shorter hours in psychological terms rather than in terms of economic income.

The Greater-Production Argument. Closely allied with, and in some respects similar to, the greater-pay argument is the greater-production argument. Decrease the length of the work day, it has been said, and production will expand. Or, what amounts to the same thing, do not increase hours or production will go down. It was the latter form that the argument generally assumed in the early 1940's. At that time the country was vigorously trying to increase its output of armaments, and the relationship between hours and output became a question of major importance. And it was at that time that the AFL executive council declared that "We must insist on maintaining the forty-hour week because it makes for greater pro-

[4] A view that is much more conservative than that expressed in Mrs. Steward's verse is contained in the following excerpt from a resolution that Ira Steward himself drafted in 1872: "That in the long run—within certain limits—less hours mean more pay, whether they work by the day or work by the piece." Quoted in *The New Encyclopaedia of Social Reform,* ed. by W. D. P. Bliss and R. M. Binder, p. 434. New York: Funk & Wagnalls Co., 1910, 3rd ed.

[5] *What Organized Labor Wants,* pp. 13-14. Pamphlet published by the Rand School Press for the Education Department of the United Automobile Workers of America (CIO), 1937.

duction." "The short work-week is an essential element in American efficiency," the council asserted. "If hours were lengthened we could not hope to maintain our high productivity."

That a reduction in the number of work hours may lead to greater production, not only per hour but also per day or per week, is a distinct possibility. It is not an invariable result, however. The whole question of the relationship between hours and output is one that cannot be discussed in brief compass. We shall defer treatment of it, therefore, until the next chapter, where we shall analyze at length several highly important issues relating to hours of work and leisure.

The Unemployment Argument. A final argument used in support of shorter hours relates to unemployment. If the length of the work day is reduced, there will be more jobs available, and hence the number of workers who are involuntarily idle will be diminished. This contention has some merit, but it is capable of gross misuse. Here again we shall postpone our detailed discussion until the next chapter.

A good summing up of the chief arguments in support of shorter hours is contained in an optimistic statement made by George Gunton, back in the 1890's. Gunton declared that the introduction of the eight-hour day by the United States, England, France, and Germany "would rapidly abolish enforced idleness and able-bodied pauperism, tend to continually extend the consumption and production of wealth, increase the comfort, education, and culture, of the masses, and permanently advance real wages, without arbitrarily disturbing existing institutions." [6]

Factors Involved in the Reduction of Hours

In trying to account for the reduction that has taken place in the length of the work day it is necessary to distinguish between initiating and fundamental causes.

Initiating Causes. The initiating causes of shorter hours are those that have exerted their influence *directly* and *immediately*. If not basically responsible for the shorter work day, they have at least made it an actuality.

[6] *Wealth and Progress,* p. 265. New York: D. Appleton & Co., 1894.

These causes have been three in number.[7] First, there has been the unenforced action on the part of employers themselves in reducing hours. Acting either because of benevolent motives or because of a belief in the economic feasibility of the policy, some employers, with little or no pressure from the outside, have reduced the length of the work day in their businesses.

A second and more important initiating influence has been the force of public opinion, operating principally in the demand for legislative control of hours. Although governmental hour regulation on a broad basis was rather slow in developing in this country, there are now important federal and state laws that place restrictions on the length of the work day. The details of these laws we shall consider in the next section.

The third and most effective initiating influence has been the unions. The remarkable reduction that has taken place in the length of the work day during the last century has in no small degree been directly due to union pressure. (At this point the reader may want to refer back to Chapter 15 where there is a brief discussion of some of the forms in which union hour demands have been expressed.)

Except during times of war the interest of workers, both organized and unorganized, in the attainment of shorter hours is continuous—though ordinarily the demand for shorter hours has not been as insistent as the demand for higher wages. Unions, acting on the basis of worker interest, carry on a more or less constant struggle for the achievement of a shorter work day. The campaign is continuous for the simple reason that in the matter of hours of work the unions have no final goal. As an AFL committee affirmed some years ago, "It is our great goal to wring as much of life from the world of toil as may be possible." Unions have immediate objectives with respect to hours, but they have no ultimate objective.

Although interest in shorter hours is generally continuous, periodically the actual struggle to win a reduction in hours becomes especially vigorous. In the 1830's, and again in the 1850's, the movement for the 10-hour day was carried on with great force; in the

[7] An extensive historical study of these three causes from the Civil War to the early 1930's will be found in Marion C. Hill, *Shorter Hours*. New York: Columbia University Press, 1932.

late 1860's the campaign for the eight-hour day was conducted with determination, as it was in the late 1880's and the early 1890's; in the 1920's the drive for the five-day week was a great issue; and in the first part of the 1930's, when unemployment was rampant, there was widespread advocacy of the 30-hour week.

Just as there have been outstanding general campaigns for shorter hours, so also have there been outstanding specific battles over the same issue. Some of the country's bitterest strikes have been waged over the question of hours, although other factors have been involved.

In their struggle for shorter hours the unions have used two principal methods of attack: the economic and the political. The former, which has been the more important, has involved direct pressure on the employers; the latter has centered around the demand for regulatory hour legislation. Both methods of attack have been supported by an immense amount of verbal argument. The unions have tried to prove that reductions in the length of the work day are desirable from the standpoint not only of the workers but of the community as well, and even from the standpoint of the employer.

Union demands relating to the general matter of hours take a variety of forms. It is not simply a question of the length of the standard work day. In collective bargaining agreements, as we noted in Chapter 15, one finds numerous hour provisions, relating to such matters as vacations, work-sharing, and shift arrangements.

Fundamental Causes. Had it not been for other developments the influences we have just discussed would have produced very little change in the length of the work day. Although these three influences initiated the reduction in hours, there were other factors that made such reductions not only possible but feasible.

The most important of these factors was progress in industrial technology. Other highly important factors were large-scale production, the corporate form of business organization, the credit system, our large volume of savings, and the abundance of our natural resources. As a result of our technological progress and the operation of these other factors, there has been a vast increase in man-hour output in industry, which, in turn, has been chiefly responsible for making the present hour standards possible. It is to be emphasized, however, that these standards would not have come into existence in any automatic fashion, certainly not as soon as they did. Pressure, from unions and the government, was needed to enforce them.[8]

Legislative Control of Hours

Attempts to exercise legislative control over hours of work go back many years. At times these attempts have been especially vigorous, as in the 1860's, for example, when under the leadership of Ira Steward a strenuous campaign was carried on for the eight-hour day. As a result of more or less continuous (though fluctuating) pressure a substantial body of hour legislation has been placed on the statute books of both the federal and the state governments. But legislation in this field had to run a long gamut of court decisions, in which the cases of Richie *v.* People, Holden *v.* Hardy, Muller *v.* Oregon, Lochner *v.* New York, and Bunting *v.* Oregon were of outstanding significance.[9]

The most important single piece of hour legislation in this country is the Fair Labor Standards Act (which, as we are already aware, is a wage law as well). The Act provides for a standard 40-hour week (to be achieved in a series of periodic jumps: 44 hours in 1937, 42 hours in 1938, and 40 hours in 1939). If a worker is employed beyond 40 hours a week, he must be paid at least time-and-a-half for the extra hours.

But the Act provides for certain complete or partial exemptions to the overtime payment rule, thus encouraging employment beyond 40 hours a week. Some employers (whom the law specifies) are wholly exempt from the overtime rule. In this category are certain employees in the dairy industry, for example. Another group of employees is completely exempt from the overtime provision, but only for a maximum period of 14 weeks a year. In this group are certain workers in the perishable or seasonable fruit and vegetable industries. Another class is partially exempt from overtime—up to 12

[8] With the extensive technological changes that have taken place in industry and the resultant changes in the physical conditions of work, it is altogether likely that many employers themselves would have realized, at least ultimately, the wisdom of reducing hours. When the processes of industry are highly mechanized and the pace of the work is fast, the output-optimum length of the work day decreases. Self-interest, therefore, would have dictated to employers the desirability of shorter hours. But the reduction would not have been as fast or as extensive.

[9] For a discussion of these cases see Glenn W. Miller, *American Labor and the Government,* pp. 148-154. New York: Prentice-Hall, Inc., 1948.

hours a day or 56 hours a week—but again for a maximum period of 14 weeks. In this class are (a) employees of industries that the Administrator of the Act has classified as of a "seasonal nature"; and (b) employees who are employed under collective bargaining agreements, involving duly certified unions, that have a guaranteed annual employment feature, or that place a limit (of 1,040 hours) on hours worked in any period of 26 weeks.

The Walsh-Healey Act (see Chapter 24) provides for an hour ceiling. Here, however, the ceiling is a double one, namely 40 hours a week and eight hours a day. Another federal law relating to hours is the so-called Eight-Hour Law. This law, which was originally passed in 1892, has been enlarged a number of times so that today it is in reality a triple statute. In general the law relates to hours of certain workers (laborers and mechanics) in connection with "public works" and "public contracts" (both as defined in the law); provides for exceptions in case of "extraordinary emergencies"; and prescribes time-and-a-half for overtime—over eight hours per day.[10]

In addition to the federal laws relating to hours of work there are numerous state laws. Most states have legislation limiting the number of hours that women may be employed. The limits vary considerably, however, though the eight-hour and/or the 48-hour week is the most common. The state laws do not have complete coverage. Women in certain occupations—agriculture and domestic work, for example—are exempt. Very few states have laws that place general limits on the hours of adult male workers.

Besides their general provisions concerning hours most of the state laws set forth specific limitations on hours in certain industries, the number of such industries running from one up. Though some of these specific limitations relate to women only, in numerous instances they cover all employees.

The employment of women and minors during certain hours of the day is ruled out by some states. Thus a law may specify that women must not be employed (except in certain industries) between 10 P.M. and 6 A.M. Most state hour laws also provide that women workers must have at least one day of rest in seven, commonly Sunday. Exemptions, however, are provided for.

[10] For a description of this law see the Prentice-Hall *Labor Course,* published annually.

28

ECONOMIC AND SOCIAL ASPECTS OF SHORTER HOURS

In this chapter we shall discuss some of the economic and social problems raised both by the actual attainment of shorter hours and by the prospect that the length of the working period will be reduced still more. Though our analysis will be primarily economic in nature, we shall not disregard noneconomic issues.

Shorter Hours and Consumption

The achievement of shorter hours inevitably involves a change in the general pattern of consumption—we "consume" relatively more leisure and relatively fewer goods. But we are now concerned with another pattern, the pattern of goods (i.e., both commodities and services) alone. The attainment of shorter hours has led to profound changes in this pattern also. Many goods have greatly increased in popularity and in importance; others have decreased. Moreover, leisure itself has called into existence goods that would not otherwise have been devised or produced.

The advent of the age of leisure, with its shorter work days, long weekends, numerous holidays, and regular vacations, has stimulated consumer demand for a wide variety of goods. If the length of the work day were 12 hours, for example, many people would not be interested in buying automobiles. There would be less interest in radios, movies, and even long novels! *Gone With the Wind* and *Anthony Adverse* would not have been nearly so popular—in terms of sales—if the standard work day had been 12 hours.

Many of the goods produced today are closely geared to the needs of a leisure society. They require for their consumption spare time on the part of the consumers. They would be produced either not at all, or else in much smaller volume, if the amount of spare time were greatly reduced.[1] Henry Ford pointed clearly to this fact when he said that we would have "a great closing down of shops" if, with our present methods of production, we returned to the 72-hour week, "because the people, regardless of their finances, would not have the leisure to consume what was being produced." [2] Not only would factories close down, but recreation centers (such as those in New Hampshire) and theaters and service stations would suffer.

The amount of satisfaction consumers receive from goods is often governed in part by the duration of the consumption period. The automobile example can again be used. Clearly a person will enjoy his car more if he works an eight-hour than if he works a ten-hour day, if he has a summer vacation than if he has not. The same is true of the satisfactions from food and clothing. In other words, leisure not only induces us to buy things we would not otherwise buy, but also enables us to get more out of many of the things we buy.

The coming of the age of leisure has brought with it a greater degree of social equality.[3] Leisure is spread more evenly over the working population than is money income. The general manager of a factory may receive a salary 10 or 20 times as large as that of an ordinary worker in the plant, but he is not likely to have 10 or 20 times the amount of leisure. The "equality principle" of distribution largely determines the matter of leisure—because of standardized work days, vacation periods, and so on. It is fortunate for the workers that this principle rather than the "productivity principle" prevails.

Shorter Hours and the Volume of Production

At least three aspects of production are affected, or may be affected, by shorter hours. These are the pattern of production, the volume of production, and the steadiness or regularity of production.

[1] An extensive study of changes in consumption expenditures will be found in J. Frederic Dewhurst and Associates, *America's Needs and Resources,* especially Part III. New York: The Twentieth Century Fund, 1947.

[2] *Moving Forward,* p. 63. Garden City: Doubleday, Doran & Co., 1930.

[3] Because leisure is now available to the poor as well as to the rich, J. L. Hammond has referred to its achievement as "the most important revolution in modern times." *New Statesman and Nation,* November 19, 1932, p. 618. For further discussion of leisure and social equality, see C. Delisle Burns, *Leisure in the Modern World,* Chap. XI. New York: The Century Co., 1932.

The general effect of shorter hours on the pattern of production is obvious from the preceding section. Let us now consider the effect of shorter hours on the volume of production. It will be recalled from the previous chapter that one argument advanced in support of a reduction in hours is that such a reduction will increase output. Is this true? Do shorter hours increase production, not per hour but per day, or per week?

Such an outcome is possible, within limits. A reduction in hours per day or per week *can* lead to an increase in output per day or per week. Sidney Webb and Harold Cox contended in their discussion of the eight-hour day that "experience shows that, in the arithmetic of labor . . . two from ten is likely to produce, not eight, but even eleven." [4] This statement is excessively strong, but queer things *may* happen in the "arithmetic of labor."

Specific Effects of Shorter Hours on Production. The possibility that shorter hours will lead to greater daily or weekly output is grounded upon a number of specific effects that such a reduction may have on the workers and on the production process.

In the first place the health of the workers may be improved because of shorter hours. Better health may lead to greater intensity of effort and less time lost owing to illness. Moreover, it may increase the length of a worker's working life. "The improvement of man," said John Rae some decades ago in speaking of the anticipated effect of the eight-hour day, "will involve an improvement of the workman." [5] This contention has some validity, though probably less now than when Rae expressed it.

Secondly, shorter hours may decrease the amount of voluntary absenteeism. If the working period is longer than the workers would like it to be, some of them may stay away from work with considerable frequency. They take the risk of possible discharge, of course, but the labor turnover involved in firing them may be harmful to production and costly to the employer. Absenteeism involves loss of production not only on the part of workers who stay away, but also on the part of those who work steadily but whose work is interrupted by the absence of some of their fellows.

Again, shorter hours may reduce both the frequency rate and the severity rate of industrial accidents. Accidents are more likely to

[4] *The Eight Hours Day,* p. 4. London: Walter Scott, 1891.
[5] *Eight Hours for Work,* p. 212. London: Macmillan & Co., 1894.

happen when the worker is tired and perhaps careless than when he is fresh and alert.

Shorter hours, if forced upon the employer, and with no change in daily pay, may lead to increased mechanization, improved methods, and possibly greater pressure on employees to be more efficient, all of which will bring about an increase in production.

There is a limit, however, to the extent to which these production-increasing influences are operative. Otherwise hours could be cut down to one or two a day without harming production. These considerations lead us to an analysis of the output optimum length of the work day.

The Output Optimum Length of the Work Day. It is true beyond question that there is a certain length of the work day that will maximize production per day. This is called by the economist the output optimum.[6] This concept is a useful one, but (as we shall see in a moment) it has its limitations when attempts are made to apply it.

The optimum length of the work day is subject to variation. Although it is theoretically possible to think of an optimum for the economy as a whole, it is also possible, and desirable, to think of separate optimums for the different industries in the economy. The length of the work day that will maximize production is not necessarily the same in the steel industry as in the gum industry. The physical conditions of work are not the same in the two industries, and hence their optimums are likely to be dissimilar.

Moreover, within each industry there are differences in the nature of the work performed, and hence again there would be different optimums. Task 23 in the steel industry may be much easier than task 97, and the optimum length of the work day for it may be considerably shorter. In addition, there are different optimums for different workers doing the same job, because of variations in their physical and mental make-up.

Since an industry ordinarily cannot set different lengths of the work day for different tasks and different persons, it is desirable to think of an "average" optimum for the industry as a whole. Some-

[6] Good discussions of this concept will be found in an article by Lionel Robbins in *The Economic Journal,* March, 1929; and in J. R. Hicks, *The Theory of Wages.* London: Macmillan & Co., 1932. See also A. C. Pigou, *The Economics of Welfare,* 2nd ed., Part III, Chap. VII. London: Macmillan & Co., 1924.

times, however, differences in production methods make it possible to apply the optimum principle to plants or enterprises within the industry.

The optimum length of the work day also varies from region to region, depending on climatic conditions. A six-hour day may maximize production in a torrid area but not in a temperate one.

The optimum varies, moreover, from one point of time to another, owing to changes in industrial methods and technology. The work day that maximized steel production in 1900 was longer than the work day that maximized steel production in 1950.[7]

Finally, the optimum length of the work day varies according to the length of the time period over which production is to be maximized. A half century ago, before the term "output optimum" was coined, J. B. Clark declared that "if you want a man to work one day, and one day only, and secure the greatest amount of work he is capable of performing, you must work him twenty-four hours." If, said Professor Clark, the work period is a week, the hours should be reduced to 20; if it is a month, to 18; if it is a year, to 15; if it is several years, to 10; and if it is a lifetime, to eight.[8]

Professor Clark's figures—except the first one of 24 hours—may no longer be applicable; but the general idea he advanced is still valid. Stating this idea formally, the optimum length of the work day varies inversely with the length of the time period over which production is to be maximized. If the time period is just a day, 24 hours is certainly the output optimum length; but if the period is longer, the length of the optimum decreases.

To illustrate this point let us consider an example. After the evacuation from Dunkirk in 1940, when the invasion of England seemed imminent, the time period over which the production of war goods was to be maximized was a few weeks. Consequently the length of the work week that was widely established was over 70 hours. However, when the invasion did not materialize, the maximizing time period became longer, and the length of the work week that was deemed desirable, in the interests of larger production, became shorter—between 50 and 60 hours.

[7] The fact, therefore, that production increases over a period of time as the length of the work day decreases is no proof that the actual length of the work day at the beginning of the period was longer than the optimum length.

[8] See *The New Encyclopaedia of Social Reform,* ed. by W. D. P. Bliss and R. M. Binder, 3rd ed., p. 430. New York: Funk & Wagnalls Co., 1910.

There is clearly a possibility that employers may work their employees excessively long hours, since the time period over which the employer wants to maximize the production of a given worker is shorter than the time period in which society is interested. The employer is concerned with the worker's output only while the worker is in his employment. Society, on the other hand, is interested in the worker's lifetime output.

For a reason that will soon be apparent, however, it is not likely that employers in many instances work their employees for periods extending beyond their lifetime output optimum. They may work them, though, beyond the "ideal" length of the work day, as we shall see in a moment.

The problem of clarifying the hours-output relationship is indeed a difficult one; and, although a few good studies of this problem have been made,[9] further investigations are desirable.

In the preceding discussion we have not mentioned the shift system. The use of this system may be very profitable to the employer and possibly to society as well. It may warrant a greater reduction in hours than would be possible under a single-shift arrangement. Our general argument, however, is not rendered invalid by the use of shifts; it is only made a little more complicated.

The Ideal Work Day

All things considered, the output optimum length of the work day is not necessarily the best length of the work day. It is best only in one sense, namely output. But workers and society at large are interested in more than output, or real wages. They are interested in leisure as well. Only at a time of great national emergency—with an invasion impending, for example—is the output optimum the best (or near the best) length of the work day. At such a time leisure is not of great importance. At other times, however, the best or ideal work day is shorter than the output optimum work day.

What, then, is the length of the ideal work day? Looking at the matter from the standpoint of a given worker, it is the amount of time that yields him the greatest amount of satisfactions in terms of

[9] See *Annual Report,* 1940, Wage and Hour Division, United States Department of Labor, Chap. I; H. R. Northrup and H. R. Brinberg, *Economics of the Work Week.* New York: National Industrial Conference Board, 1950; and William Goldner, *Hours of Work.* Berkeley: Institute of Industrial Relations, University of California, 1952.

wages obtained, unpleasant work avoided, and leisure achieved. But what, specifically, determines the ideal length of the work day? Let us consider this question in a personal manner.

Suppose you were working in a factory and had the right to say exactly how long each day you would work. What factors would you take into account in reaching a decision, assuming you went about the task of calculation in a very logical way? You would certainly give attention to the significance to you of the pay you would receive. What would each hour's wage payment mean to you, in terms of anticipated satisfactions? This would depend, in turn, on the size of the hourly wage payment; the intensity of your personal, present wants for goods; the size of your wants in the future; the number of dependents you have; and your present stock of wealth. Taking all of these into account it seems reasonable to say that as you receive more and more "hourly wage payments" each day the significance of each hour's wage to you declines, in keeping with the principle of diminishing utility.

But you would also take into account your psychological reaction to the work process: such factors as the kind of work, whether it is pleasant or unpleasant; your physical and mental make-up; and the importance you attach to leisure. Your reaction to work changes from hour to hour. The eighth hour of work would be more burdensome to you than the seventh, for example; and the seventh than the sixth. After a certain point is reached the disutility associated with each hour's work (assuming the work process is continuous) increases.

On the basis of the preceding analysis we can formulate a general "law," namely that a person seeking to get the most out of his work and wages should work each day to the point where the utility of the hour's wage is equal to the disutility of the hour's work.[10] If he did this, the length of the work day from his standpoint would be ideal. It would be the true, all-inclusive optimum.

This analysis, on first thought, may appear to be highly convincing and extremely important. Although it contains much that is valuable, we should realize its limitations. To begin with, individual workers generally do not have the right to say how long they will

[10] A graphical representation of this principle will be found in W. Stanley Jevons' pioneer discussion in his book *The Theory of Political Economy,* 2nd ed., p. 187. London: Macmillan & Co., 1879.

work each day; there is a standard work day for the whole labor force in the plant. However, if the standard is longer than the worker's ideal, he may try to remedy the situation by absenteeism. Moreover, if the standard is longer than the ideal work day of many of the workers, they may, by united action, be able to force a reduction in hours.

Again, individual workers are not the systematic "calculating machines" that our analysis suggests. They do not give careful, systematic thought to all the considerations we have indicated, nor do they establish a nice balance at the margins of utility and disutility. In Veblen's classic words, man is not "a lightning calculator of pleasures and pains, who oscillates like a homogeneous globule of desire of happiness under the impulse of stimuli that shift him about the area, but leave him intact." [11]

Man is not, however, oblivious to pleasures and pains, as anyone who has worked in a factory, especially for 10 hours a day, definitely knows. It is, perhaps, illogical for us to assume that a worker makes any exact mathematical calculation of how long he would like to work. It is not illogical, however, to assume that he has some idea whether or not the work day he is asked to work is, from his standpoint, too long or too short. And in arriving at his opinion he gives some thought to the factors that we have noted.

Our analysis suggests various conclusions, a few of which follow. (1) Other things being equal (an assumption we must make in each case) a worker prefers a shorter work day when work is unpleasant than when it is pleasant. In this connection it is pertinent to observe that the mechanization of industry has been an important influence in the advocacy of shorter hours. (2) If the worker has been able to save a sizable amount of money, a possibility that is becoming increasingly real, he prefers shorter hours to longer hours. This factor may well lead to still greater emphasis on shorter hours in the future than in the past. (3) If the worker's future needs seem small, and under our social security program they may very well seem small, he will lean toward a shorter work day.

"The practical problem which we have to decide at any given moment," Professor Lionel C. Robbins has declared, "is the problem whether our present distribution of time between work and leisure is

[11] Quoted in Paul T. Homan, *Contemporary Economic Thought,* p. 117. New York: Harper & Bros., 1928.

satisfactory."[12] This problem cannot be solved finally—for more than one person at least—by scientific methods, since it involves reliance on subjective standards of judgment, a point Professor Robbins makes. However, it is still important to examine the forces that determine the distribution of time between work and leisure.

Today's pattern of work and leisure will no longer exist 10 or 20 years from today, as the previous analysis should make plain. Writing back in 1909 S. J. Chapman said that "the ideal working-day of the future cannot be eight hours, for it must be essentially a progressive ideal."[13] The ideal work day, or work week, is indeed of a progressive character.

Shorter Hours and Regularity of Employment

In our discussion of means for coping with seasonal, technological, and cyclical unemployment we discussed the policy of shorter hours. Our emphasis was on a temporary reduction in hours as a means for dealing with unemployment, not on a permanent reduction, which we shall now discuss.

The general question can be stated as follows: Is there any reason for believing that the achievement of a shorter work day will reduce the volume of unemployment? Or, to state the question in a somewhat different form, are shorter hours necessary if we are to give employment to everyone who wants it?

The case for permanently reducing hours as a means for coping with unemployment is based, at least in popular discussions of the subject, on the belief that there is no longer enough work to go around. As the processes of industry become more and more mechanized, there is less and less work for man—so the argument runs. Hence, to provide an adequate number of jobs for the working populace hours must be reduced. On the surface this type of reasoning may seem plausible, but closer examination will show that it is fundamentally unsound, at least in its crude form.

First of all it should be noted that the argument is somewhat inconsistent with the greater-production argument. If shorter hours

[12] *The Economic Journal,* March, 1929, p. 25. Professor Robbins, after pointing out that the final solution of the problem is outside the limits of scientific inquiry, goes on to say that "a precise knowledge of the objective consequences of any variation is of material assistance in arriving at a solution."

[13] *The Economic Journal,* September, 1909, p. 358.

lead to more output, then there will be still fewer jobs available—if the basic popular assumption of the employment argument is correct.

The reasoning used in the employment argument grows out of the notion that the potential amount of work to be done is definitely fixed. Hence, in plain arithmetic, if machinery does more, man will have to do less, less not only relatively but absolutely. Now a consideration of past history, of the nature of man's wants, and of how man satisfies his wants should be enough to show that the amount of work to be done has not been fixed in the past, is not fixed at the present, and will not be fixed in the foreseeable future until man, in his consumption of goods, reaches the point of complete satiety.

The amount of work to be done is capable of immense expansion; some might say it is capable of *indefinite* expansion. As long as people want "more and more," there should be more and more work to be done. It is true, of course, that there may be obstacles in the way of making the actual amount of work available large enough to provide jobs for everyone. But these obstacles are not likely to be removed by reducing hours.

It must be granted, however, that during a period of rapid technological change a permanent reduction in hours is desirable. In the first place, with the greater productivity resulting from these changes we can "afford" shorter hours: in other words, from the standpoint of our welfare it is desirable to tip the scales more on the side of leisure and less on the side of work. Secondly, a shortening of hours under these conditions (which involve substantial labor displacement) will help to reduce the amount of unemployment.

Hours should not, however, be decreased commensurately with the increase in productivity, or material living standards will be frozen. In addition it should be borne in mind that whereas the amount of unemployment is reduced during the time the shift is made to the lower hour plateau, the influences that produce labor displacement can operate again when the new hour standards are established.

Stating the last point more generally, the influences that lead to unemployment can operate just as effectively and just as disastrously at a high hour level as at a low one. The shorter work day does not reduce the basic causes of seasonal unemployment, namely changes in the season. It does not check the introduction of new machinery and consequently reduce the volume of technological unemployment. It does not prevent unwise monetary policies, lack of balance between savings and investment, production for uncertain markets, or, one might add, spots on the sun—factors which, with the possible exception of the last, help to account for cyclical fluctuations in business and for cyclical unemployment.

If any close relationship existed between the length of the work day and the volume of unemployment, one would have some reason to expect that the average amount of unemployment would have declined over the years. The length of the work day has been cut almost in half, but there has been no such reduction.

We should not expect, therefore, that the achievement of the six-hour day or the four-hour day will solve the unemployment problem. There may be just as much unemployment with a six-hour day as with an eight-hour day. The chief reason for reducing hours is that with the increased productivity in industry we can afford a progressively shorter work day. Since we will be able to afford shorter hours in the future, from the standpoint of promoting our own welfare we should press for shorter hours.

Social Aspects of Leisure

The age of leisure has given rise to a wide range of social problems, many of which remain unsolved. Let us examine a few problems that center around the utilization of leisure time.

Writing more than a century ago Thoreau stated in his *Journal* that "a broad margin of leisure is as beautiful in a man's life as in a book." This assertion would have been more accurate if he had said "may be" instead of "is." If leisure is used properly it may indeed add beauty to man's life; it may broaden and enrich and ennoble his experience.

Viewing the matter from the standpoint of society as a whole, the wise utilization of leisure is also productive of great good. In fact Professor Irwin Edman has asserted that "The best test of the quality of a civilization is the quality of its leisure." [14] Principal L. P. Jacks, went even further. Speaking in 1931 he declared, "Today, as I see it, our civilization has to choose between two things: going to pieces altogether or finding some higher use for leisure than the pursuit of

[14] *Harper's Magazine,* January, 1928, p. 220.

external excitements and ready-made pleasures." [15] The proper use of spare time is obviously of vital significance to man considered both individually and collectively.

But what, one may ask, constitutes a proper or wise utilization of spare time? Opinions will differ on this point, but it seems clear that an excessive preoccupation with purely passive activities—with "external excitements and ready-made pleasures"—is undesirable. It is quite within the realm of possibility to devote too much time to the movies, radio, television, and car-riding, and too little time to reading books, walking, gardening, and studying the birds.

One may feel that the former activities are much more enjoyable than the latter; and, in the short run, they may be. But in the long run, and in terms of good citizenship, excessive concentration on passive activities is definitely bad. But is it possible to avoid such concentration, to improve one's use of leisure time? Some decades ago the celebrated economist Alfred Marshall pointed out that human nature improves slowly, "and in nothing more slowly than in the hard task of learning to use leisure well." [16] The number of persons who know how to work well, said Marshall, has always been larger than the number who know how to use spare time well. This view is probably as true today as when Marshall expressed it.

The age of leisure has arrived and we are not ready for it. Here is a great social problem; a whole set of problems, indeed, that society should carefully study. It is no doubt true, as Marshall went on to say, that if people are to learn how to use leisure well they must be free to use it as they see fit. They must not be *forced* to go on bird walks, to read books, to paint pictures, and to engage in esthetic dancing. But society, acting through governmental and nongovernmental agencies, can do much to encourage its members to engage in worth-while activities by sponsoring such activities and providing facilities for them. Interest should be renewed in the problem of using spare time wisely, even to the extent of calling an international conference on the subject, such as the one held 25 years ago.[17]

[15] *The Survey,* October 15, 1931, p. 75. Principal Jacks declared that a person who is educated for leisure "will be self-active and not a mere receptacle for pleasant sensations." A plea by Principal Jacks for excellence in leisure as well as in work will be found in his article "The Ethics of Leisure," *The Hibbert Journal,* January, 1929.

[16] *Principles of Economics,* 8th ed., p. 720. London: Macmillan & Co., 1925.

[17] See *Monthly Labor Review,* September, 1931. During the late 1920's and

One type of leisure "activity" that we have not mentioned is often of definite merit. This is idleness. The amount of pure loafing that is desirable varies from one person to another, but probably everyone should engage in it to some extent. The art of idleness—and it *is* an art—may have to be cultivated, but some useful guides exist.[18]

The economist, with his interest in the size of the national income, is particularly concerned with the effect of leisure activities on the productive capabilities of the worker. Does he go back to his job refreshed and interested? Or is he tired and unenthusiastic? The leisure question, it is clear, has important economic aspects, of both an individual and a social nature, that should not be overlooked; but the question is by no means simply an economic issue. It is a question of human welfare in the largest sense.[19]

---

early 1930's interest in the question of leisure utilization was at a high level. See *Monthly Labor Review*, March, 1927, pp. 167-177, for a bibliography on the subject.

[18] For a discussion of loafing see Lin Yutang, "The Importance of Loafing," *Harper's Magazine*, July, 1937.

[19] Another question is to what extent leisure activities, even of the best type, can counterbalance or redress the injury sustained by the worker in dull, uninteresting work. This matter is discussed in T. V. Smith, *The Democratic Way of Life*, rev. ed., pp. 128 ff. Chicago: The University of Chicago Press, 1939. See also C. Delisle Burns, *op. cit.*, p. 9; and L. P. Jacks, "The Ethics of Leisure," *The Hibbert Journal*, January, 1929.

PART IV

▼

SOCIAL SECURITY

29

CAUSES AND TYPES OF INSECURITY—UNEMPLOYMENT INSURANCE

In 1834 a Frenchman named Michael Chevalier visited the United States, and like many other visitors to this country he wrote a book on what he saw and learned. In his book Chevalier made the following observation. " 'Work,' says American society to the poor man; 'work, and at eighteen years of age, although a mere workman, you should get more than a captain in Europe. You shall live in plenty, be well-clothed, well-lodged, and be able to lay up part of your earnings.' "[1] It would seem from Chevalier's statement that, barring individual incapacity, all that was necessary for the achievement of economic security was a willingness to work.

Without raising the question of how accurate Chevalier's declaration was with respect to the early 1800's, it seems perfectly clear that it does not fit the situation today. To be sure, a willingness to work is a highly important contributing factor to the attainment of economic security, but it is no guarantee of security. The achievement of individual economic security today is to no small extent dependent on factors external to the individual and beyond his control. And these factors are largely a product of the industrial society that has emerged during the last century and a half.

Economic insecurity is by no means a new phenomenon; generally speaking, it has always been present. But in the pre-industrial era it was brought about to no small extent by the operation of natural forces, forces external not only to the individual but to the particular type of economic system or organization that prevailed. Such

[1] *Society, Manners and Politics in the United States,* p. 287. Boston: Weeks, Jordan & Co., 1839.

things as epidemics, crop failures, fires, and floods were the usual causes of insecurity. Since man has been able to bring these forces under some measure of control, their ravages are not as serious as they once were. At the same time, however, as we have lessened nature's influence in producing insecurity, we have built up an industrial and economic system that leads to insecurity. This is one of the paradoxes of human progress.

Characteristics of Modern Industrial Society

Modern industrial society has a number of outstanding features, five of which have a very close bearing on our present discussion. (1) To begin with our industry is highly mechanized. The extensive use of machinery has been a root cause of much of our insecurity. It has led to a vast increase in industrial accidents; it has made it increasingly difficult for the older workers to obtain new jobs if they once lose their present ones; it has tended to increase the seriousness of industrial diseases and sickness, though its great contribution to the achievement of shorter hours must be borne in mind; it has led directly to technological unemployment, and in an indirect sense it has promoted both seasonal and cyclical unemployment. Mechanized methods of production, though they are largely responsible for the higher material standards of living we have achieved and for our larger amount of leisure, neverthless have contributed greatly to economic insecurity.

(2) Modern production is specialized. There is plant specialization, in which a factory concentrates on one product, or on a number of closely related products—related in the sense that the same materials, or machines, or manpower, or market outlets are used. Plant specialization makes for high productivity, but it often exposes the plant to unstable operations, particularly if it turns out a durable product or one characterized by marked seasonality. There is also trade and job specialization. Having a worker devote all his time to one line of work, possibly to one minute task, makes for great productivity but also for insecurity. In direct contrast to the investor the worker, as we noted in an earlier chapter, cannot diversify his "holdings." He cannot follow a variety of tasks or trades. He must carry all his eggs in one basket.

(3) Another characteristic of modern industrial society, and one closely connected with the two already mentioned, is the widespread

prevalance of the roundabout, or time-consuming, method of production. This method involves the creation of capital goods: factory buildings, machines, and "machines to make machines." Thus under the roundabout method of production the capital goods industries assume a position of great importance. But these industries, as we noted in Chapter 6, are particularly vulnerable to instability; it is in them that one finds the widest fluctuations in production and employment. The roundabout method of production, it is further to be observed, involves both saving and investment. In modern industrial society these processes are ordinarily carried on by different persons, and the maintenance of a nice balance between the volume of saving and the volume of investment, which is necessary for the attainment of full employment, is not easy to achieve. This is especially true in an economy like our own in which money, in the form of deposit currency, can be easily manufactured by our commercial banks.

(4) Although the extent of "gigantomania" can be easily exaggerated, the fact remains that a very considerable fraction of the output of American industry is produced in large enterprises. The presence of these large enterprises in our economy contributes, directly or indirectly, to the degree of economic insecurity in our economy, especially since many of these enterprises produce a narrow range of products. It is not as easy as it once was for an individual, in quest of security, to go into business on his own. In an era of large-scale and medium-scale production, the individual worker must usually seek security in the employment of others, not in self-employment.

(5) In a society in which industry is highly mechanized and specialized, and in which the roundabout system of production and large-scale methods are extensively used, economic insecurity is likely to be widespread—widespread, that is, unless action is taken to cope with it or unless the people are so rich that such things as intermittent unemployment, periodic illness, and old-age retirement hold no fears for them. This condition is far from being met, however, and it is here that we see the basic "cause" of economic insecurity. The fundamental factor in such insecurity is poverty, or, to use a less extreme expression, lack of financial resources. This lack is due principally, though not wholly, to lack of income. And lack of income, viewed in terms of the population as a whole, is due to lack of production. When the output of industry is such that the great bulk of the population can enjoy a good standard of living and at the same time save

enough to constitute a bulwark against the attacks of insecurity, then, and only then, can we with any degree of propriety say (as we are wont to say) that "we have solved the problem of production." When this problem is actually solved poverty will be of very limited proportions and economic insecurity will be of relatively small significance. Insecurity is very serious in an industrial society when poverty is extensive; it is of much smaller consequence when plenty prevails.[2]

Individual and Social Responsibility

The development of society along the lines suggested in the preceding paragraphs has brought with it a shift in the *locus* of responsibility for economic insecurity. In the early stages of industrial development economic insecurity, in so far as it is not the product of natural phenomena (and excessive population growth), is largely due to individual deficiencies. The sick person or the lazy person may be exposed to privation and suffering, but not the person who is well and industrious. As society develops and becomes increasingly complex and interdependent, insecurity becomes less and less a product of individual weaknesses and more and more the result of social factors. The gap between an individual's *willingness* to earn a livelihood (and achieve security) and his *ability* to earn a livelihood increases. A technological improvement, a cyclical slump in business activity, or the attainment of economic old age may throw the willing worker out of employment and bring insecurity upon him. He is victimized by changes over which he has little or no control. Thus society must assume a large portion of responsibility for the insecurity that now exists. Society is by no means wholly responsible, of course; there is still a considerable amount of individual laziness and improvidence.

If society as a whole is primarily responsible for the insecurity that besets its individual members, it also has the responsibility of taking positive action to cope with the insecurity that it creates. This fact is now widely recognized, and society, acting through the state, has adopted a wide program to reduce the extent and lessen the im-

[2] "Poverty" is to some extent a relative matter—relative to one's desires. Such desires increase with our ability to satisfy them, but probably not as fast—certainly not when we get substantially above the subsistence level. In the discussion above the term "poverty" has been used chiefly in a physiological sense.

pact of insecurity. In this country we have government-enforced unemployment insurance, workmen's compensation, old-age and survivors' insurance, and other types of security legislation.

The extensive entry of the state into the field of social security, however, does not eliminate the need for individual initiative, foresight, and saving. If our society is to remain healthy and vigorous, its individual members must take steps themselves to guard against the economic ills that may befall them. If insecurity is to be satisfactorily controlled and at the same time a sturdy type of citizenship is to be developed, there must be both collective and individual effort. Collectively, we are indeed our brother's keeper; but our brother, acting individually, must do a great deal to keep himself. He must not shun employment when drawing unemployment insurance, nor hide assets when obtaining old-age assistance, nor feign inability to work when receiving workmen's compensation. The elimination of these undesirable practices—and we should not exaggerate their extent—is to no small degree an administrative problem; but it is also a problem of individual morality.

From what has been said it is not to be assumed that social security programs, on balance, weaken the moral fibre and individual initiative of those who benefit from them. Unfortunately they have that effect on some persons; but in general "social security is an expression of the individual's desire for a secure base on which to build a good life for himself and his family, and his desire to live in a society in which all men have the same opportunity." [3]

Social Security in the United States

The passage of the Social Security Act in 1935 marked the beginning of a new and highly important era in the history of social security legislation in this country. Before 1935 we had passed a certain amount of such legislation: of outstanding significance were the state workmen's compensation laws, which aided greatly in meeting the insecurity caused by industrial accidents. But unemployment insurance legislation was almost nonexistent, though Wisconsin had passed an unemployment insurance law in 1932, and systematic legislation providing for the hazards of old age was unknown.

It is true that certain private and public plans and agencies

[3] *Annual Report of the Federal Security Agency, 1950,* Social Security Administration, p. 15.

helped to provide security for those who needed it. A considerable number of unions had little "social security" programs of their own, covering such risks as unemployment, accidents, old age, and death. Numerous companies also had security plans in operation. And we had such things as poor houses and charity plans. But that these efforts at providing security, though useful, were very inadequate, was clearly brought out in the early years of the Great Depression.

We were experiencing, indeed, what the sociologists call a cultural lag. Changes had been occurring in our material culture—in the form of such developments as mechanization, specialization, and larger industrial units—that rendered the lot of the individual worker increasingly insecure. These changes called for adjustments in our nonmaterial, adaptive culture, particularly in the field of legislation. But these adjustments were made only after considerable delay.

The Great Depression pointed to the need for a new and greatly enlarged program of action. This need was met, not wholly but very substantially, by the Social Security Act. Compared with most other industrial countries we were rather slow in embarking upon an extensive social security program: the rapid growth of the country, the increase in the average standard of living, and the widespread trust in the effectiveness of individual initiative in meeting the economic hazards of life kept us from seeing the necessity for such a program. But these obstacles in the way of social security legislation were pushed aside by the onrush of the Great Depression, and the Social Security Act was passed. We have here a splendid confirmation of the statement Benjamin Franklin makes in his *Autobiography* that "The best public measures are . . . seldom adopted from previous wisdom, but forced by the occasion."

The Social Security Act made provision for a large-scale attack on two main types of insecurity. Indirectly it paved the way for the adoption, by the individual states, of unemployment insurance; directly it made provision for an extensive program of old-age security. The Act also contained provisions covering aid to the blind and to dependent children.

With the passage and subsequent development of the Social Security Act our defenses against the inroads of economic insecurity have been greatly strengthened. But a number of gaps in the defense ramparts still remain.

In the first place we have not established any system of family allowances, as many other countries have done; and some persons would say that this is definitely an omission. Interestingly enough, however, as we shall see shortly, in some states extra payments are made for dependents under the workmen's compensation laws and also under the unemployment insurance programs. In these states a worker with dependents gets a break if he loses a finger or becomes unemployed!

To many persons the relative absence of annual wage (or guaranteed employment) plans, which we discussed in Chapter 6, constitutes another gap in our defense against economic insecurity. Another gap is represented by our failure to provide adequate safeguards against sickness and the medical costs and loss of income resulting therefrom. This raises the question of health insurance—more accurately, medical aid insurance and disability insurance—and the question of whether such insurance should be voluntary or compulsory. These questions we shall take up in the next chapter.

Unemployment Insurance

Previous to the passing of the Social Security Act only one state, Wisconsin, had an unemployment insurance plan in actual operation, though a small number of other states had passed such legislation. The Wisconsin law was passed in 1932, after a long period of discussion. By that time the question of unemployment insurance had been taken up not only in Wisconsin and these other states but throughout the country.[4] Only after the country had experienced the most depressed years of the Great Depression, however, was a law passed by the federal government that encouraged (virtually forced) the states to adopt unemployment insurance laws.

Financing Unemployment Insurance. A very formidable obstacle in the way of the adoption of unemployment insurance laws by the individual states was the fear of competitive disadvantages in the matter of trade. The employers in a state with unemployment insurance might be undersold by employers in states without such insurance. This problem was neatly solved by the federal government

[4] A description of the "Development of Unemployment Compensation" in the United States, by Edwin E. Witte, will be found in the *Yale Law Journal,* December, 1945. This is reprinted in *Readings in Social Security,* ed. by William Haber and Wilbur J. Cohen. New York: Prentice-Hall, Inc., 1948.

when it inserted a "tax offset" provision in the Social Security Act. This particular provision, it must be emphasized, is not the one that provides for the taxes used in financing old-age pensions. Under the provision in question the federal government imposed a payroll tax on all employers who employed eight or more persons (for at least 20 days of the year, with each of these days being in a different week). The tax, which was not applicable to any income in excess of $3,000 received by any person (a figure that still prevails), was 1 per cent during 1936, 2 per cent during 1937, and 3 per cent after 1937. But the federal government said that employers could credit against their federal tax any amount they contributed to a state unemployment insurance fund, up to 90 per cent of the federal tax. Under this arrangement the states, acting in their own interests, could hardly avoid passing unemployment insurance legislation.

A refinement of the tax arrangement just described should be noted. All of the states have now introduced what is known as "experience rating" into their unemployment insurance plans. Under this scheme an employer who has very stable employment in his enterprise is able to have his taxes to the state reduced. Instead of paying a tax of, say, 2.7 per cent to the state he might pay only 1 per cent. On a payroll of $100,000 this would be $1,000. But instead of crediting only $1,000 against his federal tax (of $3,000) he may credit the amount he *would have* paid to the state had he not benefited from the experience-rating provision. Thus, in our illustration (with a state tax of 2.7 per cent) the employer would take a credit of $2,700 on his federal tax of $3,000. Consequently he would pay $300 to the federal government and $1,000 to the state. Whether or not there should be such a thing as experience rating is a very controversial issue; we shall return to it a little later.

To take full advantage of the tax offset provision the states should impose a tax of at least 2.7 per cent, this being 90 per cent of 3 per cent. A state could impose a tax of more than 2.7 per cent if it wanted to, but its employers would be denied the privilege of taking an offset credit on payments to the state over the 2.7 per cent figure. In times past a number of states had taxes higher than 2.7 per cent, but now they all adhere to that figure.

There are certain strings attached to the tax offset privilege. The unemployment insurance law of the state must provide, among other things, that all the funds collected through its unemployment insurance tax will be placed in a federal trust fund, to the credit of the state; that the funds will be withdrawn only for the payment of benefits to unemployed persons; and that the benefits will be paid through the public employment offices. There are also requirements that set forth the circumstances under which an unemployed person cannot be denied benefit payments.

To administer their unemployment insurance programs the states receive grants from the federal government. There are also conditions attached to the receipt of these grants, conditions relating to the unemployment insurance laws and to their administration. These grants, which come from annual appropriations made by Congress, do not amount to the net payments (the remaining 10 per cent) received by the federal government under the payroll tax it has imposed, and this fact has given rise to a certain amount of controversy.[5]

Unemployment insurance in this country is financed almost wholly by a tax on employers. In a few states a tax is also placed on workers (in *all* states workers covered by the federal government's pension program are subject to a tax, but that is a different tax). The principle of workers' contributions to unemployment insurance has never met with much support in this country, although arguments can be advanced in support of such an arrangement. There are no governmental contributions to unemployment insurance in this country either, though here again a case can be built up for such a scheme. In some countries a trilateral type of contributory plan is in operation; but in this country we have, for the most part, a unilateral plan. This does not mean, of course, that the employers who pay the tax are never able to shift the burden on to the consumers and workers.

The sum in the Unemployment Trust Fund at the end of 1952 was close to 8½ billion dollars, almost all of which was invested in securities of the federal government. This amount represents a sizable "cushion" against the impact of unemployment and hard times. It helps to decrease the amount of individual and family destitution

[5] In 1950 President Truman advocated, under a plan calling for the liberalization and expansion of our unemployment insurance system, that these tax payments be placed in a special account, to be used for financing the administrative costs of unemployment insurance and also for the purpose of establishing a "reinsurance" plan under which grants would be "available to States who encounter temporarily severe financial difficulties."

and at the same time acts as a partial stimulus to economic activity and employment. But it must be remembered that our unemployment insurance system has not yet been subjected to the strains of a serious depression with its mass unemployment.

Now we must pass on to a consideration of the more detailed provisions of the state unemployment insurance laws. These laws vary a great deal from state to state, and in addition they are subject to rather frequent changes. In the discussion that follows we shall not be able to give a complete and wholly up-to-date picture of the laws, but we shall deal with their more general aspects.[6]

Coverage, Eligibility, Disqualification. A number of important groups in the nation's labor force are not covered by the state unemployment insurance laws. The railroad workers are not covered, but fortunately for them they have an unemployment insurance law of their own. Other groups not covered include farm operators and employees, self-employed persons, and domestic workers. Moreover, in many states the employees of small enterprises are not covered. Although in some states employers with one or more employees are under the unemployment insurance laws, most state laws limit coverage to employers with at least several employees. (The limiting factor may be stated in terms of payroll amount also; and in some instances number of workers and payroll amount are both used, either jointly or as alternatives.) Some of the laws follow the federal government's tax provision and limit coverage to employers with eight or more employees. As time goes on the coverage of the laws, with respect to both occupational groups and small employers, will undoubtedly be broadened, just as it has been in the past. At the end of 1952 more than 37 million workers were covered by state unemployment insurance laws.

Unemployment insurance is designed for workers who are more or less regularly employed but who may occasionally become involuntarily idle. The chronically unemployed are excluded from the receipt of benefits, at least after they have exhausted their initial ben-

6 A description of actual changes, and of unadopted proposals for change, in the state unemployment insurance laws will be found periodically in the *Social Security Bulletin* and the *Monthly Labor Review*. A publication that throws light on the technical complexities of our unemployment insurance laws is *Unemployment Insurance Legislative Policy*, issued by the Bureau of Employment Security, United States Department of Labor, 1953.

efit payments. To be eligible for benefits the unemployed person must meet a number of requirements.

In the first place the worker must have been employed for a certain amount of time previous to the date on which he makes his claim for unemployment insurance; or (this is the provision in most states) he must have earned a certain minimum amount of money. Occasionally eligibility is tied up to both employment and earnings. The previous-employment and previous-earnings provisions relate to a base period (or to a fraction thereof), which is ordinarily a year in duration and precedes the "benefit year," usually with a three-month gap in between. The previous-earnings provision may be in terms of a flat amount or, more often, in terms of a certain multiple of the "weekly benefit amount" to which the unemployed worker is entitled—as "30 times wba," to cite a common rule.

To be eligible for benefits the worker, furthermore, must be "able to work" and "available for work." These two expressions are variously interpreted, but their general meaning is clear. In some states the worker not only must be available for work but must, on his own, look for work. Moreover, the benefit claimant must register at a public employment office and report there periodically. Naturally the office is interested in placing the registrant in suitable employment as soon as possible.

A problem arises concerning the meaning of "suitable" employment. In this connection it is to be noted that for the employers of a state to have the tax offset privilege, previously described, the state unemployment insurance law must provide (among other things) that benefits will *not* be withheld from an unemployed worker who refuses to accept a job where there is a labor dispute in progress, or where the wages, hours, or working conditions are substantially lower than the prevailing ones in the community.

An unemployed worker may be partially or wholly disqualified for benefits on a number of grounds. These grounds include voluntary leaving without a just reason, discharge for misconduct, the refusal of suitable employment, and participation in labor disputes. The disqualification penalty varies from state to state, extending from the postponement of benefit payments for a few weeks to outright cancellation of benefits.

Benefits. Most states in their unemployment insurance laws provide for what is known as a waiting period. The worker who becomes unemployed is not entitled at once to unemployment benefits but must wait a certain length of time before he becomes eligible. In almost all states the period is a week. In a few of these states, however, the waiting period for the partially unemployed is two weeks. In several states there is no waiting period at all. Since the unemployment insurance laws were first passed there has been a distinct decrease in the length of the waiting period. In some states it was originally three weeks, and in a few it was four weeks.

A number of reasons may be given for establishing a waiting period. For one thing, by excluding many short-period benefit claims it reduces administration costs and helps to cut down the drain on the unemployment insurance funds, thus making more money available for more serious unemployment. Moreover, a waiting period may encourage the unemployed worker to look around for a job. And what is more, unemployment lasting a few days is not likely to involve any great hardship on the worker affected.

After the waiting period has elapsed the worker becomes eligible for benefits. The size of the benefits depends on the wages the worker had received during a given period previous to the time of his becoming unemployed, except in those states that have provisions in their unemployment insurance laws for dependents' allowances. In the latter laws the previous wage is only one of the determinants of benefits.

The wage that governs the benefit amount is the wage received during the "base year," which is usually the year that precedes the benefit year. A very common rule is to take 1/26, or some larger fraction, of the wages the worker received during the quarter of the base year that his earnings were highest. Since a quarter contains 13 weeks, the benefit amount (if 1/26 is the fraction used) would amount to 50 per cent of his wage, assuming for the moment that there is no ceiling on the size of the weekly benefit. If the fraction is larger than 1/26 (say 1/20) the benefit amount would be more than half the wage, again assuming no upper limit.

In recent years an increasing number of states have introduced dependents' allowances into their unemployment insurance laws. Thus, in addition to the benefit amount calculated in the manner just described, the law may provide so much for each dependent, up to a maximum amount—perhaps $2 for each, with a limit of $6.

Nearly all states pay benefits for partial unemployment. The rule followed is to pay the partially unemployed worker an amount which, when added to the wages he earns, will amount to something more than what he would have obtained in benefits had he been completely unemployed. The "excess" is commonly two or three dollars a week.

The weekly benefit amount has both a minimum and a maximum connected with it. These exhibit marked variation from state to state, and both have changed upwards over the years. The maximum figures in most states are at such a level that for a considerable number of the unemployed workers the benefits are less than half their regular earnings. For the country as a whole the average amount paid in benefits in 1952 was $22.79 per week. This was 34 per cent of the average weekly wage.[7]

Not only do the state unemployment insurance laws place limits on the amount of benefits unemployed workers may receive; they also limit the duration of benefits during the "benefit year." The maximum duration period has increased since the laws first came into operation until it is now 20 weeks or more in most states. In some states any qualified unemployed worker may receive benefits for the maximum period; but in more than half the states the actual maximum period is governed, in each individual case, by the wages or employment of the unemployed worker during the base year. In a number of states the benefit payments for the maximum duration period are available only to workers who are entitled to the maximum weekly benefit amount. In 1952 the average duration of benefit payments (made to 4,400,000 beneficiaries) for the country as a whole was 10.4 weeks.

In California, New Jersey, and Rhode Island a system of temporary disability insurance has been established alongside the system of unemployment insurance. In these states workers who are not available for work because they are disabled are, if they meet the other eligibility requirements, entitled to benefit payments. In most states, however, unemployed workers who are disabled are not entitled to benefits, since they do not meet the availability requirement.

Unemployment insurance benefits are of immense value to a great many families each year. It should be pointed out, however, that often the benefits are exhausted before the workers are re-em-

[7] *The Labor Market and Employment Security,* March, 1953, pp. 21, 35. The average weekly wage was the average for April-June.

ployed. Thus in 1952 there were 900,000 beneficiaries who exhausted their rights to benefits, a fact that suggests the desirability of increasing (at least in some states) the duration of the benefit period.

Issues in Unemployment Insurance. There are various controversial issues in connection with the unemployment insurance program of this country. Three of these we shall examine.

(1) Some persons believe that instead of having over 50 different unemployment insurance plans, operated by the states and other political subdivisions, we should have one large plan under federal control. The establishment of a federal system of unemployment insurance would provide uniformity in the treatment of unemployed workers and probably save some administrative costs. Moreover, it would give greater protection to states in which unemployment may become particularly heavy.[8] But such a system would represent a further move in the direction of governmental centralization, and might lead to a system of unemployment insurance that was too rigid.

(2) Another issue is that of experience rating. This principle, which has received little support outside of the United States, is very popular here; every state had adopted the principle by 1948. The chief argument in favor of experience rating is that it encourages the employer to stabilize employment (since the taxes for unemployment insurance are based on his employment "experience"). One might ask, of course, why the employer has not already tried to stabilize employment to the utmost, since there are distinct advantages to him in doing so—specifically, lower labor turnover and lower overhead cost per unit of output. Certainly this incentive is present without experience rating; the possibility of lower taxes is simply a further inducement for the employer to take action.[9]

[8] The New York State Advisory Committee on Employment and Unemployment Insurance has suggested two "likely solutions" to this problem: the federalization of the unemployment insurance laws or cooperative action on the part of the states. The latter arrangement would involve the establishment of a national reinsurance fund. *The New York Times,* February 5, 1953.

[9] The notion of experience-rating had its origin in the analogy that was drawn (particularly by Professor John R. Commons) back in the 1920's between workmen's compensation and unemployment insurance (with experience-rating). When workmen's compensation was adopted and the amount the employer paid in insurance premiums geared to his accident experience, there was a marked drop in accidents. In other words workmen's compensation acted as a definite preventive of accidents. It was then argued that unemployment insurance could

In many industries there is not much the individual employer can do to stabilize his employment. Hence he may be subject to the full unemployment insurance tax. At the same time an employer in an industry that is naturally more stable will have the benefit of a lower tax. This lower tax is due not to merit on his part ("experience rating," it is interesting to note, was once called "merit rating"), but to the happy circumstances that he is engaged in a stable industry. This does not seem just. Of course, if we assume that the whole of the tax is passed on to the consumers in the form of higher prices, there is no question of unjust treatment of employers. But this shifting does not necessarily happen.

To the extent that the tax *is* passed on to consumers, however, there is another argument that can be advanced in support of experience rating. It can be maintained that since the fluctuations in employment in the various industries are to a considerable degree due to consumer buying habits, the particular consumers who are responsible for marked fluctuations (in given industries) should be willing to bear the burden resulting from this instability in their buying practices. This contention is not without some truth, but it is not universally valid. Consumers do not buy straw hats in the winter, and hence they make the straw hat industry unstable and subject to a high unemployment tax, but are they to blame for the instability?

Another argument in favor of experience rating is that it helps to maintain employer interest in unemployment insurance and hence reduces the possibility of malpractices under the system. "Without this interest," it has been claimed by the director of the Colorado Department of Employment Security, "fraud and chiseling would multiply beyond all reasonable bounds." [10]

There are also certain arguments against experience rating. For one thing the use of the principle adds to the complexity and costs of administering unemployment insurance. Also, to the degree that the costs of unemployment insurance rest upon the employers, the heaviest burden is often placed on those least able to bear it. It

---

act as a preventive of unemployment. It seems clear, however, that the individual employer can ordinarily do more to keep down accidents than to reduce unemployment.

[10] *The New York Times,* April 1, 1949.

might also be argued that experience rating tends to promote part-time work. As we noted in Chapter 4, a share-the-work plan, which involves part-time work, is desirable up to a certain point; if pushed too far, however, it may lead to a sharing of poverty. Finally, the principle is not used (or used very little) in foreign countries. If it had merit, one might expect to find it used more widely.

A final question is that of interstate competition. Employers in a state with a conservative experience-rating plan may be at a competitive disadvantage with employers in states with liberal experience-rating plans. This argument was used, for example, in New York State in 1951 when an attempt to liberalize the experience-rating plan in that state was made.[11]

(3) Another question that has been raised concerning unemployment insurance has to do with international unemployment. A few years ago a group of United Nations experts suggested a change in the International Monetary Fund to the end that the fund could serve as a pool to be used for the promotion of full employment in the Western nations.[12] The plan advanced was that if any country reduced its purchases from other nations because of a drop in its own employment and consumer demand, that country should turn over to the other nations enough money to enable them to maintain their purchases from it. This proposal reflected fears of a depression in the United States, with the disturbing international effects that such a depression would entail. The proposal was not adopted, of course, but it represents an interesting approach to a problem that the Western nations should try to handle.

There are still other issues, or at least questions, connected with unemployment insurance. For example, what is the relationship between such insurance and labor mobility? What is its effect on normal unemployment? What would be its effect if we had mass unemployment? What is its influence on the volume of savings in society? These and other questions could be discussed to advantage, but we must pass on to other topics.[13]

[11] *The New York Times*, February 5, 1951. The attempt was successful. Detailed discussions of experience rating, by R. L. Rainwater and Stanley Rector, will be found in *The Labor Law Journal*, February, May, and October, 1951.

[12] *The New York Times*, July 18, 1950.

[13] For a discussion of such question see Haber and Cohen, *op. cit.;* and Seymour E. Harris, *Economics of Social Security*. New York: McGraw-Hill Book Co., 1941.

30

OLD-AGE INSECURITY—INDUSTRIAL ACCIDENTS—SICKNESS

To cope with old-age insecurity we have a variety of pension and relief plans, both private and public, in operation. Many labor organizations have pension arrangements for their older members, and a few have homes for them. Numerous employers have pension plans in force, some established voluntarily, but many set up as a result of pressure from the unions. There are special governmental pension programs for railroad workers and for federal and other governmental employees. The most important of the governmental plans, however, are the Old-Age and Survivors' Insurance program and the Old-Age Assistance program, and we shall direct most of our attention to them.

Old-Age and Survivors' Insurance

Reasons for Old-Age Pensions. If each worker were able to save enough during his earlier years to meet all of his expenses during his later years, there would be little need for pensions or other plans for dealing with old-age insecurity. But the plain fact is that a great many persons cannot do this. Their incomes—despite all our economic progress—are not large enough to enable them to set aside any sizable amount of money for the impending "rainy days" of old age. Therefore, in the absence of a good pension program the amount of old-age dependency in the country would be large, especially during serious slumps in business activity and employment.

Why are so many workers unable to save enough to meet the expenses of their old age? (1) In the first place the regular incomes of many persons are too small to allow any surplus of savings. These low incomes are due chiefly to the low productivity of the income recipients. If we could raise the productivity of these persons—by such means as better vocational training and guidance, better methods in industrial organization and technology, improved incentives, and better health measures—we would substantially reduce old-age dependency. What is needed, therefore, is an increase in the output and the income of the low-paid workers. Simply redistributing the present total income of the nation, a process that has already been carried far as a result of progressive income taxes, will not make any large contribution to the solution of the problem. The whole national income must be raised.

(2) Many employers have established age limits for new employees. These limits, which may go even below 40 years of age, make it difficult for an older worker to shift from one employment to another or to obtain new employment once he becomes unemployed. Many companies not only have age-hiring limits but age-retiring limits, in the form of compulsory retirement plans. Although some flexibility may be provided in these plans, by which "allowances" may be made in individual cases, nevertheless many persons are forced to stop work while their productive and income-earning capacities are still at a high level.

(3) The life span of the worker has increased, and because of this increase in longevity the needs of the older person are greater than they once were. Thus at the same time that we have decreased the work span of the typical citizen we have lengthened his life span. Such is progress!

As we observed in Chapter 4 the age structure in this country is changing: the population is aging, owing to changes in the birth rate, in the life span, and in immigration. With this modification in age structure the problem of the "older worker," as it confronts society as a whole, has become increasingly serious.

(4) With the decrease in the relative importance of agriculture and the rural way of life, and the growth in the manufacturing and service industries, the economic well-being of the old workers has been endangered. An older person, if in tolerably good health, can usually perform gainful work on a farm (especially if it is his own or belongs to the family), but an older person may not have the opportunity to engage in gainful work in a factory or a store.

One important approach to the solution of the older-worker

problem is through pensions and, where pensions are inadequate or unavailable, through old-age assistance. In this country both of these steps have already been taken, and in the pages that follow we shall examine two programs that have been set up. First, we shall probe into the Old-Age and Survivors' Insurance program (OASI), which is this country's outstanding pension plan.

The present OASI program was inaugurated in 1935, with the passing of the Social Security Act. Since that time the Act has been amended a number of times (the changes made in 1939 and 1950 were especially notable). The coverage of the OASI program has been broadened greatly and the size of the benefits increased,[1] and still further changes in these two directions appear likely.

Coverage and Eligibility. OASI is applicable to persons who have worked in "covered employments." Most employments (factories, mines, stores, offices, banks, and so on) are now covered; the 1950 amendments added many self-employed persons, many domestic and agricultural workers, and many persons employed by nonprofit institutions. The chief excluded groups are farmers, the majority of self-employed professional workers, and farm and domestic workers who are not regularly employed by a single employer. Excluded from OASI but under other public pension programs are persons in the federal civil service, in the railroad and air transport industries, in the armed services, and in state and local governmental work (some of those in the last-mentioned group are now under OASI).

To possess benefit rights under OASI a person must meet certain eligibility requirements with respect to previous employment and earnings. These requirements are stated in terms of "quarters of coverage"; and a quarter of coverage is simply a calendar quarter in which a person receives (in a covered employment) at least $50 in wages, or in which he is credited with at least $100 of self-employment income. If a person receives $3,600 or more a year in a covered employment, he is credited with four quarters of coverage (even though he may have earned nothing for, say, the first quarter).

In relation to the matter of benefits there are two terms used: "fully insured" and "currently insured." A person is fully insured

[1] In December, 1951, 14 per cent of the civilian workers in the country were uncovered by public pension programs. See *Social Security Bulletin*, January, 1952, p. 3. An informative article on the first 15 years of the OASI program will be found in this issue.

if he has to his credit quarters of coverage equal to half the calendar quarters that have elapsed since 1950 or after the quarter in which he attained the age of 21, whichever is later. It should be noted that any quarter of coverage since 1936 (the Social Security Act came into operation in January, 1937) may be counted. There are two qualifying provisions relating to fully-insured status: under no circumstances is it necessary to have more than 40 quarters of coverage to meet the requirement; on the other hand, the requirement cannot be met with less than six quarters of coverage.

To be currently insured a person must have to his credit at least six quarters of coverage in the 12-quarter period preceding the quarter in which he died or in which he became eligible for benefits.[2]

Benefits. John Doe reaches the age of 65 on January 3, 1955, and applies for a pension. Since 16 calendar quarters have elapsed from the end of 1950 he must have at least eight quarters of coverage. This requirement Mr. Doe easily meets, since he has been in covered employments most of the time since January, 1937.

To ascertain the size of the pension to which he is entitled it is necessary to obtain information concerning his "average monthly wage," which is readily available (along with that of more than 80 million other persons) at the Social Security headquarters in Baltimore. The average monthly wage used in calculating the pension is, in his case, determined by adding up his earnings (subject to the Social Security tax) from January 1, 1951 to "the first day of the second full quarter" before he files his claim for a pension. The date for John Doe would be July 1, 1954.

Let us suppose Mr. Doe's average monthly pay during this period was $210.[3] To find his monthly pension it is necessary to use a two-part formula. The pension is 55 per cent of the first $100 of the average monthly wage and 15 per cent of anything over $100. The 15 per cent, however, does not apply to anything over $300 total average monthly wage since for calculating both benefits and taxes any earnings in excess of $3,600 a year are disregarded. (An esti-

[2] About 89 million persons living on January 1, 1952 had made contributions to the OASI program during the preceding 15 years. About 70 per cent were fully insured, and 25 per cent were *permanently* covered (i.e., had at least 40 quarters of coverage). See *Annual Report of the Federal Security Agency, 1952,* Social Security Administration, p. 18.

[3] Persons who have been in the armed services (since 1947) are credited with monthly earnings of $160.

mated 21 per cent of the workers in covered employments in 1951 had earnings above $3,600.) Using this formula it will be found that John Doe is entitled to a pension of $71.50 a month, for the rest of his life. This sum is known as the "primary insurance amount," and it is at present limited to $85 a month as a maximum and $25 as a minimum. The primary insurance amount is highly important, since it is the basis on which all other benefits under OASI are calculated.

If John Doe has a wife of 65 years of age or over she is entitled to a monthly pension of one-half of her husband's, or $35.75. However, if Mr. Doe dies, his wife (still assuming she is at least 65) is entitled to three-quarters of his pension, unless she remarries.

There are various other benefit provisions under the OASI program. John Doe may have dependent children, or dependent parents (these would be entitled to benefits only if there were no widow or child who could claim benefits), and the law provides benefits for them too. However the total sum going to John Doe and his family is subject to the smaller of two limiting factors: (a) 80 per cent of John's average monthly earnings and (b) $168.50. In this case the maximum amount would be the former figure.

So far in our discussion we have assumed that John Doe reached the age of 65 and was fully insured. Suppose now we imagine an example where the "currently insured" term is applicable. Let us assume that Ezra Green is a relatively new worker in a covered employment. He is married and has a young child. Two years after starting to work he dies, at the age of 24. What benefits are forthcoming to his dependents? His wife is entitled to three-quarters of his "primary insurance amount" and the child is entitled to one-half of this amount (unless the wife remarries). When the child becomes 18, however, its benefits end and so do its mother's. When she becomes 65, assuming she is still unmarried, her pension is resumed.

It might be added that a lump sum, equal to three times the primary insurance amount, is paid to the beneficiary of a deceased person who is either currently or fully insured.

There is no need to probe further into the details of the benefit features of OASI, but one or two other points should be noted. John Doe does not have to give up work completely to be entitled to a monthly pension. He can earn (in covered employments) up to $50 a month without foregoing his pension, up to the age of 75 years. If he is over 75, he can earn any amount and still obtain his pension. This provision in the law is a very good one. By encouraging older workers to engage in remunerative employment, it contributes to the psychological well-being of those who prefer to work. Moreover such employment helps to increase the size of the national income and hence is beneficial to society as a whole.[4]

If John Doe should suffer an accident before he reaches 65 years of age, he may be placed in a very insecure position. Let us suppose he is completely disabled so that he can no longer work. If his accident is caused while he is working, he will probably be entitled to workmen's compensation. If, however, it is not a work accident, no compensation will be forthcoming. Until he reaches 65 years of age he will not be entitled to an old-age pension, and even then he may not be eligible for a pension because of his long absence from gainful employment. His situation would be the same if he contracted a nonwork disease. The problem of sickness and disability arising from nonindustrial causes is a highly important one and we shall return to it later.

Before leaving the question of benefits it should be noted that in many private pension schemes set up under collective bargaining the amount actually paid by the employer in each individual case is related to the amount received under OASI. Thus the employer may agree to pay the difference between $125 and the amount (or part of the amount) coming to the worker (his primary benefit) under OASI. It should also be noted that many persons receiving OASI pensions find them inadequate and must resort to old-age assistance.[5]

Financing OASI. In the United States federal old-age pensions are jointly financed by employer and employee, except, of course, for self-employed persons covered by the plan. According to the amendments made to the Social Security Act in 1950, the tax rates are subject to periodic increase up to 1970. The various rates are

[4] One might ask why the rule concerning work after the age of 75 should not be used for those between 65 and 75. Why should a pensioner not be entitled to earn any amount he can, without foregoing his pension? For a dynamic, expanding economy (one in which the "lump-of-labor" idea is not of general significance) a strong case can be made for such an arrangement.

[5] *Social Security Bulletin,* July, 1953, p. 15. In February, 1953, 10.7 per cent of the OASI beneficiaries also received OAA.

set forth in Table 18. It will be recalled that any amount received by a worker in excess of $3,600 a year is not subject to tax.

Table 18

Tax Rates for Old-Age and Survivors' Insurance

	Tax Payable by		
Calendar Years	Employer	Employee	Self-Employed
1951-1953	1½%	1½%	2¼%
1954-1959	2	2	3
1960-1964	2½	2½	3¾
1965-1969	3	3	4½
1970 and after	3¼	3¼	4⅞

The money collected in taxes is deposited in the OASI Trust Fund. By early 1953 the fund had grown to more than 17½ billion dollars, of which more than 17 billion was invested in federal government securities. Like other funds received from individuals and organizations through the sale of government bonds, this money is used to pay the bills of the government—salaries, the cost of battleships, and so on.

The investment of the assets of the trust fund in governmental securities is quite proper (though the process has been harshly criticized). There is a danger, of course, that the government with these funds at its disposal will not use extensively enough its powers of taxation to meet its expenses, but this danger does not seem great.

As part of an extensive plan for changing our general pension program the Chamber of Commerce of the United States has come out in support of a pay-as-you-go policy. At the same time it would bring under the federal pension plan the occupational groups that are now excluded and also all persons who are 65 years of age and over (many of whom now receive old-age assistance). The Chamber's plan is strongly opposed by the unions, who feel that it would lead to inadequate pensions and to a heavier tax load on the covered workers (at the present time the latter do not contribute to our old-age assistance plans).[6]

[6] For details of the above plan, and for CIO criticism of it, see the Chamber's publication, *American Economic Security,* January-February, 1953; and the CIO's *Economic Outlook,* January, 1953.

Old-Age Assistance

There are several differences between the OASI program and our Old-Age Assistance program (OAA). In the first place OASI is a purely federal program, whereas OAA, though it receives aid from the federal government, is a state program. Next, the benefits payable under OASI are to some extent based on the earnings of the primary annuitant, whereas the benefits under OAA are in no way geared to previous earnings but are linked up with present need. Again, the benefits under OASI are not charity payments—they come to the recipient as a matter of right and from a fund that the recipient or someone in his family has helped to build up; under OAA the payments are basically, and unfortunately, of a charity character.[7] Finally, OASI is our main program for coping with old-age insecurity, whereas OAA is a fill-in program, a second line of defense. As time goes on OASI will become more and more important and OAA less and less important. However, as long as there are sizable numbers not covered by OASI and our other public and private pension plans, and as long as the benefits received by some persons under these plans are not large enough to provide a tolerably decent standard of living, OAA will remain with us.

Each state has an OAA program, partly financed by the federal government. The latter's share is as follows: three-quarters of the first $20 of the average amount paid in old-age assistance to any individual by the state, plus one-half of the remainder of the payment—except that the federal government will not participate in any payments beyond $50 a month.[8] An important provision in the 1950 amendments to the Social Security Act was the making available of federal funds for the aid of needy persons who are totally and permanently disabled, and who are not yet 65 years of age. The method of financing this aid is the same as for the aged needy. Another provision introduced in 1950 allows the federal government

[7] One might argue, with a certain amount of truth, that the aged needy have some right to share in the national income since this income has attained its present size partly as the result of achievements made by past generations. On the whole, however, old-age assistance is charity, and of a desirable type.

[8] The same plan is followed for aid to the blind and to the disabled. Beginning October 1, 1952, the federal government increased for a two-year period its public assistance aid (in these categories) by $5 a month, going up to four-fifths of the first $25.

to participate in payments made directly by state assistance agencies to persons or organizations supplying medical and remedial care to persons receiving assistance.

There are certain strings attached to the grants-in-aid of the federal government to the states for OAA. A limit is placed on the length of the "resident requirement" imposed by the states before old-age assistance is granted. It is provided that the states must take into account the income and resources of each person who applies for help. A fair hearing must be granted to a person whose request for assistance is turned down. OAA must be properly administered.

The average monthly payments under the OAA program vary a great deal from state to state. Thus, for example, during one month in 1953 the highest average was in Colorado and amounted to $78.81. California came next with $69.44. At the other extreme were Virginia with $26.55 and Alabama with $27.37. The average for the country as a whole was $48.85.[9] There are also marked differences from state to state in the relative number of recipients of old-age assistance. In the middle of 1952, 201 out of every 1,000 persons aged 65 or over in the country as a whole received assistance. In Louisiana the figure was 631 out of every 1,000, however, whereas it was only 45 out of every 1,000 in the District of Columbia.[10]

Industrial Accidents and Workmen's Compensation

A great deal of insecurity is caused by accidents—in the home, on the street and highway, and in the place of employment. We shall limit our analysis here to accidents that occur in places of employment, in other words to what are commonly called work injuries. And of these we shall consider only "disabling" work injuries. As defined by the United States Bureau of Labor Statistics disabling injuries involve a loss of time on the part of the injured worker that extends beyond the day or shift in which the injury occurs. Nondisabling injuries may be painful and involve a small loss of time, but they do not lead to serious economic loss and insecurity.

Accident Statistics. There are two terms that are often used in discussions of industrial accidents and in statistical presentations relating to these accidents. The first, "frequency rate," is "the aver-

[9] *Social Security Bulletin,* July, 1953, p. 26. The average for Puerto Rico was $7.70; for the Virgin Islands, $10.97.

[10] *Social Security Bulletin,* September, 1952, p. 23.

age number of disabling work injuries for each million employee-hours worked." The second, "severity rate," is "the average number of days lost for each 1,000 employee-hours worked." The expression of accident data in these terms is very useful in making both inter-industry and interperiod comparisons. Another term that is sometimes used, "severity average," covers the "average days lost or charged per case." [11]

Table 19 gives the injury figures for four selected industries. As one would expect there is marked variation in accident experience from one industry to another.

Table 19

Work Injuries in Selected Industries *

Industry	Frequency Rate	Severity Rate	Average Days Lost or Charged Per Case †
Dairy Products	19.1	1.1	55
Logging	98.9	10.3	103
Electrical Appliances	7.5	.7	91
Laundries	7.9	.5	63

* *Work Injuries in the United States During 1951,* pp. 19, 23, 24. Bulletin No. 1137, Bureau of Labor Statistics, United States Department of Labor.

† Of great importance in determining the figures in the last column is the accident "pattern"—i.e., the relative number of fatal accidents, accidents involving permanent partial disability, and so on.

The relative number of industrial accidents has declined over the years. For example, since the middle of the 1920's the frequency rate of accidents involving death or permanent total disability has been more than cut in half. The rates for other types of accidents—those that involve permanent partial disability, such as the loss of a finger, or temporary total disability, such as a broken leg—have fallen by approximately 40 per cent.[12]

The economic loss resulting from work injuries is very large—

[11] In figuring severity rates and severity averages a list of "standard time charges" for death and permanent disabilities is used. A fatal accident, for example, is "charged" with 6,000 days. See source quoted in Table 19, pp. 15, 17.

[12] See *Handbook of Labor Statistics,* 1950 ed., p. 179. Bureau of Labor Statistics, United States Department of Labor.

the total number of disabling work injuries in 1952 was over two million. This figure includes not only ordinary employees but the self-employed as well, and, in addition, unpaid family workers in all industries except domestic service. The number of man-days lost as a result of the 1952 injuries (lost in 1952 and in succeeding years) was placed at 206 million, the equivalent of a whole year's employment of 687,000 workers.[13] From these figures it is clear that despite all the progress that has been made in accident prevention there remains a great deal yet to be achieved.

Workmen's Compensation. The main defense the injured worker has against insecurity, apart from his own savings, is the compensation he receives under our workmen's compensation laws. These laws are now in operation in all states and are supplemented by a number of federal compensation laws as well.

When workmen's compensation legislation was first proposed in this country, its proponents encountered the strong belief that such legislation was "un-American," "socialistic," and "unconstitutional." As time went on belief in the first two of these alleged attributes decreased until it is now virtually nonexistent. And in 1917 the United States Supreme Court, in decisions relating to three compensation laws, removed all doubts of the constitutionality of such legislation.

The first state to pass a compensation law covering private employees was Wisconsin, which took the step in 1911. During the next ten years most of the other states followed suit. As in other countries legislation providing security for persons who have had industrial accidents came, in general, before laws providing security for the unemployed, the aged, and the sick. However it was not until 1948, when Mississippi passed its law, that all states had workmen's compensation legislation.

The compensation laws differ greatly from state to state, and they are subject to frequent change.[14] In the matter of coverage there is no uniformity, though in general the laws are planned to cover workers engaged in industry and commerce. Some laws cover agri-

[13] *Monthly Labor Review,* April, 1953, p. 365.

[14] Each year there is an article in the *Monthly Labor Review* dealing with recent changes in the compensation laws. Periodically the Bureau of Labor Standards of the Department of Labor publishes a detailed description of the laws—for example, Bulletin No. 125, issued in 1950.

cultural and domestic workers, but others do not. Some laws apply chiefly either to "hazardous" or to "extra-hazardous" employments, while others apply to employments in both of these categories. In many of the laws employers (at least those in nonhazardous undertakings) with fewer than a given number of employees are excluded. These numerical exemptions may run as high as 14, though in most states the figure is 2, 3, or 4. However, in most of the states with numerical exemptions provision is made for voluntary acceptance of the laws.

In about half of the states the compensation laws are compulsory; in the rest they are elective. If an employer decides not to come under the laws, he exposes himself to damage suits, which may amount to very large sums. He loses the traditional common law defenses of (a) contributory negligence, (b) fellow-servant negligence, and (c) assumed risk of employment.

Several different plans are followed in this country in the financing of workmen's compensation. Under all the laws the employer must insure, either with an outside agency or "with himself," against the risks of accidents, so that there will be adequate funds available for the payment of compensation to injured workers. The most common arrangement is for the employer to insure with a private insurance company. In a small number of states, however, the insurance must be obtained from a public "carrier"; that is, the employer must insure with the state. There is what is called an "exclusive state fund," which has a monopoly of the field. In other states the state fund competes with private carriers, and the employer has the option of choosing between them or engaging in self-insurance. In states that offer the self-insurance privilege large employers may be given the right to "insure" themselves.

One of the most controversial issues in the field of workmen's compensation is that of state funds *versus* private insurance. In many countries, such as Canada, Great Britain, and Mexico,[15] there is an exclusive state fund. But in this country various arguments have been advanced against the state-fund principle. It has been said the principle puts the state into business; that there will be political

[15] In 1949 in 28 of 57 countries having workmen's compensation laws insurance was carried and administered by a public body exclusively. See *Social Security Legislation Throughout the World,* p. 4. Bureau Report No. 16, Federal Security Agency, Social Security Administration, 1949.

interference in the administration of the funds; that the state funds will lead to unfair competition, since certain running expenses will not be charged against these funds; that there will not be enough attention given to accident prevention; that compensation payments will not be made with sufficient promptness.

In support of the state-fund principle, it has been said that workmen's compensation should be supplied at the lowest net cost; that all risks included in the law should be covered by insurance (as they are in a state fund); that the injured workers should not be exposed to economic loss owing to the failure of private insurance companies; and that state funds offer cheaper insurance, and make possible the payment of larger benefits to injured workers with no extra cost.[16]

Compensation payments may be arranged in four categories, depending on the nature of the work injury. First, for temporary disability most laws provide compensation payments of from 60 to 66⅔ per cent of wages (with a maximum weekly amount, however). In some laws this amount is payable as long as the disability lasts, but most laws set a time limit or an amount limit. In a number of laws additional payments are forthcoming if there are dependents.

For permanent total disability the amount per week is the same as for temporary disability, but there is a difference in duration. In many states the compensation is payable for life; in the majority, however, there is either a time limit or an amount limit, or both. In a few states payments are made for dependents. For permanent partial disability of a schedule or specific nature (an arm lost, for example) weekly benefits are generally the same as for total disability, but duration, in terms of weeks of benefit, varies with the nature of the disability.[17]

Finally, in case of death a fraction (up to two-thirds) of the weekly wage is payable to the widow and children. In a few states

[16] For a detailed, and sympathetic, discussion of the state-fund principle, see *Progress of State Insurance Funds Under Workmen's Compensation,* Bulletin No. 30, Division of Labor Standards, United States Department of Labor, 1939.

[17] If the permanent partial disability is of a nonschedule character (as a back injury) the benefit generally is a fraction of the amount payable under permanent total disability, the size of the fraction being governed by the extent of the loss in wages or earning capacity. Sometimes a worker who is permanently partially disabled has a second injury that totally disables him. Almost all the compensation laws make provision covering the second-injury problem.

compensation is payable to the widow for life (or until she remarries) and to the children until they reach a certain age. Most states, however, place a time limit or amount limit, or both, on the payments made. The laws vary on payments to dependent parents, brothers, and sisters. Usually the laws provide for a lump sum to cover funeral expenses.

Nearly all states provide for a "waiting period" in their compensation laws. For this period the injured worker is not entitled to compensation, though he is entitled to any medical and hospital benefits that the laws prescribe. The duration of the waiting period runs from one day to ten days, but more than half the states provide for a seven-day period. In a majority of states, compensation payments cover the waiting period if the disabling injury keeps the worker out of employment beyond a certain specified time (four weeks, for example). With a waiting period it is not necessary for the compensation authorities to bother with minor disabling injuries. A waiting period also discourages malingering.

All the compensation laws provide for medical aid to the injured worker. In somewhat less than half the states these benefits are limited; in the rest they are full. In most states the employer must supply artificial limbs and other appliances needed by the injured worker. In 1950 medical and hospitalization payments amounted to slightly less than one-third of the total workmen's compensation payments made (under the various state laws and the federal laws).

In addition to providing compensation for disabling injuries, almost all state laws provide for payments in connection with occupational diseases. In some of the states the diseases covered are limited in number and specifically mentioned; that is, there is "schedule coverage." But in more than half the states the coverage is full, and the trend is in the direction of full coverage.

Some state compensation laws provide for financial assistance to injured workers who are undergoing vocational rehabilitation. Moreover, a few states are actively interested in the actual operation of rehabilitation plans. The importance of this work is being more and more widely recognized, and activities in the field will undoubtedly spread. From the standpoint of both the individual worker and society in general vocational rehabilitation is of great value. It was stated a few years ago that of the nearly two million persons who sustain disabling work injuries each year in the United

States, at least 200,000 could benefit from "coordinated, curative services provided in rehabilitation or other specialized centers where these are available." [18] Only about 6,000 workers, however, were benefiting at that time from the state-federal program of vocational rehabilitation.

Accident Prevention and Aid. One of the interesting things about the early workmen's compensation laws was their effectiveness in reducing accidents. Since the immediate financial cost of accidents was placed on the individual employer, it was to his interest to decrease the number and the seriousness of accidents in his plant. Thus these laws not only ameliorated the lot of the injured workers but served as preventive measures as well. The same is true of the compensation laws of today. The amount of preventive work that remains to be done, however, is still large.[19]

The specific steps taken to reduce accidents in industry are many and varied. Numerous companies have safety programs. Large enterprises often have a special safety committee or division. By a variety of means, including the use of attention-catching and caution-inspiring posters, an attempt is made to make the workers safety-conscious. Steps are also taken to make the work place safer. Guards are placed around dangerous equipment; color may be used to make dangerous spots or parts more visible; ventilating devices may be used to purify the air; goggles, asbestos clothing, and shoes with steel toe-caps may be supplied to protect the worker against possible injury. Many companies have first-aid departments, possibly with full-time or part-time doctors on hand. Some have elaborate medical centers.

An agency that does a great deal to arouse interest in the serious problem of accidents, both industrial and nonindustrial, is the National Safety Council. This body collects statistics on accidents and aids in accident prevention work.

The federal government and some of the state governments are greatly interested in industrial accidents. In 1949 the first "Presi-

[18] *Proceedings,* 1950, National Conference on Workmen's Compensation and Rehabilitation, p. 3. Bulletin No. 122, Bureau of Labor Standards, United States Department of Labor. This bulletin contains an extensive discussion of the question of vocational rehabilitation.

[19] In this connection see the remarks of Max D. Kossoris in the *Monthly Labor Review,* April, 1953, pp. 365-366. This issue of the *Review* contains the first of a series of very informative articles on workmen's compensation by Mr. Kossoris.

dent's Conference on Industrial Safety" was held in Washington, and other conferences have been held since then. Following the first of these conferences a considerable number of states held governor's conferences on the subject. In addition to gatherings of this type the various governments, through their workmen's compensation departments, carry on other activities directed toward accident prevention.

Sickness and Health Insurance

The Problem. Sickness is a very effective cause of insecurity to the individual and economic loss to the nation. Each year millions of persons become ill, and in a great many instances the illness involves serious economic hardships. If a person's income is made up wholly or largely of wages, as is the income of most Americans, sickness represents a major threat, meaning as it does that little or no income is coming in. But this is just part of the story. At the same time that the ill person is without an income he may have—and probably *will* have—medical bills to pay, and possibly hospital bills in addition. If the wage earner is well and in receipt of income, he may have dependents who become ill and who require medical and hospital attention. Yet he may not be able to pay for this attention, because of either inadequate savings or low income. It requires little imagination to realize what a fruitful cause of insecurity sickness may be.

The problem of sickness is by no means wholly an individual matter. It has social aspects of a highly important nature, among them the national economic loss. One cannot say exactly how large this loss is, but a few years ago Oscar R. Ewing, the Federal Security Administrator, declared that as a result of bad health the country annually loses 4,300,000 man-years of work and 27 billion dollars in wealth.[20] From a purely economic point of view society obviously has a great stake in the health of its citizens.

But there are other considerations of a social nature to be taken into account. A nation's political strength is in part dependent on the physical condition of its people. And what is more, a "good society" (however we may define the term) is a society in which sickness is reduced as much as possible and in which adequate provision

[20] *The New York Times,* November 30, 1948.

is made for coping with the irreducible minimum. Finally, illness is a social problem, and not merely an individual one, because many persons cannot deal *financially* with illness when it befalls them; and it is neither safe, nor moral, nor economically and politically feasible, for society to disregard these persons.

What should it do about the health of its members? Should it encourage people to try to save more for the "rainy days" brought on by sickness? Should it encourage them to take out private disability insurance covering loss of income and private health insurance covering costs of medical care and hospitalization? Should it aid medical schools so that they can produce more and better doctors? These are some of the things that could be done, and it will be noted that they are all of a voluntary character. But society could adopt a very different approach: it could establish, by law, a system of compulsory insurance. Would such a step be desirable? This question has given rise to a great deal of vigorous debate. In the discussion that follows we shall first take up briefly the issue of compulsory disability insurance and then go on to a detailed analysis of the much more debatable topic of compulsory health insurance.

Compulsory Disability Insurance. A leading cause of insecurity is loss of income due to nonoccupational sickness and injury, and a strong case can be made out for the establishment of a comprehensive system of disability insurance. The insurance could cover temporary disability or permanent disability—or both. It will be recalled that under most state workmen's compensation laws some provision is made for payments in connection with *occupational* diseases. It will also be recalled, from the last chapter, that in three states (Rhode Island, California, and New Jersey) a system of temporary disability insurance exists alongside the unemployment insurance system. In addition to the temporary disability programs in these three states there is one in New York State (under the Workmen's Compensation Board) and a national program covering railroad workers.[21] Veterans, of course, are also covered by disability insurance. There are also private arrangements under which disability benefits are paid: people may purchase such protection from insurance companies, and under some of the welfare plans established in industry provision is made for the payment of disability benefits. In

[21] A detailed description of these programs, by A. M. Skolnik, will be found in the *Social Security Bulletin,* October, 1952.

1952 a total of over 38 million persons in this country were protected against loss of income due to disability.[22]

From what has been just said it is evident that at the present time we do not possess adequate safeguards against loss of income due to temporary or permanent nonwork disability. A comprehensive program of action therefore seems desirable. Such a program (in whole or in part) could be on a federal basis and integrated into our Old-Age and Survivors' Insurance plan; or it could be on a state basis and associated with the state social security programs—especially unemployment insurance—with the federal government providing grants-in-aid.

Over the years there has been considerable interest in disability insurance and in the passing of legislation providing for it. Though progress in meeting this particular type of insecurity by suitable laws has been slow in the United States, there is good reason for believing that the progress will continue, possibly at an accelerated rate. In time we shall probably have a comprehensive program of disability insurance, as many other countries have. In this connection it should be added that the American Medical Association, though strongly opposed to compulsory health insurance, is not against the principle of compulsory disability insurance.[23]

Compulsory Health Insurance. The history of the movement to establish compulsory health insurance in this country goes back several decades, and may be divided into three periods.[24] During the first of these periods, from 1910 to 1920, the American Labor Legislation Association (no longer existent) supplied much of the leadership in the movement. A considerable amount of interest was aroused in the question of health insurance, but strong opposition developed near the end of the period. Among the opponents, it is interesting to note, was Samuel Gompers, president of the AFL. Today the presidents of both the AFL and the CIO favor public health insur-

[22] *The New York Times,* September 24, 1953.

[23] For further discussion of the general problem see William Haber and Wilbur J. Cohen, *Readings in Social Security,* pp. 394-449. New York: Prentice-Hall, Inc., 1948. See also *Annual Report of the Federal Security Agency, 1952,* pp. 13-14, 30-31, 36-37.

[24] An excellent, brief article on the history of compulsory medical-care insurance in this country, by Odin M. Anderson, will be found in the *Annals of the American Academy of Political and Social Science,* January, 1951, pp. 106-113.

ance, as do the organizations they represent. During the second period, from 1921 to 1933, little in the way of outright campaigning for health insurance was carried on, but the matter was subject to study and analysis. The third period, which began in 1933 and extends down to the present time, has seen strong efforts to pass federal health insurance legislation. These efforts have met very strong opposition, particularly from the American Medical Association, which has spent large sums in advancing its point of view.[25]

During this third period numerous studies have been made of the health of the nation and many health insurance bills have been introduced into Congress. The most outstanding of these bills was the Wagner-Murray-Dingell Bill, first introduced in 1943 but reintroduced a number of times since then. The attempts to pass health insurance legislation reached a high point in 1949 when various bills were introduced, with two commanding the most attention. One of these (S. 1679) was supported by the Truman administration, and provided for compulsory health insurance; the other (S. 1970) avoided compulsory insurance but provided for federal grants to the states so that voluntary plans could be made available to all persons who were interested in coming under them.

Although a compulsory federal health insurance law has not been adopted, the principle of voluntary health insurance has been widely accepted. During recent years very rapid progress has been made in this field, partly because some groups probably think it a way to head off a compulsory insurance plan. In part, however, the progress is the result of the failure to establish compulsory insurance—many private insurance plans, for example, were established through the collective bargaining process. To some degree the progress may be looked upon as a more or less "normal" development.

The issue of compulsory health insurance cannot be discussed without giving attention to the coverage of our voluntary health insurance plans. According to a study made a few years ago,[26] it

25 In a crucial two-week period preceding the elections in 1950 the AMA spent $1,100,000 in its anti-health-insurance advertising campaign. *The New York Times,* December 8, 1950.

26 *Health Insurance Plans in the United States,* p. 2. Report of the Committee on Labor and Public Welfare, United States Senate; Report No. 359, Part I, 82nd Cong., 1st Sess. This report, including all three parts, contains a great deal of information on the general question of health and health insurance.

was estimated that at the end of 1950 over 75 million persons in the United States, out of a total population at that time of 150 million, were covered by voluntary medical-care insurance. The rapid growth in voluntary insurance of this type is evidenced by the fact that in 1939 the number was less than six million. It is important to note, however, that most of the 75 million persons who were under medical-care insurance plans in 1950 were just partly covered: 30 per cent had hospital coverage only; 42 per cent had hospital and surgical coverage; 22 per cent had hospital, surgical, and limited medical coverage; and only 6 per cent had comprehensive coverage. Since 1950 the number of persons covered by these plans has increased considerably.[27]

The most important private insurance carriers in the country are the Blue Cross, which handles hospital insurance; the Blue Shield, which affords surgical insurance and, in some instances, limited medical insurance; and the insurance companies. In addition there are a wide variety of so-called independent plans operated by consumer cooperatives, unions, employers, or unions and employers together.

These voluntary plans are serving an extremely useful purpose. But their coverage of persons, although very large, is only a fraction of the nation's population; and among those not covered are many persons who are most in need of medical care. Moreover, the coverage is very unequal geographically, with the lower-income areas less well protected than the high-income areas. Furthermore, even for the persons under such plans the risks are in most instances only partly covered.[28]

It can be argued that in terms of the national interest it is necessary that every person should be able to obtain the kind of medical aid that he needs regardless of his income, and that private insur-

[27] The Health Insurance Council has stated that in 1952 nearly 92 million persons had hospital-expense coverage; more than 73 million were under surgical-expense coverage; and nearly 36 million had medical-expense coverage. *The New York Times*, September 24, 1953.

[28] Though a considerable percentage of hospital costs are covered by voluntary insurance, it can be said, in general, that only a relatively small percentage of the total sickness cost in this country is met by insurance. For statistics relating to the percentage of the various costs met, in 1950, see *Social Security Bulletin*, December, 1951, p. 23.

ance plans are not able to achieve this objective.[29] On the other hand it might be stated in reply that the private plans have been growing very rapidly and that they will soon have a much larger coverage than they have at the present time. However it is unlikely that the private plans, unsupported by substantial federal aid, will ever grow to the size that is needed to raise the nation's health to the "optimum." In his 1954 message to Congress on health insurance, President Eisenhower proposed among other things that the federal government reinsure the health insurance plans of private companies, and two bills were introduced into Congress containing this and other suggestions. There can be no doubt that the establishment of a reinsurance plan would be a step in the right direction.

Compulsory health insurance has been opposed on the grounds that it is socialistic in nature. Such insurance is sometimes referred to by its opponents as "socialized medicine." Now a principle should never be destroyed by an epithet, but one should examine the principle to see if the epithet is appropriate. Compulsory health insurance by its very nature involves governmental interference, and it is socialistic in that sense. But so are workmen's compensation, unemployment insurance, the postal service, and police protection. We have, indeed, many socialistic undertakings in our capitalistic society. The issue of compulsory health insurance cannot be settled, therefore, by saying that it is socialistic. It must be settled on the basis of the specific results it would achieve and the general consequences that would follow from it.

A number of bills (including S. 1970, already referred to) have been introduced into Congress that would provide for the granting of public funds to aid in the promotion of voluntary insurance. Such an arrangement would avoid, at least in part, the stigma of "socialized medicine," and would undoubtedly result in a large expansion of the private plans and serve to promote the nation's health; but it is questionable whether the arrangement would achieve enough. It has been asserted that voluntary insurance of this character would be more costly and complicated, and at the same time less effective, than an outright public health insurance plan,

[29] This view is presented and discussed by Oscar R. Ewing in *The Nation's Health,* pp. 77-88. This publication, which embodies a "ten-year program," was submitted to the President in 1948, when Mr. Ewing was Federal Security Administrator.

contributory in character, decentralized in administration, and part of a broad program of social insurance.[30]

Health insurance could involve a large degree of centralized control. The supporters of such insurance have been aware of this danger, and in the bills presented in Congress an attempt has been made to avoid it. Provision has been made in the proposed measures for a large degree of local administration. While certain general matters would be decided in Washington, the day-to-day operation of the insurance plan would be determined in Oshkosh, Tallahassee, Albuquerque, and the many other towns and cities of the country.

Another possible danger of compulsory health insurance is its inflexibility and standardization. In the plans that have been proposed in Congress this danger has been circumvented, at least in part, by the provision that patients would be allowed to choose their doctors, and the doctors would be permitted to select their patients, as at present. Some of the opposition to compulsory health insurance might disappear if this fact were clearly understood. It should be added too that doctors are not compelled to come under the plan if they do not so desire.

Another danger or weakness connected with compulsory health insurance is the possible overflooding of the "health market" by persons seeking treatment, at least in the early stages of any program. To some extent this would be a good sign, since it would represent the use of medical aid by persons who previously did not have it. However, there is a real administrative problem here. Persons who do not really require medical aid would have to be prevented from using facilities and services designed for those who do require such aid.

A weakness of voluntary health insurance, relative to a compulsory system, is the possibility that it will not achieve enough in the way of *preventing* sickness. For a number of reasons, including the common practice of paying doctors on a fee basis, there is a danger that not enough attention will be given to the general promotion of the nation's health. The payment of benefits to persons who are sick is highly desirable; but it is also desirable that extensive measures be taken to prevent such persons from becoming sick

[30] *Annual Report of the Federal Security Agency, 1950,* Social Security Administration, p. 12.

in the first place. Public health insurance seems to be better able to do this than private insurance.

In general support of the principle of compulsory health insurance it may be argued that many countries have already established such insurance schemes. In 1949 the number was 36, compared with 24 ten years previously. Among these countries are not only Soviet Russia and Great Britain, but Brazil, Chile, and Venezuela. These countries provide both for medical-care benefits and for payments covering part of the wage loss.[31] The fact that other countries—many of them by no means socialistic—have adopted compulsory health insurance is certainly not a conclusive argument for our instituting such insurance, but it is a consideration of some consequence nevertheless.

It might also be argued that health insurance must be of a public character so that it can be integrated into other health plans and into our Old-Age and Survivors' Insurance program.[32] There would undoubtedly be definite advantages in a coordinated plan of this character, particularly in the matter of collecting the funds necessary to operate the joint program.

The cost of a comprehensive system of compulsory health insurance would be very large. In the late 1940's experts of the Social Security Administration placed the cost at about 4 billion dollars a year, rising to about 5⅓ billion in ten years.[33] It was also estimated that the cost of a disability insurance plan, covering in part the loss of income resulting from illness, would amount to at least 2 billion a year. The proposed costs would be met by payroll taxes. The employer and employee would each pay an estimated 1½ per cent for health insurance, and each about three-quarters of one per cent for disability insurance.

The large expenditures that would be involved have been defended (e.g., by Oscar R. Ewing) on the grounds that they do not represent wholly new costs to the economy, and that in so far as they

31 A survey of the essential features of the plans in operation in the various countries will be found in *Social Security Throughout the World*, Federal Security Agency, Social Security Administration, Bureau Report No. 16, 1949.

32 See *Annals of the American Academy of Political and Social Science*, January, 1951, p. 119, article by I. S. Falk.

33 *The New York Times*, November 30, 1948. Later the figures were raised to 5 1/3 billion and 7 1/5 billion, respectively. *The New York Times*, January 20, 1952.

represent an increase in medical service they are warranted. The American Medical Association has contended that the costs would be much larger than the figures we have cited. Back in 1948 it placed the annual cost of governmental health insurance at 18 billion dollars a year, with much larger payroll taxes than those stated above. It is with some justification that the layman exclaims: "What shall we do when the doctors—and other experts—disagree?"

INDEX

I